A NEW VARIORUM EDITION

OF

SHAKESPEARE

EDITED BY

HORACE HOWARD FURNESS, Ph.D., LL.D., L.H.D.

HONORARY MEMBER OF THE 'DEUTSCHE SHAKESPEARE-GESELLSCHAFT' OF WEIMAR

THE MERCHANT OF VENICE

[ELEVENTH EDITION]

PHILADELPHIA

J. B. LIPPINCOTT COMPANY

LONDON: 5 HENRIETTA STREET, COVENT GARDEN

Copyright, 1888, by H. H. Furness.

WESTCOTT & THOMSON,
Electrotypers and Stereotypers, Phila.

PRESS OF J. B. LIPPINCOTT COMPANY,
Phila.

IN MEMORIAM

PREFACE

As the volumes of this Edition are severally independent, it has been considered necessary hitherto to repeat in the Preface an explanation of its plan and scope. In the present volume, however, all needful information in this regard has been relegated into the Appendix, where it will be found on pp. 466 *et seq.*

Experience has deepened the conviction that for an Edition like the present the befitting Text is that of the FIRST FOLIO. Accordingly, that Text has been again adopted for *The Merchant of Venice*.

To read and to enjoy SHAKESPEARE, any text, from the *Shilling Edition* upwards, will suffice. In the familiar passages of beauty or of wisdom we find no difficulties; the text is everywhere adequately the same.

But to study SHAKESPEARE as we would a Greek Poet, dwelling on every line and syllable, weighing every phrase and every word, then we need a text as near as may be, in point of time at least, to the author's hand. With certain qualifications, such a text is that of the First Folio.

Topics, hitherto discussed in these Prefaces, are now to be found set forth in the Appendix.

It is again my high privilege to express my thanks to my Father, the REV. DR FURNESS, for the translation of many of the selections from the German.

H. H. F.

MAY, 1888.

The Merchant of Venice

The Actors Names.

The Duke of *Venice.*

Morochus, a Prince, and a Sutor to *Portia.*

The Prince of *Aragon,* Sutor alſo to *Portia.*

Baſſanio, an Italian Lord, Sutor likewiſe to *Portia.* 5

Anthonio, a Merchant of *Venice.*

Salarino, ⎫
Salanio,   ⎪ Gentlemen of *Venice,* and Compa-
Gratiano, ⎬   nions with *Baſſanio.*
Lorenſo,   ⎭   10

Shylock, the rich Iew, and Father of *Ieſſica.*

---

1. First given in Q₃.   7. Salarino] Solarino. Rowe.
3. Morochius, a Moorish Prince. Rowe.   10. Lorenzo. Rowe.

---

11. **Shylock**] STEEVENS: Our author, as Dr Farmer informs me, took this name from an old pamphlet, entitled 'Caleb *Shillocke* his prophecie, or the Jewes Prediction.' London, printed for T. P. (Thomas Pavier), no date. MALONE: If Shakespeare took the name of *Shylock* from the pamphlet mentioned by Dr Farmer, it certainly was not printed by Thomas Pavier, to whom Steevens has ascribed it, for that prototype of Curl had not commenced a bookseller before 1598. The pamphlet in question, which was not in Dr Farmer's collection (nor do I know where it is to be found), may have been printed by Thomas Purfoot. BOSWELL: Mr Bindley had a copy of this pamphlet, the date of which was 1607. 'Therefore,' says Knight, who quotes this note of Boswell, 'Farmer's theory is worthless.' HUNTER (*New Illust.* i, 307): We collect that Shylock was a Levantine Jew from the name: *Scialac,* which is doubtless the same name in a different orthography, being the name of a Maronite of Mount Libanus, who was living in 1614. See *Account of the MSS. in the Library of France,* 1782, p. 23. For this very valuable reference I am indebted to some pencil notes on this play by the late Mr F. G. Waldron. HALLIWELL (*N. & Qu.* 1st Ser. vol. i, p. 221): Upton, in 1748, remarked that *Scialac* was the generic name, and *Shylock* merely a corruption. It by no means follows that 1607 is the date of the *first edition of Caleb Shillocke,* merely because Boswell saw a copy bearing that date. M. A. LOWER (*N. & Qu.* 1st Ser. vol. i, p. 184): Was not Shylock, a proper name among the Jews, derived from the designation employed by the patriarch Jacob in predicting the advent of the Messiah,— 'until *Shiloh* come'—(Gen. xlix, 10)? The difference between *Shiloach* and Shylock is very trivial indeed. But, after all, Shylock may have been a *family name* familiar to the great dramatist. In all my researches on the subject of *English Surnames,* however, I have but once met with it as a generic distinction. In the *Battel Abbey Deeds* occurs a power of attorney to Richard Shylok of Hoo, co. Sussex. The date

Tuball, a Iew, *Shilocks* Friend.   **12**

Portia, the rich Italian Lady.

13. *the...Lady*] an Heiress of great Quality and Fortune. Rowe. an heiress. Johns. a rich Heiress. Cap.

---

of this document is 4 July, 1435. STAUNTON: This may have been an Italian name, *Scialocca*, the change of which into *Shylock* was natural. At all events, it was a name current among the Jews, for, at the end of an extremely rare tract, called ' A Jewes Prophesy, or Newes from Rome of two mightie Armies, as well footemen as horsmen,' 1607, is a piece entitled : ' Caleb Shilock his prophesie for the yeere 1607,' which begins as follows :—' Be it knowne unto all men, that in the yeare 1607, when as the moone is in the watrye signe, the world is like to bee in great danger ; for a learned Jew named Caleb Shilock doth write that, in the foresaid yeere, the sun shall be covered with the dragon in the morning, from five of the clocke untill nine and will appeare like fire,' &c. Although pretending to be a prophecy for the year 1607, this edition was a reprint of a much older copy, the date of the predicted event being altered to give interest to the publication. CLARENDON: In *Pepys's Collection of Ballads*, vol. i, p. 38, is one with the title ' Calebbe Shillocke, his Prophesie : or the Iewes Prediction. To the tune of Bragandarie.' The second verse begins, ' And first, within this present yeere, Beeing *sixteene hundreth seau'n*.' The existence of the name in the title of this ballad is sufficient to show that it was known in Shakespeare's time. CASSEL (*Literatur u. Symbolik*, 1884, p. 384): *Ock* is a termination found in many old languages, notably in the Irish, and, as it were, represents the Latin *us*. *Shyl* is the Hebrew name *Schaul;* therefore, *Saulus*.

12. **Tuball**] KARL ELZE (*Essays*, p. 383) : Tubal and Chus are taken from *Genesis*, x, 2 and 6, without change.

13. **Portia**] I have seen it somewhere stated, though I cannot now remember where or by whom, that Julius Cæsar and the characters which were grouped around him seem to have made a deep impression on the mind of Shakespeare, and that there is scarcely one of his plays wherein an allusion to them may not be found. The choice of this present name may be cited in illustration of the truth of this, together with Bassanio's direct allusion to Brutus's Portia, in I, i, 176.—ED.

TH. ELZE (*Sh. Jahrbuch*, xiii, 145): We shall hardly be contradicted when we say that every man of the North, especially a German, believes the ideal of Southern female beauty to be a slender lovely figure, an oval face, a Grecian nose, glowing dark eyes, and hair of glossy jet, flowing down over a haughty, Junonian neck. It would never occur to any poet north of the Alps in choosing an Italian heroine to represent her otherwise than with jet black hair, nor could any reader otherwise imagine a Fiormona or a Bianca Capello. In the most striking opposition to this almost universal idea, Shakespeare describes the Venetian Portia as a blonde: ' her sunny locks Hang on her temples like a golden fleece.' Is not this ' die blonde Engländerin,' or at least a blonde maiden of the North ? But before we charge Shakespeare's poetic fancy with this carelessness, we must first look around somewhat more closely in Venice. The great masters of the Venetian school in the 16th Century: Titian, Giorgione, Palma Vecchio, Paris Bordone, and others gave to their Ideal of female beauty redgolden hair. Like these great Venetian painters, the great English Dramatist arrays the ideal creature of his fancy, not only with all the wealth of intellectual and worldly gifts and graces, but also with an enchanting ornament rarely seen in Venice, sunny

Nerriſſa, her wayting-Gentlewoman.

Ieſſica, Daughter to *Shylock.*   15

Gobbo, an old man, father to *Lancelot.*

14. Nerissa, Confident to Portia. Rowe. waiting-maid to Portia. Johns. her woman. Cap.

blonde or red-golden hair. Is this noteworthy agreement of Shakespeare with Titian and Paul Veronese a happy accident, or does it not rest upon a deeper, more exact knowledge of the people of Venice and of their art? This peculiar appearance of Portia with red-golden or sunny blonde hair, Shakespeare, with deep knowledge, placed in contrast to the black locks of her waiting-gentlewoman, Nerissa. That Nerissa has black hair and is of the generally accepted type of female beauty in the South, the Poet has indicated in the finest way, which has not perhaps been generally detected—to wit, by her name. *Nerissa* is simply the Italian *Nericcia* (from *nero*), and thereby signifies 'the black-haired.' In the same way the name *Nerissa* is the most excellent opposite to the name *Biondello* (that is, the fair-haired youth) in *The Taming of the Shrew,* which C. A. Brown has mentioned as a name chosen by Shake- speare with full knowledge of the Italian tongue. RUSKIN (*Munera Pulveris,* p. 89): Shakespeare would certainly never have chosen this name had he been forced to retain the Roman spelling. Like Perdita, 'lost lady,' or Cordelia, 'heart lady,' Portia is 'fortune' lady. The two great relative groups of words, Fortuna, fero, and fors— Portio, porto, and pars (with the lateral branch, op-portune, im-portune, opportunity, &c.), are of deep and intricate significance; their various senses of bringing, abstract- ing, and sustaining being all centralized by the wheel (which bears and moves at once), or still better, the ball (spera), of Fortune.

14. HUNTER (*New Illust.* i, 309): Nerissa, or, as Shakespeare wrote the name, Nerrissa, is to be regarded not as a waiting-maid in the modern sense of the term, but as a young lady of birth and rank, such persons being often found, in the age of Shake- speare, attending on ladies of superior distinction and fortune; and therefore a suitable match for Gratiano, the friend of Bassanio. Thus Magdalene Dacre, an account of whose life was written by Richard Smith, the bishop of Chalcedon, a daughter of Lord Dacre of the North, waited on the old Countess of Bedford; and there are sixteen quarterings over the tomb of Catharine Clippesby, an attendant on the Countess of Shrewsbury of the time. That *Nerrissa,* as Shakespeare wrote, is the better reading a nice ear will perceive in this line, as well as in many others: 'Nerissa [Nerrissa] and the rest stand all aloof.'—III, ii. There are also passages in which *Anthonio,* as Shakespeare appears to have written, pleases the ear better than *Antonio,* which the modern editors have chosen to substitute. These, it may be said, are trifling remarks; but poetry is a luxury, and therefore should be as pure and perfect as may be; nor can there be any reason why we should accept at the hands of an editor a text which is even in a slight degree worse than that which the author himself has bequeathed to us.

15. Iessica] KARL ELZE (*Essays,* p. 282): To all appearance this is borrowed from *Genesis,* xi, 29, where *Iscah* of King James's translation appears in earlier edi- tions of the Bible, in 1549 and 1551, as *Jesca.* In the Hebrew it is *Jiscah,* signifying a spy, or looker-out. Has it a reference to Shylock's warning to his daughter not to 'thrust her head into the public street to gaze on Christian fools'?

16. Gobbo] STEEVENS: It may be inferred from the name of Gobbo, that Shakespeare designed this character to be represented with a hump back   ELZE (*Essays,* p. 281):

Lancelot Gobbo the Clowne.   **17**

Stephano, a Meſſenger.

Iaylor, and Attendants.

18. The following have been added: Leonardo, servant to Bassanio. Balthazar, servant to Portia. Theob. et seq. Salerio, a messenger from Venice. Steev. Coll. Wh. i, Rlfe, (a friend to Antonio and Bassanio. Cam. Glo. Cla. Wh. ii).

19. Rowe added: Senators of Venice Officers, Servants to Portia.

Rowe also added: Scene partly at Venice, and partly at Belmont, the Seat of Portia upon the Continent.

This name reminds us vividly of the Gobbo di Rialto, a stone figure which serves as a supporter to the granite pillar, of about a man's height, from which the laws of the Republic were proclaimed. This figure, as far as we know, is not mentioned by Coryat. The name of Gobbo is indeed of frequent occurrence in Italian history, and exists even now-a-days as a family name in Venice. [In BELL'S *Shakespeare's Puck* (iii, 47, 1864) are to be found fanciful derivations of the names of Shylock and Antonio, as well as several Notes on certain words and phrases in the Play.—ED.]

The Merchant of Venice.

Actus primus. [*Scene I.*]

Enter Anthonio, Salarino, and Salanio.

Anthonio.

N footh I know not why I am fo fad,   5
It wearies me : you fay it weariēs you ;
But how I caught it, found it, or came by it,
What ftuffe 'tis made of, whereof it is borne,

1. The...Venice] The Comicall History of...Venice. Qq.
  2. Actus primus.] Om. Qq.
    [Scene I. Rowe et seq.
    [A Street in Venice. Theob. et seq.
(subs.).

3. Salarino] Salaryno Q_1Q_2. Solarino
F_3F_4, Rowe+.
    Salanio] Solanio Cap. Knt.
  8. *of*] *off* Q_1.
    borne] *born* F_3F_4.

Actus primus] In the Qq there are no divisions into either Acts or Scenes. In the Ff the Acts alone are indicated. For the purposes of citation and reference I have followed the division into Scenes most commonly adopted, and have indicated by brackets that these divisions are not in the Folio. At the beginning of each Scene throughout the play ECCLES notes what, in his judgment, is the sequence of time. The discussion of 'The Duration of the Action' will be found in the Appendix, p. 332. In CHARLES KEAN's fine revival of this play at the Princess's Theatre in 1858, the curtain draws up on a scene laid in Saint Mark's Place, with various groups of Nobles, Citizens, Merchants, Foreigners, Water-Carriers, Flower-Girls, &c., passing and repassing, while a Procession of the Doge in state crosses the Square. 'This Procession was copied from a print in the British Museum by Josse Amman, who died in 1591.'—ED.

Enter . . .] A trifling difficulty in nomenclature meets us on the threshold. Anthonio enters with two friends, whose names are so nearly the same that before fifty lines are passed the compositors have fallen into a confusion over them, from which they do not recover throughout the play. In the Folios and Quartos these names appear as *Salaryno, Salerino, Slarino, Solarino, Salerio, Salanio, Salino,* and *Solanio,* with abbreviations at the beginning of the speeches correspondingly variable. Indeed, so great does the puzzle become that STEEVENS added ' *Salerio,* a messenger from Venice,' as a third character in the *Dramatis Personæ,* and has been followed therein by many an editor, even down to the conservative Cambridge Edition and to Rolfe. CAPELL was the first to attempt to solve the difficulty, and, in the belief that there were but two characters, he adopted Salerino as the name of one, and Solanio as the name of the

[Enter Anthonio, Salarino, and Salanio.]

other, 'induc'd' thereto, as he said, 'by convenience (for, in themselves, they're indifferent).' In III, ii, 230, where in F, it is three times printed *Salerio*, Capell adopts
this spelling as an abridged form of *Salerino*, which he gives in full in the stage-direction. KNIGHT approves of the distinction made by Capell, and probably thought that
he adopted it, but he did not, for he changed *Salerino* into *Salarino*. Capell's abbreviations are *Sol.* and *Sal.* Knight's are *Solan.* and *Salar.* Knight, however, does not
agree with Capell that, as to the characters 'in themselves, they're indifferent;' on the
contrary, he is of the opinion that '*Salarino* is decidedly meant for the liveliest and
the greatest talker;' wherein VERPLANCK agrees, and urges that 'this discrimination
of character, even in subordinate parts, slight as it is, is in Shakespeare's manner, and is
lost by the more equal alternation of the dialogue given by Steevens.' DYCE, STAUN-
TON, and DELIUS have followed Knight. The discussion over Steevens's third character, *Salerio*, will come more appropriately at his entrance in III, ii, 230.—ED.

5. It is not easy to see why Anthonio is represented at the outset as in this melancholy
mood. It is not his wonted mood, and yet he scarcely recovers from it throughout the
play. It is so unusual that he does not even recognize himself; nay, from being the
shrewd, long-headed merchant, the 'royal merchant,' he had become a very 'Want-
wit.' MRS GRIFFITH (p. 51) would have it that these are 'the forebodings or presentiments of evil, natural to the human mind,' which can be no more accounted for than
we can account for 'prophetic dreams.' ULRICI thinks that it is the contrast between
the real and the ideal, and the power of deceptive appearances, which have robbed
Anthonio of his gayety; he feels that 'his foreboding mind will one day fall between
the extremes of this contrast;' which I do not understand. GERVINUS says that Anthonio has the 'malady of the rich, who have been agitated and tried by nothing,' and that
he has 'the spleen.' ELZE believes that 'his wealth has blunted his feelings and made
him effeminate.' The anonymous author of *Alter Ego* (Hamburg, 1862, p. 9) would have
it that it is the prospect of losing his friend Bassanio that so weighs down Anthonio's
spirits. Bassanio had promised to tell Anthonio 'to-day' (line 131) 'the name of the
lady to whom he had sworn a secret pilgrimage;' and 'an Alpine load oppresses the
breast of Anthonio as if an irreparable loss awaited him' in thus losing his dearest
friend. MACDONALD (*The Imagination*, p. 164) points out that a melancholy disposition like Anthonio's, 'even if it be not occasioned by any definite event or object, will
generally associate itself with one; and when Antonio is accused of being in love, he
repels the accusation with only a sad "Fie! fie!" This, and his whole character, seem
to me to point to an old but ever-cherished grief.' CLARENDON says that the 'key-note
of the play' is here struck; and that this sadness without cause is a 'presentiment of
disaster: "Coming events cast their shadows before."' But this play is not a Tragedy;
it is a Comedy, wherein a tragic key-note would be falsely struck. Witches and a
blasted heath, a chilly rampart and a midnight ghost,—these are key-notes; but no
irretrievable disaster is impending here. Moreover, it is not thus that Shakespeare
deals with presentiments; he knew too well the 'lightning before death' which made
Romeo's 'bosom's lord sit lightly in his throne.' Had Shylock actually cut the flesh
from off Anthonio's breast, I doubt if Anthonio would have been here introduced as so
weighed down with sadness as to be a 'Want-wit.' I am inclined to think that the
true explanation is hinted at in a short marginal note in pencil by my lamented friend,
Prof. ALLEN, as follows: 'If Anthonio were not represented as a melancholy man and
therefore crotchety, he would not have been so extravagantly devoted to a friend, nor
would he have signed to such a bond.' Shakespeare foresaw the difficulty of represent-

I am to learne : and fuch a Want-wit fadneffe makes of
 mee,   10
That I haue much ado to know my felfe.
 Sal.   Your minde is tofsing on the Ocean,
There where your Argofies with portly faile   13

9. *I am*] As closing line 8, Ktly.
 I...learne] Sep. line, Q₃, Rowe et
seq.
 10. *mee*] Q₂.

11. *ado*] *adoe* QqF₂F₃.   *a-do* F₄.
12. Sal.] Salarino. Q₁Q₂, Wh. Rlfe.
Salar. Q₃, Var. Knt, Coll. Dyce, Sta. Glo.
Del. Ktly.

---

ing a merchant, royal among merchants, as executing a bond so hazardous in its condition that any child would shrink from signing it, and therefore introduced him as of
so changeable a mood that he was borne down by a nameless melancholy and utterly
unlike himself; and if to this we add the appellation 'Want-wit,' which he gives himself, we have the elements of character that are needed, in the scene with Shylock, to
give an air of consistency in the sealing to the bond. This melancholy, then, is, after
all, a key-note of the play, but not as portending disasters or as preluding a tragedy.—
ED.

 HUNTER (i, 299): In perusing this play we should keep constantly in mind the ideas
which prevailed in England in the time of Shakespeare of the magnificence of Venice.
Now, the name calls up ideas only of glory departed—'Her long life hath reached its
final day;' but in the age of the poet Venice was gazed on with admiration by the people
of every country, and by none with more devotion than those of England. Her merchants were princes,—her palaces were adorned with the works of Titian, and she was,
moreover, the seat of all pleasant delights—'The pleasure-place of all festivity, The
revel of the world, the masque of Italy.' Lewkenor, Moryson, and other English travellers of the age of Shakespeare, have described Venice, including Coryat, who speaks of
the palazzos of the merchants in the vicinity of the city, of the Rialto, and of the Ghetto,
one of the islands on which the Jews lived, who were in number five or six thousand.
He describes their dress; those born in Italy wearing red hats, while the Eastern or
Levantine Jews wore yellow turbans. The impression which the magnificence of Venice made upon this simple-minded but observant traveller may be judged of by the
following passage, which will at the same time serve to show how he became himself a
butt for the sharp wits of his time, so that his merit as a traveller has been too much
overlooked :—'This incomparable city, this most beautiful Queen, this untainted Virgin, this Paradise, this Tempe, this rich diadem and most flourishing garland of Christendom, of which the inhabitants may as proudly vaunt as I have read the Persians
have done of their Ormus, who say that if the world were a ring then should Ormus
be the gem thereof,—the same, I say, may the Venetians speak of their city, and much
more truly;' and he concludes with saying that 'if four of the richest manors in Somersetshire, where he was born, should have been bestowed upon him if he never saw
Venice, he would say that seeing Venice was worth them all.'

 7. **came by it**] See 'superfluity comes sooner *by* white hairs,' I, ii, 9.

 9. **I am**] ABBOTT, § 405, cites this among other ellipses after *will* and *is.* 'We
still retain an ellipsis of "under necessity" in the phrase "I am (yet) to learn."'

 12. **Ocean**] Pronounced as a trisyllable,—ABBOTT, § 479.

 13. **Argosies**] MURRAY (*New Eng. Dict.* s. v.) gives the forms of this word in
the 16th Century as *ragusye, arguze ·* from the 16th to 17th Centuries, *argose ;* in the

Like Signiors and rich Burgers on the flood,
Or as it were the Pageants of the fea,   15
Do ouer-peere the pettie Traffiquers
That curtfie to them, do them reuerence

---

14. *Burgers*] *Burgars* Q₁Q₂.
on] *of* Anon. MS (ap. Hal.) Cap.
conj. Steev. Dyce iii.
 15. *Pageants*] *Pageans* F₄.
 16. *Traffiquers*] *Traffickers* F₃F₄.

17. *curtfie*] *curfie* Q₁Q₂. *courfie* Q₃.
curt'sy'ng Allen.
   them,] *them* Q₂Q₃. *them, and*
Ktly.

17th (*rhaguse, ragosie*) *argosea, argosey, argozee ;* from the 16th to the 19th, *argosie ;* and says that it is apparently an adaptation from the Italian, *Ragusea*, plural *Ragusee*, i. e. *una* (*nave* or *caracca*) *Ragusea*, a Ragusan (vessel or carack), best represented by the earliest form *ragusye ;* the transposition in *argosea, arguze, arguzee*, &c., is no doubt connected with the fact that Ragusa (in Venetian *Ragusi*) itself appears in 16th Century English as *Aragouse, Arragouese, Arragosa*. 'That argosies were reputed to take their name from Ragusa is stated by several writers of the 17th Century; and the derivation is made inductively certain by investigations made for us by Mr A. J. Evans, showing the extent of Ragusan trade with England, and the familiarity of Englishmen with the *Ragusee*, or large and richly-freighted merchant ships of Ragusa. No reference to the ship Argo is traceable in the early use of the word.' HUNTER (i, 323): With this word Shakespeare might have become acquainted in reading Marlowe's *Jew of Malta*, in which play the word often occurs.

13–18. HUNTER (i, 324): Though this passage pleases everyone who reads it, as well by the agreeable flow of the verse as by the beautiful image it presents to the mind, of a richly laden vessel with all its sails unfurled passing in a stately manner along, it is perhaps not perfectly constructed. At least we cannot be sure that we apprehend what was the real meaning of the poet, between two meanings of which the passage admits. It may be that the argosies of Anthonio overpeer at sea the petty traffickers, just as the signiors and rich burghers do petty traffickers upon land, in which case the line, ' Or, as it were the pageants of the sea,' must be regarded as parenthetical, and as producing a slight interruption of the continuity; or it may be taken as meaning that the argosies appear upon the sea like so many signiors and rich burghers, bearing with them the ideas of wealth and abundance, and, as if that was not sufficient, he compares them again to ' pageants,' pageant ships, gorgeously decorated, such as were exhibited in the shows of the time, no longer confined to some inland lake or river, but the ' pageants of the sea ' itself, so large and so magnificent in all their apparatus.

14. on the] HALLIWELL gives a page in fac simile of extracts from a Common-place Book of the 17th Century, exhibiting some unauthorized alterations in the text of Shakespeare, and among these alterations is ' *of* the ' in this line instead of ' on the.' Capell suggests the same alteration; Steevens adopted it, as did Dyce in his third edition. Halliwell says that it is not really necessary; which is true, but I think it is really the better reading, as is shown by the very next line; just as the argosies were ' the Pageants of the sea,' so were they ' the rich Burgers of the flood.'—ED.

15. **Pageants**] DOUCE (i, 250): An allusion to those enormous machines, in the shape of castles, dragons, ships, giants, &c., that were drawn about the streets in the ancient shows or pageants, and which often constituted the most important part of them.

As they flye by them with their wouen wings.   18

   Salar.   Beleeue me fir, had I fuch venture forth,

The better part of my affections, would   20

Be with my hopes abroad.   I fhould be ftill

Plucking the graffe to know where fits the winde,

Peering in Maps for ports, and peers, and rodes:

And euery obiect that might make me feare

Misfortune to my ventures, out of doubt   25

Would make me fad.

   Sal.   My winde cooling my broth,   27

---

18. *flye*] *flie* Qq. *fly* F$_4$.
their] *theyr* Q$_2$.
19. Salar.] Salanio. Q$_1$Q$_2$, Wh. Cla.
Rlfe.   Sala. F$_2$.   Sola. F$_3$F$_4$, Rowe+.
Salan. Q$_3$, Steev. Var. Sing. Coll. Cam.
Glo. Ktly.   Sol. Cap. Solan. Dyce, Sta.
Del.
   me] *mee* Q$_2$.
   venture] *ventures* Han.
   forth] *foorth* Q$_1$.
20. *affections,*] F$_2$.

21. *abroad*] *abroade* Q$_2$. *aboard* Pope,
Han.
22. *graffe*] *graffe,* Q$_1$.
   winde] Q$_1$F$_2$Q$_3$F$_3$.
23. *Peering*] *Piering* Q$_1$. *Piring* Q$_2$
Prying Q$_3$, Pope, Han. Steev. '85.
   and peers] *for Peeres* Q$_1$. *and
piers* Johns. et seq.
27. Sal.] Salar. Qq, Steev. Mal. Var.
Knt, Sing.
   winde] Q$_1$F$_2$.

---

17. **Curtsie**] Suggested by the rocking, ducking motion in the petty traffiquers caused by the wake of the argosie as it sails past them.—ED.

21. **still**] That is, constantly. For other instances, see ABBOTT, § 69, or SCHMIDT's *Lex.*

22. **grasse**] JOHNSON cites the following from Ascham's *Toxophilus* (p. 159, ed. Arber): 'When I was in the myd way betwixt the markes whyche was an open place, there I toke a fether or a lytle lyght grasse, and so well as I could, learned how the wynd stoode,' &c.; and other instances could be cited from the same book, where the practice is frequently referred to.—ED.   KNIGHT: Though sea-weed is much more common than grass in Venice, there is enough land-vegetation in the gardens belonging to some of the palazzi to furnish the means of this experiment.

22. **sits**] ALLEN: *Sat,* (Imperf.)—by attraction,—would be normal English. 'Sits' (Pres.)—for greater vivacity is Greek.

23. **Peering**] Halliwell suggests that *Prying* of Q$_3$ was adopted to avoid the jingle with 'peers.' Unfortunately, on no other occasion does the compositor of that Qto display a similar delicacy of ear.   In one passage, however, this Qto has given us a word which several editors have adopted (see III, ii, 118, *reine* for 'raine'), and it is the sole jewel in its crown.—ED.

23. **in**] Equivalent to *into.* See ABBOTT, § 159.

23. **rodes**] CLARENDON: That is, anchorages. Cotgrave gives, '*Rade:* f. A road, an open harbor for shipping.' 'Yarmouth Roads' is the name given to the open sea off Yarmouth, where ships ride at anchor. See V, i, 304.

27. **cooling**] ABBOTT, § 452, cites two other half lines of similar scansion, viz. . 'Thy knée, | bússing | the stónes'—*Cor.* III, ·ii, 75; 'The smíle | mócking | the ս,gì '—*Cym.* IV, ii, 54, and suggests that 'the foot following the emphasized mono-

Would blow me to an Ague, when I thought   28
What harme a winde too great might doe at ſea.
I ſhould not ſee the ſandie houre-glaſſe runne,   30
But I ſhould thinke of ſhallows,and of flats,
And ſee my wealthy *Andrew* docks in ſand,   32

28. *Ague,*] ague Q₂.	32. *ſee*] see ! Ktly conj.
29. *winde*] Q₁Q₂F₃.	Andrew *docks*] Andrew *dockes* Q₁
might...ſea] Q₂FfQ₃. *at ſea,*	Arg'sie *dock'd* Han. *Andrew's decks*
might do Q₁.	Coll. conj. *Andrew, decks* Del. *An-*
30. *ſandie*] Q₂F₂Q₃.	*drew dock* Ktly. *Andrew stucke* Gould.
houre-] howre Q₁Q₂.	*Andrew dock'd* Rowe et seq.
31. *flats*] flatts Q₂.	

syllable may (as an alternative to the " pause-accent ") be regarded as quasi-trisyllabic;'
[that is, that there is an unconscious pause between the noun and its participle (here
'wind' and 'cooling'), and that this takes the place of a third syllable, whereby the
proper ictus falls on 'cooling.']

30. **houre-glaſſe**] HALLIWELL: This illustration was a very familiar one in
Shakespeare's time, when the hour-glass was an almost invariable accompaniment of
the pulpit, fixed near it on an iron stand. 'Hour-glasses for the purpose of limiting
the length of a sermon were coeval with the Reformation, as appears from the frontispiece prefixed to the Holy Bible of the Bishops' translation, imprinted by John Day,
1569. In this frontispiece, Archbishop Parker is represented with an hour-glass standing on his right hand. Clocks and watches being then but rarely in use, it was thought
fit to prescribe the length of the sermons of the Reformists to the time of an hour, that
is, the run of an hour-glass. This practice became generally prevalent, and continued
to the time of the Revolution in 1688.'—*Notes to Reprint of the Fatal Vespers*, &c.
[Halliwell subjoins a wood-cut of 'a very fine example of one still preserved in the
church of St. Alban's in Wood Street, London.']

31. **But**] ABBOTT (§ 118): A contraction for 'by-out,' and is formed exactly like
'with-out.' Hence 'but' means *excepted* or *excepting*.

32. **Andrew**] KNIGHT: Johnson explains this (which is scarcely necessary) as
'the name of the ship;' but he does not point out the propriety of the name for a
ship, in association with the great naval commander, Andrea Doria, famous through all
Italy. [This guess seems to me a little far-fetched, but none other, that I am aware
of, has ever been given. I think some proof is needed that the Italian was ever translated into English.—ED.]

32. **docks**] H. B. SPRAGUE (*Shakespeariana*, March, 1884, p. 158): Change is
needless; the meaning is more vivid, more Shakespearian, to use the present tense,
'docks,' i. e. places itself in sand as in a dock. [The alphabet contains few more
troublesome letters than *s*, whose external crookedness is typical of its internal nature
Walker, long ago, showed us how frequently it is interpolated to the marring of the
sense (see *Oth.* I, i, 31), and suggested that it might have originated in some peculiarity of Shakespeare's handwriting. It is not unlikely; but in the present play, which
in the Folio was printed from Q₂, and this again, perhaps, from a stage transcript, our
nearness to Shakespeare's own hand, with its peculiarities, is two or three times
removed. May not the confusion in this word 'docks' have arisen from the ease with
wh'ch ſ in the old Court hand can be confounded with *d* ? The top of *s* should turn

Vailing her high top lower then her ribs   33
To kiſſe her buriall ; ſhould I goe to Church
And ſee the holy edifice of ſtone,   35
And not bethinke me ſtraight of dangerous rocks,
Which touching but my gentle Veſſels ſide
Would ſcatter all her ſpices on the ſtreame,
Enrobe the roring waters with my ſilkes,
And in a word, but euen now worth this,   4C
And now worth nothing.   Shall I haue the thought
To thinke on this, and ſhall I lacke the thought
That ſuch a thing bechaunc'd would make me ſad ?
But tell not me, I know *Anthonio*
Is ſad to thinke vpon his merchandize.   45

---

33. *Vailing*] *Veyling* Q$_1$.   *Vayling*   38. *her*] *the* Q$_1$, Pope +.   *my* Anon.
Q$_2$Q$_3$.   (ap. Cam.)
     high top] *high-top* Steev.   39. *roring*] *roaring* Q$_1$Q$_3$F$_4$.
     ribs] *ribs*, Q$_1$Q$_3$F$_4$.   41. *nothing.*] *nothing ?* Q$_1$.
34. *buriall ;*] *buriall.* Q$_1$.   42. *lacke*] *lack* Q$_2$F$_3$F$_4$.
     goe] *go* Q$_1$F$_3$F$_4$.   43. *bechaunc'd*] Q$_2$.   *be-chanc'd* Q$_1$.
36. *rocks*,] *rockes*, Q$_1$F$_2$. *rocks ?* Rowe.   *bechanc'd* FfQ$_3$.

---

to the right, the top of *d* to the left; unless this turn be decided, it is not difficult to
mistake one letter for the other, which I think was done here, and that 'docks' was
really written *dockd.*—ED.]

33. **Vailing**] STEEVENS: We find in Bullokar's *Expositor*, 1621, '*Vaile bonet*. To
put off the hatte, to strike saile, to giue signe of submission.' It signifies also to *lower*,
to *let down.* Thus, in Middleton's *Blurt, Master-Constable*, 1602 [p. 248, ed. Dyce]:
'Boy, tell my love her love thus sighing spake, I'll vail my crest to death for her dear
sake.' Again, in *The Fair Maid of the West*, by Heywood, 1631 [p. 56, ed. Sh. Soc.]:
'It did me good To see the Spanish carvel vail her top Unto my maiden flag.' [Conf.
'vailed lids,'—*Ham.* I, ii, 70.]

34. **buriall**] Of course, her burial-place.

39. DYCE (ed. iii) records Lettsom's opinion that something is wanting between this
line and the next, an opinion probably founded on the difficulty of understanding the
meaning of 'this' in line 40. 'The meaning here,' says CLARENDON, 'is obscure, and
the construction abrupt, if "this" refers to the spices and silks just mentioned. As the
text stands, the actor may be supposed to complete the sense by a gesture, extending his
arms.' If this is the only explanation, and I can neither find nor offer any better, the
gesture as expressive of great wealth is, I am afraid, a little weak.—ED.

41. **thought**] That is, care, anxiety. Conf. 'pale cast of thought,' *Ham.* III. i, 85;
'Take no thought for the morrow,' *Matt.* vi, 34; 'M. Lepidus . . . who died for thought
and griefe of heart,'—Holland's *Plinie*, Bk vii, p. 186.—ED.

44. **know**] With emphasis.—ED.

45. **to thinke**] That is, *in thinking.* For an interesting and highly useful collection
of instances where '*to* is used in the sense of "for," "about," "in," "as regards," and,

Anth.   Beleeue me no,I thanke my fortune for it,   46
My ventures are not in one bottome trufted,
Nor to one place ; nor is my whole eftate
Vpon the fortune of this prefent yeere :
Therefore my merchandize makes me not fad.   50
  Sola.   Why then you are in loue.
  Anth.   Fie, fie.
  Sola.   Not in loue neither : then let vs fay you are fad
Becaufe you are not merry ; and 'twere as eafie
For you to laugh and leape,and fay you are merry   55
Becaufe you are not fad. Now by two-headed *Ianus*,
Nature hath fram'd ftrange fellowes in her time :
Some that will euermore peepe through their eyes,
And laugh like Parrats at a bag-piper.   59

46. *no,*] *no :* Q₁.
49. *yeere*] Q₂F₂.
51, 53. Sola.] Q₂Ff, Rowe+. Sala. Q₃. Sal. Cap. Salan. Mal. Steev. Coll. Sing. Ktly. Solan. Coll. iii. Salar. Q₁ et cet.
51. *Why...are*] *Then y'are* Q₁.
52. *fie.*] *fie, away !* Han.
53. *neither :*] *neither ?* Q₁. *neither !* Ff.
  let vs] *let's* Pope+, Steev. Mal.
Coll. Sing. Wh. i, Ktly, Clarke, Del. Dyce iii, Huds.
53, 55. *you are*] *you're* Pope+, Dyce iii, Clarke, Rlfe, Huds.
54. *and*] Om. Pope, Han. *an* Knt.
56. *Because you are*] *'Cause you're* Han. Dyce iii.
57. *fram'd*] *framd* Q₂.
59. *Parrats*] *Parrots* F₄.
  bag-piper] *bagpyper* Q₂. *Pagpiper* Q₃.

in a word, for any form of the gerund as well as for the infinitive,' see ABBOTT, § 356. Conf. 'make moan to be abridged,' I, i, 136, *post*, and 'To winde about my love,' &c., I, i, 164; and 'I will not shame myself to give you this,' IV, i, 451.

47. KNIGHT: This was no doubt proverbial,—something more elegant than 'all the eggs in one basket.' Sir Thomas More, in his *History of Richard III*, has : 'For what wise merchant adventureth all his good in one ship ?'

48, 49. **is . . . Vpon**] ALLEN suggests that there is no ellipsis here, but that 'is upon' may perhaps be equivalent to *exists upon*.

50. Shakespeare was such an absolute master over his slave, rhythm, that one is tempted to doubt whether there be not some subtle reason, other than rhythmical, for his frequent transpositions, as here, 'makes me not sad,' or 'touching but my gentle vessels side,' line 37.—ED.

51. **Sola.**] WHITE speaks for the majority of the editors in pronouncing Q₁ to be here right in giving the speech to Salarino, 'as the more loquacious of Anthonio's two friends, and juſ ⸱fter the entrance of Bassanio he declares that he had intended to banter Anthonio inⱶ good spirits.'

52. DYCE (ed. iii) : I have little doubt that Shakespeare wrote ' *In love !* fie, fie !'

56. **Janus**] ECCLES: He swears by that divinity, whose image exhibits a represen‐ tation of either kind of countenance, the laughing and the sad.

58. **peepe**] WARBURTON : As in laughing, when the eyes are half shut.

And other of fuch vineger afpeĉt,   60
That they'll not fhew their teeth in way of fmile,
Though *Neſtor* fweare the ieſt be laughable.

    *Enter Baſſanio, Lorenſo,*and *Gratiano.*

    Sola.   Heere comes *Baſſanio,*
Your moſt noble Kinſman,   65
Gratiano, and *Lorenſo.*   Faryewell,
We leaue you now with better company.
    Sala.   I would haue ſtaid till I had made you merry,
If worthier friends had not preuented me.
    Ant.   Your worth is very deere in my regard.   70
I take it your owne buſines calls on you,
And you embrace th'occaſion to depart.
    Sal.   Good morrow my good Lords.   (when?
    Baſſ.   Good ſigniors both, when ſhall we laugh? ſay,
You grow exceeding ſtrange : muſt it be ſo?   75

---

60. *other*] *others* Pope+.
    vineger] *vinigar* Q_2.   *viniger* Q_3.
vinegar $Q_1F_2F_4$.
61. *they'll*] *theyle* Q_2.
63. *Enter...*] After line 72, Dyce, Sta.
Clarke, Huds.
    Lorenſo] Lorenzo. Rowe.
64. Sola.] Q_2Ff.   Sala. Q_3.   Sal.
Rowe+.   Sol. Cap.   Solan. Knt, Dyce,
Sta. Del. Coll. iii, Huds.   Salan. Q_1 et cet.

66. *Faryewell*] *Fare ye well* $Q_3F_3F_4$.
Fare you well Cap. Steev. Mal. Knt,
Coll. Sing. Sta.
67. *you*] *ye* Pope, Theob. Warb.
68. Sala.] $Q_2F_2F_3$.   Salan. Q_3.   Sola.
F_4, Rowe+.   Sal. Cap.   Salar. Q_1 et cet.
71. *buſines calls*] *buſineſſe cals* Q_1.
72. *th'*] *the* Q_1.
73, 76. Sal.] Q_2Ff, Rowe+.   Salar.
Q_1 et cet.

---

60. **other**] For other instances of this singular used as a plural, see ABBOTT, § 12.

60. **aspect**] For a long list of words in which the accent was formerly nearer the end than now, see ABBOTT, § 490.

61. **in way**] For other instances of the omission of *the*, see ABBOTT, § 89.

62. **Nestor**] CLARENDON: The oldest, and therefore presumably the gravest, of heroes.

62. **swear**] ALLEN: Possibly, *sware ;* i. e. had sworn, or, should have sworn.

69. **preuented**] WORDSWORTH (*Sh. Knowl. and Use of the Bible*, p. 40): That is, anticipate. See 1 *Thess.* iv, 15 : 'We which are alive shall not prevent them which are asleep.' Also *Ps.* cxix, 148 : 'Mine eyes prevent the night-watches.'

75. **exceeding**] ROLFE: This adverbial use is frequent in Elizabethan writers. Shakespeare uses 'exceedingly' only five times, in four of which it modifies the adverb *well*, while in the fifth (*Ham.* V, ii, 103) it modifies an adjective *understood*.

75 **strange**] CLARENDON: In modern English we should say : 'You are becoming quite strangers.'

75. **Must it be so ?**] Of course the first, and perhaps the only, interpretation of these words is that they apply to the infrequency of the intercourse between Bassanio

Sul.   Wee'll make our leyfures to attend on yours.   76
Exeunt Salarino, and Solanio.
Lor.   My Lord *Baffanio,* fince you haue found *Anthonio*
We two will leaue you, but at dinner time
I pray you haue in minde where we muft meete.   80
Baff.   I will not faile you.
Grat.   You looke not well fignior *Anthonio,*
You haue too much refpect vpon the world :
They loofe it that doe buy it with much care,
Beleeue me you are maruelloufly chang'd.   85
Ant.   I hold the world but as the world *Gratiano,*
A ftage, where euery man muft play a part,   87

76. *Wee'll*] *Weele* Q₂Q₃.
77. Exeunt...] After line 81, Rowe+.
Exeunt...Solanio] Exeunt...Sa-
lanio Q₁Q₃, Mal. Steev. Coll. Wh. Cam.
Exeunt...Solar. and Sala. Rowe+.
78. Lor.] Lord. Ff. Sola. Rowe+.

78. *you haue*] *you've* Pope+, Dyce ii,
Rlfe, Huds.
81. *you.*] *you.* Exit. Q₁.
84. *doe*] *do* Q₁F₃F₄.
85. *maruelloufly*] *meruailoufly* Q₁Q₂.
mervelloufly Q₃.
87. *man*] *one* Q₁, Pope ii.

and 'the good signiors both,' but may they not refer to the leave-taking of Salarino and Solanio? As they are close to the door, or to the parting of the ways, after having actually bade Anthonio farewell, Bassanio sees how hopeless it is to detain them, and, in effect, says, 'Must you really go now?' To me this short phrase reads like one of the many which Shakespeare uses to supply the place of stage-directions.—ED.

78. **Lor.**] The misprint here in F₂ of *Lord* was repeated by F₃ and F₄, and still further sophisticated by Rowe, who changed it to *Sola.*, and was therein heedlessly followed by every editor down to Capell, and the *Exeunt* of Salarino and Solanio transferred to the end of line 81. Capell, however, restored the speech of Lorenzo, because, as he says, 'Lorenzo enters with a design of retiring, having executed the purpose he came for, to wit—the finding of Anthonio; but such a sudden and silent departure not suiting with his companion, he is kept a while 'till the other has gratify'd his passion for talking, and, that done, repeats at [line 115] his declaration in this speech, and soon after puts it in execution.'—ED.

78. **Anthonio**] One of the numberless instances of the rhythmical shortening of polysyllabic names, to which no further reference will be hereafter made,—perhaps it is needless even here. See ABBOTT, § 469.—ED.

83. **vpon**] ABBOTT, § 191: In this use of 'upon' there is an allusion to the literal meaning of 'respect.' 'You *look* too much *upon* the world.' The 'upon' is connected with 'respect,' and is not used like our *for* in 'I have no respect *for* him.'

84. **loose**] Steevens considers this a misprint for *lose*, strangely enough, because no one was better acquainted than Steevens with the fact, which Halliwell notes, that it is merely the old spelling of *lose*, and is of continual occurrence. See I, iv, 28.—ED.

84. WORDSWORTH (p. 343): This appears to be founded upon *Matt.* xvi, 25: 'Whosoever will save his life shall lose it.' ['It' refers to the opinion of the world.—ED.]

87. **stage**] STEEVENS: See Sidney's *Arcadia*, book ii: 'She found the world but a

And mine a sad one.   88

   Grati.   Let me play the foole,

With mirth and laughter let old wrinckles come,   90

And let my Liuer rather heate with wine,

Then my heart coole with mortifying grones.

Why should a man whose bloud is warme within,

Sit like his Grandsire, cut in Alablaster?

Sleepe when he wakes? and creep into the Iaundies   95

88. *mine*] *mine's* Han. Warb.	90. *wrinckles*] *wrinkles* Q₁. *wrinckes*
89. Grati.] Gra. Q₁.	Q₃.
89, 90. *foole,...laughter*] *fool...laugh-*	92. *heart*] *hart* Q₂. *heat* F₂F₃.
ter; Rowe, Pope, Han.	94. *Alablaster*] *Alabaster* Pope.
90. *let old*] *so let* Han.	95. *Iaundies*] *Jaundies* F₃. Jaundies
	F₄. *jaundice* Rowe ii.

wearisome stage to her, where she played a part against her will.' ROLFE: See the famous passage: 'All the world's a stage,' *As You Like It,* II, vii.

88. **sad**] WALKER (iii, 52): 'Sad' is *grave.* [Unquestionably. See *post,* II, ii, 193: 'Well studied in a sad ostent To please his Grandam,' and many another instance given by SCHMIDT.—ED.]

89. **foole**] WARBURTON: Gratiano desires to play the Fool's or buffoon's part which was a constant character in the old farces; from whence came the phrase, 'to play the fool.'

90. **With**] Here used causatively.

90. **old**] HALLIWELL: Gratiano here means to refer to old age, which he desires may be reached with joy and laughter; or he is possibly merely alluding to the wrinkles caused by mirth, in which case the epithet 'old' is the common augmentative. 'Some Dick, that *smiles* his cheek *in years,*' *Love's Lab. Lost,* V, ii, 465.

92. **mortifying**] Used in its literal sense, like *extravagant* in *Othello,* I, i, 149, or *fantastical* in *Macbeth,* I, iii, 139, or, perhaps as 'mortified' in the latter play, V, ii, 5. The belief that groans were 'mortifying' Shakespeare shared in common with his age; he refers to it more than once. 'Dry sorrow drinks our blood,' *Rom. & Jul.* III, v, 58; 'a spendthrift sigh, That hurts by easing,' *Ham.* IV, vii, 128; 'sighs that cost the fresh blood dear,' *Mid. N. D.* III, ii, 97; 'Look pale as primrose with blood-drinking sighs,' 2 *Hen. VI:* III, ii, 63.—ED.

94. **Grandsire**] Under this respectful appellation our German brothers seem to have detected some merry jest. Voss, Schlegel, Bodenstedt, and even Schmidt, have translated it '*Grosspapa.*'—ED.

94. **Alablaster**] MURRAY (*New Eng. Dict.*): The spelling in the 16th–17th Centuries is almost always 'alablaster;' apparently due to a confusion with *arblaster,* a cross-bowman, also written *alablaster.*—*Note* on *Oth.* V, ii, 7.

95. **Iaundies**] BUCKNILL (p. 92): In this whole passage the intimate connection between mind and body is sketched with exact physiological truth. Perhaps the most curious and undoubted instance of the mind's influence in the production of bodily disease, is jaundice caused by depressing emotion. It is not always 'crept' into, since bad news has frequently been known to cause jaundice in a few hours. In Copland's *Dict. of Medicine* it is stated that 'The most common exciting causes of jaundice are the more violent mental emotions,' and in the list of these emotions, which he adds, he specially

By being peeuifh ? I tell thee what *Anthonio*,   96
I loue thee, and it is my loue that fpeakes :
There are a fort of men, whofe vifages
Do creame and mantle like a ftanding pond,
And do a wilfull ftilneffe entertaine,   100
With purpofe to be dreft in an opinion
Of wifedome, grauity, profound conceit,

97. *it is*] *tis* Qq, Han.   100. *wilfull ftilneffe*] *wilful ftilnes* Q₄
    fpeakes :] *fpeakes.* Q₁.   102. *grauity*] *grauitie* Q₂.
99. *creame*] *dreame* Q₁.

includes 'peevishness.' In Watson's *Lectures on Physic*, that able physician states that among the causes of jaundice 'the *pathemata mentis* play their assigned part; fits of anger and fear and alarm have been presently followed by jaundice.' This curious medical fact Shakespeare has here sketched with exact fidelity. The effect of wine on the temperature of the liver, and despondency on that of the heart, are also unquestionably medical thoughts. ROLFE: The only other passage in which Shakespeare mentions the jaundice the cause is, as here, a mental one. See *Tro. & Cress.* I, iii, 2.

96. In the Folio, the page beginning with this line is wrongly numbered 162, instead of 164; so also the opposite page is 163, instead of 165; after this, the pagination is correct.—ED.

100. do] CLARENDON: That is, 'And *who* do.' Not unfrequently in Shakespeare the pronoun requires to be mentally repeated in order to complete the construction. See *1 Hen. IV:* II, iv, 279 : 'We two saw you four set on four and bound them, and were masters of their wealth.' A somewhat similar inaccuracy occurs also in the present scene, 108, 109.

100. wilfull stilnesse] MALONE: That is, an obstinate silence.

101. opinion] CLARENDON: That is, reputation for wisdom. 'Opinion' is used in the same sense in line 112.

102. grauity] HALLIWELL: This fine passage, observes Dr Dodd, always puts me in mind of a remark made by Dryden: 'There are, who wanting *wit*, affect *gravity*, and go by the name of solid men; and a *solid man* is, in plain English, a solid, solemn fool.'

102. conceit] CRAIK (*Jul. Cæs.* I, iii, 162): To *conceit* is another form of our still familiar to *conceive*. And the noun 'conceit,' which survives with a limited meaning (the conception of a man by himself, which is so apt to be one of over-estimation), is also frequent in Shakespeare with the sense, nearly, of what we now call *conception*, in general. Sometimes it is used in a sense which might almost be said to be the opposite of what it now means; as when Juliet employs it as the term to denote her all-absorbing affection for Romeo, II, v, 30. Or as Gratiano uses it here—that is, in the sense of *deep thought*. So again when Rosaline, in *Love's Lab. Lost*, II, i, speaking of Biron, describes his 'fair tongue' as 'conceit's expositor,' all that she means is that speech is the expounder of thought. The Scriptural expression, still in familiar use, 'wise in his own conceit,' means merely wise in his own thought, or in his own eyes, as we are told in the margin the Hebrew literally signifies. [Cf. the title of the First Quarto of *Rom & Jul.:* 'The Excellent conceited Tragedie,' &c.]

As who fhould fay, I am fir an Oracle,
And when I ope my lips, let no dogge barke.
O my *Anthonio*, I do know of thefe   105
That therefore onely are reputed wife,
For faying nothing ; when I am verie fure
If they fhould fpeake, would almoft dam thofe eares   108

103. *fir an*] F_2F_3. *fir, an* F_4, Rowe. *fir* Qq et cet.

104. *dogge*] *dog* $Q_1F_3F_4$.

105. *thefe*] *thofe* Q_1, Pope+.

107. *when*] *who* Rowe+, Cap. Steev. Mal. Knt, Sta. Huds.

107. *I am*] *I'm* Pope+, Dyce ii, Huds.

108. *would*] *'twould* Coll. (MS), Ktly, Dyce ii.

dam] Q_1Q_2. *dant* Q_3. *damme* F_2F_3. *doom* Clarke. *damn* F_4 et cet.

---

103. **who**] ABBOTT (§ 257, after citing *Macb.* III, vi, 42; *Rich. II:* V, iv, 8, and *Mer. of Ven.* I, ii, 45): In these passages it is possible to understand an antecedent to 'who,' 'as, or like (one) who should say.' In Early English (Morris, *Specimens*, p. xxxii) 'als *wha* say' was used for 'as *any one* may say.' Comp. the Lat. *quis* after *si*, *num*, &c. Possibly an *if* is implied after the 'as' by the use of the subjunctive. Littré explains 'comme qui dirait' by supplying 'celui.' 'Il portait sur sa teste comme qui dirait un turban; c'est-à-dire, il portait, comme dirait celui qui dirait un turban.' But this explanation seems unsatisfactory, in making a likeness to exist between 'carrying' and 'saying.' But whatever may be the true explanation of the original idiom, Shakespeare seems to have understood *who* as the relative, for the antecedent can be supplied in all passages where he uses it.

103. **sir an Oracle**] WHITE (ed. i): The absence of a capital letter in the 'sir' is remarkable in the Folio,—which, in this respect, is very carefully printed,—even if not in the Quartos. I believe the 'sir oracle' of the Quartos which has been universally adopted, to be the result of accident, and that the change in the Folio is intentional and by authority. 'Sir Oracle' is so awkward an effort in nomenclature, and a specimen of so cheap a sort of wit, that I for one am quite willing to take the testimony of the authorized edition, that it is none of Shakespeare's. But being one of those phrases which save people the trouble of thinking and finding words for themselves, it has become almost a part of the language; and to disturb the text would, under the circumstances, be a thankless work of supererogation. [I think it is a little too severe to say that the phrase is popular because it saves the trouble of thinking or of finding words. There is a certain pomposity in 'Sir Oracle' which befits the character and which speaks to all. Yet it is this very pomposity which gives it a disagreeable tone and makes me wish that the Folio were right, which it cannot be, I fear, in its present unrhythmical line, unless we suppose, with ALLEN, that the indefinite article was slurred in pronunciation: 'I am, sir, 'n Oracle.'—ED.]

106, 107. WORDSWORTH (p. 241): Conf. 'Even a fool when he holdeth his peace is counted wise; and he that shutteth his lips is esteemed a man of understanding.'—*Prov.* xvii, 28.

108. **would**] The omission of the nominative, when the sense will readily supply it, is so common that no change is needed here. See *Ham.* II, ii, 67; III, i, 8; *Lear* II, ii, 143; II, iv, 41; IV, ii, 76, V, i, 67; or ABBOTT, § 399. COLLIER (ed. ii) adopted his (MS) change *'t would*, but doubted if change were necessary. CLARENDON suggests that 'the clause "If they should speak," equivalent to "their speaking,"

Which hearing them would call their brothers fooles :
Ile tell thee more of this another time.   110
But fifh not with this melancholly baite
For this foole Gudgin, this opinion :
Come good *Lorenzo*, faryewell a while,
Ile end my exhortation after dinner.

 Lor. Well, we will leaue you then till dinner time. 115
I muft be one of thefe fame dumbe wife men,
For *Gratiano* neuer let's me fpeake.

 Gra. Well, keepe me company but two yeares mo,
Thou fhalt not know the found of thine owne tongue.

 Ant. Far you well, Ile grow a talker for this geare. 120

---

112. *foole Gudgin*] *foole Gudgion* Ff.
fool's gudgeon Pope+, Steev. Var. *fool-
gudgeon* Mal. Coll. Sing. Dyce, Sta. Wh.
i, Ktly, Rlfe, Huds.

113. Lorenfo] Lorenfo Q_2Q_3.
faryewell] *farwell* Q_1.

113. *a while*] *awhile* Coll.
116. *dumbe wife*] *dumb-wise* Huds.
118. *mo*] F_2F_3. *moe* QqF_4, Cam. Glo.
Clarke, Del. Rlfe. *more* Rowe et cet.
120. *Far you well*] Q_2. *Farwell* Q_1.
Fare you well FfQ_3. *Fare well* Pope+.

---

serves for subject to the following verb.' I think the simpler way is to suppose that
'they' is carried forward from 'should' to 'would.'—ED.

 108. **damn**] THEOBALD : That is, That some people are thought wise, whilst they
keep silence ; who, when they open their mouths, are such stupid praters, that the hearers cannot heip calling them 'fools' and so incur the judgment denounced in the Gospel [*Matt.* v, 22].

 111. **melancholly baite**] ALLEN (MS) suggests (rightly, I think) that this is a
genitive of apposition ; it should therefore be printed with a hyphen, and its meaning
would be *this bait of melancholy*, that is, *this melancholy as a bait.* The same would
apply to 'foole gudgin,' and so Malone printed it in 1790. The whole sentence is,
then, 'fish not with this melancholy as a bait for this gudgeon of the fool.' Eccles,
however, prints *fool-gudgeon*, and evidently understands 'fool' as an adjective ; 'that
is,' he says, 'a gudgeon foolish enough to be taken with such a bait,' whereby the point
is not given which I think the sentence bears. It is not the folly of the gudgeon that
is in question, but that 'this opinion' is the worthless gudgeon that only fools care to
fish for. SCHMIDT (*Lex.*) also takes 'fool' as an adjective, and there is, to be sure,
some warrant for it in the similar phrase 'fool multitude,' *post*, II, ix, 28 ; but I doubt
if the sense here admits of a similar interpretation.—ED.

 116. **dumbe wife men**] WALKER (ii, 139) : Write *dumb-wise;* for 'dumb wife
men' would be pronounced *dumb wisemen.*

 120. **Ile**] ALLEN (MS) : That is, *I will*, not *I shall.* Gratiano thanks him for the
resolution.

 120. **geare**] ECCLES : That is, 'I'll grow a talker for this time,' or 'upon this particular occasion.' NARES defines the word as meaning, in general, 'matter, subject,
or business in general ; often applied to dress also.' DYCE gives it three meanings :
dress ; matter in hand, business [as in the present instance] ; stuff.' SCHMIDT divides
its meanings under two heads : 'stuff' [as in the present instance] ; and 'affair, matter.

Gra. Thankes ifaith, for filence is onely commendable   121
In a neats tongue dri'd, and a maid not vendible.   *Exit.*

Ant. It is that any thing now.

Baf. *Gratiano* fpeakes an infinite deale of nothing,
more then any man in all Venice, his reafons are two   125

---

121. *ifaith*] *yfaith* Q₂Q₃. *i'faith* F₄.
122. *tongue*] *togue* Q₂.
  vendible] *vendable* Q₁Q₃.
  Exit.] Exeunt. Qq.
123. *It is that...now.*] *It is that.*

...*now?* Ktly. *Is that...now?* Rowe et
cet.

124. *nothing,*] *nothing* Q₂.
125. *are*] Ff, Rowe, Knt. *are as* Qq
et cet.

---

business.' [All of which confirms the truth of what Steevens said long ago—that 'it
is a colloquial expression perhaps of no very determinate import.' The sense demanded
by the context must in each case be our guide; in B. and Fl.'s *The Scornful Lady*,
II, i, Sir Roger says of tobacco, 'it is notable stinging gear indeed.' I am not sure
that our colloquial word 'stuff,' as given by Dyce and Schmidt, herein following Johnson's *Dict.*, does not very nearly correspond to 'gear.'—ED.] HALLIWELL: It has
been unnecessarily proposed to alter 'gear' to *jeer* or *year;* and another critic to *fear,*
the last one referring it to the fear of not knowing the sound of his own tongue. [See
also *post*, II, ii, 159.]

121, 122. These two lines ABBOTT, § 490, scans thus: Thanks fáith, | for sílence |
is ónly | comménd | ablé. In a néat's | tongue dríed | and a máid | not vénd | iblé.
The lines may be some jingle current at that time, but now lost.—ED.

123. JOHNSON: I suppose we should read: 'Is that anything *new?*' STEEVENS:
The sense of the old reading is, Does what he has just said amount to anything, or
mean anything? TYRWHITT: Anthonio asks: Is that *any thing* now? and Bassanio
answers, that Gratiano speaks an infinite deal of *nothing,*—the greatest part of his discourse is *not any thing.* COLLIER [whose text reads, 'It is that:—any thing now.']
says: This is the reading of Q₁, Q₂, and F₁, and it is preserved in F₂. Surely, therefore, we are not warranted in altering the text when a clear meaning can be made out
of it. Antonio's observation, 'It is that,' is addressed to Gratiano, concurring in his
remark just before he made his *exit;* and then Antonio's bad spirits return upon him,
and he adds, as if weary of Gratiano's talk, 'any thing now.' This naturally leads to
Bassanio's criticism upon Gratiano. [Collier gives the words of the Qq and Ff correctly, but the punctuation is wholly his own; there is not even a comma in the original.—ED.] LETTSOM [ap. Dyce, ed. iii]: 'It' appears to me a mere blunder for
'*I,*' i. e. *Ay!* an ironical interjection. As to the rest of this short speech, nothing can
be more awkward than 'is that any thing' for '*is there any thing in that?*' and 'now'
is worse than superfluous. On the other hand, it may be said against Johnson's conjecture *new,* that it does not so exactly accord with Bassanio's phrase, 'an infinite deal
of nothing.' It is, however, quite common for speakers to wrest the meaning of a preceding speech for the sake of a retort; when this happens in a written dialogue, it is
only an imitation of nature; but it is a fault in the writer to prepare the way for a retort
by previously introducing awkward phraseology. [I think Rowe's emendation must be
adopted. I can make nothing of the original text, which I am afraid I cannot see is
aided by Lettsom's change.—ED.]

125. **are two**] It may be that *as* of the Qq is here omitted through the compos-

graines of wheate hid in two buſhels of chaffe : you ſhall   126
ſeeke all day ere you finde them, & when you haue them
they are not worth the ſearch.

 An. Well : tel me now, what Lady is the ſame
To whom you ſwore a ſecret Pilgrimage   130
That you to day promis'd to tel me of?

 Baſ. Tis not vnknowne to you *Anthonio*
How much I haue diſabled mine eſtate,
By ſomething ſhewing a more ſwelling port
Then my faint meanes would grant continuance :   135
Nor do I now make mone to be abridg'd
From ſuch a noble rate, but my cheefe care
Is to come fairely off from the great debts
Wherein my time ſomething too prodigall
Hath left me gag'd : to you *Anthonio*   140
I owe the moſt in money, and in loue,
And from your loue I haue a warrantie
To vnburthen all my plots and purpoſes,
How to get cleere of all the debts I owe.

 An. I pray you good *Baſſanio* let me know it,   145

129. *the*] *this* Han. Sing. Ktly.   Rowe.
134. *ſomething ſhewing*] *ſhewing some-* 136. *mone*] Q₂F₂.
thing Pope+.   138. *off*] *of* Q₂.
 135. *grant*] *graunt* Q₂.   142. *warrantie*] Q₂Q₃.
 continuance] *continuance* *to* 145. *An.*] *Antho.* Q₁.

itor's carelessness, but it is doubtful if the sentence be not a little stronger without
it.—ED.

 126. **you shall**] ABBOTT, § 315 : ' You *shall* see, find,' &c., was especially common
in the meaning ' you may ;' ' you will' applied to that which is of common occurrence,
or so evident that it *cannot but be* seen. Cf. *Oth.* I, i, 44.

 129. **the same**] I cannot but think that Hanmer is here right in printing *this
same.*—ED.

 131. **That**] It is hard to say whether this refers to ' lady' or ' pilgrimage.'—ED.

 134. **Something**] See line 139 ; *Ham.* III, i, 173 ; *Lear,* I, i, 20, or ABBOTT, § 68,
for other instances of this adverbial use like *somewhat.*

 134. **port**] STEEVENS : External pomp of appearance, state.

 135. **continuance**] CLARENDON : That is, continuance *of.* Such omissions are frequent in Shakespeare. See II, vi, 11 ; III, iv, 8 ; IV, i, 406 ; and see ABBOTT, § 394.

 136. **to be**] See I, i, 45.

 139. **time**] SCHMIDT defines this simply by *life ;* but ALLEN notes that it is equivalent to ὥρα, when ὥρα means the springtime of life, youth, manhood.—ED.

 140. **gag'd**] HALLIWELL : That is, *pledged ;* not a contraction of *engaged.*

 145. **it**] That is, the plot or purpose.

And if it ſtand as you your ſelfe ſtill do,   146
Within the eye of honour, be aſſur'd
My purſe, my perſon, my extreameſt meanes
Lye all vnlock'd to your occaſions.

    Baſſ. In my ſchoole dayes, when I had loſt one ſhaft   150
I ſhot his fellow of the ſelfeſame flight
The ſelfeſame way, with more aduiſed watch
To finde the other forth, and by aduenturing both,   153

146. *ſtand*] *stands* Rowe.
147. *aſſur'd*] *aſſurd* Q₂. *aſſured* Q₁.
149. *vnlock'd*] *vnlockt* Qq.
150. *dayes, when*] *dayes. when* Q₁.
151, 152. *ſelfeſame*] *ſelfe-ſame* Q₁.
ſelfe ſame Q₂Q₃.
153. *the other forth,*] *the other foorth,*

Q₁. *the other, forth;* Han. *the other;*
Cap.

    153. *and by aduenturing*] *by ;ent'ring*
Pope+. *and, venturing* Dyce conj.
    aduenturing] *aduentring* Q₂,
Cap. Steev. '85, Mal.

---

146. **still**] That is, *constantly, always.* STAUNTON was, I think, the first to call
attention to this meaning of 'still,' instances of which are innumerable in Shakespeare.

147. **eye of honour**] ECCLES: If it be of such a nature that *honour* may be supposed to keep a continual watch over it, or, rather, perhaps, if it be such as needs not
at any time shrink from the view of *honour.* CLARENDON: That is, within the scope
of honour's vision, within the limits of that which can be regarded as honourable.
ALLEN: Cf. *1 Hen. IV:* I, i, 81, 'The theme of Honour's tongue.'

150, &c. STEEVENS: Compare Dekker's *Villanies discovered by Lanthorne and
Candlelight:* 'And yet I haue seen a Creditor in Prison weepe when he beheld the
Debtor, and to lay out money of his owne purse to free him: he shot a second arrow to
find the first.' [I have searched in vain for this passage in Grosart's edition; even if
it could be found, it would be useless; the date of the pamphlet is 1609, and therefore
subsequent to the *Mer. of Ven.* Steevens cites from the edition of 1616, wherein it is
possible the passage appears.—ED.] DOUCE cites a passage from 'P. Crescentius in
his treatise *de Agricultura,*' and another from Howell's *Letters,* where this method of
finding an arrow is referred to; and COLLIER, to the same effect, cites from *Quips upon
Questions,* published in 1600.

151. **flight**] Ascham, in his *Toxophilus* (B. p. 152, ed. Arber), lays it down, as a
rule, that 'a perfyte archer muste firste learne to knowe the sure flyghte of his shaftes.'
With this knowledge it would be possible, of course, as Bassanio says, to choose a 'fellow of the selfsame flight.' CLARENDON calls attention to another passage in Ascham
[B. p. 131, ed. Arber], where this word 'flight' is used in precisely the same sense
which it has here :' 'You must haue diuerse shaftes of one flight,' &c.—ED.

152. **aduised**] DYCE: That is, deliberate. [See II, i, 48, and 'advice,' IV,
ii, 8.]

153. **To finde**] Cf. I, i, 45.

153. **forth**] CRAIK (*Jul. Cæs.* p. 40, 2d ed.): *To find forth* may, I apprehend, be
safely pronounced to be neither English nor sense. The 'forth' has apparently been
transferred from the preceding line, which was either originally written 'The same way
forth,' or, more probably, was so corrected after having been originally written 'The
selfsame way.' STAUNTON: It may not be English of the present day, but it was

2

I oft found both.   I vrge this child-hoode proofe,

Becaufe what followes is pure innocence.   155

I owe you much, and like a wilfull youth,

That which I owe is loft : but if you pleafe

To fhoote another arrow that felfe way

Which you did fhoot the firft, I do not doubt,   159

---

156. *wilfull*] *witless* Warb. *wasteful* Coll. (MS).

---

thought good sense and good English in the time of Shakespeare.   'Forth' here
means *out*, and with this import it is used in the following, and in a hundred other,
instances : *Com. of Err.* I, ii, 37, where we have again the identical expression to
'find forth;' *Two Gent.* II, iv, 186 [and here in this play, line 153.   See Schmidt's
Lex.]

153. Various expedients have been devised to rid this line of its superfluous foot.
Capell omits 'forth;' Pope omits 'and' while contracting 'adventuring' to *vent'ring;*
Dyce proposes to omit 'by' and change 'adventuring' to *venturing;* Lloyd (ap. Cam.)
proposes to substitute *him* for 'the other;' and Abbott, § 466, would soften 'other' to
a monosyllable.   The line is unquestionably ungainly in length, but it runs throughout
smoothly, and having a pause after the third foot, I imagine that Shakespeare's ear was
satisfied; I doubt if there be need of change.—ED.

154. **child-hoode proofe**] WALKER (iii, p. 53) : Compare 'All school-days' friendship, childhood innocence,' *Mid. N. D.* III, ii, 202.   [For many other instances where
the first of two nouns may be treated as a genitive used adjectively, see ABBOTT, § 22
or § 430.]

155. **pure innocence**] DR JOHNSON interprets 'pure innocence' as 'without disguising his former faults or his present designs.'   ECCLES : 'I bring as an example in
proof of the probable success of the proposed expedient, one of the practices of *childhood*, because my designs, as to everything to come, are as *innocent* and harmless as
any of the purposes of youth in this kind of boyish amusement.'   [I think it is by no
means certain that 'pure innocence' does not here mean *pure foolishness*.   Bassanio
assuredly was aware how flimsy was his pretext for Anthonio to send more good money
after bad, and that his best argument was drawn from childish games, and therefore
does not attempt to disguise the 'innocence' (in its frequent meaning of *childishness,
foolishness*) of his proposal.   Moreover, the greater the folly of the risk, the greater
the proof of Anthonio's friendship in assuming it.—ED.]

156. **wilfull youth**] HEATH : It has happened to me, as it generally doth to a
wilful youth, I have squandered away what I am now a debtor for.   ECCLES : That is,
'that which, like a wilful youth, I owe, is lost.'   CLARENDON : 'Wilful' here means
obstinate in extravagance.   ROLFE : 'Wilful' in his prodigality.   SCHMIDT : 'Wilful,'
i. e. regardless, reckless, saucy.   In the present instance, 'like a reckless boy I confess
to you.'   [It seems to me that we need but give due weight to both syllables of 'wilful,' to have a meaning ample to fit the case.   I doubt the correctness of Schmidt's
interpretation.—ED.]

158. **selfe**] Compare 'by self and violent hands,' *Macb.* V, viii, 70; 'I am made
of that self metal as my sister,' *Lear*, I, i, 68; or ABBOTT, § 20; or for many other
instances, SCHMIDT'S *Lex.*   CLARENDON says that this use of 'self' is frequent in
Chaucer, and prevailed as late as Dryden's time.

As I will watch the ayme : Or to finde both,   160
Or bring your latter hazard backe againe,
And thankfully reſt debter for the firſt.
   An. You know me well, and herein ſpend but **time**
To winde about my loue with circumſtance,
And out of doubt you doe more wrong   165
In making queſtion of my vttermoſt
Then if you had made waſte of all I haue :
Then doe but ſay to me what I ſhould doe
That in your knowledge may by me be done,
And I am preſt vnto it : therefore ſpeake.   170
   Baſſ. In *Belmont* is a Lady richly left,

---

160. *ayme :*] *ayme* Q₁Q₂. *ayme,* Q₃,   165. *doe more*] *do to me more* Ff, Rowe.
Rowe et seq.   *do me now more* Qq et cet.
161. *hazard backe*] *hazzard bake* Q₂.   167. *waſte*] *waſt* Q₂.
164. *winde*] *wind* Q₂Ff.

---

160. **As**] ABBOTT, § 110 : '*As*, in its demonstrative meaning of *so*, is occasionally found parenthetically equivalent to 'for *so*.' See I, iii, 76 : 'As his wise mother wrought in his behalf,' i. e. '*for so* did his mother work.' [See also *Ham.* IV, iii, 58 ; *Ib.* IV, vii, 159 ; *Ib.* V, ii, 323.]

160, 161. **Or . . . Or**] See ABBOTT, § 136. This use of *or . . . or* is very frequent in B. & Fl. It is almost superfluous to call attention to the defective punctuation in line 160. The colon after 'ayme' was changed to a comma in Q₃.—ED.

164. **To winde**] That is, *in winding*. See I, i, 45.

164. **circumstance**] HALLIWELL : This line appears to have been imitated in Cooke's play of *Greene's Tu Quoque*, or *The Cittie Gallant : 'Old Geraldine.* You put us to a needless labour, sir, To run and wind about for circumstance ; When the plain word, "I thank you," would have serv'd,' [p. 283, Dodsley's *Old Plays*, ed. Hazlitt. DYCE (*Gloss.*) defines 'circumstance' by *detail*, as does also SCHMIDT ; but in Cotgrave we find '*Circuition de paroles.* A circumlocution, paraphrase, great circumstance of words, a going about the bush.'—ED.]

170. **I am**] By an error of the press, this is printed *am I* in the Var. 1778, and the error is continued in the Var. 1785. MASON (p. 73) corrected it, and in doing so quoted the phrase as, 'am I prest to serve you,' taking no note whatever of his own change of 'unto' into *to serve*, which the Cam. Ed. accredits to him as a conjectural emendation. Was it not a mere oversight ?—ED.

170. **prest**] The best definition of this word, which, although by no means uncommon in early writers, is found in Shakespeare only here and in *Pericles*, IV, Prologue, 45, is, I think, obtained from Cotgrave, who gives it as the translation of the same word in French : '*Prest : m. preste : f.* Prest, readie, full-dight, furnished, prepared, prouided, prompt, neere at hand, quick, nimble, fleet, wight.' Steevens gives several instances of its use in the sense of *ready*, and says that he could add twenty more ; but Staunton doubts (I think, needlessly) whether it is not used in this present passage in the sense of *bound* or *urged*.—ED.

·And fhe is faire, and fairer then that word,   172
Of wondrous vertues, fometimes from her eyes
I did receiue faire fpeechleffe meffages :
Her name is *Portia*, nothing vndervallewd   175
To *Cato*'s daughter, *Brutus Portia*,
Nor is the wide world ignorant of her worth,
For the foure windes blow in from euery coaft
Renowned futors , and her funny locks
Hang on her temples like a golden fleece,   180
Which makes her feat of *Belmont Cholchos* ftrond,
And many *Iafons* come in queft of her.
O my *Anthonio*, had I but the meanes
To hold a riuall place with one of them,
I haue a minde prefages me fuch thrift,   185
That I fhould queftionleffe be fortunate.

173. *vertues,*] *vertues.* Q$_1$.
    fometimes] *sometime* Theob. Han.
Cap.
174. *receiue*] *receaue* Q$_2$.
175. Portia,] Portia; Q$_1$.
    vndervallewd] *vnder-valew'd* Q$_1$.

181. Cholchos] Colchos Q$_1$.
    ftrond] *strand* Johns. Steev. et
seq.
182. *come*] *comes* Q$_1$.
184. *riuall place*] *rival-place* Pope,
Han.

172. **fairer**] ECCLES : The meaning is, that simply to declare that she was 'fair' was a commendation not adequate to the perfection of her beauty. Perhaps these words are to be considered as having a relation to those which follow; as if she was to be esteemed 'fairer' in the possession of those 'wond'rous vertues' which adorn her mind, than in that of so many personal charms.

173. **sometimes**] THEOBALD : This should certainly be *sometime*, i. e. formerly, some time ago, at a certain time; and it appears by a subsequent scene that Bassanio was at Belmont with the Marquis de Montferrat, and saw Portia in her father's lifetime. FARMER : In old English 'sometimes' is synonymous with *formerly*. Nothing is more frequent in title-pages than '*sometimes* fellow' of such a college. CLARENDON : 'Sometimes' and 'sometime' are often used by Shakespeare indifferently, with the signification *formerly, in time past*. See *Rich. II:* I, ii, 54, 'Thy sometimes brother's wife.' So also in the Authorized Version, *Ephesians*, ii, 13 : 'Ye who sometimes were far off.' [Conf. *Oth.* II, ii, 38 : 'What an eye she has! Methinks it sounds a parley to provocation;' also *Tro. & Cress.* IV, v, 55 : 'There's language in her eye.']

176. **To**] ABBOTT, § 187 : *To*, even without a verb of motion, means 'motion to the side of.' Hence 'motion to and consequent rest near.' See 'Impostors to true fear,' *Macb.* III, iv, 64. [Thus in the present passage Portia will be found not inferior when brought to the side of, and compared with, Brutus's Portia. So also *post*, II, vii, 54. Being ten times vndervalued to tride gold.']

181. **ftrond**] CLARENDON : This was once, doubtless, the pronunciation of *strana*. Another allusion to the expedition of the Argonauts is found in this play, III, ii, 254.

185. **minde presages**] For many other instances of the omission of the relative, see ABBOTT, § 244.

Anth. Thou knowſt that all my fortunes are at ſea, 187
Neither haue I money, nor commodity
To raiſe a preſent ſumme, therefore goe forth
Try what my credit can in *Venice* doe, 190
That ſhall be rackt euen to the vttermoſt,
To furniſh thee to *Belmont* to faire *Portia.*
Goe preſently enquire, and ſo will I
Where money is, and I no queſtion make
To haue it of my truſt, or for my ſake. *Exeunt.* 195

[*Scene II.*]

Enter Portia with her waiting woman Neriſſa.

Portia. By my troth *Nerriſſa*, my little body is a wearie of this great world. 3

188. *Neither*] *Nor* Pope+, Steev. '85.
189. *ſumme,*] *ſumme.* Q₁.
190. *credit*] *credite* Q₂.
[Scene II. Belmont. Rowe et seq.
[Three Caskets are set out, one of gold, another of silver, and another of lead. Rowe+. A Room in Portia's House.

Cap.
1. Enter...] Enter Portia and Nerrissa. Rowe et seq.
Neriſſa] Nerriſſa Qq.
2. Nerriſſa] Neriſſa F₃F₄.
a wearie] *awearie* Q₂Q₃. *weary* F₃F₄, Rowe+. *aweary* Cap. et seq.

188. **Neither**] For many instances where '*either, neither, whether, mother, brother,* and some other dissyllables in which the final *ther* is preceded by a vowel,—perhaps in some measure, all words in *ther*,—are frequently used either as monosyllables, or as so nearly such that in a metrical point of view they may be regarded as monosyllables,' see WALKER, *Vers.* p. 103; ABBOTT, § 466; or BROWNE, p. 10. CLARENDON says that this speech of Antonio is 'scarcely consistent with what he had previously said' (lines 46–50), that his 'whole estate' was not placed 'upon the fortunes of this present yeere.'

188. **commodity**] See SCHMIDT, s. v., for instances of the use of this word in the meanings of *convenience* (as in III, iii, 32); of *profit, advantage;* of *merchandise* (as here); and of *quantity of wares, parcels.*

193. **presently**] That is, at once, immediately.

195. **of**] ABBOTT, § 168: 'Of,' meaning *from*, passes naturally into the meaning *resulting from, as a consequence of.* ECCLES: That is, either raise it upon my credit, or obtain it on account of the affection entertained for me by the lender.

2. LADY MARTIN (p. 33): Although Portia is heart-whole, yet she is not 'fancy free.' We learn from Nerissa that in her father's time there was one visitor, a 'Venitian, a scholar, and a soldier,' whom Nerissa considered of all men the 'best deserving a fair lady.' Portia responds very briefly, but suggestively: 'I remember him well; and I remember him worthy of thy praise.' Often, no doubt, has she wondered why he has not presented himself among her suitors. Unconsciously, perhaps, the languor of hope deferred speaks in these first words we hear from her. The one who ſhe thought might possibly have been among the first comers, comes not at all.

2. **a wearie** This is, of course, merely a compositor's uncouth way of setting up

Ner.   You would be fweet Madam , if your miferies
were in the fame abundance as your good fortunes are :   5
and yet for ought I fee, they are as ficke that furfet with
too much, as they that ftarue with nothing ; it is no fmal
happineffe therefore to bee feated in the meane, fuper-
fluitie comes fooner by white haires, but competencie
liues longer.   1C

Portia.   Good fentences,and well pronounc'd.

Ner.   They would be better if well followed.

Portia.   If to doe were as eafie as to know what were
good to doe, Chappels had beene Churches, and poore
mens cottages Princes Pallaces: it is a good Diuine that   15
followes his owne inftruƈtions; I can eafier teach twentie what were good to be done, then be one of the twen-   17

---

5. *abundance*] aboundance Q₂.

6. *furfet*] furfeite Q₂.

7, 8. *it...therefore*] F₂F₃, Knt, Wh. i,
Huds. *Therefore it is no small happiness* F₄, Rowe, Pope, Han. *therefore it
is no mean happiness* Theob. Warb. Johns.

it is no mean happineffe therefore Qq et
cet.

9. *but*] *and* Han.

15. *it*] *He* Pope+.

17. *be*] *to be* Qq, Rowe, Pope, Theob.
Warb. Johns.

---

awearie.   The preposition *a*, here used as a prefix, conveys in this instance the idea
of *state.*   See MURRAY'S *New Eng. Dict.* s. v. II : 'as *a live, a sleep, a work, a jar,
a thirst, a blaze, a fright, a float, a stare.*   In these the word governed by *a* was originally a noun, e. g. *life, sleep, work, float* ("on the Mediterranean flote"—*Temp.* I, ii,
234), but being often the verbal substantive of state or act, it has been in modern times
erroneously taken as a verb, and used as a model for forming such adverbial phrases
from any verb, as *a-wash, a-blaze, a-bask, a-swim, a-flaunt, a-blow, a-dance, a-run,
a-stare, a-gaze, a-howl, a-tremble, a-shake, a-jump.*   These are purely modern and ana-
logical.'   [We have *agazed* in *1 Hen. VI:* II, iv, 126.—ED.]   ABBOTT, § 24, p. 35 ·
In *a-weary* it can scarcely be said that *weary* is a noun.   Rather '*a*-weary,' like '*of*-
walked,' means '*of*-weary,' i. e. 'tired out.'

7. **with**] ALLEN (MS): 'With' is explained by '*in* the mean' (in the next line),
and is equivalent to *apud, chez, by.*

7. **smal**] The reading of the Qq, *mean*, is much to be preferred ; in the Ff, as
CLARENDON says, the play upon the word 'mean' is lost.

9. **comes sooner by**] WRIGHT (*Bible Word-Book*): To get, acquire.   Conf. 'we
had much work to come by the boat.'—*Acts*, xxvii, 16.   'Translation it is . . . . that
remooueth the couer of the well, that we may come by the water.'—*The Translators
to the Reader.*   See also in this present play, I, i, 7, 'how I caught it, found it, or
came by it.'

9. **but**] I cannot say that I see the force of this adversative 'but;' Hanmer changed
it to *and*, which seems the more fitting word.—ED.

11. **sentences**] CLARENDON : That is, maxims.   ALLEN (MS) : *Sententiæ,* γνῶμαι.

15. **it is a good Diuine, &c.**] WORDSWORTH (p. 264) : An observation which
must find an echo in every clergyman's breast.

tie to follow mine owne teaching : the braine may de- 18
uiſe lawes for the blood, but a hot temper leapes ore a
colde decree, ſuch a hare is madneſſe the youth, to skip 20
ore the meſhe⁊ of good counſaile the cripple ; but this
reaſon is not in faſhion to chooſe me a husband : O mee,
the word chooſe, I may neither chooſe whom I would,
nor refuſe whom I diſlike, ſo is the wil of a liuing daughter curb'd by the will of a dead father : it is not hard *Ner-* 25
riſſa, that I cannot chooſe one, nor refuſe none.

    Ner. Your father was euer vertuous, and holy men 27

18. *mine*] *my* Theob. Warb. Johns.
19. *ore*] *over* Steev. Mal. Sing. Ktly.
21. *counſaile*] Q₂F₂Q₃. *counſell* Q₁.
22. *reaſon*] Ff, Rowe. *reaſoning* Qq
et cet.
    in] *the* Mason.

22. *faſhion*] Ff, Rowe. *the faſhion*
Qq et cet.
    husband :] *husband;* Q₁. *hus-*
band, Q₂Q₃.
23, 24. *whom...whom*] *who...who* Qq.
25. *it is*] *is it* QqFf et cet.
    Nerriſſa] Neriſſa Q₁F₃F₄.

18. **braine**] BUCKNILL (p. 93) : The tyranny of desire over reason is here stated physiologically : the 'blood' in this sense being always used poetically for the prompt- ings of animal passion. A better knowledge has indeed exploded the theory, and attributed both reason and passion to the brain, though to different parts of it.

22. **reason is not in**] After noting that the reading of the Qq : 'this reasoning is not in the fashion,' has been 'universally' deemed correct, WHITE adds that he is not 'prepared positively to dissent from this decision; although, had there been no Qq, the text of F₁ is sufficiently clear and sufficiently in accordance with the usage of Shake- speare's day not to have needed emendation.' On the other hand, CLARENDON pro- nounces 'reason' of F₁ 'a manifest error.' [I quite agree with White as to the need- lessness of emendation, and am inclined to go even farther and regard the reading of F₁ as being, so far from a 'manifest error,' the better of the two. 'Reason' here is not ratiocination, which is what 'reasoning' is, and what Portia, having stated merely facts, has not attempted, but is used, as in many another passage, in the sense of *speech, dis- course, talk ;* just as it is used later in this very play, where Salarino says, 'I reason'd with a Frenchman yesterday'—II, viii, meaning simply 'I talked with a Frenchman.' Thus, here, Portia exclaims, according to F₁, 'But all this talk will never pick out a husband for me.' The omission of the indefinite article, or even the definite article, in 'in fashion' for 'in *a* fashion,' or 'in *the* fashion,' is common enough; see ABBOTT, §§ 82, 90.—ED.] On the meaning of the whole passage, ECCLES remarks : Perhaps Portia designs to insinuate that maxims of prudence, such as those uttered at first by Nerissa, relative to the insufficiency of superabundant wealth to procure happiness to the possessor, and afterward expressed by herself upon the difference between specula- tive and practical wisdom, might, indeed, be of use to others, by inspiring them with caution in the choice of a husband, but could afford no advantage of such nature to her, who is precluded, by the determination of her father, from any exercise of her judgment upon that subject.

24, 25. **wil . . . will**] CLARENDON: Shakespeare, *more suo,* plays upon the twc senses of 'will.'

at their death haue good infpirations, therefore the lot-   28
terie that hee hath deuifed in thefe three chefts of gold,
filuer, and leade, whereof who choofes his meaning,   30
choofes you, wil no doubt neuer be chofen by any rightly, but one who you fhall rightly loue : but what warmth
is there in your affeĉtion towards any of thefe Princely
futers that are already come?

    Por. I pray thee ouer-name them, and as thou nameft   35
them, I will defcribe them, and according to my defcription leuell at my affeĉtion.   37

28. *lotterie*] *lottry* Q₁Q₃. *lottrie* Q₂. *lottery* Ff.   Glo. Cla. Huds. *whom you* Pope+, Coll. Clarke.

31. *wil...neuer*] *no doubt you wil neuer* Q₁.

32. *who you*] *who* Q₁, Johns. Cam.

35. *pray thee*] *prethee* Q₁. *nameſt*] *nam'ſt* Pope+.

36. *deſcription*] *deſcription,* Q₁Q₃F₃F₄.

32. The Folio here follows the Second Quarto. CLARENDON adopts the First Quarto as 'the higher authority.' I prefer it as giving us the better text, although this very passage has been cited by FURNIVALL as an instance of its inferiority to Q₂, in so far as it 'leaves out a necessary word.' (*Forewords to Q₁*, p. v.) In the text before us 'the lotterie' is nominative to 'will no doubt neuer be chosen,' and the sense is that the lottery will be sure to fall on some one whom Portia 'rightly loves;' and that this is the right meaning, says ROLFE, appears from the question which follows : 'What affection have you for any of the suitors that are *already* come?' On the contrary, I think the very point of Nerissa's comforting is lost in the present text. The very idea of the lottery was a holy inspiration, the choice of a husband is committed to Heaven, and he who is the right husband for Portia will know how to choose the right casket, he cannot choose the wrong one; no unfit husband will have the sterling qualities to choose the right one. And this is the text of Q₁. It reads : 'no doubt you wil neuer be chofen by any rightly, but one who fhall rightly loue.' 'Who' is the nominative, in sense as well as in form; not the accusative ('who' is often enough used for *whom*, but not here). That this is the true meaning Portia herself tells us, I think, in plain words, where she says to Bassanio (III, ii, 44), '*If you do love me, you will find me out.*' His capacity to find her is the very test of his 'rightly' loving her. The punctuation of Q₁ should be amended by a full stop before the sentence I have given above, thus : 'holy men .... have good inspirations, therefore [i. e. hence there is] the lottery that he hath devised .... whereof who chooses his meaning chooses you. No doubt you will never,' &c. As both the Quartos were issued in the same year and were probably printed by the same man, the question of superiority is a nice one, and can be determined only by a careful weighing of the texts. In the present instance I think the scales turn decidedly in favour of Q₁.—ED.

35. thee] For the use of *thou* and *you*, see *Oth.* II, ii, 275, in this edition, where SKEAT's general rule is given : '*Thou* is the language of a lord to a servant, of an equal to an equal, and expresses also companiouſhip, love, permission, defiance, scorn, threatening; whilst *ye* is the language of a servant to a lord, and of compliment, and further expresses honour, submission, entreaty.'—*Preface to William of Palerne*, p. xlii. Seє also ABBOTT, §§ 231, 232.

Ner.   Firſt there is the Neopolitane Prince.   38

Por.   I that's a colt indeede, for he doth nothing but
talke of his horſe, and hee makes it a great appropria-   40
tion to his owne good parts that he can ſhoo him himfelfe : I am much afraid my Ladie his mother plaid falſe
with a Smyth.

Ner.   Than is there the Countie Palentine.   44

38. *Neopolitane*] *Neapolitane* Q₁F₂.
Neapolitan F₃.   *Neopolitan* F₄.
39. *colt*] *Dolt* Theob. Han.
40, 41. *appropriation to*] *appropriation*
vnto Q₁. *approbation of* Coll. ii. (MS).
41. *him*] Om. Q₁.
42. *afraid*] *afeard* Q₁Q₂, Cap. Cam.
Glo. Cla. Wh. ii.   *afear'd* Q₃.

43. *Smyth*] *ſmith* Q₁.
44. *Than*] Q₂.
        is there] *there is* Q₁, Pope +, Cam.
Glo. Cla. Wh. ii.
        Countie] Q₂.   *County* Q₁.   *Count*
Pope +.
44, 57. *Palentine*] Q₂FfQ₃, Rowe
Palatine Q₁, Pope et seq.

37. **leuell**] That is, *aim at*.   It is here the imperative.

38. **Neopolitane**] STEEVENS : The Neapolitans, in the time of Shakespeare, were
eminently skilled in all that belongs to horsemanship.   MALONE : Though our author,
when he composed this play, could not have read the following passage in Florio's
translation of Montaigne's *Essaies*, 1603, he had perhaps met with the relation in some
other book of that time : 'While I was a young lad,' says old Montaigne, 'I saw the
prince of Salmona, at Naples, manage a young, rough, and fierce horse, and show all
manner of horsemanship ; to hold testons or reals under his knees and toes so fast as if
they had been nayled there, and all to show his sure, steady, and immoveable sitting.'

39. **colt**] JOHNSON : 'Colt' is used for a witless, heady, gay youngster, whence the
phrase is used of an old man too juvenile that he still retains his *colt's tooth*.

40. **appropriation**] COLLIER (*Notes & Emend.* p. 113) : This is altered by the
(MS) to *approbation of*, in the sense of proof,—a great *proof of* his own good parts,
&c.   *Approbation* is not unfrequently used by Shakespeare for probation ; whereas, if
'appropriation' were his word, this is the only place where he has employed it.   SINGER
(*Sh. Vind.* p. 32) : 'Appropriation to' is equivalent to *addition to* his other accomplish-
ments.   Nothing can be concluded from this being the only instance of Shakespeare's
use of the word.   DYCE called this substitution by Collier's (MS) 'cool,' but COLLIER,
in his Second Ed., adopted it and pronounced it 'excellent.'   In his Third Ed. he
silently relinquished it (as he relinquished so many other of his (MS) emendations in
his venerable age), and returned to 'appropriation.'—ED.

41. **shoo him himself**] Q₁ omits 'him,' a common enough compositor's oversight.   Rather than present all the more noticeable variations between Q₁ and Q₂ in
a dry and appalling table in the Appendix, I prefer to give a few lines to them, here
and tnere, as they occur, on the same page with the text.   In the Appendix (p. 275)
will be found a recapitulation of many of these variations, wherefrom a conclusion may
be drawn as to the relative excellence of each Qto.   I do not hesitate to avow my
preference for Q₁, albeit on the title-page of Prætorius's *Reprint of Q₂*, London, 1887,
it is stated to be that of 'The Second (and better) Quarto.'—ED.

44. **Countie Palentine**] JOHNSON : The Count here mentioned was, perhaps,
Albertus a Lasce, a P ⸱ish Palatine, who visited England in our author's lifetime, was
eagerly caressed and splendidly entertained ; but running in debt, at last stole away,

Por. He doth nothing but frowne (as who ſhould   45
ſay, and you will not haue me, chooſe : he heares merrie
tales and ſmiles not, I feare hee will proue the weeping
Phyloſopher when he growes old, being ſo full of vn-
mannerly ſadneſſe in his youth.) I had rather to be married to a deaths head with a bone in his mouth, then to ei-   50
ther of theſe : God defend me from theſe two.
Ner. How ſay you by the French Lord, Mounſier
Le Boune ?   53

---

46. *and*] Ff Q₃. *if* Q₁, Pope+, Cam.
Glo. Cla. Huds. Wh. ii. *&⁾* Q₂. *An*
Cap. et cet.

48. *Phyloſopher*] Q₂. *Philoſopher* Q₁.
49. *to be*] Ff, Rowe. *be* Qq et cet.

50. *deaths head*] *Deathſ-head* Q₃.
52. *Mounſier*] *Monſieur* Rowe.
53. Boune] QqF₂. Boun F₃F₄, Rowe+.
Bon Cap. et seq.

---

and endeavored to repair his fortune by enchantment. MALONE: County and Count
were synonymous.   The Count Alasco was in London in 1583.   CLARENDON: The
visit of Albert a Lasco, or Laski, took place when our author was still in Stratford, and
so long before the production of this play that the allusion would be unintelligible to
the audience. HALLIWELL: There was another County Palatine, who married the
daughter of James I, and who was a frequent spectator of the plays of Shakespeare,
when they were exhibited before the Court; but the present allusion, appearing in the
original editions, can scarcely be applicable to that personage, unless he had visited
England previous to the accession of his future father-in-law.

45. **as who**] See I, i, 103.

46. **and**] For 'and' equivalent to *if*, see ABBOTT, § 101, and for *and if*, see *Ib.*,
§ 105.

46. **choose**] What has *frowning* to do with an alternative choice? What is the
threat that is here implied?   I confess I do not understand the connection of thought.
Does it mean, 'If you will not have me, I don't care, take your choice?' or is it, 'If
you will not have me, let it alone?'   This is the sense in which Schlegel, endorsed by
Schmidt, translates it: 'wenn ihr mich nicht haben wollt, so lasst's !' and this same
sense Schmidt retained when, in his invaluable *Lexicon*, he gives the passage under a
meaning of the verb *to choose*, as 'to do at one's pleasure.'   Although several other
instances are there given under this head, only two of them seem to me fairly ger-
mane, viz: *Tam. of the Sh.* V, i, 48, and *Merry Wives*, I, i, 316.   In the herme-
neutical torture to which one always subjects a puzzling phrase, it has even occurred to
me that, modifying the punctuation, it might read, in view of the Countie's black looks,
'If you will not have me choose—' i. e. if you will not suffer me to make trial of the
caskets—take the consequences !—ED.

47. **weeping Phylosopher**] CLARENDON: That is, another Heraclitus.

49. **to be married**] For the infinitive after 'I had rather,' see *Oth.* I, iii, 217, in this
edition; or ABBOTT, § 349.

52. **by**] See ABBOTT, § 145, for other instances where 'by' means *about, concerning.* See also 'That many may be meant By the foole multitude,' II, ix, 28, where, as
I think, 'by' is used idiomatically after 'mean,' and is, perhaps, not exactly parallel to
the present usage.—ED.

Pro.   God made him, and therefore let him paſſe for a
man, in truth I know it is a ſinne to be a mocker, but he,   55
why he hath a horſe better then the Neopolitans, a better bad habite of frowning then the Count Palentine, he
is euery man in no man, if a Traſſell ſing, he fals ſtraight
a capring, he will fence with his own ſhadow. If I ſhould
marry him, I ſhould marry twentie husbands : if hee   60
would deſpiſe me, I would forgiue him, for if he loue me
to madneſſe, I ſhould neuer requite him.

Ner.   What ſay you then to *Fauconbridge,* the yong
Baron of *England* ?

Por.   You know I ſay nothing to him, for hee vnder-   65
ſtands not me, nor I him : he hath neither *Latine, French,*

54. Pro.] F₂.

55. *a ſinne*] *ſinne* F₂F₃. *ſin* F₄.

56. *Neopolitans*] *Neapolitans* Q₁Ff.

58. *Traſſell*] Qq. *Tarſſell* F₂. *Taſſell*
F₃. *Taſſel* F₄, Rowe. *throstle* Pope et
seq.

58. *ſtraight*] *ſtraght* Q₂.

62. *ſhould*] Ff, Rowe, Pope, Han.
ſhall Qq et cet.

63. *you*] Om. Cap. (corrected in Errata).

64. *Baron*] *Barron* Q₂.

56, 57. **better bad**] This is not a '*better-bad* habit,' as HALLIWELL thinks, whose
note is, '*better* is here used as an intensative, without the usual implication of goodness; *better bad,* that is, worse ;' but it is a 'better *bad-habit,*' and so, I think, it should
be printed in a modernized text.—ED.

58. **Trassell**] All modern editions follow Pope in changing this to *throstle,* and with
propriety; but it is not to be supposed that 'trassell' is a misprint; it is merely the
phonetic spelling of *throstle.*—ED.

59. **a capring**] For other instances of this prefix *a,* see ABBOTT, § 24.

62. **should**] Despite the editorial unanimity with which the *shall* of the Qq has been
preferred to this 'should,' I cannot but think that the Folio is right, and that in *shall*
some of the sparkle of Portia's fun is lost.   She is not foretelling the state of her
affection for a future husband, but her capacity to love twenty husbands, all of them
loving her to madness; such a multitudinous love as that, she would never be able to
requite.—ED.

65. **say**] CLARENDON : Portia playfully uses the phrase 'say to' in a different sense
from that which Nerissa meant.

66. **neither Latine**] STAUNTON : This satirical allusion to our ignorance in 'the
tongues' has not yet lost all its point.

PROELSS (*Kauf. von Ven. Erläutert,* 1875, p. 128) : It is to be inferred from this
passage that, in Shakespeare's time, a knowledge of these three languages was an indispensable requisite of a man of culture ; Portia laughs at the Baron for his ignorance
of them.   It would have been impossible for Shakespeare to hold up to ridicule this
ignorance, had he himself come under the same condemnation.   [A shrewd remark,
which will neutralize a page at least of Dr Farmer's *Essay,* which was written to prove
Shakespeare's ignorance of these very languages.—ED.]

nor *Italian*, and you will come into the Court & fweare   67
that I haue a poore pennie-worth in the *Englifh* : hee is a
proper mans picture, but alas who can conuerfe with a
dumbe fhow ? how odly he is fuited, I thinke he bought   70
his doublet in *Italie*, his round hofe in *France*, his bonnet
in *Germanie*, and his behauiour euery where.

 Ner. What thinke you of the other Lord his neigh
bour ?

 Por. That he hath a neighbourly charitie in him, for   75
he borrowed a boxe of the eare of the *Englifhman*, and
fwore he would pay him againe when hee was able : I   77

---

67. *will*] *may* Pope+.
68. *the*] Om. Rowe.

73. *other*] Ff, Rowe. *Scottifh* Qq et
cet.

77. *fwore*] *fworne* F₂.

---

 67. you will] ABBOTT, § 320: Perhaps this means 'you are willing and prepared.'
 67. Court] CLARENDON: You will bear me witness that I have but a very small
stock of English.
 69. proper mans picture] STEEVENS: 'Proper' means *handsome.* STAUNTON:
The word with this import is so common, that it is needless to give examples; they
may be found in every play of the time. ALLEN (MS) suggests that it should be
printed 'proper man's-picture;' [wherein I agree with him; in which case I think that
'proper' is to be taken in the sense of *very*, just as it is in 'though our proper son stood
in your action.'—*Oth.* I, iii, 84.—ED.]
 71. doublet . . . round hose] HALLIWELL: 'If you aske why I have put him in
rounde hose, that usually weares Venetians, it is because I would make him looke more
dapper, and plump, and round upon it.'—Nash's *Have with You to Saffron Walden*,
1596. CLARENDON: Planché (*Hist. of Brit. Costume*, p. 266) quotes from Stubbs:
'The French hose are of "two divers making; the common sort contain length,
breadth, and sideness sufficient, and they are made very *round.*"' On p. 267 Planché
describes the quilted doublet, and adds: 'These bombasted doublets formed a point in
front . . . . to this day the dress of our friend Punch, whose wardrobe of Italian origin
dates as nearly as possible from this identical period.'
 73. other] THEOBALD: This word was substituted for *Scottifh* of the Qq, for fear of
giving offence to King James's countrymen. CAPELL (ii, 59): 1598, if not earlier, is the
date of this play's birth; at which time, Portia's gentle wipe upon Scotland, and upon
France, her almost constant ally in all her quarrels with England, in which neither were
very fortunate, sounded gratefully enough in ears that had very likely been witnesses [*sic*]
to some of those 'boxes' [line 76], perhaps actors in them: but things altering shortly
after upon the Scottish accession, a change of one of the quoted words [Scottish], in
way of softening, is found in the player editor's copy [i. e. F₁]; but when made, or by
whom, we have no foundation for guessing. COLLIER (ed. ii): In the (MS) *Irish* is
substituted for 'Scottish.' 'A suggestion,' says HALLIWELL, 'which is at variance with
Portia's subsequent allusion to the Frenchman, and which would have been more appropriate to the first portion of her reply had the comedy been written after the Irish rebel
lion in 1641 '

thinke the *Frenchman* became his furetie, and feald vnder   78
for another.

Ner.   How like you the yong *Germaine*, the Duke of   80
Saxonies Nephew?

Por.   Very vildely in the morning when hee is fober,
and moft vildely in the afternoone when hee is drunke:
when he is beft, he is a little worfe then a man, and when
he is worft, he is little better then a beaft : and the worft   85
fall that euer fell, I hope I fhall make fhift to goe without him.

Ner.   If he fhould offer to choofe, and choofe the right
Casket, you fhould refufe to performe your Fathers will,
if you fhould refufe to accept him.   90

Por.   Therefore for feare of the worft, I pray thee fet
a deepe glaffe of Reinifh-wine on the contrary Casket,
for if the diuell be within, and that temptation without,   93

---

82. *vildely*] *vildlie* Q_2.   *vildly* Q_3.   *the* Han.   *an the* Cap. et cet.
83. *vildely*] *vilely* Q_1.   *vildly* Q_2.   91. *pray thee*] *prethee* Q_1.
videly Q_3.   *widely* Herr.   92. *Reinifh-wine*] *Reynifh Wine* $Q_1 Q_3$.
85. *and the*] QqFf, Rowe+.   *and,*   *Reynifhe vvine* Q_2.   *Rennifh-wine* $F_3 F_4$.

78. **Frenchman**] WARBURTON: Alluding to the constant assistance, or rather constant promises of assistance, that the French gave the Scots in their quarrels with the
English.

79. **for another**] CLARENDON: That is, for another box on the ear.   The principal
was said to 'seal to' a bond; his surety 'sealed under.'

80, &c. JOHNSON: Perhaps in the enumeration of Portia's suitors there may be some
covert allusion to those of Queen Elizabeth.

85. **and**] Equivalent to *if*, as noted by CAPELL.

89, 90. **should**] ABBOTT, § 322: *Should* is the past tense of *shall*, and underwent
the same modifications of meaning as *shall*.   Hence *should* is not now used with the
second person to denote mere futurity, since it suggests a notion, if not of compulsion,
at least of bounden duty.   But in a conditional phrase, 'If you *should* refuse,' there
can be no suspicion of compulsion.   We therefore retain this use of *should* in the conditional clause, but use *would* in the consequent clause: 'If you *should* refuse, you *would*
do wrong.'   On the other hand, Shakespeare used *should* in both clauses [as here].

92. **Reinish-wine**] Doubtless this wine is mentioned because of the young German,
but HALLIWELL gives an extract from Fynes Moryson's *Itinerary*, 1617, in which it is
said that the Germans only 'sometimes and rarely drinke Rhenish wine,' but 'commonly beere.'   In Arber's *English Garner* there is an account by Dean William Tur-
ner of the different wines drunk in England in 1568, wherein the Dean, who was also
a Doctor of Physic, says that 'the Rhenish wine that is commonly drunken in gentlemen's houses and citizens' houses is commonly a year old at the least, before it be
drunken: and therefore it is older than the common clared wine, which dureth not
commonly above one year.'—ED.

I know he will choofe it.   I will doe any thing *Nerriſſa*
ere I will be married to a fpunge.   95

Ner.   You neede not feare Lady the hauing any of
thefe Lords, they haue acquainted me with their determinations, which is indeede to returne to their home,
and to trouble you with no more fuite, vnleffe you may
be won by fome other fort then your Fathers impofiti-   100
on, depending on the Caskets.

Por.   If I liue to be as olde as *Sibilla*, I will dye as
chafte as *Diana* : vnleffe I be obtained by the manner
of my Fathers will : I am glad this parcell of wooers
are fo reafonable, for there is not one among them but   105
I doate on his verie abfence : and I wifh them a faire departure.   107

---

94. Nerriffa] Neriffa Q₁F₃F₄.
95. *I will*] *ile* Q₁.
97. *determinations*]   *determination*
Rowe, Ktly.
100. *your*] *you* F₂.

103. *chafte*] *chaft* Q₂F₄.
106. *I wiſh them*] F₂, Knt, Wh. i,
Rlfe. *wish them* F₃F₄, Rowe+. *I pray
God grant them* Qq (*graunt* Q₂) et
cet.

---

96. **the hauing**] For other instances of *the* preceding a verbal that is followed by
an object, see ABBOTT, § 93.

97. **determinations**] ALLEN (MS) : One expects (even in Shakespeare) *determination*, for it means that *one* determination which is common to all; and it is strange to
have 'home' just after, where *homes*, i. e. their respective homes, would be natural.
Cf. 'leave,' line 121.   [See Text. Notes.]

100. **sort**] WHITE : Here used in its radical sense; *sors*, a lot.   CLARENDON : It is
thus used in *Tro. & Cress.* I, iii, 376.   In the present instance the phrase means—by
some other method or manner.   ROLFE : It may be as White suggests.   [Whereto I
also agree, but possibly White, having in mind the phrase ' by lot,' may have been influenced here by the use of ' *by* some other sort.'   Conf. in Portia's next speech, ' *by* the
manner.'—ED.]

102. **Sibilla**] CLARENDON : Used erroneously as if it were a proper name.   So in
Tam. Shr. I, ii, 70: ' As old as Sibyl.'   But Shakespeare speaks of ' nine sibyls,'
I *Hen. VI :* I, ii, 56, and in *Oth.* III, iv, 74.   ROLFE : So Bacon, in *Colours of Good
and Evil,* 10, speaks of ' *Sybilla*, when she brought her three books,' and in *Adv. of
Learn.* ii, 23, 33, of ' Sybillæ's books.'   The reference here is to the Cumæan Sibyl,
who obtained from Apollo a promise that her years should be as many as the grains
of sand she was holding in her hand.   The story is told by Ovid, *Met.* xv.

103. **chaste**] WHITE : It is to be feared that a vicious and unfounded use of this
word, which has long prevailed, has produced in some minds a deplorable confusion
of thought.   Chastity and continence are far from being identical; the one is a virtue,
the other is not.   An honorable matron is as chaste as a maid; Diana was no chaster
than Penelope, and Portia as chaste after she was Bassanio's wife as before.   It is but
due to our own wives and mothers to say at least so much upon this passage.

106. **I wish**] See Textual Notes.   COLLIER : The Qq were printed befcre the Act

Ner. Doe you not remember Ladie in your Fa-   108
thers time, a *Venecian,* a Scholler and a Souldior that
came hither in companie of the Marqueſſe of *Mount-*   110
ferrat?

Por. Yes, yes, it was *Baſſanio,* as I thinke, ſo was hee
call'd.

Ner. True Madam, hee of all the men that euer my
fooliſh eyes look'd vpon, was the beſt deſeruing a faire   115
Lady.

Por. I remember him well, and I remember him worthy of thy praiſe.

Enter a Seruingman.

Ser. The foure Strangers ſeeke you Madam to take   120
their leaue : and there is a fore-runner come from a fift,

---

109. *a Scholler*] Scholler Q₁.

110. *hither*] hether Q₂.

112. *ſo was hee*] he was ſo Q₁, Pope, Cam. Glo. Cla. *ſo he was* Steev. '85.

118. *praiſe.*] Ff, Rowe, Knt, Wh. Rlfe.

praiſe. How now, what newes ? Qq et cet.

120. *ſeeke you*] Ff, Rowe. *ſeeke ſor you* Qq et cet.

Madam] Madame Q₁. *maddam* Q₂.

---

3 Jac. I, c. 21 [1605], against using the name of the Creator on the stage, Yet, else-where, the Folio has 'God forbid,' 'God rest his soul,' and other expressions where the name of the Creator occurs. WHITE: 'I wish them' of F₁ suits the occasion and Por-tia's lips better than the reading of the Qq. CLARENDON reprints the Act of 3 Jac. I, c. 21, 'to restrain the abuses of Players : For the preventing and avoiding of the great abuse of the holy Name of God, in Stage-plays, Enterludes, May-games, Shews, and such like, Be it enacted by our Sovereign Lord the Kings Majesty, and by the Lords Spiritual and Temporal, and the Commons in this present Parliament assembled, and by the authority of the same, That if at any time or times after the end of this present Session of Parliament, any person or persons do or shall in any Stage-play, Enterlude, Sew [shew], May-game, or Pageant, jestingly or prophanely speak, or use the holy Name of God, or of Jesus Christ, or of the Holy Ghost, or of the Trinity, which are not to be spoken, but with fear and reverence, shall forfeit for every such offence by him or them committed, ten pounds : The one moiety thereof to the Kings Majesty, his Heirs and Successors, the other moiety thereof to him or them that will sue for the same in any Court of Record at Westminster, wherin no Essoin, Protection or Wager of Law shall be allowed.' (Statutes at Large, ed. 1695.)

118. **praise**] See Text. Notes. KNIGHT: The questions in the Qq may well be spared; they do not belong to Portia's calm and dignified character. WHITE: It was not Portia's way to call out thus [as in the Qq] to her attendants the moment they showed themselves in her presence.

120. **foure**] HUNTER (i, 322): The recovery of the original play mentioned by Gosson would doubtless throw much light upon the composition of *The Mer. of Ven.* as we now have it. In its present state it seems to have been subjected to correction, alteration, and

the Prince of *Moroco*, who brings word the Prince his   122
Maifter will be here to night.

   Por.   If I could bid the fift welcome with fo good
heart as I can bid the other foure farewell, I fhould be   125
glad of his approach : if he haue the condition of a Saint,
and the complexion of a diuell, I had rather hee fhould
fhriue me then wiue me.   Come *Nerriſſa*, firra go before ;
whiles wee fhut the gate vpon one wooer, another
knocks at the doore.   *Exeunt.*   130

---

123. *Maiſter*] Q₂.   *Maſter* Q₁ et
cet.
   124. *good*] *good a* Q₁, Han. Cam. Glo.
Cla. Wh. ii.
   125. *farewell*] *farwell* Q₁.
   127. *complexion*] *complection* Q₁.

128. *Come*] *Come in* Ktly.
   128–130. *Come...doore*] As verse, the
first line ending *before*, Knt, Dyce, Coll.
ii. et seq. (Prose, Coll. iii.)
   129. *gate*] *gates* Q₁, Cam. Glo. Cla.
Rlfe, Wh. ii.

---

addition after it had been once completed, but doubtless all by Shakespeare's own hand,
though one passage at least remained not accommodated to the changes which were
made.   The passage is : ' The *four* strangers,' &c.; but in all the copies, beginning
with the earliest, there were *six*, namely, the Neapolitan, the County Palatine, the
French lord, the English lord, the Scottish lord, and the young German.   It may be
presumed that the number originally was only four, and that the two added on a revisal
were the English and Scottish lords, the better to please an English audience.

   124, 125. **so . . . as**] See ABBOTT, § 275, for similar instances where we should say
as . . . as.

   126. **condition**] MALONE: That is, temper, qualities.   So, in *Oth.* IV, i, 210, ' of
so gentle a condition.'

   128–130. **Come . . . doore**] KNIGHT: We have printed the conclusion of this
scene as *verse*.   [See Text. Notes.]   The doggerel line is not inconsistent with the
playfulness of the preceding dialogue.   DYCE (*Remarks*, p. 52): Knight is doubtless
right.   Many passages might be cited to show that our early dramatists frequently, at
the end of a scene, make a prose speech conclude with a couplet, the first line of which
is much shorter than the second.   COLLIER (ed. ii): The consonance of ' shrive me '
and ' wive me ' may have put Portia upon rhyming at her *exit.*

   129. **whiles**] ABBOTT, § 137: ' Whiles,' the genitive of *while*, means ' of, or during,
the time.'

[*Scene III.*]

Enter Baffanio with Shylocke the Iew.

Shy.   Three thoufand ducates, well.

Baff.   I fir, for three months.

Shy.   For three months, well.

Baff.   For the which, as I told you,   5
Anthonio fhall be bound.

Shy.   *Anthonio* fhall become bound, well.

Baff.   May you fted me? Will you pleafure me?   8

[Scene III. Rowe et seq. ...Venice.   5–11. Prose, Pope et seq.
Pope. ...a public place in Venice. Theob.   8. *fted*] *ftead* Q₁.
  2. *ducates*] ducats Q₁F₃F₄.   *pleafure me?*] *pleasure me in it?*
  4. *months*] moneths Q₁. mouths F₂.   Ktly conj.

Enter, &c.] BOOTH: Shylock enters with slow, shuffling gait; restless, half-closed eyes, and the fingers of his disengaged hand (one holds his staff) ever moving, as if from the constant habit of feeling and caressing the ducats that are passing through them. Speak with a measured and a rather gruff voice.

LEWES (p. 11): From the first moment that [Kean] appeared and leant upon his stick to listen gravely while moneys are requested of him, he impressed the audience, as Douglas Jerrold used to say, 'like a chapter of Genesis.'

2. **ducates**] HUNTER (i, 324): This is a pure Venetian piece of money, and the name is a mere abbreviation of *Ducatus Venetorum*. It was a gold coin, so that a loan of three thousand ducats must be considered a very large sum, perhaps something nearly equivalent to a loan of twenty or thirty thousand pounds, were such a transaction to take place now. The ducat bore [an abbreviated inscription]; which is to be read in full: 'Sit tibi, Christe, datus Quem tu regis, iste Ducatus.' HALLIWELL: The value of the ducat varied in different parts of the Continent. At Venice there were 'two sorts of duccats, the one currant in payment, which may bee valued ster. about 3*s*. 4*d*., and the other of banco, which may be valued about 4*s*. or 4*s*. 2*d*., as the exchange will admit, the one being twenty per cent. better than the other.'—Roberts's *Marchant's Mapp of Commerce*, 1638. A ducat means literally a coin belonging to or coined by a *duke*, and the inscriptions upon the various impressions of it are exceedingly numerous. CLARENDON: Cotgrave (ed. 1632) mentions many kinds of ducats, Venetian among them. He adds: 'all foraine coynes, of whose value (often changed by the French Kings) no certaine interpretation can be giuen, other then that they hold a rate much about v. or vj*s*. sterl. the peece.' Coryat, who visited Venice in 1608, tells us that the ducat was worth 4*s*. 8*d*.—*Crudities*, ed. 1611, pp. 228, 253. ROLFE: The value of the Venetian silver ducat was about that of the American dollar.

5. **the which**] See *Macb.* III, i, 16, or ABBOTT, § 270.

7. **bound,**] BOOTH: Here a longer pause than before, with a curious glance at Bassanio.

8. **May**] CLARENDON: 'May,' in the sense of *can*. ABBOTT, § 307: Like the German *mögen*. [Therefore, I think it is used here rather in the sense of 'Are you willing?'—ED.]

3

Shall I know your anſwere.

Shy. Three thouſand ducats for three months,   10
and *Anthonio* bound.

Baſſ. Your anſwere to that.

Shy. *Anthonio* is a good man.

Baſſ. Haue you heard any imputation to the con-
trary.   15

Shy. Ho no, no, no, no : my meaning in ſaying he is a
good man, is to haue you vnderſtand me that he is ſuffi-
ent, yet his meanes are in ſuppoſition : he hath an Argo-
ſie bound to Tripolis, another to the Indies, I vnderſtand moreouer vpon the Ryalta, he hath a third at Mexi-   20

9, 12. an∫were] aun∫were Q₂.

16. Shy.] Shylocke. Q₂.

   Ho no,] *No, no,* F₂. *No,* F₃F₄,
Rowe+. *Oh no,* Knt, Glo. Cla. Clarke,
Wh. ii.

17. ∫uffient] ∫ufficient Qq Ff.

19. *Indies,*] *Indies.* F₃F₄.

20. *Ryalta*] Qq. *Ryalto* F₂F₃. Royalto
F₄.

---

13. **good**] CLARENDON: 'Good' is opposed to *poor* in *Cor.* I, i, 16: 'We are
accounted poor citizens, the patricians good.' ROLFE: That is, 'good' in the com-
mercial ſenſe, 'having pecuniary ability of unimpaired credit.'—Webster's *Dict.*
HALLIWELL: The epithet has continued in use, in a cognate sense, to the present
day; a 'good man,' in fashionable slang, being one in actual possession of his estate.
A person who exceeds another in wealth is said to be a better man than the other.
[Shylock is his own best commentator, and fully explains the word in his next speech.
—ED.]

17. **suffient**] BOOTH: Indicate by gesture (touch your palm or the pouch you
carry) *what* you mean. All this is spoken deliberately, not too slowly, and with an
occasional shrug of the shoulders.

18. **supposition**] ECCLES: Are but *supposed*, the subject of conjecture, rather than
assurance. CLARENDON: Because exposed to the perils of the sea.

20. **Ryalta**] STAUNTON: There were in ancient Venice three distinct places properly called *Rialto*; namely, the island at the farther side of the Grand Canal; the
Exchange erected on that island; and the Ponte di Rialto, which connected the island
with St. Mark's Quarter. The first of these places, according to Daru, received the
name of *Rialto* on account of its convenience to fishermen, its height, its contiguity to
the sea, and its situation in the centre of a basin. If this conjecture be accurate, the
original name was perhaps *Riva Alta*, a high bank-shore, or *Rilevato*, an elevated margin; since the island was the highest, and probably the oldest, of those in the lagune
to which the Veneti fled. Early in the fifth century the church of San Jacopo was
erected on this spot, near the fish-market; and adjoining to it were built the *Fab-
bricche*, a series of edifices connected by arcades, employed as warehouses and custom-
houses; in the open space opposite to which was held the Exchange. Sabellicus, who
wrote on Venetian history in the seventeenth century, states that this 'most noble piazza'
was crowded from morning to night. The part where the merchants transacted the
most weighty and important affairs was near the double portico at the end of the piazza

co, a fourth for England, and other ventures hee hath   21
fquandred abroad, but fhips are but boords, Saylers but
men, there be land rats, and water rats, water theeues,
and land theeues, I meane Pyrats, and then there is the   24

21. *hath*] hath, Theob. Warb. Johns.
Cap. Steev. Mal. Knt, Sing. Sta. Cam.
Glo. Cla. Wh. ii.

22. *abroad,*] abroad. Rowe.
   boords] boards Q₁.   boordes Q₂.
boardes Q₃.

23. *men,*] men ; Q₁.
   land] lands F₂.

23. *land rats…water rats*] Hyphened
by Pope.

23, 24. *water theeues, and land theeues*]
land-thieves and water-thieves Coll. (MS),
Sing. (MS), Sta. Wh. i, Dyce iii.
   theeues] theives F₄.

24. *Pyrats,*] Pyrats ; F₃F₄.   Pyrates,
Rowe.

---

opposite San Jacopo's Church, where the *Banco Giro* was established.   The following
is Coryat's description of the Rialto, or Exchange, as it appeared when he visited Venice : 'The Rialto, which is at the farthest side of the bridge as you come from St. Mark's,
is a most stately building, being the Exchange of Venice, where the Venetian gentlemen
and the merchants doe meete twice a day, betwixt eleven and twelve of the clocke in
the morning, and betwixt five and sixe of the clocke in the afternoone.   This Rialto is
of a goodly height, built all with bricke as the palaces are, adorned with many faire
walkes or open galleries that I have before mentioned, and hath a pretty quadrangular
court adjoining to it.   But it is inferior to our Exchange in London, though indeede
there is a farre greater quantity of building in this than in ours.'—*Crudities*, 1611,
p. 169.   CLARENDON : 'As it were, Rivo Alto, a high shore . . . . An eminent place in
Venice where Marchants commonly meete.'—Florio, *Ital. Dict.* 1611.   The bridge
called Ponte di Rialto was first built in 1591, but the existing bridge is a more recent
structure.   [See *post*, line 111.]

   20. **Mexico**] See TH. ELZE, III, ii, 284.

   21. **hath**] Note Theobald's judicious punctuation.—ED.

   22. **squandred**] KNIGHT : In a letter published by Waldron, in Woodfall's 'Theatrical Repertory,' 1801, it is stated that 'Macklin, mistakenly, spoke the word with a
tone of reprobation, implying that Antonio had, as we say of prodigals, unthriftly squander'd his wealth.'   The meaning is simply *scattered ;* of which Waldron gives an example from Howell's *Letters : '* The Jews, once an elect people, but now grown contemptible, and strangely squander'd up and down the world.'   In Dryden's *Annus Mirabilis*
we have the same expression applied to ships : 'They drive, they squander, the huge
Belgian fleet.'   HALLIWELL : Still used in Warwickshire, and, according to Wilbraham,
p. 80, still used in Cheshire in the sense of *scattered, dispersed.*

   23, 24. **water . . . theeues**] ECCLES : It seems that these ought to change places,
i. e. 'land thieves and water thieves,' for the purpose of connecting 'water thieves' with
'pirates.'   STAUNTON : There can be little doubt that the reading in the old copies was
a printer's or transcriber's error.   HALLIWELL : Shylock is intended to speak somewhat
disjointedly, otherwise one would be induced to adopt the change suggested by Eccles.
[See note on 'warmed . . . . summer,' III, i, 57.—ED.]

   24. **Pyrats**] HALLIWELL : 'Water-rats,' a jocular term for pirates, is not peculiar to
Shakespeare.   [The instances cited are from 'a rare tract: *The Abortive of an Idle
Hour*, 1620;' Massinger's *A Very Woman*, 1655 [1624 is probably its earliest date],
and *land-pirate* in *The Wandering Jew telling Fortunes*, &c., 1649—all subsequent to
The Merchant of Venice.—ED.]

perrill of waters, windes, and rocks : the man is notwith-   25
ftanding fufficient, three thoufand ducats, I thinke I may
take his bond.

 Baf. Be affured you may.

 Iew. I will be affured I may : and that I may be affured, I will bethinke mee, may I fpeake with *Antho-*   30
nio ?

 Baff. If it pleafe you to dine with vs.

 Iew. Yes, to fmell porke, to eate of the habitation
which your Prophet the Nazarite coniured the diuell   34

---

25. *perrill*] Q₂F₂F₃.   *perill* Q₁Q₃.   29, 33, 41. Iew.] Q₂FfQ₃.   Shy. Q₁.
28, 29. *affured*] *affurd* Q₂. *affur'd*   30. *mee,*] *me ;* Rowe.
Q₃.   34. *Nazarite*] *Nazarit* Q₂.

---

26. **three thousand ducats**] BOOTH : Very slowly, as if calculating the chances
of loss or gain.

29. **I will**] BOOTH : With emphasis on '*will*,' and with a chuckle.

32. **dine**] HALLIWELL : This invitation was of an unusual character under any circumstances of business, and intended evidently as a very great compliment.

33. **porke**] BOOTH : Doggett, doubtless, made a strong 'point' here, but be very
careful that you do not; a too strong emphasis or expression of disgust might cause a
laugh; the whole speech must be spoken impressively. [The rest of this sentence,
down to 'I will buy with you,' Dr Johnson silently omitted.—ED.]

34. **Nazarite**] HALLIWELL : According to some critics, Shylock is here speaking in
contempt of Christ, the Nazarenes being mentioned in the Scriptures as having been in
low estimation with the Jews; but the better interpretation is that the speaker wishes
merely to indicate more strongly his intense horror of pork, by recalling it to mind as
the material into which the devils were driven, thus ridiculing Bassanio by implying
how foolish he and other Christians were in eating of the flesh of the animal which
was selected by their own prophet for the proper habitation of evil spirits. The great
prophet himself was not regarded contemptuously by the Jews of Venice, and Shylock
would be speaking out of character were he to be represented as ridiculing him. A
Jew whom Coryat met in that city told him 'that Christ forsooth was a great prophet,
and in that respect as highly to be esteemed as any prophet amongst the Jewes that
ever lived before him; but derogated altogether from his divinitie, and would not
acknowledge him for the Messias and Saviour of the world, because he came so con-
temptibly, and not with that pompe and majestie that beseemed the redeemer of man
kind.'—*Crudities*, 1611, p. 215. [The use of this word instead of *Nazarene* is at first
sight puzzling. The distinction between a 'Nazarite' and a *Nazarene* is of the broadest. Samson was a Nazarite, and is always correctly so called by Milton in his *Samson
Agonistes*. And John the Baptist was a Nazarite. Shylock must have known perfectly
well that the Prophet who conjured the devil into the swine was not a Nazarite, but a
Nazarene. While still lost in questionings over the passage I mentioned the difficulty
to my friend, Dr THOMAS CHASE, late President of Haverford College, who at once in
the simplest and most obvious way solved it, in the following note : 'You say well that
" Shakespeare is always right," and he was right in saying " your prophet the Nazarite."

into : I will buy with you, fell with you, talke with   35
you, walke with you, and fo following : but I will
not eate with you, drinke with you, nor pray with you.
What newes on the Ryalta, who is he comes here ?

Enter Anthonio.

Baff.   This is fignior *Anthonio.*   40
Iew.   How like a fawning publican he lookes.

35. *into :*] *into ?* Theob.
37, 38. *pray...here ?*] *pray with you,*
that's flat. Lans.

38. *Ryalta*] *Ryalto* Q₁Q₂ Ff. *Rialto* Q₃.
is he] Om. Rowe.
41. [Aside. Rowe et seq.

The word "Nazarite" was, in his day, the proper (and probably the only) appellation for
"a man of Nazareth." Thus, in Tyndale's version (1534), we find "He shalbe called
a Nazarite." In the same passage it is *Nazarite* in Myles Coverdale's translation
(1535); Matthews's (1537); Taverner's (1539); Cranmer's (1539); the Bishops' Bible
(1568) [which Ginsburg has shown to be that used by Shakespeare—ED.]; in the
Geneva version (1587); and in the Rheims, or Roman Catholic, version (1582). What
else then could Shakespeare call him in the *Mer. of Ven.*? especially as King James's
Version, in which, as far as I know, the word *Nazarene* appears for the first time, was
not published till 1611.'—ED.]

41. **publican**] CLARENDON: A 'fawning publican' seems an odd combination.
The Publicani, or farmers of taxes, under the Roman government, were much more
likely to treat the Jews with insolence than with servility. Shakespeare perhaps
remembered that in the Gospels 'publicans and sinners' are mentioned together as
objects of the hatred and contempt of the Pharisees. KARL ELZE (*Sh. Jahrbuch*, xi,
276): 'Clarendon' overlooks the fact that in the parable related in *Luke* xviii, 10–14,
the Publican is represented as 'fawning' not on man, but on God. Such humility and
contrition before God as is there expressed in 'God be merciful to me, a sinner!' Shylock—nay, the Mosaic Law itself—neither knows nor comprehends; there the Phari-
see is the exact representative of his faith. On the other hand, Shylock repeatedly
refers to his rights, not only as before man but as before God; as before them both he
stands upon his bond. 'What judgment shall I dread doing no wrong?' and 'My
deeds upon my head!' he exclaims in Act IV. So, too, Marlowe's Barabas says, 'The
man that dealeth righteously shall live.' From this point of view the publican fawning
on God and begging for mercy was most repugnant to Shylock, just as Portia's exquisite plea for mercy rebounded from him without effect. The only objection which can
be urged against this explanation is, that a reference to the New Testament is put in
the mouth of the Jew Shylock; but this reference lies in the word 'publican,' interpret
'fawning' as we please. ALLEN (MS): Shakespeare must have made Shylock, as a
Jew, speak of a 'publican' as his forefathers did in the New Testament; and yet the
epithet he used shows that he conceived of him as an English innkeeper. In various
dialects (see Halliwell's *Archaic Dict.*) 'public' is equivalent to an inn. So in Scotland, as in Scott's novels. So *now* in Ireland: 'The *publicans* are in terror at Father
Mathew's approach.'—*Life of Mother McAuley*, p. 380, New York, 1866. In Webster's *Dict.*, under 'publican,' in the sense of innkeeper, this very passage is cited.
WHITE (ed. ii): A strange and either heedless or ignorant use of 'publican.' That

I hate him for he is a Chriſtian :   42
But more, for that in low ſimplicitie
He lends out money gratis, and brings downe
The rate of vſance here with vs in *Venice*.   45
If I can catch him once vpon the hip,

<hr>

43. *more,*] *more* F₄.

Shylock means an innkeeper is hardly possible.   [I incline to agree with Elze that the
thought uppermost in Shylock's mind was the publican of the parable, but cannot go
as far as he does in attributing Shylock's contempt for humility to the Jewish race in
general.   The parable itself was told by a Jew.—ED.]

42. **for**] For instances of 'for' in the sense of 'because of,' see ABBOTT, § 151.

45. **vsance**] DOUCE (i, 251) : 'It is almoste incredyble what gaine the Venetians
receiue by the vsury of the Jewes, both pryuately and in common.   For in euerye citee
the Jewes kepe open shops of vsurie, taking gaiges of ordinarie for .xv. in the hundred
by the yere : and if at the yeres ende, the gaige be not redemed, it is forfeite, or at the
least dooen away to a great disaduantage : by reason whereof the Jewes are out of
measure wealthie in those parties.'—Thomas's *Historye of Italye*, 1561, fol. 76 b.
[Several Editors call attention to the interchangeable use of *interest, usance*, and *usury*,
and some refer to Bacon's *Essay of Vsurie*.   In the opening sentences of that Essay
there is an allusion which seems noteworthy, not alone because of the mention of the
'orange-tawney bonnets,' but because we may infer that in 1625, when this Essay was
first published, the presence of Jews in England was not so unfamiliar as on historical
grounds might be supposed.   'Many haue made Wittie Inuectiues against *Vſurie*.
They ſay, that it is Pitie, the Deuill ſhould haue Gods part, which is the *Tithe*.   That
the *Vſurer* is the greatest Sabbath Breaker, becauſe his Plough goeth euery Sunday
That the *Vſurer* is the *Droane*, that Virgil ſpeaketh of : *Ignauum Fucos Pecus à præ-
ſepibus arcent*.   That the *Vſurer* breaketh the *Firſt Law*, that was made for Man-
kinde, after the Fall ; which was, *In Sudore Vultûs tui comedes Panem tuum ;* Not,
In Sudore Vultûs alieni.   That *Vſurers* ſhould haue Orange-tawney Bonnets, becauſe
they doe *Iudaize*.   That it is againſt Nature, for *Money* to beget *Money ;* And the like.
I ſay this onely, that *Vſury* is a *Conceſſum propter Duritiem Cordis ;* For ſince there
muſt be Borrowing and Lending, and Men are ſo hard of Heart, as they will not lend
freely, *Vſury* muſt be permitted.'   Bacon goes on to recommend that '*Vſury*, in generall be reduced to Fiue in the Hundred,' and frequently employs the word *Intereſt*
instead of *Vſury*.   See line 112, *post*.—ED.]

46. **vpon the hip**] Here, at IV, i, 350, and in *Oth*. II, i, 338, are the only passages
in Shakespeare where this phrase is found.   Johnson (*Oth*. II, i, 338) says that it is a
phrase from the art of wrestling, but in his *Dict*. he derived it from hunting ; with
more probability, says Dyce (*Remarks*, 52), and cites several passages in proof, none
of which seems to me conclusive, and one seems decidedly to point to wrestling.   Since
compiling the note in *Oth*. I have found, in *Notes & Qu*. vol. vii, p. 375, the following
remarks on ᵗʰe phrase by W. R. ARROWSMITH, which, with its citation from Sir John
Harington, settles its meaning beyond a peradventure : ' "On the hip," at advantage.
A term of wrestling.   So said Dr Johnson at first ; but, on second thought, referred it to
venery, with which Mr Dyce consents ; both erroneously. . . . . The hip of a chase is
ℭ term of woodman's craft ; the haunch is.   Moreover, what a marvellous expression
ꞇo say, A hound has a chase *on* the hip, instead of *by !*   Still more prodigious to say,

I will feede fat the ancient grudge I beare him.   47
He hates our facred Nation, and he railes
Euen there where Merchants moft doe congregate
On me, my bargaines, and my well-worne thrift,   50
Which he cals interreft : Curfed be my **Trybe**
If I forgiue him.
    Baff.   Shylock, doe you heare.
    Shy.   I am debating of my prefent ftore,
And by the neere geffe of my memorie   55
I cannot inftantly raife vp the groffe
Of full three thoufand ducats : what of that?
Tuball a wealthy Hebrew of my Tribe
Will furnifh me; but foft, how many months
Doe you defire ? Reft you faire good fignior,   60

---

47. *ancient*] *auncient* Q₂.   53. Shylock] *Shyloch* Q₂.
    grudge] *grudg* F₄.   55. *geffe*] Q₂F₂. *gueffe* Q₁Q₃. *guefs*
50. *well-worne*] F₂F₃. *well-wone* Q₂.   F₃.
well-worn F₄. *well-won* Q₁Q₃ et cet.   60. *defire ?*] *desire ?* [To Ant.] Rowe
    51. *interreft*] Q₂F₂. *intereft* Q₁.   et seq.

---

that a hound *gets* a chase *on* the hip. . . . . To the examples alleged by Mr Dyce, the three following may be added; whereof the last, after the opinion of Sir John Haring-ton, rightly refers the origin of the metaphor to wrestling. . . . . "Full oft the valiant Knight his hold doth shift, And with much prettie sleight, the same doth slippe; In fine he doth applie one speciall drift, Which was to get the Pagan on the hippe : And having caught him right, he doth him lift, By nimble sleight, and in such wise doth trippe : That downe he threw him," &c.—Harington's trans. of *Orlando Furioso*, Booke xlvi, Stanza 117.' The two other examples, cited by Arrowsmith, in no wise explain the phrase, but merely repeat it; and moreover they are *post*-Shakespearian —ED.

    51, 52. **Cursed . . . him**] BOOTH : This in a lower tone, almost growled *sotto voce.* Turning your back on Antonio as he enters, and pretending to be lost in calcu-lation of your 'present store.'

    54. **of**] For other instances where 'of' means *as regards, concerning, about,* see ABBOTT, § 174; also, V, i, 421.

    58. **Tuball**] CASSEL (*Literatur u. Symbolik,* 1884, p. 381) says that this name is not to be found in Jewry. [It is no disgrace to be inferior to Shakespeare in any wise, not even in the reading of the Bible; in *Genesis* x, 2, Tubal is enumerated among the sons of Japheth, and Chus or Cush, afterwards mentioned by Jessica, is among the sons of Ham. See Actors Names, *ante.*—ED.]

    60. **desire**] This is one of the many instances cited by WALKER (*Vers.* 144) where words ending in *ire* suffer dissolution, as the grammarians call it. 'This, like many other archaic modes of pronunciation, occurs more frequently in Shakespeare's earlier plays than in his later, and even in them he is more sparing of it, or, at any rate, ap-plies it to a smaller number of words, than Marlowe, Greene, &c.' ABBOTT'S corre-

Your worſhip was the laſt man in our mouthes.   61
   Ant.   *Shylocke,* albeit I neither lend nor borrow
By taking, nor by giuing of exceſſe,
Yet to ſupply the ripe wants of my friend,
Ile breake a cuſtome : is he yet poſſeſt   65
How much he would?

61. *mouthes*] *mouth's* F₃.
62. *albeit*] *although* Q₁, Pope+, Cam.
Glo. Cla. Wh. ii.
   borrow] *borrow,* Q₁.
65, 66. *is he...he would*] Ff, Rowe,
Pope, Han. *are you reſolu'd, How much*

he would haue? Q₁. *is he...ye would* '
Q₂Q₃, Dyce, Cam. Glo. Del. Cla. Wh. ii.
Are you...he would? Coll. (MS). *is he
...we would?* Walker, Dyce ii, Huds.
Is he...you would? Theob. et cet.

sponding paragraph is 480; in Browne's *Notes,* &c, that invaluable condensation, see
p. 15.   Booth: Here turn, and with pretended surprise at Anthonio's presence,
uncover, and address him obsequiously, but with a touch of irony in voice and face.

   61. worship] Morris: We retain the same meaning in the title of 'your worship'
(i. e. worth-ship), addressed to the magistrate on the bench.

   63. By . . . of] Abbott, § 178, 'of' naturally followed a verbal noun.   In many
cases we should call the verbal noun a participle, and the 'of' has become unintelligible
to us.   'Here stood he mumbling of wicked charms,'—*Lear* II, i, 39.   In most cases,
however, a preposition is inserted, and thus the substantive use of the verbal is made
evident.   As in this present passage.

   63. excesse] Clarendon: That which, when the loan is repaid, is paid in excess
of the sum lent, i. e. interest.

   64. ripe] Johnson: That is, wants come to the height, wants that can have no
longer delay.   Perhaps we might read—*rife* wants, wants that come thick upon him.
Malone: So afterwards, 'stay the very riping of the time.'

   65. possest] Steevens: That is, acquainted, informed.   So in *Twel. N.* II, iii,
149: 'Possess us, possess us.'   See also *post,* IV, i, 39.

   65, 66. is . . . would] That 'he' in line 66 is a misprint, is clear.   As we know
that this text was printed from Q₂, the misprint is probably due to the compositor's mistaking the *ye* in that Quarto for 'he.'   Theobald changed *ye* into *you,* and has been
followed by the majority of editors.   This involves the supposition that Anthonio
breaks off in his talk to Shylock, and asks Bassanio the question.   Yet Bassanio does
not answer, and Shylock, who was doing all he could to gain time, would, I think,
have willingly resigned the conversation to Bassanio had the chance occurred.   Nor
is it Bassanio who says, 'And for three months,' but Anthonio.   Bassanio does not
speak for some time, not until after Shylock has made his offer.   This address to Bassanio is therefore apparently purposeless; nothing is called forth by it.   As a general
rule, this is not Shakespeare's style; but it might be urged that we have it here, and
must understand it as best we can.   Happily, we have a resource in an appeal to Q₁.
The text there reads : 'are you resolu'd How much he would haue?'   This is plain and
clear.   The only objection to it that I can see lies in the scansion, and this is but trifling
in comparison with the objection to Q₂ with its change of address, to which no heed is
paid by Bassanio; and the scansion is very far from irregular : a pause in the third
foot is common enough.   'Ile breák | a cústom; | ′ | are yóu | resólv'd.'   In the Fifth
Act Gratiano says, 'That shé | did gíve me | ′ | whose pó | sy wás.'   There is even

Shy. I, I, three thouſand ducats.   67
Ant. And for three months.
Shy. I had forgot, three months, you told me ſo.
Well then, your bond : and let me ſee, but heare you,   70
Me thoughts you ſaid, you neither lend nor borrow

67. *I, I,*] *J, I,* Q₂. *Ay, ay,* Rowe.
68. *months*] *moneths* Q₁.
69. *you*] *he* Han.
70. *and let*] *but let* F₃F₄, Rowe. *and,*

let Cap. Mal. Steev. Sing. Sta. Ktly.
71. *Me thoughts*] Q₂Ff. *Me-though.*
Q₁. *Me thought* Q₃. *Methoughts* Rowe,
Cap. *Methought* Pope et cet.

reason for a pause in Anthonio's line; there is a change of thought. Nor is the scansion in line 66 any more difficult. Just as in line 65, *I will* is contracted into ' I'll,' so
here ' he would ' may be contracted into *he'd :* ' How múch | he'd háve ? | Ay, áy |
three thoú | sand dúcats.' For the rest, *resolv'd* is quite as Shakespearian as ' possest.'
On the whole, the text of Q₁ seems to me preferable to that of Q₂; it is perfectly intelligible, its metre is irreproachable, and it obviates a change of address which needs
explanation. But FURNIVALL pronounces it (*Forewords to Q₁,* p. v) ' *the* [Italics,
his] test-passage ' in deciding that Q₂ is superior to Q₁. ' And though,' continues Furnivall, ' you can mend the metre without introducing *yet,* by printing : " Are you
' " resoluĕd how much he would have ?" yet few students will doubt that the Heyes
' Quarto [Q₂] has Shakspere's reading—revisd, if not original,—when it makes
' Antonio turn to Bassanio, and say " is hee yet possest How much ye would ?" This
' change cannot have been a copier's or printer's doing, but must have been got
' from Shakspere directly or thru his MS.' In a foot-note : ' This may involve the
' change of *Bass.* for *Ant.* in the " And for three months," with Shylock answering
' Bassanio, " I had forgot, three months, you told me so," and then turning to Antonio
' with " Well, then, your bond." I prefer this change [first suggested by Capell.—
' ED.], but of course the Heyes text may stand as it is.' Merely that the question of
a change as great as that of a redistribution of speeches can be raised in Q₂, is in itself
a plea for the superior simplicity and clearness of the text of Q₁. If, however, the
text of Q₂ is to be preferred, I should certainly change the *ye,* not into *you,* as Theobald changed it, but into *we,* as suggested by WALKER and adopted by DYCE and
HUDSON.—ED.

68. **Ant.**] CAPELL (p. 60, *a*) : Had the moderns [by this term all the editors from
Rowe to Johnson are designated] set the name of Bassanio here, the speech's own fitness, and a word of the line immediately answering it, had gone far to have justify'd
them : but not quite far enough : for Antonio had learnt in conversation, before his
entry, as well the term as the sum; and the Jew—whose brain is then working upon
matters that break out afterwards,—thinks Bassanio the speaker, and frames his first
line accordingly; his next addresses Antonio, and his whole speech is the language
of one absent. [However broadly we may smile at Capell's uncouth style, if we will
but have the patience to penetrate the rough rind, we shall find the kernel generally
sound and at times wholesome. In this present passage ' you told me so ' might have
been uttered δεικτικῶς, as the grammarians say, that is pointing to Bassanio.—ED.]

70. **and let me see**] BOOTH : Slowly; with a slight pause and a searching look at
Antonio.

71. **Me thoughts**] This form occurs elsewhere in the Ff and Qq; it is found twice
in Clarence's dream in *Rich. III :* I, iv; and also in *Wint. T.* I, ii, 154. It is perhaps

Vpon aduantage.   72

   Ant.   I doe neuer vſe it.

   Shy.   When *Iacob* graz'd his Vncle *Labans* ſheepe,

This *Iacob* from our holy *Abram* was   75

(As his wiſe mother wrought in his behalfe)

The third poſſeſſer ; I, he was the third.   77

---

73 *doe*] *did* Rowe.   77. *third.*] *third,*— Dyce, Cam. Glo.
75. Abram] Abraham F$_4$, Rowe et seq.   Ktly, Cla. Clarke, Del. Rlfe, Huds. Wh.
77. *poſſeſſer*] *poſſeſſor* Q$_3$.   ii.

---

formed, as WALKER suggests (*Vers.* 284), 'by *contagion* from *methinks.*' ' Me thought '
and ' me thoughts ' are always printed as two words in F$_1$. It is to be borne in mind
that the word ' think,' in ' methinks,' comes from the Anglo-Saxon *thincan,* to seem
to appear, and not from *thencan,* to think. See notes in *Ham.* V, ii, 63.—ED.

   74. **Iacob**] GINSBURG (*Athenæum,* 28 April, 1883) : Every item in this remarkable
dialogue exhibits Shakespeare as one of the most original interpreters of the Bible
Jacob is selected because he was not only preferred by God himself to his brother
Esau, but because his additional name was Israel,—the name from which Shylock and
his race obtained the appellation *Israelites.* The paraphrase 'the eanlings which were
ſtreak'd and pied' is Shakespeare's own, and beautifully reflects the sense of the original. The reply which he puts into the mouth of Anthonio, that it was God's wonderful interposition, and must not be adduced as justifying foul play, shows that Shakespeare has not only carefully studied the Biblical naꞧative, but that he has based it
upon the remark in the margin against the passage (*Gen.* xxx, 37) in the Bishops'
Bible (1568), which is as follows: ' It is not lawefull by fraude to seke recompence of
iniurie: therefore Moyses sheweth afterwarde that God thus instructed Jacob.' (*Gen.*
xxxi, 9.) But the most remarkable part of this remarkable transaction is the crushing
manner in which the attempt 'to clothe the naked villainy with old, old ends stolen
forth from Holy Writ' is brought home to the villain. Shakespeare makes Anthonio
meet this device by appealing to another Scriptural event showing that 'the devil can
cite Scripture for his purpose.' But as this fact is recorded in *Matt.* iv, 6, and as Shylock the Jew does not believe in the New Testament, Anthonio is made to address it
to his Christian friend Bassanio. [In this valuable letter Ginsburg shows from the use
of the word 'charity' in *Love's Lab. Lost,* IV, iii, 364, that the version which Shakespeare used was the Bishops' Bible (1568), the only version of the eight then extant
wherein this word is found; all the other seven read ' love.' The present passage, as
Ginsburg shows us, also points to his use of that same version.]

   76. **As**] That is, For so. See I, i, 160.

   77. **third**] FARREN (p. 12): Actors have misunderstood one of the finest allusions
in the play. The reader will remember the part taken by Rebecca, the wife of Isaac
and the mother of Jacob, to obtain his father's blessing for him in preference to Esau,
the elder son (*Gen.* xxvii). It was by this act of hers that Jacob *became* the *third* possessor; and for this deceit Shylock thinks her entitled to great praise, not only as it
showed the superior cunning of the woman on behalf of her favorite son, but as it was
the means through which the greatness of the Israelites was accomplished; for it drove
Jacoꞇ to Laban, and from Jacob the whole of the tribes were descended. Shylock,
therefore, says with greꝺ exultation: ' Ay, he was the third,' whereas the actors have

Ant.   And what of him, did he take interreſt ?   78

Shy.   No, not take intereſt, not as you would ſay

Directly intereſt, marke what *Iacob* did.   80

When *Laban* and himſelfe were compremyz'd

That all the eanelings which were ſtreakt and pied

Should fall as *Iacobs* hier, the Ewes being rancke,

In end of Autumne turned to the Rammes,

And when the worke of generation was   85

Betweene theſe woolly breeders in the act,

The skilfull ſhepheard pil'd me certaine wands,   87

80–91. *marke...Iacobs*] *You know the story.* Lansdowne.

80. *did.*] In the original, this period may be a comma.

81. *were*] *vvas* Q₃.

compremyz'd] *compremyzd* Q₁Q₂. *comprimyz'd* F₂F₃. *compremiz'd* Q₃. *comprimiz'd* F₄. *compromis'd* Rowe.

82. *eanelings*] *euelings* F₄. *Ewelings* Rowe. *yeanlings* Pope+.

83. *hier*] *hire* F₄.

84. *In end*] *In th' end* Q₁, Pope+. *In the end* Steev. Var. Sing. Cam. Ktly, Glo. Wh. ii.

85. *And*] *Then* Han.

86. *woolly*] *wolly* Q₂.

87. *pil'd*] *pyld* Q₁Q₂. *peel'd* Pope+ Steev. Mal. Coll. Dyce, Cam. Del. Glo. Wh. ii. *pill'd* Knt, Sing. Sta. Ktly. *pile'd* Wh. i.

---

uttered the line as if Shylock doubted whether Jacob were the third, or a subsequent possessor,—a point of genealogy, not only thoroughly well known to Shylock, but to every Jew who has lived from the time of Jacob to the present hour.   CLARENDON : That is, reckoning Abraham himself as the first.   BOOTH : Antonio should break in, impatiently.

79. WORDSWORTH (p. 64) : The use here made of the history of Jacob and Laban appeared, I conclude, objectionable to Mr Bowdler, for he has omitted the entire passage, amounting to thirty-two lines ; but to me it appears so far otherwise, that I venture to cite almost the whole of it, as a remarkable instance of the tact with which Shakespeare could apply with perfect accuracy a passage of Scripture open to misconception, and yet divest its application of all dangerous tendency.   A close knowledge of the Bible may be traced also in the use of the word 'falsehood' [line 106] for *knavery* or *dishonesty.*

81. comrpemyz'd] CLARENDON : That is, had come to a mutual agreement.

82. eanelings] HALLIWELL : Lambs just born.   From the Anglo-Saxon *eanian,* to bring forth, and the old English verb *eane,* of the same meaning.   '*Chordi agnes,* lames eaned after their tyme.'—Elyote's *Dict.,* 1559.

84. In end] The definite article, which Q₁ adds here, is scarcely needed ; it can be but slightly indicated in pronunciation.   In regard to 'turned,' WALKER (*Vers.,* p. 40) is inclined to think that in all words, where *rm, rn* are followed by *-ed,* the *e* in *-ed* is not suppressed.—ED.

87. pil'd] KNIGHT : This is usually printed *peel'd.*   The words are synonymous ; but in the old and the present translations of the Bible we find *pill'd,* in the passage of *Genesis* to which Shylock alludes.   BOOTH : Use your staff to illustrate the acts of peeling and sticking the wand in the ground.

87. me] For other instances of this ethical dative, see ABBOTT, § 220, or Shakespeare *passim.*

And in the dooing of the deede of kinde,   88
He ſtucke them vp before the fulſome Ewes,
Who then conceauing, did in eaning time   90
Fall party-colour'd lambs, and thoſe were *Iacobs*.
This was a way to thriue, and he was bleſt:
And thrift is bleſſing if men ſteale it not.
    Ant. This was a venture ſir that *Iacob* ſeru'd for,
A thing not in his power to bring to paſſe,   95
But ſway'd and faſhion'd by the hand of heauen.
Was this inſerted to make interreſt good?
Or is your gold and ſiluer Ewes and Rams?
    Shy. I cannot tell, I make it breede as faſt,
But note me ſignior.   100
    Ant. Marke you this *Baſſanio*,
The diuell can cite Scripture for his purpoſe,   102

---

90. *eaning*] *yeaning* F₃F₄, Rowe+.
93. *And*] *This* Var. '21 (misprint).
   bleſſing if] *Bleſſing, if* Q₃. *bleſſing if*, F₄.
94. *ſeru'd*] *ſer'ud* Q₁. *ſerud* Q₂.

97. *inſerted*] *inferred* Coll. (MS).
99. *breede*] *breeds* F₂.
101-106. [Aside to Bass. Ktly, Coll. iii.
102. *diuell*] Q₁F₂. *deuill* Q₂.

---

89. **fulſome**] LATHAM (*Johnson's Dict.*, s. v.) says that it is difficult to determine in this passage whether the root of this word is *full* or *foul*. SKEAT (*Dict.* s. v.) defines the word 'cloying, satiating, superabundant,' and adds that it is '*not* derived from *foul.*' He does not cite this passage. Whatever its original meaning, its later usage certainly conveys a meaning akin to foulness, and in the present passage it seems to be nearly synonymous with 'rancke,' line 83. See *Oth.* IV, i, 45.—ED.

91. **Fall**] For other instances of intransitive verbs converted into transitive verbs, see ABBOTT, § 291.

92. ALLEN: These two propositions are independent; the second is equivalent to 'Jacob was the one that received Isaac's blessing.' ECCLES: In Shylock's defence of usury, drawn from the example of Jacob's conduct, there seems to be little appositeness or ingenuity; indeed, it is not easy to discover in what the parallelism of the two cases consists. However exorbitant the demands of the money-lender may be, the utmost extent of the profits accruing to him is defined by mutual stipulation between him and the borrower; whereas the advantage obtained by Jacob was the result of a stratagem, practised after the compact, of which Laban had no suspicion, and the success of which was by no means certain. Moreover, the money is to be considered as the property of the lender; the ewes were a part of the possessions of Laban; in short, the only circumstance of resemblance seems to be, a supposed earnest appetite for gain in each, and a diligent exercise of the means of obtaining it; and of these, Shylock evidently wishes to establish the justification upon the authority of so venerable a character. This objection may appear in some measure to have been anticipated by Anthonio's reply.

102. **diuell**] GREY (i, 131): See *Matthew* iv, 6, where the devil quotes *Pſalm* xci.

An euill foule producing holy witneſſe,   103
Is like a villaine with a ſmiling cheeke,
A goodly apple rotten at the heart.   105
O what a goodly outſide falſehood hath.
  Shy.   Three thouſand ducats, 'tis a good round ſum.
Three months from twelue, then let me ſee the rate.
  Ant.   Well *Shylocke*, ſhall we be beholding to you?
  Shy.   Signior *Anthonio*, many a time and oft   110

---

106. Transpose, to follow 102, reading *Or* for *A*, line 105, Johns. conj. (withdrawn).

    goodly outſide] *godly outside* Rowe, Pope, Theob. Han. Huds. *comely outside* Bailey.

108. *then...rate*] *then, let me see; the rate—* Cam. (Lloyd conj. ap. Cam.) Glo. Cla. Dyce iii, Huds. Wh. ii.

109. *beholding*] *beholden* Pope+, Knt, Sing. Sta. Ktly.

11, 12. BOOTH : Hearing this, Shylock shows his true feeling in his face as he turns from them ; then, just loud enough for them to hear, calculates the rate, &c.

106. WARBURTON : But this is not true, that falsehood hath always a goodly outside. Nor does this take in the force of the speaker's sentiment, who would observe that that falsehood which quotes Scripture for its purpose has a goodly outside. We should therefore read *outside's falsehood*, i. e. outside *his* falsehood, Shylock's. HEATH (p. 112) : These words must be understood as spoken in an ironical, contemptuous manner, by which they are peculiarly applied and confined to the instance which had just then presented itself to observation. They are not intended to express a general maxim, which holds universally ; so that Warburton's first objection is beside the purpose. Still more so is his other objection ; since this is the very circumstance which gave occasion to this sarcasm, and is particularly alluded to in it. JOHNSON : *Falsehood*, which, as *truth* means *honesty*, is taken here for *treachery* and *knavery*, does not stand for *falsehood* in general, but for the dishonesty now operating. [When Walker, whose library was small, suggested (*Crit.* i, 303) that 'goodly' should be *godly*, he did not know that several editors had followed Rowe in so reading. To me it is a *lectio certissima* on its own merits, even without the many instances which Walker cites where *goodly* and *godly* have been interchangeably misprinted, or without, as Dyce suggests, supposing that it had been caught by the printer from the preceding line.—ED.]

109. **beholding**] See ABBOTT, § 372. [A form very common in our early writers. We have 'beholdingness' in B. and Fl., *The Faithful Friends*, IV, iii, p. 281, ed. Dyce.—ED.]

110. BOADEN (*Memoir of Mrs Siddons*, i, 119) : Henderson set out in the play with a reading which I should recommend for effect to the actor, but carefully keep from the text of Shakespeare. . . . . The compound adverb *many-a-time-and-oft* is one of those clustered pleonasms which have passed unquestioned into common speech ; absurd enough, like the aldermanic toast, 'a speedy peace and soon ;' but it was the phraseology of Shakespeare, and should never be suspected of corruption. Henderson divided it, for the sake of strengthening his impression, ' *Many a time*,'—(as if he had implied many *places*,)—' and oft on the RIALTO !' (the place where merchants most do congregate, and therefore that where his vituperation would be most injurious,) ' you have rated me.' I persuade myself that Shakespeare, with our present feeling of the value

In the Ryalto you haue rated me   111
About my monies and my vſances :
Still haue I borne it with a patient ſhrug,
(For ſuffrance is the badge of all our Tribe.)
You call me misbeleeuer, cut-throate dog,   115

111. *In*] *On* Cap. conj. Coll. ii, iii.   Q₁F₃F₄ et cet.
      Ryalto] Rialto F₄.   114. *badge*] *badg* F₄.
112. *monies*] *moneyes* Q₂.   115. *call*] *call'd* Rann, Coll. (MS).
114. *ſuffrance*] Q₂F₂Q₃. *ſufferance*

of character upon the Royal Exchange, would have thanked an actor for a discrimination so emphatic and judicious. BOOTH : Pause before turning to him, and show great self-restraint; turn slowly, and, beginning with rising inflection of voice, address Antonio reproachfully. ROLFE : 'Many a time and oft' is an old phrase still familiar; equivalent to many and many a time—that is, many times, and yet again many more times. RUSHTON (*Sh. a Lawyer*, p. 49) points out that Shakespeare uses the phrase again in *1 Hen. IV:* I, ii; *2 Hen. VI:* II, i; *Timon*, II, i; and in *Jul. Cæs.* I, i.

111. **In the Ryalto**] HALLIWELL : Shakespeare uses indifferently *in, on,* and *upon* the Rialto. The Rialto was, in fact, in the general style of its construction, very similar to the Bourse at Antwerp, the model of the original London Exchange. 'The foure square market-place of Rialto is compassed with publike houses, under the arches whereof, and in the middle part lying open, the merchants meet.'—Moryson's *Itinerary*, 1617. [See *supra*, line 20.]

112. **vsances**] See the quotation from Bacon at line 45, *supra*. MALONE : This term occurs three times in the sense of *interest* in the present drama. REED : 'I knowe a gentleman borne to five hundred pounde lande, did never receyve above a thousand pound of nete money, and within certeyne yeres ronnynge still upon usurie and double usurie, the merchants termyng it *usance* and *double usance*, by a more clenly name, he did owe to master usurer five thousand pound at the last, borowyng but one thousande pounde at first, so that his land was clean gone, beynge five hundred poundes inherytance, for one thousand pound in money, and the usurie of the same money for so fewe yeres; and the man now beggeth.'—*Wylson on Usurye*, 1572, p. 32.

113. **Still**] That is, always.

113. **shrug**] MALONE : So in Marlowe's *Jew of Malta* [II, ii p. 269, ed. Dyce], 'I learn'd in Florence how to kiss my hand, Heave up my shoulders when they call me dog.'

114. HALLIWELL : According to a memorandum, the source of which is unknown to me, Shylock 'should assuredly wear a large red cross, embroidered upon his shoulder, the Senate of Venice having passed an edict to mortify the Jews,—many of whom quitted their territory to avoid its infliction,—that no Israelite should appear upon the Rialto without the emblem or badge above specified.' [In Booth's Acting Copy there is a stage-direction here : 'Showing his yellow cap.' In MS he notes : 'I prefer the yellow cap to the cross upon the shoulder which other actors have worn, my Father among them. Cooke used the cap, and said that Macklin also used it.']

115. **call**] Rann's emendation : 'Call'd' is, to me, more than plausible. Shylock is rehearsing what Anthonio has done to him in the past, and then contrasts it with his

And ſpet vpon my Iewiſh gaberdine,   116
And all for vſe of that which is mine owne.
Well then, it now appeares you neede my helpe :
Goe to then, you come to me, and you ſay,
Shylocke, we would haue moneyes, you ſay ſo :   120
You that did voide your rume vpon my beard,
And foote me as you ſpurne a ſtranger curre
Ouer your threſhold, moneyes is your ſuite.
What ſhould I ſay to you ? Should I not ſay,
Hath a dog money ? Is it poſſible   125
A curre ſhould lend three thouſand ducats ? or
Shall I bend low, and in a bond-mans key
With bated breath, and whiſpring humbleneſſe,   128

---

116. *ſpet*] Qq F₂, Cap. Knt, Sing. Sta.
Wh. Rlfe. *spat* Rann. *ſpit* F₃F₄ et
cet.
120. *moneyes*,] *monies*, Q₁Q₃. *moneys*,
F₃F₄. *monies;* Rowe.
121. *rume*] *rheume* F₂.
123. *threſhold*,] *threshold;* Rowe.
moneyes] *money* Q₁, Pope +.

123. *is*] *are* Eccles conj.
125. *money*] *monies* Ktly.
126. *ſhould*] Ff, Rowe, Wh. i.   *can*
Qq, Pope et cet.
127. *bond-mans*] *bondmans* F₄.
128. *bated*] *'bated* Cap. Steev. Mal.
Knt, Coll. Sing.

---

present conduct, ' Well then, it *now* appears,' &c.   He afterward refers to Anthonio's
treatment of him in the past, ' You that did void,' ' You spurn'd me such a day,' ' You
call'd me dog.'   This change occurred also to Allen, independently.—ED.

116. **spet**] DYCE: The Folio has 'spit' in *Meas. for Meas.* II, i; *As You Like It*,
III, ii; IV, i; *Tam. Shr.* III, i; *Wint. Tale*, IV, ii, &c. &c.   ROLFE: 'Spet' is used
by Milton in the one instance (*Comus*, 132) in which he employs the word.   [Halli-
well, who erroneously refers the word to *Lycidas*, says that Milton himself wrote it
' spits.'—ED.]

116. **gaberdine**] KNIGHT: Shylock speaks of ' his *Jewish* gaberdine;' but independently of Vecellio's assurance that no difference existed between the dress of the
Jewish and Christian merchants save the yellow bonnet, the word ' gaberdine' conveys
to us no precise form of garment, its description being different in nearly every Dictionary, English or foreign.   In German, it is called a rock or frock, a mantle, coat, petti-
coat, gown or cloak.   In Italian, *palandrano*, or great coat, and *gavardina*, a peasant's
jacket.   The French have only *gaban* and *gabardine*,—cloaks for rainy weather.   In
Spanish, *gabardina* is rendered a sort of cassock with close-buttoned sleeves.   In English, a shepherd's coarse frock or coat.   HALLIWELL: A kind of large, loose cloak.
' Furst, a gawlberdyne of russett welvett for my lord, gardytt with green cloth of golde,
and lyned with black sarsnett.'—MS temp. Hen. VIII.   ' A gabbardine, tunica
casatica vel rustica, a sort of double mill'd Kersy, such as was formerly given for
livery cloaks; vid. plura apud Skinnerum.'—MS Gl.   STAUNTON: It does not appear
that this habiliment, as worn by the Jews, was in any respect different from that in
ordinary use

Say this : Faire fir, you fpet on me on Wednefday laft ;
You fpurn'd me fuch a day ; another time   130
You cald me dog : and for thefe curtefies
Ile lend you thus much moneyes.

    Ant.   I am as like to call thee fo againe,
To fpet on thee againe, to fpurne thee too.
If thou wilt lend this money, lend it not   135
As to thy friends, for when did friendfhip take
A breede of barraine mettall of his friend ?   137

---

129. *Say this*] Separate line, Steev. '93 et seq. (except Ktly).

    fpet] Qq Ff, Rowe, Cap. Knt, Sta. Wh. Rlfe. *spat* Rowe ii. *spit* Pope et cet.

    on...laft] *last Wednesday* Pope+, Eccles. *Wednesday last* Cap. *Wednefday*] *wendfday* Q₁.

  130. *You*] *Your* F₂. *day ; another*] *day another* Qq.

131. *me dog*] *me dogge* Q₂Q₃. *me—dog* Cap. Steev. Mal. Sing. Sta.

134. *fpet*] Qq Ff, Cap. Knt, Sta. Wh. i, Rlfe. *spit* Rowe et cet. *thee too*] *thee to* Qq.

136. *friends*] *friend* Ff, Rowe+.

137. *breede of*] Ff, Rowe+, Knt, Hal. Wh. i. Del. Rlfe, Huds. *breed for* Qq et cet. *barraine*] Q₂F₂. *barren* Q₁.

---

129. From the Text. Notes it will be seen that Steevens was the first to resolve this Alexandrine into regular verse. For many other instances of similar dealing with Alexandrines, both apparent and real, see ABBOTT, § 499. This scansion, however, is wholly for the eye.—ED.

    131. BOOTH : Sarcastically,—with a pause and a gulp before ' dog,' as Kean is said to have uttered it. [See Text. Notes, which show that the credit of suggesting this pause before ' dog ' is due to Capell. Its effectiveness, as employed by Kean, remains, 'o he says, still vivid in my Father's memory.—ED.] Utter ' courtesies ' with strong emphasis—looking up, as you ' bend low,' with a devilish grin into Antonio's face. Antonio should stand erect, looking contemptuously at Shylock till the end, when he moves, as if stung, a few paces from his position, to return and angrily reply, but not too violently, yet sufficiently to cause Shylock to pretend alarm and regret at the ' storm ' he has raised.

    137. **breede of barraine**] THEOBALD (Nichols's *Lit. Hist.* ii, 305) : Will ' barren' metal ' breed '? I rather think the Poet wrote ' A breed of *bearing* metal,' i. e. producing an increase by usury, or interest. Consonant to this, you know, the Latins explained interest thus : *fœnus, fœtum accepti ;* and the Greeks called it τόκος. Both which expressions take in our Poet's idea of a ' breed.' WARBURTON : A *breed*, that is, interest money bred from the principal. By the epithet *barren*, the author would instruct us in the argument on which the advocates against usury went, which is this : that money is a *barren* thing, and cannot, like corn and cattle, multiply itself. And to set off the absurdity of this kind of usury, he put *breed* and *barren* in opposition. POPE having said that ' the old editions (two of 'em) have it, A bribe of barren metal,' CAPELL remarks that ' this is perhaps a mistake : and that the word which follows *breed* in this copy differ'd from the word he has follow'd, for this is true of *four* old ones : and had he been pleased to restore it, he had purg'd his author of a glaring absurdity (for what else is—breed *of* things that are barren ?) that runs through all his other editions, old

But lend it rather to thine enemie,   138
Who if he breake, thou maiſt with better face
Exaĉt the penalties.   140
   Shy.   Why looke you how you ſtorme,
I would be friends with you, and haue your loue.
Forget the ſhames that you haue ſtaind me with,   143

---

139. *Who*] *Then* Eccles conj.   Qq et cet.
140. *penalties*] Ff, Knt,Wh. i. *penalty*   141. *looke you*] Om. Pope+.

---

and new :—*breed* conveys in that place it's generical idea, i. e. encrease; but *breed* is chose to express it by, that it's opposition to "*barren*" may set off and heighten the unfitness of such usury.' FARMER : Old Meres says : 'Usurie and encrease by gold and silver is unlawful, because against nature; nature hath made them *sterill* and *barren*, usurie makes them procreative.' HOLT WHITE: The honour of starting this conceit belongs to Aristotle. See *De Republica*, lib. i. GRANT WHITE (ed. i) : 'Of,' for *for* in the Qq, is not only authoritative, but very happy. 'A breed of barren metal' is an increase of barren metal; but, in Lucina's name, what is 'a breed *for* barren metal'? [White apparently found an answer somewhere to his question before he published his Second Edition, wherein he followed the Qq without comment. I prefer the Ff decidedly. Anthonio is merely repeating the very phrase of Shylock, who had just boasted that he made his gold and silver 'breed as fast' as sheep. Anthonio's contemptuous use of 'barren' casts a slur on Shylock's well-won thrift, which assuredly was felt. If the reading of the Qq: 'a breed *for* barren metal' is equivalent to 'a breed for the use of that which cannot breed,' it is, to me, much inferior to that of the Ff.—ED.]

   139. **Who if he**] ALLEN : *Qui si fidem franget;* a proof of Shakespeare's grammar-school instruction; he *translates* as he was taught. 'Who—he' may be taken as *one* subject separated by *if.* Or else 'who' is used for the *From whom*, which Shakespeare *would* have written if he had foreseen how he was to end. ABBOTT, § 249: The Supplementary Pronoun is generally confined to cases where the relative is separated from its verb by an intervening clause, and where, on this account, clearness requires the supplementary pronoun. The present passage seems at first as though it could be explained [by supposing 'who' to be like *which*, when the latter approximates the vulgar idiom so familiar to the friends of 'Sairey Gamp']; but 'who' is put for *whom*, and 'exact the penalty' is regarded as a transitive verb. [This explanation cannot, I think, be ranked among the happiest of Dr Abbott's.—ED.]

   141. BLACKWOOD'S MAGAZINE (Dec. 1879) : When Shylock changes from reproach to fawning in this speech, he [IRVING] comes close up to Antonio and touches him on the breast with an air of familiar entreaty. Antonio recoils from him with contemptuous scorn, and Shylock bows low, while he winces at the rebuke. This has been praised as a fine stroke of truth. But is it so? Antonio has just told Shylock that he is 'as like to spit on him again, to spurn him too.' Would Shylock, with these words fresh in his ears, forget himself so far as to lay a finger on the haughty merchant, never haughtier than at that moment when asking a loan from a man he despised. Again, is such an action conceivable in one who feels the pride of race so strongly as Shylock? For one of 'the sacred nation' like himself to touch the Christian merchant would, in his mind, be viewed as nothing less than contamination and defilement.

   143. **shames**] ALLEN : Shylock compares the *words* of shame (*probra*) which

4

Supplie your prefent wants, and take no doite
Of vfance for my moneyes, and youle not heare me,   145
This is kinde I offer.
 Baff. This were kindneffe.
 Shy. This kindneffe will I fhowe,
Goe with me to a Notarie, feale me there
Your fingle bond, and in a merrie fport   150

---

145. *vfance*] *usage* Rowe.
145, 146. *and...offer*] One line, Coll.
Wh. Walker, Dyce iii.
145. *me,*] *me :* Q₃. *me ;* F₄.
146. *This is*] *This sure is* Han.

146. *I offer.*] *I offer you.* Ktly. *that I
offer* Ktly conj.
147. *Baff.*] Q₁Q₂ Ff, Rowe, Cap. Dyce,
Cam. Glo. Cla. Hal. Rlfe. Ant. Q₃ et cet.
This] *Ay, this* Cap.

Antonio had been wont to utter against him, to the *spittle* which he had voided
on him.

144. doite] HALLIWELL: A Low Country coin in Shakespeare's time of exceedingly small value, and hence the term came generally to be used for a very trifle, a
mere fraction. According to Coryat, the Dutch 'use to stampe the figure of a maide
upon one of their coynes that is called a doit, whereof eight goe to a stiver, and ten
stivers do make our English shilling.'—*Crudities*, 1611, p. 642. FAIRHOLT (ap. Halliwell) says that these 'coins are now of extreme rarity, their small intrinsic value con-
ducing to their loss; and our National collection contains no examples of them . . . .
the meanest coin which received a current stamp in the Middle Ages.' SKEAT derives
it from the 'Dutch *duit*. Remoter origin unknown.'

149. Dr M. JASTROW (*Young Israel*, Mai, 1876): Does Shylock really intend to
carry out the forfeiture of his bond? Hardly; he intends merely to humiliate, to torture his enemy, to see him at his feet, and then to heap coals of fire on his head by a
magnanimous revenge. What a triumph for the 'dog' that to him, to the dog, the great
man should owe his life. What a degradation, worse than death, for the 'royal merchant,' to drag round ever after like a chain, the gift of his very life at the hands of a
Jew! [Dr Jastrow goes on to show that it was Jessica's flight and robbery that changed
all this.—ED.]

150. From this line to line 172 the verses do not begin with capitals, but with lower
case, in Q₂.—ED.

150. Your] ABBOTT, § 219: *Your, our, their,* &c. are often used in their old signification, as genitives, where we should use 'of *you*,' &c.

150. single bond] 'An obligation, or bond, is a deed whereby the obligor obliges
himself, his heirs, executors, and administrators, to pay a certain sum of money to
another at a day appointed. If this be all, the bond is called a single one, *simplex
obligatio;* but there is generally a condition added, that if the obligor does some particular act, the obligation shall be void, or else shall remain in full force: as payment
of rent; . . . . repayment of a principal sum of money borrowed of the obligee. . . . .
In case this condition is not performed, the bond becomes forfeited, or absolute at law,
and charges the obligor.'—BLACKSTONE'S *Commentaries*, iv, 340. LORD CAMPBELL
says that this 'bond to Shylock is prepared and talked about according to all the forms
observed in an English attorney's office. The distinction between a "single bill" and
a "bond with a condition" is clearly referred to.' For this latter hasty assertion, LORD

If you repaie me not on fuch a day,   151
In fuch a place, fuch fum or fums as are
Expreft in the condition, let the forfeite
Be nominated for an equall pound   154

153. *forfeite*] *forfaite* Q₂.

Campbell was properly criticised by RUSHTON (*Testamentary Language*, p. 51), and
the technical distinction pointed out between 'a single bond' and 'a bond with a condition,' to which latter class, I should say, Antonio's bond pretty decidedly belongs.
The simplest explanation, to me, is that 'single' is used neither in its legal sense nor
as applied to the bond. SCHMIDT (*Lex.*) says that it here means 'no more than mere,
only,' and refers to *Temp.* I, ii, 432: 'What wert thou, if the King of Naples heard
thee? A single thing, as I am now.' But I am inclined to think that it means
'separate, alone,' just as it is used in 'single combat.' Shylock wanted the bond of
Anthonio, of him alone, and hence 'single' refers to Anthonio, and not to the bond.
CLARENDON says that Shylock means 'a bond with your own signature alone attached
to it, without the names of sureties.' I doubt if 'single' in this sense can be properly
applied to a bond. Whatever difference the presence or absence of sureties would
make in a bond with such a condition as Shylock was seeking, the difficulty of finding sureties might make much difference in the ease with which Anthonio could
execute it. Practically, therefore, I agree with Clarendon, merely withholding, on
technical grounds, the application to the bond of the term 'single.' ROLFE says
(*Shakespeariana*, Jan., 1886) that he has sometimes been inclined to explain 'single'
here as used craftily by Shylock in its technical sense, because Shylock 'wants to make
the "condition" appear like none at all,—merely the "merry sport" he calls it; as if
he had said, "Give me your bond without any condition,—at least none worthy of the
name or to be legally enforced,—though for the joke of the thing we will say that I
am to have a pound of your flesh if you fail to pay up at the appointed time."' I
think we need place no limit to Shylock's craftiness, and if a legal acceptation of the
term 'single,' as applied to the bond, be here insisted on, Rolfe's explanation is pat.
(Rolfe himself thinks that 'single' is used as Clarendon interprets it.) When, however, we undertake to discuss the term 'single' in its legal bearings, there is no end to
the quiddities and quillets we may sound shrilly and to no purpose. Here, and in the
Trial scene, Shakespeare accepted what of law there is, as he found it either in the old
play, mentioned by Gosson, which he rewrote, or in Ser Giovanni's novel, and as far as he
considered it effective for dramatic purposes. It was enough that the scene was laid in a
far-off foreign land, and in former times, to lend acquiescence on the part of his English
audiences in any apparent misuse of legal terms or violation of legal procedure.—ED.

150-152. BOOTH: Jocosely. Keep up this expression and chuckle until Bassanio
interferes, then suddenly change it to disappointed rage,—but only for a moment; then,
at 'O father Abram,' &c., assume a look and tone of pity.

154. nominated] ALLEN: Not *nominated-for*, but *forfeit-for*, i. e. 'the forfeit
(nominated) shall be for,' &c. This, therefore, may be one of Shakespeare's frequent
transpositions. In fact, 'nominated' really belongs much earlier: 'and (in a merry
sport) let it be nominated, that if . . . . the forfeit [shall] be for,' &c. This is the way
'nominated' is used in IV, i, 273. ABBOTT, § 148: *For* is nearly redundant in this
passage. [Which I do not think Abbott would have said had Allen's interpretation
occurred to him.—ED.]

Of your faire flesh, to be cut off and taken   155
In what part of your bodie it pleaseth me.
    Ant.   Content infaith, Ile seale to such a bond,
And say there is much kindnesse in the Iew.
    Bass.   You shall not seale to such a bond for me,
Ile rather dwell in my necessitie.   160
    Ant.   Why feare not man, I will not forsaite it,
Within these two months, that's a month before
This bond expires, I doe expect returne
Of thrice three times the valew of this bond.
    Shy.   O father *Abram*, what these Christians are,   165

---

156. *it pleaseth*] Ff, Rowe, Wh. i. *it shall please* Pope+. *pleaseth* Qq et cet.

157. *infaith*] Q₂F₂Q₃. *ifaith* Q₁, Cap. *in faith* F₃F₄ et cet.

Ile] *yle* Q₂.

158. *the Iew*] *a Jew* or *thee, Jew* Cap. conj.

161. *forsaite*] Q₂. *forfet* Q₁. *forfeite* F₂. *forfeit* Q₃ et cet.

164. *valew*] Q₂F₂. *value* Q₁ et cet.

165. Abram] Qq F₂F₃, Wh. Cam. Glo. Del. Cla. Abraham F₄ et cet. *these*] *the* Cap. (corrected in Errata).

---

154. equall] CLARENDON, ROLFE, and HUDSON interpret this as 'equivalent for the debt,' but I prefer SCHMIDT's definition of 'exact,' 'just the weight,' where the beams of the scales are exactly, equally counterpoised, as in *Ham.* I, ii, 13, 'In equal scale weighing delight and dole.' ELZE (*Jahrbuch*, xi, 277) also adopts this view, and appositely cites not only Portia's parallel use of 'just' in IV, i, 343, but also the title-pages of the First and Second Quartos, where Shylock's extreme cruelty is mentioned in cutting a 'just pound' of flesh.—ED.

155. faire flesh] This suggests Shylock's darker, Oriental hue.—ED.

155, &c. SALAMAN (*Jews As They Are*, p. 215): Jews are commanded by their immutable divine Law to love their neighbors as themselves, and to treat all living creatures with kindness, mercy, and humane consideration. When slaughtering animals required for food, they are forbidden to torture them or to subject them to prolonged suffering. To mutilate any living creature, much less [Qu. more?] a human being, is strictly opposed to the merciful spirit of the Jewish Law, as it would be abhorrent to the Jewish nature. It may be confidently averred that no Jew that ever had existence, beyond the inflamed imagination of a romancer or a balladmonger, was ever justly charged with the abominable crime of animal mutilation, or even with the barbarous disposition to mutilate which is ascribed to Shylock. The mere suggestion that so horrible a desire might be possible, has been viewed by all Jews as a foul libel upon Jewish character. Cruelty to the person has never been a Jewish vice.

157, 158. Ile . . . Iew] COLLIER (ed. ii): These words are addressed to Bassanio, and not to Shylock; consequently, Bassanio immediately answers. In the (MS) 'the Jew' is changed to '*thee*, Jew,' which might have been right if Antonio had been speaking to Shylock. [See Text. Notes.—ED.]

165–167. O . . . others] BOOTH: My Father uttered this as an aside, and I rather think he was right; but in that case the tone and look should express disgust.

165. what] ABBOTT, § 256.

Whofe owne hard dealings teaches them fufpe&t   166
The thoughts of others : Praie you tell me this,
If he fhould breake his daie, what fhould I gaine
By the exa&tion of the forfeiture ?
A pound of mans flefh taken from a man,   17n
Is not fo eftimable, profitable neither
As flefh of Muttons, Beefes, or Goates, I fay
To buy his fauour, I extend this friendfhip,
If he will take it, fo : if not adiew,
And for my loue I praie you wrong me not.   175
    Ant.   Yes *Shylocke*, I will feale vnto this bond.
    Shy.   Then meete me forthwith at the Notaries,
Giue him dire&tion for this merrie bond,   178

---

166. *dealings*] *dealing* Ff, Rowe, Cap. Sing. Dyce iii.

    teaches them fufpect] *teach them to fufpect* Pope +.

167. *Praie*] F₁.

171. *profitable neither*] *or profitable* Pope +.

172. *Goates,*] *Goats.* Rowe.

174. *it, fo :*] *it fo,* Q₁.

---

166. **teaches**] For other instances of this Northern Early English plural in -*s*, see ABBOTT, § 333.

166. **suspect**] For other instances of the omission of *to* before the infinitive, see ABBOTT, § 349.

168. **breake his daie**] HALLIWELL: The word *day* was frequently used by our old writers in the generic sense of *time*, and the verb *to break* in the sense of not keeping an appointment on a contract. In the old ballad of *Gernutus*, the usurer recommends his wife to 'keep your day,' that is, adhere strictly to the terms of your loans. Conf. Heywood's *The Fayre Maide of the Exchange*, II, ii, 1607 : 'If you do break your day, assure yourself That I will take the forfeit of your bond.' [Many other examples are given, and many more could be added.—ED.]

171. WALKER (*Vers.* p. 274): We sometimes find two unaccented syllables inserted between what are ordinarily the fourth and fifth [as here] or the sixth and seventh, the whole form being included in one word : 'Is nót | so ést ima | ble, pró | fitá | ble neither | .' ABBOTT, § 495, to the same effect. ALLEN suggests the following punctuation : 'Is not so estimable, profitable, neither As,' &c. That is, perhaps, is not so estimable (i. e. profitable) as that of either muttons, beefs, or goats.

172. **Beefes**] CLARENDON: In *1 Hen. IV:* III, iii, 199, the Prince calls Falstaff 'O, my sweet beef!' Cotgrave explains *bœuf* to mean 'An Ox; a Beefe; also beefe.' The plural occurs in *2 Hen. IV:* III, ii, 253. [MURRAY (*New Eng. Dict.*) gives the plural as *beeves*.—ED.]

175. **for my loue**] CLARENDON: Not 'in return for my love,' but 'for my love's sake.' [Does Shylock mean 'for my love's sake, do not, in this matter, impute unworthy motives to me,' or (he has just spoken of 'buying Anthonio's favour') 'do not, for my love's sake, hereafter maltreat me' ?—ED.]

177. BOOTH : Eagerly.

And I will goe and purſe the ducats ſtraite.
See to my houſe left in the fearefull gard   180
Of an vnthriftie knaue : and preſentlie
Ile be with you.   *Exit.*

 Ant. Hie thee gentle *Iew.* This Hebrew will turne
Chriſtian, he growes kinde.

  Baſſ. I like not faire teames, and a villaines minde.   185

 Ant. Come on, in this there can be no diſmaie,
My Shippes come home a month before the daie.

            Exeunt.

---

179. *ſtraite*] *ſtraight* Q₁.
180. *See*] *Look* Cap. (corrected in Errata).
 fearefull] *fearless* Warb.
182. *Ile*] *I'le* F₃F₄. *I will* Theob. ii et seq.
183. *Hie...Iew*] As closing line 182, Q₃, Pope et seq.

183, 184. *This...kinde*] Prose, Q₄Q₂ Ff.
Separate line, Q₃ et cet.
183. *This*] *The* Qq, Pope, Han. Cap. Coll. Cam. Glo. Cla. Rlfe, Huds. ᵛ⁻...
ii.
184. *growes*] *growes* ſᵣ Q₁.
185. *teames*] *termᵪᵄ* or *tearmes* or *terms* Qq Ff.

---

180. **fearefull**] JOHNSON: A guard that is not to be trusted, but gives cause of fear. ABBOTT, § 3 : Adjectives, especially those ending in *full, less, ble,* and *ive,* have both an active and a passive meaning.

183. **This, &c.**] BOOTH : Shylock overhears this, and grins at it as a pleasant joke, and, moving slowly up the stage, turns as they exeunt, and looks after them with intense hatred.

185. **teames**] JOHNSON : Kind words, good language. [Of course a misprint for *termes.* But does it mean no more than 'kind words, good language'? May it not refer to the bond?—ED.] LLOYD : The thoughtful rejoinder of Bassanio marks apprehension, and this is the very cautiousness that besteads him in his venture on the caskets, when he comments on the deceptiveness of ornament, 'The seeming truth, which cunning time puts on To entrap the wisest.'

Actus Secundus.   [*Scene I.*]

*Enter Morochus a tawnie Moore all in white, and three or
foure followers accordingly, with Portia,
Nerriſſa, and their traine.
Flo. Cornets.*

Mor.   Miſlike me not for my complexion,   5
The ſhadowed liuerie of the burniſht ſunne,
To whom I am a neighbour, and neere bred.
Bring me the faireſt creature North-ward borne,
Where *Phœbus* fire ſcarce thawes the yſicles,
And let vs make inciſion for your loue,   10
To proue whoſe blood is reddeſt, his or mine.

[Scene I. Belmont. Rowe.   A Room
n Portia's House. Cap.
    1. Morochus] Morochius Ff, Rowe+.
Prince of Morocco. Cap.
    all in white] all white Ff.
    3. their traine.] her train. Rowe.

4. Flo. Cornets] Om. Qq.
5. Mor.] Moroc. Q_2Q_3. Morocho. Q_2.
6. *burniſht*] *burning* Coll. (MS).
8. *Bring me*] *Bring* Q_1.
10. *inciſion*] *incyzion* Q_3.

1. **tawnie Moore**] It is well to remember that it is this phrase in this place on which stress is laid by those who maintain that Othello, although a Moor, was not black. Note, too, the misprint of the Ff: '*a tawnie Moore all white.*'—ED.

4. **Flo. Cornets.**] See Appendix, p. 274.

5. KOENIG (*Ueber Sh.*, p. 103): Conf. *The Song of Solomon*, i, 6: 'Look not upon me, because I am black, because the sun hath looked upon me.'

6. **burnisht**] COLLIER, in his *Notes*, &c. (1853, p. 114), thinks that *burning*, of the (MS), 'seems much more proper, when the African Prince is speaking of his black complexion as the effect of the sun's rays. To speak of the sun as artificially "burnished" is very unworthy.' In a Review of Collier's *Notes* in *Blackwood* (Aug., 1853), the Reviewer denies that the African Prince speaks thus, and asserts that 'he is merely throwing brightness and darkness into picturesque contrast,—as the sun is bright or "burnished," so am I, his retainer, dark, or "shadowed."' 'Shakespeare speaks of the sun as *naturally* burnished; and so far is this from being "unworthy," it is, in the circumstances, highly poetical.' COLLIER, in his ed. ii, records the reading of his (MS), but is not 'so confident that "burnished" is wrong as to exclude it' and adopt *burning*.

7. **whom**] For other instances where *who* personifies irrational antecedents, see ABBOTT, § 264.

8. **Bring me**] Q_1 omits 'me,' somewhat to the detriment of the metre, but not to the sense; it is probably merely a compositor's oversight.—ED.

11. **reddest**] JOHNSON: To understand how the tawny prince, whose savage dig-ity is very well supported, means to recommend himself by this challenge, it must be

I tell thee Ladie this aſpeᶜt of mine   12
Hath feard the valiant, (by my loue I ſweare)
The beſt regarded Virgins of our Clyme
Haue lou'd it to : I would not change this hue,   15
Except to ſteale your thoughts my gentle Queene.

13. *feard*] Q₂ Ff. *fear'd* Q₁Q₃. *scar'd*   15. *Haue*] *Hath* Q₁.
Stockdale conj.   *to*] *too* Q₁ Ff Q₃.
  14. *beſt regarded*] *best-regarded* Steev.

---

remembered that *red* blood is a traditionary sign of courage. Thus, Macbeth calls one
of his frighted soldiers a *lily-liver'd* boy; again, in this play, cowards are said to have
livers as white as milk; and an effeminate and timorous man is termed a milksop.
DOUCE (i, 254): Dr Johnson's observation derives support from our English Pliny,
Bartholomew Glantville, who says, after Isidorus, 'Reed clothes ben layed upon deed
men in remembrance of theyr hardynes and boldnes, whyle they were in theyr bloudde.'
On which his commentator, Batman, remarks: 'It appereth in the time of the Saxons
that the manner over their dead was a red cloath, as we now use black. The red of
valiauncie, and that was over kings, lords, knights and valyaunt souldiers : white over
cleargie men, in token of their profession and honest life, and over virgins and matrons.'
MONCK MASON (note on Fletcher's *Humorous Lieutenant*, IV, iv, p. 511, ed. Dyce):
It was the fashion in Fletcher's time for the young gallants to stab themselves in the
arms, or elsewhere, in order to drink the healths of their mistresses, or to write their
names, in their own blood. The custom is particularly described in Jonson's *Cynthia's
Revels* [and mentioned or alluded to in innumerable passages of early writers—DYCE.]
Morochius alludes to this practice in the *Mer. of Ven.* See ABBOTT, § 10, for the
superlative.

  12. **aspect**] For a long list of words where the accent is nearer the end than at
present, see ABBOTT, § 490.

  13. **feard**] ABBOTT, § 291 : This is not an intransitive verb converted into a transitive verb. It had the signification of *frighten* in Anglosaxon and Early English.

  16. **steale**] CLARENDON : Except I might steal your affections by disguising myself,
as thieves do. KOENIG (p. 103) : Morocco, in order to counteract the judgment that
may be passed on him for his color, appeals to what is, to be sure, somewhat of an
internal quality, but which is of a purely physical nature, and therefore, in reality, external—namely, his blood; then he refers to his exterior, and tells how his 'aspect'
has 'feared the valiant,' and how the 'best regarded virgins of his clime' have fallen
in love with his face. Thus far in six verses he has mentioned 'love' three times, and
twice his love for Portia, whom he has just seen, evidently for the first time. What he
calls 'love,' therefore, is nothing but a desire to possess Portia for her wealth and her
fair reputation,—a purely superficial affection, not an honest love down deep in the
heart. Then he goes on to talk of the devotion of true love, and he declares, with a
jingling of his sabre, that to win Portia he is ready to confront perils and engage with
lions and bears. Portia's assurance that he stood as fair as any other of her suitors
conveys to us, who know what her feelings toward those others are, a keen satire,
which becomes extremely comic when Morocco thanks her for it. In the choice itself,
true to his whole character, Morocco passes by the lead casket solely on account of its
homely exterior, and hesitates between the silver and gold solely with reference to his
own merits; and finally chooses the gold entirely in accordance with its exterior and

Por.   In tearmes of choife I am not folie led   17
By nice direction of a maidens eies :
Befides, the lottrie of my deftenie
Bars me the right of voluntarie choofing :   20
But if my Father had not fcanted me,
And hedg'd me by his wit to yeelde my felfe
His wife, who wins me by that meanes I told you,
Your felfe (renowned Prince) than ftood as faire
As any commer I haue look'd on yet   25
For my affection.
Mor.   Euen for that I thanke you,   27

---

17. Por.] Portia. Q₂.

folie] *foly* Q₁Q₂F₂F₃. *foelly* F₄. *folely* Q₃.

19. *deftenie*] Q₂. *deftiny* Q₁.

22. *wit*] *will* Han. Cap. Steev. '85, Rann, Mal. Dyce iii, Huds. Coll. iii

24. *than*] Q₁Q₂. *then* F₂.

---

its inscription, as he wishes to have that which all the world desires, and more than he deserves.

17, 18. **In tearmes . . . By nice**] Conf. 'in way of smile,' I, i, 61, and 'In way of marriage,' line 48 of this present scene, and many other instances of the omission of the definite article, in ABBOTT, §§ 89, 90.

17. **tearmes**] KARL ELZE (*Jahrbuch*, vi, 166): The terms for the choice of the caskets were devised to frighten off unworthy and unlovable wooers, like the French jumping-jack, the German toper, and the Neapolitan dilettante in the noble art of horse-shoeing. In plain prose, Portia's Father did not wish that she should become the prize of a wooer who should choose her for the sake of her gold and silver, one who should in marriage seek outward show not inward worth, one who should love her fortune not herself. And yet—strange contradiction !—Bassanio it was who set out for Belmont on purpose to win the 'Golden Fleece;' while to the Princes of Arragon and of Morocco, with their royal wealth, this mercenary motive could not be imputed. . . . . We learn to know afterwards that Bassanio, in spite of his prodigality and too swelling port, is at heart a sound, manly character, and does not love Portia's wealth more than her very self.

18. **nice**] DYCE: Scrupulous, precise, squeamish.

20. **Bars**] ABBOTT, § 198 : Verbs of ablation, such as *bar, banish, forbid*, often omit the preposition before the place or inanimate object.

22. **wit**] THEOBALD (*Nichols's Ill. of Lit.* ii, 305): I would read, *will*. So in l, ii, 25, 'the will of a dead father;' *Ib.*, line 89, 'you should refuse to perform your Father's will;' *Ib.*, line 104, 'by the manner of my Father's will.' JOHNSON : I suppose we may safely read *will*. Confined me by his will. STEEVENS : As the ancient signification of 'wit' was sagacity, or power of mind, I have not displaced the original reading. STAUNTON : 'Wit' is *knowledge, foresight, wisdom*.

23. **His**] ABBOTT, § 218 : *His, her*, &c. being genitives of *he, she*, &c., may stand as the antecedent of a relative.

24. **stood**] The same construction as 'had scanted' just above.

24. **as faire**] CLARENDON : A reference to the complexion of the Moor.

Therefore I pray you leade me to the Caskets   28
To trie my fortune : By this Symitare
That flew the Sophie, and a Perſian Prince   30
That won three fields of Sultan Solyman,
I would ore-ſtare the ſterneſt eies that looke :
Out-braue the heart moſt daring on the earth :
Plucke the yong ſucking Cubs from the ſhe Beare,
Yea, mocke the Lion when he rores for pray   35
To win the Ladie.   But alas, the while

29. *Symitare*] Q₂Q₃.   *Semitaur* Qₓ.
Symitar Ff.
    30. *Sophie*] Fₓ.   *Sophy* Qₓ et cet.
    Prince] *Prince,* Rowe.
    32. *ore-ſtare*] Q₂FfQ₃, Rowe, Cap.
Knt, Sta. Wh. i, Rlfe.   *out-ſtare* Qₓ et
cet.

    34. *ſucking*] *suckling* Ktly.
    35. *he*] *a* Q₂Q₃.
    pray] *prey,* Rowe.
    36. *the Ladie.*] *thee, lady.* Rowe ii et
seq.
    while] *while !* Pope.

---

30. **Sophie**] JOHNSON : Shakespeare seldom escapes well when he is entangled with geography.   The Prince of Morocco must have travelled far to kill the Sophy of Persia. TYRRWHITT : It were well if Shakespeare had never ' entangled ' himself 'with geography' worse than in the present case.   If the Prince of Morocco be supposed to have served in the army of Sultan *Solyman* (*the Second,* for instance), I see no *geographical* objection to his having killed the Sophi of Persia.   (See D'Herbelot in Solyman Ben Selim.)   HALLIWELL : The Prince, however, clearly means to say that he won three fields *from* Solyman.   CLARENDON : In 'The Table' at the end of *The History of the Warres betweene the Turkes and the Persians,* written in Italian by J. T. Minadoi, and translated by Abraham Hartwell, London, 1595, we read : ' *Soffi,* and *Sofito,* an auncient word signifying a wise man, learned and skilfull in Magike Naturall.   It is growen to be the common name of the Emperour of Persia.'   The first monarch who bore the name was Ismael Sophi, the founder of the Suffavian dynasty, at the beginning of the 16th Century.   So says Mill in his *British India,* but Minadoi, p. 48, affirms that he did rather renew it in his own person.   It is not necessary to suppose that Shakespeare was at all careful of historical accuracy ; but probably he refers, in the next line, to the unfortunate campaign which Solyman the Magnificent undertook against the Persians in 1535.   [The 'Sefi of Persia' is mentioned in *Der Jud von Venedig,* performed during Shakespeare's lifetime by English comedians on the Continent.   See Appendix, ' Source of the Plot.'—ED.]

    33. **ore-stare**] A majority of editors have decided, and, I think, rightly, that Qₓ has here decidedly the better word.   Again, in line 35, I think ' he ' of Qₓ and Ff is better than the colloquial *a* of Q₂.—ED.

    36. **alas, the while**] STAUNTON : The vernacular phrase *alas,* or *woe the while,* appears to have been a parenthetical ejaculation of sorrow, with no more determinate meaning than Pistol's ' lament therefore,' or our ' it's sad to think.'   It occurs again in *Hen. V :* IV, vii, 78, and in *Jul. Cæs.* I, iii, 82.   ROLFE : This expression seems originally to have meant, ' Alas for the present state of things !' but it came to be used as indefinitely as the simple ' alas !'   CLARENDON : Compare *Ezekiel,* xxx, 2 : ' Woe worth the day !'

If *Hercules* and *Lychas* plaie at dice   37
Which is the better man, the greater throw
May turne by fortune from the weaker hand:
So is *Alcides* beaten by his rage,   40
And ſo may I, blinde fortune leading me
Miſſe that which one vnworthier may attaine,
And die with grieuing.
  Port. You muſt take your chance,
And either not attempt to chooſe at all,   45
Or ſweare before you chooſe, if you chooſe wrong
Neuer to ſpeake to Ladie afterward
In way of marriage, therefore be aduis'd.   48

38. *man,*] *man ?* Rowe.   Theob. et cet.
40. *rage*] Qq Ff, Rowe, Pope i. *page* 44, 49. *chance*] *chaunce* Q₂.

---

40. **rage**] THEOBALD (*Sh. Restored*, p. 166): Tho' the whole Set of Editions con-cur in this Reading, I am very well assur'd, and I dare say the Readers will be so too anon, that it is corrupt at Bottom. Let us look into the Poet's Sentiment, and the His-tory of the Persons represented. If *Hercules* (says he) and *Lichas* were to play at Dice for the Decision of their Superiority, *Lichas*, the weaker Man, might have the better Cast of the Two. But how then is *Alcides* beaten by his Rage? To admit This, we must suppose a Gap in the Poet, and that some Lines are lost in which *Hercules*, in his Passion for losing the Hand, had thrown the Box and Dice away, and knock'd his own Head against the Wall for meer Madness. Thus, indeed, might he be said, in some Sense, to be beaten by his *Rage*. But SHAKESPEARE had no such Stuff in his Head. He means no more than, if *Lichas* had the better Throw, so might *Hercules* himself be beaten by *Lichas*. In short *Lichas* was the poor unfortunate Servant of *Hercules*, who, unknowingly, brought his Master the envenom'd Shirt, dipp'd in the Blood of the Cen-taur *Nessus*, and was thrown headlong into the Sea for his Pains. [Ovid's *Metam.* ix, 155.] The Poet has alluded to some Parts of this Fable in another of his Plays; [*Ant. & Cleop.* IV, xii, 43] and there indeed a reasonable Intimation is made of *Hercules* worsting himself thro' his own Rage. Can we desire more than to know this one Cir-cumstance of *Lichas's* Quality to set us right in the Poet's Meaning, and put an End to all the present Absurdity of the Passage? Restore it, without the least Scruple, only with cutting off the Tail of a single Letter; So is *Alcides* beaten by his PAGE. . . . . . The very excellent Lord Lansdowne, in his Alteration of this Play, tho' he might not stand to make the Correction upon the Poet, seems at least to have understood the Pas-sage exactly as I do; And tho' he changes the Verse, retains the Sense of it in this Manner; 'So were a Giant worsted by a Dwarf.' Tho' I had made the *Emendation*, before I thought to look into his *Lordship's* Performance, it is no small Satisfaction to me, that I have the Authority of such a *Genius* to back my Conjecture.

48. **In way**] See 'In tearmes,' line 17.

48. **aduis'd**] JOHNSON: Therefore be not precipitant; consider well what you are to do. 'Advis'd' is the word opposite to *rash*. [See I, i, 152.]

Mor.   Nor will not, come bring me vnto my chance.

Por.   Firſt forward to the temple, after dinner   50
Your hazard ſhall be made.

Mor.   Good fortune then,   *Cornets.*
To make me bleſt or curſed'ſt among men.   *Exeunt.*   53

49. *come...vnto*] *therefore bring me to*   52. Cornets.] Om. Qq.
Γope+.   53. *bleſt*] *bless't* Steev. '93.
  vnto] *to* Q₁, Pope+.   *curſed'ſt*] *curſedſt* Q₁.
50. *temple*] *table* Ktly.

---

49. **Nor will not**] For other instances of double negatives, see ABBOTT, § 406, also above I, ii, 26 : 'nor refuse none.'

49. **vnto**] F₁ here wisely followed Q₂, to the improvement of the metre.—ED.

50. **temple**] ECCLES : Where. I suppose, the oath she spoke of was to be administered to the suitors.   KEIGHTLEY (*Exp.* p. 149) : Surely 'temple' has no meaning here.   Must not the poet have written *table?*   In *Lucrece* (St. 168), in the Var. Shakespeare, 'Her sacred *temple*' is printed 'Her sacred *table*.'   I am not aware that any critic has observed this palpable error.   The term *table*, it may be observed, was much more used by our forefathers than by us.   CLARENDON : The mention of a temple instead of a church seems odd here.   Perhaps Portia's Roman name led Shakespeare momentarily to forget that she was a Christian, or the mention of Hercules and Lichas may have given his thoughts a classical turn.

52. **Good**] ECCLES : Morochius cannot mean that *good* fortune, as opposed to *bad*, should *make* him *cursed;* 'good' is here only an epithet of respect applied to Fortune in his address to her : 'Thou, O good Fortune ! it will be thy task, or office, to make me blest, or,' &c.

53. **blest**] STEEVENS : That is, blessed'st.   WALKER (*Crit.* i, 218) gives many instances, not alone from Shakespeare, but from the Elizabethan poets, with whom, as he says, the idiom is not unfrequent, of 'attaching terminations to one adjective, which affect others.'   Thus, 'The generous and gravest citizens,'—*Meas. for Meas.* IV, vi, 13; 'The humble as the proudest sail doth bear,'—*Sonn.* lxxx.   We have the adverbial termination in 'Why do you speak so startingly and rash,'—*Oth.* III, iv, 94.   Again, the usage, whereby the *latter* of two superlatives copulated with *and* is changed into a positive, is frequent in Shakespeare and his contemporaries.   Conf. 'The *best* condition'd and *unwearied* spirit,'—*Mer. of Ven.* III, ii, 310.   The corresponding section in ABBOTT is 398.   ECCLES remarks that the present passage will be 'good sense enough, though we should suppose "blest" only in the positive degree;' which is true, but the number of instances alleged by Walker show that the superlative applies to both adjectives; moreover, in this present line, there is the *sound* of a superlative in 'blest,' which satisfies the ear.—ED.

[*Scene II.*]

Enter the Clowne alone.

Clo.   Certainely, my confcience will ferue me to **run**
from this Iew my Maifter : the fiend is at mine elbow,   3

[Scene II. Venice. Rowe.   Venice. A   2. *will*] *will not* Hal.
Street. Cap.   3. *Maifter*] Q₂.
  1. Enter...] Enter Launcelot alone.   *mine*] *my* Rowe i.
Rowe.

---

  1. The lack in the Qq of any division into Acts and Scenes is made use of by EC-
CLES to re-arrange the order, whereby the First Act ends with the discomfiture of the
Prince of Morocco, and the Second with that of Arragon.   It is not altogether for the
sake of sensational effect that he thus closes the Acts, but for reasons connected with
the dramatic time of the action, reasons which will be found more fully discussed in
the Appendix.   At the first blush there seems to be a degree of propriety in this re-arrangement; in each of the first three Acts we have a Casket scene, with all its attendant bravery, and the charm and fragrance of Belmont dominate the Ghetto; but the
Master is wiser than all of us.   The play hereby becomes three different stories, at the
end of each we draw a long breath, instead of keeping our suspense locked up to the
very close.   Portia has just told Morocco that his hazard must be made after dinner;
Eccles accordingly takes the Seventh Scene of Act Second, wherein Morocco makes
his choice, and transfers it to this First Act, and closes the Act with it.   The First
Scene of the Second Act, according to Eccles, now opens at Venice, with Launcelot
Gobbo.   'The particular time of the day,' he says, 'is undetermined; Bassanio, however, upon his entrance, desires that "supper may be ready by five of the clock."'—ED.

  1. **Clowne**] DOUCE (i, p. 271): There is not a single circumstance through the
whole of this play which constitutes Launcelot an *allowed Fool* or *Jester;* and yet there
is some reason for supposing that Shakespeare intended him as such, from his being
called *a patch*, *a fool* of Hagar's offspring, and in one place *the* fool.   It is not reasonable, however, to conclude that a person like Shylock would entertain a domestic of
this description; and it is possible that the foregoing terms may be designed merely as
synonymous with the appellation of *clown*, as in *Love's Lab. Lost.*   On the whole we
have here a proof that Shakespeare has not observed that nice discrimination of character in his clowns for which some have given him credit.

  2. **will serue**] ECCLES: He must be understood to mean that his conscience will
finally be induced to acquiesce in, or even be assistant to, his purpose of running away
from the Jew.   HALLIWELL: The particle *not*, a word frequently omitted in early editions of plays, seems essential to the sense of what follows.   The fiend beats the conscience, but the latter is represented as firmly inveighing against the desertion of his
master.   ALLEN: Read either 'will *not*' with Halliwell, or 'will *forbid*,' which is not
so very remote from the *ductus literarum.*   'Will not' is more plausible for modern,
than for Old, English.   *Will*, in Shakespeare, is oftener equivalent to *veut, intends.*
Now 'it is clear (from what it has been saying and continues to say) that my conscience intends to forbid my running away' is exactly consistent with the fact, as stated
by Launcelot himself.

and tempts me, faying to me, *Iobbe, Launcelet Iobbe,* good
Launcelet, or good *Iobbe,* or good *Launcelet Iobbe,* vfe   5
your legs, take the ftart, run awaie : my confcience faies
no ; take heede honeft *Launcelet,* take heed honeft *Iobbe,*
or as afore-faid honeft *Launcelet Iobbe,* doe not runne,
fcorne running with thy heeles ; well, the moft coragi-   9

4. *tempts*] *attempts* F$_3$F$_4$, Rowe i.   Launcelot Rowe.
4, &c. Iobbe] Q$_2$F$_2$Q$_3$, Rowe ii. Job   9. *heeles*] *bells* Anon. ap. Hal.
F$_3$F$_4$, Rowe i. Gobbo Q$_1$, Pope et seq.   *coragious*] Q$_2$Q$_3$. *couragious* Q$_1$ Ff.
Launcelet] Qq Ff. (Lancelet Q$_1$.)   *contagious* Coll. (MS).

---

4. **Iobbe, &c.**] This spelling, repeated half a dozen times, is apparently one of those
wild and inexplicable freaks to which the old compositors were subject, and familiar
enough to the readers of old plays.   Or it may be an indication of the piecemeal composition whereby these plays were set up.   Launcelot's father enters a few lines lower
down, and his name is consistently spelled *Gobbo* throughout; and Launcelot's speeches
are at once indicated by *Lan.* or *Laun.* for over a hundred lines, when, at line 143, they
are again indicated by *Clo.* (See the Text. Notes for the way in which this *Iobbe* misled
F$_3$F$_4$ and Rowe.)   I am afraid we must echo Bottom : ' man is but an ass, if he go about
to expound this.'—ED.

4. **Launcelet**] WHITE (ed. i): This invariable spelling in the QqFf,—the English
diminutive of *Launce,*—warrants the belief that such was its original form.   But as the
nomenclature of the Dramatis Personæ is purely Italian, as the diminutive in that language is formed in *otto,* and as the present name has been in the text for a hundred and
fifty years, it is not worth while to make a change in so trivial a matter.

9. **with thy heeles**] STEEVENS : Launcelot was designed for a wag, but, perhaps,
not for an absurd one.   We may therefore suppose no such expression would have been
put in his mouth as our author had censured in another character.   When Pistol says,
' he hears with ears,' Sir Hugh Evans very properly is made to exclaim, ' The tevil and
his tam ! what phrase is this, *he hears with ears ?* why it is affectations.'   To talk of
running with one's heels has scarcely less of absurdity.   It has been suggested that we
should read and point the passage as follows : ' Do not run ; scorn running ; *withe* thy
heels :' i. e. connect them with a *withe* (a band made of osiers), as the legs of cattle
are hampered in some countries to prevent their straggling far from home.   I think
myself bound, however, to add that in *Much Ado,* the very phrase, that in the present
instance is disputed, occurs : ' O illegitimate construction ! I scorn that with my heels ;'
i. e. I recalcitrate, kick up contemptuously at the idea, as animals throw up their hind
legs.   Such also may be Launcelot's meaning.   [I do not for a minute suppose that
Steevens, that ' Puck of Commentators,' was serious when he started this laughable
emendation.   I think he chuckled in anticipation over the grave and didactic refutation which it would receive from Malone, as it did.   No one knew better than Steevens, with his retentive memory and extensive reading, that the phrase was proverbial ;
but the fiend was at his elbow, he took a good start, and has led the commentators a
very pretty chase ever since.   Had there been anything indelicate in the allusion, his
note would have been signed Amner or Collins ; as it is, he says simply, ' It has been
suggested,' and in citing the passage from *Much Ado,* he knew well enough that he
gave all the explanation needed.—ED.]

ous fiend bids me packe, *fia* faies the fiend, away faies   10
the fiend, for the heauens roufe vp a braue minde faies
the fiend, and run; well, my confcience hanging about   12

10. fia] Qq Ff. *Via* Rowe.
11. for] *'fore* Coll. iii (MS).
    heauens] Qq Ff, Rowe+, Sta.
heavens; Cap. Steev. Mal. Knt, Sing.

Ktly. *heavens,* Coll. Dyce, Wh. i, Clarke, Rlfe. *haven;* M. Mason.
11. roufe] *rofe* F₄.
12. run;] *run.* Rowe.

---

10. **fia**] NICHOLSON (*N. & Qu.* 6th Ser. vol. i, p. 333): Why was this Italian word in not uncommon use in Shakespeare's England, and why does Shakespeare think it congruent to put it into the mouth of certainly a quick-witted and town-living, but country bred, clown? The answers, I think, lie in the fact, told us by Capt. John Smith in his *Seaman's Grammar*, that *via*, or, as he spells it by pronunciation, *vea*, a nautical term, from the Italian, like some others, was a word of exhortation used by a boat's crew when redoubling their stroke or pulling more vigorously. It was apparently spoken unanimously, and, like the paviors' 'Hoh!' after each stroke, for he gives it thus, 'Vea, vea, vea, vea, vea, vea.' Hence it was doubtless in common use among the Thames watermen. IBID. (*Ib.* vol. ii, p. 305): Since writing my former note, I think it right to add that I have found 'via' was used contemporaneously in England to horses. Gervase Markham, in his *Country Contentments*, 1615, twice gives 'via, how, hey' at pp. 40 and 45, as terms of encouragement from their riders to horses. Also in his *Cavalariæ*, 1617: 'But if you crie *Hoa, Ho,* or *Hey, Hey,* or *Via, Via,*' &c. [HALLIWELL had already called attention to Markham's reference to it in *Cheap and Good Husbandry*, p. 15, as a word to be used in encouraging a horse.]

11. **heauens**] CAPELL (ii, 60 *b*): Signal changes in sense, made by punctuation can rarely be lay'd before a reader in any other way than that we are now taking:— 'for the heavens' is in all prior copies connected with 'rouse' &c., having no point between them; and some moderns mark such it's connection still stronger, by changing *fiend's* comma into a semicolon: How they understood them, or whether they understood them at all, matters not; pointed as they are at this present, the words have no difficulty; and by giving voice to this passage, through four sentences, we shall feel in the only cadence and run of them the pointing's rectitude: the words are found in the mouth of some other characters and (particularly) in that of Beatrice at II, i, of that play. But what impropriety, says some objecter, in making the '*fiend*' speak them! True; and in that very impropriety lyes the wit: blunders and false conclusions of all sorts, join'd with numberless oddities and an innate honesty, make up this character; some choice flowers in his way the moderns rob him of towards the speech's end, by adopting the readings of a quarto. GIFFORD (*Every Man Out of His Humour*, II, i, p. 68, ed. 1816): The words, 'for the heavens!' are merely a petty oath; and where soever they occur, in this manner, and by whomsoever they are spoken, mean neither more nor less than—by heaven! .... That no future doubts may arise on the subject, I will subjoin two or three of as many score examples which I could instantly produce; the first shall be from Jonson himself: 'Come on, Sir Valentine, I'll give you a health, for the heavens, you mad Capricio.'—*The Case is Altered*. The second from his old enemy Dekker: 'A lady took a pipefull or two (of tobacco) at my hands, and praised it, for the heavens!'—*Untrussing the Humorous Poet*. And, to conclude, Tweddle, the drunken piper in *Pasquil and Katharine*, exclaims, 'I must goe and clap my mistress' cheekes (his tabor) there, for the heavens.'

the necke of my heart, ſaies verie wiſely to me : my ho-   13
neſt friend *Launcelet*, being an honeſt mans ſonne, or rather an honeſt womans ſonne, for indeede my Father did   15
ſomething ſmack, ſomething grow too ; he had a kinde of
taſte ; wel, my conſcience ſaies *Lancelet* bouge not, bouge
ſaies the fiend, bouge not ſaies my conſcience, conſcience
ſay I you counſaile well, fiend ſay I you counſaile well,
to be rul'd by my conſcience I ſhould ſtay with the *Iew*   20
my Maiſter,(who God bleſſe the marke)is a kinde of di-

16. *too*] *to* Q₂Q₃, Pope et seq.   *ill* Theob. Warb. Johns.
17. *taſte*] *taſt* Q₂Q₃.   19. *fiend ... well*] *Fiend ... ill* Q₁,
   Lancelet] Om. Q₁, Pope+.   Pope+.
17, 18. *bouge*] *budge* F₃. *budg* F₄.   21. (*who God*] Q₂Q₃. *who* (*God* Q₁
18, 19. *conſcience...well*] *conſcience...*   et cet.

16. **smack**] ECCLES : *Of a knave*, he may be understood to mean. Whether we take 'smack' as signifying *tinctured* or as *smacking the lips*, with either acceptation, 'he had a kind of taste' may agree; the difference will not be great respecting the morality of old Gobbo. To 'grow to' I suppose to have been a cant phrase, but which it seems not very easy precisely to define; it may be designed to express a pretty strong *natural bias* to knavish tricks, cheating practices; or all taken together may imply nothing more than the old man's original propensity to certain conjugal infidelities as opposed to his wife's honesty. CLARENDON : 'Grow to.' A household phrase applied to milk when burnt to the bottom of the sauce-pan, and thence acquiring an unpleasant taste. 'Grown,' in this sense, is still used in Lincolnshire. (Brogden's *Dict. of Provincial Words*, &c.)

17, &c.] DOUCE (i, 255) thinks it not improbable that 'this curious struggle between Launcelot's conscience and the fiend might have been suggested by some well-known story in Shakespeare's time, grafted' on a monkish fable, which Douce proceeds to set forth, wherein a woman's laziness argues with her conscience about getting up in the morning to go to mass. [How inexhaustible and untiring was Shakespeare's industry in collecting materials wherefrom to compose his patchwork plays !—ED.]

19. **fiend . . . well**] FURNIVALL (*Forewords to Quarto 1*) : Q₁ misses Lancelot's point by making him say, 'Fiend say I you counsel *ill*,' where we *must* [*sic*] have the Heyes 'well,' to match the 'Conscience say I you counsell well,' and Lancelot's following the Fiend's advice by budging from Shylock. [On what compulsion *must* we believe that logic or reason rules in anything that is said by Launcelot, 'whose nose fell a bleeding on black Monday last, at six o'clock in the morning, falling out that year on Ashwednesday was foure years in the afternoon' ? It may be that Q₂ is right, but that Gobbo's words are here illogical does not, I think, prove Q₁ wrong; certainly not so wrong as that the passage can be cited, as Furnivall cites it, in conclusive proof that Q₂ is the more correct text. POPE, THEOBALD, HANMER, WARBURTON, and DR JOHNSON all preferred in this passage the text of Q₁.—ED.]

20. **to be rul'd**] See ABBOTT, § 356, for instances of infinitives indefinitely used.

21. **marke**] CLARENDON : This phrase is used as a parenthetic apology for some profane or vulgar word. ROLFE : The origin and meaning of it are alike obscure. [Prof. F. J. CHILD suggests to me that it may have been derived from the mark set

uell; and to run away from the *Iew* I fhould be ruled by   22
the fiend, who fauing your reuerence is the diuell himfelfe: certainely the *Iew* is the verie diuell incarnation,
and in my confcience, my confcience is a kinde of hard   25
confcience, to offer to counfaile me to ftay with the *Iew*;
the fiend giues the more friendly counfaile : I will runne
fiend, my heeles are at your commandement, I will
runne.

Enter old Gobbo with a Bafket.   30

Gob. Maifter yong-man, you I praie you, which is the
waie to Maifter *Iewes*?
Lan. O heauens, this is my true begotten Father, who
being more then fand-blinde, high grauel blinde, knows
me not, I will trie confufions with him.   35

---

24. *diuell*] *Devil's* Ktly conj.
  incarnation] *incarnall* Q₁, Pope,
Ec. Cam. Glo. Cla. *in-carnation* Rann.
25. *is a*] Ff, Knt. *is but a* Qq et cet.
26. Iew;] Iew. Q₁.
28. *commandement*] *command* Q₁,
Cam. Cla. Glo. Wh. ii. *commandment*
Rowe et cet.

31, &c. *Maifter*] Q₂. *Mafter* Q₁ et
cet.
31. *yong-man*] F₂. *yong man* Q₁.
young-man Q₂Q₃F₃F₄, Rowe+.
33. [Aside. Johns. et seq.
35. *not*,] *not ;* Q₃.
  confufions] *conclufions* Q₁, Johns.
Steev. Mal. Var. Knt.

---

upon idolaters, in *Ezekiel*, ix, 6. In the misplaced parenthesis before 'who,' one of
the many proofs is afforded that the Folio was printed from Q₂.—ED.]

23. **sauing your reuerence**] This phrase is used in much the same way as 'God
bless the mark.'—ED.

24. **diuell**] If it be desirable to spoil this speech by making sense of its nonsense,
KEIGHTLEY's emendation, 'Devil's incarnation' will serve the turn.—ED.

32. **Iewes**] KNIGHT: [The Jews' Quarter] is situated on the canal which leads to
Mestre. There are houses there old enough to have been Shylock's, with balconies
from which Jessica might have talked; and ground enough beneath, between the
houses and the water, for her lover to stand, hidden in the shadow, or under a 'penthouse.' Hence, too, her gondola might at once start for the mainland, without having
to traverse any part of the city.—(M). [Miss Martineau?—ED.]

34. **sand-blinde**] CAPELL: That is, purblind; a vulgar phrase for it, as *stone-blind*
is for those who are quite so : Launcelot finds a blind between these, which he calls
'gravel-blind.' MALONE: So in Latimer's First Sermon on the Lord's Prayer: 'The
Saintis be purre-blinde and sand-blinde.' CLARENDON: Cotgrave has '*Berluè*: f.
The being sand-blind, or pur-blind.' HALFS (*Notes & Essays*, p. 193): Probably the
sand, as has been suggested, is the Anglosaxon *sám* (the Latin *semi*, Greek ἡμι), as in
sám-cwic, sám-wis, &c.

35. **confusions**] COLLIER: The printer of Q₁ did not understand the joke of Launcelot, which he carries into effect immediately afterward by misdirecting his father 'the

5

Gob. Maifter yong Gentleman, I praie you which is the waie to Maifter *Iewes*. 36

Laun. Turne vpon your right hand at the next turning, but at the next turning of all on your left; marrie at the verie next turning, turne of no hand, but turn down indirectlie to the *Iewes* houfe. 40

Gob. Be Gods fonties 'twill be a hard waie to hit, can you tell me whether one *Launcelet* that dwels with him, dwell with him or no.

Laun. Talke you of yong Mafter *Launcelet*, marke me now, now will I raife the waters; talke you of yong Maifter *Launcelet*? 45

Gob. No Maifter fir, but a poore mans fonne, his Fa- 48

---

38. *vpon*] Ff, Knt, Hal. Sta. *up, on* Pope+. *vp on* Qq et cet.
39. *all*] all, Theob. et seq.
41. *to the*] *vnto the* Q₁, Johns.
42. *Be*] *By* F₄ et seq.
43. *whether*] *whither* Q₁.
44. *no.*] *no ?* Q₁F₄.

45. Launcelet,] Lancelet? Q₁. Launcelot ? [Aside] Johns. et seq.
47, 55. *Maifter*] M. Q₁.
48. *Maifter*] *Master*, Rowe et seq.
48–50. Four lines, ending *fonne...fay't ...man...liue.* Q₁.

---

way to Master Jews.' CLARENDON: Launcelot would not have given a hard word [like 'conclusions' of Q₁] so correctly.

38. THEOBALD calls attention to similar perplexing directions given by the slave Syrus to the old man Demea in Terence's *Adelphi*, IV, ii, 42. There is a feeble attempt at a similar misdirection in the *Jud von Venedig*. See Appendix.—ED.

40. **of no hand**] ABBOTT, § 165 : 'Of' is here used where we should use *on*.

42. **sonties**] STEEVENS: I know not of what oath this is a corruption. I meet with 'God's-santy' in Dekker's *Honest Whore* [I, xii, p. 315, ed. Dodsley]. Again, in *The Longer thou Livest the more Fool thou Art*, bl. l. without date: 'God's santie, this is a goodly book indeed.' Perhaps it was once customary to swear by the *santé*, i. e. health, of the Supreme Being, or by his *saints*, or, as Ritson observes to me, by his sanctity. Oaths of such a turn are not unfrequent among our ancient writers. All, however, seem to have been so thoroughly convinced of the crime of profane swearing, that they were content to disguise their meaning by abbreviations which were permitted silently to terminate in irremediable corruptions. ALLEN: 'By God's dear Saints.' 'Saint' = (as in Scotch) *saunt; sauntie* (as in Scotch), diminutive ὑποκοριστικῶς. Conf. By'r *Lakin*.

45. **yong**] CAPELL (ii, 61 *a*): We should observe from the Son's *young's*, which are emphatical, that 'Launcelot' was his father's name too: His *ergo's* the pronouncer should sound—*argo;* and he uses them for—talk logically, let us keep to our *ergo's*.

48. **Maister**] In the *Trans. of the New Shakspere Soc.*, Part I, p. 103, FURNIVALL gives a quotation from Smith's *Commonwealth of England* to show that ' Master is the tytle which men giue to esquires, and other gentlemen.'

ther though I fay't is an honeft exceeding poore man,
and God be thanked well to liue.   50

   Lan.   Well, let his Father be what a will, wee talke of
yong Maifter *Launcelet.*

   Gob.   Your worfhips friend and *Launcelet.*

   Laun.   But I praie you *ergo* old man, *ergo* I befeech you,
talke you of yong Maifter *Launcelet.*   55

---

49. *fay't*] Q₂FfQ₃, Hal. Wh. Rlfe.   *fir* Qq et cet.
fay it Q₁ et cet.   55. Launcelet.] Q₁Q₂F₂F₃, Knt, Sing.
51. *a*] *he* Pope+, Cap. Steev. Mal.   Sta. Wh. Ktly.   Launcelet? Q₃F₄ e·
53. Launcelet] Ff, Knt.   Launcelet   cet.

---

50. **well to liue**] The meaning of this phrase, which we all understand at once as implying 'with every prospect of a long life,' appears to have escaped all the German translators from Wieland down to Bodenstedt. Eschenburg translates it 'noch ganz munter;' Schlegel, 'recht wohl auf;' Max Moltke, 'befindet sich recht wohl;' and Hager, as well as Schmidt (to whom we owe the *Lexicon*), 'es geht ihm gut.'—Ed.

53. This line is obscure. I cannot see that the reading of the Qtos: 'Launcelet, Sir,' helps it much, if any. Steevens reports Dr Farmer as of the opinion that 'we should read *Gobbo* instead of Launcelet; and observes that phraseology like this occurs also in *Love's Lab. Lost*, V, ii, 574, where Costard says, "Your servant, and Costard;"' but this instance is not parallel; 'your servant' refers to 'Pompey,' the character Costard was acting. Capell's explanation we have just had, that the Father and Son bore the same name, and that here old Gobbo refers to himself. Malone's explanation, which White also adopts, is perhaps the best—that is, 'plain Launcelot; and not, as you term him, *master* Launcelot.'—Ed.

55. Knight: This sentence is usually put interrogatively, contrary to the punctuation of all [*sic*] the old copies; which is not to be so utterly despised as the modern editors would pretend. Dyce: So says Mr Knight, forgetting that this is a repetition of Launcelot's preceding *interrogation*, 'Talk you of young Master Launcelot?' White: This is imperative, not interrogative. The misapprehension of the passage by more than one modern editor justifies an explanation of it. Launcelot whimsically takes his father to task for disrespect to himself—Launcelot, and says, in reply to old Gobbo's statement of their condition in life, 'Well, let his father be what he will, we talk of young Master Launcelot.' The father, still unable to dub his son 'Master,' replies deprecatingly, 'Your worship's friend, and Launcelot,' i. e. 'Ay, we speak of your worship's friend, who is Launcelot.' To this, Launcelot, who evidently, like the Gravedigger in *Hamlet*, understands, after a fashion, the Latin word he uses, rejoins, 'But I pray you, *ergo*, old man, *ergo*, I beseech you, talk you of young Master Launcelot,' i. e. 'And therefore, because I am "your worship" and he is my friend, you should speak of him as Master Launcelot.' Cambridge Editors: Dyce's remark that the sentence is a repetition of the preceding interrogation, seems conclusive as to the sense. Nothing is more frequent than the omission of the note of interrogation in the older editions, apparently from a paucity of types. [I cannot see that White's explanation would not justify an interrogation quite as well as an imperative: 'And therefore, because I am "your worship" and he is my friend, are you, I beseech you, talking of young Master Launcelot?' 'Of Launcelot,' replies the old man, which surely seems a response fitter to a question than to a command.—Ed.]

Gob.   Of *Launcelet,* ant pleafe your maifterfhip.   56

Lan. Ergo Maifter *Lancelet,* talke not of maifter *Lance-let* Father, for the yong gentleman according to fates and deftinies, and fuch odde fayings, the fifters three, & fuch branches of learning, is indeede deceafed, or as you   60 would fay in plaine tearmes, gone to heauen.

Gob.   Marrie God forbid, the boy was the verie ftaffe of my age, my verie prop.

Lau.   Do I look like a cudgell or a houell-poft, a ftaffe or a prop : doe you know me Father.   65

Gob.   Alacke the day, I know you not yong Gentle-man, but I praie you tell me, is my boy God reft his foule aliue or dead.

Lan.   Doe you not know me Father.

Gob.   Alacke fir I am fand blinde, I know you not.   70

Lan.   Nay, indeede if you had your eies you might

---

56. *ant*] *an't* Q_1F_4 et seq.	Dyce iii.
60. *is*] *in* F_2.	65. *you know*] *you not know* Dyce iii,
62. *verie*] *verey* F_4.	Ktly.
64, 65. *Do...prop*] As an Aside, Coll.	67. *God*] *GOD* Q_1Q_2.

---

57. **Ergo Maister**] STAUNTON: The humour here, which consists in Launcelot's determination to be dignified by the title of *master,* and the old man's unwillingness so to honor him, is less apparent in writing than in acting, where the *Master* Launcelot can be rendered sufficiently emphatic. [Theobald was the first to change the comma after Launcelot to a semicolon; Collier, rightly, I think, changed it to a full stop. Launcelot has gained his point, his father has called him 'your mastership.'—ED.]

61. MONTÉGUT (*Commentaire,* &c. p. 461) : It is noteworthy that after a sort Laun-celot is a rustic *bel esprit;* a servant who has picked up, here and there, scraps and orts of learning. He uses Latin words, which he places higgledy-piggledy in his sen-tences; we shall find him displaying a knowledge of palmistry; he criticises mytho-logical expressions and metaphors used by the learned; he plays on words sharply enough to drive Lorenzo mad, and loses no opportunity to discourse. Before entering the Jew's service he must have been the domestic of some savant of the Renaissance or of some canon of Venice, or have been a choir-boy under the curate of the village where he was born.

64. **houell-post**] Cotgrave gives : *Escraigne,* A little houell made of poles set round with their ends meeting at the top, and couered with turues, sods, &c. so thicke, that no weather can pierce it.—ED.

65. **you know**] DYCE (ed. iii) : *Not* is here omitted in the old eds., but is abso-lutely necessary : and compare Launcelot's next speech.

65. **Father**] WHITE : Twice Launcelot calls Gobbo father, and yet the old man does not even suspect with whom he is talking; the reason of which is the ancient custom, almos universal among the peasantry, of calling all old people father or mother.

faile of the knowing me : it is a wife Father that knowes   72
his owne childe. Well, old man, I will tell you newes of
your fon, giue me your bleffing, truth will come to light,
murder cannot be hid long, a mans fonne may, but in the   75
end truth will out.

Gob. Praie you fir ftand vp, I am fure you are not
Lancelet my boy.

Lan. Praie you let's haue no more fooling about
it, but giue mee your bleffing : I am *Lancelet* your   80
boy that was, your fonne that is, your childe that
fhall be.

Gob. I cannot thinke you are my fonne.

Lan. I know not what I fhall thinke of that : but I am
Lancelet the *Iewes* man, and I am fure *Margerie* your wife   85
is my mother.

Gob. Her name is *Margerie* indeede, Ile be fworne if
thou be *Lancelet,* thou art mine owne flefh and blood :
Lord worfhipt might he be, what a beard haft thou got ;
thou haft got more haire on thy chin, then Dobbin my   90
philhorfe has on his taile.

---

74. *son,*] *son.* [kneels] Coll. [kneels,
with his back to Gobbo] Dyce iii.
  74, 76. *truth*] *trueth* Q₁Q₂.
  75. *murder*] *Murther* Q₁. *muder* Q₂.
  75, 76. *in the end*] *at the length* Q₁,
Cam. Glo. Cla. Wh. ii.
  76. *out*] *not* Ff, Rowe et seq.
  89. *Lord*] *Lord !* Coll. Wh. i.
    worfhipt] *worfhip* F₄.
    might] Om. Cap. (corrected in

Errata).
  89. *got.*] *got !* [feeling the back of his
head] Hal. Dyce (subs.).
  91. *philhorfe*] Q₂ Ff. *pilhorfe* Q₁. *philhorfe* Q₃, Rowe, Pope i, Mal. *Thill-horse*
Theob +, Steev. *fill-horse* Pope ii, Dyce,
Cam. Glo. Cla. Wh. ii. *fil-horse* Cap.
phill-horse Var. et cet.
    has] *hafe* or *hafe* Q₂.
    taile] *tale* Q₁.

---

83. **you**] Note Gobbo's respectful 'you,' until he recognizes Launcelot, and then
his change to 'thou.'—ED.

89. **Lord . . . be**] Rev. JOHN HUNTER, whose text reads, 'Lord-worshipped,' explains the phrase by, 'He might be a lord worshipful,' and adds : 'This refers to the
supposed beard, and the arrogated *mastership*.' HUDSON : This expression does not
occur again in Shakespeare. The Rev John Hunter means, apparently, that he has
beard enough to receive the title of lordship. But I doubt both his printing and his
explanation. ABBOTT, § 313, interprets 'might' as an optative.

89. **beard**] STAUNTON : Stage tradition, not improbably from the time of Shakespeare himself, makes Launcelot, at this point, kneel with his back to the sand-blind
old Father, who, of course, mistakes his long back hair for a beard, of which his face
is perfectly innocent.

90, 91, 93, 94. **on . . . on . . . of . . . of**] ABBOTT, § 175 : *Of,* signifying proximity of any kind, is sometimes used locally in the sense of *on.*

Lan. It ſhould ſeeme then that Dobbins taile   92
growes backeward. I am ſure he had more haire of his
taile then I haue of my face when I loſt ſaw him.

Gob. Lord how art thou chang'd : how dooſt thou   95
and thy Maſter agree, I haue brought him a preſent ; how
gree you now ?

Lan. Well, well, but for mine owne part, as I haue ſet
vp my reſt to run awaie, ſo I will not reſt till I haue run   99

93. *of his*] *on his* Rowe+, Steev.   94. *loſt*] Q₂. *laſt* Qₓ et cet.
Mal.   95. *dooſt*] Q₂F₂. *doeſt* Qₓ. *doſt* F₃ et
94. *of my*] *on my* F₃F₄, Rowe+, Steev.   seq.
Mal.   97. *gree*] *agree* Qₓ, Pope+, Coll.

91. **philhorse**] THEOBALD: This must be restored ' *Thill*-horse ;' i. e. the Horse
which draws in the *Shafts*, or *Thill*, of the Carriage. HALLIWELL: Theobald's
change is unnecessary; both *phill-horse* and *thill-horse* were certainly in use. *Fill-
horse, filler*, the horse which goes in the shafts.—Forby's *East Anglia*. WHITE :
' Phill-horse,' as a corruption of ' *thill*-horse,' the synonym for ' shaft-horse,' is now in
common use in the rural districts of New England [and of Pennsylvania.—ED.].
CLARENDON : Shakespeare uses 'fills' in *Tro. & Cress.* III, ii, 48, 'An you draw
backward, we'll put you i' the fills.'

97. **gree**] For many instances of dropped prefixes, see ABBOTT, § 460.

98. **set vp my rest**] There seems to be some obscurity in regard to the origin of
this phrase, although there is general agreement that it means ' to be resolved, to be
determined.' Steevens maintained at one time that the expression is taken from the
manner of firing a matchlock, which was so heavy that a supporter called a *rest* was
fixed in the ground before the piece was levelled to take aim. Collier adopted this
derivation ' in spite of Gifford,' whose name carries more weight than any other, perhaps, of those who maintain that ' the metaphor is taken from play, where the highest
stake the parties were disposed to venture was called the *rest*.' Nares restricted ' the
play ' to the ' once fashionable and favorite game of *Primero*,' and said that it meant to
stand upon the cards you have in your hand, in hopes they may prove better than those
of your adversary. Hence, ' to make up your mind, to be determined.' Keightley com-
bines both definitions, and to that extent gives the more plausible explanation. He says
(*Expositor*, p. 419) that the phrase ' is derived from gaming, chiefly from the game of
Primero. As this game came from Spain, it brought, like Ombre, its terms with it, and
"rest" was the Spanish *resto*, which meant, not as is usually supposed, the stake, but the
bet or wager, which appears to have been made by the players only. "What shall we
play for?—one shilling *stake* and three *rest*."—Florio, *First Fruites*. The Spanish
phrase for laying a wager, or making a bet at play, was *echar el resto*, put or throw
down the sum betted ; and this became the English *set up the rest*. The reason, perhaps, was because this phrase was already in use in a military sense, as the matchlock
guns, on account of their weight and mode of firing them, required a *rest* or support.'
It is to be regretted that the only authority which Keightley cites for a Spanish phrase
is an Italian Phrase-book, and even the passage cited I have been unable to find in
Florio's *First Fruites*, 1578. Moreover in Minsheu's *Spanish Dict.* 1623, the phrase
echar el resto is not given under either the verb or the noun. In one *Dialogues* at the

fome ground; my Maifter's a verie *Iew*, giue him a pre-   100
fent, giue him a halter, I am famifht in his feruice.   You
may tell euerie finger I haue with my ribs : Father I am
glad you are come, giue me your prefent to one Maifter
Baffanio, who indeede giues rare new Liuories, if I ferue
not him, I will run as far as God has anie ground.   O rare   105
fortune, here comes the man, to him Father, for I am a
Iew if I ferue the *Iew* anie longer.

Enter Baffanio with a follower or two.

Baff.   You may doe fo, but let it be fo hafted that
fupper be readie at the fartheft by fiue of the clocke :   110
fee thefe Letters deliuered, put the Liueries to making, and defire *Gratiano* to come anone to my lodging.

Lan.   To him Father.

Gob.   God bleffe your worfhip.   115

Baff.   Gramercie, would'ft thou ought with me.

---

102. *my*] *your* Anon. ap. Cam.
105. *not him*] *him not* Rowe+.
108. Enter...] Enter Bassanio with
Leonardo, and a follower or two more.
Theob. et seq. (subs.).

112. *anone*] *anon* Q_1F_3 et seq.
113. [Exit one of his men. Q_1.
116. *would'ft*] *woul'd* F_3.   *would* F_4.
ought] *aught* Knt et seq.

---

end of the *Dict.*, there is (p. 26) a dialogue during a game of *priméra*, where we find :
' Que ha de ser el tanto ?   *What is the summe that we play for ?*   Quatro reáles y dies
y seis de saca.   *Two shillings stake, and eight shillings rest.*'   Where, as we see, the
English sustains Keightley, but the Spanish does not.   Further on occurs ' Yo enbido
mi resto.   *I set my rest.*'   Perhaps *embidar* is near enough to *echar.*   See the notes
on the phrase in *Rom. & Jul.* IV, v, 6.—ED.

103 **giue me**] The Ethical Dative.   If need be, see ABBOTT, § 220.

105. **ground**] KNIGHT (*Illust.*) : A characteristic speech in the mouth of a Venetian.   Ground to run upon being a scarce convenience in Venice, its lower orders of
inhabitants regard the great expanse of the mainland with feelings of admiration which
can be little entered into by those who have been able, all their days, to walk where
they would.—(M.) [Miss Martineau ?]

111. **to making**] ABBOTT, § 349 : There are many cases in which the terminations
of the infinitive and present participle have been confused together, and the *-ing* in
this construction represents the old infinitive inflection *-en.*   Perhaps, also, *-ing*, as in
the present instance, was added as a reminiscence of the old gerundive termination
-ene.

113. Note the stage-direction of Q_1 as another indication of its superiority over Q_2.
—ED.

116. **Gramercie**] French, *grand merci.*

Gob. Here's my ſonne ſir, a poore boy. 117

Lan. Not a poore boy ſir, but the rich *Iewes* man that would ſir as my Father ſhall ſpecifie.

Gob. He hath a great infeƈtion ſir, as one would ſay 120
to ſerue.

Lan. Indeede the ſhort and the long is, I ſerue the *Iew*, and haue a deſire as my Father ſhall ſpecifie.

Gob. His Maiſter and he (ſauing your worſhips reuerence) are ſcarce catercoſins. 125

Lan. To be briefe, the verie truth is, that the *Iew* hauing done me wrong, doth cauſe me as my Father being I hope an old man ſhall frutifie vnto you.

Gob. I haue here a diſh of Doues that I would beſtow 129

117, 119, 123, 128. *boy.* ...*ſpecifie.* ...
ſpecifie. ...*you.*] *boy,— ...ſpecify,— ...*
ſpecify,— ...you,] Theob. et seq.
119. *ſir*] *ſir,* Q₁Q₃F₄.
124. *ſauing*] *ſavin* F₃.

125. *catercoſins*] *cater-cousins* Rowe et
seq.
127, 128. *Father...hope*] *Father, ...*
hope, Q₁.
128. *frutifie*] *fruitify* Cap. Hal.

---

119. **specifie**] THEOBALD (Nichols's *Illust.* ii, 306): Considering that Launcelot is here upon his game and knocking all words out of joint, Mr Bishop imagines this should be *spicifie*. Just as he a little after says 'fruitifie' (*fruit* and *spice*). [Is it stage tradition here also which makes Launcelot not only interrupt his father, but turn him swiftly round, and after the delivery of his speech to Bassanio turn him as swiftly back again, and keep up these gyrations until the amazed Bassanio says, 'One speak for both'?—ED.]

125. **catercosins**] JOHNSON (*Dict.*): A corruption of *quatre-cousin*, from the ridic-
ulousness of calling cousin, or relation, to so remote a degree. CLARENDON: No such phrase is, or apparently ever was, known in French as 'quatre-cousin.' This is the only passage in Shakespeare in which it occurs. Halliwell (*Arch. and Prov. Dict.*) gives 'caper-cousins' as a Lancashire expression for 'great friends.' This is evidently a corruption of our phrase. The sense required here is 'barely on speaking terms.' HALES (*Notes & Essays*, p. 177): Is it impossible that the *cater* is connected with *cate* or *cake, cater, acater, caterer*, &c., and that the word means simply *mess-fellow?* This explanation has been offered before; it still requires confirmation. [I do not find the word either in Wedgwood, or Skeat.—ED.]

129. **dish of Doues**] C. A. BROWN (p. 109): The Merchant of Venice is a mer-
chant of no other place in the world. Everything he says or does, or that is said or done about him, except when the scene changes to Belmont, is, throughout the play, Venetian. Ben Jonson, in his *Volpone*, gives no more than can be gathered from any one book of travels that has ever been published; nothing but the popular notion of the city. Shakespeare, in addition to the general national spirit of the play, describes the Exchange held on the Rialto; the riches of the merchants; their argosies 'From Tripolis, from Mexico, and England; From Lisbon, Barbary, and India:' some with 'silks' and 'spices,' 'richly fraught;' he represents 'the trade and profit of the city' as consisting 'of all nations;' he talks familiarly of the 'masquing mates,' with their

vpon your worſhip, and my ſuite is.   130
  Lan.   In verie briefe, the ſuite is impertinent to my

---

130. *is.*] *is*—— Q₁, Rowe et seq.

'torch-bearers' in the streets; of 'the common ferry which trades to Venice,' where
Portia is to meet Balthazar, after he has delivered the letter to Doctor Bellario, at
Padua, the seat of law; and 'In a gondola were seen together Lorenzo and his amorous Jessica.' All this is written with a perfect knowledge of the place. So magical
is the painting, that a lover of Shakespeare, as he enters Venice, looks about him with
the air of a man at home, and almost expects to see some merchants talking with a
Shylock on the Rialto, till he spies the poverty of the people, and sighs to himself,—
'Alas! how changed since the days of the Republic!' Shakespeare might have read
of the 'strict Court of Venice' on commercial questions, and of the reasons for such
strictness; he might also have found authority in books for—'You have among you
many a purchased slave;' but where did he obtain his numerous graphic touches of
national manners? where did he learn of an old villager's coming into the city with a
'dish of doves' as a present to his son's master? A present thus given, and in our
days too, and of doves, is not uncommon in Italy. [In Dixon's *Story of Lord Bacon's
Life*, p. 98, Lady Anne Bacon tells her son Anthony that she sends him 'xij pigeons,
my last flight, and one ringdove beside, and a black coney taken by John Knight this
day, and pigeons, too, to-day.' This incident I am sure that I have seen, in some
attempted proof that Bacon wrote Shakespeare's plays, cited, in conclusive answer to
C. A. Brown's question, as the genuine dovecote whence issued Gobbo's doves. I
mistrust the fitness of spending any time in search for it. My editorial conscience is
rendered placid by the simple allusion; merely begging to be allowed to remark that if
Bacon wrote this passage, I fully respond to Pope's estimate of Bacon's baseness, and
find herein even a lower depth, in thus introducing his Mother as a prototype of old
Gobbo. One is sometimes inclined to say to those who dispute the auſhorship of these
plays, as the Cockney did to the eels, 'down, wantons, down!' but a little calm reflection reveals to us that this attempt to dethrone Shakespeare, so far from being treason,
or *lèse majesté*, is, in fact, most devout and respectful homage to him. In our ſallad
days, when first we begin to study Shakespeare, who does not remember his bewilder-
ing efforts to attribute to mortal hand these immortal plays? Then follows the fruitless
attempt to discern in that Stratford youth, the Emperor, by the grace of God, of all Literature. In our despair of marrying, as Emerson says, the man to the verse, we wed
the verse to the greatest known intellect of that age. Can homage be more profound?
But, as I have said, this we do when we are young in judgement. The older we grow
in this study, and the farther we advance in it, the clearer becomes our vision that, if
the royal robes do not fit Shakespeare, they certainly do not, and cannot, fit any one
else. Wherefore, I conceive that we have here a not altogether inaccurate gauge of
the depth, or duration, or persistence of Shakespearian study, and, measuring by a scale
of maturity, or growth, in this study, I have come to look upon all attempts to prove that
Bacon wrote these dramas, merely as indications of youth, possibly, of extreme youth,
and that they find their comforting parallels in the transitory ailments incident to
childhood, like the chicken-pox or the measles. The attack is pretty sure to come,
but we know that it is neither dangerous nor chronic, that time will effect a cure, and
that, when once well over it, there is no likelihood whatever of its recurrence.—ED.]

  130. is] The long dash following this word in Q₁ is an instance of the unusual care
with which that edition was set up.—ED.

felfe, as your worſhip ſhall know by this honeſt old man,   132
and though I ſay it, though old man, yet poore man my
Father.

 Baſſ. One ſpeake for both, what would you?   135
 Lan. Serue you ſir.
 Gob. That is the verie defect of the matter ſir.
 Baſſ. I know thee well, thou haſt obtain'd thy ſuite,
Shylocke thy Maiſter ſpoke with me this daie,
And hath prefer'd thee, if it be preferment   140
To leaue a rich *Iewes* ſeruice, to become
The follower of ſo poore a Gentleman.
 Clo. The old prouerbe is verie well parted betweene
my Maiſter *Shylocke* and you ſir, you haue the grace of
God ſir, and he hath enough.   145
 Baſſ. Thou ſpeak'ſt it well; go Father with thy Son,
Take leaue of thy old Maiſter, and enquire
My lodging out, giue him a Liuerie   148

143, 150. Clo.] Clowne. Q₂Q₃. Lan. Q₁. 148. *out,*] out. Q₁. *out:* Q₃F₄.

---

140. **prefer'd**] CRAIK (789, p. 344): 'To prefer,' Reed observes, 'seems to have been the established phrase for *recommending a servant.*' And he quotes [this present passage]. But to *prefer* was more than merely to recommend. It was rather to transfer, or hand over. That it had come to imply also something of promotion, may be seen from what Bassanio goes on to say. The sense of the verb *to prefer* that we have in Shakespeare, continued current down to a considerably later date. . . . . At an earlier date, again, we have Bacon, in the Dedication of the first edition of his *Essays* to his brother Anthony, thus writing:—'Since they would not stay with their master, but would needs travail abroad, I have preferred them to you, that are next myself,' &c.

143. **prouerbe**] STAUNTON: The proverb referred to is 'The grace of God is better than riches;' or, in the Scot's form, is 'God's grace is gear enough.'—[Ray's *Proverbs,* p. 295, ed. 1670,—ap. Clarendon.]

145. **enough**] THEOBALD (Nichols's *Illust.* ii, 306): Now here, indeed, methinks, this is a little too serious for Launcelot; and he delivers the proverb more justly than the Poet intended. It would be very satirical, both to his old and his new master, with relation both to their *religion* and *circumstances*, if we might imagine a small transposition in the words: '*He* hath the *Grace of God*, Sir, and *you* have *enough.*' For Launcelot to say the Jew, whom he thought a Devil, had the grace of God, or that Bassanio had enough, whom he knew to be a borrower, is very droll. And then there is much humour, too, in the ironical reply of Bassanio: 'Thou speak'st it well.' Or, as we read it: 'Thou split'st it well.' [This emendation Theobald did not allude to in his subsequent edition; but Warburton, in his edition, put it forth in a note, and the Camb. Edd. have accorded its authorship to him, an error for which Theobald should surely be grateful. The harshness of 'split'st it' would be much less likely to offend Warburton's ear than Theobald's.—ED.]

More garded then his fellowes : fee it done.

Clo.   Father in, I cannot get a feruice, no, I haue nere   150
a tongue in my head, well : if anie man in *Italie* haue a
fairer table which doth offer to fweare vpon a booke, I   152

149. *garded*] Qq Ff, Rowe i, Cap.
guarded Rowe ii et cet.

150. *no,*] Qq Ff.   *no ?* Rowe ii+.   *no !*
Knt, Hal.   *no ;* Rowe i et cet.
    haue] *ha* Q₁.

151. *tongue*] *tong* Q₂Q₃.
    head, well :] Q₂.   *head : Well,*

Q₃, Rowe i.   *head well :* F₂F₃.   *head well,*
F₄.   *head ? well,* Rowe ii+.   *head !—*
well ; Knt, Hal. Ktly.   *head.   Well,* Q₁,
Cap. et cet. (subs.).

151. [Looking on his own hand. Han.
...palm. Johns.

---

149. garded] HANMER (*Gloss.*) : A *guard*, the hem or welt of a garment ; also, any lace or galloon upon the seams or borders of it.   *To guard*, to lace over, to adorn. STAUNTON : So called from its guarding the stuff from being torn.

152. table] STAUNTON : The *table line*, or *line of fortune*, is the line running from the forefinger, below the other three fingers, to the side of the hand.   *The natural line* is the line which curves in a different direction, through the middle of the palm ; and the *line of life* is the circular line surrounding the ball of the thumb.   The space between the two former lines being technically known as *the table*.   [Whoever is interested in Chiromancy may find diagrams, ancient and modern, of the hand, and abundant authorities on the subject, in Knight, and in Halliwell.   I have selected Staunton's note as the earliest which really gives all needful illustration of the text in shortest compass.—ED.]

152. table which doth] WARBURTON in his text indicated an omission after these words, and supplies the 'lost sense,' which he says is 'easy enough,' thus : 'If any man in Italy have a fairer table, which doth *promise good luck, I am mistaken.   I durst almost* offer to swear,' &c.   JOHNSON : 'Table' is the palm of the hand extended. Launcelot congratulates himself upon his dexterity and good fortune, and, in the height of his rapture, inspects his hand, and congratulates himself upon the felicities in his table.   The act of expanding his hand puts him in mind of the action in which the palm is shown, by raising it to lay it on the book, in judicial attestations.   'Well,' says he, 'if any man in Italy have a fairer table, that doth offer to swear upon a book—.' Here he stops with an abruptness very common, and proceeds to particulars.   HEATH (p. 114) : Considering Launcelot's humourous and fantastical language, the place will very well bear the following interpretation : 'If any man in Italy have a fairer table, which pronounces that I shall have good fortune, with as much assurance as if it were ready to swear it upon a book—.'   Here the sentence breaks off, and we must supply 'I am mistaken,' or some other expression of like import.   KENRICK (*Rev. of Dr Johnson*, &c., p. 50) : None of these commentators, though very sensible of the break in this passage, seems to know where it lies ; but if I might be allowed to take the most trifling liberty in the world with the text, I dare say the reader would see the whole meaning and propriety of it at one view : 'Well, if any man in Italy have a fairer table !—Why, it doth offer to swear upon a book I shall have good fortune,— Go to,' &c.   TYRWHITT : Launcelot, looking into the palm of his hand, breaks out : 'Well ; if any man in Italy have a fairer table ; which doth offer to swear upon a book, I shall have good fortune'—i. e. *a table* which doth (*not only* promise, *but*) offer to swear (*and to swear* upon a book *too*) *that* I shall have good fortune.   (He omits the

fhall haue good fortune; goe too, here's a fimple line 　153
of life, here's a fmall trifle of wiues, alas, fifteene wiues
is nothing, a leuen widdowes and nine maides is a fim- 　155
ple comming in for one man, and then to fcape drow-

153. *fortune ;*] *fortune.* Q$_1$.　　　　　Rlfe, Huds. *a 'leven* Cam. *eleuen* Q$_2$
155. *a leuen*] Q$_2$. *a leven* Q$_3$F$_2$. *a leaven*　　et cet.
F$_3$F$_4$. *aleven* Hal. Sta. Wh. i, Dyce iii, 　　156. *comming in*] *coming-in* Theob.
　　　　　　　　　　　　　　　　　　　　fcape] *efcape* Q$_1$.

conclusion of the sentence, which might have been) *I am much mistaken ;* or, *I'll be
hanged,* &c. KNIGHT: The table (palm) which doth offer to swear upon a book, is
not very different from other palms; but the palm which doth offer to swear that the
owner shall have good fortune, is a fair table to be proud of. [Tyrwhitt's explanation,
whose punctuation Knight also adopted in his text.] HALLIWELL: Launcelot means
to say: 'Well; if any man in Italy, who doth offer to swear upon a book, have a fairer
table,' a vernacular form of speech, implying that no one has a fairer table. [White
(ed. i) adopted this explanation.] CLARENDON: If the text be as Shakespeare wrote
it, Launcelot seems to have left the sentence imperfect at 'table,' with an ellipsis of
'I'll be hanged,' or some such phrase. ROLFE follows Johnson's punctuation and
explanation as opposed to Tyrwhitt's, that is, that it is the man, not the table, which
doth offer to swear. [My own decided preference is for Kenrick's punctuation, and
for an explanation I am indebted to a MS note of ALLEN's : 'Well, if any man in Italy
have a fairer table! which doth (equivalent, as in Greek or Latin, to *for it doth*) offer
to swear,' &c. That is, there is no hand so fair in its indications of fortune as mine,
because it offers to swear that I shall have good luck; which is virtually the same paraphrase as Kenrick's, and Tyrwhitt's, the difference being merely that they apparently
failed to note that 'which' is here used like the Latin causal relative.—ED.]

153. **fortune**] MALONE: I am persuaded that the author wrote: 'I shall have *no*
good fortune.' These words are not, I believe, connected with what goes before, but
with what follows; and begin a new sentence. Shakespeare, I think, meant that Launcelot, after this abrupt speech—Well, if any man *that* offers to swear upon a book, has
a fairer table than mine—(I am much mistaken)—should proceed in the same manner
in which he began:—I shall have *no* good fortune; go to; here's a *simple* line of life!
&c. [Malone did not venture to adopt this in his text. Eccles did.]

153. **goe too**] ABBOTT, § 185: 'To' is still used adverbially in 'to and fro' and
nautical expressions, such as 'heave *to*,' 'come *to*.' This explains 'Go to.' 'Go' did
not, in Elizabethan or Early English, necessarily imply motion *from*, but motion generally. Hence, 'go *to*' meant little more than our stimulative 'come, come.'

153. **simple line**] KNIGHT: A simple or complex line of life were indications that
made even some of the wise exult or tremble. Launcelot's 'small trifle of wives' was,
however, hardly compatible with the *simple* line of life. There must have been too
many *crosses* in such a destiny. CLARENDON: 'A simple line of life,' i. e. 'a poor,
mean line,' is ironical for the converse.

154. **trifle of wiues**] HALLIWELL: 'Long and deep lines from the Mount of Venus
[the ball of the thum̃] towards the line of life, signifieth so many wives. . . . . These
lines visible and deep, so many wives the party shall have.'—Saunder's *Chiromancie.*

155. **a leuen**] HALLIWELL: *Aleven* is a common vulgarism in Shakespeare's time,
It is also archaic.

ning thrice, and to be in perill of my life with the edge   157
of a featherbed, here are fimple fcapes : well, if Fortune
be a woman, fhe's a good wench for this gere : Father
come, Ile take my leaue of the *Iew* in the twinkling.   160
Exit Clowne.

Baff.   I praie thee good *Leonardo* thinke on this,
Thefe things being bought and orderly beftowed
Returne in hafte, for I doe feaft to night
My beft efteemd acquaintance, hie thee goe.   165
Leon.   My beft endeuors fhall be done herein. *Exit. Le.*
Enter Gratiano.

Gra.   Where's your Maifter.
Leon.   Yonder fir he walkes.
Gra.   Signior *Baffanio.*   170
Baf.   *Gratiano.*
Gra.   I haue a fute to you.
Baff.   You haue obtain'd it.
Gra.   You muft not denie me, I muft goe with you to
Belmont.   175

160. *twinkling.*] *twinkling of an eye.* Q₁, Pope et seq.
163. *beftowed*] *beftow'd* Q₁, Cap. et seq.
164. *night*] *night,* Q₁.
165. *beft efteemd*] *best-esteemed* Theob. ii.
thee] *thee,* Q₁Q₃.
goe] *go* Q₁. *gon* F₂. *gone* F₃F₄, Rowe.
166. Exit Le.] Exit. Q₁.   Exit Leon-

ardo. Q₂.   Exit Leonato. Ff, Om. Rowe. After line 169, Theob. et seq.
167. [Scene III. Pope, Han. Warb
171. Gratiano.] Gratiano? Q₁.   *Signior Gratiano!* Han.
172. *a fute*] *fute* Q₂.
174. *You*] *Nay, you* Han. Cap. Dyce iii, Huds.
174, 175. *with...Belmont*] Separate line, Han. Cap. Dyce iii, Huds.

---

158. **featherbed**] WARBURTON : A cant phrase to signify the danger of marrying.

159. **gere**] See I, i, 120.

160. **twinkling**] Every editor from the days of Pope has followed the completer text of Q₁.

163. **bestowed**] Of course, on board the ship.

166. **Exit. Le.**] This Exit of Leonardo, inserted before he actually leaves the scene, indicates that the copy from which the Folio was printed, and, in fact, the copy of which the Qq were transcripts, had been used as a stage-copy.—ED.

172. **a sute**] Again may be noted the accuracy of Q₁.—ED.

173, 176.] you . . . you . . . thee] ABBOTT, § 231 : Mark the change of pronoun as Bassanio assumes the part of a friendly lecturer.

174. See Hanmer's text and division of lines in Text. Notes, which Dyce adopts because 'this speech was, beyond all doubt, originally verse.'

Baſſ. Why then you muſt : but heare thee *Gratiano*,   176
Thou art to wilde, to rude, and bold of voyce,
Parts that become thee happily enough,
And in ſuch eyes as ours appeare not faults;
But where they are not knowne, why there they ſhow   180
Something too liberall, pray thee take paine
To allay with ſome cold drops of modeſtie
Thy skipping ſpirit, leaſt through thy wilde behauiour
I be miſconſterd in the place I goe to,   184

176. *muſt : but*] Ff. *muſt but* Q₂. *muſt, but* Q₃. *muſt. But* Q₁, Johns. et seq.

   thee] *me* Q₃.

177. *to...to*] Q₂. *too...too* Q₁ et cet.

179. *faults ;*] *faults* Q₂.

180. *they are*] Ff, Rowe, Knt, Rlfe. *thou art* Qq et cet.

180. *knowne, why*] *knowne. Why* Q. *knowne ; why* Q₂.

181. *liberall,*] *lib'rall :* Q₁.

   pray thee] *prethee* Q₁.

183. *leaſt*] *leſt* Q₁F₄.

184. *miſconſterd*] *miſconſtred* Qq. *miſconſter'd* F₄, Hal. Sing. Sta. Wh. Ktly. *misconstrued* Rowe et cet.

---

176. **heare thee**] ABBOTT, § 212: Verbs followed by *thee* instead of *thou*, have been called reflexive. But, though ' haste *thee* ' and some other phrases with verbs of motion may be thus explained, and verbs were often thus used in Early English, it is probable that ' look *thee*,' ' hark *thee*,' are to be explained by euphonic reasons. *Thee*, thus used, follows imperatives, which, being themselves emphatic, require an unemphatic pronoun. The Elizabethans reduced *thou* to *thee*. We have gone further, and rejected it altogether.

181. **liberall**] JOHNSON : That is, mean, gross, coarse, licentious. [Are not these adjectives, which have been adopted by many subsequent editors, too strong for Bassanio's friendly remonstrance ? Would not our modern ' free and easy ' something better correspond ? Rolfe gives ' free, reckless,' which are certainly better than ' licentious ' in any sense.—ED.]

181. **paine**] In printing a modernized text of this play, I should not hesitate to change this to the plural, *pains*. Although Shakespeare may have used the singular elsewhere (which is doubtful), the plural is certainly used twice subsequently in this play, viz. IV, i, 10, and V, i, 201. And no one, I think, can thoughtfully examine the instances given in Walker (*Crit.* i, 233) of the final *s* both interpolated and omitted in the First Folio, without becoming convinced that an editor has ample discretionary power in making a change like this, whereby the phrase conforms to sense or usage. Numerous as are the instances given in Walker's thirty pages and more, the list is by no means complete. In a note on *Oth.* I, i, 31, two additional examples were given not noticed by Walker, in that play alone. See ' multitudes,' II, ix, 35, *post.*—ED.

182. **cold**] STEEVENS: So in *Ham.* III, iv. 123: ' Upon the heat and flame of thy distemper Sprinkle cool patience.'

182. **modeſtie**] ALLEN: That is, moderation (est *modus* in rebus).

183. **spirit**] For similar contractions into monosyllables, see WALKER, *Vers.* 64, or ABBOTT, § 463, or BROWNE, p. 12, § 5.

184. **misconsterd**] This form, for the modern *misconstrued*, is common, says DYCE (*Remarks*, p. 54), in our early writers. See also the note on *conster* of the Qq in *Oth.* IV, i, 118.

And loofe my hopes.   185
   Gra.   Signor *Baſſanio*, heare me,
If I doe not put on a fober habite,
Talke with refpeᴄᴛ, and fweare but now and than,
Weare prayer bookes in my pocket, looke demurely,
Nay more, while grace is faying hood mine eyes   190
Thus with my hat, and figh and fay Amen:
Vfe all the obferuance of ciuillitie
Like one well ftudied in a fad oftent
To pleafe his Grandam, neuer truft me more.
   Baſ.   Well, we fhall fee your bearing.   195
   Gra.   Nay but I barre to night, you fhall not gage me
By what we doe to night.
   Baſ.   No that were pittie,
I would intreate you rather to put on
Your boldeft fuite of mirth, for we haue friends   200

185. *loofe*] Q₂F₂. *loſe* Q₁ et cet.   189. *pocket*] *pockets* Rowe, Pope,
  hopes] *hope* Q₃.   Theob. Han. Johns.
187. *If I*] *If* F₂.   196. *barre*] *bar* F₄.
188. *than*] Q₁Q₂.

187. **habite**] Eᴄᴄʟᴇs: That is, conduct, behaviour.

190. **is saying**] Probably *in* or *a-* has been omitted. See Aʙʙᴏᴛᴛ, § 372, or Wʜɪᴛᴇ (*Words and their Uses*, chap. xi, 'Is being done,' p. 334). Rᴏʟғᴇ cites Marsh, *Lect. on English Lang.*, p. 649.

190. **hood**] Mᴀʟᴏɴᴇ: It should be remembered that in Shakespeare's time they wore their hats during the time of dinner. Sᴛᴀᴜɴᴛᴏɴ: The practice of wearing the hat at meals, and especially at ceremonial feasts, was probably derived from the age of chivalry. In the present day, at the installation banquet of the Knights of the Garter, all the Knights Companions wear their hats and plumes. It appears to have been usual formerly for all persons above the rank of attendants to keep on their hats at the dinner-table. Lilly, in his Autobiography, gives an edifying account of his wooing of his widowed mistress, who finally signified her acceptance of his suit by making him sit down with her to dinner with his hat on. And the custom may be inferred from the following: 'Roger the Canterburian, that cannot Say Grace for his meat with a low-crowned hat before his face: or the character of a prelatical man affecting great heighths. Newly written by G. T. Lond.' As also from the Recipe for Dressing a Knuckle of Veal, sent by Dr Delany to Swift: 'Then skimming the fat off Say Grace with your hat off.'

192. **ciuillitie**] Cʟᴀʀᴇɴᴅᴏɴ: That is, civilization, refinement.

193. **sad ostent**] Jᴏʜɴsᴏɴ: Grave appearance; show of staid and serious behaviour. Sᴛᴇᴇᴠᴇɴs: 'Ostent' is a word very commonly used for *show* among the old dramatic writers. Bᴏswᴇʟʟ: See *post*, II, viii, 47.

200. **suite**] Eᴄᴄʟᴇs: Probably referring to the 'sober habit' of line 187.

That purpofe merriment : but far you well,   201
I haue fome bufineffe.

Gra.   And I muft to *Lorenfo* and the reft,
But we will vifite you at fupper time.   *Exeunt.*

[*Scene III.*]

Enter Ieffica and the Clowne.

Ief.   I am forry thou wilt leaue my Father fo,
Our houfe is hell, and thou a merrie diuell
Did'ft rob it of fome tafte of tedioufneffe ;
But far thee well, there is a ducat for thee,   5
And *Lancelet*, foone at fupper fhalt thou fee
Lorenzo, who is thy new Maifters gueft,
Giue him this Letter, doe it fecretly,
And fo farwell : I would not haue my Father
See me talke with thee.   10

Clo.   Adue, teares exhibit my tongue, moft beautifull
Pagan, moft fweete Iew, if a Chriftian doe not play the   12

---

201. *far you well*] *faryewell* Q$_1$. *fare you well* F$_2$ et seq.
  [Scene IV. Pope+. Scene III. Cap. et seq.
2. *I am*] *I'm* Pope+, Dyce iii, Huds.
3. *merrie*] Om. F$_3$F$_4$.
5. *far*] Q$_2$. *fare* Q$_1$ et cet.
9. *farwell*] *farewell* F$_2$.

10. *talke*] *in talke* Qq, Cap. Knt, Coll. Hal. Dyce, Sta. Wh. Cam. Del. Glo. Cla. Rlfe.
11. Clo.] Lance. Q$_1$. Clowne. Q$_2$Q$_3$.
11, 13, 15. *Adue*] F$_2$. *Adew* Q$_1$. *Adiew* Q$_2$Q$_3$. *Adieu* F$_3$F$_4$ (line 15, *adieu* Q$_1$).
12. *doe*] Qq, Steev. Mal. Coll. i, Verp. Hal. Clarke. *did* Ff et cet.

---

3. **hell**] ALLEN: A 'hell' to Jessica in her state of 'strife' (line 21) between her *love* and her *religion*, between duty to her father and passion for her lover. She is *now* in a morbid state. Her gift of a ducat to Launcelot may have been a rebellion against her father's maxims of thrift, due to this state, or she may have been so constituted as to have an instinctive disposition to lavishness. The reaction, at any rate, was a most violent one.

6. **soone**] As this supper was to be ready at farthest at five of the clock, it is not impossible that 'soon' may be here used in its ordinary sense; but I think it more likely that its meaning is the same as in *Oth.* III, iv, 229 and 231 : at night-fall, 'ad primam vesperam.'—ED.

11. **exhibit**] ECCLES: My tears express what my tongue should, if sorrow would permit it. HALLIWELL suggests that the word is one of Launcelot's blunders for *prohibit*. CLARENDON remarks that Launcelot means *inhibit*. [I prefer Eccles's interpretation. —ED.]

12, 13. **doe . . . get**] The Text. Notes show how general has been the preference for

knaue and get thee, I am much deceiued ; but adue, thefe   13

---

the change from 'do' to *did*, first started by F₂. Of course, if we accept *did*, we must
suppose that 'get' is used for *beget*. Malone upholds F₁, and maintains that Launcelot
is not talking about Jessica's father, but about her future husband. 'I am aware,' he
adds, 'that in a subsequent scene he says to Jessica : " Marry, you may partly hope
your *father got you not ;*" but he is now on another subject. [In his edition of 1790
Malone suggests that it is the love-letter to Lorenzo which starts the current of Launcelot's thoughts.] Moreover, a Christian may be said to play the knave if he should
steal the Jew's daughter, as Lorenzo himself expresses it in Scene vi : " When you shall
please to *play the thieves* for wives," &c.' Steevens suspects that the 'waggish Launcelot designed this for a broken sentence,' and that after 'get thee—' there is a subaudition of 'into trouble,' or the like. The subaudition Cowden-Clarke supplies is : 'get
thee for a wife.' Verplanck asserts that it is the poor joke conveyed by casting a slur on
Jessica's birth which has made the reading of F₂ popular. On the other hand, Monck
Mason has 'no doubt but that *did* is the true reading. Launcelot is not foretelling the
fate of Jessica, but judging from her lovely disposition that she must have been begotten by a Christian, not by such a brute as Shylock ; a Christian might marry her without playing the knave, though he could not beget her.' Halliwell begins his note by
saying that although *did* has been generally adopted, he thinks it erroneous, and then
argues so earnestly for interpreting 'do' in the sense of *did*, just as in *King John* we
have 'waft' for *wafted*, 'heat' for *heated*, &c., that at the close of his note he says that
'unless "do" is a grammatical usage for *did*, the latter word should be substituted ;'
and that, on the whole, it is most probable that Launcelot means to imply that Jessica
is too beautiful and good to be the daughter of Shylock, and to this Jessica seems to
allude in the next speech when she laments the sin of 'being ashamed to be my father's
child.' Dyce (*Remarks*, p. 54) thinks Launcelot plainly means that he cannot believe
Jessica to be Shylock's daughter ; and White adds, 'beside this "get thee" had a well-
settled meaning in Shakespeare's day.' [I also think that *did* here conveys Launcelot's
meaning. I very much doubt if those who saw no harm in Jessica's theft of her father's
money, would have seen any knavery in stealing the girl herself. Moreover, the character of Jessica is so complex, not to say apparently inconsistent, that at times I am
almost tempted to think that in her we have an outcropping of the old original play,
wherein it may perhaps have been that she was not the Jew's own daughter. Can we
point to a single trait in her that stamps her not only as a daughter of Shylock, but
even as a Jewess? She is lavish of money to Gobbo, and profusely lavish of it on her
own pleasures ; she has fallen in love with a gay Christian, and longs to change her
religion ; she shows no respect for her dead mother, and not an atom of regard for her
living father ; her very complexion is not oriental, but fair. In the next scene her
hand is spoken of as whiter than paper, and the contrast between Shylock and her is
declared by Salarino to be greater than between jet and ivory. Lastly, is the Jessica
out-nighting Lorenzo in moonlit Belmont the same Jessica who can find amusement in
the merriment of a Gobbo? In thus supposing Jessica to be no child of Shylock, I
confess the wish to be, for Shylock's sake, the father to the thought. Of course it is
evident, as Macdonald and others have pointed out, that for dramatic purposes the profoundest depths of Shylock's nature must be stirred against Anthonio and the Christians ; and this is done when he believes that they have induced his 'own flesh and
blood to rebel' against him.—Ed.]

6

foolifh drops doe fomewhat drowne my manly fpirit :
adue.   *Exit.*   15
   Ief.   Farewell good *Lancelet.*
Alacke, what hainous finne is it in me
To be afhamed to be my Fathers childe,
But though I am a daughter to his blood,
I am not to his manners : O *Lorenzo,*   20
If thou keepe promife I fhall end this ftrife,
Become a Chriftian, and thy louing wife.   *Exit.*

---

14. *fomewhat*] *fomething* Qq, Cap.
Sta. Cam. Glo. Cla. Wh. ii.
  16. *Farewell*] *Farell* Var. '21 (misprint).
  17. *hainous*] *heynous* Q₁Q₂.

18. *childe,*] *child?* Rowe+.   *child,*
Steev. et seq.
  20. *O*] δ Q₂Q₃.
  21. *If*] *Yf* Q₂.
  22. Exit.] Om. Ff.

---

17. **what**] ROLFE suggests that 'possibly this is one of the instances in which
"what" is used for *what a,*' and refers to Abbott, § 86. [But by the omission of *a,*
'sin' becomes a collective noun, and suggests many an occasion when Jessica has been
ashamed to be her father's child. —ED.]

20. **Lorenzo**] MACDONALD (*The Imagination,* p. 165): Into the original story
upon which this play is founded, Shakespeare has, among other variations, introduced
the story of *Jessica* and *Lorenzo,* apparently altogether of his own invention. [See
Appendix, 'Source of the Plot.'] What was his object in doing so? Surely, there
were characters and interests enough already! It seems to me that Shakespeare
doubted whether the Jew would have actually proceeded to carry out his fell design
against Antonio, upon the original ground of his hatred, without the further incitement
to revenge afforded by another passion, second only to his love of gold—his affection
for his daughter; for in the Jew, having reference to his own property, it had risen to
a passion. Shakespeare therefore invents her that he may send a dog of a Christian
to steal her, and, yet worse, to tempt her to steal her father's stones and ducats.

21. **strife**] ECCLES: This inward conflict of opposite affections.

[*Scene IV.*]

Enter Gratiano, Lorenzo, Slarino, and Salanio.

Lor.   Nay, we will flinke away in fupper time,
Difguife vs at my lodging, and returne all in an houre.
   Gra.   We haue not made good preparation.
   Sal.   We haue not fpoke vs yet of Torch-bearers.   5

[Scene V. Pope+. Scene IV. Cap.   1. Salanio.] Solania. Ff.   Solanio and
et seq.   Salerino. Cap.
   Enter...Slarino] F₁.   5. *vs yet*] *as yet* F₄, Rowe, Pope, Han.
                                              Johns.

---

2. TH. ELZE (*Sh. Jahrb.* xiv, p. 167): Of the public entertainments and festivities of
the Venetians, of their political and popular observances, of their theatres, of their religious music, of their hunting and their games, Shakespeare makes no mention, but
only of a single amusement which was peculiarly Venetian, and more favoured in the
city of lagoons than anywhere else. To him who is unacquainted with the old customs
of the Venetians, it must seem to be a very extraordinary, nay almost fantastic, invention of the Poet to represent Lorenzo as slinking away with his friends from a supper
whereto they had been invited by Bassanio, to go to a masquerade, when it was not
even carnival time. Such an idea could be conceived of in no other country, not even
in any other state of Italy, except in Venice, although the custom of wearing masks
was at that time very common; but here in Venice it was practised universally, and at
all seasons of the year. It was thus that the Doge, who appeared in public only on
State occasions, visited the Opera, attended by only a single servant; he was then incognito. The Officers of State and the Magnificoes appeared in masks, in the Reception Hall of the Republic, on the evenings when new Ambassadors were received.
Thus, the dignitaries of the Church and State wore at least half-masks, whereby all
formal ceremonials were avoided, and a freer, unforced intercourse took place instead.
Thus, a Venetian lady had her mask at hand, just like her fan and handkerchief, as
Shakespeare has intimated in *Othello* (IV, ii). And thus, then, among the gay and
livelier young people, a play with masks was not unusual. That torch-bearers were
also needed arose from the fact that the streets were a tangle and the street-lighting
deficient.

   2. in] ABBOTT, § 161: Here used for *during* or *at*. See also the many repetitions
of 'in,' with this sense, in V, i, 1, &c.

   5. spoke vs] CAPELL: This phrase may be—bespoke us; but being oddly follow'd by 'of,' part of it may have been a printer's mistake for *as*. WALKER (*Crit.* iii,
53): Until 'spoke us' can be shown to be English, I would read, with Pope, 'spoke
as.' ABBOTT, § 220: 'Us' seems equivalent to *for us*. That is, 'spoken for ourselves
about torch-bearers.' [Which does not seem to me much more intelligible than the
original phrase. When, in the preceding Scene, for the sake of a clown's joke we
were all so ready to change 'do' into *did*, I cannot see why we should be in anywise
reluctant here to change 'us' into *as*, which clears away all difficulty and gives us
English.—ED.]

   5. Torch-bearers] See *Rom. & Jul.* I, iv, 11.

Sol.   'Tis vile vnleſſe it may be quaintly ordered,   6
And better in my minde not vndertooke.

Lor.   'Tis now but foure of clock, we haue two houres
To furniſh vs ; friend *Lancelet* what's the newes.

Enter Laucelet with a Lettər.   10

Lan.   And it ſhall pleaſe you to break^e vp this, ſhall it
ſeeme to ſignifie.

Lor.   I know the hand, in faith 'tis a faire hand
And whiter then the paper it writ on,
I the faire hand that writ.   15

Gra.   Loue newes in faith.

Lan.   By your leaue ſir.

Lor.   Whither goeſt thou *?*

Lan.   Marry ſir to bid my old Maſter the *Iew* to ſup
to night with my new Maſter the Chriſtian.   20

Lor.   Hold here, take this, tell gentle *Ieſſica*

---

6. Sol.] Ff.   Solanio. Q₂.   Salanio.
Qₗ.   Salan. Q₃.
8. *of clock*] Q₂F₂Q₃, Hal.   *a clocke*
QₗF₃F₄, Rowe.   *a-clock* Pope+, Steev.
o'clock Cap.
10. Enter...] After line 8, Qₗ.
with a letter.] Om. Qq.
11. *And it ſhall*] Q₂FfQ₃, Rowe, Pope.

If it Qₗ.   *An it ſhall* Theob. et cet.
11, 12. *ſhall it ſeeme*] *it ſhall ſeeme*
Qq Ff et seq.
14. *whiter*] *whither* F₂.
on,] *on* Q₂.
15. *I*] Ff.   *Is* Qq et cet,
16. *Loue newes*] *Loue newes,* Qₗ.
Loue, newes Q₂Q₃.   *Love-news* Ff et cet.

---

6. **quaintly**] DYCE: Ingeniously, cleverly, artfully.

7. **vndertooke**] For other 'curtailed forms of past participles common in Early
English,' see ABBOTT, § 343.

11. **breake vp**] STEEVENS: A term in carving. So in *Love's Lab. Lost*, IV, i, 56,
'you can carve Break up this capon.' [It would be rash to assert that there is no reference here, in Launcelot's speech, to carving, yet the mere use of the phrase 'break up'
is insufficient to sustain the assertion. If the gentle and elegant speech of Dame Juliana
Berners still obtained in Elizabethan days, a 'dere was *broken*, a gose *reryd*, a chicken
fruſhed,' &c., but 'break up' is common enough in passages where it cannot refer to
carving, and where it does refer to opening a sealed letter. Surely there is no reference to carving by Horatio when he says, 'Break we our watch up.' It is equally sure
that Leontes could have had no such thought in that solemn moment when the oracle
was received from Delphos and he commands : 'Break up the seals, and read.'—ED.]

14. **paper it writ**] Hanmer added 'paper *that* it writ,' an emendation which I am
inclined to think is *certissima*, when it is considered how easy it would have been for
the compositor to omit the *that*, if in the MS it were spelled with the Anglosaxon *y*,
and followed as it is by another word almost exactly like it. Dyce adopted it in his
text in his Third Edition, saying that, 'without this addition, which is Hanmer's, the
accent (as Mr W. N. Lettsom observes) would be placed wrong in the line.' Hudson
alſo adopted it.—ED.

I will not faile her, ſpeake it priuately :   22
Go Gentlemen, will you prepare you for this Maske to
    night,
I am prouided of a Torch-bearer.   *Exit. Clowne.*   25
    Sal. I marry, ile be gone about it ſtrait.
    Sol. And ſo will I.
    Lor. Meete me and *Gratiano* at *Gratianos* lodging
Some houre hence.
    Sal. 'Tis good we do ſo.   *Exit.*   30
    Gra. Was not that Letter from faire *Ieſſica* ?
    Lor. I muſt needes tell thee all, ſhe hath directed
How I ſhall take her from her Fathers houſe,
What gold and iewels ſhe is furniſht with,
What Pages ſuite ſhe hath in readineſſe :   35
If ere the *Iew* her Father come to heauen,
It will be for his gentle daughters ſake ;
And neuer dare misfortune croſſe her foote,   38

---

23. *Go*] Closing line 22, Cap. Steev. Mal. Knt, Sing. Hal. Dyce i, Ktly, Del. Clarke.

    Gentlemen] Separate line, Cap. Steev. Mal. Knt, Sing. Hal. Dyce i, Ktly, Del. Clarke.

    Go Gentlemen] Qq Ff, Pope. *Go, Gentlemen,* Rowe, Han. Cam. Glo. Cla. Wh. ii. *Go.—Gentlemen,* Theob. Warb.

Johns. Coll. Sta. Dyce iii, Rlfe, Huds As a separate line, Coll. Wh. Cam. Glo. Cla. Dyce iii, Rlfe, Huds.

    23. *prepare you*] *prepare* Q₁, Pope +. *this*] *th'* Han.

    25. Exit...] After line 22, or after *Go* line 23, Cap. et seq.

    27. Sol.] Q₂ Ff. Salan. Q₁Q₃.

    30. Exit.] Exeunt. Cap.

---

23. **Go Gentlemen**] The Textual Notes will show that here, as in many another place, the correct arrangement of the lines is due to Capell.—ED.

25. **of a**] ABBOTT, § 171 : 'Of' is, hence, used not merely of the agent, but also of the instrument. This is most common with verbs of construction, and of filling; be-cause in construction and filling the result is not merely effected *with* the instrument, but proceeds out *of* it. We still retain *of* with *verbs* of construction and *adjectives* of fulness; but the Elizabethans retained *of* with *verbs* of fulness also, as in this present passage; see also 'You are not satisfied *Of* these events,' V, i, 324; 'Supplied *of* kernes and gallowglasses,' *Macb.* I, ii, 13.

29. **Some houre**] ABBOTT, § 21 : 'Some' being frequently used with numeral adjec-tives qualifying nouns of time, as '*some* sixteen months,' *Two Gent.* IV, i, 21, is also found, by association, with a singular noun of time. As here; see also 'some month or two,' III, ii, 10.

32. **needes**] For other 'adverbs ending in *s,* formed from the possessive inflection of Nouns,' see ABBOTT, § 25.

38. **dare**] ROLFE: Either the 'subjunctive used imperatively' (see Abbott, § 364), or the Third Person of the Subjunctive. [It might also be the future continuing the conſtruction of the preceding line : ' And ne'er [will] dare Misfortune,' &c.—ED.]

Vnleſſe ſhe doe it vnder this excuſe,
That ſhe is iſſue to a faithleſſe *Iew* :   40
Come goe with me, pervſe this as thou goeſt,
Faire *Ieſſica* ſhall be my Torch-bearer.   *Exit.*

---

40. **faithleſſe**] CLARENDON: Unbelieving. See *Matt.* xvii, 17 ; *Mark*, ix, 19.

42. **shall**] ABBOTT, § 315 : *Shall*, meaning *to owe*, is connected with *ought*, *must*, *it is destined*. Thus, here, 'Fair Jessica *is to be* my torchbearer.' Hence, *shall* was used by the Elizabethans with all three persons to denote inevitable futurity without reference to 'will' (desire). ECCLES: It is not rendered very apparent whether it was designed that this frolic of a masking party should continue no longer than while they were absent from the company, and that they should return to it in their proper habits, or whether they were to enter in masquerade, as a surprise to the rest of Bassanio's guests. The circumstance of Jessica's being expected to accompany them in her flight must incline us to imagine the latter to have been the case ; for, that it was not proposed that Lorenzo and she should separate themselves from the others, is sufficiently evident from what is said of her being 'a torch-bearer,' and from their being 'to return *all* in an hour.' The manner of their intended disguise was, doubtless, happily calculated to favour the lady's escape, and, possibly, they had this end in view when the masking scheme was first concerted, though that particular be not expressly declared. From Gratiano's lodging, the scene of their rendezvous, all matters being previously settled, we may conclude they were to proceed to supper with Bassanio.

[*Scene V.*]

Enter Iew, and his man that was the Clowne.

Iew. Well, thou fhall fee, thy eyes fhall be **thy iudge,**
The difference of old *Shylocke* and *Baſſanio*;
What *Ieſſica*, thou fhalt not gurmandize
As thou haft done with me : what *Ieſſica*?   5
And fleepe, and fnore, and rend apparrell out.
Why *Ieſſica* I fay.
   Clo. Why *Ieſſica.*
   Shy. Who bids thee call? I do not bid thee **call.**
   Clo. Your worſhip was wont to tell me   10
I could doe nothing without bidding.
                Enter Ieſſica.
   Ieſ. Call you? what is your will?   13

[Scene VI. Pope+. Scene V. Cap. et seq.
  1. Enter...] Enter the Iew and Lance-let. Q$_1$.
  2. *ſhall ſee*] F$_2$. *ſhalt ſee* Q$_1$ et cet.
  4. Ieſſica,] Qq Ff. *Jessica!* Rowe.
     gurmandize] Q$_2$Ff. *gourmandize* Q$_1$.

  5. Ieſſica?] Q$_1$. Ieſſica, Q$_2$Q$_3$.
  6. *apparrell*] Q$_1$. *apparaile* Q$_2$.
  8. Clo.] Clowne. Qq.
  9. *do*] *did* Rowe+.
  10, 11. As prose, Q$_1$, Pope et seq.
  11. *I*] *that I* Q$_1$, Theob. Warb. Johns. Coll. Cam. Glo. Cla. Wh. ii.

  1. ECCLES: Shylock appears just before to have received a summons to the entertainment provided for the friends of Bassanio before the latter starts for Belmont. After Shylock's recent kindness to him and to Anthonio, it was naturally imagined a proper mark of gratitude to invite the Jew as one of the guests. The invitation, according to modern ideas, appears to have been sent rather late to one who was in no special degree his friend. Lorenzo, a little while before, had taken notice: '' Tis now but four o'clock; we have two hours To furnish us.' Possibly this message might have been designed only to remind him of a former engagement, and not to invite him for the first time. [The difficulty which Eccles encounters here arises from Shakespeare's use of double time. See Appendix, 'Duration of the Action.'—ED.]

  2. thy iudge] KEIGHTLEY (p. 149): It might be better to read '*the* judge.' Even at the present day printers confound these words.

  4. What] CLARENDON: 'What,' 'why,' and 'when' were all used as exclamations of impatience.

  4. gurmandize] ALLEN: Launcelot had said (II, ii, 101) that he was 'famished,' &c.; but this must have been merely for effect, speaking to his father; for in his soliloquy he makes no such complaint. On the other hand, Shylock must not be taken too literally; to him, with his thrifty habits, any self-indulgence would appear to be excess; and it is not likely that, in a household governed by so strict and systematic a master, anything like what he complains of would be allowed.

Shy. I am bid forth to ſupper *Ieſſica*,
There are my Keyes : but wherefore ſhould I go?   15
I am not bid for loue, they flatttr me,
But yet Ile goe in hate, to feede vpon
The prodigall Chriſtian. *Ieſſica* my girle,
Looke to my houſe, I am right loath to goe,
There is ſome ill a bruing towards my reſt,   20
For I did dreame of money bags to night.
     Clo. I beſeech you ſir goe, my yong Maſter
Doth expeꞔt your reproach.
     Shy. So doe I his.
     Clo. And they haue conſpired together, I will not ſay   25
you ſhall ſee a Maske, but if you doe, then it was not for
nothing that my noſe fell a bleeding on blacke monday   27

22. *I...goe*] One line, Q₁.

18. **Christian**] STEEVENS: Shylock forgets his resolution. In a former scene he declares he will neither *eat, drink,* nor *pray* with Christians. Of this circumstance the poet was well aware, and meant only to heighten the malignity of the character, by making him depart from his most settled resolve, for the prosecution of his revenge.

18. **Iessica my girle**] BOOTH: These are the only words that Shylock speaks which in the least degree approach gentleness, and they mean nothing.

20. **ill**] CLARENDON: 'Some say that to dreame of money, and all kinde of coyne is ill.'—Artemidorus, *The Iudgement, or Exposition of Dreames,* p. 99, ed. 1606. [Probably on the principle that dreams go by contraries.—ED.]

20. **a bruing**] For this *a,* which still exists in *alive, afoot, asleep,* see ABBOTT, § 140; see also § 24, or 'aweary,' I, ii, 2.

21. **to night**] ABBOTT, § 190: 'To' was used without any notion of 'motion toward the future' in *to-night* (*last* night). See also *2 Hen. VI:* III, ii, 31. So in Early English, '*to* year' for *this year;* '*to* summer,' &c. Perhaps the provincial 'I will come *the* night, *the* morn,' &c., is a corruption of this 'to.' It is, indeed, suggested by Mr Morris that *to* is a corruption of the demonstrative. [And if so, it well explains, it seems to me, the sense, either past or future, which the provincial usage can convey.—ED.]

24. BOOTH: Significantly. Launcelot's mistake should not be too marked, as is frequently done; it seems too much like helping Shylock to his little joke.

25. **And**] The GLOBE and CLARENDON read *an,* but the editors suggest that this spelling, making 'and' equivalent to *if,* is of doubtful propriety.

27. **a bleeding**] HALLIWELL: An unexpected bleeding of the nose was formerly considered an omen that either something wonderful would happen, or that some mischance would ensue. See examples quoted by Brand. When Charles II was concealed at Boscobel House on the Sunday, 'his majesty, coming down into the parlour, his rose fell a bleeding, which put his poor faithful servants in a fright,' till he reassured them by saying it was a circumstance of frequent occurrence.

laſt, at ſix a clocke ith morning, falling out that yeere on   28
aſhwenſday was foure yeere in th'afternoone.

Shy.   What are their maskes ? heare you me *Ieſſica*,   30
Lock vp my doores, and when you heare the drum
And the vile ſquealing of the wry-neckt Fife,
Clamber not you vp to the caſements then,
Nor thruſt your head into the publique ſtreete
To gaze on Chriſtian fooles with varniſht faces :   35

28. *ith*] *in the* Q₁.   *ith'* F₃.   *i'th'* F₄.
29. *aſhwenſday*] *Aſhwedneſday* F₃ et
seq.

th'afternoone] *thafternoone* Q₂. *the
afternoon* F₄.
30. *What are their*] Ff, Rowe. *What
are there* Q₂Q₃. *What, are there* Q₁, Cap.
Dyce, Cam. Glo. Cla. Huds. Wh. ii. *What*

are these Pope, Han.   *What ! are there*
Theob. et cet.
30. *heare you*] *Heare* Q₁.
32. *ſquealing*] *ſqueaking* Q₁, Pope+,
Steev. Mal. Coll. i, ii, Hal. Dyce i, Clarke,
Del.

Fife] *Fiffe* Q₂Q₃.

---

27. **blacke monday**] PECK (*Memoirs of Milton*, p. 229): Black Monday is a movable day. It is Easter Monday; and was so called on this occasion : 'In the 34 Edw. III (1360.) the 14. of April, & the morrow after Easter-day, K. *Edwarde* with his hoast lay before the cittie of *Paris ;* which day was full darke of mist & haile, & so bitter cold, that many men died on their horses backs with the cold. Wherefore unto this day it hath beene called the *Blacke monday.*'—Stow, p. 264 b.

32. **wry-neckt Fife**] MALONE: 'Primâ nocte domum claude; neque in vias Sub cantu querulæ despice tibiæ.'—Horace, III, Od. vii. MONCK MASON: It appears from hence that the fifes in Shakespeare's time were formed differently from those now in use, which are straight, not wry-necked. BOSWELL: The 'fife' does not mean the instrument, but the person who played on it. So in Barnaby Rich's *Aphorismes* at the end of his *Irish Hubbub*, 1616 : 'A fife is a wry-neckt musician, for he always looks away from his instrument.' PYE (p. 72): During Queen Anne's wars an old country gentleman, in the *Spectator*, expresses surprise at his son, in a letter from the army, mentioning a saucy trumpet and a drum that carried messages. KNIGHT: Yet we are inclined to think that Shakespeare intended the instrument. We are of this opinion principally from the circumstance that the passage is an imitation of the lines in Horace, cited by Malone, in which the instrument is decidedly meant. But, independent of the internal evidence derived from the imitation, the form of the old English flute,— the fife being a small flute,—justifies, we think, the epithet 'wry-neck'd.' This flute was called the *flute à bec*, the upper part or mouth-piece resembling the beak of a bird. And this form was as old as the Pan of antiquity. The terminal figure of Pan, in the Townley Gallery, exhibits it. HALLIWELL gives a wood-cut of a 'wry-necked fife,' copied by 'Mr Fairholt from a curious sculpture at Rheims upon a building of the thirteenth century known as *La Maison des Musiciens*, in which there is a representation of a musician with a tabor hung on his neck who is playing on a fife either end of which is angulated.' BOOTH: My father illustrated this by turning his head as it is held when one plays upon the fife.

35. **varnisht faces**] HALLIWELL: 'For varnisht faces and gay and painted cloths, Are but to tempt fooles ; every man this knowes.'—*The Newe Metamorphosis*, c. 1600,

But ftop my houfes eares, I meane my cafements,   36
Let not the found of fhallow fopperie enter
My fober houfe.   By *Iacobs* ftaffe I fweare,
I haue no minde of feafting forth to night:
But I will goe : goe you before me firra,   40
Say I will come.
   Clo.   I will goe before fir.
Miftris looke out at window for all this ;
There will come a Chriftian by,
Will be worth a Iewes eye.   45

---

36. *ftop*] *shut* Cap.

42. *I…fir*] *Sir, I will go before* Han.
I'll…you, sir. Walker.

42, 43. Prose, Coll. Dyce i, Wh. Cam.
Glo. Del. Cla. Rlfe.

43. *at*] *at a* Q₁, Rowe ii, Pope, Han.

45. *Iewes*] Qq F₂, Wh. i. *Jew's* F₃F₄.
Rowe. *Jewès* Ktly. *Jewess'* Pope et
cet.

[Exit Laun. Rowe et seq.

MS. 'The cortezans . . . . adulterate their faces. . . . . A thing so common amongst
them, that many of them which have an elegant naturall beauty, doe varnish their faces
. . . . with these kinde of sordid trumperies.'—Coryat's *Crudities*, 1611, p. 266. CLAR-
ENDON: Shylock alludes also to Christian duplicity.   Conf. *Timon*, IV, ii, 36: 'But
only painted, like his varnish'd friends.'   WALKER (*Crit.* iii, 54) refers to a Review in
The Athenæum, 15 March, 1845, of Mrs Merrifield's translation of Cennini's *Treatise
on Painting*, &c., in which the Reviewer suggests that the painting of the face was
practised by masqueraders in Italy.

   36. **stop**] To Capell's reading *shut* I can find no reference throughout his *Notes,
Various Readings*, or *Errata ;* although it is not impossible that in that 'rudis indi-
gestaque moles' some reference may lie perdu; yet, after my search, I think it unlikely.
Thus far it is the only uncorrected misprint which I have found in his text.—ED.

   38. **Iacobs staffe**] CLARENDON: See *Gen.* xxxii, 10, and *Heb.* xi, 21.   It is in this
sense, no doubt, that Shakespeare understands the phrase, but it was familiarly used in
the sense of a pilgrim's staff, because St James (or Jacob), the patron of pilgrims, was
represented with one in his hand.   See Spenser, *Faerie Queene*, I, vi, 35: 'And in his
hand a Iacobs staffe, to stay His weary limbs upon.'   BOOTH: Speak these two lines
very solemnly, with a slight pause before and after.

   39. **of**] For many other instances where we should use *for* in place of 'of,' see
ABBOTT, § 174.   Also, *Ib.* § 41, for examples of 'forth' used 'without a verb of motion
(motion being implied).'

   45. **Iewes eye**] WHALLEY: 'It's worth a Jew's eye' is a proverbial phrase.
KNIGHT: That worth was the price which the persecuted Jews paid for immunity
from mutilation and death.   When our rapacious King John extorted an enormous sum
from the Jew of Bristol by drawing his teeth, the threat of putting out an eye would
have the like effect upon other Jews.   The former prevalence of the saying is proved
from the fact that we still retain it, although its meaning is now little known. COLLIER
(ed. ii): It may be a question whether Shakespeare did not mean that Launcelot should
merely repeat the phrase, 'with a Jew's eye,' leaving 'Jewés' to be pronounced as a
dissyllable.   WALKER (*Crit.* iii, 54): The proverb, in Shakespeare's days, perhaps,

Shy. What faies that foole of *Hagars* off-fpring?   46
ha.

Ief. His words were farewell miftris, nothing elfe.

Shy. The patch is kinde enough, but a huge feeder: 49

---

was still pronounced 'a Jewĕs eye.' WHITE: All the editors read 'a Jew-*ess*' eye,'
none of them having observed, or all having forgotten, that 'Jew*ess*' is quite a modern word, 'Jew' having been applied of old to Hebrews of both sexes. It is only
in the Scene but one previous that Launcelot calls Jessica 'most sweet Jew.' DYCE,
after quoting this note of White, adds: 'Not "quite a modern word," surely: "Felix
came with his wife Drusilla, which was a *Jewess*," *Acts*, xxiv, 24 (Tyndale's Bible 1525
or 1526 having there the spelling "iewes," the Bible of 1599 and the Bible of 1629 the
spelling " *Iewesse*,"—not to mention other Bibles).'

46. **Hagars off-spring?**] FARREN (p. 24): This allusion is very appropriate to
the departure of his servant; Hagar having been *bondswoman* to Sarah, the wife of
Abraham, and having quitted her, as Launcelot does Shylock, under the supposed
grievance of too little indulgence (*Genesis*, xvi).

47. **ha**] In a modernised text, should not this be printed *Hey?*—ED.

49. **patch**] DOUCE (i, 257): It has been supposed that this term originated from
the name of a fool belonging to Cardinal Wolsey, and that his parti-coloured dress was
given to him in allusion to his name. The objection to this is, that the motley habit
worn by fools is much older than the time of Wolsey. Again, it appears that *Patch*
was an appellation given not to one fool only that belonged to Wolsey. There is an
epigram by Heywood, entitled *A saying of Patch my Lord Cardinal's foole;* but in
the epigram itself he is twice called *Sexten*, which was his real name. In a manuscript *Life of Wolsey*, by his gentleman usher, Cavendish, there is a story of another
fool belonging to the Cardinal, and presented by him to the King. A marginal note
states that 'this foole was called *Master Williames*, otherwise called *Patch*.' In Hey-
lin's *History of the Reformation* mention is made of another fool called *Patch* belonging to Elizabeth. But the name is even older than Wolsey's time; for in some household accounts of Henry the Seventh there are payments to a fool named *Pechie* and
Packye. It seems, therefore, more probable that fools were nicknamed *Patch* from
their dress; unless there happen to be a nearer affinity to the Italian *pazzo*, a word that
has all the appearance of a descent from *fatuus*. But although in the above instance,
as well as in a multitude of others, a *patch* denotes a fool or a simpleton, and, by corruption, a clown, it seems to have been occasionally used in the sense of *any low* or
mean person. Thus, in *Mid. N. D.* III, ii, Puck calls Bottom and his companions 'a
crew of patches, rude mechanicals,' certainly not meaning to compare them to pam-
pered and sleek buffoons. KNIGHT: The usurper in *Hamlet*, the 'vice of kings,' was
'a king of shreds and patches.' It is probable that in this way the word 'patch' came
to be an expression of contempt; just as we say still, *cross-patch*. SKEAT (s. v.): The
supposition that 'patch' is a nickname from the dress is most probably right. It is independent of Italian *pazzo*, a fool, a madman, which is used in a much stronger sense.
A derivative is *patch-ock*, a diminutive form (cf. *bull-ock, hill-ock*); 'as very *patchokes*
[clowns] as the wild Irish,'—Spenser, *View of the State of Ireland*, Globe ed. p. 636;
this is the word spelt 'pajock' in *Ham.* III, ii. S. L. LEE (*The Academy*, 27 Nov
1880): If further proof be required to show that Shakespeare has portrayed in Shylock the humane side of the Jewish character, the touching allusion to Leah's turquoise

Snaile-flow in profit, but he ſleepes by day   50
More then the wilde-cat : drones hiue not with me,
Therefore I part with him, and part with him
To one that I would haue him helpe to waſte
His borrowed purſe.   Well *Ieſſica* goe in,
Perhaps I will returne immediately ;   55
Doe as I bid you, ſhut dores after you, faſt binde, faſt
          finde,   57

50. *but he*] Pope, Theob. Warb. Johns.   56. *Doe...after you*] One line, Q₁, Cap.
but Ff, Rowe.   *and he* Qq et cet.   Coll. et seq.
56. *Doe as I bid you*] Om. Pope, Han.   *ſhut*] *shut the* Pope +.
Separate line, Theob. Warb. Johns. Steev.   *faſt...faſt*] *safe...safe* Coll. (MS).
Mal. Knt, Sing.

should be supplemented by the present passage.   Launcelot has arranged with Jessica
for her elopement, and she, by a series of barefaced falsehoods, has evaded her father's
enquiries as to his business with her.   Jessica declares that his final words are : ' " Farewell, mistress ;" nothing more ;' and induces Shylock to believe that Launcelot is throughout paying her merely the ordinary courtesies of service.   It can only be an appreciative
kindliness of disposition, which certainly could not belong to a man always ' grinning
with deadly malice ' (as Shylock has often, on and off the stage, been represented), that
can induce the Jew to reply : ' The patch is kind enough,' and then to add, half blam-
ing himself having parted with a servant who shows such befitting respect to his beloved
child, ' but a huge feeder,' &c.   Very effective are the first words of the speech in their
pathos, when we remember how very, very little Launcelot at the moment deserved them,
or how they were suggested by the cruel deceptions of the Jew's unworthy daughter.
Introduced where they are in the play, they are in themselves almost sufficient to prove
that Shakespeare saw in Shylock a man ' more sinned against than sinning.'

50. **profit**] ECCLES : In the performance of those duties whence profit might be
expected to arise to his master.   ALLEN suggests that *perhaps* it might mean ' in
improvement.   He is the same ignorant, awkward country lad he was.'   For such
compounds as ' snail-slow,' see ABBOTT, § 430.

50. **but**] Clearly a misprint for *and ;* caught by the compositor from the preceding
line.—ED.

51. **wilde-cat**] CLARENDON : The wild cat, which prowls and preys by night
sleeps during the day.

55. **Perhaps I will**] ABBOTT, § 319 : Some passages which are quoted to prove
that Shakespeare used ' will ' with the first person, without implying *wish, desire*, &c., do
not warrant such an inference. . . . . There is a difficulty in the expression ' perchance
I *will ;*' but, from its constant recurrence, it would seem to be a regular idiom.   Compare the following passages : '*Perchance*, Iago, I *will* ne'er go home,'—*Oth.* V, ii, 246
[of this ed.] ; '*Perchance* I *will* be there as soon as you,'—*Com. of Err.* IV, i, 39 ;
and this present passage.   In all these, ' perchance ' precedes, and the meaning seems
to be in Shylock's speech, for instance : ' My purpose may, perhaps, be fulfilled,' and
' my purpose is to return immediately,' or, in other words, ' If possible, I intend to
return immediately.'   In all these cases the ' perhaps ' stands by itself.   It does not
qualify ' will,' but the whole of the following sentence.   BOOTH : It would seem from
this remark that Shylock had not perfect confidence in her.

A prouerbe neuer ftale in thriftie minde.   *Exit.*   58

   Ief. Farewell, and if my fortune be not croft,

I haue a Father, you a daughter loft.   *Exit.*   60

---

56. **dores**] Malone, whose name was originally Maloney, having made the harm-less, if needless, remark that '*doors* is here a dissyllable,' Ritson, from whose acerbity ninety years have evaporated the cruelty, observed that, 'a previous acquaintance with the Irish howl must be of infinite service in the perusal of this harmonious edition.' —Ed.

56, 57. **fast . . . finde**] WALKER (*Crit.* iii, 54): In Middleton the former line of the concluding couplet is frequently a short one; in Shakespeare, very seldom. [See Dyce, I, ii, 128.] DYCE (*Notes*, &c. p. 64): Collier's (MS) seems to have made a change 'for variation's sake.'—Compare Cotgrave's *Dict.* sub *Bon.* '*Bon guet chasse malaventure :* Pro. Good watch preuents misfortune; *fast bind, fast find,* say we.' COLLIER (ed. ii): The correction in the (MS) may only denote a difference of reci-tation. The usual form occurs in Fletcher's *Spanish Curate*, II, ii, a better authority than Cotgrave. It also occurs in S. Rowland's *Paire of Spy-Knaues.*

60. Oxberry's Edition professes to give 'the Stage Business and Stage Directions, as performed at the Theatres Royal' (*circa* 1820). In that edition this scene closes with an outburst of song from Jessica, as follows:

'Haste, Lorenzo, haste away,
  To my longing arms repair,
With impatience I shall die;
  Come, and ease thy Jessy's care;
Let me, then, in wanton play
Sigh and gaze my soul away.'

[*Scene VI.*]

Enter the Maskers, Gratiano and Salino.

Gra.　This is the penthoufe vnder which *Lorenzo*
Defired vs to make a ftand.

Sal.　His houre is almoft paft.

Gra.　And it is meruaile he out-dwels his houre,　　5
For louers euer run before the clocke.

Sal.　O ten times fafter *Venus* Pidgions flye　　7

[Scene VII. Pope, Han. Warb. Johns. Omit, Hal. Dyce, Huds. Scene VI. Cap. et cet.

1. Salino.] Ff. Salerino. Q₂Q₃, Cap. Salanio. Rowe+, Steev. Salarino. Q₁ et cet.

2, 3. Prose, Rowe+.

3, 4. *Defired...houre*] One line, Wh. 1.
3. *to make a*] Om. Steev. conj.
　　a ftand] Ff, Rowe+, Wh. i. *ftand* Qq et cet.
7. *Pidgions*] Q₂F₂Q₃. *pigeons* Q₁. *Widgeons* Warb.

There is really no new Scene here, and no change could be made even on the modern stage, but Shakespeare indicated to his audience in almost the only way he could, with his limited resources of traverses, by the rhyming couplets with which both Shylock and Jessica retire, that a new paragraph in the Story was beginning and that our attention must be shifted to a new group. We should bear in mind that these rhyming couplets, mere jingles as they may be to us, were of importance to the audience of Shakespeare's day. See Text. Notes, for the Editors who have continued the Scene. —ED.

3, 4. To cure the defective metre of these two lines, when read as one, Steevens proposed to omit 'to make a,' as an evident interpolation, and Grey (i, 135) would omit 'almost,' because Gratiano immediately says that Lorenzo 'out-dwells his hour.' [In view of the shortness of life, I am afraid it behooves us to forego the pleasure of adjusting the rhythm of fragments of lines. As long as each fragment is in itself rhythmical, I doubt if Shakespeare troubled himself to piece them together. It is not difficult to read these fragments thus: Desi | red us | to make | a stand ‖ His ho | ur's al | most past.—ED.]

7. **Venus Pidgions**] Warburton detected a rich joke here which had been 'murder'd by the ignorance or boldness of the first transcribers.' 'The image of Venus's pidgeons flying to seal the bonds of Love is very odd.' He therefore 'doubts not but Shakespeare wrote *Venus' Widgeons*.' 'For,' he continues, in Ornithology's despite, 'Widgeon is not only one species of Pidgeons, but signified likewise, metaphorically, a *silly fellow*, as *Goose*, or *Gudgeon* does now. The joke consists in the ambiguity of the signification. And the calling love's votaries, *Venus's Widgeons*, is in high humour.' Although the Bishop's 'high humour' failed to tickle Dr Johnson, yet this note so far misled him that he thought the pigeons were the 'lovers,' and 'as in poetry they were always called *turtles* or *doves*, in lower language they might be called *pigeons*.' HEATH (p. 115) set them both right. 'It is not the pigeons,' said he, 'who are understood to "seal the bonds of love," any more than "to keep obliged faith unforfeited;" but it is Venus herself (who is drawn by them, and regulates their flight according to her own good pleasure) who is supposed to be assistant in both.'

To fteale loues bonds new made, then they are wont	8
To keepe obliged faith vnforfaited.
   Gra. That euer holds, who rifeth from a feaft	10
With that keene appetite that he fits downe?
Where is the horfe that doth vntread againe
His tedious meafures with the vnbated fire,
That he did pace them firft : all things that are,
Are with more fpirit chafed then enioy'd.	15
How like a yonger or a prodigall
The skarfed barke puts from her natiue bay,
Hudg'd and embraced by the ftrumpet winde :
How like a prodigall doth fhe returne	19

8. *fteale*] Ff, Rowe. *feale* Qq et cet.
10. *holds,*] Ff. *holds :* Qq. *holds.* Rowe.
13. *meafures...fire,*] *meafures, ...fire* Q₁Q₃.
14. *firft :*] *firft ?* Q₁F₃F₄.
16. *yonger*] F₂. *younger* Qq F₃F₄, Cap.

Knt, Wh. i, Rlfe. *Younker* Rowe et cet.
18. *Hudg'd*] *Hugd* Q₁Q₂. *Hug'd* F₂
F₄. *Hugg'd* Q₃F₃.
19. *like a*] *like the* Qq, Pope+, Sing.
Ktly, Cam. Glo. Cla. Rlfe.
    doth fhe] *fhe doth* F₃F₄, Rowe.

9. obliged] CLARENDON : Faith bound by contract.

11. sits downe] For other instances where the preposition is omitted, see I, i, 135, or ABBOTT, § 394.

12. vntread] CLARENDON : That is, tread in reverse order, retrace. So in *King John*, V, iv, 52 : 'We will untread the steps of damned flight.' The allusion seems to be to a horse trained to perform various feats, such as we now see only in a circus.

16. yonger] Although Shakespeare's printers use the form *younker* elsewhere, change is needless here. '*Younker* exactly expresses,' says CLARENDON, 'the Greek νεανίας.' HENLEY calls attention to the imitation of this passage by Gray in *The Bard* in those familiar lines : 'Fair laughs the morn,' &c. Coleridge (*Biog. Lit.* i, chap. 1) criticised the imitation adversely on the ground that it depends on the printer's use of small capitals (as in 'YOUTH at the prow, and PLEASURE at the helm') 'whether the words should be personifications or mere abstractions.'—ED.

17. skarfed] STEEVENS : That is, the vessel decorated with flags. So in *All's Well*, II, iii, 214 : 'The scarfs and bannerets about thee, did manfully dissuade me from be- lieving thee a vessel of too great a burthen.' ECCLES, from the definition of 'scarf,' both the noun and the verb, in Johnson's *Dict.*, thinks that the allusion is to 'a ship under full sail.' CLARENDON : Or is it that a ship in full sail is compared to a woman dressed in scarfs? From the passage in *All's Well*, it would seem that a scarf was a decoration of a pleasure vessel.

19. a] COLLIER : There seems to be no particular allusion to the Prodigal Son, and '*a* younker' and '*a* prodigal' are spoken in the earlier part of the simile. HALLI- WELL : The particle *the*, if correct, is of course used with reference to the prodigal previously mentioned. CLARENDON refers to *Luke*, xv, 11–32, and calls attention to the text of the Qq, where in line 16 it is '*a* prodigal,' and here '*the* prodigal.' [To me it is immaterial whether the article be definite or indefinite, the allusion seems mani- fest to the Scriptural Prodigal.—ED.]

With ouer-wither'd ribs and ragged failes,   20
Leane, rent, and begger'd by the ftrumpet winde?

Enter Lorenzo.

Salino.   Heere comes *Lorenzo,* more of this hereafter.

Lor.   Sweete friends, your patience for **my** long **a-**   25
  bode,
Not I, but my affaires haue made you wait:
When you fhall pleafe to play the theeues for wiues
Ile watch as long for you then: approach
Here dwels my father Iew.   Hoa, who's within?   3c

---

20. *ouer-wither'd*] Ff, Rowe. *ouer-
wetherd* Q₁Q₂. *over-weatherd* Q₃ et cet.
22. Enter...] After line 24, Dyce, Cam.
Glo. Cla. Rlfe, Wh. ii.
23. Salino.] Ff. Sal. Q₁Q₂. Saler. Q₃.

29. *you then:*] *you. Come then,* Ritson.
approach] *approach;* Rowe. *Come,
approach* Pope+, Cap.
30. *Hoa*] Ff. *Ho* Q₁. *Howe* Q₂. *Hoe* Q₃.
who's] *whofe* Qq.

---

19. **she**] STEEVENS: Surely the bark ought to be of the *masculine* gender, otherwise the allusion wants somewhat of propriety. This indiscriminate use of the personal for the neuter at least obscures the passage. A ship, however, is commonly
spoken of in the feminine gender. WHITE: But here there is no poetical personification of the bark; it is only compared to a prodigal. [Is there not some corruption in
these lines? There seems to be something wrong in the repetition of 'the strumpet
wind.'—ED.]

28. **you shall please**] See ABBOTT, § 297, *ad fin.*

29. CLARENDON considers Ritson's emendation of this metrically-defective line as
more satisfactory than Pope's.

30. **Hoa**] WHITE: 'Ho,' 'hoa,' and 'how' were pronounced alike. [These words
'Hoa, who's within,' are omitted in Oxberry's Edition, and in their place Lorenzo, not
to be outdone by Jessica, responds as follows:

> 'My bliss too long my bride denies;
>   Apace the wasting summer flies;
>   Nor yet the wint'ry blasts I fear,
>   Nor storms nor night shall keep me here.

> 'What may for strength with steel compare?
>   O, love has fetters stronger far!
>   By bolts of steel are limbs confin'd;
>   But cruel love enchains the mind.

> 'No longer, then, perplex thy breast;
>   When thoughts torment, the first are best;
>   'Tis mad to go, 'tis death to stay;
>   Away, my Jessy, haste away.'

Shall we assume that these 'songs' were inserted to make up to us the loss of Shakespeare's 'Tell me where is fancy bred,' which, in this Edition, is omitted?—ED.]

Ieſſica aboue.   31

Ieſſ.   Who are you? tell me for more certainty,
Albeit Ile ſweare that I do know your tongue.
  Lor.   *Lorenzo,* and thy Loue.
  Ieſ.   *Lorenzo* certaine, and my loue indeed,   35
For who loue I ſo much? and now who knowes
But you *Lorenzo,* whether I am yours?
  Lor.   Heauen and thy thoughts are witneſs that thou
        art.
  Ieſ.   Heere, catch this casket, it is worth the paines,   40
I am glad 'tis night, you do not looke on me,
For I am much aſham'd of my exchange:
But loue is blinde, and louers cannot ſee   43

---

31. aboue.] above in Boys Cloths.
Rowe et seq. (cloaths. Pope+, Cap.
Steev. Mal. clothes. Steev. '93).
  36. *who*] *whom* Johns. Coll. Wh. i,
Clarke, Huds.

40. *Heere*] Q₂F₂. *Here* Q₁.
it is] *tis* Q₁.
  41. *I am*] *I'm* Pope+, Dyce iii, Huds.
  42. *aſham'd*] *aſhamde* Q₂.

---

33. **your**] ALLEN: Qu. *that—yt* mistaken for *yr*? Cf. *Rom. & Jul.,* 'My ears have
not yet drunk a hundred words Of *that* (Q₁) tongue's uttering.'
  36. **who**] For manifold instances of 'who' for *whom,* see ABBOTT, § 274.
  38. **thy thoughts**] ECCLES: It is impossible that she, any more than Heaven itself,
to which our hearts lie open, can in reality harbour a doubt of the sincerity of his professions. ALLEN: Perhaps '*my* thoughts.' In that case, the meaning is: 'Not I alone
know it—Heaven witnesses *with* my thoughts.' Emphasize, therefore, *and* (as in 'Ye
cannot serve God *and* Mammon'). 'Heaven,' by the way, is a compulsory euphemism
for *God* (in answer to 'who knows').
  40. **LLOYD**: Elopement, in Jessica's case, it must be said, is a virtue; and the ela-
tion at exchanging freedom for degraded oppression explains and excuses the dry eyes,
—nay, laughing lips—with which she departs. If we care to apologize for the casket
she carried off, we may say she helped herself, perhaps not exorbitantly, to her dowry;
but we shall do better to mark the incident as the last seal of the truth worth laying to
heart, how utterly unkindness, cruelty, sordidness, and distrust can at last erase the
faintest traces of natural duty and affection in hearts that by nature are disposed to be
their hallowed home. ELZE (*Essays,* Trans. p. 92): Jessica appropriates the ducats,
all of which must necessarily fall to her after her father's death, as she is his only child.
Gervinus considers her to be an 'ethereal being, naïve, and inexperienced as a child,
and perfectly unacquainted with the value of money.' This last assertion is, however,
contradicted by her own words here. She tells her lover that the casket is worth the
pains, and she hurries back to 'gild' herself with more ducats.
  41. **you**] ECCLES: I suspect that this should be, '*yet* do not look on me,' the darkness not being sufficient entirely to conceal the transformation of which she is ashamed.
ALLEN: Either: 'I'm glad (since 'tis night) you do not look on me;' or: 'I'm glad 'tis
night (so that) you do look on me.'
  7

The pretty follies that themſelues commit,
For if they could, *Cupid* himſelfe would bluſh   45
To ſee me thus transformed to a boy.
    Lor. Deſcend, for you muſt be my torch-bearer.
    Ieſ. What, muſt I hold a Candle to my ſhames?
They in themſelues goodſooth are too too light.
Why, 'tis an office of diſcouery Loue,   50
And I ſhould be obſcur'd.

---

48. *ſhames*] *ſhame* Ff, Rowe.   Sing. Ktly. *too-too* Hal. Dyce, Sta. Wh.
49. *too too*] *too, too*, Johns. *too, too*   i, Rlfe, Huds.

---

45. **Cupid**] ECCLES: That Cupid does not blush is, in a confused manner, considered as the consequence of the blindness of his votaries, rather than of his own ALLEN: For if they could (and I were Cupid), Cupid himself, &c.

47. **must**] ABBOTT, § 314: This is sometimes used by Shakespeare to mean no more than definite futurity, like our 'is to' in 'He is to be here to-morrow.'

49. **too too**] NARES pointed out the intensive effect of this reduplication, giving instances from Holinshed and Spenser. Halliwell (*Sh. Soc. Papers*, 1844, i, 39) shows that 'too-too' is a provincial word recognized by Ray, and explained by him as meaning 'very well, or good,' and that Watson, a few years afterward, says it is 'often used to denote *exceeding*.' In proof '*that* TOO-TOO, *as used by our early writers, is one word, denoting "exceedingly," and that it ought to be so printed,*' Halliwell gives twelve instances from the poets, from Skelton down to *Hudibras*, and refers to over thirty other passages where the phrase is found. HUNTER doubts if this reduplication be emphatic. It appears to him to have been, in sense, neither more nor less than *too*, and he cites many instances from prose writers. Palsgrave, he adds, has beside *to-much, to-little*, &c., *to to much, to to little, to to great, to to small*, answering to *par trop trop peu, par trop trop grant, par trop trop petit*. The pronunciation was *too-toó*, as appears by this line of Constable's: 'But I did too-too inestimable wey her.' [That this accent can be shifted, see 'Whence it appears, this too-too to frequent.'— Sylvester's *Du Bartas*, p. 576, *a*, ed. 1632.—ED.] WHITE thinks that it was used with intensifying iteration, from the similar iteration of other adverbs and adjectives in Elizabethan literature; for instance: 'Thy wit dost use still still more harmes to finde,'— Sidney's *Arcadia*, ii, 225, ed. 1603; 'While he did live far, far was all disorder,'—*Ib.* v, 430; 'Your lesson is Far far too long,'—*Astrophel and Stella*, St. 56, *Ib.* p. 537; 'Stop you my mouth with still still kissing me,'—*Ib.* St. 81, *Ib.* p. 547; 'Even to thy pure and most most loving breast.'—Shakespeare's *Sonn.* 110. In any case the compound epithet must have originated in the frequent iterative use of the word. [Note on *Ham.* I, ii, 129, of this edition.—ED.]

50. **discouery**] HUNTER (i, 325): This is a military term. Sir John Smith, in his *Instructions and Orders Military*, 1595, p. 51, speaks of 'great intelligence by discoverers and espials.' 'Obscured' is disguised. SINGER: I do not think such a sense was thought of here. ABBOTT, § 439: This is often used for *uncovering*, i. e. *unfold*, whether literally or metaphorically. 'So shall my anticipation prevent your discovery.' —*Ham.* II, ii, 305.

51. **should**] ABBOTT, § 323: 'Should,' the past tense, not being so imperious as *shall*, the present, is still retained in the sense of *ought*, applying to all three persons.

 Lor.　So you are fweet,　　　　　　　　　　　　52
Euen in the louely garnifh of a boy: but come at once,
For the clofe night doth play the run-away,
And we are ftaid for at *Baſſanio's* feaft.　　　　　55
 Ieſ.　I will make faft the doores and guild my felfe
With fome more ducats, and be with you ftraight.　　57

---

52. *you are*] *are you* Qq, Pope et
seq.
 53, 54. *Euen...run-away*] Three lines,
ending *boy...night...run-away* Q₁.
 53. *louely garniſh of a*] *garnish of a*

lovely Coll. (MS).
 53. *but...once*] Separate line, Pope et
seq.
 57. *more*] *mo* Q₁Q₂.　*moe* Q₃.
[Exit from above. Theob. et seq

In the Elizabethan authors, however, it was more commonly thus used, often where we should use *ought*. As here: 'A torch-bearer's office reveals the face, and mine *ought to* be hidden.' See 'Should sunder,' &c., *post*, III, ii, 127.

 53. **louely**] ECCLES: That is, rendered 'lovely' because she had assumed it.

 54. **run-away**] See *Rom. & Jul.* III, ii, 6. CLARENDON: The secret night is stealing away.

 55, 56. SPEDDING (*Cornhill Maga.*, March, 1880): The moral sensibilities of a modern spectator receive here a little shock, from which a judicious adapter might relieve him by the omission of a few lines. Not that I would debar Jessica from seeking relief from her Jewish disabilities by the nearest way. We are all glad to see her at liberty to choose her husband and her religion for herself; to escape from a house which was to her a hell, with only the 'merry devil' Launcelot to cheer it; from a father of whose manners she was (not without reason and to her credit, though to her regret) ashamed; and from the chance, should it suit *him*, of having to take 'any of the stock of Barrabas' for a husband; nor do many of us object to see advantage taken by Antonio of the pressure which the law enables him to put on Shylock for the purpose of securing a comfortable provision for her. But we all feel that she ought to have left the jewels and the ducats behind; and the fact that Shakespeare allowed her to carry them off without a hint of disapprobation from anybody (there being no dramatic necessity for it) suggests a doubt whether in those early days he was fully alive to the impropriety. Perhaps the easy morality of the comic theatre in all such questions,—the large privilege which the young lovers have always enjoyed of deceiving and overreaching the stern parent,—had become so familiar as to hide from him the true nature of the transaction; which in so tragic a business as Shylock's revenge cannot be regarded with the levity which comedy permits. But, however that may be, I cannot doubt that the effect would be much better in modern eyes if Jessica were allowed to escape without the treasure. The loss of his daughter to her race and faith would supply Shylock with as fair a motive for vengeance; he could make as much noise about it; and the secret that he really cared more for the ducats than the daughter would not be forced upon the knowledge of his admirers, who regard paternal tenderness as one of his most conspicuous virtues. Two lines struck out from Jessica's part in the Sixth Scene of the Second Act, a few from Salanio's in the Eighth, and a few more in the interview with Tubal, would (without at all disturbing the action of the play) remove completely our only remaining scruple as to the poetic justice of the final settlement.

Gra.   Now by my hood, a gentle, and no Iew.   58
Lor.   Befhrew me but I loue her heartily.
For fhe is wife, if I can iudge of her,   6c
And faire fhe is, if that mine eyes be true,
And true fhe is, as fhe hath prou'd her felfe :
And therefore like her felfe, wife, faire, and true,
Shall fhe be placed in my conftant foule.

Enter Ieffica.   65

What, art thou come ? on gentlemen, away,
Our masking mates by this time for vs ftay.   *Exit.*   67

---

58. *gentle*] Q₂, Cap.   *Gentile* Q₁FfQ₃   66. *gentlemen*] *gentleman* Q₂.
et cet.   67. Exit.] Exit with Jessica and Sa-
59. *Befhrew*] *Befhrow* Q₂Q₃, Cap.   lerino. Cap.

---

58. **hood**] MALONE: Gratiano is in a masqued habit, to which it is probable that
formerly, as at present, a large cape or hood was affixed. STEEVENS: He alludes to
the practice of friars, who frequently swore by this part of their habit. [This assertion
Steevens possibly took from Capell, who says : ' The speaker's oath is of monkish original.']   HALLIWELL gives a MS note by O. Gilchrist, to the effect that ' the allusion is
to the practice in single combat, where the accused threw down his hood as a challenge
against the impeachment of the accuser. See Holinshed, vol. 3, p. 5.' [As the edition
of Holinshed is not given, I have searched my copy of 1587 in vain for the passage.—
ED.]   WHITE : I had always understood this ancient oath here and elsewhere to be,
' by my self,' i. e. ' by my estate '—manhood, kinghood, knighthood, or whatever the
hood or estate the protester might be. CLARENDON : It is found nowhere else in
Shakespeare.

58. **gentle**] JOHNSON : A jest arising from the ambiguity of *Gentile*, which signifies
both a *heathen* and *one well born.*

59. **Beshrew**] STAUNTON : To ' beshrew ' is to *imprecate sorrow* or *evil* on any per
son or thing, to *curse*, &c.   See ' *Museragno*, a kinde of mouse called a shrew, deadlie
to other beasts if he bite them, and laming any bodie if he but touch them, of which
that curse came, I beshrew thee.'—Florio's *Worlde of Wordes*, 1598.

59. **but**] ABBOTT, § 126: ' But ' is not adversative, but means ' if not,' after ' be-
ſhrew me,' &c.

63. **true**] ELZE (*Essays*, Trans. p. 94): It is lucky that there was no Brabantio
near to whisper into the confiding lover's ear : ' She did deceive her father, marrying
thee !'

67. **Exit**] Where is ' die tragische Schuld ' of our German brothers, that relentless
fate which pursues the guilty and ensures their downfall, here in Jessica's career ?
From the hour of the cruel deception of her father onward, smooth success is strewed
before her little feet, until they trip into bliss and Belmont under patines of bright gold.
Why was a fate so different allotted to poor Desdemona, who yielded to her old father,
after her first offence, all the tender devotion that a married daughter can bestow ? I am
afraid the doctrine of ' die tragische Schuld ' in Shakespeare needs patching.—ED.

Enter Anthonio. 68

   Ant. Who's there?
   Gra. Signior *Anthonio?* 70
   Ant. Fie, fie, *Gratiano*, where are all the reſt?
'Tis nine a clocke, our friends all ſtay for you,
No maske to night, the winde i s come about,
Baſſanio preſently will goe aboord,
I haue ſent twenty out to ſeeke for you. 75
   Gra. I am glad on't, I deſire no more delight
Then to be vnder ſaile, and gone to night.   *Exeunt.*

---

69. *Who's*] *VVhoſe* $Q_2 Q_3$.
71. *Fie, fie*] *Fie*, Pope+.
75. *I...you*] Om. Q_1. Transposed to

follow line 72, Han.
   76. *Gra.*] Om. Q_1, continuing to Anth.
    I am] *I'm* Pope+, Dyce i:i, Huds.

---

73. winde] See III, ii, 284, TH. ELZE.

75, 76. The omission of a whole line here in Q_1, and continuing Gratiano's speecn to Anthonio, is an inexcusable defect in that edition.—ED.

[*Scene VII.*]

Enter Portia with Morrocho, and both their traines.

Por.   Goe, draw afide the curtaines, and difcouer
The feuerall Caskets to this noble Prince :
Now make your choyfe.

    Mor.   The firft of gold, who this infcription beares,   5
Who choofeth me, fhall gaine what men defire.
The fecond filuer, which this promife carries,
Who choofeth me, fhall get as much as he deferues.
This third, dull lead, with warning all as blunt,
Who choofeth me, muft giue and hazard all he hath.   10
How fhall I know if I doe choofe the right ?

Scene III. Belmont. Rowe. Scene VIII. Pope+. Scene VII. Cap. Steev. Mal. Sta. Cam. Wh. Scene VI. Hal. Dyce, Huds.

    A Room in Portia's House. Flourish. Cap.

    1. Morrocho] Morrochius. Rowe+. Prince of Morocco. Cap.

4. [Three caskets are discovered. Rowe.

    5. *who*] *which* Pope+, Dyce iii, Huds. Coll. iii.

    6. *what*] *what many* Qq, Rowe et seq.

    6, 8, 10. In Italics Q_3.

    11. This line is repeated only in F_1F_2.

The Scene which follows, marked in the majority of modern editions Scene vii, is transposed by ECCLES to the First Act, and there termed Scene v. See II, ii, 1.

    2. **curtaines**] KEIGHTLEY (*Exp.* 150): As in Scene ix, it is ' curtain.' I ascribe the *s* to the printer.

    5. **who**] DYCE (ed. iii): This is plainly an error for *which*, occasioned by the ' Who's ' which follow; and compare the third line of the speech. ABBOTT, § 264 : *Who* personifies irrational antecedents. . . . . The slightest active force or personal feeling attributed to the antecedent suffices to justify *who*. Perhaps in this way we may distinguish ' The first of gold, *who* this inscription bears ;' ' The second silver, *which* this promise carries '—that is, ' the first of gold, *and it* bears this inscription; the second (silver), *which* carries,' &c. In the first the *material*, in the second the *promise*, is regarded as the *essential quality*. (Or does euphony prefer *which* in the accented, *who* in the unaccented, syllables ?)

    6, 8, 10. ABBOTT, § 501 : This trimeter couplet is often used by the Elizabethan writers in the translation of quotations, inscriptions, &c.

    6. **what men**] WHITE : That the omission of *many* is due to accident, its presence in the Qq and its occurrence in the inscription (which, of course, was always the same) when it is read by the Prince of Arragon, are sufficient evidence.

    9. **blunt**] JOHNSON : That is, as gross as the dull metal. HALLIWELL : I should read—not as gross as the metal is dull, but as blunt as the dull metal is gross.

    11. In the Folio this line is the last on the page, with the catchwords ' *Por.* The ' beneath it. At the head of the next page the line is repeated (but with a period,

Por. The one of them containes my picture Prince, 12
If you choofe that, then I am yours withall.
   Mor. Some God direct my iudgement, let me fee,
I will furuay the infcriptions, backe againe : 15
What faies this leaden casket ?
Who choofeth me, muft giue and hazard all he hath.
Muft giue, for what ? for lead, hazard for lead ?
This casket threatens men that hazard all
Doe it in hope of faire aduantages : 20
A golden minde ftoopes not to fhowes of droffe,
Ile then nor giue nor hazard ought for lead.
What faies the Siluer with her virgin hue ?
Who choofeth me, fhall get as much as he deferues.
As much as he deferues ; paufe there *Morocho*, 25
And weigh thy value with an euen hand,
If thou beeft rated by thy eftimation
Thou dooft deferue enough, and yet enough
May not extend fo farre as to the Ladie :
And yet to be afeard of my deferuing, 30
Were but a weake difabling of my felfe.
As much as I deferue, why that's the Lady.
I doe in birth deferue her, and in fortunes,
In graces, and in qualities of breeding :
But more then thefe, in loue I doe deferue. 35

---

13. *withall*] *with all* Coll. i.
18. *hazard for lead*] Om. F_3F_4, Rowe i.
19. *threatens men*] *threatens. Men* Rowe et seq.
22. *nor giue*] *not giue* Rowe ii+.
   ought] *aught* Mal.
25. *deferues ;*] *deserves ?* Pope.

25. Morocho] Morrochius. Rowe+.
   Morocco. Cap.
27. *thy*] *the* F_4, Rowe i.
30. *afeard*] *afraid* Q_3, Rowe+.
32. *deferue,*] *deserve—* Rowe.
35. *deferue*] *deserve her* Cap. conj. Coll. ii, Ktly.

---

inftead of an interrogation, at the end). That it is merely a compositor's oversight is shown by the catchwords. I have not deemed it worth while to reproduce it here. —ED.

23. **her**] ALLEN: He says 'her' of silver because he already had in mind 'virgin' as its analogue.

27. **beest**] ROLFE: This must not be confounded with the subjunctive *be*. It is the Anglosaxon *bist*, 2d pers. sing. Pres. Ind. of *beón*, to be.

35. **deferue**] Capell's emendation 'deserve her' is, to me, most certain. It is not only a repetition of the very phrase two lines before, but it is easy to see that the printer was misled by the 'here' in the line following. Eccles suggests two interpretations of this line : ' either "more than these *deserve*," the word "these" being a nominative, or,

What if I ſtrai'd no farther, but choſe here?   36
Let's ſee once more this ſaying grau'd in gold.
Who chooſeth me ſhall gaine what many men deſire:
Why that's the Lady, all the world deſires her :
From the foure corners of the earth they come   40
To kiſſe this ſhrine, this mortall breathing Saint.
The Hircanion deſerts, and the vaſte wildes
Of wide Arabia are as throughfares now
For Princes to come view faire *Portia*
The waterie Kingdome, whoſe ambitious head   45
Spets in the face of heauen, is no barre
To ſtop the forraine ſpirits, but they come
As ore a brooke to ſee faire *Portia*.
One of theſe three containes her heauenly piĉture.
Is't like that Lead containes her? 'twere damnation   50
To thinke ſo baſe a thought, it were too groſe

---

41. *mortall breathing*] Hyphened, Dyce.

42. *Hircanion*] *Hircanian* F₂ et seq. *vaſte*] F₂. *vaſt* F₃F₄, Rowe. *vaſtie* Q₂Q₃, Pope+. *vaſty* Q₁ et cet.

43. *throughfares*] *thoroughfares* Rowe +, Dyce iii.

45. *waterie*] *watry* Q₁.

46. *Spets*] Qq Ff, Cap. *Spits* Rowe et cet.

50. *containes*] *contain* Rowe i.

"more than *I deserve in* these, in love I do deserve," the preposition *in* being understood.' As confirming the latter interpretation, I think we might suppose that the *in* has been absorbed in 'then.' 'But more then' these, in love I do deserve her.—ED.

41. shrine] The use of this word, instead of *image*, here and in: 'for feature, lamng The shrine of Venus,' *Cym.* V, v, 164, WALKER (*Crit.* i, 66) cites as instances of 'an inaccurate use of words in Shakespeare.' Similar instances ('eternal' for *infernal*) we have had in *Ham.* I, v, 21, and *Oth.* IV, ii, 154. I am afraid Walker is right, but it costs a pang to give up the lowly kiss merely on the shrine that holds the saint.—ED.

42. Hircanion] CLARENDON: Hyrcania was a name given to a district of indefinite extent south of the Caspian. Shakespeare three times mentions the tigers of Hyrcania: *3 Hen. VI:* I, i, 156; *Macb.* III, iv, 101; *Ham.* II, ii, 428. In Holland's *Plinie*, viii, cap. 18, we find: 'Tygres are bred in Hircania and India.'

42. vaste] For many another instance of the confusion, in the old copies, of *e* and *ie* final, see WALKER (*Crit.* ii, 48). CLARENDON: Waste, desolate. It has almost an active sense in *Hen. V:* II, iv, 105: 'War opens his vasty jaws.' So 'vastness' is used for desolation in Bacon's *Advancement of Learning*, II, vii, 7: 'Because their excursions into the limits of physical causes hath bred a vastness and solitude in that tract.'

44. to come] For instances of the omission and of the insertion of 'to,' see ABBOTT, § 349.

To rib her fearecloath in the obfcure graue :   52
Or fhall I thinke in Siluer fhe's immur'd
Being ten times vndervalued to tride gold ;
O finfull thought, neuer fo rich a Iem   55
Was fet in worfe then gold / They haue in England
A coyne that beares the figure of an Angell
Stampt in gold, but that's infculpt vpon :   58

52. *rib*] *ribb* Q₂Q₃.   58. *Stampt*] *Stamped* Rowe ii et seq.

---

52. **rib**] STEEVENS : That is, to enclose. See *Cym.* III, i, 19 : 'Neptune's park, ribbed and paled in With rocks unscaleable, and roaring waters.'

52. **searecloath**] CLARENDON : See Cotgrave, ' *Cerat :* A Plaister made of Waxe, Gummes, &c., and certaine oyles ; Wee also, call it, a cerot or seare-cloth.'

54. **vndervalued**] CLARENDON : In the beginning of Elizabeth's reign, gold was to silver in the proportion of 11 to 1 ; in the forty-third year of her reign (i. e. 1600, the year in which this play was first printed) it was in the proportion of 10 to 1 (*Encycl. Brit.*, Art. ' Coinage '). The ratio at present is nearly 15 to 1.

54. **to**] See *ante,* I, i, 176.

57. **coyne**] KNIGHT : ' To come now unto the cause of the general calling of our Ancestors by the name of *Englishmen,* and our Country consequently by the name of *England.* . . . . This King [Egbert] considering that so many different names, as the distinct Kingdoms before had caused, was now no more necessary, and that as the peo-ple were all originally of one Nation, so was it fit they should again be brought under one name ; and although they had had the general name of *Saxons,* as unto this day they are of the *Welsh* and *Irish* called, yet did he rather chuse and ordain that they should be all called *English-men,* as but a part of them before were called ; and that the Coun-try should be called *England.* To the affectation of which name of *English-men*, it should seem he was chiefly moved in respect of Pope *Gregory,* his alluding the name of *Engelisce* unto *Angel-like.* The name of *Engel* is yet at this present in all the *Teu-tonick* Tongue, to wit, the high and low *Dutch,* &c. as much to say, as *Angel,* and if a *Dutch-man* be asked how he would in his Language call an *Angel-like-man,* he would answer, *ein English-man ;* and being asked how in his own Language he would or doth call an *English-man,* he can give no other name for him, but even the very same that he gave before for an *Angel-like-man,* that is, as before is said, *ein English-man, Engel* being in their Tongue an *Angel,* and *English,* which they write *Engelsche, Angel-like.* And such reason and consideration may have moved our former Kings, upon their best Coin of pure and fine Gold, to set the Image of an *Angel,* which may be supposed, hath as well been used before the *Norman* Conquest, as since.'—Verstegan's *Restitution of Decayed Intelligence,* &c. [p. 161, ed. 1673]. DYCE : This gold coin, an ' angel,' at its highest value was worth ten shillings. CLARENDON : It has supplied Shakespeare with many puns.

58. **insculp**] STEEVENS : To 'insculp' is to *engrave.* DOUCE : It is here put in oppo-sition to *engrave,* and simply denotes to *carve in relief.* The angel on the coin was *raised ;* on the casket *indented.* The word *insculp* was, however, formerly used with great latitude of meaning. ECCLES : It seems as if Morochius, at first view, imagined that he had found out the subject of an ingenious and refined compliment, which, at the next moment, he discovers to be incapable of producing the effect he expected from

But here an Angell in a golden bed
Lies all within.   Deliuer me the key :   60
Here doe I choofe, and thriue I as I may.
  Por.   There take it Prince, and if my forme lye there
Then I am yours.
  Mor.   O hell ! what haue we here, a carrion death,
Within whofe emptie eye there is a written fcroule ;   65
Ile reade the writing.

> *All that glifters is not gold,*
> *Often haue you heard that told ;*
> *Many a man his life hath fold*
> *But my out fide to behold ;*   70

---

63. [Unlocking the gold casket. Rowe   64–66. Three lines, ending *here,* ...
et seq. (subs.).   *eye...writing.* Cap. et seq.
                                            66. *Ile...writing*] Om. Ff, Rowe.

---

it. [Dyce long ago said (*Remarks*, p. 96) that 'except those explanatory of customs,
dress, &c., the notes of Douce are nearly worthless;' which is so true that I never repeat Douce's notes unless they have been, in whole or in part, used by subsequent editors; in that case the scope of this present edition requires their insertion.   The above
note is in point.   Douce apparently thought that a distinction was made by Morocco
between *relievo* and *intaglio;* whereas the Angell, lying all *within*, in a golden bed,
was the portrait of Portia, as is pointed out by the Cowden-Clarkes.   Eccles also apparently fails to see the meaning.—ED.]

60, 61. **key . . . may**] WALKER (*Crit.* ii, 167): A rhyme.   'Key,' in Shakespeare's
time, was almost always pronounced *kay*.   ELLIS (*Early Eng. Pron.*, p. 957): It is
not quite certain whether this is meant for a rhyme.   [This difference of opinion between two excellent authorities teaches us caution in drawing conclusions from the
abundance or the lack of rhymes in these plays.—ED.]

63–65. I see no absolute necessity for changing the division of the lines here.   Surely,
after the broken line 'Then I am yours,' the time which elapses while the Prince is opening the casket is enough to make the ear forget the exigencies of an iambic trimeter.—ED.

67. **glisters**] ROLFE: *Glisten* does not occur in Shakespeare nor in Milton.   In
both we find 'glister' several times.

69, 70. Eccles is the only editor, as far as I know, who finds any difficulty here, and
I sympathize with him.   The general drift is clear enough, and is contained in the very
first line, in the old proverb; but it is not so clear that many a man has sold his life
merely for the sake of looking at gold.   Eccles thinks that, perhaps, since gold possesses 'no essential, inherent utility beyond inferior metals, the extraordinary fondness
for it may be considered as arising from the gratification men feel in *looking at it ;*'
which I doubt.   Perhaps it is enough to suppose that in days when wealth was kept
locked up in chests, to see the gold was to own it.   Or it may be that men are willing
to sell their lives merely for the outside glitter of wealth, its gewgaws and frippery.   Or
there may be no reference to gold at all; as it is the skull that speaks, it may refer to
beauty.—ED.

> *Guilded timber doe wormes infold:*   71
> *Had you beene as wiſe as bold,*
> *Yong in limbs, in iudgement old,*
> *Your anſwere had not beene inſcrold,*
> *Fareyouwell, your ſuite is cold,*   75

Mor. Cold indeede, and labour loſt,
Then farewell heate, and welcome froſt: 77

71. Guilded] Gilded Rowe et seq.　　　*may* Pope+. *woods do* Ktly. *tombs do*
71. timber doe] Q₂F₃. timber do Q₁F₂ Johns. conj. Cap. et cet.
F₄, Rowe, Hal. Timber doe Q₃. *wood*

---

71. JOHNSON: 'Gilded wood may worms infold' is a line not bad in itself, but not so applicable to the occasion as that which, I believe, Shakespeare wrote: 'Gilded *tombs* do,' &c. A tomb is the proper repository of a *death's head*. CAPELL (p. 62): 'Tombs' (or, as written formerly, *tombes*) we can very readily imagine, of either printer or copyer, to have been mistaken for 'timber:' but that *wood* should be so, and, over and above that, *may* for 'doe,' never enter'd yet into head that had just conceptions of criticism; yet into both those words are *timber* and *doe* converted by the second modern [Pope], and his conversion adher'd to by all his successors: *Tombs*, richly gilded, are the ornaments of many old churches at this day. STEEVENS: Conf. Sidney's *Arcadia*, i: 'But gold can guild a rotten piece of wood.' MALONE: Dr Johnson's emendation is supported by Shakespeare's 101st *Sonnet:* 'It lies in thee To make thee much outlive a gilded tomb.' KNIGHT: Without any violation of grammatical propriety, 'timber' might be used as a plural noun. Gilded timber — timbers — *coffins* — do infold worms. Still the original reading is harsh and startling. STAUNTON: If 'timber' is right, then the redundant 'do' is an interloper, and should be omitted. HALLIWELL: 'Timber' is here a plural noun, and the redundant syllable is no sufficient reason for adopting Dr Johnson's plausible alteration. It may be questioned whether Shakespeare is referring either to a coffin or a tomb, but rather to the gilded chest which contained 'the carrion death.' COLLIER (ed. ii): Johnson's suggestion of 'tombs' is countenanced by the (MS), and there can be no doubt about it. DYCE (ed. iii): 'Timber' is a sheer misprint.

73. ABBOTT, § 275: It would seem that '*as . . . . so*' are both to be implied from the previous line. '(*As*) young in limbs, (*so*) in judgement old.'

74. **Your**] JOHNSON: Since there is an answer 'inscrol'd,' or *written* in every casket, I believe for 'your' we should read *this*. When the words were written *yʳ* and *yˢ*, the mistake was easy. ECCLES: '*Your* answer' may signify, 'such an answer as you have now received.'

74, 75. HOLT WHITE proposed that between these lines, 'All that glitters is not gold' should be inserted. 'The inscription on the gold casket will then be comprised in the same number of lines which the inscription on the silver one contains.'

77. HALLIWELL: This is a paraphrastical inversion of the common old proverb: 'Farewell, frost,' which was used on the absence or departure of anything that was unwelcome or displeasing. 'Farewell, frost, will you needes be gone,'—Wapull's *Tyde Taryeth No Man*, 1576. 'Therefore are you so foule, and so, farewell, frost.'— Lilly's *Mother Bombie*, and elsewhere.

Portia adew, I haue too grieu'd a heart   78
To take a tedious leaue : thus loofers part.   *Exit.*
   Por.   A gentle riddance : draw the curtaines, go :   80
Let all of his complexion choofe me fo.   *Exeunt.*

---

79. Exit.] Exit with his train. Cornets. Dyce.

---

79. **part**] CLARENDON : That is, depart.   *Depart* was also used where we should say 'part,' as in the Marriage Service 'till us do part' is a corruption of 'till death us depart.'

79. **Exit.**] M. D. CONWAY : Standing before the dull leaden casket which holds the portrait of Portia, the unsuccessful Prince might justly say to it : ' Leaden box, you are a lie!   You are not the fair and honest setting for such a pearl as Portia!'   The box might reply : ' No, I am not exactly a lie, but a stratagem for getting at the truth amid a lying world.   An old man wanted his daughter to marry a man who had the wit to look below the surface of things.'   ' Well,' the Prince might retort, ' you will succeed in getting a deeper fellow than I am; but you may find, when Bassanio has paid his debts with your gold, that there is such a thing as being too deep.'   [See Cam. Edd. note on ' Flo. Cornets ' in line 2 of the next Scene.]

81. JOHNSON : This play having been probably divided without authority by the publishers of the First Folio, lies open to a new regulation, if any more commodious division can be proposed.   The story is itself so wildly incredible and the changes of scene so frequent and capricious, that the probability of action does not deserve much care; yet it may be proper to observe, that, by concluding the Second Act here, time is given for Bassanio's passage to Belmont.

[*Scene VIII.*]

Enter Salarino and Solanio.

Flo. Cornets.

Sal.   Why man I faw *Baſſanio* vnder fayle,
With him is *Gratiano* gone along;
And in their ſhip I am ſure *Lorenzo* is not.   5
  Sol.   The villaine *Iew* with outcries raiſd the Duke,
Who went with him to ſearch *Baſſanios* ſhip.
  Sal.   He comes too late, the ſhip was vnderſaile;
But there the Duke was giuen to vnderſtand
That in a Gondilo were ſeene together   10
Lorenzo and his amorous *Ieſſica.*
Beſides, *Anthonio* certified the Duke
They were not with *Baſſanio* in his ſhip.
  Sol.   I neuer heard a paſſion ſo confuſd,
So ſtrange, outragious, and ſo variable,   15

Scene IV. Venice. Rowe.   Scene IX.
Pope. Scene VI. Eccles. Scene VIII.
Steev. Scene VII. Hal.
  1. Salarino] Solarino Rowe.
    Solanio] Salanio Q$_1$.
  2. Flo. Cornets.] Om. Qq, Rowe+.
  5. *I am*] *Ime* Q$_1$.   *I'm* Pope+, Coll.
Wh. i, Dyce iii, Huds.

6. Sol.] Salan. Q$_1$.
8. *comes*] Ff, Rowe.   *came* Qq et cet.
10. *Gondilo*] *Gondylo* Qq.   *Gondalo*
Rowe.   *Gondola* Theob.
11. *amorous*] *armorous* Q$_1$.
14, 27, 36, 53. Sol.] Salan. Q$_1$.
15. *ſtrange, outragious*] *strange-out-*
rageous Dyce iii.

---

2. **Flo. Cornets.**] CAMBRIDGE EDITORS: This Stage-direction Capell [and Dyce]
transferred to the beginning of Scene vii. Dyce added 'Cornets' at the end of the
Scene also. We have adopted the suggestion, as the Prince's leaving the stage would
naturally be accompanied with the same pomp as his entrance.

10. **Gondilo**] Staunton and Halliwell give a long account by Tom Coryat (*Crudi-*
ties, p. 170, 171, ed. 1611) of the gondola as it was in Shakespeare's day, whereby
it appears that it differed little from that of the present time; then, as now, 'if the
passenger meaneth to be private, he may draw down' 'the faire black cloth,' 'and
after row so secretly that no man can see him.' Wherefore, if Lorenzo and the
amorous Jessica were 'seen,' it was because they chose to be, as Knight suggests.—
ED.

14, &c. ELZE (*Essays*, p. 95): This is the only Scene in which Shylock might
appear in a ridiculous light, and the poet very wisely does not bring it before us on the
stage, but merely describes it by hearsay.

15. **strange, outragious**] WALKER (*Crit.* i, 32): Read, undoubtedly, *strange-out-*
rageous; οὕτως ἀτόπως ἔκθυμον. The awkwardness of the common reading is the same
as in *Jul. Cæs.* I, iii, 'Most bloody-fiery, and most terrible.'

As the dogge _Iew_ did vtter in the ſtreets ;   16
My daughter, O my ducats, O my daughter,
Fled with a Chriſtian, O my Chriſtian ducats !
Iuſtice, the law, my ducats, and my daughter ;
A ſealed bag, two ſealed bags of ducats,   20
Of double ducats, ſtolne from me by my daughter,
And iewels, two ſtones, two rich and precious ſtones,
Stolne by my daughter : iuſtice, finde the girle,
She hath the ſtones vpon her, and the ducats.

Sal.   Why all the boyes in Venice follow him,   25
Crying his ſtones, his daughter, and his ducats.

Sol.   Let good _Anthonio_ looke he keepe his day
Or he ſhall pay for this.

Sal.   Marry well remembred,
I reaſon'd with a Frenchman yeſterday,   30
Who told me, in the narrow ſeas that part
The French and Engliſh, there miſcaried
A veſſell of our countrey richly fraught :
I thought vpon _Anthonio_ when he told me,
And wiſht in ſilence that it were not his.   35

Sol.   Yo were beſt to tell _Anthonio_ what you heare.

17, 18. _O_] _ô_ Q₂Q₃. | Johns.   _too ! two_ Coll. ii, iii (MS).
22. _two ſtones, two_] _two_ Ff, Rowe. _two_ | 36. _Yo_] F₁.
stones Pope, Theob. Han. _too, stones_, Warb.

---

17. WALKER (_Crit._ iii, 54) : Sidney, _Arcadia_, ii, 178 (describing the death of 'the old bad Chremes '),—' But one thing was notable for a conclusion of his miserable life, that neither the death of his daughter, who (alas, poor gentlewoman !) was by chance slain among his clowns, while she overboldly for her weak sex sought to hold them from me, nor yet his own shameful end, was so much in his mouth as he was led to execution, as the loss of his goods and burning of his house : which often, with more laughter than tears of the hearers, he made pitiful exclamations upon.' [See also, _Wily Beguiled_, in Appendix.]

27. keepe] For the subjunctive in subordinate sentences, see ABBOTT, § 368.

30. reason'd] CAPELL : An arrant Gallicism ; us'd, as do the French their _Je raisonnois_, for—I talk'd, simply.

31. the narrow seas] See _post_, III, i, 4.

36. Yo were best] WALKER (_Crit._ ii, 204) : _Thou wert, you were, I was_, &c. occur freqiently, both in Shakespeare and contemporary dramatists, in places where it is clear they must have been pronounced as one syllable, in whatever manner the contraction was effected. [See _Ham._ IV, v, 14 ; _Oth._ I, ii, 34, &c. Walker cites _2 Hen. VI :_ V, i : 'You were best to go to bed, and dream again,' as under this rule, 'unless,' he adds, 'Shakespeare wrote " You were _best go_," ' &c., which gives a hint of anticipating ALLEN's conjecture here—viz. 'You were _best tell_ Antonio,' &c. According to Allen

Yet doe not fuddainely, for it may grieue him.   37
 Sal. A kinder Gentleman treads not the earth,
I faw *Baffanio* and *Anthonio* part,
Baffanio told him he would make fome fpeede   40
Of his returne : he anfwered, doe not fo,
Slubber not bufineffe for my fake *Baffanio*,
But ftay the very riping of the time,
And for the *Iewes* bond which he hath of me,
Let it not enter in your minde of loue :   45
Be merry, and imploy your chiefeft thoughts
To courtfhip, and fuch faire oftents of loue
As fhall conueniently become you there ;
And euen there his eye being big with teares,   49

---

37. *doe*] *do't* Heath.
 for] *left* Cap. (Erratum).
42. *Slubber*] *flumber* Q₂Q₃.

46. *imploy*] *employ* Q₁F₃F₄. *apply*
Dodd, Coll. ii (MS).
48. *there ;*] *there.* Q₁. *there,* Q₂Q₃.
49. *there*] *then* Dyce iii.

---

this is an instance of the absorption of the 'to' in the *t* of '*best*.' '*Best to*,' he says, 'is against the *ear* of that age.'—ED.] See ABBOTT, § 230, for the whole phrase, with 'other ungrammatical remnants of ancient usage.' Also *post*, V, i, 196; *Lear*, I, iv, 93; III, iv, 99.

45. **enter in**] See ABBOTT, § 159, for other instances of the use of *in* with verbs of motion; see also, V, i, 65.

45. **minde of loue**] JOHNSON suspects some corruption here. HEATH (p. 116): There ought to have been a comma after 'mind;' the sense is : Let me entreat you by our mutual love, that you take not the least thought of it. CAPELL (p. 62): It was once fancy'd that another sense was intended, inconsistent with this pointing; namely,— '*in your mind* that is and should be engag'd by *love* and love-matters:' but as this anticipates somewhat the thoughts that follow, the other meaning (which moreover has pathos to recommend it) is rather preferable : 'of love' is every day us'd by us in the sense of—for love's sake. STEEVENS : 'Your mind of love' may, however, in this instance, mean *your loving mind.* STAUNTON : 'Mind of love' may be correct, but *bond of love* would be more in Shakespeare's manner, and is countenanced by a passage in *Twelfth N.* V, i, 159, where it occurs, and also in *Wint. Tale*, IV, iv, 584. ABBOTT, § 169, adopts Heath's interpretation. CLARENDON adopts Steevens's interpretation, and cites *Meas. for Meas.* II, iv, 179: 'Such a mind of honour.' So, likewise, ROLFE. [It is difficult to decide where both interpretations, Heath's and Steevens's, are so evenly balanced. The weight of authority, however, is on the side of Steevens. —ED.]

46. **imploy**] DODD (*ap.* Eccles): The sense seems here, evidently, to require we should read *apply*.

48. **conueniently**] CLARENDON: Fitly, suitably. See *Proverbs*, xxx, 8: 'Feed me with food convenient for me.'

49. **there**] DYCE: This is repeated by mistake from the preceding line. [See Text. Notes, where Dyce's change had occurred to me independently.—ED.]

Turning his face, he put his hand behinde him,   50
And with affection wondrous fencible
He wrung *Baffanios* hand, and fo they parted.
 Sol. I thinke he onely loues the world for him,
I pray thee let vs goe and finde him out
And quicken his embraced heauineffe   55
With fome delight or other.
 Sal. Doe we fo.   *Exeunt.*

---

51. *fencible*] Q₂.   55. *embraced*] *unbraced* Anon. ap.
54. *pray thee*] *prethee* Q₁.   Hal.

---

55. **embraced**] WARBURTON: This unmeaning epithet would make me choose, rather, to read: *enraced*, from the French *enraciner*. JOHNSON: When I thought the passage corrupted, it seemed to me not improbable that Shakespeare had written *entranced*, musing, abstracted, moping melancholy. But I know not why any great efforts should be made to change a word which has no incommodious or unusual sense. We say of a man now that 'he *hugs* his sorrows,' and why might not Anthonio *embrace* heaviness? STEEVENS: See *post*, III, ii, 115: 'doubtful thoughts and rash-embrac'd despair.'

[*Scene IX.*]

Enter Nerriſſa and a Seruiture.

Ner . Quick, quick I pray thee, draw the curtain ſtrait,
The Prince of Arragon hath tane his oath,
And comes to his election preſently.   4

Scene IX. Steev. Scene V. Rowe.   1. Enter...Seruiture] Enter...Servitor.
Scene X. Pope. Scene VII. Ec. Scene $Q_1F_3F_4$. Enter...Serviter. F_3.
VIII. Dyce.   3. Arragon] Arrogon Q_2.

SCENE IX.] FREYTAG (*Technik des Dramas*, 1876, p. 71, &c.), in dealing with rep
etitions of the same or similar dramatic situations, which must always either afford some
agreeable relief as a foil to exciting scenes, or else, as the drama proceeds, conduce to a
heightening of the interest, cites as a happy instance of the former, the drowsiness of
Lucius during the conspiracy in Act II of *Jul. Cæs.*, and a repetition of his drowsiness
in Act IV, in the tent of Brutus; and, as an instance of the latter, Romeo's fatal duel
with Tybalt, and his second fatal duel with Paris. 'But Shakespeare is not always
equally happy. The repetition of the Witches' incantation scene in Macbeth adds
nothing to the dramatic effect of the tragedy; nor does the threefold choice of caskets
here in the *Mer. of Ven.;* the dramatic movement in the first two elections is but
small, and there is a lack of exquisite elegance in the speeches of the first two suitors.'
'But,' Freytag adds, 'Shakespeare could permit himself to indulge in such rhetorical
delicacies because his solid, substantial public found especial pleasure in courtly addresses.' [Freytag is not the only offender in failing to give Shakespeare credit for
consummate skill in the mere artistic construction of his dramas. There is a feeling
abroad that Shakespeare's success in this regard was merely a lucky hit, a kind of
inspiration, of whose operation he himself was not conscious. Proofs of this are
afforded in the freedom with which critics do not hesitate to rearrange Shakespeare's
scenes. It is strange that it does not occur to them that any sequence of scenes, as it
arranged itself in a mind as through and through dramatic as Shakespeare's, must be
better than it possibly can be in any mind less dramatic. If the structure of any of
his dramas appear incomprehensible to us, it is our duty to study until light dawns on
us. It never occurred to Freytag, able critic as he is, that there is in the very framework of this play a dramatic necessity of making three months equivalent to a watch
in the night, and that powerful, essential aids to this end are the succession of days at
Belmont, and the succession of suitors which come and go, and all the weeks which
have to pass to fill up three months, while Bassanio is journeying by night only twenty
miles from Venice. No soliloquies, no dialogues can give to an audience a 'realizing
sense' of this flight of time but the actual passing of the events before their eyes upon
the stage. Yet of this necessity Freytag appears to have caught never a hint.—ED.]

2. draw] STEEVENS: That is, draw it open. So in an old Stage-direction in *Hen.
VIII:* 'The king draws the curtain and sits reading pensively.' [It can evidently
mean either to open or close the curtain. At the conclusion of this Scene, line 88,
Portia again tells Nerissa to 'draw the curtain,' of course to close it, after Arragon's
choice.—ED.]
8

Enter Arragon, his traine, and Portia.   5
Flor . Cornets.

Por.   Behold, there ſtand the caskets noble Prince,
If you chooſe that wherein I am contain'd,
Straight ſhall our nuptiall rights be ſolemniz'd :
But if thou faile, without more ſpeech my Lord,   10
You muſt be gone from hence immediately.

Ar.   I am enioynd by oath to obſerue three things ;
Firſt, neuer to vnfold to any one
Which casket 'twas I choſe ; next, if I faile
Of the right casket, neuer in my life   15
To wooe a maide in way of marriage :
Laſtly, if I doe faile in fortune of my choyſe,
Immediately to leaue you, and be gone.

Por.   To theſe iniunctions euery one doth ſweare
That comes to hazard for my worthleſſe ſelfe.   20

Ar.   And ſo haue I addreſt me, fortune now

6. Flor. Cornets] Om. Qq.
9. *Straight*] *Srraight* Q₁.
   rights] *rites* Pope et seq.
10. *thou*] *you* Qq, Rowe et seq.
17. *Laſtly*] *Last* Pope+. Closing line

16, Cap. et seq. (except Sta. Wh. i, Rlfe).
Separate line, Cam. Glo. Del. Cla. Wh. ii.
17. *I doe*] *I* Pope+.
21, 22. *me*, ...*hope :*] *me ; ...hope :* Q₅.

9. **solemniz'd**] WALKER (*Vers.* p. 194) called attention to the shifting accent of
this word.   Here and in III, ii, 199, the accent is the same, but in *Love's Lab. Lost,*
II, i, 42, it is *solémnizéd.*   ABBOTT, § 491, thinks that the emphasis which *-ised* now
has is due to the present broad pronunciation of *i.*   Polysyllables with this termination
'generally have now two accents, the principal accent coming first.   But in Shakespeare's time it would seem that the *i* approximated in some of these words to the
French *i,* and, the *-ed* being pronounced, the *i* in *-ised* was unemphatic.'

16, 17. **in way . . . in fortune**] See I, i, 61; II, i, 17; or ABBOTT, § 89, for omission of the definite article.

16. **marriage**] A trisyllable.   See WALKER (*Vers.* 175); ABBOTT, § 479.

17. **Lastly**] The Cambridge Editors rightly regard this word as an interjectional
line.   For other instances, see ABBOTT, § 511.

20. **to hazard**] CLARENDON: Here a substantive.   SCHMIDT (*Lex.*) considers it
a verb.   It is not easy to determine, but considering the frequency with which the definite article is absorbed or elided, Clarendon's view seems the more likely.—ED.

21. **addrest**] STEEVENS: To 'address' is to *prepare.*   That is, I have prepared
myself by the same ceremonies.   TYRWHITT: I believe we should read, 'And so have
I.   Address me, Fortune, now To my heart's hope.'   So in the *Merry Wives,* III, v,
135, 'I will then address me to my appointment.'

21. **fortune, &c.**] ECCLES: 'Be propitious !' or some such words, seem to be understood.   CLARENDON: That is, 'May good fortune second my heart's hope.'   Or, sup-

To my hearts hope : gold, filuer, and bafe lead. 22
Who choofeth me muft giue and hazard all he hath.
You fhall looke fairer ere I giue or hazard.
What faies the golden cheft, ha, let me fee : 25
Who choofeth me, fhall gaine what many men defire :
What many men defire, that many may be meant
By the foole multitude that choofe by fhow,
Not learning more then the fond eye doth teach,
Which pries not to th'interior, but like the Martlet 30
Builds in the weather on the outward wall,

23, 26. Italics, Q_3.

27. *defire,*] *desire—* Rowe.

many may] Many, *may* Rowe. *may* Pope +.

28. *By the foole*] *Of the full* Pope, Han. *Of the fool* Theob. Warb. Johns. Cap. Steev. '85.

28. *foole multitude*] *foole-multitude* Q_n, Theob. Warb. Johns. Ktly.

30. *pries*] *payes* F_3. *pays* F_4. *pry* Theob. Warb.

pries not to] *prize not* Coll. (MS).

th'interior,] *th'interiour;* Q_1, Han. *thinteriour,* Q_2. *th'inheritour,* Q_3.

but] Om. Han

---

posing the speaker to invoke the goddess, we might point thus : 'Fortune! now To my heart's hope.' Now let me try my luck.

28. **By**] MALONE : That is, by that many may be meant the foolish multitude [which WHITE suggested as a possible reading]. So in Plutarch's *Life of Cæsar*, translated by North, 1575 : 'These fat long-heared men made him not affrayed, but the lean and whitely-faced fellows ; meaning that by Brutus and Cassius.' Again, in Sir Thomas More's *Life of Edward the Fifth*, Holinshed, p. 1374 : 'That meant he by the lordes of the queenes kindred.' Again, *Ib*. p. 1371 : 'This meant he by Catesby, which was of his near secrete counsaile.' Again, Puttenham's *Arte of Poesie*, 1589, p. 157 : 'The good old gentleman would tell us that were children, how it was meant [in an enigma] by a furr'd glove.' Again, *Ib*. p. 161 : 'Any simple judgement might easily perceive by whom it was meant, that is, by lady Elizabeth, Queene of England.' [In this note of Malone I have omitted the paraphrase which he carefully gives after each instance except the last, to show the different construction of the present day. It is strange that it never seems to have occurred, either to Malone or to any one else except ALLEN, that these instances, and they might be greatly multiplied, reveal the fact that while we now say, 'I mean this epithet *for* you,' Shakespeare and his contemporaries said, 'I mean this epithet *by* you.' Abbott, § 145, includes this present instance under the same section with 'How say you *by* the French lord,' I, ii, 52. It may be that they are parallel, but to me it seems simpler to hold it as an idiom that *by* was used commonly after the verb *to mean*.—ED.]

28. **foole multitude**] Unquestionably, 'foole' here is used adjectively, and is so cited by Schmidt (*Lex.*). See 'foole gudgin,' I, i, 112.—ED.

30. This line is one of those, of which ABBOTT, § 495, gives several instances, where two syllables are inserted at the end of the third or fourth foot : 'Which pries | not to | th'inte*rior*, | but like | the Mart*let*.'

30. **Martlet**] See Rowe's emendation, *Macb*. I, vi, 4.

Euen in the force and rode of cafualtie.   32
I will not choofe what many men defire,
Becaufe I will not iumpe with common fpirits,
And ranke me with the barbarous multitudes.   35
Why then to thee thou Siluer treafure houfe,
Tell me once more, what title thou dooft beare ;
Who choofeth me fhall get as much as he deferues :
And well faid too ; for who fhall goe about
To cofen Fortune, and be honourable   40
Without the ftampe of merrit, let none prefume
To weare an vndeferued dignitie :
O that eftates, degrees, and offices,
Were not deriu'd corruptly, and that cleare honour
Were purchaft by the merrit of the wearer ;   45
How many then fhould couer that ftand bare ?
How many be commanded that command ?
How much low pleafantry would then be gleaned   48

---

32. *force*] *course* Bailey.
    rode] Qq Ff. *road* Rowe.
35. *barbarous*] *barbarious* F$_4$.
    multitudes] Walker, Dyce iii.
38, 52, 60. Italics, Q$_1$Q$_3$.
39. *too*] *to* Q$_2$Q$_3$.
41. *merrit,*] *merit ?* Rowe.

44. *and*] Om. Pope +.
45. *purchaft*] *purchac'd* Q$_1$.
48. *pleafantry*] *pezantry* Q$_1$. *peafantry*
Q$_2$Q$_3$, Rowe et seq.
48, 50. *gleaned … Pickt*] *fann'd …*
Gleaned Daniel.

---

32. **force**] Steevens: That is, the power. Allen: Perhaps equivalent to *in vi et via*, exposed to the attack of.

35. **multitudes**] Walker (*Crit.* i, 254). *Multitude*, surely; 'the fool multitude that choose by show,' a few lines above. [In this very valuable chapter, No. XXXVIII, Walker gives a great number of instances of the frequent interpolation, and of the frequent omission, of the final *s* in the First Folio. So large is the number that Walker himself (p. 237) says that 'the fact of the same error being so often repeated leads me to doubt whether it is an error after all.' See 'gossips,' III, i, 7; 'flints,' IV, i, 35; 'Masters,' IV, i, 55; 'Messengers,' IV, i, 116. Also, *Oth.* I, i, 31; *Lear*, V, iii, 258.]

43. **estates**] Not property, but dignity, status.

44. **cleare**] Eccles: That is, bright, splendid; or, perhaps, unsullied. Dyce (*Gloss.*): Pure, innocent, free from evil. [See 'the clearest gods,' *Lear*, IV, vi, 73, and notes.—Ed.]

46. **couer**] Clarendon: Wear their hats, as masters. See *As You Like It*, III, iii, 78: 'Pray be covered.' [See also, III, v, 51.]

48. **gleaned**] Johnson: The meaning is, How much meanness would be found among the great, and how much greatness among the mean. But since men are always said to *glean* corn though they may *pick* chaff, the sentence had been more agreeable to the common manner of speech if it had been written: 'How much low pleasantry would then be *pick'd* . . . . how much honour *glean'd*,' &c.

From the true ſeede of honor ? And how much honor
Pickt from the chaffe and ruine of the times,   50
To be new varniſht : Well, but to my choiſe.
Who chooſeth me ſhall get as much as he deſerues.
I will aſſume deſert ; giue me a key for this,   53

---

49. *And*] Om. Pope+.
50. *chaffe*] *chaft* Q₂.
51. *varniſht:*] *verniſh'd?* Q₁. *varniſt;*
Q₂.   *vanned* Warb.

53. *I...this*] *A Key for this; I will
assume deſert,* Han.
deſert ;] *deſert.* Q₁.

---

50. chaffe and ruine] STAUNTON: The same as *chaff and bran.* 'Ruin' meant
refuse, rubbish. 'But,' asks ALLEN, 'is *bran* more rubbish than *chaff ?* Perhaps "ruin"
is the Latin *ruina,* a heap, and perhaps the phrase, by hendiadys, a heap of chaff.'

51. varnisht] WARBURTON: This confusion and mixture of metaphors makes me
think that Shakespeare wrote *vanned,* i. e. winnow'd, purged, from the French *vanner.*
This alteration restores the metaphor to its integrity.   STEEVENS: Shakespeare is perpetually violating the integrity of his metaphors, and the emendation proposed seems to
me to be as faulty as unnecessary; for what is already *selected from the chaff* needs not
be new *vanned.*   I wonder Dr Warburton did not think of changing the word 'ruin'
into *rowing,* which in some counties of England is used to signify the second and inferior crop of grass which is cut in autumn.   HEATH (p. 116): The confusion of metaphors was introduced by adding 'ruins' to 'chaff,' and it is to the former of these
words that 'new *varnish'd'* is adapted.   ECCLES: The connection between the 'chaff'
and 'ruins' is not extremely obvious, but 'honour,' having been recovered thence, is,
upon the metaphorical allusion being suddenly dropped, to be considered in a new
point of view, more suitable to its true nature and character, and, possibly, with reference to those armorial insignia and types of nobility, which, having been painted, are
liable by time to be sullied and defaced, but, by being *new varnished,* may be restored
to their primitive splendor.   BAILEY (ii, 206) devotes six octavo pages to the justification of his emendations in this passage, and no one will think them too many when he
sees the alterations which Bailey says give a 'clear meaning' to Shakespeare and render Shakespeare's metaphorical language 'consistent throughout.'   'How much low
peasant's rye would then be *screen'd* From the true seed of honour! and how much
seed Pick'd from the chaff and *strewings* of the *temse,* To be new *garner'd !*'   'Temse,'
which appears to be a kind of sieve, Bailey acknowledges is not to be found in Shakespeare, nor indeed in any other writer, except in Tusser, and then only as a compound
with 'loaf.'   It also appears from a book called 'The Wheat Plant,' published in Cincinnati, in 1860, that 'formerly' (Bailey does not tell us when) it was 'usual' (Bailey
does not tell us where) to sow rye and early wheat together; the harvested grain was
termed *meslin.*   'It is a probable supposition,' concludes Bailey, 'that Shakespeare, in
forming his metaphor, had this *meslin* in his mind, and it is pretty clear why he spoke
of *peasant's rye.*   It may be added, that "peasantry" is a word not to be found in his
dramas.'—ED.

53. assume] SCHMIDT: That is, claim. [Perhaps it is even stronger than 'claim.'
It is used, I think, in its original Latin meaning of *taking to one's self ;* just as Hamlet
tells his mother to 'assume a virtue, if she have it not,' or as Bassanio uses it in III,
ii, 87.—ED.]

53. for this] DYCE (ed. iii): Hanmer, Ritson, and Steevens were, I believe, right in

And inftantly vnlocke my fortunes here.

    Por.   Too long a paufe for that which you finde there.   55

    Ar.   What's here, the portrait of a blinking idiot

Prefenting me a fcedule, I will read it :

How much vnlike art thou to *Portia* ?

How much vnlike my hopes and my deferuings *?*

Who choofeth me, fhall haue as much as he deferues.   60

---

55. As an aside, Cap.
56. [Unlocking the silver casket. Rowe.
   here,] *here !* Q₃.
   portrait] *pourtrait* Q₂Q₃.

57. *fcedule,*] *fedule ?* Q₁. *fhedule,* Q₂ *fchedule ?* F₄.
59. *deferuings*] *deferving* F₄, Rowe.
60. *haue*] *get* Knt, Dyce iii.

---

regarding these words as an interpolation. [Against which I beg to enter a deferential protest. To me, these words are both important and emphatic. After he has got as far as to assume desert, Arragon makes so long a pause that Portia (although, perhaps, in an Aside) even calls attention to it. Now, while we do not need this pause, as we frequently do need one, to supply the lack of missing syllables, yet the line is undeniably broken, and in broken lines I think that all the requirements of rhythm are met if both fragments run smoothly. Of course, there is a limit in all things. It is not to be supposed that we should accept fragments composed of four feet each. In that case we may suspect corruption and, perhaps, set to work at restoration. But here the fragments are of only three feet each, and when joined together merely form an Alexandrine; and however much we may slur over syllables and compress full-grown words into dwarfs, yet Alexandrines are to be found in Shakespeare, and Alexandrines they will remain, not alone to the eye, but to an ear which prefers a clear and clean enunciation to an abnormal one. Arragon says, 'give me the key *for this ;*' to me the words are indispensable. We could even better spare 'give me,' or even 'the key,' which is involved in the word 'unlock.' But there is no necessity for any omission, and not a syllable can be spared, as I think. In a modernized text, might it not be proper to print this in a parenthesis? Unless this request for the key be parenthetical, how are we to understand the construction? This 'give' is an imperative addressed to Portia. With the customary punctuation, 'unlock' is an imperative also, and is Portia to unlock the casket? If 'give me a key for this' be put in a parenthesis, then 'unlock' is future, and in the same construction with 'I will assume desert.'—ED.]

   55. I cannot find that any editor has noticed Capell's plausible reading of this line as an Aside. (There is no reference to it in the Cam. Ed.) It is to me, beyond a peradventure. As addressed to Arragon these words have the sound of twitting him, which is not, to me, quite in character. To be sure, it may be said that Portia is so delighted at his failure that she cannot restrain her merriment, but the open expression of it, even to a deliberate fool, is not exactly in harmony with that sympathetic tenderness of hers which was like the gentle rain from heaven.—ED.

   60. **haue**] DYCE (ed. i) : This (if not an oversight of the poet) is a mistake of the scribe or printer for *get ;* see this line [where it has been previously given]. WHITE (ed. i) : But as this line is read from 'a schedule,' there is little warrant and less need to change it. [From aught that the context shows, it does not follow that Arragon did read the line. This very change in phraseology may have been meant as a hint to us that he was repeating it from memory.—ED.]

Did I deferue no more then a fooles head,   61
Is that my prize, are my deferts no better?
　Por.　To offend and iudge are diftinct offices,
And of oppofed natures.
　Ar.　What is here?   65

> *The fier feauen times tried this,*
> *Seauen times tried that iudement is,*
> *That did neuer choofe amis,*
> *Some there be that fhadowes kiffe,*
> *Such haue but a fhadowes bliffe :*   70
> *There be fooles aliue I wis*
> *Siluer'd o're, and fo was this :*
> *Take what wife you will to bed,*
> *I will euer be your head :*
> *So be gone, you are fped.*   75

61, 62. *head, ...prize,*] *head?...prize?*
Q₁Q₃.
62. *prize*] *price* Cap. conj.
65. *What is*] *VVhat* Q₁.
　[*Hee reads.* Q₁.
66. *fier feauen*] Q₂. *fire feuen* Q₁.
67. *iudement*] Q₂. *iudgement* Q₁.

70. *fhadowes bliffe*] *shadow'd Bliss*
Rowe.
71. *I* wis] *Iwis* Q₂.
75. *be gone*] *be gone fir* Ff, Rowe+,
Steev. Mal. Dyce iii, Huds. *farewell, sir*
Cap. *begone* Knt, Coll. Sing. Hal. Wh. i,
Sta. Ktly.

---

63. ECCLES : There is surely an obscurity in this reply. She seems to consider him as having *offended* by the injudicious choice he had made; he ought not, therefore, to assume the character of a *judge* in deciding upon his own merits, which, indirectly, he may be said to do by this indignant inquiry.

63. **distinct**] See ABBOTT, § 492, for a list of words in which 'the accent was nearer the beginning than with us.'

65. **What is here?**] Again another careless omission in Q₁.

71. **I wis**] CAMBRIDGE EDITORS : Mr Staunton, in a note to *Tam. Shr.* I, i, mentions, on Sir F. Madden's authority, that 'I wis' is undoubtedly derived from the Saxon adverb 'gewis,' but in the 13th century 'ge' was changed to 'y' or 'i,' and in the latter end of the 15th it was probably held to be equivalent to the German 'Ich weiss.' There can be no doubt that Shakespeare spelt it 'I wis,' and used it as two words, pronoun and verb. [See also ABBOTT, § 345.]

73. JOHNSON : Perhaps the poet had forgotten that he who missed Portia was never to marry any woman. HALLIWELL : The best solution of this difficulty is to suppose that the oaths were enjoined by Portia, and not by the father who prepared the caskets. CLARENDON : Johnson is hypercritical when he finds fault with this doggerel.

74. CLARENDON : There is here, perhaps, a reference to the text: 'The husband is the head of the wife.'—*Ephesians*, v, 23.

75. **gone**] The *sir* of F₂, BOSWELL says was added 'unnecessarily;' HALLIWELL thinks because the editor of that edition did not 'understand the metrical system followed by the author;' and COLLIER would 'prefer *for*, if it were wanted at all.'

Ar. Still more foole I fhall appeare   76
By the time I linger here,
With one fooles head I came to woo,
But I goe away with two.
Sweet adue, Ile keepe my oath,   80
Patiently to beare my wroath.
    Por. Thus hath the candle fing'd the moath:
O thefe deliberate fooles when they doe choofe,
They haue the wifdome by their wit to loofe.
    Ner. The ancient faying is no herefie,   85
Hanging and wiuing goes by deftinie.
    Por. Come draw the curtaine *Nerriffa.*

Enter Meffenger.

Mef. Where is my Lady?
    Por. Here, what would my Lord?   90

76. Ar.] Om. Q₁. Arrag. Q₂Q₃.
81. wroath] Q₁Q₂Ff, Cap. Var. Hal.
wrath Theob. ii, Warb. Johns. roth Dyce
i. wroth Q₃ et cet.
    [Exit. Rowe.

82. *fing'd*] *findg'd* Q₁. *fingd* Q₂.
    moath] Moth Q₁F₃F₄.
84. the] their Q₁Q₃.
86. goes] go Han. Hal.

81. **wroath**] CAPELL (p. 63): This, and a word that follows it, 'moath,' at the end of Arragon's speech, are strange perversions of spelling (but authentic perversions) caus'd by rime. But *wroath* is open to yet another objection, after we have discover'd that *wrath* is meant by it, viz. that there is no seeming sense in it: the best, and the only one (perhaps) that invention can put on it, is—misfortune which wrath has brought down, the wrath of the gods. STEEVENS: 'Wroath' is used in some of the old books for *misfortune;* and is often spelt like *ruth,* which at present signifies only *pity,* or *sorrow for the miseries of another.* WHITE: *Wroth* seems here to be used somewhat in its radical sense, which connects it with the idea of suffering. See Richardson's *Dict.* s. v. 'Wrath.' COWDEN-CLARKE: It is an old word for that which causes writhing: 'misfortune,' 'calamity,' 'disaster.'

82. **moath**] This is, as Capell intimates in the preceding note, evidently a merry rhyme of Portia to the 'oath' and 'wroath' of Arragon, howsoever these two words were pronounced. I cannot find that either Grant White or Ellis has anywhere noted this rhyme, yet that the former would accept it as such I have but little doubt.—ED.

86. Halliwell gives very many references to this proverb, which, as he truly says, is 'so exceedingly common.' In fact, its commonness might well be presupposed from Nerissa's calling it 'the ancient saying.'—ED.

87. **curtaine**] ALLEN suggests, *metri gratiâ,* 'curtaine *to,*' i. e. to close it. Or *good* Nerissa,' although Portia uses no epithet elsewhere with Nerissa.

88. **Messenger**] COLLIER, in his first edition, inferred from Portia's address that this was a 'person of rank,' but omitted the note in his Second Edition.

90. **my Lord?**] TYRWHITT: Would not this speech to the servant be more proper

Mef.   Madam, there is a-lighted at your gate   91
A yong Venetian, one that comes before
To fignifie th'approaching of his Lord,
From whom he bringeth fenfible regreets ;
To wit (befides commends and curteous breath)   95
Gifts of rich value ; yet I haue not feene
So likely an Embaffador of loue.
A day in Aprill neuer came fo fweete
To fhow how coftly Sommer was at hand,
As this fore-fpurrer comes before his Lord.   100
  Por.   No more I pray thee, I am halfe a-feard
Thou wilt fay anone he is fome kin to thee,   102

---

91. *a-lighted*] *alighted* F₄.
95. *curteous*] *courteous* Q₁. *curtious*
Q₂. *curious* Q₃.
99. *Sommer*] *Summer* Q₁.
100. *fore-fpurrer*] *fore-spurrier* Cap.
(Corrected in Errata.)

101. *a-feard*] Q₂F₂Q₃. *a-fear'd* Q₁.
a feard F₃. *afraid* Pope+. *afeard* F₄
et cet.
102. *Thou wilt*] *Thou'lt* Pope+, Dyce
iii, Huds.
  anone] *anon* Q₁.

---

in the mouth of Nerissa ? 'No,' replies RITSON (p. 53), 'very impertinent, in the pres
ence of her lady.' DYCE (*Remarks*, p. 55) : Portia was not herself of sufficient rank
to have 'persons of rank' among her attendants. Her reply here is nothing more than
a sportive rejoinder to the abrupt exclamation of the Messenger. Compare :

> '*Hostess.* O Jesu ! *my lord*, the prince.
> *P. Henry.* How now, *my lady*, the hostess.'—*1 Hen. IV :* II, iv.

> '*Groom.* Hail, royal *prince !*
> *King Richard.* Thanks, noble *peer.*'—*Rich. II :* V, v.

> '*Enter Peter with a candle.*
> *Peter.* Where are you, *my Lord ?*
> *Hog.* Here, *my Lady.*'—*The Hogge hath Lost his Pearle*, 1614, sig. H.

STAUNTON : A dozen instances may be cited, where a similar expression is used by an
individual of station to one of very inferior rank. [But Staunton, while citing those
already alleged by Dyce, unfortunately adds none to them.—ED.]

94. **sensible**] CLARENDON : Evident to the senses, substantial. See *Macb.* II,
i, 36.

94. **regreets**] STEEVENS : That is, salutations, as in *King John*, III, i, 241.

95. **commends**] ABBOTT, § 451, gives this in a list of words used as nouns, to which
we should at the present time append *-ation* or *-ition*, *-ure* or *-ing*.

96. **yet**] See ABBOTT, § 76, for other instances of the use of 'yet' before a negative,
meaning 'up to this time.'

97. **likely**] ROLFE : In the Yankee sense of *promising* [or *good-looking ?*—ED.].

99. **costly**] ALLEN suggests 'costly *a.*' Here equivalent to German *köstlich*, precious.

Thou ſpend'ſt ſuch high-day wit in praiſing him :   103
Come, come *Nerryſſa,* for I long to ſee
Quicke *Cupids* Poſt, that comes ſo mannerly.   105
  Ner. Baſſanio Lord, loue if thy will it be.   *Exeunt.*

103. *high-day*] *high day* Qq F₄.
104. Nerryſſa] Q₂Q₃. Nerriſſa Q₁.
105. *Quicke* Cupids] *Cupid's quick*
Coll. (MS).
106. Baſſanio *Lord, loue*] Q₁Q₂F₂F₃.
Baſſanio, *Lord, Love* Q₃. Baſſanio *Lord,*

love, F₄. *Bassanio lord, Lord!* Pope.
Bassanio, Lord Love! Theob. Han. Coll.
ii. *Bassanio, Lord Love,* or *Bassanio,
lord love,* Rowe et cet.
106. Exeunt] Exit. Q₁.

---

103. **high-day**] STEEVENS : So *Merry Wives,* III, ii, 69 : 'he speaks holiday.
ECCLES : It seems here to have a sense pretty similar to *high-flown, extravagant.*

106. THEOBALD (Nichols's *Illust.* ii, 307) : Mr Pope certainly conceives ' Bassanio
lord ' to stand for *Lord Bassanio.*   I take the liberty to alter the pointing : ' Bassanio,
—Lord Love ! if,' &c. ALLEN : Thus scan : Bassá | nió | Lord Lóve | if thy | will't
bé.

Actus Tertius.

[*Scene I.*]

Enter Solanio and Salarino.

Sol.   Now, what newes on the Ryalto?

Sal.   Why yet it liues there vncheckt, that *Anthonio*
hath a ſhip of rich lading wrackt on the narrow Seas; the
Goodwins I thinke they call the place, a very dangerous   5

Actus Tertius] Om. Qq.

  1. Solanio] Salanio Q₁, Rowe+, Cam.
Glo. Cla.

1. Salarino] Solarino F₄, Rowe+.

2, &c. Sol.] Salan. Q₁. Solanio Q₀.
    Now,] Now Q₂Q₃.

---

4. the narrow Seas] CLARENDON: The English Channel. In the 'prologe of
the processe of the *Libell of Englishe Policye*' [ed. Hertzberg] we find: 'Cherish
marchaundyes keep th' amiraltee That we be maysteres of the narow see.'   And again
of Calais and Dover: 'Keep thees two townes, sire, to your magestee As your twein
eyen, to keep the narow see.'   Sir John Hawkins, writing to Lord Burghley, Nov. 30,
1593, 'sends a note of the pay for the ships serving in the Narrow seas.'—*Calendar
of State Papers*, 1591–1594, p. 389. [The foregoing extracts from the *Libell of English Policy*, Clarendon takes from Hakluyt's *Voyages*, i, p. 387, ed. 1599, but they are
given above from the admirably-edited edition by Hertzberg. In this *Libell*, which,
dating from 1436, is probably the very earliest Protectionist plea extant, there are several other allusions to 'the narowe see,' especially one which occurs just before the first
example cited by Clarendon, which, by 'exhortyng alle England to keep the see envi-
roun, and namely the narowe see,' also shows that the English Channel is unquestionably meant. Yet in every instance the 'sea' is in the singular, and not in the plural,
as Shakespeare uses it. The citation from Sir John Hawkins, therefore, is exactly
apposite.—ED.]

  5. I thinke they call the place] There is a fine passage in *1 Hen. IV:* I, iii, 241,
where Hotspur, in his headlong fury, cannot recall the name of Berkeley Castle: 'What
do you call the place?—A plague upon it—it is in Gloucestershire,—'Twas where the
madcap duke his uncle kept—His uncle York—where I first bow'd my knee Unto
this king of smiles, this Bolingbroke,—'Sblood!—When you and he came back from
Ravensburgh.' So true to nature is Hotspur's annoyance, that I cannot divest myself
of the belief, first suggested to me by my father, that Shakespeare in the hurry of
composition, could not, himself, at that instant, recall the name. Thus here, I was
inclined at first to think that Shakespeare might have been himself a little in doubt as
to the correctness of the name 'Goodwins,' but I yield to the Cowden-Clarkes and to
Elze, who rightly, as I now think, interpret it as uttered by Salarino for the sake of giving local colour, and to make us believe that we are in Venice, where Venetians, and
not Englishmen, are speaking. 'By such touches as these,' say the COWDEN-CLARKES,

flat, and fatall, where the carcaffes of many a tall fhip, lye   6
buried, as they fay, if my goffips report be an honeft woman of her word.

    Sol. I would fhe were as lying a goffip in that, as euer
knapt Ginger, or made her neighbours beleeue fhe wept   10
for the death of a third husband : but it is true, without
any flips of prolixity, or croffing the plaine high-way of
talke, that the good *Anthonio,* the honeft *Anthonio* ; ô that
I had a title good enough to keepe his name company !
    Sal. Come, the full ftop.   15
    Sol. Ha, what fayeft thou, why the end is, he hath loft
a fhip.
    Sal. I would it might proue the end of his loffes.
    Sol. Let me fay Amen betimes, leaft the diuell croffe   19

---

7. *goffips report*] Q₁ Ff, Rowe. *gossip,* | 9. *lying a*] *a lying* Q₁.
report, Coll. Wh. i, Clarke. *goffip report*
Q₂Q₃, Pope et cet.
    honeft] *honft* F₂.

13. *honeft* Anthonio;] Q₂. *honeft* Anthonio, Q₁. *honeft* Antho. Ff.

' Shakespeare keeps perpetually before us the circumstance that the scene of his play is
abroad.' And, furthermore, the distance from Venice of this remote locality insensibly
conveyed to the hearer the idea of ' Long Time.' See Appendix, ' Duration of Action.'
—ED.

    7. **gossips**] See WALKER, II, ix, 35.

    8. **of**] See ABBOTT, § 173, where instances are given of ' of ' applied not merely
to the agent and the instrument, but to any influencing circumstance, in the sense of
' as regards.'

    10. **knapt Ginger,**] STEEVENS : To ' knap' is to *break short.* The word occurs in
The Common Prayer : ' He knappeth the spear in sunder.' HALLIWELL : That is, to
snap, or break off short. ' *Breusté* for *Brousté ;* Broused, or knapped off.'—Cotgrave.
' He knapped the staffe of the darte asunder.'—North's *Plutarch,* 1579. [Other in
stances of this meaning of ' knap' are given by Halliwell and White, and I doubt not
many more could be added. But, as White truly remarks, ' ginger is a tough root ;'
and so impressed was he with this objection, that in his First Edition he hinted that ' a
ginger cake must be meant, and probably of the sort even now called " ginger snaps." '
In his Second Edition all doubts have vanished ; he says, without qualification, that
' knapp'd ginger' is equivalent to ' snapped ginger nuts.' I think, however, that Cotgrave will help us to a better definition of ' knap,' in this present passage, than to *break
off short,* a meaning it undoubtedly bears in the passages cited above. As the translation of *Ronger* and its five derivatives, Cotgrave gives invariably ' to gnawe, knap or
nible off ;' so also of *Brouter, Broust, Brouteur,* &c., he gives to ' brouze, knap or nible
off.' Whence, I think, we may be justified in paraphrasing ' knapt ginger' by *nibbled
ginger.* That old women were fond of ginger is to be inferred from *Meas. for Meas.*
IV, iii, 8, a passage which I think must have escaped White ; the reference there is to
old ginger,' which is not likely to mean ' old *ginger nuts.*'—ED.]

my praier, for here he comes in the iikenes of a *Iew*. How   20
now *Shylocke*, what newes among the Merchants?

Enter Shylocke.

Shy.   You knew none fo well, none fo well as you, of
my daughters flight.

Sal.   That's certaine, I for my part knew the Tailor   25
that made the wings fhe flew withall.

Sol.   And *Shylocke* for his own part knew the bird was
fledg'd, and then it is the complexion of them al to leaue
the dam.

Shy.   She is damn'd for it.   30

Sal.   That's certaine, if the diuell may be her Iudge.

Shy.   My owne flefh and blood to rebell.

Sol.   Out vpon it old carrion, rebels it at thefe yeeres.

Shy.   I fay my daughter is my flefh and bloud.

Sal.   There is more difference betweene thy flefh and   35
hers, then betweene Iet and Iuorie, more betweene your

---

20. *my*] *thy* Warb. Theob. Johns.
Steev. '85.

    iikenes] Misprint.

21. *Merchants*] *Marchants* Q₁.

22. Enter...] After *Iew* line 20, Q₁,
Cap. et seq.

23. *knew*] *know* Q₁.

23, 24. *of...flight*] Separate line, Q₁.

26. As verse, Q₁.

28. *fledg'd*] *flidge* Q₂Q₃. *fledge* Cap
Mal.'90.

33. *yeeres*] *times?* Rowe ii.

34. *bloud*] *my blood* Q₂Q₃, Cap.

36. *hers*] *hirs* Q₁.

---

20. **my praier**] WARBURTON: But the prayer was [Salarino's]. We must therefore
read '*thy* prayer.'   HEATH (p. 116): It is somewhat wonderful this reverend gentleman should not have recollected that the people pray as well as the priest, though the
latter only pronounces the words, which the people make their own by saying 'Amen'
to them.   It is after this needless to add that the Devil, in the shape of a Jew, could
not cross [Salarino's] prayer, which, as far as it was singly his, was already ended.
CAPELL (p. 63): Meaning the prayer of his companion, which he would make his
own by saying 'amen' to it; for this, in all prayers congregational, is the force of that
formula.   The changers of '*my*' to *thy* seem to have thought 'amen' a conjuring formula, that sanctify'd the prayer and prevented the devil's crossing it.   [Heath is right,
of course.   'Amen' was Solanio's own prayer.—ED.]

25, 26. In Q₁ these two lines are printed as verse, divided as they stand here in the
Folio.   Although they have been held to be prose (and rightly) by all editors, yet they
are metric prose, and by giving them as verse the transcriber of that Quarto shows a
more excellent ear than the transcribers of the other texts.—ED.

28. **complexion**] CLARENDON: That is, nature, disposition, temperament.   Cotgrave translates the French *complexion*, thus: 'The complection, making, temper, constitution of the bodie; also, the disposition, affection, humors, or inclination of the
mind.'

bloods, then there is betweene red wine and rennifh : but   37
tell vs, doe you heare whether *Anthonio* haue had anie
loffe at fea or no?

Shy.   There I haue another bad match, a bankrout, a   40
prodigall, who dare fcarce fhew his head on the Ryalto,
a begger that was vfd to come fo fmug vpon the Mart:
let him look to his bond, he was wont to call me Vfurer,
let him looke to his bond, he was wont to lend money
for a Chriftian curtfie, let him looke to his bond.   45

Sal.   Why I am fure if he forfaite, thou wilt not take
his flefh, what's that good for?

Shy.   To baite fifh withall, if it will feede nothing
elfe, it will feede my reuenge ; he hath difgrac'd me, and
hindred me halfe a million, laught at my loffes, mockt at   50

---

37. *rennifh*] *rhennifh* F_3F_4.
38, 39. *anie loffe at*] *at loffe a* Q_I.
40. *bankrout*] Qq Ff, Knt, Hal. *bankrupt* Rowe et cet.
40, 41. *a prodigall*] *for a prodigal* Warb.
41. *dare*] *dares* Rowe ii+.

41. *Ryalto*] *Ryalta* Ff.
42. *was vfd*] *us'd* Rowe ii+, Steev. Var. Coll. Sing. Ktly.
46. *forfaite*] Q_2F_2. *forfet* Q_I. *forfeit* Q_3.
50. *halfe*] *of half* Theob. ii, Warb. Johns. Steev. Var. Ktly.

38, 39. **anie losse at sea**] The text in Q_I, 'at losse a sea or no,' is not a very serious blunder; it is merely a transposition of words, instead of *a losse at sea ;* and is probably due to the compositor, not to the transcriber.—ED.

41. **prodigall**] WARBURTON: This is spoke of Anthonio.   But why a 'prodigal'? His friend Bassanio had indeed been too liberal, and with this name the Jew honours him when he is going to sup with him : 'I'll go in hate to feed upon The prodigal Christian.'   But Anthonio was a plain, reserved, parsimonious merchant; be assured, therefore, we should read : 'a bankrupt *for* a prodigal,' i. e. he is become bankrupt by supplying the extravagancies of his friend Bassanio.   JOHNSON: There is no need of alteration.   There could be, in Shylock's opinion, no prodigality more culpable than such liberality as that by which a man exposes himself to ruin for his friend.   EDWARDS (p. 121): His lending money without interest was reason enough for the Jew to call him prodigal, and this Shylock upbraids him with immediately after.

42. **was vsd**] COLLIER (ed. ii): In the (MS) it is 'that *was wont to*,' consistently with 'was wont to call' and 'was wont to lend,' just below.   The poet may have had reason to vary the expression, although actors may have reiterated it.

49. **disgrac'd**] ALLEN: To *grace* a person is to show favour to him by some act of kindness or help.   To *disgrace*, therefore, may be to show *dis*favour to (to be *un*gracious to) by doing him some wrong.   SCHMIDT gives this passage under the meaning 'to dishonour.'   It would be better placed, I think, under the meaning, of which he gives instances, of 'to lower in estimation.'—ED.

50. **halfe a million**] See ABBOTT, § 198 *a*, for other instances of the omission of the preposition after some verbs and adjectives that imply *value, worth,* &c.

my gaines, fcorned my Nation, thwarted my bargaines, 51
cooled my friends, heated mine enemies, and what's the
reafon? I am a *Iewe*: Hath not a *Iew* eyes? hath not a
Iew hands, organs, dementions, fences, affections, paffions, fed with the fame foode, hurt with the fame wea- 55
pons, fubiect to the fame difeafes, healed by the fame
meanes, warmed and cooled by the fame Winter and
Sommmer as a Chriftian is: if you pricke vs doe we not
bleede? if you tickle vs, doe we not laugh? if you poifon
vs doe we not die? and if you wrong vs fhall we not re- 60
uenge? if we are like you in the reft, we will refemble you
in that. If a *Iew* wrong a *Chriftian*, what is his humility, 62

52, 53. *the reafon*] Ff, Rowe. *his*
reafon Qq et cet.
53. *Hath not*] *Hath nos* Q₁.
54. *dementions*] Q₂. *dimenfions* Q₁.

57. *meanes*] *medicines* Warb. conj.
57, 58. *Winter and Sommmer*] *sum-*
mer and winter Han.

---

53. **I am a Iewe**] HAWKINS (*Life of Kean*, i, 150): How beautifully did Kean
express these last four words! A slight approach to deprecation on account of his
unmitigated injuries passed away in a moment when he reflected that the dignity of his
race must not be hurt by his exciting commiseration in a *Christian*. In this single speech
he was worth, Hazlitt states, 'a wilderness of monkeys that have aped humanity.'

54. **affections, passions**] See IV, i, 54, where there is an excellent citation by
Steevens from Greene's *Never Too Late*, which shows that the distinction formerly
drawn between these two words is, that 'affections' were objective and 'passions' subjective. 'Affections' are influenced through the eyes, 'passions' are stirred from the
heart. GOULD (*The Tragedian*, p. 75): Cooke, when he came to the word 'affections,'
so informed it with human feeling, so contrasted it with the context, that it remains as
the marked point of his performance.

57, 58. **warmed . . . Sommmer**] An instance of the construction called by the
old grammarians a *chiasm*. (If under 'warmed' and 'cooled' were written 'winter'
and 'summer,' and the words which refer to each other joined by a line, the Greek
letter *chi* would be formed.) It is the same as in I, iii, 23, 'land rats and water rats,
water thieves and land thieves,' although it may be doubted if the order of the words
be there correct.'—ED.

62. **humility**] SCHMIDT (*Lex.*): That is, kindness, benevolence, humanity. Thus,
'plant in tyrants mild humility,—*Love's Lab. Lost*, IV, iii, 349; 'in peace there's
nothing so becomes a man as modest stillness and humility,'—*Hen. V:* III, i, 4; 'I
thank God for my humility,—*Rich. III:* II, i, 72. [This excellent distinction in the
use of this word is original, I think, with Schmidt, and was given first in the *Sh. Jahrb.*
(1868) iii, 346; where, furthermore, by examining every instance of Shakespeare's use
of the word, Schmidt shows that *humanity* was always used by Shakespeare in the
sense of the *nature of man*, and never in our modern sense of universal benevolence.
Wherefore, when in the foregoing citation from *Love's Lab. Lost*, Collier's (MS) substituted *humanity* for 'humility,' Schmidt considers it as a conclusive proof that the
(MS) was modern, almost modern enough to date from our own days. Of course

reuenge? If a *Chriſtian* wrong a *Iew*, what ſhould his ſuf-   63
ferance be by Chriſtian example, why reuenge? The vil-
lanie you teach me I will execute, and it ſhall goe hard   65
but I will better the inſtruction.

Enter a man from Anthonio.

Gentlemen, my maiſter *Anthonio* is at his houſe, and
deſires to ſpeake with you both.

Sal. We haue beene vp and downe to ſeeke him.   70

Enter Tuball.

Sol. Here comes another of the Tribe, a third cannot
be matcht, vnleſſe the diuell himſelfe turne *Iew*.

Exeunt Gentlemen.   74

---

64. *by*] *by a* F$_3$F$_4$, Rowe.
    example, why reuenge?] *example?*
why revenge. Ff (subs.).
    67. Enter...] Enter a Servant. Rowe.

68. *Gentlemen*] Ser. *Gentlemen* Rowe.
71. Enter...] Repeated, after line 74,
Q$_2$.   After line 74, Coll.

'humility' in many cases has its usual meaning, but for the present passage and for those cited above, Schmidt has, I think, given its true definition.—ED.]

64. **reuenge**] COWDEN-CLARKE: To those who, like the present editors, can remember Edmund Kean's delivery of this superb speech of wild wrath pleading its claim to some show of justice, there is excitement in recalling the wonderful eyes flashing out their red sparkles, the body writhing from head to foot, the arm thrown upward as witness to the recorded oath of vengeance. The attitude, as the voice, rose to a sublime climax when these words were uttered; then there was a drop, both of person and tone, as he hissed out the closing sentence of deep concentrated malignity.

66. FRANÇOIS VICTOR HUGO (p. 41): This sublime imprecation is the most eloquent plea that the human voice has ever dared to utter for a despised race. Whatsoever be the dénoûment, it is hereby justified. Let Shylock be as implacable as he may, assuredly he will no more than equal his instruction. Even granting that he obtains it, a pound of Antonio's flesh will never outweigh, in the scales of reprisal, the millions of corpses heaped in the Christian shambles by a butchery of thirteen centuries.

HONIGMAN (*Sh. Jahrb.* xvii, 221): Here it is that Shylock figures as the deputy and avenger of his whole shamefully-maltreated race. In his tones we hear the protest, crying to heaven, of human rights trodden under foot, against the love of humanity paraded by the hypocritical mouths of his oppressors; and if his towering revenge mounts to fanaticism, it is verily of a different stamp to the fanaticism of usury and greed which the critics are fain to find in his character.

71. **Tuball**] BOOTH: Tubal should wear a yellow cap,—not necessarily of the same shape as Shylock's.

72, 73. COLLIER (ed. i): This should be spoken as Tubal is approaching, and before he actually comes upon the stage; because the instant that he appears, Shylock ought to put the question to him, 'How now, Tubal?' &c.   Hitherto the entrance of Tubal has been wrongly placed, preceding what Salanio says, and keeping Shylock, who must naturally be all eagerness, waiting until Salanio has concluded his observation. [See Text. Notes.]

Shy. How now *Tuball*, what newes from *Genowa*? haſt   75
thou found my daughter?

Tnb.   I often came where I did heare of ſter, but cannot finde her.

Shy.   Why there, there, there, there, a diamond gone
coſt me two thouſand ducats in Franckford, the curſe ne-   80
·uer fell vpon our Nation till now, I neuer ſelt it till now,
two thouſand ducats in that, and other precious, precious iewels : I would my daughter were dead at my foot,   83

---

75. Genowa] Geneva F₄.   *Genoua*   77. *ſter*] F₁.
Rowe.   80. *Franckford,*] *Frankford* Q₁F₄.

---

75. The COWDEN-CLARKES call attention here to the artistic use of indications of Long Time. At the opening of the scene Shylock's vehement words to Solanio, and Salarino, give the effect of Short Time, uttered as they seem to be in the first fury of his discovery of Jessica's flight, and thereby the Third Act is linked to the period of the previous Acts. But here in his talk with Tuball every sentence serves to aid an impression of Long Time, and to advance the period when the date of the bond shall have expired and the forfeiture become due.

75. Genowa] White (ed. i) finds in this spelling a proof that the pronunciation was *Ge-no′a*, although in the *Tam. of the Shr.*, as he notes, ‘the rhythm enables us to determine that the pronunciation is plainly *Gen′o-a*.’ He has no note in regard to this in his Second Edition; I think his inference is scarcely justifiable. Could we not equally well from this spelling infer that the pronunciation was, in New England style, Gén-o-way? In Howell's *Instructions for Forraine Travel*, 1642, the distinction in spelling between the name of the city and an inhabitant of it is curious. On p. 41 (Arber's *Reprint*) occurs the following : ‘Having put foot ashoare in *Genoa*, I will not wish him stay. . . . . When a Jew meeteth with a *Genoway*, and is to negotiat, &c.—ED.

77. BOOTH: Before replying to Shylock's questions, shake your head sorrowfully and speak slowly.

83, &c. HEINEMANN (*Shylock and Nathan*, 1886, p. 10) : What Hebrew father is there, what Hebrew mother, that does not know these words of Shylock to be false, nay, impossible? How happens it then that Shakespeare, this greatest searcher of the human heart, has erred so grievously in regard to Jews and Jewry? It is because he has overlooked, and he could not but overlook, one element which has entered most largely into the history of Jewry—viz. that ideal blessing which Israel carried with it into its sorrowful night of exile, and to which it has always remained steadfast and true : its Doctrine, its Religion. Shakespeare could not know how, by our Sabbaths and High-days, a pure and secluded life was cherished around our hearthstones, which blossomed forth in the narrow houses of the Jewish quarter, and transformed the gloomy Ghetto into a Paradise. He could not know how the Jew, albeit scorned and despised by the outer world, retired to his humble home, and there refreshed himself with the strains which once flowed from the harp of his Poet-king, or else strengthened himself with the consoling promises of the Prophets, or lost himself in the intricacies of a discussion over the Talmud, or over the deepest problems of humanity, and that amid such an elevating and intellectual life he never cherished for the outer world and

and the iewels in her eare : would fhe were hearft at my
foote, and the duckets in her coffin : no newes of them,   85
why fo? and I know not how much is fpent in the fearch :
why thou loffe vpon loffe , the theefe gone with fo
much, and fo much to finde the theefe, and no fatisfa-
&tion, no reuenge, nor no ill luck ftirring but what lights
a my fhoulders, no fighes but a my breathing, no teares   90
but a my fhedding.

 Tub. Yes, other men haue ill lucke too, *Anthonio* as I
heard in Genowa?   93

---

84. *would*] Q₂Ff. *O would* Q₁, Pope
+. *'would* Cap. Steev. Mal. Knt, Sing.
Sta. Ktly.

 85. *duckets*] *ducats* Qq F₃F₄.

 85, 86. *them, why fo ?*] Q₂F₂Q₃F₃. *them,
why fo :* Q₁. *them ; why fo ?* F₄. *them—
why, so !* Johns. *them ? Why, so ;* Cap.

 86. *how much is*] Ff, Rowe, Knt. *what*
Han. *whats* Qq, Pope et cet. (subs.).

 87. *thou*] *then* Ff, Rowe, Pope, Han.
Hal. Wh. i, Dyce iii. *thou—* Coll. Sing,

Ktly. *there !* Lloyd (ap. Cam.).

 89, 90. *lights a*] Q₂FfQ₃, Rowe ɪ.
lights on Q₁, Cam. Glo. Cla. Wh. ii. *lights
o'* Rowe ii et cet.

 90, 91. *but a*] Q₂FfQ₃, Rowe i. *but of*
Q₁, Cam. Glo. Cla. Wh. ii. *but o'* Rowe
ii et cet.

 93. *heard in*] *heard, is in* Q₃.
Genowa ?] *Genoway.* Q₁. *Genowa,*
F₂. *Genowa.* F₃. *Genoua.* F₄. *Genoua—*
Rowe et seq.

---

its scorn feelings of hate, but only of pity. Shakespeare could never know how the
Jew, from the heights of this spiritual life, looked down upon those who could fetter
his body indeed, but never his soul.

 85. **coffin**] HONIGMAN (*Jahrb.* xvii, p. 222) : This passage is always cited to prove
that the love of gold had eradicated all human affection from Shylock's heart. This
opinion is wrong and exaggerated. If the passage is taken in connection with the rest
of the dialogue, it will be found to be merely a masterstroke of the poet in depicting as
powerfully as possible the unbridled passion of a volcanic nature, like Shylock's, whose
violence forces his speech beyond the bounds of genuine feeling. This language reminds us of the exaggerated expressions of King Lear against his daughters. Reflect
for a minute on the profound bitterness of the injury to the wounded old man : his
daughter, lost to all propriety or shame, had eloped with a Christian ; a thief, and her
own father the victim ; despising the souvenirs of her mother and forswearing her religion
—and for the loss of such a creature as this is he to grieve ? Never ; so low has she
fallen in his esteem that, even were she lying dead before him, regret for her loss would
be far inferior to that for the money she had stolen. It is the very strongest expression
of scorn which his wrath can suggest.

 86. **why so ?**] Is not this better marked as an interrogation than as an exclamation ? 'Why is there no news of them ? after I have spent, I know not how much, in
the search.'—ED.

 86. **how much is**] See in Text. Note an unusual variation in the Folio from
the Qq.

 87. **thou**] I cannot find that any of those Editors who have here followed F₁ have
given any reason for so doing. I cannot but think that 'thou' is a misprint for the
then of the Ff.—ED.

Shy-   What, what, what, ill lucke, ill lucke.

Tub.   Hath an Argofie **caſt** away comming from Tri-   95
polis.

Shy.   I thanke God, I thanke God, is it true, is it true?

Tub.   I fpoke with fome of the Saylers that efcaped
the wracke.

Shy.   I thanke thee good *Tuball*, good newes, good   100
newes : ha, ha, here in Genowa.

Tub.   Your daughter fpent in Genowa, as I heard, one
night fourefcore ducats.

Shy.   Thou ftick'ft a dagger in me, I fhall neuer fee my
gold againe, fourefcore ducats at a fitting, fourefcore du-   105
cats.

Tnb.   There came diuers of *Anthonios* creditors in my   107

---

94. *What, what, what*] What, what,
Rowe, Pope, Han.
  lucke.] *lucke?* Q₁F₄.
97. *is it...is it*] *iſt...iſt* Q₁.
99. *wracke*] Qq Ff (subs.).

100. *thee*] *the* Q₁.
101. *here*] Ff. *heere* Qq. *where?* Rowe
et cet.
102. *one*] *in one* Q₁, Cam. Glo. Cla.
Rlfe, Wh. ii.

---

97. **God**] Booth : Clapping his hands high in the air.

97. **is it true?**] Booth : Eagerly, almost a shriek. Tubal's answer should be
spoken quickly.

98. **escaped**] See Abbott, § 198, for the omission of the preposition.

101. **here**] This Scene opens with the rumour, which lives unchecked on the Rialto,
that one of Anthonio's rich ships had been wrecked on the distant coast of England.
Shylock must have heard it, but had evidently not allowed himself to trust it, and when
Salarino asks about it he is too wily to give the insolent young fellow an additional chance
to jeer. But when Tubal refers positively to the wreck of an argosy, thus verifying the
rumour, Shylock shrieks out 'is it true?' and laughs aloud at the thought that the loss
which is reported as fallen on Anthonio has happened, not far off, in England, but is
known 'here' in Italy, 'in Genoa.' Is this interpretation too forced? If it be not,
then we can adhere to the authority of the Qq and Ff. But if otherwise, then I see
no way for it but to accept Rowe's text, and reading *where*, turn it into a question, to
which, be it observed, Tubal makes no reply.—Ed.

102. Booth : Nod several times affirmatively before replying, and speak the line
slowly, with the least shade of wickedness in your look. Shylock's expression
gradually changes from joy to agony while this line is spoken, therefore speak it
slowly.

102. **as I heard**] Eccles : It may be doubted whether this account by Tubal of
Jessica's extravagance was intended by the poet as truth, or as only a vague, uncertain
rumour, with little or no foundation.

102. **one night**] Q₁ here supplies the missing word *in*, which, although not absolutely necessary, is good, and will serve to offset some of its previous omissions.—Ed.

107. Booth : This with a cheerful tone, and quickly.

company to Venice, that fweare hee cannot choofe but   108
breake.

Shy. I am very glad of it, ile plague him, ile torture   110
him, I am glad of it,

Tub. One of them fhewed me a ring that hee had of
your daughter for a Monkie.

Shy. Out vpon her, thou tortureft me *Tuball*, it was
my Turkies, I had it of *Leah* when I was a Batcheler : I   115
would not haue giuen it for a wildernesse of Monkies.

Tub. But *Anthonio* is certainely vndone.

Shy. Nay, that's true, that's very true, goe *Tnball*, fee
me an Officer, befpeake him a fortnight before, I will
haue the heart of him if he forfeit, for were he out of Ve-   120

---

108. *to*] *vnto* Q₁.
   hee] *that hee* Q₁.
110. *very*] Om. Rowe+, Steev. '85.
111. *of it,*] *on't.* Q₁. *of it.* Q₂ et cet.

114. *tortureft*] *tortur'ft* Q₁.
115. *Turkies*] *Turkis* Ff. *Turquoise* Rowe.
118. *Tnball*] Om. Pope+.
   fee] *see* Var.'21 (misprint).

---

115. **Turkies**] STEEVENS: As Shylock had been married long enough to have a daughter grown up, it is plain he did not value this turquoise on account of the money for which he might hope to sell it, but merely in respect of the imaginary virtues formerly ascribed to the stone. It was said to fade or brighten as the health of the wearer increased or grew less. To this Ben Jonson refers in his *Sejanus*, I, i : 'And, true as turquoise in my dear lord's ring, Look well or ill with him.' [In a note on this passage in *Sejanus*, Gifford says that 'to this supposed quality of the stone our old writers have innumerable allusions.'] Again, Edward Fenton, in *Secrete Wonders of Nature*, 1569 : 'The Turkeys doth move when there is any perill prepared to him that weareth it.' [There is a long account in Holland's *Plinie*, ii, 619, *a*, of Turquoises which 'be found in ycie cliffes hardly accessible,' and which 'the people of that country reach afar off with slings, and so drive them down;' and it occurs in the paragraph immediately following one which I cannot but think that Shakespeare once read, and from which he took the allusion to 'one entire chrysolite' in *Oth.* V, ii, 179.--ED.]

115. **I had, &c.**] Le Tourneur (1781) thus translates : 'Je l'achetai de Lee, étant encore garçon.'—ED.

116. HAZLITT (p. 273) : We may collect from a few sentences the history of Shylock's life,—his descent and origin, his thrift and domestic economy, his affection for his daughter, whom he loves next his wealth, his courtship and his first present to [?] Leah, his wife ! 'I would not have parted with it' (the ring which he first gave her) 'for a wilderness of monkeys !' What a fine Hebraism is implied in this expression ! KNIGHT : Shakespeare here, with marvellous art, shows us the betrayed and persecuted Shylock, at the moment when he is raving at the desertion of his daughter, and panting for a wild revenge, as looking back upon the days when the fierce passions had probably no place in his heart.

nice, I can make what merchandize I will : goe *Tuball*, 121
and meete me at our Sinagogue, goe good *Tuball*, at our
Sinagogue *Tuball*.   *Exeunt*.

121. *I will : goe*] Q_2 Ff Q_3, Cap. Knt. *go*, Johns. et cet.
I will go : go Q_1. *I will : go : go* Pope+. 122, 123. *Sinagogue*] $Q_2 F_2$. *Synagogue*
I will : go, go, Warb. *I will. Go*, Coll. Q_1 et cet.
Hal. Dyce, Sta. Huds. Wh. i. *I will. Go*, 123. *Exeunt*.] Om. F_4.

---

121. **I will : goe**] The misplaced colon here in Q_1 ('I will goe :') is a typographical
error, of so common and slight a kind that it scarcely deserves to be reckoned among
the variations which are to be counted as proofs of its inferiority to Q_2.—ED.

122. **Sinagogue**] CLARENDON : Shakespeare probably intended to add another
shade of darkness to the character of Shylock by making him still formally devout
while meditating his horrible vengeance. FRANÇOIS VICTOR HUGO (p. 43) : The Jew
invokes the Ancient of Days, who spoke unto Moses aforetime : 'If a man cause a
blemish in his neighbour; as he hath done, so shall it be done to him; breach for
breach, eye for eye, tooth for tooth; as he hath caused a blemish in a man, so shall it
be done to him again.' In entering his synagogue Shylock entrusts his hatred to the
safeguard of his Faith. Henceforward his vengeance assumes a consecrated character.
His bloodthirstiness against the Christian becomes sacerdotal. The expiation of Anthonio
is but a holocaust offered to the Omnipotent Avenger. Shylock is bound by irrevoca-
ble vows. And when he appears before the tribunal his bearing is the indomitable
impassiveness of a priest about to sacrifice an expiatory lamb to the God of Sabaoth.

[*Scene II.*]

Enter Baſſanio, Portia, Gratiano, and all their traine.

Por. I pray you tarrie, pauſe a day or two
Before you hazard, for in chooſing wrong
I looſe your companie ; therefore forbeare a while,
There's ſomething tels me (but it is not loue)   5
I would not looſe you, and you know your ſelfe,
Hate counſailes not in ſuch a quallitie;
But leaſt you ſhould not vnderſtand me well,
And yet a maiden hath no tongue, but thought,   9

[Scene II. Rowe.	6. *looſe*] *loſe* Q₁.
1. traine.] Traines. Q₁. traynes. Q₂.	7. *counſailes…quallitie;*] *counſels …*
4. *therefore*] Om. Pope, Han.	*quality.* Q₁.

---

2. GEO. FLETCHER (*Fraser's Maga.*, May, 1850, p. 506) : Why at this moment does
Portia wish to stay Bassanio from election ? Because, though she has no doubt whatever of his personal liking for her, and his readiness to marry her, she feels not yet
assured that he really *does* love her with that perfect devotion which alone can or ought
to content a spirit like hers in such a union. Bassanio, we must observe, is no Romeo,
quite a novice in the world; on the contrary, he is a man of the world and of pleasure,
as well as a scholar and a soldier. Nevertheless, with the high instinct of her noble
heart and intelligence, she doubts not that a man of his endowments will not fail to
love her truly if he once but know her thoroughly.

3. **in choosing**] ABBOTT, § 372 : That is, 'in the event of *your* choosing wrong,
I lose your company.'

7. This line presents a noteworthy proof that what is so often loosely spoken of as
'Shakespeare's spelling,' is merely that of a compositor. Here in the Folio the spelling is archaic simply because the compositor followed his copy, which happened to be
Q₂. In Q₁, printed in the same year with Q₂, the spelling and punctuation are, as a
general rule, as modern as in Dyce's Third Edition.—ED.

9. SEYMOUR : Does this mean that she utters nothing but what her heart suggests,
and that, therefore, she ought not to be misunderstood ? or that, being a maiden, she
cannot speak freely, and must only think ? I believe the first is the sense. CLAREN-
DON : Portia means : 'And yet, since a maiden may only think and not speak her
thoughts, you will not understand me, however long you stay.' A. CAMERON (*Shakespeariana*, Dec. 1886) gives a discussion of the meaning of this line, with a class composed chiefly of young women from fifteen to eighteen years of age, where the first interpretation offered was that Portia loved Bassanio, but felt herself restrained from telling
him so by maidenly modesty and social conventionality. Thus, in *The Temp.* III, i,
Miranda feels the restraining force of 'bashful cunning' as much as Portia feels it, but,
being untrammelled by the acquired bonds of conventionality, can say, 'Hence, bashful
cunning! And prompt me, plain and holy innocence! I am your wife, if you will
marry me.' A second suggestion was that 'a maiden speaks just what she thinks,—
tells the plain truth.' This was considered to fit in well with the previous line, 'But

I would detaine you here fome month or two   10
Before you venture for me.   I could teach you
How to choofe right, but then I am forfworne,
So will I neuer be, fo may you miffe me,   13

---

10. *month*] *moneth* Q$_1$Q$_2$.   Steev. '85, Cam. Glo. Cla. Wh. ii.
12. *then I am*] *I am then* Q$_1$, Pope +,   13. *be,*] *be ;* Theob. et seq.

---

lest you should not understand me well.' 'And yet, why shouldn't you understand
me? I'm telling you the simple, honest truth.' To this it was objected that Portia
had just told Bassanio, 'There's something tells me, but it is not love, I would not lose
you.' Whereas it is quite apparent from her whole speech and conduct that she is passionately in love with him. A more general objection was ungallantly insinuated by
the question: 'Does a maiden's tongue always speak just what is in her thought?' In
affirmation only one quotation was forthcoming,—Rosalind's 'Do you not know that
I am a woman? When I think I must speak.'—*As You Like It*, III, ii, 263. In
denial, Chaucer, Byron, and Allan Ramsay were cited. From *The Gentle Shepherd:*
'When maidens, innocently young, Say often what they never mean, Ne'er mind their
pretty, lying tongue, But tent the language o' their e'en.' Byron testifies: 'The charming creatures lie with such a grace There's nothing more becoming to the face.' But
the Wife of Bath blurted out: 'Half so boldely can ther no man Sweren and lyen as
a woman can.' The third interpretation was that Portia thinks what she would like
Bassanio to know, but is unable to clothe her thoughts with speech; like the Laureate's,
'Oh, that my tongue could utter The thoughts that arise in me!'—and that perhaps she
is even a little lovingly angry with him for not at once divining her thoughts. The
proposer of this view thought there should have been such perfect sympathy of soul
between the lovers that, as Tennyson says, 'Thoughts leapt out to wed with thought,
Ere thought could wed itself with speech;' and that he should have been able to read
her thoughts as clearly as Venus read those of Adonis: 'His meaning struck her ere
his words begun.' We had to finish our discussion just as we began it: Is there any
generally-accepted interpretation of this line? [The most probable interpretation of
line 8 is, undoubtedly, as it seems to me, that which Fletcher and Clarendon suggest:
that Portia wishes Bassanio to learn to know her better before he hazards. But is it not
also possible to interpret the whole passage, as follows: If I beg you to forbear a while,
you are not to construe this wish into a confession of love, and yet at the same time
you know it cannot be hate; wherefore, since I cannot explain myself more fully, but
am restricted to maiden meditation, and since I do not wish you to misunderstand me,
let me beg you simply to stay here a month or two before you choose? Thus far Portia
intended to be, and was, absolutely non-committal. She did not wish to reaffirm her
'fair speechless messages' of aforetime, and she could not deny them. She had had
'no tongue' then; she had none now; she wished him simply to stay a while. It seems
to me, that in the somewhat broken sentences may be detected her maidenly embarrassment at asking Bassanio to pause 'a day or two' (which as she goes on grows into 'a
month or two'); and 'lest he should not understand her well' in preferring such a
request, she urges her incapacity as a tongue-tied maiden to explain herself more fully,
and can only reiterate her wish to detain him. In the interesting discussion in *Shakespeariana*, I should be inclined to think that 'the first interpretation offered' is the true
one.—ED.]

10. **some**] See II, iv, 29.

But if you doe, youle make me wifh a finne,
That I had beene forfworne : Befhrow your eyes,   15
They haue ore-lookt me and deuided me,
One halfe of me is yours, the other halfe yours,
Mine owne I would fay : but of mine then yours,
And fo all yours ; O thefe naughtie times
Puts bars betweene the owners and their rights.   20
And fo though yours, not yours (proue it fo)

---

15. *Befhrow*] Q₂F₂, Cap. *Befhrew* Q₁ F₃F₄, Rowe et cet.

16. *deuided*] Q₂F₂. *diuided* Q₁ et cet.

17. *halfe yours*] *halfe* Ff, Rowe, Pope, Han. *yours* Cap.

18. *of*] *firft* Ff, Rowe. *if* Qq, Pope et seq.

19. *yours ;*] *yours.* Q₁.

19. *O*] *ô* Q₂. *Alas!* Pope+.

20. *Puts*] *Put* F₂F₃, Rowe ii et seq.

21. *not yours*] *not yours*, Rowe i, Warb. *not yours ;* Rowe ii, Pope, Theob. Han. *not yours.*— Johns. et seq. *I'm not yours* Johns. conj.

proue] *but prove* Han.

it fo)] *it not so!* Cap. *it so,* Rowe +, Steev. et seq.

---

15. Beshrow] Undoubtedly spelled as it was pronounced. WALKER (*Crit.* i, 159) says that 'Shrewsbury' is still pronounced by some *Shrowsbury*.

16. ore-lookt] ECCLES : That is, *bewitched* me, in allusion to the superstitious notion of the influence of malignant and envious eyes. Portia seems to consider her present agitation as the consequence of a supposed fascination. MALONE : So, in *Merry Wives*, V, v, 87 : 'Vile worm, thou wast o'erlook'd even in thy birth.'

17. the other] See ABBOTT, § 462, for words contracted in pronunciation. [I suppose Portia in reality said 't'other.'—ED.]

18. of mine] See Text. Notes for the correct reading of the Qq.

20. Puts] For other instances of this Northern plural form in *s*, see ABBOTT, § 332.

21. yours, not yours] MALONE : The first is a monosyllable, and the second a dissyllable. WALKER (*Vers.* 137, 138) gives many other instances of this use of the same word as a monosyllable and as a dissyllable in the same line in Shakespeare and in his contemporaries. See also ABBOTT, § 480, who says it is a matter of taste which 'yours' should receive the emphasis. See also §§ 475, 476.

21. proue it so] CAPELL (p. 63) : These words are, by old editions of all sorts, put in parenthesis ; their putting so indicates a disjunction or sentence apart, and the words shew themselves a wish : a consistent wish they cannot be, without a negation ; and exactly that negative which they are now [see Text. Notes] furnish'd with, perfects the verse's measure. Her last expressions—'not yours'—are look'd upon by the speaker as expressions of ill omen ; and this wish, or this petition, is put up to avert it : A pause ensues upon it ; and then other expressions, indicating a renewal of former struggles between her love and her oath, in which the latter has victory ; they are the result of her fears, that, in this affair of the choice, 'fortune' might prove perverse ; in which case she bids fortune 'go to hell' for her perverseness ; for herself she meant not to hazard it by infringing her oath ; 'it' relates to the choice, which she had then been debating internally how it should be decided, whether by fortune's act or her own. HEATH (p. 117) : The meaning is, 'If the worst I fear should happen, and it should prove ir the event that I, who am justly yours by the free donation I have made you

Let Fortune goe to hell for it, not I.   22
I ſpeake too long, but 'tis to peize the time,
To ich it, and to draw it out in length,
To ſtay you from election.   25
   Baſſ.   Let me chooſe,
For as I am, I liue vpon the racke.
   Por.   Vpon the racke *Baſſanio*, then confeſſe
What treaſon there is mingled with your loue.
   Baſſ.   None but that vglie treaſon of miſtruſt.   30
Which makes me feare the enioying of my loue:
There may as well be amitie and life,   32

---

22. *goe to hell*] *pay the due* C. Clarke.   *itch* F_4. *eche* Rowe+. *eke* Johns. et seq.
for it] Om. Q_3.   24. *ich it*] *eche it out* Pope ii.
not I] *not me* Han.   *to draw it out*] *to dravv out* Q_1.
23. *peize*] *poize* Rowe i. *peece* Rowe ii   *draw it out* Ff, Rowe i.
+. *piece* Johns. Cap. Ktly, Dyce iii, Wh.   28. Baſſanio,] Baſſanio? Rowe ii et
ii. *peiſe* Dyce i, Del. Huds. *pauſe* Coll.   seq.
(MS).   31. *the enioying*] *th' inioying* Qq.
24. *ich*] F_2F_3. *eck* Q_1. *ech* Q_2. *eech* Q_3.   32. *life*] *lief* Daniel.

---

of myself, should yet not be yours in consequence of an unlucky choice, let fortune go
to hell for robbing you of your just due, not I for violating my oath.'

   22. not I] See ABBOTT, § 216, where instances are given (among them, *Ham.* III,
ii, 231, and *Ib.* I, iv, 54) of *I, thou,* and *he* used for *me, thee,* and *him,* 'when they
stand quasi-independently at some distance from the governing word or preposition.'

   23. peize] STEEVENS: From the French *peser,* and therefore means *to retard by
hanging weights.* See *Rich. III:* V, iii, 105.   HENLEY: To 'peize' is to weigh or
balance; and figuratively, to keep in suspense, to delay.   So, in Sir Philip Sidney's
Apology for Poetry: 'Not speaking words as they changeably fall from the mouth, but
peyzing each sillable.'   COLLIER (ed. ii): The change to *pause* of the (MS) is by no
means required, although it is very likely the word of some old performer in the part
of Portia.   KEIGHTLEY (*Exp.* p. 150): Rowe's correction, *piece,* is, I think, right.
CLARENDON: The word is used in the sense of *poise* in *King John,* II, i, 575.   ALLEN
cites Arthur Brooke's *Romeus and Juliet:* 'Which thing when he had wayde, and
when he understoode That the agreement twixt them twayn was lawfull, honest, good,
And all thinges peysed well,' &c.—line 2927.

   24. ich] HALLIWELL; The Editors have not noticed the readings of the Qq and
Ff here, which, though possibly misprints in this case, are genuine archaic forms.
Eche, from Anglosaxon *ēcan,* is found in mediæval English; and *ich,* to eke out, is
given by Kennett in MS Lansd., 1033, as a provincialism.

   30. mistrust] ECCLES: Possibly, 'mistrust,' extreme diffidence, or anxiety as to his
choice, is as destructive to his peace as actual 'treason' is to the tranquillity of a state.

   31. feare the] ABBOTT, § 200, gives instances where the preposition *for* is omitted
after 'fear' and other verbs, a simpler explanation than that of Eccles, who says that
not is to be understood before 'enjoying,' like, as Allen suggests, the Lat. *vereor ut.*—
ED.

   32 life] In one of Walker's valuable chapters he gives a large number of instances

'Tweene fnow and fire, as treafon and my loue.   33
   Por. I, but I feare you fpeake vpon the racke,
Where men enforced doth fpeake any thing.   35

---

35. *doth*] *do* or *doe* Qq et cet.

---

where a word has been corrupted by its proximity to another word much resembling it,
either in sound or spelling. In the present instance Walker suggests that the true word
is *league,* and that it was perverted by the printer through its nearness to 'life,' four
lines farther on. So highly did Dyce approve of this suggestion, that, conservative as
he professed to be, he adopted *league* in his text in his Third Edition, as did also Hudson. It may be right, but two objections to it are possible. First: Is not change needless? 'Life' may be here, as in many another case (see Schmidt), equivalent to *living;* secondly, and this objection lies to not a few of Walker's instances, are the two
words so near together that the first, which is under the compositor's eye, could have
been affected by the second, which we can scarcely presume that he has yet seen?
Where the second is affected by the first, which has preceded it in the mind of the
compositor, the case is different, and several lines may intervene, even five or six, especially if they are in the same speech. But when the reverse is the case, the nearness
of the second to the first must be close, closer, I fear, than in the present instance,
before we can, I think, admit of a substitution through proximity.—ED.

   34, 35. HUNTER (i, 326): It is an admirable quality of Shakespeare's free and noble
spirit that in all questions of politics and morals he is ever on the side of justice and
humanity. He has here given us what is the great argument against the use of torture,
folded up, as his manner is, in small space, fit to circulate from hand to hand, and thus
produce a combination of sentiment and judgement in the whole community against
what was a common but iniquitous practice of the time. Let us observe, also, to the
honour of this great teacher of truth, that such a sentiment as this, which in the reign
of Victoria would find a respondent and approving voice from all, in the reign of Elizabeth would be coldly received by those at least who guided the public counsels or conducted private examinations, if they found not sedition in it, and matter for a Star Chamber inquiry. At the very time when Shakespeare's actors were repeating these words
at the Black Friars, or on the Bankside, the secret chambers of the Tower were actually echoing the groans of suspected persons who were subjected to this unreasonable
mode of extorting information. Shakespeare must have known this, and I hope that
it was because he knew it that he sent the thrilling words through the crowds that
resorted to his theatre. He has at least taken care that they should be connected with
the idea of treason. [See lines 29, 30, and 33.] Portia is throughout a little sententious, and in line 37 gives a counterpart expression to one of our English stock-prov-
erbs: 'Confess, and die.' I cannot quit this passage without again calling attention
to the boldness as well as to the wisdom of it. In Jardine's *Essay on the Use of Torture in England,* 1836, we have sufficient proof of the frequent use of it in the reigns
of Elizabeth and James, but we have not evidence that either the Law or the Church
remonstrated against what he shows to be a new practice in England. Is it too much
to claim for Shakespeare that he was the first who raised his voice expressly against it,
and, heedless of the consequences to himself, showed the iniquity and the folly of what
they were doing, to the politicians who commanded the application of it? Let some
other person produce an earlier instance. I know of none. [In Silvayn's *Orator* (see
Appendix), which contained a ' Declamation ' ' of a Jew who would for his debt haue

Baſſ. Promiſe me life, and ile confeſſe the **truth.** 36
Por. Well then, confeſſe and liue.
Baſſ. Confeſſe and loue
Had beene the verie ſum of my confeſſion :
O happie torment, when my torturer 40
Doth teach me anſwers for deliuerance :
But let me to my fortune and the caskets.
Por. Away then, I am lockt in one of them,
If you doe loue me, you will finde me out.
Nerryſſa and the reſt, ſtand all aloofe, 45
Let muſicke ſound while he doth make his choiſe,
Then if he loofe he makes a Swan-like end,
Fading in muſique. That the compariſon
May ſtand more proper, my eye ſhall be the ſtreame
And watrie death-bed for him : he may win, 50
And what is muſique than ? Than muſique is
Euen as the flouriſh, when true ſubiects bowe
To a new crowned Monarch : Such it is,
As are thoſe dulcet ſounds in breake of day, 54

---

47. *Then*] (Aside) *Then* Anon. (ap.   49. *proper*] *just* Pope+.
Cam.).   51. *than*] *then* Q₁ Ff.
   looſe] *loſe* Q₁.   *Than*] *Then* Q₂Q₃ Ff.
48, &c. *muſique*] *muſicke* Q₁.   53. *crowned*] *crownd* Q₁.

---

a pound of the flesh of a Christian,' Shakespeare might have found more than one
illustration of the effects of the 'racke.' The '26 Declamation' reads : 'A Iudge
. . . . caused two men suspected of murther to be racked : they confesse the fact, and
are put to death. Some certaine time after their execution, he which was suppoſed to
be murthered returned home ; wherevpon the kinsman of those that were executed
accused the iudge, saying,' &c. Again, the 58th Declamation is 'of a sorceress, which
poysoned her son in law, ... and is not onely suspected for his death but accused and
conuinced thereof ; wherefore she being laid vpon the racke . . . . accused her owne
daughter, so that she was adiudged to be burned with her mother.' See also the trial
of Dr Lopez, in Appendix, p. 398.—ED.]

47. **Swan-like**] See DOUCE (i, 262) ; or *Oth.* V, ii, 309, of this Edition.

48. ECCLES : I cannot but think that the cadence of the foregoing line, and the
pause in this, have a fine effect in impressing the idea communicated to the mind.
ALLEN : The 'the' after 'that' must be absorbed. Thus scan : Fáding | in Mú | sic.
Thát' | compá | rison.

52. **flourish**] CLARENDON : At the coronation of English sovereigns, the moment
of putting on the crown is announced by a flourish of trumpets. [See Appendix,
'Date of the Play.'—ED.]

54. **dulcet sounds**] HALLIWELL : An allusion to the custom of playing music
under the windows of the bridegroom's bedroom on the morning of his marriage.

That creepe into the dreaming bride-groomes eare,   55
And fummon him to marriage.   Now he goes
With no leffe prefence, but with much more loue
Then yong *Alcides*, when he did redeeme
The virgine tribute, paied by howling *Troy*
To the Sea-monfter : I ftand for facrifice,   60
The reft aloofe are the Dardanian wiues :
With bleared vifages come forth to view
The iffue of th'exploit : Goe Hercules,
Liue thou, I liue with much more difmay   64

---

59. *virgine*] *virgin* Q₁.
  virgine tribute] *Virgin-tribute* F₃
F₄, Rowe +.
  paied] *payd* Q₁.   *payed* Q₂.
62. *bleared*] *bleated* Johns. (misprint).
64. *thou, I liue*] *thou, I liue,* F₃F₄,

Rowe i. *thou, I live.*— Johns. *thou, I
live ;* Rowe ii et cet. (subs.).
  64. *much*] Q₁F₄, Wh. i, Rlfe. *much
much* Q₂F₂F₃, Cam. Glo. Cla. Wh. ii.
much-much Dyce, Sta. *much, much* Q₃,
Rowe et cet.

---

57. **presence**] JOHNSON : With the same dignity of mien.

57. **more loue**] CLARENDON : Because Hercules rescued Hesione not for love of
the lady, but for the sake of the horses promised him by Laomedon.   MALONE : See
Ovid, *Metamorph.* xi, 199 et seqq.

60–63. HUNTER (i, 327) : There is something very Greekish in this ; something
which seems to show that Shakespeare was acquainted with the structure of the Greek
drama, and he shows his acquaintance with it at the proper time, when Portia compares
herself to the virgin devoted by Laomedon to the sea-monster.

64. **Liue thou**] Through an oversight the CAMBRIDGE EDITORS attribute to Halliwell an assertion that Roberts's Quarto reads *then* for 'thou ;' whereas Halliwell
merely quotes Johnson's note as it stands in the Variorum of 1821, and, in fact, in
every Variorum after Steevens's of 1793, where the note first appeared in its present
shape.   The Cambridge Editors add : ' It [i. e. *then*] is not so in our copy.'   Nor is
it so in mine, nor, if I am right, was it so in the copy of Dr Johnson, in whose note,
as I believe, *then* is a misprint.   The point of that note was to call attention to other
readings in this and the following line, and not to any variation between *thou* and *then*.
—ED.

64. **Liue thou**] See ABBOTT, § 361, for other instances of where the subjunctive
is indicated by placing the verb before the subject.   See also 'Live Roderigo,' &c.,
Oth. V, i, 17.

64. **much**] WHITE (ed. i) : The repetition 'much much' in Q₂ has been universally
followed.   The repetition is tame and prosaic to a degree ; and the fact that while it
occurs in the edition from a copy of which the Folio was printed, it is omitted in the
Folio itself, instead of justifying the restoration, proves, if it prove anything, that the
omission was intentional.   Had the word been found in Q₁, but not in Q₂, and did it
enhance as much as it deforms the beauty of the passage, its absence might be reasonably attributed to a mere perpetuation of an error left uncorrected in the copy furnished
to the printer.   The pause which a proper reading of the passage requires after ' Live
thou, I live,' entirely perfects the elocutionary rhythm of the line ; and Shakespeare,

I view the fight, then thou that mak'ft the fray.   65
            Here Muficke.

   A Song the whilft Baffanio *comments on the*
             Caskets to himfelfe.

   Tell me where is fancie bred,   69

65. *I*] *To* Q₁.
66. Here Muficke] Om. Qq. Music   within. Rowe.
                                                69. is] his Warb.

---

who thought only how his verse would sound in an actor's mouth, not how it would look to a critic's eye, often used this freedom. [Before putting forth his Second Edition, White may have read Walker's chapter (*Crit.* ii, 141) on the 'Omission of Repeated Words,' and the numerous examples there given may have converted him; but, however this may be, certain it is that in his later edition he silently adopts the text of Q₂. Yet is the testimony in his First Edition valuable as showing that at least this line cannot be cited as an unquestionable proof of the inferiority of Q₁ to Q₂. The full text of the two Quartos is as follows: Q₁ has, 'Liue thou, I liue with much more difmay To view the fight, then thou that mak'ft the fray.' Q₂ has, 'Liue thou, I liue with much much more difmay, I view the fight, then thou that mak'ft the fray.' Although the punctuation in both is defective, yet with its bad punctuation, Q₁ after all, gives a meaning, which can scarcely be said of Q₂; the transcriber of the text for Q₂ gives us the better text, but he did not understand it, and hence his ill-placed commas. The transcriber of Q₁, being more intelligent than the other, saw that something was wrong and did his best to correct it, either by punctuation or by changing 'I' to 'To.' With proper punctuation, such as Rowe (ed. ii) supplied (see Text. Notes), Q₂ gives us the better text.—Ed.]

   65. **that mak'ft**] Eccles: To consider Bassanio as a spectator of the combat waged by himself, though but metaphorical, would be a very unusual mode of thinking and speaking. The objection might be obviated by a change of this sort, 'than thou *maintain'ft* the fray.'

   69–74. Rushton (*N. & Qu.* 4th, xii, p. 304): In the *Euphues* of Lily is the following: 'For as by Basill the Scorpion is *engendred,* and by meanes of the same hearb destroyed: so love, which by time and *fancie is bred* in an idle *head,* is by time and fancie banished from the *heart:* or as the Salamander which being a long space *nourished* in the fire, at the last quencheth it, so affection having taking holde of the fancie, and living as it were in the minde of the lover, in tract of tyme altereth and changeth the heate, and turneth it to chilnesse' [*Euphues and his England,* 1580, p. 298, ed. Arber]. Weiss (p. 312): Portia bids the music play. Bassanio must be attempered to his choice; the song's key must have an instinct for the proper casket's key. Unconsciously she breaks her oath; for what benign influence selected the song that is now sung? Some star, whose tenant was her father? Or was it Nerissa's doing, who determined to convey a hint to the lover? [The maid gave a hint in the *Pecorone.*—Ed.] Or did Gratiano hit upon it, who had got from Nerissa a promise of her love if the choice went to suit her? A hint indeed! It is the very breadth of broadness, and a lover is not dull. A song that did good sexton-service, for fancy's knell is rung indeed. The strain reminds Bassanio of notices in his experience: that error hides its grossness in ornament; vice assumes some mark of virtue; beauty is for sale

Or in the heart, or in the head :   70
How begot, how nourished.   *Replie, replie.*
It is engendred in the eyes,
With gazing fed, and Fancie dies,
In the cradle where it lies :   74

70. Or in] In Johns.
71. nourished.] nourished ? Qq.
   Replie, replie] Om. Rowe. *Reply*
(as a stage direction) Han Johns. Steev.
Mal. '90, Huds. As a separate line, Pope

+, Var. Knt et cet.
72. engendred] engendered Q₁.
   eyes] eye Qq, Pope, Theob. Han.
Warb. Cam.
73. fed,] fed ; Cap. et seq.

by weight, and is a show which cunning puts on to entrap wise men ; in short, as the song says, fancies (which sometimes in Shakespeare mean genuine passion, but here it hints only a passing sentiment) come by gazing, have no life deeper than the eyes where they are born. ' So may the outward shows be least themselves.' This fortune hunter, after all, is Portia's counterpart. The melody woven out of air glides into his hand, and becomes a clew to bliss. Oh, the woman thrills ! in touching the lead his hand has clutched her heart, and forces from her words that are outbreaks of that which is everlastingly the Woman. They assail, they challenge man to say what is so great as love. This polished, clear, sagacious, gifted, balanced woman dares man to say love is not greatest of all.

   69. **where**] ABBOTT, by referring to § 136, apparently understands this as a contraction for *whether*, which, I think, it is ; as far as the sense is concerned, it is immaterial.—ED.

   69. **fancie**] STEEVENS : Love. GEORGE FLETCHER (*Fraser's Maga.*, May, 1850, p. 507) : ' Fancy,' we must observe, in the writings of Shakespeare, and in the language of his time, signifies that uneasy season of love which precedes the certainty of its thorough requital. Thus, in any case, ' Fancy dies In the cradle where it lies,' since it either expires on finding itself hopeless of requital, or becomes merged in the perfect enjoyment of mutual love. CLARENDON : Fancy, here, seems to be censured as a feeling neither bred in heart nor in brain, but in the eye only, penetrating no deeper, and lasting only while its object is in sight.

   71. **Replie, replie**] JOHNSON : These words, in all the old copies, stand as a marginal direction. [Capell printed this Song in two stanzas, which he calls ' 1. V.' and ' 2. V.,' and ' reply, reply ' as the last line of the first stanza, and added this note :] For this Song's form the present Editor is accountable : the words ' reply, reply ' shew it to be a song in two parts, or by two Voices : [therefore Capell's ' 1. V.' and ' 2. V.' mean *First Voice* and *Second Voice*] follow'd by a Chorus of divers assistant voices, which ' all ' indicates. KNIGHT : These words are unquestionably part of the song ; the mutilation whereof, in the belief that the words were a stage-direction, is certainly one of the most tasteless corruptions of the many for which the Editors of Shakespeare are answerable. CAMBRIDGE EDITORS : These words seem to be required, as part of the song, by the rhythm, and (if we read *eye* with the Qq) by the rhyme also.

   72. **eyes,**] In a modern text I think there should be a semicolon after this word, which is, to me, better in the plural than in the singular ; the singular, common as it is, always conveys to me more or less the idea of mayhem.—ED.

   74. CAPELL : The matter of this song is both pleasing and suitable, and, in one place, satirical ; for the sentence, beginning—' and fancy dies ' is expressive of love's

> *Let vs all ring Fancies knell.*   75
> Ile begin it.
> *Ding, dong, bell.*
>   All.   *Ding, dong, bell.*

Baff. So may the outward fhowes be leaft themfelues
The world is ftill deceiu'd with ornament.   80
In Law, what Plea fo tanted and corrupt,
But being feafon'd with a gracious voice,
Obfcures the fhow of euill? In Religion,
What damned error, but fome fober brow
Will bleffe it, and approue it with a text,   85
Hiding the grofeneffe with faire ornament:
There is no voice fo fimple, but affumes
Some marke of vertue on his outward parts;
How manie cowards, whofe hearts are all as falfe
As ftayers of fand, weare yet vpon their chins   90

---

76. Roman in QqFf, Rowe, Pope, Theob. Han. Warb.
76, 77. As one line, Johns. Cap. et seq.
81. *tanted*] *tainted* QqFf.
87. *voice*] Q$_1$. *voyce* Q$_2$Q$_3$. *vice* Ff,

Rowe et seq.
88. *marke*] Om. Q$_1$.
    his] *its* Theob. Warb. Johns.
90. *ftayers*] Q$_2$Q$_3$, Knt, Huds. *ftaiers* Q$_1$. *ftayres* F$_2$F$_3$. *ftairs* F$_4$, Rowe et cet

---

changeableness, which has both its birth in the *eye* from one object, and its extinction or death from others. Eccles: This line cannot refer to the *eye* or *eyes*, in which *fancy* is *engendered*, but rather to the shortness of its duration, as *dying* while still in its *cradle*, i. e. in infancy.

77. Halliwell: This burthen was formerly a serious one, appropriately significant of a knell.

79. Johnson: He begins abruptly; the first part of the argument has passed in his mind. Eccles: Or perhaps this line refers to the subject of the Song; that the objects of *fancy* afford only that short-lived enjoyment just alluded to.

82. **season'd**] Clarendon: This carries on the metaphor suggested by 'tainted' in the preceding line.

85. **approue**] Dyce (*Gloss.*): That is, ratify, confirm.

88. **marke**] Through the compositor's carelessness this word is omitted in Q$_1$; it can be scarcely called a different text.

90. **stayers**] Knight: The propriety of the image appears to us to justify the restoration of the original word in this passage. Cowards in their falseness,—their assumption of appearances without realities,—may be compared to *stairs* of sand, which betray the feet of those who trust to them; but we have here cowards appearing ready to face an enemy with 'beards of Hercules and frowning Mars;' they are false as *stayers* of sand—banks, bulwarks of sand,—that the least opposition will throw down,—vain defences,—feeble ramparts. Dyce (*Remarks*, p. 55) calls attention to the shifting and uncertain spelling of 'stairs' in Taylor's *Workes*, and adds that

The beards of *Hercules* and frowning *Mars*,   91
Who inward fearcht, haue lyu ers white as milke,
And thefe affume but valors excrement,
To render them redoubted.   Looke on beautie,
And you fhall fee 'tis purchaft by the weight,   95
Which therein workes a miracle in nature,
Making them lighteft that weare moft of it :
So are thofe crifped fnakie golden locks
Which makes fuch wanton gambols with the winde
Vpon fuppofed faireneffe, often knowne   100
To be the dowrie of a fecond head,

98. *crifped*]   *crispy* Theob. Warb.   99. *makes*] Ff Q₃, Rowe.   *maketh* Q₁
Johns.   Q₂.   *make* Pope et cet.

Knight's 'defence and explanation of "stayers" is of more than Warburtonian subtlety,
and will assuredly never carry conviction to a single Englishman,—though, perhaps, it
may receive the commendation of Tieck, with his imperfect knowledge of the language, and in gratitude for the respect with which Mr Knight has treated *his* vagaries.'
HUDSON, nevertheless, retains the old spelling, and explains it 'in the sense of *props,
supports,* or *stays.* The word is to be pronounced, here, as one syllable ; as " cowards "
also is.' ALLEN : I wonder if there be not here an allusion to the *mirage* in the *sandy
desert ?*

93. excrement] MALONE : That is, what a little before is called the '*beard* of
Hercules.' See *Wint. Tale,* IV, iv, 734. STAUNTON : A brave man's beard. The
meaning is,—cowards, who inwardly are false and craven, by the assumption of what
is merely the excrescence of true valour, think to be considered indomitable.

94. beautie] HEATH (p. 117) : By ' beauty,' I apprehend, is meant only artificial
beauty, which is procured by painting, and is mere adventitious show and ornament
superinduced upon true and real nature, like that false hair the mention of which immediately follows. This factitious beauty, though purchased by weight, the more it is
laid on, the more lightness it indicates in the wearer.

98. crisped] STEEVENS : That is, curled. ROLFE : Milton (*Comus,* 984) speaks
of ' crisped shades and bowers,' referring to the leaves waved and curled by the
wind.

99. Which makes] ABBOTT (§ 247) : The relative (perhaps because it does not
signify by inflection any agreement in number or person with its antecedent) frequently
takes a *singular* verb, though the antecedent be *plural.*

100. Vpon supposed fairenesse] CLARENDON connects this with the ' snakie
golden locks,' and paraphrases it, ' surmounting fictitious beauty.' But ROLFE paraphrases it, ' on the strength of their fictitious beauty,' and thinks that it is ' closely connected with the preceding line.'

101. MRS FURNESS (MS) : Conf. *Sonnet,* 68, 7 : ' To live a second life on second
head,' where, in the preceding line, the word ' sepulchre ' also occurs.

101. dowrie] MALONE : The prevalence of this fashion in Shakespeare's time is
evinced by the following passage in an old pamphlet, entitled : *The Honestie of this*

The fcull that bred them in the Sepulcher.   102
Thus ornament is but the guiled fhore
To a moft dangerous fea : the beautious fcarfe   104

---

103. *guiled*] *guilded* Ff.   *gilded* Rowe, Pope, Han. Cap.   *guilty* Warb.

Age, proving by good Circumstance that the World was never honest till now, by Bar-
nabe Rich, 1615 :—'My lady holdeth on her way, perhaps to the tire-maker's shop,
where she shaketh her crownes to bestow upon some new fashioned attire, upon such
artificial deformed *periwigs,* that they were fitter to furnish a theatre, or for her that in
a stage-play should represent some hag of hell, than to be used by a Christian woman.'
Again, *ibid :* 'These attire-makers within these fortie yeares were not known by that
name; and but now very lately they kept their lowzie commodity of *periwigs,* and their
monstrous attires closed in boxes;—and those women that used to weare them would
not buy them but in secret.   But now they are not ashamed to set them forth upon
their stalls,—such monstrous mop-powles of haire, so proportioned and deformed, that
but within these twenty or thirty yeares would have drawne the passers-by to stand
and gaze, and to wonder at them.'   STEEVENS, in a note on *Timon,* IV, iii, 144, has
collected many references to this practice.   He says that Stowe informs us that
'women's periwigs were first brought into England about the time of the massacre of
Paris.'

103. guiled] STEEVENS: That is, treacherous.   'Guiled' stands for *guiling.*   CA-
PELL: *Gilded* [of the Ff] is a well-chosen epithet; expressing the glitter of cliffs and
rocks, and of the sea's beach, when the sun lyes upon them.   ECCLES: If *gilded* be
the right word, it may, perhaps, bear an allusion to the *golden locks* just before mentioned.   COLLIER: The (MS) alters *guilded* to *guiling ;* it may have been the custom
to use the word *guiling* in the old Corrector's time; but as Shakespeare and other
writers of that period often employed the passive participle instead of the active, and
vice versâ, we have introduced no alteration; by '*guiled*' Shakespeare certainly meant
guiling,—of that there is no question.   WALKER (*Crit.* i, 291): For 'guiled,' compare: 'To me came Tarquin armed; so beguiled With outward honesty, but yet defiled
With inward vice,' &c.—*R. of L.* 1544.   Still I suspect 'guiled.'   LETTSOM [foot-note
to Walker]: I believe the verb *to guile* was unknown to Shakespeare.   However that
may be, I have little doubt that the poet was thinking of Raleigh's '*Discovery of Gui-
ana,*' and wrote *guilded.*   CLARENDON: That is, full of guile, deception, treacherous.
So IV, i, 196, 'blest,'—i. e. endowed with blessing; and in *1 Hen. IV:* I, iii, 183:
'Revenge the jeering and disdain'd contempt Of this proud King,' where 'disdain'd'
means full of disdain.   So probably in *Meas. for Meas.* III, i, 121: 'the delighted
spirit' means the spirit capable of delight.   ABBOTT, § 294, gives a list of participles
formed from adjectives, and of participles derived from nouns, with respective modifications of meaning.   ROLFE: Marsh (*Lect. on Eng. Lang.,* p. 655) gives examples
of 'passive participles with active meaning,' as *well-spoken, fair-spoken,* &c.   'Well
read' is similar.   [Clarendon's interpretation, sustained by Abbott, is, to me, unquestionably correct, and we need not suppose that a passive participle is here used for an
active one.   Just as 'delighted' in *Meas. for Meas.* and in *Oth.* I, iii, 320, means
endowed with delights, 'deliciis exornata' as Sidney Walker gives it, so here 'guiled'
means *endowed, infested with guiles.*   It is the same construction in 'Your loop'd and
window'd raggedness,' *Lear,* III, iv, 31.—ED.]
10

Vailing an Indian beautie ; In a word,   105

105. *an Indian beautie*] *an* Indian
beauty F₄, Rowe+, Cap.   *an Indian
dowdy* Han.   *Deformity* Lansd.   *an Indian : beauty*, Coll. ii, iii (MS).   *an Indian feature* Ktly, Huds.   *an Indian
beauty* Qq F₂F₃, Steev. et cet.   *an Indian*

idol Cartwright.   *an Indian gipsy* Walker.
an Indian favour Lettsom.   *an Indian
swarthy*, or *Indian sooty* Herr.   *an Indian deity* Schmidt.   *an Indian bosom*
Parry.

---

105. **Indian beautie**] THEOBALD (Nichols's *Illust.* ii, 307) : There is a glaring
contrast betwixt *gilded shore* and *dang'rous sea ;* but is there the same betwixt *beauteous
scarf* and *Indian beauty ?* I suspect both the pointing and the text wrong. Read : ' the
beauteous scarf Veiling an Indian.—Beauty's, in a word, The seeming truth which cunning *Dames* (or *tires*, or *trims*) put on,' &c. [This reading, ' Indian ; beauty's,' was
adopted by HARNESS, and COLLIER'S (MS) reads ' Indian : beauty,'] CAPELL : If we
lay stress upon ' Indian,' we shall have no occasion to back it with the Oxford editor's
dowdy. ECCLES : One of the causes, no doubt, for suspecting a corruption here is that
the words ' beauteous ' and ' beauty ' come so close together, but in that the writer
might have designed something like an antithesis.   A. E. BRAE (*N. & Qu.* 1852,
1st, v, 483) gives the following reasons for retaining ' beautie ' : First, The argument
of Bassanio is directed against the deceptiveness of ornament in general, of which seeming beauty is only one of the subordinate illustrations.   These illustrations are drawn
from *law, religion, valour*, and *beauty ;* all of which are finally summed up in the
passage in question, beginning ' Thus ornament,' &c.   Therefore this summing up
cannot refer singly to *beauty*, no more than to any other of the subordinate illustrations,
but it must have general reference to adventitious ornament, against which *the collected*
argument is directed.   Secondly, The word ' beauty ' is necessarily attached to ' Indian '
as designative of *sex :* ' an Indian,' unqualified by any other distinction, would imply a
male ; but an ' Indian beauty ' is at once understood to be a female.   Thirdly, The repetition, or rather *the opposition*, of ' beauteous ' and ' beauty ' cannot seriously be objected
to by any one conversant with the phraseology of Shakespeare.   ' The beauteous scarf '
is the deceptive ornament which leads to the expectation of something beneath it *better*
than an *Indian* beauty !   ' Indian ' is used adjectively, in the sense of *wild, savage,
hideous*,—just as we, at the present day, might say a ' Hottentot beauty ;' or as Shakespeare himself in other places uses the word ' Ethiop.'   BLACKWOOD'S MAGAZINE
(Aug. 1853) : We still confess a partiality for the old text, both in words and in pointing. ' An Indian beauty ' may mean the worst species of ugliness, just as ' a Dutch nightingale ' means a toad.   HALLIWELL : *Idol* has been suggested for ' beauty.'   DYCE (ed.
i) : [Harness's punctuation] may be dismissed at once as erroneous, because it utterly
subverts the whole construction of the passage.   The word ' beauty ' in which the difficulty lies, would seem to be a misprint caught from the preceding ' beauteous ;' unless
we suppose (and it is difficult to suppose so) that ' an Indian beauty ' may mean—what
is a beauty among the Indians, but nowhere else.   STAUNTON : I have always suspected
an error of the press in this passage.   The printer appears to have caught the word
' beauty,' of all others the most inappropriate here, from the ' beauteous ' of the preceding line, and permitted it to usurp the place of the original expression ; but what
that was must be left to the reader's sagacity to determine.   WHITE : Ornament, not
beauty, is here the subject of Bassanio's reflection.   ' Indian ' is used in a derogatory
sense ; and the occurrence of ' beauteous ' and ' beauty ' in the same sentence is not at
all unlike Shakespeare's manner.   BAILEY (i, 157) : I propose to read ' an *Indian's*

[105. Vailing an Indian beautie ;]

blackness,' which expresses in the most direct way what was manifestly in the author's mind. [But by the time Bailey reached his second volume this manifestness was not quite so manifest. He says, ii, 214]: It has since occurred to me that the word *body* would form an emendation equal at least in point of appropriateness, and more easily changed into the received text. KEIGHTLEY (*Expositor*, p. 150): Unless we take it ironically—which is unworthy of the poet—'beauty' here is nonsense. It plainly owes its origin to the preceding 'beauteous.' Hanmer read *dowdy ;* Sidney Walker, *gipsy*—both bad. I read, with the utmost confidence, *feature* as the only word suited to the place. [Keightley had already proposed this, in *N. & Qu.* 1863, 3d, iv, 121.] E. L. SWIFTE (*N. & Qu.* 1863, 3d, iv, 203): Let me attempt to restore the antithesis of the passage : 'Veiling an Indian *Deity,*' the Oriental idols being, as travellers tell us, gaudily attired and awfully ugly. [As WHITE did not himself, in either of his editions, allude to the explanation which he gave in his *Shakespeare's Scholar,* it is not worth while to do more than allude to it here. In his Second Edition he explains 'Indian beauty' as 'one with thick lips and a black skin.'] COWDEN-CLARKE: It is just possible that Shakespeare may have written 'suttee' (spelt, perhaps, 'sutie' in the MS, and the printer, being unacquainted with the word, made it out 'beautie'), having met with the name in the works of his day; as Diodorus mentions an instance of a suttee three hundred years before the Christian era. By the term 'suttee' is now meant a Hindoo woman, who performs the sacrifice of burning herself on her deceased husband's funeral pile ; but formerly it may have been known merely as a name for an Indian woman. However, we merely suggest the possibility of Shakespeare's having used the word 'suttee' here; as we have always taken the passage as it stands to be merely another form of 'a brow of Egypt,' which he employs to signify a dark-complexioned, ill-favoured woman. CLARENDON: Various guesses have been made as to the word which we should substitute for 'beauty,' [among others] 'visage,' 'beldam;' but it is impossible to pronounce positively which is the right, if any. Perhaps 'bosom' may be better than all these, if we consider how a scarf is worn. ALLEN: We require some word like *poisoner,* or one that fascinates, or kills with the evil eye, or the like. Shakespeare must (in that case) have read or heard of some such veiled danger to his countrymen in their plantations among the Indians. It is unnecessary to confine one's self to the *ductus literarum,* for 'beauty' was probably brought down by the compositor from the preceding line. REV. JOHN HUNTER: Montaigne (*Essays,* ii, 12, Florio's Translation) says of beauty: 'The Indians describe it black and swarthy, with blabbered thick lips, with a broad and flat nose.' [If Shakespeare read this in Montaigne, he read it in French; Florio's translation was not published until 1603. One thing is clear to us all in this passage, and it is, that the antitheses which have preceded must be kept up. We have uniformly had the outward shows of ornament contrasted with the thing itself, the sham with the reality, from a gracious voice seasoning a tainted plea down to a beauteous scarf ornamenting —something repulsive; what that something is each student will have to decide for himself; for me, the original suffices. An Indian beauty is assuredly not an English beauty. 'In the estimation of Europeans,' says Sydney Smith, in his *Lectures on Moral Philosophy*, Lecture xii, 'part of the beauty of a face is the color of the cheek; not that there is something in that particular position of red color, which, I believe, is of itself beautiful,—but habit has also connected it with the idea of health. An Indian requires that his wife's face should be the color of good marketable sea-coal; another tribe is enamoured of deep orange; and a cheek of copper is irresistible to a

The feeming truth which cunning times put on   106
To intrap the wifeft.   Therefore then thou gaudie gold,
Hard food for *Midas*, I will none of thee,
Nor none of thee thou pale and common drudge
'Tweene man and man : but thou, thou meager lead   110
Which rather threatneft then doft promife ought,
Thy paleneffe moues me more then eloquence,   112

---

107. *Therefore then*] Q₂. *Then* Pope+.
Therefore Q₁, Ff, Rowe, Cap. et seq.
  108. *food*] *foole* Q₁.
  109. *pale*] *stale* Farmer, Dyce iii.
     drudge] *drudg* F₄.

111. *threatneſt*] *threatenſt* Q₂.
112. *paleneſſe*] *palenes* Q₂.   *plainneſs*
Warb. Theob. Han. Johns. Cap. Steev.
Mal. '90, Dyce i, Sta. Wh. i, Del. Rlfe,
Huds.

---

fourth.'   In the foregoing discussion, allusion is made by Brae, Singer, and Dyce to
an Anonymous edition of Shakespeare, printed by Scott and Webster in 1833.   This
is one of the many reprints of Harness's edition, wherein the note on this passage
reads : ' I have deviated slightly from the Folio, [where the text] by no means serves
to illustrate the reflexion which Bassanio wishes to enforce.'   Collier's (MS) reads
' beauty,' herein differing slightly from the 'beauty's ' of Theobald and Harness, a difference which escaped the notice of some of the critics.—ED.]

  107, 108. If in line 108 Q₁ is inferior to Q₂ in printing *foole* for *food*, it is superior
to Q₂ in line 107 by omitting the 'then' which mars the metre.

  108. Midas] WALKER (*Crit.* i, 152) devotes a Chapter to Ovid's influence on
Shakespeare, and cites this allusion to Midas, and to Thisbe, and to Medea in Act V,
as among the many examples.   But I do not find that Walker has anywhere noted
that it was chiefly Golding's Translation that was impressed on Shakespeare's memory
See note on V, i, 1.—ED.

  109. pale] FARMER : I would rather give the character of silver, ' Thou *stale,* and
common drudge 'Tween,' &c.   WALKER (*Crit.* i, 305) : From this punctuation it
would seem that Farmer makes *stale* a substantive.   HALLIWELL : It may be mentioned, that *stale* and *common* appear together in the context in a passage in *Hen. IV;*
and that *stale* is misprinted *pale* in the first edition of *Tro. and Cress.*   DYCE (ed. iii) :
The words *stale* and *pale* are frequently confounded by early transcribers and printers.
[It is the drudge's overwork between man and man that makes him 'pale.'—ED.]

  112. palenesse] WARBURTON : Bassanio is displeas'd at the golden casket for its
gaudiness, and the silver one for its *paleness;* but, what! is he charm'd with the leaden
one for having the very same quality that displeas'd him in the silver?   The poet certainly wrote, ' Thy *plainness;*' this characterizes the lead from the silver, which 'paleness' does not, they being both *pale.*   Besides, there is a beauty in the antithesis
between *plainness* and *eloquence;* between *paleness* and *eloquence* none.   So it is
said before of the leaden casket : ' This third, *dull* lead,' &c.   FARMER : The 'paleness' of lead is for ever alluded to.   ' Diane declining, pale as any ledde,' says Stephen
Hawes.   In Fairfax's *Tasso,* we have—' The lord Tancredie, pale with rage as lead.'
Again, Sackville in his *Legend of the Duke of Buckingham :* ' Now pale as lead, now
cold as any stone.'   And in the old ballad of *The King and the Beggar :* ' She blushed
scarlet red, Then straight again as pale as lead.'   As to the antithesis, Shakespeare has
already made it in *Mid. N. D.:* ' When,' says Theseus, ' I have seen great clerks look

And here choofe I, ioy be the confequence.   113
Por.   How all the other paffions fleet to ayre,
As doubtfull thoughts, and rafh imbrac'd defpaire:
And fhuddring feare, and greene-eyed iealoufie.
O loue be moderate, allay thy extafie,   117

114-120. [Aside. Lansdowne, Cam. 117. *O...moderate*] *Be moderate, love!*
Glo. Cla. Rlfe, Wh. ii.   Han.
 116. *fhuddring*] *fhyddring* Qq.   *O loue*] Separate line, Glo. Wh. ii.

---

pale, I read as much as from the rattling tongue Of saucy and audacious *eloquence.'*
CAPELL: Opposition between the terms that compose it appearing manifestly an intention in [line 112], 'palines' (the word of the original Quarto) must have been a corruption, and that for *plainness*, in the manuscript—*plaines*. MALONE: By laying an
emphasis on 'Thy,' ('*Thy* paleness,' &c.) Warburton's objection is obviated.   Though
Bassanio might object to silver, that 'pale and *common drudge*,' lead, though *pale* also,
yet not being in daily use, might, in his opinion, deserve a preference.   A. E. BRAE
(*N. & Qu.* 1852, 1st, vi, 59) : I am convinced that Warburton's suggestion of *plainness* is right.   There is no relation between 'paleness' and 'eloquence,' in the sense
required by the context.   'Paleness' can only move 'more than eloquence' when the
feeling to be excited is *compassion;* but *plainness* has just that sort of opposition to
eloquence, which the tenour of the passage requires.   Moreover, *plainness* has an
obvious reference—which paleness has not,—to the preceding line : 'Which rather
threat'nest than doth promise aught.'   And it is also an appropriate continuation of
meagre, in the sense of poor, barren, unassuming.   STAUNTON : We admit Warburton's
emendation, but demur to the reasoning by which he sought to establish it.   The *plainness* which moves Bassanio *more than eloquence* is clearly not alone the unpretending
appearance of the leaden coffer, as Warburton seems to have thought, but the plain
speaking of the inscription on it,—'Which rather threat'nest,' &c., contrasted with the
tempting labels of its neighbours.   BAILEY (ii, 215) not only adopts 'plainness' on the
score of antithesis, but 'being of opinion,' he says, 'that "eloquence" is in this case
exceptionable, because utterly misplaced, I propose that it should be exchanged for a
word resembling it, which makes as perfect an antithesis as can be desired.   Let us
read : "Thy *plainness* moves me more than *elegance*," and we obtain a line which
perfectly expresses all that is wanted.   The last word is certainly not frequent in our
author's writings ; he uses it, in fact, only once in his dramas' [an error ; Shakespeare
uses 'elegancy' in *Love Lab. L.*, but never *elegance*.   From Capell we can infer with
what ease the mistake of 'paleness' for *plainness* might arise, and Brae and Staunton
show that threats lie in *plainness*, but not in 'paleness;' and therefore, I think, Warburton's emendation should be adopted.   The single dead fly in this ointment is that
Capell is not quite right in saying that *palines* is the original word in the Qto. Q_1 and
Q_3 are the same as F_1; Q_2 has *palenes*.   Capell's own copy of Q_1 is now before me,
wherein he has laboriously marked in red ink the variations between it and Q_2.   In
the present word 'palenesse,' he has erased the three final letters, *sse*, and written
above them the single letter *s*.   The *e* he has not changed to *i*.   The presumption is,
therefore, that his spelling, *palines*, is an oversight.—ED.].

 115. **As**] That is, to wit, namely.   See WALKER (*Crit.* i, 127), or ABBOTT, § 113
Conf. *Ham.* I, iv, 25.

 117. **O loue**] To avoid an Alexandrine, WALKER (*Vers.* 268) and ABBOTT (§ 512)

In meafure raine thy ioy, fcant this exceffe,   118
I feele too much thy bleffing, make it leffe,
For feare I furfeit.
    Baf. What finde I here?
Faire *Portias* counterfeit. What demie God   122

---

118. *raine*] Q_2F_2. *range* Q_1. *reine* Q_3.	*surfeit in't* Anon. (ap. Cam.).
rein Sing. Coll. ii, iii, Cam. Glo. Wh. ii.	121. *What...I*] *What do I find* Han.
rain F_3F_4, Rowe et cet.	*Ha! what find I* Cap.
120. *furfeit*] *surfeit me* Steev. conj.	122. *demie God*] *demy-god* F_4.

---

would read this as an interjectional line by itself 'in spite of the rhyme,' says the former. Unquestionably, there is abundant propriety in this treatment of interjections, exclamations, &c., but is it not, after all, only scansion for the eye? The voice must make the pause whether the exclamation be in a separate line or not. As long as the rhythm is smooth, I cannot believe that Shakespeare's ear was offended by an Alexandrine. —ED.

118. **raine**] JOHNSON: I once believed Shakespeare meant *rein*. The words 'rain' and *rein* were not in these times distinguished by regular orthography. There is no difficulty in the present reading; only, where the copies vary some suspicion of error is always raised. MALONE: 'Rain' is supported by 'It rain'd down fortune show'ring on thy head.'—*1 Hen. IV: V,* i, 48. TOLLET: Compare the following, which approaches very near to the present reading, if we adopt *rein :* '—being chaf'd, he cannot Be rein'd again to temperance.'—*Cor.* III, iii, 27. COLLIER (ed. i): It may reasonably be doubted whether we ought to read 'rain' or *rein*. DYCE (*Remarks*, p. 57): To doubt that 'rain' is the right reading, appears to me most *un*reasonable. COLLIER (ed. ii): I was formerly for 'rain;' but Portia, I am convinced, means only *curb* your joys, restrain them, and she therefore follows up the exclamation by 'scant this excess.' DYCE (*Strictures,* &c. p. 66): Is it usual to talk of *reining* anything 'in measure'? and do not the words 'scant this excess,' which Mr Collier adduces in support of *rein,* distinctly prove that it is the wrong reading? CLARENDON: Most editors after Malone [among them Clarendon.—ED.] print 'rain;' but *rein* rests on higher authority and makes good sense. [To me, *rein* is much to be preferred. Portia adjures love to be moderate, to allay its ecstasy, to rein in its joy by due restraint, lest she die in this excess. If *rein* be the right word, then Q_2 comes nearer to it than the *range* of Q_1, yet the latter is not wholly meaningless. Clarendon speaks of *rein* as resting on a 'higher authority' than that of many modern editors. I find it hard to consider a compositor as of any authority here whatsoever, least of all, far least of all, the compositor who set up the Third Quarto for Laurence Hayes.—ED.]

120. To complete the rhythm of this line and the next, Steevens proposed to add *me* after 'surfeit.' Hanmer and Capell both added a syllable to line 121. If the attempt to adjust broken lines to the full measure of whole ones be not waste time, then it seems to me that Lettsom's conjecture, given by Dyce (ed. iii), of *on't* after 'surfeit,' is the most plausible. The fact should never be lost sight of that these plays were written to be spoken and acted, not to be read and studied, nor even printed.—ED.

122. **counterfeit.**] STEEVENS: A *likeness,* without comprehending any idea of fraud. [For other instances in Shakespeare, see SCHMIDT. HUNTER (i, 328) gives an instance from Haringtoi s *Life of Ariosto,* in his translation of the *Orlando* · 'His counterfeit was taken by Tytiano, that excellent drawer,' &c]

Hath come ſo neere creation ? moue theſe eies?   123
Or whether riding on the bals of mine
Seeme they in motion ? Here are ſeuer'd lips   125
Parted with ſuger breath, ſo ſweet a barre
Should ſunder ſuch ſweet friends : here in her haires
The Painter plaies the Spider, and hath wouen
A golden meſh t'intrap the hearts of men
Faſter then gnats in cobwebs : but her eies,   13c
How could he ſee to doe them ? hauing made one,
Me thinkes it ſhould haue power to ſteale both his
And leaue it ſelfe vnfurniſht : Yet looke how farre   133

---

124. *whether*] *whither* Q₁Q₂.   Glo. Cla. Rlfe, Wh. ii.
       bals] *ball's* Q₁.   132. *Me   thinkes*]   *Me-thinks* Q₁
126. *ſuger breath*] *sugar'd breath* Pope,   *Methinks* F₄.
Han.   *sugar-breath* Dyce iii.   133. *vnfurniſht*]   *unfinish'd* Rowe,
127. *haires*] *hair* Han.   Pope, Theob. Warb. Coll. iii (MS). *half-*
129. *t'intrap*] *tyntrap* Q₂.   *to entrap*   *furnish'd* Anon. (ap. Hal.).
Cap. Steev. Mal. Knt, Dyce i, Sta. Cam.

---

124. **Or whether**] See ABBOTT, § 136, for other instances of the use of 'whether' after 'or,' where 'we should omit one of the two.'

127. **Should**] In the sense of *ought*, as in 'I should be obscured,' *supra*, II, vi, 51

131. **hauing**] ABBOTT, § 466, cites this as one of the instances where the *v* is soft ened in pronunciation and the word pronounced as a monosyllable. 'It may seem difficult for modern readers to understand how the *v* could be dropped. But it presents no more difficulty than the *v* in *ever, over*.' See also Walker (*Vers.* 103). [The Scotch find no difficulty in dropping the *v* in *have, love, brave*, &c. See note on 'pov-erty,' IV, i, 285; and also on 'riveted,' V, i, 188.—ED.] CLARENDON: The nomina-tive is changed, leaving the words 'having made one' without a verb to follow.

133. **vnfurnisht**] JOHNSON: Perhaps it might be, 'leave *himself* unfurnish'd.' MONCK MASON: 'Unfurnished' must mean 'unfurnished with a companion or fellow.' Conf. this passage in Fletcher's *Lover's Progress* [II, i, p. 47, ed. Dyce] where Alci-don says to Claringé, on delivering Lydian's challenge : 'You are a noble gentleman, Will't please you bring a friend? we are two of us, And pity either, sir, should be un-furnish'd,' i. e. unfurnished with an antagonist. HENLEY: Dr Johnson's emendation would altogether subvert the poet's meaning. If the artist, in painting *one* of Portia's eyes, should lose both his own, that eye which he had painted must necessarily be *left unfurnished*, or destitute of his fellow. MALONE: That is, it must leave itself incom-plete; unaccompanied with the other usual component parts of a portrait—viz. another eye, &c. STEEVENS: A hint for this passage appears to have been taken from Greene's *History of Faire Bellora*, afterward published under the title of *A Paire of Turtle Doves* : 'If Apelles had beene tasked to have drawne her counterfeit, her two bright-burning lampes would have so dazled his quicke-seeing sences, that quite despairing to express with his cunning pensill so admirable a worke of nature, he had been inforced to have staid his hand, and left this earthly Venus unfinished.' BAILEY (i, 159) : 'Un-furnished' seems exceedingly vague, if not entirely destitute of sense, and could scarcely

The ſubſtance of my praiſe doth wrong this ſhadow
In vnderpriſing it, ſo farre this ſhadow   135
Doth limpe behinde the ſubſtance. Here's the ſcroule,
The continent, and ſummarie of my fortune.

> *You that chooſe not by the view*
> *Chance as faire, and chooſe as true :*
> *Since this fortune fals to you,*   140
> *Be content, and ſeeke no new.*
> *If you be well pleaſd with this,*
> *And hold your fortune for your bliſſe,*
> *Turne you where your Lady is,*
> *And claime her with a louing kiſſe.*   145

Baſſ.   A gentle ſcroule : Faire Lady, by your leaue,
I come by note to giue, and to receiue,
Like one of two contending in a prize
That thinks he hath done well in peoples eies :
Hearing applauſe and vniuerſall ſhout,   150
Giddie in ſpirit, ſtill gazing in a doubt
Whether thoſe peales of praiſe be his or no.   152

135. *vnderpriſing it*] *vnderprizing it*
Q₁. *vnderpryſing it* Q₂. *underpriſing*
F₃F₄.
142. pleaſd] Q₂Q₃. pleas'd Q₁. pleaſed
Ff.

146. [Kissing her. Rowe.   After line
147, Coll. Wh. i.
151. *ſtill...a*] *gazing still in* Pope+.
152. *peales*] *pearles* Q₁.

---

have proceeded from any writer who had a passable command of language. Fortunately
there is a word used by Shakespeare elsewhere, which so exactly expresses what he evidently meant to say here, that I have little doubt it was the epithet which 'unfurnished'
has 'pushed from its stool.' It is *unfellowed*. If I mistake not, to name this emendation is to ensure its reception.

133. **how**] ABBOTT, § 46, gives the following additional instances of the use of
'how' for *as :*— *V. and A.* 815; *Ib.* 67; similarly, Gascoigne (Mätzner) has: '*How*
many men, *so* many minds.'

137. **continent**] DYCE: That which contains anything.

147. **note**] HALLIWELL: This seems to be an allusion to a bill or note for money
or anything lent, which is both given and received, or, possibly, to an ordinary receipt.
The metaphor is also carried out afterwards, '—until confirm'd, sign'd, ratified by you.'
CLARENDON: To give a kiss and receive the lady.

151. Pope's reading certainly gives a smoother rhythm to this line, and the temptation is strong to adopt it. As the line now stands there seems no way but to make
'spirit' a monosyllable : 'Gíddy in spirít | still gáz | ing ín | a doúbt;' where, in addi-
tion, the accen̄ falling on *in* is objectionable.—ED.

So thrice faire Lady ſtand I euen ſo,   153
As doubtfull whether what I ſee be true,
Vntill confirm'd, ſign'd, ratified by you.   155
   Por.   You ſee my Lord *Baſſiano* where I ſtand,
Such as I am ; though for my ſelfe alone
I would not be ambitious in my wiſh,
To wiſh my ſelfe much better, yet for you,
I would be trebled twenty times my ſelfe,   160
A thouſand times more faire, ten thouſand times
More rich, that onely to ſtand high in your account,
I might in vertues, beauties, liuings, friends,
Exceed account : but the full ſumme of me
Is ſum of nothing : which to terme in groſſe,   165

---

156. *ſee my*] F₂F₃. *ſee, my* F₄, Rowe,
Pope, Han. Knt. *ſee me* Qq et cet.
   Baſſiano] F₂.
   162. *More rich,*] Separate line, Mal.
Steev. Knt, Dyce i, Cam. Glo. Clarke,
Cla. Wh. ii. Closing line 161, Coll. Sing.
Hal. Sta. Wh. i, Ktly, Del. Rlfe, Huds.
   onely] Om. Ff, Rowe+, Cap.

165. *ſum of nothing :*] Ff. (*ſumme* F₃),
Rowe, Pope, Han. Knt, Coll. Sing. Dyce,
Sta. Wh. Ktly, Clarke, Del. Rlfe. *ſumme
of ſomething ;* Q₁Q₃. *ſume of ſomething :*
Q₂. *ſum of ſomething,* Theob. Warb. Johns.
Cap. Steev. Mal. Rann, Hal. Cam. Glo.
sum of—something, Cla. *sum of—something ;* Huds.
   terme] *ſum* Daniel.

---

156. **my**] Assuredly the Qq are right here.—Ed.

162. **More rich**] To avoid the Alexandrine which those two syllables, as the line stands, render inevitable, Malone printed them in a line by themselves, and he has a highly respectable following.   Collier accepts an Alexandrine, but prefers to inflict the black disgrace on line 161 ; he therefore transferred 'More rich' to the end of that line, whereby he not only gained in smoothness, but by avoiding an awkward cæsura after 'to,' he gives Abbott (§ 501) the chance to say that the line, 161, thus amended, is only an 'apparent Alexandrine' after all, and to call it 'a trimeter couplet.'—Ed.

163. **liuings**] Dyce : Possessions, fortune.   [An ecclesiastical meaning of this word is not as likely to occur to us Americans as to an Englishman.—Ed.]

165. **sum of nothing**] Warburton : We should read '*some* of something,' i. e. only a piece, or part of an imperfect account ; which she explains in the following line. Heath : The common reading is, 'sum of something.'   The meaning, I apprehend, is this : The full sum of me is (to express myself in gross) the sum of what may be expected to be found in an unlessoned girl.   Capell : After telling us, in expressions of great warmth, what she *would* be if wishes could make her such, and on what account she would be, she descends with exquisite modesty to what she *is ;* and in these expressions asserts a title to 'something,' or to be something, was any estimate made of her ; and, that even this may not appear too much, the *something* which she pretends to is defin'd and ascertain'd by her presently in terms of the greatest sweetness. Steevens : The purport of the text [of the Qq] seems to be this : —the full sum of me—Is sum of something ;' i. e. is not entirely ideal, but amounts to as much as can be found in—'an unlesson'd girl,' &c.   Monck Mason : I prefer the Folo, as it is

Is an vnleſſoned girle, vnſchool'd, vnpractiz'd,   166
Happy in this, ſhe is not yet ſo old
But ſhe may learne : happier then this,   168

166. *vnleſſoned*] *vnleſſon'd* Q₁Q₃. *vn-*
leſſond Q₂.
168. *happier then this*] Qq. *happier*
then in this Ff, Rowe, Coll. iii. *more*

happy then in this Pope+. *happier than*
this in that Cap. Ec. *then happier in this*
Dyce iii, Huds. *happier than this* Johns.
et cet.

Portia's intention in this speech to undervalue herself. HALLIWELL: The reading
of the Folio appears, at first view, to be the most obvious; but having regard to the
author's fondness for a jingle, and to the circumstance that 'nothing' will scarcely
suit the passage immediately following it, the other and older lection may be preferred.
The sum (or whole) of me is sum (or whole) of something, which, to term in gross,
&c. There should only be a comma after *something*. WHITE: Portia enumerates, so
modestly and yet with dignity and self-respect, traits and conditions all of which are
negative. She is an *un*lesson'd girl, *un*school'd, *un*practis'd, *not* yet so old but she
may learn, *not* bred so dull but she *may* learn, mistress of herself and her belongings
before, ' but now this house, these servants, and this same myself, are yours, my lord.'
Here, indeed, is sum of nothing; but how sum of something? But even were not
the first expression so appropriate, and the second so inappropriate, were their fitness
for the context equal, the appearance of one in forty Quartos would, as against the
appearance of the other in the one authentic Folio, only show that an error, or a passage
in an unrevised form had been repeated forty times. There must be some other reason
for deviating from the authorized text than the mere preference of any editor, or the
occurrence of a variation in other editions. CLARENDON: We have retained the Qq
reading, introducing a dash after 'of.' We understand Portia to hesitate for a word
which shall describe herself appropriately. The Folio reading, 'nothing, which to
term in gross,' &c., would be a singular anti-climax if it were not a direct self-contradiction. HUDSON (ed. iii): The dash before *something* is to indicate that the fair
speaker hesitates for a term with which to describe herself modestly, yet without any
affectation of modesty. ROLFE: The Folio reading is more in keeping with the negative characteristics which follow than the Qq reading. KNIGHT, SINGER, COLLIER,
and STAUNTON all agree substantially with Monck Mason. [Whether we read 'something' or 'nothing,' I think a dash should precede it. Then the choice of the word
will depend on the light in which we here regard Portia. If she is speaking with
deliberation and choosing her words, she probably said 'sum of—something,' which
clearly and rationally any *sum* whatever must imply. Nor does the expression lack
a certain archness in keeping with the occasion. But if, on the other hand, we see
Portia, brimming over with joy, and in wild, careless, exuberant exaggeration, wishing herself twenty times trebled, and a thousand times fairer, and ten thousand times
richer, and in virtues, beauties, livings, friends beyond all calculation, then, I think, we
shall know of a surety that in such a mood Portia would exclaim that the full sum of
her was the 'sum of—nothing.'—ED.]

165. which] ECCLES: Perhaps Shakespeare here, as elsewhere, considered 'which'
both as nominative and accusative.

168, 169. But] ABBOTT, § 127: Sometimes *but* follows an adjective qualified by
the negative with *so*, as in the present two instances. So Chaucer: 'I *nam but* dede,
—*Knights' Tale*, where, omitting the negative *n*, we should say, 'I am *but* dead.'

Shee is not bred fo dull but fhe can learne;
Happieft of all, is that her gentle fpirit   170
Commits it felfe to yours to be directed,
As from her Lord, her Gouernour, her King.
My felfe, and what is mine, to you and yours   173

169. *bred*] *bread* F_3.   Dyce iii, Rlfe, Huds.
170. *is*] *in* Coll. ii, iii (MS), Wh. i,   172. *King*.] *King*, Rowe.

168. **happier then this**] CAPELL pronounces his emendation ('happier than this
in that') 'necessary for sense as for measure;' to which CLARENDON assents. MA-
LONE tried to mend the metre in the line as it stands, by saying that 'learn' is here a
dissyllable. Whereupon STEEVENS: Till the reader has reconciled his ear to the dis-
syllabical pronunciation of 'learn,' I beg his acceptance of *and*, a harmless monosyllable which I have ventured to introduce for the sake of obvious metre. [To me it
seems clear that we have here, in reality, but one and the same reading in all the Ff
and Qq. The 'in' of $F_2F_3F_4$ is present to the ear in F_1 in the final *n* sound of 'then,'
an absorption to which the Elizabethan ear was more accustomed than ours, so accustomed, indeed, that the compositors of the Qq and F_1 omitted the *in* altogether. If this
be so, the full text of the later Ff supplies all that Capell found 'necessary for sense as
for measure,' without his emendation, which is to my ear harsh.—ED.]

170. **is**] COLLIER (ed. ii): The emendation *in* of the (MS) is comparatively trifling,
but happy and elegant. Portia means that she is happiest of all, in as much as her gen
tle spirit will in future be directed by Bassanio. WHITE (ed. i): There can be no
reasonable doubt [of the correctness of Collier's (MS) emendation]. Portia first says
that she is 'happy *in* this, she is not yet so old,' &c., which is equivalent to 'happy in
that she is not yet so old,' &c. Next, when speaking in the comparative, she uses a
similar ellipsis of 'she is not bred' for '*in that* she is not bred.' But in the last clause
no such ellipsis can be supposed; and yet the conditional form 'in that' is required by
the structure of the sentence and the sequence of the thoughts; and it is restored to
the text by the correction of a highly probable typographical mistake of a single letter.
CLARENDON supports the QqFf by making 'Happiest' neuter: 'The happiest thing
of all is,' &c.; and ABBOTT, § 404, explains the old text by supposing an ellipsis:
'Happiest of all is (*it* or *this*)' &c. [But both of these methods are to me unsatisfactory; a shifting of the construction is always more or less awkward, and to be avoided;
here it is needless when we have as trifling a change as is offered by Collier's (MS).—
ED.]

172. WEISS (p. 322): Does this language seem to you slavish and old-fashioned?
And do you, madam, declare that you never saw the man yet for whom you would so
demean yourself? Then I shall know that just at present you are not in love. Perhaps you never have been; for it is the perfect language of a woman's first hours which
follow love's declaration, when she feels that her life and soul are to be made complete
by marriage. She storms herself with questions never before suggested. What could
he see in her? What has she got to repay this exquisite flattery, this shuddering
delight at being summoned out of millions of her sex? The first impulse is to spill
the soul in a libation to the deity of the hour; let the whole of it drench my lover; let
me not dare to reserve a portion to teach me a first selfish lesson. All, all is yours, my
king! Come, drain it at the chalice of my lips!

Is now conuerted.   But now I was the Lord
Of this faire manfion, mafter of my feruants,   175
Queene ore my felfe : and euen now, but now,
This houfe, thefe feruants, and this fame my felfe
Are yours, my Lord, I giue them with this ring,
Which when you part from, loofe, or giue away,
Let it prefage the ruine of your loue,   180
And be my vantage to exclaime on you.
    Baff.   Maddam, you haue bereft me of all words,
Onely my bloud fpeakes to you in my vaines,
And there is fuch confufion in my powers,
As after fome oration fairely fpoke   185
By a beloued Prince, there doth appeare
Among the buzzing pleafed multitude,
Where euery fomething being blent together,   188

174. *But now I*] *I but now* Pope, Han.   *even now ;* Rowe.
   the Lord] *the Lady* Rowe.   *Lady*   178. *Lord*] *Lords* Q$_2$.
Pope, Han.   179. *loofe*] *lofe* Q$_1$.
175. *mafter*] *mistress* Rowe, Pope,   182. *Maddam*] *Madame* Q$_1$.   *Madam*
Han.   Q$_3$F$_3$F$_4$.
176. *felfe : and euen now,*] *self, and*   183. *vaines*] Q$_2$.   *veines* Q$_1$.

174. **conuerted**] ABBOTT, § 472: *Ed* following *d* or *t* is often not written (this
elision is very old), and when written, often not pronounced.   [An additional illustration of that absorption by the ear of similar final sounds of which we have just had
an example in line 168.   See also 'riveted,' V, i, 188, and Shakespeare *passim.*—ED.]

174, 175. **Lord . . . master**] CAPELL: [Rowe's change] is injurious; the former
of these terms seeming to have been chosen intentionally to express the greater
dominion.   ECCLES: Portia's words will have a more natural effect if stress be laid
upon the pronoun : 'but now *I* was the lord,' &c.

176. **euen now**] ABBOTT, § 38: '*Even* now,' with us, is applied to an action that
has been going on for some long time and *still* continues, the emphasis being laid on
'now.'   In Shakespeare the emphasis is often to be laid on 'even,' and '*even* now'
means '*exactly* or *only* now,' i. e. 'scarcely longer ago than the present :' hence '*but*
now.'   Often 'but *even* now' is used in this sense: *Mer. of Ven.* I, i, 40.   On the
other hand, both '*even* now' and '*but* now' can signify 'just at this moment,' as in
the present instance.   See also V, i, 296.

181. **vantage**] DYCE: Opportunity.   CLARENDON: The position of one who is
'master of the situation.'

183. **Onely**] ABBOTT, § 420, refers to this as an instance of the transposition of the
adverb.   But I doubt if it be an adverb here.   Is it not an adjective?   Bassanio's
tongue is silent; only his blood, his blood alone, in his happy blushes, can speak, &c.
It is, perhaps, not unworthy of note, that the spelling, almost invariable, of this word,
'n the Folio, reflects the probable Shakespearian pronunciation of *one*, i. e. like the
present *own.*—ED.

185. **spoke**] See ABBOTT, § 343, for instances of curtailed forms of past participles.

Turnes to a wilde of nothing, faue of ioy
Expreſt, and not expreſt : but when this ring   190
Parts from this finger, then parts life from hence,
O then be bold to ſay *Baſſanio*'s dead.
   Ner.   My Lord and Lady, it is now our time
That haue ſtood by and ſeene our wiſhes proſper,
To cry good ioy, good ioy my Lord and Lady.   195
   Gra.   My Lord *Baſſanio,* and my gentle Lady,
I wiſh you all the ioy that you can wiſh :
For I am ſure you can wiſh none from me :   198

---

189. *wilde*] *void* Coll. conj.   192. Baſſanio's] Baſſanio *is* Q₁.
192. O] *ô* Q₂.

---

194. **our**] ALLEN: I conjectured *your*,—a very easy and unobjectionable change, considering that *our* and *your* are so frequently interchanged in Shakespeare and his fellow-dramatists (cf. Walker, *Crit.* ii, 7), and felt *very* confident I was right, at first, because I referred 'our' to the wiſhes of Nerissa and Gratiano for their *own* connection ; and that would give a sense too grossly selfish to be tolerated,—i. e. we wish you joy, *because* your success makes *us* successful. Whereas, *your* indicates that the *main* interest (in the mind even of Nerissa and Gratiano) lay in the wishes and hopes of Portia and Bassanio ; that is, it is now time that *we,* who have seen your hopes realized, should follow up your mutual congratulations (for which we have been giving you time) with *our* wishing of joy. For 'our' is certainly emphatic ; and the emphasis appears to indicate that *we* are now to do what *you* have been doing before. But it *now* occurs to me, that Nerissa *may* be understood to have a less selfish,—in fact, a very generous and delicate—sentiment in her mind, and that 'our' is the happiest expression of it, viz. that she and Gratiano felt Portia and Bassanio's cause to be their own, (out of affection and not out of self-interest,) and that to indicate such unselfish interest on their part they said : We have stood by and seen our wishes prosper. The objection to this last interpretation (apparently happy as it may be) is, that it makes the subordinates too patronizing. It would do very well in the case of parents, especially where the parents had been contriving a match,—but not so well in that of even a lady in a rank so far inferior to that of the noble and world-renowned heiress. I am still inclined, therefore, to adhere to my emendation. [To my thinking, the text needs no change. The unselfish sense in which Prof. Allen says 'our' *may* be interpreted, is the unselfish sense in which I think it must be interpreted, if we catch here an echo of that heartsome, fervent wish of Nerissa with which the Second Act closed : 'Bassanio, lord Love, if thy will it be !'—ED.]

198. **from**] HANMER: That is, distinct from me and my wishes. CAPELL: That is, you can wish for nothing, the obtaining of which would rob me of joy. JOHNSON: That is, none *away from* me ; none that I shall lose, if you gain it. STAUNTON: Rather, it means : none beyond what I wish you. ABBOTT, § 158: That is, none differently *from* me ; none which I do not wish you. This is probably the correct interpretation. CLARENDON: Being all-sufficient to each other, you cannot wish to deprive me of any joy to add to your own. ROLFE: That is, none *away* from me, ſince you have enough yourselves.

And when your Honours meane to folemnize
The bargaine of your faith : I doe befeech you   200
Euen at that time I may be married too.
   Baff.   With all my heart, fo thou canft get a wife.
   Gra.   I thanke your Lordfhip, you gaue got me one.
My eyes my Lord can looke as fwift as yours :
You faw the miftres, I beheld the maid :   205
You lou'd, I lou'd for intermiffion,
No more pertaines to me my Lord then you ;
Your fortune ftood vpon the caskets there,
And fo did mine too, as the matter falls :
For wooing heere vntill I fwet againe,   210
And fwearing till my very rough was dry

---

201. *too.*] *to.* Qq.
203. *gaue*] *haue* Qq Ff.
206. *lou'd for intermiffion,*] Q₁Q₂F₂F₃. *lov'd for intermiffion.* Q₃F₄, Rowe, Pope, Cam. Glo. Wh. ii. *lov'd for intermission;* Sta. *loved, for intermission* Cla. *lov'd: for intermission* Theob. et cet.
208. *caskets*] *Casket* Q₁Q₃, Pope+,

Cam. Glo. Ktly, Cla. Wh. ii.
209. *too,*] *to* Q₂Q₃.
210. *heere*] *heete* F₂. *heat* F₃F₄. *Herd* Rowe i. *Her* Rowe ii. *here* Pope et seq. *fwet*] *fweat* F₃F₄.
211. *rough*] Q₂Ff. *roofe* Q₁. *tongue* Coll. (MS).

---

202. **so**] ABBOTT, § 133 : 'So' is used with the future and the subjunctive to denote *provided that.* See also line 217, *post.*

205. **maid :**] WHITE : Nerissa was no servant-maid, according to modern notions, but an attendant friend, as well born and bred, perhaps, though not as wealthy, as Portia herself. Such a relation was common of old. It existed between Gratiano and Bassanio, whose intercourse is that of equals, and the former of whom is evidently a gentleman in every sense of the word. Bassanio says to him and to Nerissa : 'Our feast shall be *much honour'd* in your marriage.' [See HUNTER on The Actors' Names, *ante*, p. xii.]

206. **intermission**] THEOBALD : This passage has been nonsensically pointed thro' all the Editions. If *loving for intermission* can be expounded into any sense, I confess I as yet am ignorant, and shall be glad to be instructed in it. But till then I must beg leave to think the sentence ought to be thus regulated : 'You lov'd, I lov'd :—For Intermission No more pertains,' &c., i. e. standing idle ; a Pause, or Discontinuance of Action. And such is the signification of *intermissio* amongst the Latines. STAUNTON [see Text. Notes] : If 'intermission' is not used, as I think it probably is, for *pastime,* Gratiano may mean 'for *fear of* intermission,' i. e. to avoid delay or loss of time. [In spite of Staunton's good plea for the old text, I cannot but think that Theobald's punctuation and interpretation are right.—ED.]

207. **No more, &c.**] STAUNTON : I owe my wife as much to you as to my own efforts. [To understand this we must bear in mind Staunton's punctuation in the preceding line : 'You lov'd, I lov'd for intermission ;']

210. **heere**] Note in Text. Notes the evolution of *here* into *heat.*—ED.

210. **swet**] For the form, see ABBOTT, § 341.

211. **rough**] HALLIWELL : If the ordinary reading be incorrect, perhaps we may

With oathes of loue, at laſt, if promiſe laſt,   212
I got a promiſe of this faire one heere
To haue her loue : prouided that your fortune
Atchieu'd her miſtreſſe.   215

   Por.   Is this true *Nerriſſa?*

   Ner.   Madam it is ſo, ſo you ſtand pleas'd withall.

   Baſſ.   And doe you *Gratiano* meane good faith?

   Gra.   Yes faith my Lord.

   Baſſ.   Our feaſt ſhall be much honored in your mar-   220
riage.

   Gra.   Weele play with them the firſt boy for a thouſand ducats.

   Ner.   What and ſtake downe?

   Gra.   No, we ſhal nere win at that ſport, and ſtake   225
downe.
But who comes heere? *Lorenzo* and his Infidell?
What and my old Venetian friend *Salerio?*   228

---

217. *is ſo, ſo*] Ff, Rowe. *is, ſo* Qq,
Pope et seq.
224–226. In sens. obsc.

228, 229, 238. Salerio] Qq Ff. Salanio
Rowe+. Solanio Knt, Hal. Dyce, Sta.
Clarke, Del. Huds. Coll. iii.

---

substitute *mouth.* [Let the better spelling of Q₁ be noted in its favour. Is it not
strange that this word has not as yet attracted that winsome band of readers who say
(as Grant White has somewhere said that they say), 'Come, let's sit down and amend
Shakespeare'? Halliwell's suggestion is good, but the list of words which can be
substituted for 'rough' is not exhausted ; no pent-up Quarto need contract our powers,
the whole boundless Dictionary is ours.—ED.]

   220. shall] This means more, I think, than the mere future.—ED.

   227. Infidell] THEOBALD (Nichols's *Illust.* ii, 310): How comes it to pass, that
there is no more notice taken of Jessica, and that Bassanio and Portia take no notice
of her at all? Was she still in the habit of a boy, and appeared as Lorenzo's page?
[Theobald forgets Jessica's junketings at Genoa.—ED.] That there might be no occasion of taking notice of her, and hearing her story, which could not be so properly done
if Bassanio [*sic*] had a letter to deliver of such consequence, and that required so much
haste ; and much less, if Bassanio had read it. But then again, if she was in man's
cloaths, how comes Gratiano to say to Nerissa—Bid her welcome, without intimating
at least that she was a woman in man's apparel? And again is it not a little odd that
Jessica [afterwards] mixes herself in discourse about the Jew her father's desire of
revenge on Antonio, and still not one civil word is addressed to her by Bassanio or
Portia? [See Theobald's note, line 250.]

   228. Salerio] The question here is whether this Salerio represents a new character
or is merely the compositor's sophistication of Solanio or Salarino. Rowe and his followers treated it apparently as a mere misprint, and silently changed it to Salanio.
Capell retains it, but believes it to be an abbreviation for Salerino, which, in the Stage·

Enter Lorenzo, Ieſſica, and Salerio.

Baſ. *Lorenzo* and *Salerio,* welcome hether,   230
If that the youth of my new intereſt heere
Haue power to bid you welcome : by your leaue   232

Scene III. Pope +.   *Salerio* ? from Venice. Q$_3$.   Enter...Sale-
229. Enter...Salerio.] Enter...Salerio   rino. Cap.
a meſſenger from Venice Q$_1$Q$_2$. Enter...   230. *hether*] Q$_2$.   *hither* Q$_1$ et cet.

---

direction, he prints in full.   Steevens and his followers not only retain it in the text,
but, induced by the Stage-direction in the Qq, add it as a distinct character to the Dramatis Personæ, in addition to Salanio and Salarino.   Knight changed it to Solanio.
'Gratiano,' he says, 'calls this Salerio "my old Venetian friend;" and there is no reason whatever for not receiving the name as a misprint of Solanio or Salanio.'   'It
appears to us,' Knight continues, 'not only that there is no necessity for introducing a
new character, Salerio, but that the dramatic propriety is violated by this introduction.
In the First Scene of this Act the servant of Antonio thus addresses Solanio and Salarino : "Gentlemen, my master Antonio is at his house, and desires to speak with you
both."   To the unfortunate Antonio, then, these friends repair.   What can be more
natural than that, after the conference, the one should be dispatched to Bassanio, and
the other remain with him, whose "creditors grow cruel"?   We accordingly find in the
Third Scene of this Act that one of them accompanies Antonio when he is in custody
of the gaoler.   In the confusion in which the names are printed, it is difficult to say
which goes to Belmont and which remains at Venice.   We have determined the matter by the metre of this line, and of the subsequent lines in which the name is mentioned.'   Dyce agrees with Knight in regarding 'Salerio' as a decided error,—and in
thinking it altogether unlikely that Shakespeare would, without necessity and in violation of dramatic propriety, introduce a new character, 'Salerio,' in addition to Solanio
and Salarino.   'The name of the friend who remains at Venice is rightly given in Q$_1$,
Salarino;' see III, iii, 1.   The Cambridge Editors follow Steevens and add 'Salerio'
to the Dramatis Personæ.   To Knight's and Dyce's objection that the introduction of
this new character would be in violation of dramatic propriety, they urge that : 'tried
by this standard Shakespeare's violations [where?—ED.] of dramatic propriety are
frequent indeed, and it is no part of an Editor's duty to correct them.'   [Writing for a
company of actors so few in number that an attendant cannot be spared for the task,
but a Prince of Denmark must himself drag a dead body off the stage, it does not seem
likely that a prudent playwright (whatever else he might have been) would, without
excellent reason, add to the number of the Dramatis Personæ.   If, however, a new
character must be introduced late in the play, that playwright is, indeed, poverty-
stricken in nomenclature who to avoid confusion can think of no name sharply different from any with which the audience is already familiar.   Furthermore, granting
that a new character is introduced here, at this late day, when the play is mcre than
half over, does it not add to the confusion, or to the patchiness, to term him 'an old
friend'?   Wherefore, in view of all the circumstances, I agree with Rowe and Capell
in the supposition that we have here either *Solanio* or *Salarino,* more likely the former,
and for the reason given by Dyce.—ED.]

231. If that] For *that* as a conjunctional affix, see ABBOTT, § 287.

I bid my verie friends and Countrimen   233
Sweet *Portia* welcome.

    Por.   So do I my Lord, they are intirely welcome.   235

    Lor.   I thanke your honor ; for my part my Lord,
My purpoſe was not to haue ſeene you heere,
But meeting with *Salerio* by the way,
He did intreate mee paſt all ſaying nay
To come with him along.   240

    Sal.   I did my Lord,
And I haue reaſon for it, Signior *Anthonio*
Commends him to you.

    Baſſ.   Ere I ope his Letter
I pray you tell me how my good friend doth.   245

    Sal.   Not ſicke my Lord, vnleſſe it be in minde,
Nor wel, vnleſſe in minde : his Letter there
Wil ſhew you his eſtate.

                  Opens the Letter.

    Gra.   *Nerriſſa*, cheere yond ſtranger, bid her welcom.   250

---

233. *verie*] Om. Q$_3$.

235. *they … welcome*] Separate line,
Cap. et seq.

    intirely] *entirely* Q$_1$.

242. *I haue*] *haue* Ff.

    for it] *for't* Pope+, Dyce iii,
Huds.

243. [Gives Bassanio a letter. Theob.

244. *his*] *this* F$_3$F$_4$, Rowe, Coll. ii.

248. Opens…] He opens… Q$_1$.   open
… Q$_2$Q$_3$.   Bassanio opens… Rowe.

250, 257. *yond*] Q$_2$Ff.   *yon* Q$_1$, Knt,
Hal. Sta. Cam.   *yon'* Cap. Steev. Mal.

---

233. **verie**] BIBLE WORD-BOOK : In the phrases ' very and eternal God ;' ' very God
of very God ;' ' art thou my very son Esau ?' *very* has its original sense of *true ;* from
French *vrai*, Old French *verai*, which again are referred by Diez to the Lat. *veracus*,
not *verax*.

237. **to haue seene**] See ABBOTT, § 360, for other examples of the Complete
Present Infinitive.

240. **along**] See ABBOTT, § 30.

247. **vnlesse in minde**] ECCLES : Unless he is comforted and supported by forti-
tude.

248. **estate**] BIBLE WORD-BOOK : This word in the Bible and Prayer-book, and in
old writers generally, is not restricted to the meaning now usually put upon it, but has
the same breadth of signification which is still given to the word *state*. Queen Elizabeth, in a letter to Sir Thomas Heneage (*Leycester Corr.* p. 241), speaks of a ' counsell
of *estate* ;' and Lord Bacon constantly uses this form of the word in the sense in which
it is used in the Collect for Good Friday, ' for all *estates* of men.' Latimer defines as
part of the duty of a king, ' To see to all *estates* ; to provide for the poor ; to see victuals
good cheap.'—*Serm.* p. 215.

249. **Opens, &c.**] See Appendix, ' The Text,' p. 275.

250. THEOBALD : The Poet has shewn a singular art here in his conduct with rela-
  11

Your hand *Salerio*, what's the newes from Venice?   251
How doth that royal Merchant good *Anthonio*;
I know he vvil be glad of our fucceffe,
We are the *Iafons*, we haue won the fleece.

     Sal. I would you had vvon the fleece that hee hath   255
loft.

     Por. There are fome fhrewd contents in yond fame
Paper,   258

---

255. *I would*] *Would* Pope+, Huds.   257. *fhrewd*] *fhrowd* Q₂, Cap.
' Would Steev. '93, Var. Knt, Sing.

---

tion to Jessica. As the audience were already apprized of her story, the opening it
here to Portia would have been a superfluous repetition. Nor could it be done properly while a letter of such haste and consequence was to be delivered, and on which
the main action of the play depended. Jessica is, therefore, artfully complimented in
dumb shew; and no speech made to her, because the Scene is drawn out to a great
length by more important business. [Thus Theobald has answered his own questions
at line 227.]

     252. **royal Merchant**] WARBURTON: In the beginning of the 13th Century the
Venetians gave liberty to any subject of the Republic, who would fit out vessels, to
make themselves masters of the isles of the Archipelago, and other maritime places;
and to enjoy their conquests in sovereignty; only doing homage to the Republic for
their several principalities. By virtue of this license, the Sanudos, the Justiniani, the
Grimaldi, the Summaripos, and others, all Venetian merchants, erected principalities in
several places of the Archipelago (which their descendants enjoyed for many generations), and became thereby truly and properly *royal merchants.* Which, indeed, was
the title generally given them all over Europe. JOHNSON: This epithet was, in our
poet's time, more striking and better understood, because Gresham was then commonly
dignified with the title of the *royal merchant.* HUNTER (*New Illust.* i, 308): Shakespeare did not use this term without having an eye to the peculiar force of the expression. This is remarked by Warburton, who does not appear to have caught its precise
effect. A 'royal merchant' in the Middle Ages was a merchant who transacted business for a sovereign of the time. Thus King John calls Brand de Doway, 'homo noster et dominicus mercator noster.' See a protection granted to him, *Rotuli Selecti*
1834, p. 23.

     254. **Iasons**] DOUCE (i, 264): The meaning is, Antonio, with his *argosie*, is not
the successful Jason; we are the persons who have won the fleece.

     255. I would | you'd won | the fleece, | &c.

     255. **fleece**] DANIEL (p. 37): Salerio brings the news that all Antonio's ships have
been lost, and here, I believe, puns on the words *fleece* and *fleets.* Qy. print *fleets,* in
future, in Salerio's speech?

     257. **shrewd**] SKEAT (*Dict.* s. v.): Malicious, wicked; cunning, acute. The older
sense is malicious, mischievous, scolding or shrew-like, as in *Mid. N. D.* III, ii, 323.
Middle English, *schrewed, shrewed,* accursed, depraved, wicked; 'schrewed folk,' i. e.
wicked people, Chaucer. *Schrewed* is, literally, 'accursed,' past participle of *schrewen,*
to curse, beshrew; and the verb is formed from the Middle English adjective *schrewe,*
evil, malicious

That ſteales the colour from *Baſſianos* cheeke,

Some deere friend dead, elſe nothing in the world　　260

Could turne ſo much the conſtitution

Of any conſtant man.　What, worſe and worſe?

With leaue *Baſſanio* I am halfe your ſelfe,

And I muſt freely haue the halfe of any thing

That this ſame paper brings you.　　265

　　Baſſ.　O ſweet *Portia*,

Heere are a few of the vnpleaſant'ſt words

That euer blotted paper.　Gentle Ladie

When I did firſt impart my loue to you,

I freely told you all the wealth I had　　270

Ran in my vaines : I was a Gentleman,

And then I told you true : and yet deere Ladie,

Rating my ſelfe at nothing, you ſhall ſee

How much I was a Braggart, when I told you

My ſtate was nothing, I ſhould then haue told you　　275

That I vvas worſe then nothing : for indeede

I haue ingag'd my ſelfe to a deere friend,

Ingag'd my friend to his meere enemie　　278

---

259. *ſteales*] Qq Ff, Rowe, Cap. Steev. '85, Sta. Cam. Glo. Rlfe, Cla. Wh. ii. *steal* Pope et cet.

　　Baſſianos] F₂.

264. *I muſt freely*] *muſt freely* Ff, Rowe. *I muſt* Q₃, Pope +, Dyce iii, Huds.

268, &c. *Ladie*] *Lady* Qq Ff.

271. *vaines : ... Gentleman,*] *veins. ... gentleman,* Rowe. *veins, ...gentleman ;* Pope et seq.

　　vaines] Q₂. *veines* Q₁ et cet.

274. *Braggart*] *beggar* F₄.

275. *haue*] *baue* F₃.

277. *haue*] *had* Allen.

---

262. **constant**] DOUCE : Grave.　CLARENDON : Steady, even-minded, self-possessed.　CRAIK (*Jul. Cæs.* II, iv) : Firm, resolute.

264. As this line stands here in the Folio, it contains unquestionably, to the eye cf flesh, twelve syllables, and is therefore (I turn pale while I write it) an Alexandrine. Pope, believing that there was no way but this, cut out 'freely' and breathed so afterwards, let us hope.　Dyce applauded the deed, and was upheld by Lettsom, who observed to him that 'freely' had 'crept in here from the fifth line below,'—a crablike feat which always fills me with amaze.　On the other hand, instructed by Abbott, § 494, I can only say,—I would request you,—or I would entreat you,—not to fear, not to tremble; my life for yours.　If you think this is a real Alexandrine, it were pity of my life; no, it is no such thing; it is only an 'apparent Alexandrine;' it is really a respectable Iambic pentameter, like all the rest, only, 'the last foot contains, instead of one extra syllable, two extra syllables, one of which is slurred.　And I′ | must freé | ly háve | the hálf | of *ánything.*'—ED.

267. **vnpleaſant'ſt**] For similar instances of this contraction, see ABBOTT, § 473.

278. **meere**] Unqualified.　See Shakespeare *passim.*

To feede my meanes.   Heere is a Letter Ladie,
The paper as the bodie of my friend,   280
And euerie word in it a gaping wound
Iffuing life blood.   But is it true *Salerio*,
Hath all his ventures faild, what not one hit,
From Tripolis, from Mexico and England,
From Lisbon, Barbary, and India,   285
And not one veffell fcape the dreadfull touch
Of Merchant-marring rocks?
   Sal.   Not one my Lord.
Befides, it fhould appeare, that if he had   289

279. *Heere is*] *Heer 's* Q₁.
280. *as*] *is* Pope, Han.
282. *life blood*] *life-blood* Rowe.
283. *Hath*] *Have* Rowe et seq.

283. *what*] *what*, Q₁F₄.
284. *and*] *from* Rowe+.
286. *And*] *Has* Eccles conj.
      fcape] *'scaped* Pope+, Ec.

---

280. as] Walker (*Crit.* iii, 55), not knowing that he was anticipated by Pope, suggested *is*. But Dyce (ed. iii) says that he prefers the old reading, and I think he speaks for all of us. 'The paper [being] as the body,' &c., is one of Allen's adversaria.—Ed.

282. **Issuing**] CLARENDON: The verb is generally neuter, except in the phrases, 'to issue an edict,' 'issue a proclamation.'

284. **Mexico**] TH. ELZE (*Sh. Jahrbuch*, xiv, 178), after a thorough and searching examination of this play for the purpose of detecting in it violations of local manners and customs, discovers barely three or four. The first is the reason assigned for Bassanio's hasty departure at nine in the evening (II, vi, 73), because 'the wind is come about.' 'This reason is not applicable,' says Elze, 'to a passage through the lagoon to the mouth of the Brenta; it applies only to a seacoast.' Next, the allusion to Mexico here and at I, iii, 20, is English, not Venetian. 'The Republic never had any direct communication with Mexico, nor even with America.' Lastly, the organization of the Court in the Trial Scene is not exactly correct. See Elze's note, IV, i, 1, and also *Oth.* I, ii, 51. 'These,' he says in conclusion, 'are all the instances which I have been able to find in the *Merchant of Venice* and in *Othello* that deviate from local truth. Little enough, indeed! And when we consider that even historians, and travellers like Tom Coryat, rarely are free from far worse errors of this kind, it is astounding that the Poet, untrammelled by restrictions laid on writers of travels, has not often offended against reality, but has been so exactly true to it. Shakespeare's knowledge of Venice and of Padua seems inconceivable, his fidelity in depicting them, marvellous; assuredly it may be said that the *Merchant of Venice* and the First Act of *Othello* have not merely Venice for their background, but are actually played in the very city.'

286. **scape**] ROLFE: Not to be printed ''scape.' It is found in prose.

288. ECCLES: The supposed universality of Anthonio's losses is not a little injurious to the probability of the fable.

289. **should**] It is not easy to define this 'should;' as the past tense of *shall* there seems to be somewhat too much compulsion in it; Abbott, § 324, suggests a verb *shall*, like the German *sollen*, which means *is to*, not quite *ought*. Perhaps it is of this *shall*

The prefent money to difcharge the Iew,   290
He would not take it : neuer did I know
A creature that did beare the fhape of man
So keene and greedy to confound a man.
He plyes the Duke at morning and at night,
And doth impeach the freedome of the ftate   295
If they deny him iuftice.   Twenty Merchants,
The Duke himfelfe, and the Magnificoes
Of greateft port haue all perfwaded with him,
But none can driue him from the enuious plea
Of forfeiture, of iuftice, and his bond.   300
    Ieffi.   When I was with him, I haue heard him fweare
To *Tuball* and to *Chus*, his Countri-men,   302

---

300. *forfeiture, of*] *forfeiture of* F_3 302. *Countri-men*] F_1F_2. *Country-men*
F_4. Q_1Q_2. *countrey-men* Q_3. *countrimen* F_3.
   301. *heard him*] *heard hiw* Q_3.   *countrymen* F_4.

---

that 'should' is here the past tense.   Rolfe refers to Abbott, § 322, where instances
are given of 'should' as the past tense of the usual *shall;* he may be right.   The
Elizabethan use of *should* is to me always difficult to analyze.   Compare Stephano's
question about Caliban : 'Where the devil should he learn our language ?'—ED.

   291. **He**] Note the facile shifting of the subject.—ED.

   292, 293. **man**] Where are our happy emenders of Shakespeare that they have not
sat down before these two lines, each ending (dreadful thought!) with the same word?
What arguments founded on logic, propriety, *ductus literarum*, &c., &c., might there
not be alleged to prove that the former line should read: 'A creature that did bear
the human shape'!—ED.

   293. **confound**] Clarendon explains this word by examples from *Macb.*, *King John*,
Jeremiah, and *Isaiah*.   It somehow seems to me that my Yankee ears have, at times,
detected the sound of a word, which I thought was the same as this, in one of the
verses of 'God Save the Queen,' on which I have not hitherto supposed that Britons
needed a commentary.—ED.

   295. **impeach the freedome**] CLARENDON : That is, denies that strangers have
equal rights in Venice.   ROLFE : Compare, however, IV, i, where Shylock says : 'If
you deny me, let the danger light Upon your charter and your city's freedom,' as if
the freedom depended upon a charter, which might be revoked by the power that had
granted it.   The thought here may be the same.

   297. **Magnificoes**] 'The chiefe men of *Venice* are by a peculiar name called *Mag-
nifici*, i. Magnificoes.'—Minsheu, *Guide into Tongues*, 1617, s. v. Magnificent.

   298. **perswaded with**] ABBOTT, § 194: That is, argued with.   ROLFE : It is the
only instance in which Shakespeare joins 'with' to this verb.

   299. **enuious**] DYCE : Malicious.

   302. **Countri-men**] WALKER (*Crit.* ii, 141) calls attention to this spelling in the
Folio, as also to puppi-dog, ladiship, ladi-bird, honisuckle, peniworth, not indeed peculiar to it, being common to all the publications of that age, but which he notes as use-
fu. for the purposes of collation, &c.

That he would rather haue *Anthonio*'s flefh,   303
Then twenty times the value of the fumme
That he did owe him : and I know my Lord,   305
If law, authoritie, and power denie not,
It will goe hard with poore *Anthonio*.
    Por. Is it your deere friend that is thus in trouble ?
    Baff. The deereft friend to me, the kindeft man,
The beft condition'd, and vnwearied fpirit   310
In doing curtefies : and one in whom
The ancient Romane honour more appeares
Then any that drawes breath in Italie.
    Por. What fumme owes he the Iew ?
    Baff. For me three thoufand ducats.   315
    Por. What, no more ?
Pay him fixe thoufand, and deface the bond :
Double fixe thoufand, and then treble that,
Before a friend of this defcription
Shall lofe a haire through *Baffano*'s fault.   320
Firft goe with me to Church, and call me wife,
And then away to Venice to your friend :
For neuer fhall you lie by *Portias* fide
With an vnquiet foule.   You fhall haue gold   324

---

310. *condition'd, and*] *condition'd: An*
Warb. Johns.   *condition'd, most* Lansd.
    vnwearied] *unweary'd* Rowe+.
unwearied'st Hunter, Coll. ii, iii (MS).
    316, 317. One line, Qq.

319. *this*] *his* Walker.
320. *Shall*] *Should* Cap. Var.
    through] *through my* Ff, Rowe+.
thorough Steev. '78, '85, Sta. Coll. iii.
Baffano's] F$_1$.

---

310. **vnwearied**] See II, i, 53.

313. **Then any**] ALLEN: Read 'Than' any' [where '*Than*' represents the absorp
tion of the preposition *in*.   See line 168 above].

319. **this**] After seeing the many instances which WALKER (*Crit.* ii, 219) has gathered from the Folio where *this* and *his* have supplanted one another, I think we shall
be inclined to accept his change in this passage of 'this' into *his*.—ED.

320. To aid the scansion, Malone tells us that 'hair' is used as a dissyllable; and
Steevens printed 'thorough.'

320. **Shall**] BOSWELL says that this is '*should* in the folio and quarto H [i. e.
Q$_2$]; *shall* in quarto R.' [i. e. Q$_1$].   A serious misprint; how it arose it is difficult to
say.   Perhaps Boswell found some note by Capell which he misinterpreted.   Capell
has *should;* it is unusual for him to adopt a reading differing from all authorit.s without a word of comment, but I can find none here.   As is indicated in the Tex Notes,
the four Folios and the three Quartos have all the same word : 'shall.'—ED.

321. **Church**] CLARENDON: Not 'temple,' as in II, i, 50.

To pay the petty debt twenty times ouer.   325
When it is payd, bring your true friend along,
My maid *Nerriſſa*, and my ſelfe meane time
Will liue as maids and widdowes ; come away,
For you ſhall hence vpon your wedding day :
Bid your friends welcome, ſhow a merry cheere,   330
Since you are deere bought, I will loue you deere.
But let me heare the letter of your friend.

Sweet Baſſanio, *my ſhips haue all miſcarried, my Credi-*
tors grow cruell, my eſtate is very low, my bond to the Iew is
forfeit, and ſince in paying it, it is impoſſible I ſhould liue, all   335
debts are cleerd betweene you and I, if I might ſee you at my
death : notwithſtanding, vſe your pleaſure, if your loue doe not
perſwade you to come, let not my letter.

Por.   O loue! diſpach all buſines and be gone.   339

---

329. *your*] *my* Rowe.
330, 331. In margin by Pope, Han.
331. *deere bought*] *dear-bought* Dyce.
333. Sweet] Baff. [reads] *Sweet* Rowe
et seq.
336. and I,] *and me*, Pope+, Cap.
Steev.'85.   *and I.* Harness (with a dash

before *notwithstanding*).
336. fee] Ff, Rowe, Rlfe.   but fee Qq
et cet.
at] as Q₂.
337. death :] death. Q₁.
339. Por.] Om. Q₁.
diſpach] F₁.   *dispatch* Q₁.

---

325. **twenty times**] WHITE (ed. ii) : In her enthusiasm and her love, Portia talks
largely.   In Shakespeare's time sixty thousand ducats were equal to at least one million
of dollars now.

330. **cheere**] STEEVENS: Countenance.   [Cotgrave gives : *Chere :* f. The face, visage, countenance, fauour, looke, aspect of a man ; also, cheere.]

331. ECCLES : Portia could not possibly intend by these words ungenerously to remind
Bassanio of the benefits she had conferred upon him.   They must, I think, relate to that
anxiety and distress of mind which she had undergone during the time that his fate was
in suspense ; possibly, too, to the grief she was now about to suffer in his absence.   [Not
only during the time that Bassanio's fate was in suspense, but during the time when her
own fate hung on the chance decision of her suitors, when her little body was aweary
of the world.—ED.]

336. **you and I**] ABBOTT, § 205 : Sometimes euphony and emphasis may have
successfully contended against grammar.   This may explain *I* in 'and I,' 'but I,' frequently used for *me*.   ''Tween you and I' seems to have been a regular Elizabethan
idiom.   The sound of *d* and *t* before *me* was avoided.   See several examples in § 209.
HARNESS : According to the general way of printing this passage, the seeing Bassanio
at his death has been made the condition of Antonio's forgiving him his debt.   Such
a want of generosity is inconsistent with the tenderness and nobleness of Antonio.
The present punctuation [see Text. Notes] was suggested by Mr Charles Kemble.

339. CAPELL (ii, 66) : To the exclamation that follows the letter, the name (Portia)

Baſſ.   Since I haue your good leaue to goe away,   340
I will make haſt ; but till I come againe,
No bed ſhall ere be guilty of my ſtay,
Nor reſt be interpoſer twixt vs twaine.   *Exeunt.*

343. *Nor*] *No* Q₁, Theob. Warb. Johns.   ii.
Steev. Mal. '90, Hal. Cam. Glo. Cla. Wh.   343. *twaine*] *two* Rowe i.

---

is prefix'd in all editions but one, Q₁ ; it's absence from that Quarto, and the absence
from every Quarto and Folio too of the words that direct a *reading* by the person she
speaks to, create suspicion—that she herself is the *reader*, for all her 'hear,' having the
letter put into her hands by Bassanio, who found himself incapable to obey her in that :
persons of feeling will be apt to think, with the editor, that there is in this a propriety,
as well as a good dramatic effect, and her instant exclamation when over does certainly follow more naturally and with better grace than at present.   [It was while at
the harmless drudgery of collation, and long before I had read Capell's excellent note,
that I was struck with the omission in the Qq and Ff of any intimation that it falls to
Bassanio to read the letter, as is his wont on the stage.   Add to this that in Q₁ Portia's name is not prefixed to line 339; although the letter is in Italics and this line in
Roman, yet the suggestion was unavoidable that it is Portia who reads the letter. (Such
suggestions, let me add, are more likely to arise with the full text in view than when it
is looked at piecemeal in Textual Notes.)   But Portia says, ' Let me *hear* the letter of
your friend,' which is, doubtless, the reason why Rowe inserted the Stage-direction to
Bassanio to read it.   Whereupon it occurred to me that all difficulties would disappear
if Bassanio, in obedience to Portia, were to begin the letter, and, when he falteringly
reaches the words ' if I might see you at my death,' were to pause,—unable to master
his emotion.   Portia then tenderly takes the letter from him, finishes it aloud, and, in
a transport of agony, cries, ' O love ! dispatch all business and begone.'—ED.]

[*Scene III.*]

Enter the Iew, and Solanio, and Anthonio,
and the Iaylor.

Iew.   Iaylor, looke to him, tell not me of mercy,
This is the foole that lends out money *gratis*.
Iaylor, looke to him.   5
    Ant.   Heare me yet good *Shylok*.
    Iew.   Ile haue my bond, ſpeake not againſt my bond,
I haue ſworne an oath that I will haue my bond :
Thou call'dſt me dog before thou hadſt a cauſe,
But ſince I am a dog, beware my phangs,   10
The Duke ſhall grant me iuſtice, I do wonder
Thou naughty Iaylor, that thou art ſo fond   12

Scene IV. Pope+. Scene III. Rowe et cet.
    1. Enter...Solanio] F₂F₃, Cap. Hal. Enter...Salarino Q₁, Knt, Dyce, Sta. Cam. Glo. Clarke, Cla. Huds. Coll. iii, Wh. ii. Enter...Salerio Q₂Q₃. Enter...Salanio F₄, Steev. Mal. Coll. i, Sing. Wh. i, Ktly. Enter...Solarino Rowe+.
    3, 5, 12. *Iaylor*] QqFf. *Goaler* Rowe +. *Gaoler* Johns. *Jailor* Cap.
    3. *not me*] *me not* Rowe i.
    4. *lends*] Ff, Rowe, Knt, Hal. Wh. i, Rlfe, Huds. *lent* Qq et cet.
    8. *I haue*] *I've* Pope+, Dyce iii, Huds.
    9. *call'dſt*] *call'ſt* F₄, Rowe i.
    10. *phangs*] *phanges* Q₂. *fangs* Q₁.
    11. *iuſtice,*] *iuſtice;* Q₁. *Justice.* Rowe.

    1. GENTLEMAN (*Dram. Censor*, i, 285) : In this Scene we are certain our author might have very much improved both characters, had extending them occurred to his imagination ; characters of importance should never be brought on for trifling purposes.
    3. LORD CAMPBELL : It appears from this Scene that the action on the bond had been commenced and Antonio had been arrested on *mesne process*. In lines 12, 13, Shylock threatens the Jailer with an action for 'escape,' for allowing Antonio to come for a short time beyond the walls of the prison.
    4. lends] COLLIER : Now that Antonio is ruined and in prison, it is more propei for Shylock to speak in the past with the Qq, than in the present with the Folio. An tonio has nothing now to lend.   HALLIWELL : On the supposition that Shylock is here speaking with a violent sneer, the present tense seems preferable ; although, of course, as a strict matter of fact the past tense is correct.
    12. naughty] STAUNTON : In the present day this is commonly employed to express some venial or childish trespass. In old language it bore a stronger meaning, and was used indifferently with *wicked, bad, base*, &c. Thus, Leonato says of the villain Borachio,—'this *naughty* man shall face to face be brought to Margaret.'—*Much Ado*, V, ii. And Gloster, in *King Lear*, addresses the savage and relentless Regan, when she plucks his beard, as : ' *Naughty* lady.'
    12, 13. so fond To] ABBOTT, § 281 : As sometimes the antecedent and sometimes the relative may be omitted without injury to the sense, so in relative constructions,

To come abroad with him at his requeſt.   13
    Ant.   I pray thee heare me ſpeake.
    Iew.   Ile haue my bond, I will not heare thee ſpeake,   15
Ile haue my bond, and therefore ſpeake no more.
Ile not be made a ſoft and dull ey'd foole,
To ſhake the head, relent, and ſigh, and yeeld
To Chriſtian interceſſors : follow not,
Ile haue no ſpeaking, I will h aue my bond.   *Exit Iew.*   20
    Sol.   It is the moſt impenetrable cur re
That euer kept with men.
    Ant.   Let him alone,
Ile follow him no more with bootleſſe prayers :
He ſeekes my life, his reaſon well I know ;   25
I oft deliuer'd from his forfeitures
Many that haue at times made mone to me,
Therefore he hates me.
    Sol.   I am ſure the Duke will neuer grant
        this forfeiture to hold.   30

14. *pray thee*] *prethee* Q₁.
15. *bond,*] *bond :* Q₁.
17. *dull ey'd*] *dull-ey'd* Q₁.
25. *life,*] *life ;* Rowe.

26. *from*] *him* Q₃.
29. *I...Duke*] Separate line, Pope ⊔ seq.
29, 30. *I...hold*] Prose, Ff, Rowe.

---

e. g. *so* . . . . *as, so* . . . . *that*, &c., one oſ the two may be omitted.   Thus, here : so fond (as) to come abroad,' &c.

    12. **fond**] STEEVENS: That is, so foolish.   KNIGHT: We are inclined to think that it here means *indulgent,* tender, weakly compassionate.

    17. **dull ey'd**] In my copy of Q₁ there is between these words a hyphen, faint, it is true, but distinct enough to have attracted my notice, and the notice of Capell, who was not dull eyed ; he underscored it with red ink as a *varia lectio.*   In Ashbee's faithful Facsimile it may still be detected as a dot.   In my copy of Grigg's photographic Facsimile it has vanished.—ED.

    17. **foole**] COWDEN-CLARKE: By the way in which the Jew uses this term here,—twice in this short Scene, and each time in conjunction with benevolence,—Shakespeare well marks Shylock's characteristic idea, that kindness, compassion, and good feeling are synonymous with folly.

    18. **the**] ABBOTT, § 92 : French influence is perceptible here in this use of the article, instead of the possessive pronoun.

    22. **kept**] SINGER : That is, dwelt.   In some of the midland counties in England, the common dwelling-room is still called the keeping-room.   STAUNTON : To 'keep,' in the sense of *to live* or *dwell,* is still preserved at the University ; 'Where do you *keep ?*' being frequently heard with the meaning of 'Where do you *reside ?*'

    29, 31. LORD CAMPBELL : All this has a strong odor of Westminster Hall.

    30. **forfeiture to hold**] To the instances which he alleges where a noun and

An.   The Duke cannot deny the courſe of law :   31

31. *law:... Venice,*] *law,... Venice:* Theob. conj. (subs.), Cap. Ec. Knt, Sta. Ktly, Huds.

---

infinitive are used as subject or object, ABBOTT, § 354, says that perhaps this present example may be added, 'though "forfeiture" may be personified, and "grant" used like *allow*.'

31, &c. THEOBALD, in a letter to Warburton, dated 1729 (Nichols's *Illust.* ii, 310), suggested a comma after 'law,' a full stop after ' Venice,' and to read '*Twill* for ' Will.' WARBURTON : As the reason here given seems a little perplexed, it may be proper to explain it.   If, says he, the duke stop the course of law, it will be attended with this inconvenience, that stranger merchants, by whom the wealth and power of this city is supported, will cry out of injustice.   For the known stated law being their guide and security, they will never bear to have the current of it stopped on any pretence of equity whatsoever.   CAPELL (ii, 66) : In this division and reading [of the Folio], the nominative to 'impeach' is 'commodity;' which, whatever sense shall be put on it, cannot rationally be said—to impeach a State's justice.   In the next place, 'denied' is a repetition of the term [two lines above], and the relative by which it is govern'd should have reference (in course) to the terms which 'deny' governs, i. e. 'course of law,' which are not its reference under the punctuation [of the Folio].   There are such objections to that punctuation and the former reading ['Will,' line 34], that it is not seen by the Editor how they can be maintained : and as the minute alterations that he has made in those articles [see Text. Notes] remove both these objections, and (withal) develop the speaker's reasoning with great clearness, they are given into by him with much readiness, and ('tis fancy'd) will be by others.   ' For ' has its common sense of— by reason of; and 'commodity' is—commodious privileges : and the words in which Antonio declares his reason why a denial of law's course would impeach the State's justice, imply—that the State was bound to let the law have its course with all nations, as its profits rose out of all.   MALONE : That is, for the denial of those rights to strangers which render their abode at Venice so commodious and agreeable to them, would much impeach the justice of the State.   The consequence would be, that strangers would not reside or carry on traffic here; and the wealth and strength of the State would be diminished.   In *The Historye of Italye*, by W. Thomas [1561, fol. 85], there is a chapter on ' The libertee of straunger's in Venice ' [in which he says : ' Al men, specially strangers, haue so muche libertee there, that though they speake very ill by the Venetians, so they attempt nothinge in effect against theyr astate, no man shal control theim for it. . . . . And generally of all other thynges, so thou offende no man priuately, no man shal offende the: whyche vndoubtedly is one principall cause, that draweth so many straungers thither.'—ap. Clarendon].   KNIGHT : The construction of this passage, as it stands in all the old copies, is exceedingly difficult; and the paraphrases of Warburton and Malone do not remove the difficulty.   In their reading, which is ordinarily followed, 'commodity' governs 'impeach.'   But 'commodity' is used in the sense of traffic—commercial intercourse ; and, although the traffickers might impeach the justice of the State, the traffic cannot.   Capell, neglected and despised by all the commentators, has, with the very slightest change of the original, supplied a text which has a clear and precise meaning, and this we have followed : The Duke cannot deny the course of law *on account of* the interchange which strangers have with us in Venice ; if it be denied, '*twill* much impeach the justice of the State.   COLLIER (ed. i) : The sense of these lines is quite clear, though the construction may be a little involved. Antonio says that if the commodity or advantage which strangers enjoy in Venice be

For the commoditie that ſtrangers haue   32
With vs in Venice, if it be denied,
Will much impeach the iuſtice of the State,
Since that the trade and profit of the citty   35
Conſiſteth of all Nations.   Therefore goe,
Theſe greefes and loſſes haue ſo bated mee,
That I ſhall hardly ſpare a pound of fleſh
To morrow, to my bloudy Creditor.   39

---

34. *Will*] ' *Twill* Theob. conj. Cap. Ec.   Cla. Wh. ii.
Knt, Sta. Ktly, Huds.   36. *Therefore*] *Thereforr* F$_4$.
    the State] *his ſtate* Q$_1$, Cam. Glo.   37. *haue*] *hath* Q$_3$.

---

denied, that denial will much impeach the justice of the State, which derives its profit from all nations.   No change of the ancient text seems necessary.   SINGER : It must be borne in mind that Antonio was a citizen of Venice, and Shylock one of the *strangers*.   HALLIWELL: The grammatical construction of this passage is exceedingly involved, but the meaning seems to be : for the privilege which strangers have in Venice, if the letter of the law be denied, will call into question the justice of the State, which derives its trade and profit from commerce with all nations.   Strangers were especially favoured in Venice.   STAUNTON : We adopt the slight alteration proposed by Capell; for the construction of the original is so perplexed that it seems impossible to extract from that any clear sense.   Possibly, ' For the commodity that strangers have '—is in the same predicament with other lines in these plays ; and being intended by the author to be cancelled, was carelessly inserted by the old printers, together with the better expression of the same idea which follows it : ' Since that the trade and profit of the city Consisteth of all nations.'   Without this unaccommodating line, the passage is perfectly logical and easy : ' The duke cannot deny the course of law With us in Venice ; if it be denied, 'Twill much impeach the justice of the State ; Since,' &c.   WHITE (ed. i) : It is more in Shakespeare's free style to repeat ' deny ' with reference to another subject (i. e. ' the commodity,' &c.), than to write so precise a passage as Capell's text gives.   CLARENDON : For the refusal of the usual facilities enjoyed by strangers in Venice will bring in serious question the justice of the State. DYCE (ed. iii) : The proper punctuation of this passage is very doubtful.   ALLEN : Capell must be right.   [The difficulty in this puzzling passage lies in determining to what ' it,' in ' if *it* be denied,' refers.   It can refer either to ' course of law ' or to ' commoditie.'   Capell referred it to the former ; Malone to the latter ; and under these two leaders all subsequent commentators have, in effect, ranged themselves.   At present, I prefer Malone.—ED.]

34. **iustice**] KEIGHTLEY (*Exp.* p. 151) : I am rather dubious of ' justice,' and should prefer *interest* or *traffic*.

35. **Since that**] See ABBOTT, § 287 ; or *Macb.* IV, iii, 106 ; or *Oth.* I, i, 75 ; or *Lear*, IV, vi, 215.

37. **bated**] ROLFE : Reduced, lowered.   Cf. ' bated breath,' I, iii, 128.   It should not be printed '*bated;* it is not a mere metrical contraction of *abated,* but a distinct word (cf. *wake* and *awake*, &c.), often found in prose writers.   See examples in Webster's *Dict.*

Well Iaylor, on, pray God *Baffanio* come   40
To fee me pay his debt, and then I care not.   *Exeunt.*

[*Scene IV.*]

*Enter Portia, Nerriffa, Lorenzo, Ieffica, and a man of
    Portias.*

Lor.   Madam, although I fpeake it in your prefence,
You haue a noble and a true conceit
Of god-like amity, which appeares moft ftrongly   5
In bearing thus the abfence of your Lord.
But if you knew to whom you fhew this honour,
How true a Gentleman you fend releefe,
How deere a louer of my Lord your husband,
I know you would be prouder of the worke   10
Then cuftomary bounty can enforce you.
    Por.   I neuer did repent for doing good,
Nor fhall not now : for in companions
That do conuerfe and wafte the timetogether,   14

---

40. *on,*] *on ;* F₄ et seq.

   Scene V. Pope+.   Scene IV. Rowe,
Cap. et seq.

   1. a man of Portias] a servant of Portia's. Rowe.

   3. *your*] *you* F₂.

5. *god-like*] *gold-like* Q₃.

   moft] Om. Pope, Han.

7. *fhew*] *fhow* Q₂.

8. *releefe*] *relief to* Rowe+.

12, 13. *for...Nor*] *of...And* Pope+.

---

   5. **amity**] WALKER (*Vers.* 201): The *i* in *ity* is almost uniformly dropt in pronunciation. [Where see many examples; see also ABBOTT, § 467. As ALLEN says, this
'amity' is as betweén Bassanio and Anthonio.—ED.]

   8. **Gentleman**] CLARENDON: This is in the dative case. We, in modern English,
use such a dative, i. e. without the preposition *to*, only when it comes between the verb
and its accusative, as 'you send the gentleman relief.' [See also ABBOTT, § 394, for
the omission of the preposition in relative sentences; and I, i, 135; II, vi, 11; and
IV, i, 406.]

   9. **louer**] MALONE: In Shakespeare's time this was applied to those of the same
sex who had an esteem for each other. Ben Jonson concludes one of his letters to Dr
Donne by telling him : 'He is his true lover.'   See our author's *Sonnets*, passim ; also
'bosom lover,' line 19 in this Scene.

   11. ECCLES: Than such common acts of bounty as you are in the continual habit
of performing can incline you *to be*.   CLARENDON: You would be prouder of the work
than ordinary benevolence can constrain you to be.

   14. **waste**] HALLIWELL: Here used in its primitive sense, to consume, spend, pass,
not necessarily with any idea of unprofitableness.   ROLFE: Cf. Milton (*Sonnet to Mr*

Whofe foules doe beare an egal yoke of loue,   15
There muft be needs a like proportion
Of lyniaments, of manners, and of fpirit ;
Which makes me thinke that this *Anthonio*
Being the bofome louer of my Lord,
Muft needs be like my Lord.   If it be fo,   20
How little is the coft I haue beftowed
In purchafing the femblance of my foule ;
From out the ftate of hellifh cruelty,
This comes too neere the praifing of my felfe,   24

15. *egal*] F₂, Cap. Dyce, Coll. iii. *egall*
Q₂. *equal* Q₁ et cet.
17. *lyniaments,*] Q₂F₂Q₃. *lineaments,*
Q₁F₃F₄. *lineaments* Warb. Johns.
19. In parenthesis, Q₁.

19. *bofome louer*] *bofome-louer* Q₁,
Pope+, Ktly.
22. *foule ;*] *foule,* Q₁. *foul* F₄.
23. *cruelty,*] *cruelty.* Rowe. *cruelty ?*
Pope. *cruelty !* Coll. *misery.* Q₁, Cam.
Glo. Cla. Wh. ii.

Lawrence) : 'Help waste a sullen day ;' where, however, the idea of 'killing time' is
more evident than here.

15. **egal**] STEEVENS : Commonly used for *equal* in Shakespeare's time. [See Text.
Notes.]

16. **needs**] See ABBOTT, § 25.

17. **lyniaments, of manners,**] WARBURTON : The wrong pointing has made this
fine sentiment nonsense ; as implying that friendship could not only make a similitude
of manners, but of *faces*.   The true sense is,—*lineaments of manners*, i. e. form of the
manners, which, says the speaker, must needs be proportionate.   STEEVENS : The poet
only means to say,—that corresponding proportions of body and mind are necessary for
those who spend their time together.   So in *2 Hen. IV* : '*Dol.* Why doth the prince
love him so then ?   *Fal.* Because *their legs are both of a bigness*,' &c.   Every one will
allow that the friend of a toper should have a strong head, and the intimate of a sports-
man such an athletic constitution as will enable him to acquit himself with reputation
in the exercises of the field.   The word 'lineaments' was used with great laxity by
our ancient writers.   In *The learned and true Assertion of the Original, Life*, &c. *of
King Arthur*, translated from the Latin of John Leland, 1582, it is used for the human
frame in general.   Speaking of the removal of that prince's bones, he calls them 'Arthur's lineaments three times translated ;' and again, 'all the lineaments of them remaining in that most stately tomb, saving the shin bones of the king and queen,' &c.   Again
in Greene's *Farewell to Follie* [vol. ix, p. 255, ed. Grosart], 'Nature had so curiously
performed his charge in the lineaments of his bodie.'   Again in Chapman's *Fifth Iliad :*
'Took the weariness of fight From all his nerves and lineaments.'   Again in the *Twenty-
third Iliad :* 'So overlabour'd were His goodly lineaments with chase of Hector.'

23. **From out**] See ABBOTT, § 157.

23. **cruelty**] I cannot but think that *misery* of Q₁ is the purer text.   Is it not too
soon for Portia to know the full depth of Shylock's 'cruelty' ?   The utter bankruptcy
of a Royal Merchant is *misery* enough.—ED.

24. **the praising**] For the substantive use of the verbal with *the* before it and *of*

Therefore no more of it : heere other things   25
Lorenſo I commit into your hands,
The husbandry and mannage of my houſe,
Vntill my Lords returne ; for mine owne part
I haue toward heauen breath'd a ſecret vow,
To liue in prayer and contemplation,   30
Onely attended by *Nerriſſa* heere,
Vntill her husband and my Lords returne :
There is a monaſtery too miles off,   33

25. *heere other things*] *here other things,*	26. Lorenſo] Q₂. Lorenzo Q₁.
F₃F₄, Pope. *Here are other things.* Rowe.	hands,] *hands* F₄.
Hear other things. Thirlby, Theob. et	27. *mannage*] Q₂. *manage* Q₁.
seq.	29. *ſecret*] *sacred* Coll. (MS).

after it, see ABBOTT, § 93, where it is said that it seems to have been sometimes regarded as colloquial.

24, 25. **This comes . . . of it**] COWDEN-CLARKE: There is exquisite subtlety and refinement of modesty in this passage. There is the delicacy of a mind that dreads even to disclaim merit lest it seem to imply that there exists merit to be disclaimed; and there is the sensitiveness of a profound love, which feels it a kind of egoism to laud that being who is but another self.

25. **heere**] THEOBALD: Portia, finding that her reflections come too near self-praise, says, She'll say no more of that sort; but call a new subject. This was also suggested by Dr Thirlby. [See Nichols's *Lit. Hist.* ii, 225.]

27. **husbandry**] See 'Borrowing dulls the edge of husbandry,'—*Ham.* I, iii, 77; and, 'There's husbandry in heaven,' *Macb.* II, i, 4. CLARENDON: Stewardship; οἰκονομία in the literal sense.

27. **mannage**] See ABBOTT, § 451, for a list of words used as nouns by Shakespeare, to which ' we should append *-ation* or *-ition, -ure* or *-ing*. Almost all of these words come to us through the French.'

29. **secret**] COLLIER (ed. ii) : *Sacred*, says the old (MS); perhaps he himself mis-heard the word, or perhaps it was a variation by the actor whom he saw. There is no reason for disturbing the old text.

32. **her husband and my Lords**] Compare ' As soul and body's severing,'—*Hen. VIII :* II, iii, 16; 'Shall be your love and labour's recompense,'—*Rich. II :* II, iii, 62, cited by ABBOTT, § 397, who says that ' probably this idiom arises partly from the readiness with which a compound phrase connected by a conjunction is regarded as one and inseparable.' See also Walker (*Crit.* i, 218), or Schmidt (*Lex.* p. 1419, § 6).

33. **monastery**] TH. ELZE (*Sh. Jahrb.* xiii, p. 143): Monasteries there were in abundance at that time everywhere in Italy, but as it happens there really was a Con-vent not far from the locality selected by the poet for Belmont. About three English, or Italian, miles from Strà, landwards from the right bank of the Brenta, lay the village of Saonara. Here, in the 16th Century, stood a Benedictine Convent, whose occupants, it is true, in 1558 united with the Nuns of the same order at St Anna's in Padua, but the Convent buildings survived down to the present century. [Dr Karl Elze maintains that Belmont must have been on the banks of the Brenta; and Th. Elze, in this learned

And there we will abide.   I doe defire you
Not to denie this impofition,   35
The which my loue and fome neceffity
Now layes vpon you.
    Lorenf.   Madame, with all my heart,
I fhall obey you in all faire commands.
    Por.   My people doe already know my **minde**,   40
And will acknowledge you and *Ieffica*
In place of Lord *Baffanio* and my felfe.
So far you well till we fhall meete againe.
    Lor.   Faire thoughts & happy houres attend on you.
    Ieffi.   I wifh your Ladifhip all hearts content.   45
    Por.   I thanke you for your wifh, and am well pleas'd
To wifh it backe on you : faryouwell *Ieffica.*   *Exeunt.*
Now *Balthafer*, as I haue euer found thee honeft true,
So let me finde thee ftill : take this fame letter,
And vfe thou all the indeauor of a man,   50
In fpeed to Mantua, fee thou render this

    34. *we will*] *will we* Q₁, Cam. Glo.
Cla. Rlfe, Wh. ii.
    37. *layes*] *lay* Han. Hal.
    you] *me* Q₃.
    41. *acknowledge*] *acknowledg* F₄.
    43. *So...well*] Q₂. *So fare you well*
FfQ₃. *And fo farewell* Q₁, Cam. Glo.
Cla. Wh. ii.
    46. *pleas'd*] *'pris'd* Warb. conj.
    47, 48. Lines end *you :...Baltaser, ...*

true Walker.
    47. *faryouwell*] *farewell* Q₁.
    48. *Now* Balthafer] Separate line, Pope
et seq.
    Balthafer] Balthazar Ff.
    honeft true] *honeft-true* Dyce, Cam
Ktly, Glo. Del. Cla. Rlfe, Wh. ii.
    50. *the indeauor*] *th' indeuour* Qq,
Pope +.
    51. *Mantua*] *Padua* Theob. et seq.

Essay, narrows the locality to the neighbourhood of Dolo, around which, from La Mira
to Strà, on both banks of the Brenta, the magnificoes of Venice had, and still have,
their palatial residences. Belmont, therefore, must be supposed to have been not far
from the high road between Padua and Fusina, because Lorenzo met Salerio on the
road from Venice with the letter from Anthonio, and the park gate where Portia's
coach awaited her, must have been on or near a highway fit for travel.   Hence, Th.
Elze's allusion to Strà in the extract which I have just given.—ED.]

    48. thee] Note the instant change of address, to a servant.   Portia uses chiefly
thou to Nerrissa, but Nerrissa invariably, I think, addresses Portia as *you.*   See I, ii,
35.—ED.

    48. honest true] WALKER (*Crit.* i, 23) : Write *honest-true.*   See also ABBOTT,
§ 2, for parallel instances where 'two adjectives are combined, the first being a kind of
adverb qualifying the second.'

    51. Mantua] THEOBALD : 'Tis evident to any diligent reader that we must restore,
as I have done,—' In speed to *Padua ;*' it was there, and not at ' Mantua,' Bellario
liv'd.   So afterwards : ' A messenger, with letters from the Doctor, new come from

Into my cofins hand, Doctor *Belario,*   52
And looke what notes and garments he doth giue thee,
Bring them I pray thee with imagin'd fpeed
Vnto the Tranect, to the common Ferrie   55

52. *cofins*] *cofin* Q₂.   Ktly, Del. **Coll. iii,** Wh. ii.
55. *Tranect*] *Traject* Rowe+, Sing.

Padua.'   And again: 'Came you from *Padua,* from Bellario?'   And again: 'It
comes from *Padua,* from Bellario.'   Besides, *Padua,* not 'Mantua,' is the place of
education for the Civil Law in Italy.

52. **cosins**] KEIGHTLEY: This word was used, in its primitive sense of *consan-*
guineus, of any one that was akin.

54. **imagin'd**] STEEVENS: That is, with celerity like that of imagination.   So in
the Chorus before *Hen. V:* III: 'Thus with imagin'd wing our swift scene flies.'
Again, in *Ham.* I, v, 30: 'Wings as swift As meditation.'   ECCLES: Here, however,
I incline rather to think it is put for *imaginable.*   ABBOTT, § 375: The passive participle is often used to signify not that which *was* and *is,* but that which *was,* and, therefore, *can be hereafter.*   In other words, *-ed* is used for *-able.*

55. **Tranect**] STEEVENS: This appears to be derived from *tranare,* and was probably a word current in the time of Shakespeare, though I can produce no example of
it.   CAPELL (*Gloss.*): A Ferry- or Passage-boat: possibly from some provincial Italian
Word of that Import, springing of—*tranare,* to swim or pass over, that does not appear
in their Dictionaries.   [In his *Notes,* p. 67, CAPELL says:] Of this word's sense, and
derivation you have the Editor's opinion at large in the *Glossary;* to which integrity
calls upon him to add that no example is found of it: notwithstanding which, the word
must be adher'd to, and not it's substitute—*traject,* a word that has some examples, but
not many, and signifying—place of passage; whereas 'tranect' is—vehicle, and explain'd so by the Poet himself in the very words it is follow'd by.   MALONE: Twenty
miles from Padua, on the river Brenta, there is a dam or sluice to prevent the water of
that river from mixing with that of the marshes of Venice.   Here the passage-boat is
drawn out of the river, and lifted over the dam by a crane.   From hence to Venice
this distance is five miles.   Perhaps some novel-writer of Shakespeare's time might
have called this dam by the name of the 'tranect.'   See DuCange in v. *Trana.*
KNIGHT: No other example is found of the use of this word in English, and yet there
is little doubt that the word is correct.   *Tranare* and *trainare* are interpreted by Florio
not only as *to draw,* which is the common acceptation, but as *to pass* or *swim over.*
Thus, the 'tranect' was, most probably, the *tow-boat* of the ferry.   IBID. (*Illust.*): If
Shakespeare had been at Venice (which, from the extraordinary keeping of the play,
appears the most natural supposition), he must surely have had some situation in his
eye for Belmont.   There is a 'common ferry' at two places, Fusina and Mestre.   The
Fusina ferry would be the one if Portia lived in perhaps the most striking situation,
under the Euganean Hills.   But the Mestre ferry is the most convenient medium between Padua and Venice.   There is a large collection of canal-craft there.   It is eighteen English miles from Padua, and five from Venice.   Supposing Belmont to lie in the
plain N.-W. from Venice, Balthazar might cut across the country to Padua, and meet
Portia at Mestre, while she travelled thither at a lady's speed.—M[artineau?].   HUN-
TER (i, 328): The ferries at Venice were called *traghetti, trajects,* as we learn from
Coryat (*Crudities,* i, 210): 'There are in Venice thirteen ferries or passages, which

12

Which trades to Venice ; wafte no time in words,　　　　　56
But get thee gone, I fhall be there before thee.
　　Balth.　Madam, I goe with all conuenient fpeed.
　　Por.　Come on *Neriffa*, I haue worke in hand
That you yet know not of; wee'll fee our husbands　　　60
Before they thinke of vs ?
　　Nerriffa.　Shall they fee vs ?
　　Portia.　They fhall *Nerriffa* : but in fuch a habit,
That they fhall thinke we are accomplifhed
With that we lacke ; Ile hold thee any wager　　　　65
When we are both accoutered like yong men,

---

56. *words*] *word* Q₃.
57. *get thee*] *get hee* F₂.
58. [Exit. Q₁.

65. *that*] *what* Rowe ii+, Steev. Mal.
66. *accoutered*] *apparreld* Q₁, Pope+.
accoutred Rowe, Cap. et seq.

---

they commonly call Traghetti.'　Halliwell: 'And that men may passe speedily, besides this bridge, there are thirteen places called *traghetti*, where boats attend called *gondole*, which, being of incredible number, give ready passage to all men.'—Moryson's *Itinerary*, i, 77.　'Tranect' is probably a corruption.　Singer: I adopt Rowe's alteration, which corresponds with *traghetto*, as explained by Florio, in v. 'a *ferrie*, a passage, or gozell over, or from, shore to shore;' and with the Latin *trajectus*, which is quite in Shakespeare's manner to have in mind.　Staunton: 'Tranect' is probably a misprint for *traject*.　White: '*Traject*' may be correct on the authority of Coryat. Keightley (*Exp.* 152): Rowe, I think properly, reads *Traject*.　Collier: The (MS) makes no change, and none is necessary.　Dyce and Clarendon: Rowe's *traject* is, perhaps, the right reading.　Cowden-Clarke: The Italian *tranare* or *trainare* also means to draw or drag; and it is possible that the Venetian ferry-boat was drawn through the water by a process still in use in some places.　One of the present Editors saw a ferry-boat at Rotterdam made to traverse the stream, from the man on board laying hold of a rope strained across the canal for the purpose.　Karl Elze (*Essays*, 1873, p. 279): The ferry to Venice was at that time at Fusina, at the mouth of the Brenta. The nonsensical word 'tranect' proves that copyist and compositors possessed no knowledge of this word, and still less of the thing itself.　Even the word *traject*, correctly restored by Theobald, is not a genuine English word, otherwise the poet would not have added the explanation, 'the common ferry,' which he surely did, only to make the meaning clear to his readers and hearers.　What visitor does not here at once recognize the Venetian traghetto (tragetto)?　And whence did the poet get a knowledge of the traghetto?　Coryat is out of the question, and Vecellio, even if we knew that Shakespeare had read the book, which we do not, has not a word about the traghetto, so that the disbelievers in an Italian journey of Shakespeare cannot account for his knowledge by any other means than by oral communication.　[Elze contends, in this fine *Essay*, on *The Supposed Travels of Shakespeare*, that the simplest of all explanations of this exact local knowledge of Italy is that Shakespeare had himself journeyed thither.—Ed.]

66. **accoutered**] Although this word has been generally adopted since the days of Capell, I am not sure that *apparreld* of Q₁ is not the more satisfactory word.　If Portia

Ile proue the prettier fellow of the two,   67
And weare my dagger with the brauer grace,
And ſpeake betweene the change of man and boy,
With a reede voyce, and turne two minſing ſteps   70
Into a manly ſtride ; and ſpeake of frayes
Like a fine bragging youth : and tell quaint lyes
How honourable Ladies ſought my loue,
Which I denying, they fell ſicke and died.
I could not doe withall : then Ile repent,   75

---

70. *minſing*] *mincing* Q₁.   +, Cap. Steev. Mal.'90. *withal* F₄, Rowe
75. *withall*] Qq F₂F₃. *with all* Rowe ii   i, Var. et seq.

---

had in mind the Doctor's cap and gown which Dr Bellario was to send her, I doubt if
she would speak of them as *accoutrements*.   On the other hand, she refers, almost in
the same breath, to her dagger and as though she were to be dressed like a bragging
Jack.   Hence I am inclined to prefer Q₁, which obviates all difficulties.

The Elizabethan audiences seemed to find especial pleasure in seeing female characters disguised as men, to judge from the lightness with which, throughout the drama,
women slipped into doublet and hose.   Rosalind and Imogen occur to us at once; in
Beaumont and Fletcher there are many more of these disguises than in Shakespeare,
e. g.: Aspatia in *The Maid's Tragedy*, Euphrasia in *Philaster*, Alathe in *The Night-
Walker*, and in *Love's Pilgrimage* Theodosia retains her disguise from her first entrance
down to the Fifth Act, and Leocadia from her first entrance down to the very last scene
of the Fifth Act.—ED.

72. **quaint**] DYCE : Ingenious, artful, clever.

75. **doe withall**] In a note on *Meas. for Meas.* Steevens, under the pseudonym,
Collins, shows that this phrase was at times used indelicately.   In a note on this
present passage, 'Collins' refers to his former note with the implication that Portia so
uses the phrase here.   Whereupon GIFFORD, in a note on Jonson's *Silent Woman*, V,
1, 39, thus vindicates the phrase, and Portia, with such proof as has been accepted by all
editors and commentators ever since : ' In one of the prettiest speeches surely that ever
was penned, that of Portia to Nerissa, she describes the appearance she shall make and
the language she shall hold when " accoutred like a man."   The line " I could not do
withal," or rather, a corruption of it, the commentators, who are always routing in the
mire of impurity, explain in the most indecent manner.   I will not say of Portia, as of
Desdemona, that her " motion blushed at herself," yet she was assuredly a woman of
modesty, and therefore little likely to use the language of a brothel, or to attribute the
manners of one to the " *honourable ladies* who sought her love."   The fact is, that the
phrase, so shamelessly misinterpreted, is, in itself, perfectly innocent, and means neither
more nor less than, I COULD NOT HELP IT.   In *Morte Arthur*, where Guinever is
accused of poisoning one of the Knights of the Round Table, the King says to her,
" None of them will say well of you, nor none of them will doe battle for you, and
that shall be great slaunder for you in this court.   Alas ! said the queen, *I cannot doe
withall*," (I cannot help it,) " and now I miss sir Launcelot," Part III, c. 108.   In
the trial of Udall, lord Anderson says : " You had as good say you were the author.
Udall. " That will not follow, my lord : but if you think so, *I cannot do withal*" (I

And wifh for all that, that I had not kil'd them ;   76
And twentie of thefe punie lies Ile tell,
That men fhall fweare I haue difcontinued fchoole
Aboue a twelue moneth : I haue within my minde
A thoufand raw tricks of thefe bragging Iacks,   80
Which I will practife.

     Nerrif.   Why, fhall wee turne to men ?
     Portia.   Fie, what a queftions that ?
If thou wert nere a lewd interpreter :

78. *I haue*] *I've* Pope+, Dyce iii,   82. *Why*] Om. Pope+.
Huds.   83. *queftions*] *question's* $Q_1 F_3$ et seq.
79. *moneth*] *month* Q_1.   84. *nere*] *near* Rowe et seq.
   I haue] *I've* Dyce iii, Huds.   *interpreter :*] *interpreter ?* Rowe
   within] *in* Pope+.   *interpreter !* Theob.

---

cannot help it).—*State Trials,* fol. vol. I, p. 162. And in that excellent old play, the *Little French Lawyer,* Dinant, who is reproached by Clerimont for not silencing the music, which endangered his safety, replies : "*I cannot do withal ;*" (I cannot help it ;) "I have spoke and spoke ; I am betrayed and lost too." I make no apology for this long note. Shakespeare is in every hand ; and it is therefore incumbent on all those who feel a due respect for youth and innocence, to take every opportunity of removing the impurities with which his pages are wantonly overcharged. As the sense of the words is now fully ascertained, we have a right to expect that the stupid and indecent comments of Collins and others on it shall be henceforth omitted. "*Withal,* the reading of the old copies," Mr Malone tells us, "was *corrected*" (corrected, with a vengeance !) "to *with all* by Mr Pope." Notwithstanding this cheering assurance, the future editors of Shakespeare will do well to let him speak his own language, and to print the line as it stands above, and as it ought always to have stood : "I could not do withal." ' DYCE (*Remarks,* p. 57) : Though after Gifford's decisive note, this phrase is not likely to be again misinterpreted, I may cite the following passage from Palsgrave's *Lesclarcissement de la Lang. Fr.* 1530 : 'I can nat *do withall,* a thyng lyeth nat in me, or I am nat in faulte that a thyng is done,' Fol. clxxx (Table of Verbes). HALLIWELL : A very common phrase, equivalent to I could not help it, it was not my fault. 'If he beare displeasure agaynst me, I can nat do withal. *Sil indigne contre moy, je nen puis mays.*'—Palsgrave, 1530. The phrase occurs more than once in Florio's *Second Frutes,* 1591. 'Beare witnes, my masters, if hee dye of a surfet, I cannot doo withall ; it is his owne seeking, not mine,'—Nash's *Have with You to Saffron Walden,* 1596. See further examples in Middleton's *Works,* iv, 26, ed. Dyce ; Webster's *Works,* iii, 215, ed. Dyce. There is a proverbial phrase : 'to look as if one could not do withal,' which has a different signification. See instances of it in Pick's *Festum Voluptatis,* 1639, p. 37 ; Heywood's *Late Lancashire Witches,* 1634.

78. **That**] For other instances of the omission of *so* before *that,* see ABBOTT, § 283, or *Lear,* IV, vii, 47 ; *Ham.* IV, vi, 211.

80. **Iacks**] MALONE : In our author's time, a term of contempt. See *Much Ado,* I, i, 186.

But come, Ile tell thee all my whole deuice   85
When I am in my coach, which ftayes for vs
At the Parke gate ; and therefore hafte away,
For we muft meafure twentie miles to day.   *Exeunt.*

85. *my*] *my my* Q₂.

---

85. **all my whole**] CLARENDON: A similar pleonasm occurs in *1 Hen. VI:* I, i,
126.

86. **coach**] HALLIWELL: Coaches had become exceedingly common at the time
this present Comedy was written; and in 1601 was introduced into Parliament a bill
'to restrain the excessive use of coaches within this realm of England.'   It should be
recollected that Portia is not speaking of Venice.   In that city there were no coaches.
See Coryat's *Crudities*, 1611, p. 225.   [From the following note of TH. ELZE (*Sh.
Jahrbuch*, xiii, 148), it would seem that Shakespeare is a better authority than the 'Od-
combian Legge-stretcher,' as Tom Coryat called himself: 'In 1562 there were coach-
makers (*carrozzeri*) in Venice, who with the Saddlers formed a branch of the Guild
of Upholsterers.   By a law of Venice of 8 October 1562 no coaches were allowed to
have silk cushions or covers, or any lavish expense of gold or silver, except for the
handles of the coach-doors, under penalty of 20 ducats fine for every infraction of the
law.']

88. **twentie miles**] ECCLES: This is, it may be presumed, nearly the whole dis
tance from Belmont to Venice.   ELZE (*Essays*, p. 279): This may be spoken at ran-
dom, and she wishes, perhaps, by a vague statement to conceal the true state of things.
Twenty, like forty, very frequently indicates an indefinite number.   It is however, an
exceedingly remarkable coincidence that the distance between Venice and Dolo [one
of the possible localities of Belmont] is exactly twenty Italian miles, and the Italian
mile is the same as the English.   Can Shakespeare have known this, and is his statement, after all, to be taken literally?   [Portia just before speaks of telling '*twenty* puny
lies.'   Halpin contends that Venice is only ten miles away, and that 'twenty miles'
means to Venice and back again.   See 'Duration of the Action' in Appendix.—ED.]

[Scene V.]

Enter Clowne and Ieſſica.

Clown. Yes truly ; for looke you, the ſinnes of the Father are to be laid vpon the children, therefore I promiſe you, I feare you, I was alwaies plaine with you, and ſo now I ſpeake my agitation of the matter : therfore be of   5
good cheere, for truly I thinke you are damn'd, there is but one hope in it that can doe you anie good, and that is but a kinde of baſtard hope neither.

Ieſſica. And what hope is that I pray thee ?

Clow. Marrie you may partlie hope that your father   10
got you not, that you are not the Iewes daughter.

Ieſ. That were a kinde of baſtard hope indeed, ſo the ſins of my mother ſhould be viſited vpon me.

Clow. Truly then I feare you are damned both by father and mother : thus when I ſhun *Scilla* your father, I   15

Scene VI. Pope+.   Scene V. Cap. et
seq.
  1. [A garden. Cap.
    Enter Clowne...] Enter Launcelot
... Rowe.
  2, &c. Clo.] Laun. Rowe.
  3, 4. *promiſe you*] *promiſe ye* Q₁, Cam.

Glo. Cla. Huds. Wh. ii.
  5. *be of*] *be a* Q₁Q₂.   *be o'* Cap.
  6. *there is*] *ther is* Q₁.
  8, 12. *baſtard hope*] *baſtard-hope* F₄,
Rowe.
  15. *I ſhun*] *you ſhun* Rowe+.
  15, 16. *I fall*] *you fall* Rowe.

---

4. **feare you**] For other instances of the omission of the preposition, see ABBOTT, § 200.

5. **agitation**] ECCLES : *Cogitation* is probably the word about which Launcelot blunders here.

12. **ſo**] STAUNTON : ' So ' means *in that case.*

12, &c.] CHARLES COWDEN-CLARKE (*Sh. Characters*, p. 406) : I have no desire to hypercriticise, or to see more in our poet than he himself intended ; but the very circumstance of Jessica's trifling with the Clown upon her conversion from the faith of her fathers, strikingly harmonizes with her general tone of character. She would have turned Mohammedan, or Buddhist, or Spinning Dervish, or Spinning Jenny, or spinning *anything*, and danced a polka at her new faith ; flimsy, thoughtless, and unstable.

15. **Scilla**] MALONE : Alluding to the well-known line of a modern Latin poet, Philippe Gualtier, in his poem entitled Alexandreis : ' Incidis in Scyllam, cupiens vitare Charybdim.' STEEVENS : Philip Gualtier de Chatillon (afterward bishop of Megala) was born toward the latter end of the 12th Century. In the fifth book of his heroic Poem, Darius (who, escaping from Alexander, fell into the hands of Bessus) is thus apostrophized : ' Quo tendis inertem Rex periture fugam ? nescis, heu ! perdite, nescis Quem fugias, hostes incurris dum fugis hostem : Incidis in Scyllam, cupiens vitare Cha-

fall into *Charibdis* your mother ; well, you are gone both   16
waies.

Ief.   I fhall be fau'd by my husband, he hath made me
a Chriftian.

Clow.   Truly the more to blame he, we were Chrifti-   20
ans enow before, e'ne as many as could wel liue one by a-
nother : this making of Chriftians will raife the price of
Hogs, if wee grow all to be porke-eaters, wee fhall not
fhortlie haue a rafher on the coales for money.

Enter Lorenzo.   25

Ief.   Ile tell my husband *Lancelet* what you fay, heere
he comes.

Loren.   I fhall grow iealous of you fhortly *Lancelet*,
if you thus get my wife into corners ?

Ief.   Nay, you need not feare vs *Lorenzo, Launcelet*   30
and I are out, he tells me flatly there is no mercy for mee
in heauen, becaufe I am a Iewes daughter : and hee faies
you are no good member of the common wealth, for
in conuerting Iewes to Chriftians, you raife the price
of Porke.   35

Loren.   I fhall anfwere that better to the Common-

---

21. *enow*] *enough* Rowe.
e'ne as] *in as* Q$_2$.
26. Lancelet] Launcelet Q$_2$Q$_3$.
27. *comes.*] *come ?* Q$_2$.

28. *iealous*] *iealious* Q$_2$.
36–38. An overlooked fragment of the
Old Play which Sh. rewrote. ED. conj.

---

rybdim.'   The author of the line in question (who was unknown to Erasmus) was first
ascertained by Galeottus Martius, who died in 1476, and we learn from Henricus Gan-
davensis *de Scriptoribus Ecclesiasticis* (i. e. Henry of Gaunt) that the Alexandreis had
been a common school-book.   HALLIWELL gives many examples of the proverbial use
of this allusion, which Vergil has made familiar to every school-boy, and adds : 'There
is an old Somersetshire proverb of a similar effect : " He got out of the muxy, and fell
into the pucksy." '

18. **husband**] HENLEY : From St. Paul, *1 Corinthians*, vii, 14 : 'The unbelieving
wife is sanctified by the husband.'

21. **enow**] CLARENDON : 'Enow' seems to be generally used of numbers, *enough*
of quantity.   The same distinction holds in some provincial dialects where both forms
are still current.

24. **coales**] HALLIWELL : A 'rasher on the coals' was a favourite article of food
in Shakespeare's time, and is mentioned with the red-herring as a capital incentive for
the lover of wine in Nash's *Pierce Penilesse*, 1592.   'The mystical hieroglyphick of
rashers o' th' coals.'—Decker's *Gull's Hornbook*, 1609.

36–41. See Appendix, p. 321.

wealth, than you can the getting vp of the Negroes bel-   37
lie : the Moore is with childe by you *Launcelet*?

Clow.   It is much that the Moore fhould be more then
reafon : but if fhe be leffe then an honeft woman, fhee is   40
indeed more then I tooke her for.

Loren.   How euerie foole can play vpon the word, I
thinke the beft grace of witte will fhortly turne into filence, and difcourfe grow commendable in none onely
but Parrats : goe in firra, bid them prepare for dinner ?   45

Clow.   That is done fir, they haue all ftomacks ?

Loren.   Goodly Lord, what a witte-fnapper are you,
then bid them prepare dinner.

Clow.   That is done to fir, onely couer is the word.   49

---

38. *Moore is*] *Moore's* Q₁.

42. *the word*] *a word* Han.

44. *onely*] Om. Rowe ii+.

47. *Goodly*] *Good* Pope+, Coll. iii.

Good my Anon. (ap. Hal.).

48. *then*] *than* Q₂.

49. *That is*] *That's* Q₁.

to fir] *too fir* F₂ et seq.

---

39. more] STEEVENS : So in *The Fair Maid of the West*, 1631 : 'And for you
Moors thus much I mean to say, I'll see if more I eat the more I may.'

40. lesse] CAPELL (ii, 68) : A change of 'less' into *more* makes the jingle fuller.
HALLIWELL : The original better expresses the speaker's amusing way of blundering.
STAUNTON : The quibble here on 'more' and 'less,' petty as it is, has been repeated in
Tit. And.: 'Nurse. O, tell me, did you see Aaron the Moor ? *Aaron.* Well, *more* or
less, or ne'er a whit at all, Here Aaron is,' &c.

45. ELZE (*Essays*, p. 110) : This conversation is unquestionably the prelude to
the penalty imposed on Shylock in the Trial scene ; it gives, as it were, the chord
and key-note to it. Herein lies its importance, otherwise it would be an idle excrescence. But what is the key-note ? When we remember Launcelot's ridiculous allusions to cheiromancy and to dreams, it might not, perhaps, be easy to difcern here in
his talk with Jessica anything deeper than witty derision of Theology and the conversion of Jews. As far as the conversion of the Jews is concerned, it is not impossible
that some contemporary incident may have given point to Shakespeare's wit and fun.
Be this, however, as it may, the serious correlative to this humorous treatment of the
subject can scarcely be other than that here, under the jingling of the Clown's bells,
Shakespeare expresses his own personal disapproval of the religious conversion imposed
on Shylock. And, moreover, no baptism will help the Jew in the least ; spite of his
assumed Christianity, he is, and will remain, damned. To Shakespeare the main
spring of religion is the practice of duty and morality, not dogmas. Hence, he could
not possibly have approved of Shylock's treatment, either by the State or by society.

47. Goodly] TYRWHITT : Surely this should be corrected, as it is by Pope. FAR-
MER : It should be : *Good yᵉ Lord!* HALLIWELL : There does not appear to be any
clear necessity for alteration. ALLEN : I have heard in New England : 'O, *goody*
Lord !' and 'O, *goody !*' (Lord or God euphemistically suppressed.) Farmer may,
therefore, be nearly right—i. e. *Goody Lord* may be right.

Loren. Will you couer than fir?   50
Clow. Not fo fir neither, I know my dutie.
Loren. Yet more quarrellng with occafion, wilt thou
fhew the whole wealth of thy wit in an inftant ; I pray
thee vnderftand a plaine man in his plaine meaning : goe
to thy fellowes, bid them couer the table, ferue in the   55
meat, and we will come in to dinner.
Clow. For the table fir , it fhall be feru'd in , for the
meat fir , it fhall bee couered , for your comming in to
dinner fir, why let it be as humors and conceits fhall go-
uerne.   *Exit Clowne.*   6o
Lor. O deare difcretion, how his words are futed,
The foole hath planted in his memory   62

50. *than*] *then* F₄.   61. *futed*] *suited* Rowe.
53. *inftant ;*] *inftant ?* Q₁.

---

50. couer] See II, ix, 46.

52. occasion] ECCLES: That is, opportunity afforded by another speaker to play
upon his words.   CLARENDON: Quibbling on every opportunity, taking every oppor
tunity to make perverse replies.   SCHMIDT: At odds with the matter in question,
turning it into ridicule without reason.

61. deare discretion] ECCLES: That faculty of the mind most opposite to, and
inconsistent with, this disposition to quibble, for which Launcelot was so remarkable.
CLARENDON: Faculty of discrimination, which Launcelot's misapplied words shewed
him to lack.   See *Ham.* II, ii, 490: 'Well spoken, with good accent and good discretion.'   SCHMIDT: Good sense, common sense, reason, wisdom.

61. suted] JOHNSON: I believe the meaning is, What a *series* or *suite* of *words* he
has independent of meaning; how one word draws on another without relation to the
matter.   MONCK MASON: Lorenzo expresses surprise that a fool should apply his
words so properly.   ECCLES: I doubt whether Lorenzo does not mean how *badly*,
rather than how *well*, 'his words are suited,' that is, in how unnatural a manner those
'good words' were connected with matter of so frivolous a character.   CAPELL: To
Lorenzo's reflections the reader is wish'd to pay some attention : after which, it is possible he may be of opinion that the poet's 'play upon words,' which he may have often
arraign'd him for, is less a matter of choice in him than of indulgence to what appears
from these very passages to have been the taste of his times.   HALLIWELL: This is
spoken ironically, Launcelot's words being anything rather than 'suited,' or agreeing
with the context ; or, perhaps, 'suited' may here mean simply *arranged ;* or, how they
are matched to suit a perverted meaning.   ALLEN: Lorenzo pities 'discretion' (sound,
sober sense, and fair meaning) for the way in which it is 'defied' [or *defeated* = dis-
featured] by the 'tricksy words' [fantastically *suited*, or dressed up] by the fool.
'Suited' is equivalent to either: First, dressed-up (as an operation performed upon the
words themselves), tricked-out; or, secondly, matched (here ill-matched) with the
matter.

62. ALLEN suggests the excellent punctuation: 'The fool hath planted in his mem-

An Armie of good words, and I doe know   63
A many fooles that ftand in better place,
Garnifht like him, that for a trickfie word   65
Defie the matter:how cheer'ft thou *Ieffica,*
And now good fweet fay thy opinion,
How doft thou like the Lord *Baffiano's* wife?

    Ieffi.   Paft all expreffing, it is very meete
The Lord *Baffanio* liue an vpright life   70
For hauing fuch a bleffing in his Lady,
He findes the ioyes of heauen heere on earth,
And if on earth he doe not meane it, it   73

65. *Garnifht*] *Garnifh'd* Q₁.

66. *Defie*] *Defeat* Allen conj.

    cheer'ft] *cherft* Q₂. *far'ft* Q₁, Pope+.

    Ieffica,] Ieffica? Q₁.

68. Baffiano's] F₂.

70. Baffanio] Baffianio F₂.

73, 74. *meane it, it Is*] F₂. *mean it, it Is* F₃F₄, Rowe, Cap. Steev. Rann, Mal. Knt, Wh. *meane it, it in* Q₂. *meane, In* Q₃. *merit it, In* Pope+, Dyce ii, iii, Huds. Coll. iii. *earn it, it Is* Bailey. *meane it, then In* Q₁ et cet.

---

ory, An army,' &c., and calls attention to a corresponding punctuation which he proposes in IV, i, 383: 'Thou hast not, left, the value of a cord.'—ED.

64. **A many**] ABBOTT, § 87 : *A* was frequently inserted before a numeral adjective for the purpose of indicating that the objects enumerated are regarded collectively as *one.* We still say 'a score,' 'a fo(u)rt(een)-night.' The *a* in 'a many men,' 'a few men,' is, perhaps, thus to be explained. Compare '*This* nineteen *years,*'—*Meas. for Meas.* I, iii, 21, with '*This* many *summers,*'—*Hen. VIII;* III, ii, 360.

66. **cheer'st**] According to Schmidt's *Lex.* this is the only instance in Shakespeare of *cheer* used intransitively, and, although this of itself would not be any reason for discarding it, yet when we have a word in Q₁ against which not only no possible objection can be made, but which is also a usual, familiar mode of address, I think we may be allowed to regard *cherft* with suspicion, especially when the *ductus literarum, far'ft* and *cherft,* suggests a probable misreading.—ED.

73. **meane it**] HALLIWELL: This may be, possibly, an error for '*find* it,' or some word of like import. STAUNTON: Both the Quarto and Folio are equally unintelligible. What can be made of 'mean it'? Mean what? The commentators afford us no assistance here, although the sense is more ambiguous than in many passages on which they have expended whole pages of comment. The allusion applies to the belief that suffering in this life is a necessary preparation for happiness hereafter. Haply we should read, '*he do not moan, it is* In reason,' &c. The meaning of Jessica appears to be this: It is meet Bassanio live virtuously; for, possessing, with such a wife, the joys of Paradise, he could not plead suffering here as an atonement for his errors, and, in reason, therefore, would be excluded from heaven. WALKER whose library was small, did not know, when he conjectured (*Crit.* iii, 110), '*merit* it, '*Tis,*' that he had been anticipated by Pope as far as *merit* is concerned. '*Merit,*' says Walker, 'in the sense of *mereri.* The word was, perhaps, written *merite,* which comes nearer to "meane" in appearance. At any rate, the text, as it stands, is wrong.' In a foot-note,

Is reaſon he ſhould neuer come to heauen?
Why, if two gods ſhould play ſome heauenly match,   75

LETTSOM, Walker's admirable editor, remarks, after giving the various readings of the
Qq and Ff, and after stating that Pope had anticipated Walker, 'I should say that
Heyes's quarto [Q₂] gives the unsophisticated nonsense of the MS from which it was
printed; Roberts's [Q₁] boldly altered the second *it* to *then*, to gain an empty shadow
of sense; while F₁ played the same game with the text of Heyes's quarto by substituting *is* for *in* at the beginning of the second line. An early transcriber seems to
have corrupted *merit* into "mean it;" this vitiated all succeeding copies. The neo-
phyte Jessica had evidently been reading the parable of Lazarus and Dives. She
preaches up a righteous life, with her father's ducats in her pocket.' GRANT WHITE:
Heyes's quarto differs from Roberts's by having *it* instead of *then ;* a partial correction
which makes nonsense, until it is completed in the Folio by changing '*In*' to '*Is.*'
KEIGHTLEY: Here '*it*' seems to mean 'to live an upright life;' rather a harsh construction. It is not likely that the poet used 'mean' in the sense of *mener*, Fr., yet it
seems to be used so sometimes in Piers Ploughman. CLARENDON: The reading of F₁
is evidently a conjectural emendation. There is some corruption in this passage for
which no satisfactory emendation has been proposed. That of Pope is, perhaps, the
most plausible. *Earn it, then*, or *merit them*, might be suggested. But we rather
require a word with the sense of *appreciate*. HUDSON [reading *merit it*] : 'It' refers
to *blessing*, in the second line above. ROLFE: 'Mean it,' i. e. intend to *live an upright
life*. [I have reserved CAPELL to the last, because he gives, what is to me, emphatically the true interpretation. It was first set forth in his *Glossary*, as follows : 'to *mean*
it, observe the Mean, enjoy Blessings moderately,' and was afterward thus alluded to in
his *Notes*, p. 68 : 'As unfit a choice as the last [that is, Pope's change of "accoutered,"
in the preceding Scene, to *apparelled*] is made by the same gentlemen in this [present
passage] ; but their operations on this line set them high in the rank of critics; for,
instead of weighing the speaker's reasoning, and collecting (as had been easily done
from that reasoning) the undoubted and proper sense of her "mean it," change is proceeded to; and their phrase of alteration is—*merit it, In* beginning their next line :
How consequential this is to what has preceded, will not escape the considerer; but
the present and true reading, he will find so abundantly ; and though he may see some
extravagance in the sᵉntiment that is convey'd by that reading, he will not be apt to
condemn it, taking with it the occasion and speaker, and it's affinity in extravagance to
the thought that comes from her next.' The same interpretation occurred to Prof. COR-
SON, who says, in a privately-printed Note, that ' "mean" is the noun in the sense of
middle between two extremes, as in "golden mean" (as a noun it occurs in I, ii, 8 :
"to be seated in the meane"), and in the passage before us is used as a verb, and
the pronoun "it" is used indefinitely, as was very commonly done after intransitive
verbs, and *especially after nouns used as verbs. . . . .* This passage therefore means that
"if on earth he do not observe a mean in his pleasures, it is reason," &c.' If this be
the true interpretation of 'meane,' and I think it is, it may be noted to its credit that
Q₁ affords us an irreproachable text : 'And if on earth he doe not meane it, then In
reason he should neuer come to heauen.' This line occasioned a discussion in *Notes
& Qu.* 1877, 5th, viii, pp. 5, 1 4, &c., which, perhaps, let me add in all due humility,
would not have arisen had there been a new Variorum Edition at that date, wherein
all the notes of the Commentators could have been found on the same page with the
text and its various readings.—ED.]

And on the wager lay two earthly women,   76
And *Portia* one : there muſt be ſomething elſe
Paund with the other, for the poore rude world
Hath not her fellow.

  Loren. Euen ſuch a husband   80
Haſt thou of me, as ſhe is for a wife.

  Ieſ. Nay, but aske my opinion to of that?

  Lor. I will anone, firſt let vs goe to dinner?

  Ieſ. Nay, let me praiſe you while I haue a ſtomacke?

  Lor. No pray thee, let it ſerue for table talke,   85
Then how ſom ere thou ſpeakſt 'mong other things,
I ſhall digeſt it?

  Ieſſi. Well, Ile ſet you forth.   *Exeunt.*

---

78. *Paund*] *Pawn'd* Q₁.
80, 81. *Euen…me*] One line, Q₁.
81. *for a*] *for* Q₁Q₂.
82. *to of*] *too of* F₂ et seq.
83. *anone*] *anon* Q₁.
85. *pray thee*] *prethee* Q₁.

86. *how ſom ere*] F₂. *how ſo mere* Q₂. *how ſo ere* Q₃. *howſom ere* F₃. *howſome're* F₄. *howſoere* Q₁, Pope et seq.
'mong] *mong* Qq. *'mongſt* F₄, Rowe.
87. *digeſt*] *diſgeſt* Qq.

---

78. **Paund**] ECCLES : That is, staked.

81. **of me**] ABBOTT, § 172 : *Of* is used metaphorically with verbs of construction, as in the modern—'They make an ass of me.'—*Twelfth N.* V, i, 19. But *of* is also thus found without verbs of construction [as here, and in many other examples].

87. Note throughout this Scene the poverty of the compositor's 'case,' in the substitution of interrogation marks for periods.—ED.

Actus Quartus.

[*Scene I.*]

Enter the Duke, the Magnificoes, Anthonio, Baſſanio, and
  Gratiano.

Duke.   What, is *Anthonio* heere?

Ant.   Ready, ſo pleaſe your grace?

Duke.   I am ſorry for thee, thou art come to anſwere   5
A ſtonie aduerſary, an inhumane wretch,

Actus Quartus] Om. Qq.

[Scene I. Rowe.

[The Senate-house in Venice. Theob.
Venice. A Court of Justice. Cap.

  1. Enter...Magnificoes] Enter...Sena-
tors Rowe. Enter, in state, ...Magnificoes,
Officers of the Court, &c., and seat themselves; then, Enter Antonio, guarded.
Cap.

  2. Gratiano.] Gratiano, at the Bar.
Theob. Gratiano, Salerino, Solanio, and
others. Cap.

  5. *I am*] *I'm* Pope+, Dyce iii, Huds.
  6. *inhumane*] *inhumaine* Q₂.

In CHARLES KEAN'S revival of this play in 1858, the Doge was represented as
attended by six Senators in red; the authority for this is a picture at Hampton Court
Palace, where the Doge of Venice in state is receiving Sir Henry Wootton, ambassador
from James the First. The picture is by Odoardo Fialletti, better known as an
engraver than as a painter, who was living in Venice at the time.

TH. ELZE (*Sh. Jahrbuch*, xiv, 178): Although this Scene is correctly laid in a Court
of Justice, it is incorrect that Senators should appear as Judges, and the presence of the
Doge, as presiding officer at least, is an anachronism. If a civil case, the proceedings
would have been before one of the Supreme Courts, of which, at that time, Venice had
two, each composed of Forty Judges, hence the names: *Quarantia al civil vecchia*, dating from 1425, and *nuova*, dating from 1462. Over neither of these did the Doge preside. But if a criminal case, then it lay before a Supreme Court, likewise of Forty
Judges, entitled *Quarantia al criminal*. Over this latter Court the Doge did originally
preside, but from the time of the Doge Marco Cornaro (1365–67) his place was supplied
by three Counsellors. But who would ever think of criticising Shakespeare, even if
Shakespeare knew these facts, for introducing the Doge for the sake of mere scenic
effect?

HUDSON (p. 77): The Trial Scene, with its tugging vicissitudes of passion and its
hush of terrible expectation,—now ringing with the Jew's sharp, spiteful snaps of malice, now made musical with Portia's strains of eloquence, now holy with Antonio's tender breathings of friendship, and dashed, from time to time, with Gratiano's fierce jets
of wrath and fiercer jets of mirth,—is hardly surpassed in tragic power anywhere; and
as it forms the catastrophe proper, so it concentrates the interest of the whole play.

  4. **Ready**] The answer, to this day, when cases are called in Court.

  6, 7. **inhumane . . . Vncapable**] ABBOTT, § 442: *Un-* for modern *in-*; *in-* for
un-. We appear to have no definite rule of distinction even now, since we use

Vncapable of pitty, voyd, and empty   7
From any dram of mercie.

   Ant. I haue heard
Your Grace hath tane great paines to qualifie   10
His rigorous courfe : but fince he ftands obdurate,
And that no lawful meanes can carrie me
Out of his enuies reach, I do oppofe
My patience to his fury, and am arm'd
To fuffer with a quietneffe of fpirit,   15
The very tirann y and rage of his.

   Du. Go one and cal the Iew into the Court.

   Sal. He is ready at the doore, he comes my Lord.

         Enter Shylocke.

   Du. Make roome, and let him ftand before our face.   20
Shylocke the world thinkes, and I thinke fo to

10, 11. Three lines, ending *paines...*
courfe...obdurate Q₁.

  10. *tane*] ta'ne F₄. ta'en Rowe.

  18. *He is*] QqFf, Cap. Sing. Dyce i,

Cam. Ktly, Glo. Rlfe, Cla. Wh. ii. *He's*
Pope et cet.

  21. *fo to*] *fo to*, Q₁Q₃. *fo too* F₂ et seq.

---

*un*grateful, *in*gratitude; *un*equal, *in*equality. *Un-* seems to have been preferred by
Shakespeare before *p* and *r*, which do not allow *in-* to precede except in the form *im-*.
In- seems also to have been in many cases retained from the Latin, as in the case of
'*in*gratus,' '*in*fortunium,' &c. ROLFE: Shakespeare uses both *incapable* (six times)
and *uncapable* (twice).

   8. From] CLARENDON: Elsewhere Shakespeare always uses *of* as we do, with
'void' and 'empty.' ALLEN: We still say 'clear *from*,' 'free *from*.'

   8. dram] ALLEN: Any very minute quantity, applicable equally to what is liquid
and to what is solid. But as 'mercy' is spoken of afterward by Portia as liquid, it is
probable that Shakespeare, when he here used the word 'dram,' had in his mind a
drop.

   10. qualifie] DYCE: To soften, to moderate, to abate, to weaken. [Cf. Cassio's
'craftily qualified' cup,—*Oth*. II, ii, 56.]

   11. obdurate] See ABBOTT, § 490, for a long list of words wherein the accent is
nearer the end than with us.

   12. And that] See ABBOTT, § 285, for other instances like the present, where *that*
is omitted and then inserted, e. g. 'Were it not thy sour leisure gave sweet leave, And
that thou teachest.'—*Son*. 39.

   13. enuies] STEEVENS: It here means *hatred* or *malice*. KNIGHT: See *Mark*,
xv, 10, 'He knew that the chief priests had delivered him for envy.'

   16. tiranny] SCHMIDT (*Lex.*): Cruelty, injurious violence.

   19. Enter] BOOTH: Slowly, until in front of the Duke, then bow to him. Show
great deference to the Duke throughout the Scene, but to none else, except, of course,
to Portia, while she seems to favour your suit.

That thou but leadeſt this faſhion of thy mallice   22
To the laſt houre of act, and then 'tis thought
Thou'lt ſhew thy mercy and remorſe more ſtrange,
Than is thy ſtrange appʳant cruelty ;   25
And where thou now exact'ſt the penalty,
Which is a pound of this poore Merchants fleſh,
Thou wilt not onely looſe the forfeiture,
But touch'd with humane gentleneſſe and loue :
Forgiue a moytie of the principall,   30
Glancing an eye of pitty on his loſſes
That haue of late ſo hudled on his backe,
Enow to preſſe a royall Merchant downe ;
And plucke commiſeration of his ſtate
From braſſie boſomes, and rough hearts of flints,   35

22. *mallice*] Q₂. *malice* Q₁.

24. *Thou'lt*] *thowlt* Q₂. *Thouw'lt* Q₃.

25. *ſtrange apparant*] *ſtrange apparent* F₃. *strange-apparent* Walker, Dyce ii.

26. Om. Rowe.
exact'ſt] *exacts* Qq.

28. *looſe*] *loſe* F₄, Rowe+, Ec. Var.

Knt, Coll. i, ii, Hal. Sta.

29. *humane*] *humaine* Q₂. *human* Rowe.

30. *moytie*] *moiety* F₃F₄.

33. *Enow*] QqFf, Coll. Dyce, Hal.Wh. Rlfe, Clarke. *Enough* Rowe et cet.

34. *his ſtate*] *this ſtates* Q₂.

35. *flints*] Q₂. *flint* Q₁ et cet.

24. **remorse**] Pity. See *Oth.* III, iii, 426 and 532.

25. **apparant**] JOHNSON : That is, *seeming;* not real.

26. **where**] JOHNSON : For *whereas.* For other instances, see ABBOTT, § 134.

28. **loose**] COLLIER : Perhaps we ought to take this in the sense of *release.* BARRON FIELD (*Sh. Soc. Papers*, iii, 133) : Certainly, ' Loose ' is right. It is a bond ; and *to loose* is the correlative of *to bind.* See *Matt.* xvi, 19. But *lose* and *loose* are the same word, and both are generally in the old Editions *loose.* See, in this play, I, i, 84. HALLIWELL : The spelling is of no importance. To ' loose,' to release, makes good sense ; but *lose,* that is, give up in your own loss, lose it by your own will, seems the more likely reading. WALKER (*Crit.* iii, 55) : Shakespeare would have written ' *consent to* lose,' or the like. Write *loose,* i. e. *release, remit.* The ' loose ' of F₁ may be either the one or the other. Jonson, *Epigram* lviii, ' And so my sharpness thou no less disjoints, Than thou didst late my sense, *losing* my points.' Read *loosing;* a play upon words. [Hereupon LETTSOM, in a foot-note : ' It would seem from this that the words were not merely spelt, but pronounced, alike.'] DYCE (ed. iii) : That is, remit, release.

30. **moytie**] Used by Shakespeare to express any portion. In *1 Hen. IV:* III, 1, 96, it means a third ; and it may also mean a third in *Lear,* I, i, 6. One of the many advantages of having the original text before us is that, as here, the spelling guides us to the scansion. We see at once that *moiety* is a dissyllable.—ED.

33. **Enow**] See ' Christians enow before ' in the preceding Scene.

33. **royall Merchant**] See III, ii, 252.

35. **flints**] See ' multitudes ' II, ix, 35.

From ſtubborne Turkes and Tarters neuer traind   36
To offices of tender curteſie,
We all expeƈt a gentle anſwer Iew?
　　Iew.   I haue poſſeſt your grace of what I purpoſe,
And by our holy Sabbath haue I ſworne   40
To haue the due and forfeit of my bond.
If you denie it, let the danger light   42

---

36. *Tarters*] *Tartars* Q₁Q₃F₄ et seq.   40. *Sabbath*] *Sabaoth* Q₂, Cap.　*Sab-*
39. Iew.] Shy. Rowe.   *baoth* Q₃.

---

38. **gentle**] CLARENDON: A pun on Gentile is doubtless here intended.　[To me,
this is doubtful.　I do not forget how dearly Shakespeare loved a pun, and how, at
times, its attractions are irresistible to him, or that, in this very Scene, Anthonio puns
in his dying farewell to Bassanio.　Dr Johnson says that a quibble had 'a malignant
power over Shakespeare's mind,' and that it was to him 'the fatal Cleopatra for which
he lost the world, and was content to lose it;' so that I do not object to a pun here as
beneath the dignity of the Doge or of the occasion, but because it seems to mar the
gracious urbanity, and, more than all, the exquisite tact of this speech, and defeat its
very purpose.　The present is not the first occasion when the Doge has talked with
Shylock about the bond, and ta'en great pains to qualify his rigorous course; and he
therefore must have known Shylock's temper and temperament well enough by this
time to be convinced that any disparaging allusion to the Hebrew faith (which, as a pun,
this would be) would instantly evoke a bitter spirit of implacable antagonism.—ED.]

39. **possest**] See *ante*, I, iii, 65.　BOOTH: These first eight lines should be spoken
firmly, but with great respect in tone and manner.　At the allusion to his oath by his
'holy Sabbath,' the right hand should be raised with palm upward, and with an inclination of the head.

40. **Sabbath**] WHITE: *Sabaoth* of Q₂ has no such peculiar fitness that the word
of the authentic Edition should be set aside for it; for *sabaoth* is merely the Hebrew
for *hosts* or *armies*.　But it is possible that Shakespeare might have been misled by
the expression, 'Lord God of Sabaoth,' which occurs in the New Testament, into the
supposition that 'sabaoth' signified something peculiarly high and holy to the Jews.
CLARENDON: The same mistake occurs in Bacon's *Advancement of Learning*, Bk. ii,
24: 'Sacred & inspired Diuinitie, the Sabaoth and port of all men's labours and pere-
grinations.'　Spenser also confounds the signification of the two words: 'But thence-
forth all shall rest eternally With him that is the God of Sabbaoth hight: [O Thou great
Sabbaoth God, graunt me that Sabaoth's sight.]'—*Faerie Queene* [Bk. vii, c. 8, *vnperfite*.　It is not perfectly clear to me that Spenser has here confounded the two words.
Clarendon does not cite the line in brackets.　But it is a matter of small moment; the
canto is very 'vnperfite,' and consists of only eighteen lines.—ED.] Dr Johnson, in the
First Edition of his *Dictionary*, treated Sabbath and Sabaoth as identical words; and
Sir Walter Scott has, *Ivanhoe*, ch. x: 'The gains of a week, ay, the space between
two Sabaoths.'　But the error has been corrected in later editions.

41. **due and forfeit**] ALLEN: Hendiadys; the forfeit which is due.

42, 43. GOULD (*The Tragedian*, p. 79): These two lines were given [by the elder
Booth] with an outreaching and arching motion of the arm and hand, palm downward,
like the stoop of a bird of prey.

Vpon your Charter, and your Cities freedome. 43
You'l aske me why I rather choofe to haue
A weight of carrion flefh, then to receiue 45
Three thoufand Ducats? Ile not anfwer that:
But fay it is my humor; Is it anfwercd?
What if my houfe be troubled with a Rat,
And I be pleas'd to giue ten thoufand Ducates 49

44. *You'l*] *Youle* Q₂.
45. *then*] *than* F₄.
46. *Ducats ?...that :*] *Ducats ?...that,*

Q₁. *Ducats :...that ?* Q₂.
47. *But fay it is*] *But, say, it is* Cap.
anfwercd] F₁.

---

43. **Charter, and your Cities freedome**] WHITE: Here Shakespeare puts a threat into Shylock's mouth which would have little terror for the Doge of Venice. But, according to his habit, he availed himself of associations which were familiar and significant to his audience.

46, 47. **Ile . . . humor**] WARBURTON: This Jew is the strangest Fellow. He is asked a question; says he will not answer it; in the very next line says he has answered it, and then spends the nineteen following lines to justify and explain his answer. Who can doubt, then, but we should read: 'I'll *now* answer that, *By saying* 'tis,' &c.? HEATH: The common reading means: 'I will not give a direct answer to the question you ask, nor give you a particular account of the motives of my present proceeding; But suppose it is my particular fancy to act thus; Will you accept that for an answer?' He must be almost as strange a man as Mr Warburton represents the Jew, who thinks a serious expostulation of a supreme magistrate, on a most extraordinary proceeding, in any measure answered by the person addressed telling him, 'Tis my humour, or particular fancy, to act thus. Every man of common sense immediately sees that refusing to give any answer, and the giving such an answer as this, amount to the same thing. Nor doth the Jew throughout the nineteen lines which follow, assign any other reason for a conduct so shocking than a settled hatred of, and antipathy to, Anthonio, which is just the same with what he here calls his 'humour,' and, therefore, he may be justly said to persist in his declared resolution not to answer the Duke's question. Accordingly, Bassanio immediately replies, 'That is no answer.' JOHNSON: The Jew being asked a question which the law does not require him to answer, stands upon his right, and refuses; but afterwards gratifies his own malignity by such answers as he knows will aggravate the pain of the enquirer. I will not answer, says he, as to a legal or ferious question, but since you want an answer, will this serve you? SIR WALTER SCOTT (ap. Singer): The worthy Corporal Nym hath this apology usually at his fingers' ends, and Shylock condescends to use his extravagant cruelty as a *humour*, or irresistible propensity of the mind. The word 'humour' is not used in its modern signification, but for a peculiar quality which sways and masters the individual through all his actions. In Rowland's *Epigrams*, No. 27 amply illustrates this phrase: 'Aske *Humors* why a fether he doth weare? It is his humour (by the Lord) heele sweare,' &c. HALLIWELL: 'Humour' is probably here employed in the sense attached to the word as commonly used in Shakespeare's time, an indescribable exaggeration of its meaning as applied to whim, caprice, or any propensity. Any peculiar quality or turn of mind was a 'humour.'

To haue it bain'd ? What, are you anfwer'd yet ?   50
Some men there are loue not a gaping Pigge:
Some that are mad, if they behold a Cat:
And others, when the bag-pipe fings i'th nofe,   53

50. *bain'd*] *baind* Qq. *brain'd* Rowe.   51. *Pigge*] *pig* Q₁.
bane'd Pope.   53. *i'th*] *ith* Q₂Q₃.

---

51. **loue**] For many other examples of the omission of the relative, see ABBOTT, § 244.

51. **gaping Pigge**] STEEVENS: So in Webster's *Dutchess of Malfi* [III, ii, p. 240, ed. Dyce]: 'He could not abide to see a pig's head gaping; I thought your grace would find him a Jew.' See *Hen. VIII:* V, iv, 3 [where Steevens interprets 'gaping' as *shouting* or *roaring*, and adds that 'perhaps the "gaping pig" mentioned by Shylock has been misinterpreted']. MALONE: By 'gaping pig,' Shakespeare, I believe, meant a pig prepared for the table. So in Fletcher's *Elder Brother* [II, ii]: 'Ask 'em anything Out of the element of their understanding, And they stand gaping like a roasted pig.' Again, in Nashe's *Pierce Penilesse* [p. 55, ed. Grosart] (a passage which perhaps furnished our author with his instance): 'The causes conducting vnto wrath are as diuers as the actions of a man's life. Some will take on like a mad man, if they see a pigge come to the table.' KNIGHT: We are inclined to think that Shylock alludes to the squeaking of the living animal. He is particularizing the objects of offence to other men; and he would scarcely repeat his own dislike to pork, so strongly expressed in the First Act. [Knight cites a passage from Donne's *Devotions*, 'in which the doctrine of antipathies is put in a somewhat similar manner.'] HALLIWELL quotes 'a curious enumeration of antipathies given in the *Newe Metamorphosis*, a poem written early in the Seventeenth Century.' GRANT WHITE: Shakespeare may have meant either the roasted or the living, squealing pig; and let not the doubt which, disturb our souls.

53. **bag-pipe**] WARBURTON: This incident Shakespeare seems to have taken from J. C. Scaliger's *Exot. Exercit.* against Cardan,—a book that our author was well read in, and much indebted to for a great deal of his physics, it being then much in vogue. In his 344 *Exercit.*, Sect. 6, he has these words: 'Narrabo nunc tibi jocosam *Sympathiam* Reguli Vasconis Equitis. Is dum viveret, audito phormingis sono, urinam illico facere cogebatur.' And to make this jocular story still more ridiculous, Shakespeare, I suppose, translated 'phorminx' by 'bag-pipe.' But what I would chiefly observe from hence is this, that as Scaliger uses the word 'sympathiam,' which signifies, and so he interprets it, 'communem affectionem duabus rebus,' so Shakespeare translates it by 'affection;' which shows the propriety of the full stop after that word in the next line. FARMER: In an old translation from the French of Peter de Loier, entitled, *A Treatise of Spectres, or Strange Sights, Visions*, &c., we have this identical story from Scaliger; and, what is still more, a marginal note gives us, in all probability, the very fact alluded to, as well as the *word* of Shakespeare: 'Another gentleman of this quality lived of late in Devon, neere Excester, who could not endure the playing on a *bag-pipe*.' We may justly add that 'affection,' in the sense of *sympathy*, was formerly technical, and so used by Lord Bacon, Sir K. Digby, and many other writers. MALONE: The story of the Devonshire gentleman, I believe, first appeared in the margin of De Loier's book in 1605, some years after this play was printed; but it might have been current in conversation before, or it may have found its way into some other book of that age.

Cannot containe their Vrine for affection.
Mafters of paffion fwayes it to the moode   55

54, 55. *Vrine...of*] Qq Ff (*Maifters* Q₂F₂), Warb. Mal. Var. Coll. i, Wh. i. *urine for affection*. *Masterless* Rowe, Pope, Theob. Han. *urine, for affection; Master of* Johns. *urine; for affection, Mistress of* Thirlby, Cap. Steev. '93, Var. '03, Var. '13, Cam. Glo. Ktly, Dyce iii. *urine. For affection, Masters of* Steev. '70.

urine: for affections, Masters of Hawkins, Steev. '78, '85. *urine; for affection, Master of* Rann, Knt, Sing. Dyce i, ii, Hal. Coll. ii, iii, Sta. Clarke, Del. Wh. ii.

55. *fwayes it*] *sways us* Han. *sway it* Warb. Hawkins, Steev. '70, '78, '85, Mal. Var. Coll. i, Wh. i.

54, 55. **Cannot . . . moode**] The earliest critical attempt at emending this passage is almost the best of all, and in its substitution of a comma after 'affection,' has been adopted by a large majority of Editors since, and including, Capell.   In Nichols's *Illust. of Lit.* ii, 225, there is, under date of 1729, the list of changes which DR THIRLBY sent to Theobald.   The list is a bare one; the changes are proposed without comment.   In it there stands, at this passage : ' for affection, Master (or Mistress) of passion, sways it,' &c.   THEOBALD, in his subsequent Edition, speaks with praise of this emendation, but does not adopt it.   He had mildly suggested it to Warburton in his correspondence (p. 311 of Nichols), and, although Warburton's reply has not been preserved, I cannot but think that Theobald was brow-beaten out of it by his 'most affectionate friend,' who, in his own Edition, thus dogmatically decides the question : ' " Masters of passion." This is certainly right,' says WARBURTON.   ' He is speaking of the power of sound over the human affections, and concludes, very naturally, that the " masters of passion " (for so he finely calls the musicians) sway the passions or affections as they please, alluding to what the ancients tell us of the feats that Timotheus and other musicians worked by the power of music.   Can anything be more natural ?' HEATH : I have no doubt but the old reading is the genuine one; it undoubtedly means : ' The masters of passions, that is, such as are possessed of the art of engaging and managing the human passions, influence them by a skillful application to the particular likings and loathings of the person they are addressing; this is a proof that men are generally governed in their conduct by those likings or loathings; and, therefore, it is by no means strange or unnatural that I should be so, too, in the present case.   RITSON (*Remarks*, p. 54) : [The punctuation of the Folio] is surely defensible.   The meaning is, that some men, when they hear the sound of a bag-pipe, are *so affected therewith,* that they cannot, &c.   For those things which are masters over passion make it like or loath whatever they will.   MALONE (who also preferred the old text, or, at least, merely a colon after 'affection') : These lines mean, I believe,—Cannot, &c., on account of *their being affected* by the noise of the bag-pipe; or, in other words, on account of an involuntary antipathy to such a noise.   In the next line, which is put in apposition with that preceding, the word 'it' may refer either to 'passion' or 'affection.'   '*It*' ('sway it'), in my opinion, refers to 'affection,' that is, to the sympathetic feeling.   STEEVENS : That *affections* and *passions* anciently had different significations, may by known from the following instance in Greene's *Never Too Late* [p. 174, ed. Grosart.   See also III, i, 54, of the present play] : ' His hart was fuller of *passions* than his eyes of *affections.*' *Affections*, as used by Shylock, seems to signify *imaginations* or *prejudices.*   A passage somewhat similar is in *Oth.* I, iii, 251.   CAPELL : The terms *affection* and *passion* are of philosophic precision, intimating—the impressing and the impress'd.   *Mistress* has its justness, being spoken of mind; nor is the word it sprang out of so remote from it

[54, 55. for affection. Masters of passion]

as a modern reader will think, for the form that *mistress* wears in old books is not un-frequently—*maistres*. COLMAN: I must confess that I cannot discover on what prin-ciple all the Editors since Theobald and Hanmer have followed the punctuation of Thirlby. It is impossible, I think, for any reader accustomed to the manner of our old writers, not to feel a certain harshness in the new regulation of the text, or, indeed, to doubt for a moment that the old books gave the line correctly as at that time spoken on the stage, and originally written by the author. I never heard, excellent and very Shylock as he is, Macklin's full stop in the middle of the line without a shock; and the following words of the line not only soften the expression, but are most easy and natural. We still apply the verb *affect* in the same sense that Shylock here uses the noun derived from it. [This affection, Colman thinks, must be *sympathy* and it is brought in as a contrast to the 'gaping pig' and to the 'cat,' where *antipathy* predom-inates; the 'grand Desideratum,' therefore, is some word, or phrase, or line expressive of an irresistible influence over our *likings* and *loathings*, as well as governing the verb 'sways.' Colman continues:] On the whole, therefore, I conceive that the original punctuation should be maintained, the word *Maisters* in the old copies should be read *Mistress*, and that the imperfection in the sense, according to that reading, arises from a line or two lost or dropt at the press, in which the words *Sympathy* and *Antipathy*, so congenial to the argument, had most probably a place. [This line Colman accord-ingly supplies, and reads the passage thus:] 'Cannot, &c., for affection. *Sovereign*, *Antipathy*, or *Sympathy*, Mistress of passion, sways it,' &c. KNIGHT: Shylock himself, in a previous Scene, has distinguished between *affection* and *passion* [III, i, 54]. The distinction, indeed, is a very marked one in the original use of the words. *Affection* is that state of the mind, whether pleasant or disagreeable, which is produced by some *external* object or quality. *Passion* is something higher and stronger—the *suggestive* state of mind—going to a point by the force of its own will. The distinction is very happily preserved in Greene's *Never Too Late*. Keeping in view this distinction, we have a key to this very difficult passage, whose meaning then, is, that *affection*, either for love or dislike,—sympathy or antipathy,—being the *master of passion*,—sways *it* (*passion*) to the mood of what *it* (*affection*) likes or loaths. If we were to adopt the reading which Malone prefers: '*Masters* of passion sway *it*, &c., of what *it* likes,' &c., the second *it* would be inconsistent with the sense, and we ought to read—'Of what *they* like or loath.' COLLIER (ed. i): This passage has occasioned a good deal of con-troversy, but the difficulty seems to be to find a difficulty; in the old copies 'sway' is printed *sways*, making a false concord, the nominative case being 'masters;' the pro-noun 'it,' of course, in both instances, agrees with 'passion.' Shylock, in the preced-ing lines, speaks of those who are not 'masters of passion.' DYCE (*Remarks*, p. 57): The preceding part of the passage clearly shews that there must be a pause at 'urine;' as also that 'for affection' must be connected with the next line. Shylock states three circumstances: first, that some men dislike a gaping pig; secondly, that some are mad if they see a cat; thirdly, that some, at the sound of a bag-pipe, cannot contain their urine; and he then accounts for these three peculiarities on a general principle. Knight's alteration [in reality, Rann's,—ED.] is greatly preferable [to Thirlby's] be-cause it deviates from the old Editions only by omitting a single letter. With respect to Collier's reading, I have further to observe, that 'Masters of passion' (if we under-stand the words in the sense which, as his note shews, he supposes them to bear) were the very persons of whom Shylock would carefully avoid all mention. COLLIER (ed. ii): I formerly punctuated this line differently, but I am now satisfied that I was in

Of what it likes or loaths, now for your anfwer :   56
As there is no firme reafon to be rendred
Why he cannot abide a gaping Pigge?
Why he a harmleffe neceffarie Cat?
Why he a woollen bag-pipe : but of force   60

---

56. *it*] *she* Ktly.

    loaths,] *loathes* · Q$_1$. *loaths.* F$_4$.

58, 59. *Pigge?...Cat?*] *pig,...cat,* F$_4$.

60. *woollen*] *wollen* F$_4$. *wawling* Cap. conj. *swollen* Hawkins, Steev. Var. '03,

'13, Sing. Ktly, Clarke. *bollen* Dyce, Coll. ii, iii. *wauling* Huds. *wailing* Cartwright. *swelling* Hawkins. *waullen* Brae. *wilean* or *willne* Oliver (*N. & Qu.* 5th, viii, 63).

---

error. 'Affection,' here meaning sympathy, is the nominative to 'sways,' 'Master of passion' being, as it were, in parenthesis. The only variation from the old Editions is reading *Master* for 'Masters.' The (MS) makes no change. STAUNTON : The true source of the difficulty, however, may lie neither in 'masters' nor 'affection,' but in the comparatively insignificant preposition 'of.' If 'of' is a misprint for *our*, the passage would run : 'For affection Masters *our* passion, sways it,' &c. [Staunton notes also that the F$_1$ omits 'it' after 'sways.' I think this must be a misprint. The 'it' is present in the copy of the Cambridge Editors, in my copy, and in Staunton's own Photo-lithographic Edition.—ED.] WALKER, who (*Crit.* i, 252) cites 'Masters' in this line as an instance of the interpolated *s* (see II, ix, 35), says, 'point undoubtedly, and, I think, read as follows : " For affection, Master of passion, sways it," &c. At any rate, there is no necessity, as far as the *s* is concerned, for reading *maistresse ;* which spelling, moreover, occurs nowhere else in the Folio, as far as I recollect.' GRANT WHITE : Change is unnecessary, and comment would seem superfluous. The Folio accidentally omits 'it' [after 'sways.' I am afraid this assertion was taken, without due verification, from Staunton.—ED.] The difficulty seems to have arisen entirely from a misapprehension of the meaning of 'masters of passion ;' by which Shylock does not mean *men* who are able to control the passions of themselves or others, but such *agencies* as those of which he has just been speaking. 'Passion' is used in its more radical sense, and not with reference to any one of the passions, a common use in Shakespeare's day. 'Affection' means, of course, 'the being affected,' in this case, by the sound of the bag-pipe—also, of old, a common use of the word ; and thus the masters of passion are those things or occurrences that move either the sympathy or antipathy of any man, and 'sway' it to the mood of what it likes or loaths. KEIGHTLEY (*Exp.* p. 152) : For 'Of what it likes,' &c., I read, 'Of what *she* likes,' &c. ; the 'it' was evidently caused by that in the preceding line. ABBOTT (p. 481, Note 10), in regard to the confusion of *Masters* and *Mistress,* refers to *Temp.* II, i, 5, and to 'Where be thy *mastres,* man? I would speak with *her.*'—Beau. & Fl., *The Coxcomb,* II, iii, 9 [which is, perhaps, scarcely parallel, because the speaker is disguised as an Irish footman, and gabbles nonsense. In the margin of my copy of Dyce's *Remarks,* Lettsom has written, with pencil, 'for affection's Master of passion, sways it,' &c. I follow Thirlby, as modified by Rann.—ED.].

    58, 59, 60. **he**] ALLEN : Like ὁ μὲν, ὁ δὲ, ὁ δὲ.

    60. **woollen**] JOHNSON : As all the editors agree with complete uniformity in reading '*woollen,*' I can hardly forbear to imagine that they understood it. But I never saw a 'woollen bag-pipe,' nor can well conceive it. I suppose the author wrote *wooa'en,* meaning that the bag was leather, and the pipe of *wood*. [HEATH made independently

Muſt yeeld to ſuch ineuitable ſhame,   61
As to offend himſelfe being offended :

61. *ſhame*] *sway* Bailey.   *himſelf*, F₄, Rowe, Cap. Steev. Sta. *offend,*
62. *offend himſelfe*] Q₂F₂F₃Q₃. *offend*   *himſelfe* Q₁, Pope et cet.

---

the same conjecture.] CAPELL: Why, in the rudeness of ancient poverty, the bag should not have been of *wool* (that is—cloth of extream coarseness) in some places, the editor sees not. ROBINSON: Perhaps it is called 'woollen' from the bag being generally covered with woollen cloth. STEEVENS: As the aversion was not caused by the outward appearance, but merely by the sound, I have adopted *swollen* in the text. RITSON (p. 54): It is not unusual to see the large skin or bladder of the bag-pipe covered with *flannel;* and, it is possible the word was only used as a descriptive epithet. MONCK MASON (p. 76): I consider *swol'n* as one of those amendments which carry conviction the moment they are suggested. DOUCE (i, 264): We have here one of the too frequent instances of *conjectural* readings; but it is to be hoped that all future editors will restore the original 'woollen,' after weighing not only what has been already urged in its support, but the additional and accurate testimony of Dr Leyden, who, in his edition of *The Complaynt of Scotland*, p. 149, informs us that the Lowland bagpipe commonly had the bag covered with *woollen cloth* of a green colour, a practice which, he adds, prevailed in the northern counties of England. COLLIER (ed. ii): *Bollen* is from the (MS) and is doubtless the epithet of the poet, who had used it in his *Lucrece* [line 1417]: 'Here, one being throng'd, bears back, all boll'n and red.' *Bollen* is swelled or inflated. 'Woollen' is a corruption of *bollen*, of which *swollen* is merely a translation. DYCE (ed. ii) [see Text. Notes]: In the first place, what writer ever used such an expression as *a woollen bag-pipe* in the sense of *a bag-pipe covered with woollen cloth?* (Might he not, with almost equal propriety, talk of *a woollen lute* or *a woollen fiddle?*) And, in the second place, can anything be more evident than that Shylock *does not intend the most distant allusion to the material which either composed or covered the bag-pipe?* I adopt the (MS's) emendation. (I have repeatedly met with old handwriting in which the initial *b* bore such a resemblance to *w*, that a compositor might easily have mistaken it for the latter.) GRANT WHITE: No one who has seen a bagpipe, or who knows that the bag is generally, if not always, covered with baize or some other cloth, will think either *swollen* or *bollen* worth consideration. CAMBRIDGE EDITORS: In an illuminated copy of an *Office de la Vierge* in the library of Trinity College, there is a representation of a bagpipe which appears to be of sheepskin with the wool on. We incline, however, to think that Capell's conjecture *wawling* approaches nearest the truth. STAUNTON in his *Addenda and Corrigenda* having adduced in support of the old reading, a line from Massinger's *The Maid of Honour,* IV, iv: 'Walks she on woollen feet?' DYCE (ed. iii) replied that ' "woollen *bag-pipe*" (if right) means a bag-pipe *actually covered with woollen cloth*, while "woollen feet" is *a purely metaphorical expression*.' ALLEN: The logic of the passage requires an indifferent or innocent epithet (as in line 59), not *wawling* nor *mewling*. [The dispute again burst forth in *Notes & Queries*, 5th, vol. viii, pp. 4, 63, 182, 423, but surely the bulk of the notes and comments, already given, is sufficiently *bollen.*—ED.]

61. Must] For the omission of the nominative, compare I, i, 108, or see ABBOTT, § 399.

62. himselfe] STAUNTON: Modern editors point this line: 'As to offend, himself being offended,' which renders it near akin to nonsense. [To the same effect, WALKER

So can I giue no reafon, nor I will not,   63
More then a lodg'd hate, and a certaine loathing
I beare *Anthonio*, that I follow thus   65
A loofing fuite againft him? Are you anfwered?

   Baff.   This is no anfwer thou vnfeeling man,
To excufe the currant of thy cruelty.

   Iew.   I am not bound to pleafe thee with my anfwer.

   Baff.   Do all men kil the things they do not loue?   70

   Iew.   Hates any man the thing he would not kill?

   Baff.   Euerie offence is not a hate at firft.

   Iew.   What wouldft thou haue a Serpent fting thee
twice?

   Ant.   I pray you thinke you queftion with the Iew: 75

---

64. *lodg'd*] *lodgd* Q₂. *lodged* Q₁.
66. *loofing*] *lofing* Q₁.
   him?] *him;* Q₁.
67. *anfwer*] *anfwer,* Q₁.
68. *currant*] *current* F₃F₄.
69, 71, 73. Iew.] Shy. Q₁.
69. *anfwer.*] *anfwers?* Q₂. *anfwers.*

Q₃, Cap. Cam. Glo. Cla. Wh. ii.
70. *things*] *thing* Ff, Rowe+.
75. *you thinke*] Qq Ff, Rowe, Pope.
you, think, Theob. ii, Warb. Johns. *you think :* Sing. *you, think* Theob. i, et cet.
the Iew] *a Jew* F₃F₄, Rowe+.

(*Crit.* iii, 56), KEIGHTLEY (*Expofitor*, p. 152), and ALLEN. To me also, this punctuation, that of F₄, is the better, but CLARENDON thinks that 'both the context and the rhythm of the verse seem to favour' a comma after 'offend.'—ED.]

64. **a certaine**] ALLEN: Dele 'a,' and read 'certain,' i. e. sure, fixed. 'Certain loathing' repeats 'lodgèd hate.' (The 'a' was inserted by the compositors under the impression that 'a certain' was equivalent to τὶς, quidam, a kind of.)

66. **a loofing suite**] CLARENDON: A suit in which I have nothing to gain. [Or is it, a suit in which I lose my money? Does not Shylock hope to gain the forfeit of his bond?—ED.]

66. **answered?**] BOOTH: Bow to the Duke. At Bassanio's exclamation draw yourself up, your back toward him, and speak contemptuously, without looking at him.

72. ECCLES: This reply seems to be somewhat foreign to the question of Shylock; besides, Bassanio seems to forget that the Jew's charge against Anthonio, in their first interview after the opening of the play, was that he had 'many a time and oft' affronted him. CLARENDON: 'Offence' means resentment of the injured party [i. e. Subjective] as well as the injury itself [i. e. Objective]. Bassanio uses the word in the former sense, Shylock's reply alludes to the latter.

73. BOOTH: Turn on him sharply.

75. KNIGHT: The construction of this line appears to us elliptical,—we believe it should be understood thus: 'I pray you think [if], you question with the Jew.' [For me, a comma after 'I pray you,' removes all difficulty.—ED.] KEIGHTLEY (*Exp.* p. 153): I cannot but adhere to *stint your* for 'think you,' as I have given it in my Edition. It seems to me so much more forcible, and more suited to the calm resignation of Anthonio; while in the other reading there is something of sneer or irony that is unpleasant. Nothing was easier than for the printer to read *stint*, the more unusual

You may as well go ſtand vpon the beach, 76
And bid the maine flood baite his vſuall height,
Or euen as well vſe queſtion with the Wolfe,
The Ewe bleate for the Lambe: 79

---

77. *baite*] *bate* Qq F₂. *be at* F₃F₄. *'bate*
Theob.
78. *Or...well*] Ff, Rowe. *vvell* Q₂.
You may as well Q₁Q₃, Pope et cet.
79. *The...Lambe:*] *the Ewe bleake for
the Lambe:* Q₂. *Why he hath made the*

Ewe bleake for the Lambe: Q₁. *The Ewe
bleate for the Lambe: when you behold,*
Ff, Rowe. *When you behold the ewe bleat
for the lamb;* Han. *Why he hath made
the Ewe bleat for the Lambe:* Q₃ et cet

---

term, as 'think,' and then to make *your* 'you' for the sake of sense, and as they are
pronounced nearly alike. However, *judicet lector.* BOOTH: Shylock listens to all
this with an expression of mockery.

75. question] STEEVENS: That is, converse. To *reason* had anciently the same
meaning. CLARENDON: Remember you are arguing with Shylock, whose cruel nature
is known.

77. baite] Note the ingenious change made by F₃F₄, which, if it were in the *editio
princeps,* would find, probably, many an advocate whom nothing could persuade that
'baite' was the true word.—ED.

78, 79. It is scarcely beyond the bounds of probability that these two lines when
heard from the stage would be adequately intelligible; the connection of thought would
tide us over the obstruction: the ocean will be governed by its own laws, the wolf will
be true to his cruel nature, the ewe will bleat for its lamb, the mountain pines will sway
to the tempest; the words are uttered, our interest is absorbed, the speech hurries forward, and we see no difficulty. But with the printed page before us we see the havoc
with the sense that some accident at the printing-press has made. These lines have
evidently been fretted by a gust of some kind. It was not, however, at the press where
the Folio was printed; there has been even an attempt at repairing it by the printers
of that Edition. The accident happened with the unfortunate Q₂, from which the
Folio was printed, and the result is another of the many indications of the haste with
which the Heyes's Quarto was issued. According to the Cambridge Editors, Halliwell has seen a copy of this Qto. in which line 79 was omitted altogether. In
Ashbee's Facsimile, the lines run thus: 'and bid the maine flood bate his vſuall
height, ‖ vvell vſe queſtion with the Woolfe, ‖ the Ewe bleake for the Lambe:' ‖ The
very defective copy, then, which Halliwell has seen, shows that there were gradations
in the accident, or in the repairs of it. It may, therefore, have happened that the copy
which the compositors of the Folio used, actually read as the text in the Folio gives it;
or these same compositors may have attempted to amend the passage, and considered
that they had done their duty by adding, 'Or euen as,' and by changing *bleake* into
'bleat.' However this may be, we have, happily, Q₁ to refer to, and here again we
find another proof of its superiority to the copy of Q₂, which the compositors of the
Folio used. Lines 78, 79, there read: 'You may as well vſe queſtion with the Wolfe, ‖
Why he hath made the Ewe bleake for the Lambe:' This is the text which has
been adopted, with only two or three exceptions, by all Editors. In dealing with the
Quartos (and it might almost be affirmed of the Folios also) it is necessary to specify
the particular copies which are cited, so much do copies of the same date differ. I
haᵥe been particular iust now in speaking of the copy of Q₂ which was used for the

You may as well forbid the Mountaine Pines   80
To wagge their high tops, and to make no noife
When they are fretted with the gufts of heauen:
You may as well do any thing moft hard,
As feeke to foften that, then which what harder?
His Iewifh heart.   Therefore I do befeech you   85
Make no more offers, vfe no farther meanes,
But with all briefe and plaine conueniencie
Let me haue iudgement, and the Iew his will.
 Baf.   For thy three thoufand Ducates heereis fix.   89

---

80. *Mountainé*] *mountaine of* Qq.
81. *no noife*] *a noise* Han. Warb.
82. *fretted*] *fretten* Qq, Coll. Sing. Hal. Wh. i, Cam. Glo. Ktly, Dyce iii, Huds.
84. *then*] *than* Ff.

84. *what harder ?*] F$_2$F$_3$, Wh. i. *what harder*, F$_4$, Rowe. *what's harder :* Qq et cet.
86. *more*] *moe* Q$_1$Q$_2$.

Folio. This copy was probably like that in the Duke of Devonshire's library (which was used by Prætorius in his Reproduction), and also like that from which Ashbee made his Facsimile. But it is clearly different from the Q$_2$ in Capell's library, which, I presume, was the one used by the Cambridge Editors, because they make special note of the text in the Duke of Devonshire's copy, and say that 'Lord Ellesmere's copy agrees with Capell's *literatim;*' in Capell's Q$_2$, therefore, the lines must be almost exactly as they are in Q$_1$. The copy of Q$_1$ which is now before me, and which I have used throughout for collation, formerly belonged to Capell, and in it he has, in his painful chirography, recorded the *variæ lectiones* of Q$_2$ and of Q$_3$; his only note on these lines is that 'bleake' is changed to *bleat* in Q$_3$. This long note on a trifling matter must find its justification in the lesson, which this passage affords, that Quartos and Folios may all alike be treated as proof-sheets, out of which we may, with what power of insight Nature has vouchsafed us, prepare our own text, with an abounding charity for those who do not agree with us,—which, in all likelihood, will comprise the rest of mankind.—ED.

 80. **Pines**] STEEVENS: This image seems to have been caught from Golding's *Ovid* [1567, Bk xv, p. 195]: 'Such noyse as Pynetrees make what tyme the heady easterne wynde Dooth whiz amongst them.'

 81. **to make**] ABBOTT, § 382: The Elizabethan authors objected to scarcely any ellipsis, provided the deficiency could be easily supplied from the context. Thus the present line may be explained, by implying from 'forbid' a word of speaking, *bid*, and not by a double negative: 'To wag their high tops, and [bid them] to make no noise.' [See line 168, *post*, 'no impediment.']

 82. **fretted**] COLLIER: There seems no reason to abandon the form *fretten*, probably adopted by Shakespeare; if *fretten* were not the original word, it is singular that it should be found in both Qq, which were evidently printed from different manuscripts. GRANT WHITE: It is most probable that Shakespeare wrote *fretten*, and that 'fretted' was a printer's conformity to the custom of the day; but this canno* be assumed as absolutely certain. See ABBOTT, § 344, for other instances of irregular participial formations, like *fretten.*

Iew. If euerie Ducat in fixe thoufand Ducates   90
Were in fixe parts, and euery part a Ducate,
I would not draw them, I would haue my bond?
    Du. How fhalt thou hope for mercie, rendring **none**?
    Iew. What iudgement fhall I dread doing no **wrong?**
You haue among you many a purchaft flaue,   95
Which like your Affes, and your Dogs and Mules,
You vfe in abiect and in flauifh parts,
Becaufe you bought them.   Shall I fay to you,
Let them be free, marrie them to your heires?
Why fweate they vnder burthens? Let their beds   100
Be made as foft as yours : and let their pallats
Be feafon'd with fuch Viands : you will anfwer
The flaues are ours.   So do I anfwer you.
The pound of flefh which I demand of him
Is deerely bought, 'tis mine, and I will haue it.   105
If you deny me ; fie vpon your Law,
There is no force in the decrees of Venice ;
I ftand for iudgement, anfwer, Shall I haue it?
    Du.   Vpon my power I may difmiffe this Court,
Vnleffe *Bellario* a learned Doctor,   11U

---

96. *your Affes*] you *Affes* F₂.   105. *'tis*] *tis* Q₁. *as* Q₂Q₃. *is* Cap.
97. *parts*] *part* Ff, Rowe+.   Mal. '90, Steev. Hal.
98. *you bought*] *your bought* F₂.

90–92. BOOTH : Slowly, with great determination, in subdued tones.

92. **draw**] ALLEN : We now speak of *drawing* money only from a bank, or place of deposit. Was it then used of accepting or receiving money in any way? 'Draw' may be equivalent to choose, that is, if offered at the same time with the bond.

94. BOOTH : With a look and tone of surprise.

95. JOHNSON : This argument, considered as used to the particular persons, seems conclusive. I see not how Venetians or Englishmen, while they practise the purchase and sale of slaves, can much enforce or demand the law of ' doing to others as we would that they should do to us.'

103. **So . . . you**] BOOTH : Respectfully but firmly, and at line 108, bow as you ask.

109. **Vpon**] ABBOTT, § 192 : *Upon* from meaning superposition, comes to mean *in accordance with* (like 'after'), as here.

110. **Bellario**] JOHNSON : The doctor and the Court are here somewhat unskillfully brought together. That the Duke would, on such an occasion, consult a doctor of great reputation, is not unlikely; but how should this be foreknown by Portia? TYRWHITT : I do not see any necessity for supposing that *this* was *foreknown by Portia*. She consults Bellario as an eminent lawyer, and her relation. If the Duke had not consulted him, the only difference would have been, that she would have come into

Whom I haue ſent for to determine this,   111
Come heere to day.
   Sal.   My Lord, heere ſtayes without
A Meſſenger with Letters from the Doctor,
New come from Padua.   115
   Du.   Bring vs the Letters, Call the Meſſengers.
   Baſſ.   Good cheere *Anthonio.* What man, corage yet :   117

---

113. Sal.] Saler. Q₁.   Salerio Q₂.   116. *Meſſengers*] *Meſſenger* Qq.
116. *Letters,*] *letters ?* Q₂. *Letters.* Q₃.   117. *corage*] *courage* Qq F₃F₄.

Court as an advocate, perhaps, instead of a judge. KENRICK (*Rev. of Johnson's Ed.,* p. 52): Is it not very natural to suppose that, after Bassanio was called away in such haste to Venice, his bride Portia would send a messenger to her cousin Bellario, in order to ask his opinion of so extraordinary a case, or to interest him in Anthonio's behalf? And can anything be more probable than that he should inform her, on receiving such a message, that he was actually sent for to Venice on that very account? For it is to be observed that the Duke speaks as if he had sent for him some considerable time before; for he says, 'unless Bellario, ... come here *to-day.*' His power of dismissing the Court also, on his not coming, seems founded on some physical or moral impediment, that might very naturally occur, to prevent his arrival within the time; so that he must be supposed either at such a distance as made it necessary to give him a considerable timely warning, or that the extraordinary nature of the cause might make him require so much the more time to prepare himself equitably to determine it. This being the case, was not here a very apt foundation on which to build Portia's plot of officiating for the doctor? which design she no doubt concerted with him by letter, before she sent for the notes and clothes mentioned in III, v. And that this was really the case seems evident from what Portia says to Lorenzo *during* the *absence* of Bassanio, and *before* she sends Balthazar to Bellario. Lorenzo compliments her on her noble conduct 'in bearing thus the absence of her lord.' A sufficient intimation, I think, that Bassanio must have been gone some time. Again, in Portia's reply to this compliment, we find her speaking very peremptorily and certainly of Anthonio's deliverance, and of the cost already bestowed to effect it. Is it reasonable to think that she would express herself thus confidently on a mere suggestion of her own? Besides, what cost could she have bestowed? Her having bid her husband pay the bond thrice over was nothing; because she could not be sure the money would be taken. Nay, she evidently does not intend to trust to that acceptance. It is therefore, I think, very evident that she had, even at this time, concerted the scheme with her cousin Bellario. It is true that the formality with which Portia introduces her charge to Balthazar, when she sends him for the notes and clothes, seems to favour the supposition that this was the first time she had sent to Bellario, in which case there would be some grounds for Dr Johnson's remark; but we must observe that Balthazar is now to be entrusted with a more important charge than he had before been, in merely carrying and bringing back a letter; or, it is not unlikely, that Portia entrusted that business with a servant of less importance. [See Th. Elze in Appendix : 'Dr Bellario;' and Lady Martin.—ED.]

112. BOOTH : Shylock shrugs his shoulders, and retires apart from the others.

116. **Messengers]** Another instance of the superfluous *s* noted by WALKER (*Crit.* 1, 233) and alluded to II, ix, 35, which see.

The Iew ſhall haue my flesh, blood, bones, and all,   118
Ere thou ſhalt looſe for me one drop of blood.

  Ant.   I am a tainted Weather of the flocke,   120
Meeteſt for death, the weakeſt kinde of fruite
Drops earlieſt to the ground, and ſo let me ;
You cannot better be employ'd *Baſſanio,*
Then to liue ſtill, and write mine Epitaph.

          Enter Nerriſſa.   125

  Du.   Came you from Padua from *Bellario* ?
  Ner.   From both.
My Lord *Bellario* greets your Grace.
  Baſ.   Why doſt thou whet thy knife ſo earneſtly ?
  Iew.   To cut the forfeiture from that bankrout there.   130
  Gra.   Not on thy ſoale : but on thy ſoule harſh Iew

---

120. *Weather*] *wether* Steev.
122. *earlieſt*] *soonest* Cap. (erratum).
    and] Om. Ff, Rowe.
[Scene II. Pope +.
125. Enter...] Enter...dress'd like ·a
Lawyer's Clerk. Rowe.
127, 128. One line, Qq, Pope et seq.
127. *both.   My Lord*] Ff. *both, my
L.* Q₁. *both ? my L.* Q₂. *both : my L.*

Q₃. *both.   My Lord,* Rowe.   *both : my
lord* Pope.   *both, my lord :* Theob. et seq.
  130. *forfeiture*] *forfeit* Rowe ii+,
Dyce iii, Coll. iii, Huds.
  131. *ſoale...ſoule*] F₂.   *ſoule...ſoule*
Qq.   *ſoale...ſoul* F₃F₄, Theob. Warb.
soal...soul Rowe, Johns. Cap. Steev. '85,
Mal. '90.   *soul !...soul* Pope.   *sole...soul*
Han. et cet.

118, 119. BOOTH: Shylock smiles scornfully, and slowly drawing his knife, at line 124, kneels, to whet it.

129. **whet**] MURDOCH (*The Stage*, 326): When a young man, acting Shylock, Mr Forrest was in the habit of carrying in his gaberdine a small whetstone for sharpening the knife. This I never saw, but I was told of it by an old actor of the Bowery Theatre, New York, who vouched for its truth. BOOTH: Whet the knife on the sole of the shoe,—not too rapidly.

130. **forfeiture**] RITSON: Read *forfeit*. It occurs repeatedly in the present scene for 'forfeiture.' ALLEN: Although 'forfeiture' can be scanned, the shorter and sharper word is *required* for Shylock. (The several *t*s are all most cuttingly expressive.)

131. **soale . . . soule**] THEOBALD (in his *Shakespeare Restored*, p. 168,—that criticism of Pope's Edition which Pope answered by making 'Tibbald' the original hero of *The Dunciad*): I dare venture to restore Him, from the Authority of some of the Folio Editions; tho' I am obliged at the same Time to restore such a Sort of Conceit, and Jingle upon two Words, alike in Sound but differing in Sense, as our Author ought to have blush'd for. But be That upon his own Head. If I restore his Meaning, and his Words, he himself is accountable to the Judges for writing them. 'Not on thy SOLE, but on thy SOUL, harsh Jew.' That is, Tho' thou thinkest that thou art whetting thy Knife on the *Sole* of thy Shoe, yet it is upon thy *Soul*, thy immortal Part, that Thou doest it, mistaken, inexorable Man! The bare intention of thy Cruelty is so unpardonable, that thou must bring thy very *Soul* into Hazard. I dare affirm, This is the

Thou mak'ft thy knife keene : but no mettall can,   132
No, not the hangmans Axe beare halfe the keenneffe

132. *but*] *for* Pope+.   132. *mettall*] *mettell* Q₂. *mettle* Q₃.

---

very *Antithesis* of our Author; and I am the more confident, because it was so usual
with him to play on Words in this manner; and because in another of his Plays he
puts the very same Words in Opposition to one another, and That from the Mouth of
one of his serious Characters.   See *Rom. & Jul.* I, iv, 15 : 'You have dancing shoes
With nimble soles; I have a soul of lead.'   WARBURTON : This lost jingle Mr Theobald found again; but knew not what to make of it when he had it, as appears by his
paraphrase. [which Warburton quotes, and exclaims] Absurd ! the conceit is, that his
soul was so hard that it had given an edge to his knife.   STEEVENS : So in *2 Hen. IV :*
IV, v, 108 : 'Thou hid'st a thousand daggers in thy thoughts; Which thou hast whetted
on thy stony heart.'   ECCLES : To me, Theobald and Warburton seem to mean pretty
much the same thing.   Both admit that the Jew's *soul* is supposed, by the figure, to be
the instrument of rendering the edge more keen.   The jingle may incline us to an
opinion that the vulgar, diphthongal pronunciation of the word 'soul' was in use, even
among polite speakers, in Shakespeare's days.   [It is possible that the difference of
spelling in the Folio indicates a difference of pronunciation between the two words,
but with which of the two our modern pronunciation better agrees it is hard to decide.
The spelling of the same words in *Rom. & Jul.* gives us no help, but rather adds to
the perplexity : 'You haue dancing fhooes With nimble foles, I haue a foale of Lead;'
nor is *Jul. Cæs.* I, i, 15, any clearer, where the Cobbler says that he is 'a Mender of
bad foules.'   As the present Irish pronunciation is supposed to represent in many words
the pronunciation of Shakespeare, it may be that Eccles, who was an Irishman, has
given us the true hint, and that *soul* was pronounced almost dissyllabically *sowl*.   This
was confirmed, I thought, by finding in *Com. of Err.* II, i, 22 : 'Indued with intellectuall
fence and foules Of more preheminence then fifh and fowles;' but the strength of this
example was immediately weakened by observing only a few lines before it : 'The
beafts, the fifhes and the winged fowles Are their males subjects and at their controules,'
which goes to show, even if other evidence were wanting (which is not), that *fowl* approached more nearly to our pronunciation of *soul*, than *soul* to *fowl*.   On turning to
ELLIS (*Early Eng. Pron.*, Part III, p. 903), I find that Gill (*Logonomia*, 1621, pp.
77, 117) gives *sool* as the pronunciation of 'sole,' and (*Ib.* 20, 136) *sooul* as that of
'soul.'   This, by making the latter dissyllabic, would leave some slight difference to be
detected by a nice ear.   But Hodges, 1643, who, on the score of delicacy of pronunciation, is not rated by Ellis as high as Gill, in his list of words 'alike in sound and
unlike both in signification and writing,' gives 'the *sole* of a shoo, the *soule* and body.
the *soles* of his shoos, he *soleth* his shoos, *soules* and bodies bought and *sold*, the shoos
are *sol'd;'* (Ellis, p. 1021), wherein it is apparently intimated that there is no difference
whatever in pronunciation.   If I remember rightly, Mrs Kemble gave to 'soul' the
slightly dissyllabic sound mentioned by Gill, with a narrower sound to the *oo*, almost
like a very broad *aa*.   I once thought that peradventure the *s* in 'sole,' in memory of
the close connection between soles and shoes, might have had the sound of *sh* which
we still retain in *sure, sugar*, and, until recently, in *sewer*.   But the search was fruitless.—ED.]

133. **hangmans**] DYCE (*Gloss.*) : An executioner.   So in Fletcher's *Prophetess*,
III, i, Dioclesian, who had *stabbed* Aper, is called 'the hangman of Volusius Aper;'

Of thy ſharpe enuy.　Can no prayers pierce thee?

　Iew.　No, none that thou haſt wit enough to make.　　**135**

　Gra.　O be thou damn'd, inexecrable dogge,

And for thy life let iuſtice be accus'd:

Thou almoſt mak'ſt me wauer in my faith;

To hold opinion with *Pythagoras,*

That ſoules of Animals infuſe themſelues　　**140**

Into the trunkes of men.　Thy curriſh ſpirit

Gouern'd a Wolfe, who hang'd for humane ſlaughter,　　**142**

---

135. *haſt*] *hoaſt* F₂.

136. *inexecrable*] Qq F₂, Knt, Cam. Glo. Cla. Wh. ii. *inexorable* F₃F₄ et cet.

138. *faith;*] *faith,* Rowe.

142. *humane*] *humaine* Q₂.

---

and in *Jacke Drum's Entertainment,* Brabant Junior, being prevented by Sir Edward from *stabbing* himself, declares that he is too wicked to live: 'And therefore, gentle knight, let mine owne hand Be mine own hangman,' 1616; compare, too, a play of a much later date, the Duke of Buckingham's *Rehearsal,* where Bayes says: 'I come out in a long black veil, and a great huge hangman behind me, with a furr'd cap, and his sword drawn; and there tell 'em plainly, that if, out of good nature, they will not like my play, I'gad, I'll e'en kneel down, and he shall cut my head off.'—*Works,* i, p. 21, ed. 1775.

134. Scan, for the sake of emphasising the proper words: 'Of thý | sharp énvy. | ′ | Can nó | prayers piérce *thee* ?'—Ed.

135. Booth: *No*—doggedly, without looking up.

136. **inexecrable**] Malone: This was, perhaps, unnecessarily changed in F₃. *In* was sometimes used, in our author's time, in composition, as an augmentative or intensive particle.　Dyce (*Remarks,* p. 58): Richardson has given 'inexecrable' a place in his *Dictionary.* I agree with Collier [and Capell, too, Dyce might have added] in considering it a misprint.　Clarendon: That is, that cannot be execrated enough.　Abbott: Compare *invaluable.* [Apart from the fact that 'inexecrable' is found nowhere else in the language, *inexorable* is so very appropriate after Gratiano's vain prayers, that I cannot but think that the former word is a misprint. I do not quite see the parallelism of Abbott's *invaluable* (a word, by the way, not to be found in Shakespeare); a thing that cannot be valued enough is invaluable; a thing that cannot be execrated enough is, what?—*inexecratable ?*—Ed.]

137. **for thy life**] Capell: His meaning is, that as he had before invok'd *damnation* upon him, so now he would have 'justice' (executive justice) take away his 'life;' though it were in wrong and to that justice's impeachment.　Eccles: Is it not as likely he may intend to say that 'justice' itself merits *accusation* for permitting a person of so unworthy and cruel a character any longer to *live ?*

138. **wauer in my faith**] Booth: Shylock now looks up at him with mocking wonder. During the rest of this speech he slowly takes from his bosom the bond, and at its close, points to the seal, still kneeling.

142. **who . . . slaughter**] Clarendon says that this is another instance of what is called *nominativus pendens* in Latin, and refers to I, iii, **139**: 'Who if he break,' &c.　Abbott, § 376, considers it a case of Nominative Absolute.　Steevens: This allusion might have been caught from some old translation of Pliny, who mentions a

Euen from the gallowes did his fell foule fleet ;   143
And whil'ft thou layeft in thy vnhallowed dam,
Infus'd it felfe in thee : For thy defires   145
Are Woluifh, bloody, fteru'd, and rauenous.

Iew.   Till thou canft raile the feale from off my bond
Thou but offend'ft thy Lungs to fpeake fo loud :
Repaire thy wit good youth, or it will fall
To endleffe ruine.   I ftand heere for Law.   150

---

144. *whil'ft*] *whilft* Q₁. *whileft* Q₂Q₃.   150. *endleffe*] Ff, Rowe, Wh. i. *care-*
146. *fteru'd*] Ff, Knt, Sing. Sta.   *less* Pope. *cureleffe* Qq et cet.
ftaru'd Q₁Q₂. *ftarv'd* Q₃ et cet.   *heere*] Om. Q₃.

Parrhasian turned into a *wolf*, because he had eaten part of a child that had been consecrated to Lycæan Jupiter.   See Goulart's *Admirable Histories*, p. 390.   [With what ridicule Steevens would have greeted this note had it been put forth by luckless Theobald !   The passage referred to in Goulart, contains merely an account of Lycanthropy, and not a syllable, that I can find, which has any bearing on these words of Gratiano, except that the word 'wolf' is common to both.   Allen notes that 'it is singular, that while Gratiano *says* a *wolf*, he shews he is *thinking* of a *wolvish man*, a murderer.' To me it is so singular that (coupled with its grammatical difficulty), I am inclined to suspect that there is some corruption here.   If Mr S. L. Lee is correct (see his noteworthy article on 'The Jews in England' in the Appendix) in surmising a connection between this play and the fate of Dr Lopez, the Jew, who was hung at Tyburn in 1594, the allusion here, vague as it is, is quite pointed enough to have been caught by an audience in whose minds the event was so recent.   It is not inconceivable that this is one of those actor's additions which Hamlet denounces, and this would measurably account for its grammatical awkwardness.   The whole passage from 'Thy currish spirit,' line 141, to 'Infus'd itself in thee,' line 145, can be omitted without injury either to the sense or to the rhythm.   Thus : 'That souls of animals infuse themselves Into the trunks of men.   For thy desires Are wolvish, bloody, sterv'd, and ravenous.'—ED.]

144. **layest**] DOUCE : Is not this a very common misprint for *lay'dst*, where the preterite is intended ?   [A query which ALLEN aptly characterizes as 'a curious piece of *deliberate* bad grammar.'—ED.]

146. **steru'd**] COLLIER : The meaning of 'sterv'd' and *starv'd* is the same ; if there were a difference, it might be fit to mark it with a difference of spelling.   ROLFE : The word is the Anglosaxon *steorfan*, Old Eng. *sterven* (frequent in Chaucer), Ger. *sterben*. It originally meant to die, but in the latter part of the 16th Century came to be used in the narrower sense of perishing with *cold*,—a meaning which it still has in the North of England (see also *2 Hen. VI* : III, i, 343, &c.)—or with *hunger*.   [How did Pope pronounce it ?   'But still the *Great* have kindness in reserve, He help'd to bury whom he help'd to starve.'—*Epistle to Dr Arbuthnot.*—ED.]

147. BOOTH : Now rise, and, after 'I stand here for the law,' turn contemptuously from Gratiano.

147. **raile**] My Father says that the prolonged, grating, guttural tone of utter contempt with which Edmund Kean dwelt on this word has never left his memory.—ED

150. **endlesse**] I am by no means sure that *cureless* of the Qq is the better word here.—ED.

Dn. This Letter from *Bellario* doth commend   151
A yong and Learned Doctor in our Court;
Where is he?
   Ner. He attendeth heere hard by
To know your anſwer, whether you'l admit him.   155
   Du. With all my heart.   Some three or four of you
Go giue him curteous conduct to this place,
Meane time the Court ſhall he are *Bellarioes* Letter.

Y Our Grace ſhall vnderſtand, that at the receite of your
   Letter I am very ſicke : but in the inſtant that your meſ-   160
ſenger came, in louing viſitation, was with me a young Do-
ctor of Rome, his name is Balthaſar : *I acquained him with*
the cauſe in Controuerſie, betweene the Iew and Anthonio
the Merchant : We turn'd ore many Bookes together : hee is
furniſhed with my opinion, which bettred with his owne lear-   165
ning, the greatneſſe whereof I cannot enough commend, comes
with him at my importunity, to fill vp your Graces requeſt in   167

152. *in our*] Ff, Rowe, Pope. *to our*   162. *Balthaſar*] Balthazer Q₁Q₂.
Qq et cet.   acquained] F₁.
159–171. Roman, Q₂Q₃.   163. cauſe] caſe F₃F₄, Rowe.
159. [Clerk. [reads] Cap.   165. bettred] *bettered* Q₂Q₃F₃F₄.
160. in the] at the Rowe+, Steev. '85.

158, 159. **shall**] ABBOTT, § 315 : Used to denote inevitable futurity without reference to *will* (desire).   See also 'Fair Jessica shall be my torch-bearer,' II, iv, 42.

159. BOOTH : Shylock gives deep attention to this letter, and looks quickly and curiously at Portia until she is on the dais R. H., then he turns to the Duke.

159. **receite**] ECCLES : It is probable that Bellario received the Duke's summons to
attend this cause about the time, or rather, perhaps, a little before, his cousin made her
application to him by letter.   Whether the doctor's illness was real, or pretended, is of
no moment to the business of the play; it is sufficient that it coincided better with Portia's project that he should be absent upon this occasion.

165. **opinion**] KENRICK (*Rev. of Dr Johnson*, p. 52) : I have known some spectators impute the device, by which Anthonio evades the penalty of the bond, to the
ingenuity of Portia.   Perhaps this is the case, indeed, with the audience in general.
But, as I think it a little out of character, in a young lady of her education, to be so
well versed in the quirks and quibbles of the law, so I conceive there is sufficient
reason given in the play to suppose that evasion to have been suggested by Bellario.
For she expressly mentions to the messenger the *notes* and *clothes*.   These 'notes'
were, doubtless, the brief or hints for her pleading.   And Bellario says in his letter
'he is furnished with my opinion.'

167. **fill vp**] CLARENDON : 'Up' intensifies the verb to which it is attached, like
κατά in Greek.   '"As true as Troilus," shall crown up the verse,'—*Tro. and Cress.*
III, ii, 189.   On the other hand, in *Meas. for Meas.* I, ii, 168, 'up' is almost redundant :
'Whether the tyranny be in his place, Or in his eminence that fills it up.'

my sted.   I beseech you, let his lacke of years be no impedime nt   168
to let him lacke a reuerend estimation : for I neuer knewe so
yong a body, with so old a head.   I leaue him to your gracious   170
acceptance, whose trial shall better publish his commendation.

Enter Portia for Balthazar.

Duke.   You heare the learn'd *Bellario* what he writes,
And heere(I take it)is the Doctor come.
Giue me your hand : Came you from old *Bellario?*   175
   Por.   I did my Lord.
   Du.   You are welcome : take your place;
Are you acquainted with the difference
That holds this present question in the Court.
   Por.   I am enformed throughly of the cause.   180
Which is the Merchant heere? and which the Iew?
   Du.   *Anthonio* and old *Shylocke*, both stand forth.
   Por.   Is your name *Shylocke*?   183

---

168. sted] F$_1$.   stead Qq Ff.
172. Enter...] Enter Portia dress'd like
a Doctor of Laws. Rowe.
175. *Came*] *come* Qq, Cam. Cla. Glo.
Wh. ii.

177. *You are*] *You're* Pope+, Dyce iii,
Huds.
180. *throughly*] *thoroughly* Steev. '85,
Ktly.
   cause] *Case* F$_3$F$_4$, Rowe+.

---

168. **no impediment**] CLARENDON : That is, no hindrance to his receiving.   So
μή is used in Greek, after words signifying to 'hinder,' 'forbid,' &c., a usage which
sprang originally from a confusion of thought, similar to that in line 81 of the present
Scene : 'Forbid . . . . to make no noise.'   SCHMIDT (p. 1420) : This is equivalent
either to 'let his lack of years be no motive to let him lack,' or 'be no impediment to
let him have.'

171. **whose**] See ABBOTT, § 263, for other instances of ' "who" used for "and
he," "for he," &c.'   Thus here, 'whose trial,' that is, '*for his* trial.'

173. **Bellario what**] ABBOTT, § 414 : Instead of saying 'I know what you are,'
in which the object of the verb 'I know' is the clause 'what you are,' Shakespeare
frequently introduces before the dependent clause another object, so as to make the
dependent clause a mere explanation of the object.   [One of WALKER'S chapters
(*Crit.* i, p. 68) is devoted to examples of this redundancy, which, as he says, corresponds to the Greek idiom; *e. g. Il.* B. 409 : ἤδεε γὰρ κατὰ θυμὸν ἀδελφεὸν, ὡς ἐπονεῖτο.]

175. **Came**] Portia's reply, 'I did,' as suggested by Clarendon, shows that this is
better than *Come* of the Qq.

177. **place**] STAUNTON : In the representation of this scene, pictorially or on the
stage, it seems never to be remembered that Portia, throughout the trial, appears as a
judge, not an advocate, and that her proper place, therefore, is on the judgement-seat,
below the Duke's throne, rather than on the supposed floor of the Court, in front of the
stage.   BOOTH : Portia goes to a table on dais R. H., facing the Duke.

182. BOOTH : Antonio and Shylock advance and bow to the Duke.

   14

Iew.   *Shylocke* is my name.

Por.   Of a ſtrange nature is the ſute you follow,   185
Yet in ſuch rule, that the Venetian Law
Cannot impugne you as you do proceed.
You ſtand within his danger, do you not?

Ant.   I, ſo he ſayes.

Por.   Do you confeſſe the bond?   190

Ant.   I do.

Por.   Then muſt the Iew be mercifull.

Iew.   On what compulſion muſt I ? Tell me that.   193

187. *impugne*] *impunge* Q₁.   188. [To Anthonio. Rowe.
188. *you not*] *ye not* Q₁.

---

184. BOOTH: After a look of surprise, he replies doggedly.

185. CAMPBELL (p. 60): The trial is conducted according to the strict forms of legal procedure. Portia, the PODESTA or judge, called in to act under the authority of the Doge, first inquires if there be any plea of *non est factum*.

186. **in such rule**] ALLEN: So *regular*.

187. **impugne**] STEEVENS: That is, to oppose, to controvert.

188. **danger**] TYRWHITT (*Cant. Tales*, v. 665): That is, within his reach or control. HENLEY: There are frequent instances in *The Paston Letters* of the use of this phrase in the same sense; whence it is obvious, from the common language of the time, that to be in *debt* and to be in *danger* were synonymous terms. GIFFORD (Massinger's *Fatal Dowry*, I, ii): That is, to be in your debt, a common expression in our old writers. MALONE: Again, in *V. & A.* 639: 'Come not within his danger by thy will.' KNIGHT: The phrase is not used by Portia in the limited and secondary sense of being in debt. COLLIER (ed. ii): 'Within his danger' was, in Shakespeare's time, and long before, equivalent merely to *indebted to him:* the phrase has no necessary reference to the peril of Anthonio's position. HALLIWELL: The phrase seems to be partially retained in the still common proverb, 'out of debt, out of danger.' STAUNTON: Ducange explains the term as follows: '*Danger*, quidquid juri stricto, atque adeo confiscationi obnoxium est.' WEDGWOOD (s. v.): To be in the danger of any one, *estre en son danger*, came to signify to be subjected to any one, to be in his power, or liable to a penalty to be inflicted by him or at his suit, and hence the ordinary acceptation of the word at the present day. 'In danger of the judgement—in danger of Hellfire.' SKEAT (s. v.): Old French, *dangier* (modern French, *danger*), absolute power, irresponsible authority; hence, power to harm, as in [the present passage. Gairdner's Index to *The Paston Letters* supplies us with the following: 'I truste right well all the aldermen, except Broun and sech as be in his dawnger.'—*John Jenney to John Paston*, vol. i, p. 340, ed. Gairdner.—ED.]

190. BOOTH: Shylock darts a glance at Anthonio.

192. **must**] ABBOTT, § 314: Sometimes used by Shakespeare to mean no more than definite futurity, like our 'is to' in 'He *is to* be here to-morrow.' [See II, vi, 47.] Somewhat similar, without the notion of compulsion, is the use of it in [the present passage. Abbott is, of course, right in saying that Portia uses 'must' without any notion of compulsion, yet it is exactly in that sense that Shylock takes it.—ED.].

193. BOOTH: With great assurance, and contemptuously turning away.

Por.   The quality of mercy is not ftrain'd,
It droppeth as the gentle raine from heauen   195
Vpon the place beneath.   It is twice bleft,
It bleffeth him that giues, and him that takes,   197

195. *raine*] *dew* Lansdowne.

194. BOOTH: When Portia begins to speak she descends from the dais and advances. DOUCE: In composing these beautiful lines it is probable that Shakespeare recollected the following verse in *Ecclesiasticus*, xxxv, 20: 'Mercy is seasonable in the time of affliction, as clouds of rain in the time of drought.' [There is a tendency, I think, in repeating this familiar line, to lay the chiefest emphasis on 'mercy.' Is this right? In reply to Shylock's demand for a proof of his compulsion to be merciful, Portia exclaims that the very characteristic of mercy is that there can be no compulsion in its exercise. Its very nature is to fall like the rain. Should not 'quality,' then, receive the greater, and 'mercy' a secondary, emphasis?—ED.

In the *Jahrbuch*, ix, p. 195, there is a learned article by Wm. Koenig, *Ueber die Entlehnungen Shakespeare's*,' &c. In that article (p. 218) passages are cited from Rabelais, from Cicero, from a tragedy by Leonoro Verlato, called *Rodopeia*, and elsewhere, which bear certain resemblances to some of the lines and ideas in this speech. It is not always easy to take interest in the detection of parallelisms like these, which lead us nowhere. In view of Shakespeare's myriad-mindedness, our wonder is not that there are so many, but that there are no more.—ED.]

HAZLITT (p. 274): This speech about 'mercy' is very well; but there are a thousand finer ones in Shakespeare. [See in Appendix Charles Cowden-Clarke's explanation of the unsympathetic mood which seemed to rule Hazlitt throughout his criticism of Portia.—ED.]

194. **strain'd**] R. S. DAVIES: That is, confined by laws, restricted to a few persons. 'You are as free to use it as any one. The rain does not favour the king's garden any more than the peasant's. It waters all places alike, and mercy should descend as equally and impartially.' [I suppose this is the best possible defence of an erroneous interpretation, which overlooks in 'strain'd' the answer to Shylock's question of compulsion.—ED.]

196. **twice blest**] ECCLES: 'Mercy' is made both the *blesser* and the *blessed*. The verb is twice used in the same general sense of, *to make happy*, varying only from passive to active. In its first application, however, 'mercy' is the representative both of the person who exercises that virtue, and also of him who is the object of it; in its second, it is made a distinct agent from both, and regarded as conferring happiness upon each. It may, perhaps, help to solve this perplexity if we consider 'mercy' as personified, and 'blest,' inasmuch as she enjoys the power of *blessing*, i. e. of rendering happy both the giver and receiver; or we may understand the word 'blest' in a signification which it frequently bears, that of *addressed* or *saluted with benediction;* in the first place, on the part of *him that gives* for the pleasure which he derives from having acted mercifully, and again, on the part of *him that takes* for the benefit conferred by the mercy shown him. SEYMOUR (i, 125): Would not the sense be better expressed if we should read 'twice-blessing'? Yet I cannot approve this: 'twice-blessed' certainly does not mean blessed in repetition, as our actresses most vilely utter it, but blessed augmentedly, blessed supremely, or in a great degree, as we say, *thrice happy*, withovt any idea of repetition. 'Blessed' here is *holy*. ALLEN refers to III,

'Tis mightieft in the mightieft, it becomes   198
The throned Monarch better then his Crowne.
His Scepter fhewes the force of temporall power,   200
The attribute to awe and Maieftie,
Wherein doth fit the dread and feare of Kings :
But mercy is aboue this fceptred fway,
It is enthroned in the hearts of Kings,
It is an attribute to God himfelfe ;   205
And earthly power doth then fhew likeft Gods

206. *likeft*] *lik'ft* Q₁.

ii, 103, 'the guiled shore,' where, if 'guiled' means endowed with *guiles*, then 'blest'
may be here equivalent to endued with the capacity to bless.

201. **awe and Maiestie**] ALLEN : 'Awe,' properly, of the subject ; 'majesty,' of
the king, the cause of 'awe.'   By hendiadys, both might be taken together, equivalent
to *awful majesty*.   The subject 'dreads and fears' the king, because of that awe-breed-
ing majesty which is associated with his *temporal* power.   It is implied in what follows,
that the God-like quality of *mercy*, on the other hand, being seated in the *heart* of the
king, evokes from the subject a corresponding affection of the heart, even *love*.

204. **hearts**] ECCLES : This, I think, should be spoken with particular emphasis.

206, 207. WHALLEY (p. 65) : Compare *Tit. And.* I, i, 117, tho' there is a proba
bility it might not come from Shakespeare : 'Wilt thou draw near the nature of the
gods ?   Draw near them then in being merciful.'   Which is directly the sense and
words of a passage in one of Cicero's finest Orations : 'Homines ad Deos nulla re
proprius accedunt quam salutem hominibus dando.'—*Orat. pro Ligar. sub fin.*
MALONE : So, in *King Edward III*, 1596, V, i, 41 : 'And Kings approch the nearest
vnto God By giuing life and safety vnto men.'   So Sir J. Harrington [*Orlando Furioso*,
1591, B. xxiv, st. 30—*Collier*] : 'This noble vertue and divine, Doth chiefly make a
man so rare and od, As in that one he most resembleth God.'   So Thomas Achely,
also quoted in *England's Parnassus*, under the same head 'Mercie :' 'Then come
we nearest to the gods on hie, When we are farthest from extremitie, Giving forth sentence of our lawes with Mercie.'   BLACKEWAY : There is something extremely like
this in the petition of the Convocation to Queen Elizabeth, in 1580, praying her to
pardon Archbishop Grindal : 'Nihil est tam populare quam bonitas : atque principes ad
præpotentem Deum nullâ re propius accedunt quam offensionibus deponendis et obli-
viscendis injuriis,'—Fuller's *Church Hist. sub ann.*   HUNTER (i, 328) : It was one of
the common-places of the time, and might, no doubt, be found in innumerable writers ;
but it may be doubted whether it is anywhere exhibited in a manner so impressive as
here.   Such sentiments, so far as they respect the course of public punishments, it was
of more importance to urge in Shakespeare's time than now ; when the single mind
of the monarch, unswayed by counsel, and with no very determinate principles, often
decided the fate of persons convicted of crimes, of which a very remarkable instance
occurred in the time of Shakespeare, when James I secretly determined to save the lives
of the Lords Grey and Cobham, convicted of treason, when every one beside thought
that their execution was certain.   CLARENDON : It is possible that Shakespeare in writing this passage intended to compliment Elizabeth, whose rule (whatever be the judgement of recent historians) was certainly held by her subjects to be mild and merciful.

When mercie feafons Iuftice.   Therefore Iew, 207
Though Iuftice be thy plea, confider this,
That in the courfe of Iuftice, none of vs
Should fee faluation : we do pray for mercie, 210
And that fame prayer, doth teach vs all to render
The deeds of mercie.   I haue fpoke thus much
To mittigate the iuftice of thy plea :
Which if thou follow, this ftrict courfe of Venice
Muft needes giue fentence 'gainft the Merchant there. 215
  Shy.   My deeds vpon my head, I craue the Law,
The penaltie and forfeite of my bond.
  Por.   Is he not able to difcharge the money ?
  Baf.   Yes, heere I tender it for him in the Court, 219

214. *courfe*] *Court* Qq, Pope et seq.

---

206. **Gods**] BOOTH : At the mention of the sacred name, Shylock bows reverently, which none of the Christians do.   Cooke, when commended for this, said it was Macklin's 'business,' and, according to my belief, Burbage did it,—perhaps at Shakespeare's suggestion.

208. **Iuftice**] Shylock's plea was 'judgement,' not justice.—ED.

210, 211. BLACKSTONE : Portia, referring the Jew to the Christian doctrine of salvation and the Lord's Prayer, is a little out of character.   R. T. (*Anon. ap.* SEYMOUR, i, 125) : Besides that it is supposed the Lord's Prayer consists of expressions in use among Jews, their Scriptures abound with passages recommending mercy, particularly *Ecclesiasticus*, xxviii.   WORDSWORTH (p. 111) : The learned judge was probably not aware that the Lord's Prayer was not composed by our Lord as containing anything which would be new and strange to His disciples, but as putting together, in a short form, all that was most valuable in the Jewish liturgies already known to them.   See Lightfoot, ii, 159, 439 ; Grotius on S. Matthew, vi, 9 ; who also refers to *Ecclesiasticus*, xxviii.   The Biblical critics, therefore, who, like Burkitt, except the particular clause which Portia refers to—viz. 'As we forgive them that trespass against us,' from the foregoing representation in regard to the origin of the several petitions of the Lord's Prayer, have, in all probability, made that single exception without sufficient reason. Besides, it is to be borne in mind that many of the Jews, though they did not accept Christ as their Messiah, yet they did accept Him as 'a teacher come from God.'   And certainly it is not correct to suppose that the Christian *doctrine* of salvation is not alfe the doctrine of salvation to the faithful Jew.

211. **that same prayer**] Dunlap's *Life of Cooke :* Shakespeare here makes Portia, in her zeal, quote *the Lord's Prayer*, but the great actor, by his look and the shake of his head and of his hand, gives a comment on the text, by rejecting the application to himself, or to those of his belief.

216. BOOTH : After a pause.   HENLEY : An imprecation adopted from that of the Jews to Pilate : 'His blood be on us, and our children.'

216. **Law,**] In a modern text there should be here either a dash, as Allen suggests, or a colon, to indicate that what follows in the next line is what the law gives him.—ED.

Yea, twice the fumme, if that will not fuffice,   220
I will be bound to pay it ten times ore,
On forfeit of my hands, my head, my heart :
If this will not fuffice, it muſt appeare
That malice beares downe truth.   And I befeech you
Wreſt once the Law to your authority.   225
To do a great right, do a little wrong,
And curbe this cruell diuell of his will.
    Por.   It muſt not be, there is no power in Venice
Can alter a decree eſtabliſhed :
'Twill be recorded for a Preſident,   230
And many an error by the fame example,
Will ruſh into the ſtate : It cannot be.
    Iew.   A *Daniel* come to iudgement, yea a *Daniel*.   233

---

220. *twice*] *thrice* Ritson, Coll. iii.   230. *Preſident*] Ff, Rowe. *precedent*
229. *alter*] *altar* Q₂.   Qq.

---

220. **twice**] CAPELL (ii, 70) : When Portia, towards the page's bottom, mentions this offer, she calls it—an offer of 'thrice' the sum ; and this *thrice* is the sum accepted by Shylock ; from whence some might be apt to infer an error in the term of this passage : but Portia had ground enough for her *thrice* from what Bassanio says afterwards, and the Jew (as was right) catches at the term in her offer.   COLLIER : Portia afterward speaks of '*thrice* thy money.'   This may have been a mere inadvertence, a mishearing, or a misprint.   CLARENDON : As Bassanio offers ten times the sum, Portia is authorized to offer thrice the sum in his name, as *omne majus continet in se minus*. Or Bassanio here may be supposed to offer twice the sum *in addition* to his previous tender of the sum itself; thrice the sum in all.   ROLFE : We see no necessity for bringing the two passages into mathematical agreement.

224. **truth**] THEOBALD (*Sh. Restored*, p. 167) : How does Malice bear down Truth in this process ?   What one circumstance is there in the cause whereby Truth or Falsehood can come into question ? . . . . I make not the least question but our poet made Bassanio say, ' That malice bears down *ruth*.'   HEATH (p. 121) : I apprehend that the word ' truth' here denotes that supreme rule of right and equity by which all human actions ought to be directed.   JOHNSON : ' Malice' oppresses honesty ; a *true man*, in old language, is an *honest man*.   We now call the jury *good men and true*.   [In his Edition, Theobald says that, ' upon more mature advice,' he believes ' the text needs no alteration.   Truth may mean here *reason ;* the reasonable offers of accommodation which we have made.']

228, &c. BOOTH : Shylock's face expresses joy and astonishment.   Portia utters ' It cannot be,' line 232, with great decision ; lines 233, 234, Shylock utters almost wildly (not too loud), and kisses the hem of Portia's gown.

231. **error**] SCHMIDT (*Translation*) : Portia's point of view is not that of the moraⱥ ist, but of the statesman ; and ' error' is here not a *mistake*, but a departure from the prescribed path.   Compare *Oth.* V, ii, ' It is the very error of the moon ; she comes more nearer earth than she was wont,' &c. ; also *Mid. N. D.* V, i, 250.

O wife young Iudge, how do I honour thee.
   Por.   I pray you let me looke vpon the bond.   235
   Iew.   Heere 'tis moſt reuerend Doĉtor, heere it is.
   Por.   *Shylocke,* there's thrice thy monie offered thee.
   Shy.   An oath, an oath, I haue an oath in heauen :
Shall I lay periurie vpon my foule ?
No not for Venice.   240
   Por.   Why this bond is forfeit,
And lawfully by this the Iew may claime
A pound of fleſh, to be by him cut off
Neereſt the Merchants heart ; be mercifull,
Take thrice thy money, bid me teare the bond.   245
   Iew.   When it is paid according to the tenure.

---

234 and throughout. *Iudge*] *Judg* F₄.   237. *offered*] *offer'd* Pope.
    do I] *I do* Qq, Cap. Coll. Hal.   240. *No not*] *Not not* Q₂.
Dyce, Cam. Glo. Cla. Huds. Wh. ii.   246. *tenure*] *tenour* Q₁.
    235. *let me*] Om. F₃F₄.

---

233. THEOBALD (Nichols, *Illust.* ii, 312) : There is no fault in sense here ; I think
the pointing is not exactly as the poet designed it. I like it better, ' A Daniel ! Come
to judgement :—yea, a Daniel !' For this reading not only extols the advocate, but
expresses the Jew's impatience for a sentence. [This was not repeated in Theobald's
Edition.—ED.] HUNTER (i, 329) : One would rather have expected to have found
Solomon in this place. [Solomon is added in Lansdowne's Version.—ED.] But see
the *Story of Susannah and the Elders ;* and also *Ezekiel,* xxviii, 3, and *Daniel,* vi, 3
WORDSWORTH (p. 87) : Daniel, according to the *History of Susannah and the Elders,*
v. 45, was a ' young youth ' when he convicted the Elders ' of false witness by their own
mouth.' His detection also of the imposture of the priests of Bel, as we read in the
Apocryphal *History of Bel and the Dragon,* may have contributed to suggest the propriety of the allusion.
    234. thee] ABBOTT, § 233 : *Thou* is the rhetorical, *you* the conversational, pronoun.
This explains the apparent liberty which Shylock takes here.
    236. BOOTH : With great haste he draws forth both the bond and his knife. Portia
utters the next line impressively, and Shylock replies as solemnly.
    238–240. HAWKINS (*Life of Kean,* i, p. 151) : Kean replaced the conventional, sol-
emn severity of manner with a tone of humour bordering on the ludicrous ; it was the
bitter ironical joke of a man who saw no obstacle standing between him and the con-
summation of his cherished purpose.
    244. Neerest . . . heart] HALLIWELL : This seems, at first sight, at variance with
what is stated in the First Act : ' To be cut off and taken in what part of your body
pleaseth me ;' but it may be presumed that the selection of the part was made by Shylock before the bond was actually drawn up.
    244. be mercifull] BOOTH : Shylock shrugs his shoulders and shakes his forefingeɪ
after the Italian custom. Line 246 he speaks quickly, preventing the act.
    246. Dunlap's *Lṛ⸱ of Cooke* (i, 122) : The audience were surprised and delighted
by the abruptness of his reply to Portia's request that he would permit the bond to be

It doth appeare you are a worthy Iudge :   247
you know the Law, your expofition
Hath beene moft found.   I charge you by the **Law**,
Whereof you are a well-deferuing pillar,   250
Proceede to iudgement : By my foule I fweare,
There is no power in the tongue of man
To alter me : I ftay heere on my bond.
    An.   Moft heartily I do befeech the Court
To giue the iudgement.   255
    Por.   Why then thus it is :
you muft prepare your bofome for his knife.
    Iew.   O noble Iudge, O excellent yong man.
    Por.   For the intent and purpofe of the Law
Hath full relation to the penaltie,   260
Which heere appeareth due vpon the bond.
    Iew.   'Tis verie true : O wife and vpright Iudge,
How much more elder art thou then thy lookes ?
    Por.   Therefore lay bare your bofome.
    Iew.   I, his breft,   265
So fayes the bond, doth it not noble Iudge ?
Neereft his heart, thofe are the very words.
    Por.   It is fo : Are there ballance heere to weigh the
flefh ?   269

250. *pillar*] *piller* Q₂Q₃.
262, 265, 270, 273, 276. Iew.] Shy.
Q₁.
264. *your*] *thy* F₄, Rowe.

268. *It...weigh*] One line, Cap. et seq.
(except Hal. Sta.).
    ballance heere] *ballances here*
Rowe.   *scales* Pope +.

---

torn : ' When it is *paid* according to the tenour,' he replies, indicating a degree of
apprehension lest she *should* tear it, and, at the same time, a malignant recognition
of the penalty due.

253. on] ABBOTT, § 180 : Metaphorically for *in dependence on.*

259-261. ECCLES : The intention and meaning of the law, framed for the determination of similar cases, is clearly applicable to, and strongly in favour of, Shylock's
right to exact the penalty.   BOOTH : Shylock watches the effect of Portia's words on
the faces of the Duke and Senators.

263. more elder] For double comparatives, see ABBOTT, § 11.

265. BOOTH : Shylock takes the bond eagerly from Portia, and, when returning it
to her after 'those are the very words,' looks at Anthonio.

268. ballance] HALLIWELL gives several instances where 'balance' was used in
Shakespeare's time as a plural noun.   CLARENDON : This is the only instance where
it is thus used by Shakespeare.   It is common to find a confusion in the Number of
nouns ending in a sibilant.   [See *Oth.* I, iii, 357; WALKER'S *Vers.* 243; ABBOTT,

Iew.   I haue them ready.   270

Por.   Haue by fome Surgeon *Shylock* on your charge
To ftop his wounds, leaft he fhould bleede to death.

Iew.   It is not nominated in the bond?

Por.   It is not fo expreft : but what of that?
'Twere good you do fo much for charitie.   275

Iew.   I cannot finde it, 'tis not in the bond.

---

270. [Producing scales. Coll. ii.   273. *It is not*] Ff, Rowe, Wh. i.   *Is*
272. *fhould*] Ff, Rowe+, Knt, Wh. i.   *it fo* Qq et cet.
do Qq et cet.

---

§ 471.   Difficult as is the scansion of this line as it stands in the Folio, I prefer it to the 'running-on' scansion of Capell, which here strikes me as peculiarly unhappy. If the line must be divided, I should prefer to consider ' It is so ' as the first fragment, and supply any defect in metre by a pause after it.   Thus says Coleridge (*Table Talk*, p. 80, ed. Morley) : ' Shakespeare's rhythm is so perfect that you may be almost sure that you do not understand the real force of a line, if it does not run well as you read it. The necessary mental pause after every hemistich, or imperfect line, is always equal to the time that would have been taken in reading the complete verse.'—ED.]

273. Whether it is better to read this, despite the interrogation mark, as an assertion, with the Folio, or as a question, with the Quartos, I, for one, cannot decide.   Booth's Shylock ' places the scales on the dais and takes the bond from Portia.'   In this case Shylock must ask, ' Is it so nominated ?' before he examines the bond.   If he examines the bond first, he must say, ' It is not so nominated ' at the conclusion of his examination and as he returns the bond to Portia.   It is, however, immaterial, and may be safely left to the actor.—ED.

275. 'Twere . . . do] ABBOTT, § 370, explains the irregular sequence of tenses here by supposing that a present tense is implied : ' It were *and is* good.'   At the word ' charity,' says BOOTH, ' Shylock rivets his gaze on Anthonio until he has returned the bond to Portia,' which he does while uttering line 276.

276. HAWKINS (*Life of Kean*, i, 152) : Kean substituted a chuckle of transport for the savage sneer with which the line had been rendered by Cooke and Macklin.   This was a fine touch of nature.   ' The most ferocious and deadly passions,' writes one of the critics in justification of this innovation, ' relapse into an almost paroxysm of joy when the victims are placed in their power; as the poet has made death grin horribly a ghastly smile at the prospect of an abundant food for his savage appetite.'

276. LADY MARTIN (p. 43) : At this point I have always felt in the acting that my desire to find extenuations for Shylock's race and for himself leaves me, and my heart grows almost as stony as his own.   I see his fiendish nature fully revealed.   I have seen the knife sharpened to cut quickly through the flesh; the scales brought forward to weigh it; have watched the cruel, eager eyes, all strained and yearning to see the gushing blood welling from the side ' nearest the heart,' and gloating over the fancied agonies and death-pangs of his bitter foe.   This man-monster, this pitiless, savage nature, is beyond the pale of humanity; it must be made powerless to hurt.   I have felt that with him the wrongs of his race are really as nothing compared with his own remorseless hate.   He is no longer the wronged and suffering man; and I longed to pour down on his head the ' justice ' he has clamoured for, and will exact without pity.

Por. Come Merchant, haue you any thing to fay ? 277
Ant. But little : I am arm'd and well prepar'd.
Giue me your hand *Baſſanio*, fare you well.
Greeue not that I am falne to this for you : 280
For heerein fortune ſhewes her ſelfe more kinde
Then is her cuſtome. It is ſtill her vſe
To let the wretched man out-liue his wealth,
To view with hollow eye, and wrinkled brow
An age of pouerty. From which lingring penance 285
Of ſueh miſerie, doth ſhe cut me off :
Commend me to your honourable Wife,
Tell her the proceſſe of *Anthonio's* end :
Say how I lou'd you ; ſpeake me faire in death :
And when the tale is told, bid her be iudge, 290
Whether *Baſſanio* had not once a Loue :

277. *Come*] *You* Qq, Coll. i, ii, Cam.
Glo. Cla. Rlfe, Wh. ii.
282. *her cuſtome*] *his cuſtome* Ff.
286. *ſueh*] *ſuch a* Ff, Rowe+, Cap.
Steev. '93, Knt, Coll. iii, Dyce iii, Huds.

such deep Ktly. *sordid* Lloyd (ap. Cam.).
so much Cam. Edd. conj. *such-like*, or
searching Cla. conj.
291. *Loue*] *lover* Coll. ii, iii (MS),
Dyce iii, Huds.

---

285. **pouerty**] A dissyllable, as in the Scotch *purtye*, at this day. Whenever *v* comes between two vowels, Shakespeare's printers, almost invariably, use a *u*, an indication, I think, that the *v* sound in such cases was, in pronunciation of the very lightest, so light as to be practically absent. That this practice has survived in several common words is familiar enough, e. g. *e'er*, *ne'er*, *de'il*, &c. Note also, the Scotch *lo'e*. See also note on 'hauing,' III, ii, 131, and 'riueted,' V, i, 188. This fact explains, I think, the confusion which is found in the Folio in the use of 'lie' for *live*, on which Walker has a chapter, but does not detect what I am here, with much diffidence, proposing as its cause. The printers, accustomed to pronounce *live* almost like *li'e*, occasionally even so spelt it. If I am right in thus suggesting this vanishing sound of *v* between vowels, we can understand a pun of Mercutio's, which is otherwise lost ; he accuses Benvolio (III, i, 12) of being 'as soon moved to be moody and as soon moody to be moved.' Is it not clear that he said 'as soon mo'ed to be moody and as soon moody to be mo'ed'?—ED.

286. **sueh miserie**] The Textual Notes show the attempts that have been made to cure the scansion of this line. Clarendon would accent 'misery' on the second syllable, citing as a precedent the use of a similar accent in *King John*, III, iv, 35 : 'And buss thee as thy wife. Misery's love.' But Abbott, § 490, says that this line from *King John* proves nothing, that the pause-accent is sufficient to justify *misery*, and thinks it more probable, wherein I quite agree with him, that in the present line the 'a,' which is supplied by F_2 has dropped out after 'such.'—ED.

289. **speake me faire**] An omission, not unusual, of the preposition, which, in this case, as the context shows, is *of*. In the same phrase, as ABBOTT, § 200, points out, in *Rom. & Jul.* III, i, 158, 'Romeo that spoke him fair,' the preposition is *to*.

291. **Loue**] Collier says that the use of this word in the sense of *lover* is not com-

Repent not you that you ſhall looſe your friend, 292
And he repents not that he payes your debt.
For if the Iew do cut but deepe enough,
Ile pay it inſtantly, with all my heart. 295
  Baſ. *Anthonio,* I am married to a wife,
Which is as deere to me as life it ſelfe,
But life it ſelfe, my wife, and all the world,
Are not with me eſteem'd aboue thy life.
I would looſe all, I ſacrifice them all 300
Heere to this deuill, to deliuer you.
  Por. Your wife would giue you little **thanks for that**
If ſhe were by to heare you make the offer.
  Gra. I haue a wife whom I proteſt I loue,
I would ſhe were in heauen, ſo ſhe could 305

---

292. *not you*] *but you* Qq, Hal. Cam.
Glo. Cla. Wh. ii.
295. *inſtantly*] *preſently* Q₁, Cam. Glo.
Cla. Wh. ii.

300. *I ſacrifice*] *I'd ſacrifice* Rowe.
ay, ſacrifice Pope et seq.
302, 303. [Aside. Hal.
304. *whom*] *who* Qq.

---

mon. As Anthonio has been once before (III, iv, 19) styled the 'lover' of Bassanio, it seems extremely probable that that is the true word here.—ED.

292. **not**] COLLIER prefers this 'not' to 'but' of the Qq as perhaps more consistent with what Anthonio says above. HALLIWELL: Either reading can be supported. The Qq—only repent, give but a tear for the loss of your friend; the Ff,—obliterate me from your memory, let not my death interfere at all with your happiness, and I shall give up my life without a sigh. CLARENDON: Surely Anthonio would wish his friend to regret his loss. In both lines 'repent' is used in the sense of *regret, sorrow for;* as in *Mid. N. D.* II, ii, 111: 'I do repent The tedious minutes I with her have spent.'

295. **instantly**] Synonymous with '*presently*' of Q₁; see I, i, 193, and line 404 of this present scene; also *Oth.* V, ii, 66.—ED.

295. **with all my heart**] CLARENDON: A jest like this enhances the pathos. Men at the point of death have a natural tendency to beguile the misery of the time by playing upon words. Compare the death scene in *King John,* V, vii. So Shake-speare makes Gaunt jest on his name in *Rich. II:* II, 73. So also Sophocles makes Ajax 'play nicely with his name,' line 430.

297. **Which**] ABBOTT, § 266: Where *so dear, such,* &c. is implied in the antece dent, we may expect, as here, 'which' (§ 278) in the relative.

300, 304. DR JASTROW (*Young Israel,* Mai, 1876): This braggadocio dealing with the dearest relationship of life sounds to Shylock like rank blasphemy. He could use the half, or the whole, of his wealth as a make-weight to his friendship, but to put wife, or child, in the balance—at this very hour, it sounds like sacrilege.

301. BOOTH: Shylock manifests impatience during these speeches,—smiles grimly at mention of his cutting deep enough, and contemptuously at the Christians' willing-ness to sacrifice their wives for friendship; give a scarcely-audible sneer at each of their protestations.

Intreat fome power to change this currifh Iew.   306

   Ner. 'Tis well you offer it behinde her backe,

The wifh would make elfe an vnquiet houfe.   (ter

   Iew. Thefe be the Chriftian husbands : I haue a daugh-

Would any of the ftocke of *Barrabas*   310

Had beene her husband, rather then a Chriftian.

We trifle time, I pray thee purfue fentence.

   Por. A pound of that fame marchants flefh is thine,

The Court awards it, and the law doth giue it.   314

307, 308. Aside. Hal.   310. Barrabas] *Barabbas* Coll. i, iii.
309. [Aside. Rowe et seq. (generally).   313. *marchants*] *merchants* Qq.
   I haue] *I've* Pope+.

---

309. **haue**] ALLEN : I *feel* that Shylock *must* have said 'I *had* a daughter.' A similar misprint occurs in III, ii, 277 [q. v. Text. Notes].

309. **daughter**] The Second Quarto and the first three Folios have no punctuation after this word. The First and Third Quartos have a comma (I am not quite sure that it is not a full stop in Q₃), and are followed therein by F₄, Rowe, and Pope. Theobald increased this comma to a semicolon, and has been followed, I think, with but one exception, by all Editors to the present time ; Dyce, in his Third Edition, puts a comma and a dash after it. It is of no great moment, because the sense is clear under any punctuation ; but by introducing a semicolon we obliterate an example of what Walker (*Crit.* i, 55) describes as 'an instinctive striving after a natural arrangement of words, inconsistent indeed with modern English grammar, but perfectly authorized by that of the Elizabethan age.' Among many instances, Walker gives the following : ' No, no, my lord, This milky gentleness and course of yours Though I condemn it not, yet, under pardon, You are much more at task for want of wisdom,'—*Lear*, I, iv, 335 ; ' But if I thrive, the gain of my attempt The least of you shall share his part thereof.' —*Rich. III :* V, iii, 267.—ED.

309-311. BOOTH : With intense hate in look, and subdued tones ; between your teeth, as it were.

310. **Barrabas**] DYCE (*Remarks*, p. 59) : The word, I believe, was invariably made short in the second syllable by the poetical writers of Shakespeare's days : in Marlowe's *Jew of Malta*, ' Barrăbas ' occurs *seventy-eight times*. ALLEN : Shakespeare followed the pronunciation of his day, and that was the Reuchlinian, that is, he pronounced by the Greek, not by the Latin, accents, Βαραββᾶς. CLARENDON : It is thus spelt in Tyndale's and Coverdale's versions. STEEVENS : Our poet might otherwise have written : ' Would any of Barabbas' stock had been Her husband, rather than a Christian !'

312. **trifle time**] CAPELL : These words seem to betray a consciousness in the poet that he had a little wander'd from the τὸ πρέπον of character, in these several reflections preceding that begin with one from Bassanio : but desire (and some necessity indeed) of throwing into his dialogue something that should enliven it just at that time, begat this small trespass ; which, the necessities of his piece's nature consider'd, may be pardon'd even by the severest.

312. **pursue**] See ABBOTT, § 492, for a list of words in which ' the accent is nearer the beginning than with us.'

Iew.   Moſt rightfull Iudge.   315
Por.   And you muſt cut this fleſh from off his breaſt,
The Law allowes it, and the Court awards it.
Iew.   Moſt learned Iudge, a ſentence, come prepare.
Por.   Tarry a little, there is ſomething elſe,
This bond doth giue thee heere no iot of bloud,   320
The words expreſly are a pound of fleſh :
Then take thy bond, take thou thy pound of fleſh,   322

---

320. *iot*] *iote* Q₁Q₂.   *jot* F₂ et seq.   Mal. Steev. '93, Coll. Hal. Dyce. Sta.
322. *Then take*] *Take then* Qq, Cap.   Cam. Rlfe, Wh. ii.

---

315. BOOTH : With back to audience, and knife raised high above his head.

318. BOOTH : 'Most learned Judge' is uttered with an exultant voice, not too loud, and 'A sentence' is spoken with a low bow to the Duke.   COLLIER (ed. ii) : At the exclamation, 'Come, prepare !' the actor is directed by the (MS) to *show the scales again*.   This may only explain the manner of a particular actor, in order to give greater effect to his part.

319–326. HAYNES (*Outlines of Equity*, p. 19) : The popular belief that the law exacts a literal fulfillment of contracts has ever been deeply rooted.   We trace it distinctly in the drama and in works of fiction.   Perhaps one of the most remarkable instances is that of Shylock's bond. . . . . And how is the intended victim rescued ?   By the merest verbal quibble.   I should be sorry to profane Shakespeare or to approach the creations of his genius in the same spirit that I should a Report in Meeson and Welsby.   Considerable latitude is to be allowed to the dramatist ; but when I see Antonio saved by a species of construction, according to which, if a man contracted for leave to cut a slice of melon, he would be deprived of the benefit of his contract unless he had stipulated, in so many words, for the incidental spilling of the juice, one cannot help recognizing in the fiction of the immortal poet an intensified representation of the popular faith—that the *law* regarded the *letter*, not the *spirit*.   As to the tender coming too late, that was in strict historical accordance with the law.   At Common Law, if a bond was once forfeited by non-payment of principal and interest on the day stipulated, the whole penalty must have been paid. . . . . It is clear that, had the scene of Shakespeare's play been laid in England, and not in Venice, the proper advice for Portia to have given would have been to file a bill in Chancery.   But I confess I cannot say that the play would have been improved.   C. K. DAVIS (*Law in Shakespeare*, p. 117) : It may be observed here that the law language of Shakespeare is that of the Common Law, and not of the Equity Jurisprudence.   No word peculiar to Chancery is, as far as I am aware, used by him.   Yet he wrote after the time when Waltham had enjoined the Shylocks of his day from exacting their penalties, and compelled them to take their principal ; after Wolsey had expanded the jurisdiction of that Court ; and after More had administered its benevolent justice in such cases.   He was contemporary with Ellesmere, and with that memorable contest between the Courts of Equity and Law, in which the former insisted upon its power to give relief, against the strict letter of the Common Law, from penalties and forfeitures, even after judgement.   Had Shakespeare been a Chancery lawyer he might have caused an injunction to be served on Shylock, and avoided the unsatisfactory and quibbling process by which Portia rescued the Merchant from the knife of the Jew.

But in the cutting it, if thou doſt ſhed   323
One drop of Chriſtian bloud, thy lands and goods
Are by the Lawes of Venice confiſcate   325
Vnto the ſtate of Venice.

  Gra.   O vpright Iudge,
Marke Iew, ô learned Iudge.

  Shy.   Is that the law?

  Por.   Thy ſelfe ſhalt ſee the Act :   330
For as thou vrgeſt iuſtice, be aſſur'd
Thou ſhalt haue iuſtice more then thou deſireſt.

  Gra.   O learned Iudge, mark Iew, a learned Iudge.

  Iew.   I take this offer then, pay the bond thrice,
And let the Chriſtian goe.   335

  Baſſ.   Heere is the money.

  Por.   Soft, the Iew ſhall haue all iuſtice, ſoft, no haſte,
He ſhall haue nothing but the penalty.

  Gra.   O Iew, an vpright Iudge, a learned Iudge.

  Por.   Therefore prepare thee to cut off the fleſh,   340

327, 328. One line, Pope et seq.   *337. Soft,*] *Soft ;* (as a separate line)
334. *this*] *his* Q₃, Cap. Walker, Dyce   Cap. et seq.
iii, Huds.   *340. cut off*] *cut of* Q₂.

---

323. **the cutting it**] See I, ii, 96; III, iv, 24, or Abbott, § 93.

325. **confiscate**] See ABBOTT, § 342, for a list of verbs ending in *-te, -t*, and *-d*, which, on account of their already resembling participles in their terminations, do not add *-ed* in the participle or past tense. Words like *miscreate, consecrate, confiscate*, being directly derived from Latin participles, stand on a different footing, and may themselves be regarded as participial adjectives, without the addition of *d*.

326. BOOTH : Shylock staggers backward and drops the knife.

329. BOOTH : In a choked tone of amazement to the Duke, bowing. His opinion of Portia is now changed; all he says is addressed to the Duke, except ' I am content,' when he looks steadily at Portia.

334. **this offer**] CAPELL (in his note on line 220, having approved of Portia's offer of 'thrice,' continues) : The Jew (as was right) catches at the term in her offer, whom he mistakes for a doctor : who, being now out of favour with him, he calls it—' *his offer* ' with marks of signal displeasure, when *his* is utter'd in tone, action, and look. STEEVENS : Perhaps we should read *his,* i. e. Bassanio's, who offers *twice* the sum. MASON : *This* offer is right. Shylock specifies the offer he means, which is : 'to have the bond paid thrice.' MALONE : He means, I think, to say, ' I take *this* offer that has been made me.' Bassanio had offered at first but *twice* the sum, but Portia had gone further—'there's *thrice* thy money,' &c. The Jew naturally insists on the larger sum. ALLEN : Capell *must* be right. DYCE (ed. iii) : Malone's attempt to reconcile the inconsistency of the old Eds. is very far from happy. [I much prefer *his.*—ED.]

337. **all iustice**] ALLEN : Namely, that wh'ch is wholly justice, unmixed with either equity or mercy.

Shed thou no bloud, nor cut thou leſſe nor more   341
But iuſt a pound of fleſh : if thou tak'ſt more
Or leſſe then a iuſt pound, be it ſo much
As makes it light or heauy in the ſubſtance,
Or the deuiſion of the twentieth part   345
Of one poore ſcruple, nay if the ſcale doe turne
But in the eſtimation of a hayre ,
Thou dieſt, and all thy goods are confiſcate.
   Gra.   A ſecond *Daniel*, a *Daniel* Iew,
Now infidell I haue thee on the hip.   350
   Por.   Why doth the Iew pauſe, take thy forfeiture.

---

342. *tak'ſt*] *cutſt* Q₁, Cam. Cla. Glo. Wh. ii.

343. *be it*] Ff, Rowe, Coll. Wh. i. *be't but* Pope+, Dyce iii, Huds. *be it but* Qq et cet.

345. *Or*] *On* Theob. Warb. Johns. Cap. *Of* Ktly.

   deuiſion] *diuiſion* Q₁Q₃.

346. *doe*] Om. Pope+, Steev. '85.

350. *thee*] *you* Qq, Cap. Cam. Cla. Glo

351. *thy*] *the* Pope+.

---

343. **just pound**] ABBOTT, § 14 : That is, *exact*, as in Latin. [It is a '*just* pound in the title-pages of the Qq and in Silvayn's *Declamation*.]

343. **be it**] On rhythmical grounds I prefer this reading to the *be it but* of the Qq. *Be it but* must be contracted *be't but*, which is, to me, cacophonous. Moreover, the *but* is scarcely needed ; it comes with much force two or three lines further on, where its strength may, perhaps, be a little weakened by its anticipation here.—ED.

344. **substance,**] COLLIER : *Balance* according to the (MS), which may be right ; but as 'scale' is mentioned just afterwards, we make no change. REV. JOHN HUNTER (who omits the comma) : In the amount of a twentieth, or even the fraction of a twentieth. The twentieth part of a scruple is a grain. CLARENDON : That is, in the mass, in the gross weight. There is a climax in Portia's threat : first, if it be lighter or heavier, i. e. according to ordinary tests ; then, if it weigh less or more by a single grain ; thirdly, if the scale be uneven by a single hair's breadth. The turning of the scale is estimated in the first instance by the eye. Possibly, however, it may mean that the *weight* of a hair would redress the balance. [I think it refers to *weight*.—ED.]

351. **pause**] In this 'pause' does Shakespeare intimate to us that the balance is trembling between Tragedy and Comedy ? The choice between them lies in Shylock's power. Is he debating it ? The end is not yet ; he can yet make that end Tragic, and I am rash enough to say that I am not altogether sure he should not so make it. Up to this point it cannot be said that Shylock's character excites our admiration. Socially, he is grossly ill-treated, and for that we pity him ; otherwise he is simply a cruel and vindictive creditor, highly intellectual, of course, as all of Shakespeare's chief characters are, but a persecuted Jew he is not ; that, however, he at once becomes, and compels our sympathy, when the law, which ought to have supported him, crushes him. Nothing convinces me more clearly that this is not a 'tendenz-drama,' wherein is infused a subtle plea of toleration for the Jews, than that, instead of a Jewish Tragedy, Shylock suffers it to end as a Christian Comedy. Shylock had sworn by his holy Sabbath to fulfil the bond, and, if the representative of a

Shy.   Giue me my principall, and let me goe.   352
Baſſ.   I haue it ready for thee, heere it is.
Por.   He hath refus'd it in the open Court,
He ſhall haue meerly iuſtice and his bond.   355
Gra.   A *Daniel* ſtill ſay I, a ſecond *Daniel*,
I thanke thee Iew for teaching me that word.
Shy.   Shall I not haue barely my principall?
Por.   Thou ſhalt haue nothing but the forfeiture,
To be taken ſo at thy perill Iew.   360
Shy.   Why then the Deuill giue him good of it:
Ile ſtay no longer queſtion.   362

355. *He*] *And* Q₁.   360. *taken ſo*] Ff. *ſo taken* Qq et cet.
358. *haue barely*] *barely haue* Pope +.   362. *longer*] *longer heere in* Q₁.

race, no perjury must taint his soul; cureless ruin has fallen on him; his life is gone, since there is no law for him in Venice; a Christian, worse than if of the stock of Barrabas, claims his daughter; to his ancient grudge is added the curse of his nation; since his fall, then, is inevitable, let him redeem his vow and drag down Anthonio with him. Anthonio's gushing blood will hide all former stains on the Jewish gaberdine. When, therefore, after the 'pause' for making up his mind, Shylock drops the knife to clutch the money, we see that his oath was hollow, and that he is still willing to wear the badge of sufferance and to be footed over the threshold like a stranger cur. No one of course can say with assurance why at this dividing of the ways Shakespeare decided in favour of comedy. If he objected to the many corpses on the stage, he got well over that aversion by the time he had written *Hamlet*. In my secret heart I like to believe that Shakespeare had fallen in love with Portia, as why should he not, with the most perfect of his creations? and though he might have thought that as a work of art the play should be a tragedy, yet that the vision of Portia's troubled, agonised face was more than he could bear, and her streaming eyes were more intolerable to him than Anthonio's streaming breast; it is to Portia, in more ways than one then, that I hope the Merchant owes his life. And as for Shylock, I find relief in the assurance, which a knowledge of his character as revealed on the Trial affords, that it cannot be long before his financial prospects are as fair as ever. One half of his present property, which he is allowed to retain, is probably a much larger sum than he started with in life; and the wide-spread notoriety which will accrue to him from this trial, and which is believed in these modern days of advertising to be 'the soul of business,' cannot but stand him in admirable and remunerative stead.—ED.

352. BOOTH: After a brief struggle. Bassanio offers the bag of money; Shylock takes it, but Gratiano seizes it from him.

354, 355. BOOTH: As Portia says this she descends from the dais, gives the bond to Shylock, and goes to the table. As Shylock replies he throws the bond at Anthonio's feet. Or Portia may throw the bond at Shylock's feet, who stamps on it with impotent rage. When Portia says that the law hath yet another hold on him, Shylock shows great alarm.

362. If it were not for the metre, the reading of Q₁ seems to me an improvement: Ile stay no longer here in question.' If 'question' be pronounced as a trisyllable,

Por. Tarry Iew,   363
The Law hath yet another hold on you.
It is enacted in the Lawes of Venice,   365
If it be proued againſt an Alien,
That by direct, or indirect attempts
He ſeeke the life of any Citizen,
The party gainſt the which he doth contriue,
Shall ſeaze one halfe his goods, the other halfe   370
Comes to the priuie coffer of the State,
And the offenders life lies in the mercy
Of the Duke onely, gainſt all other voice.
In which predicament I ſay thou ſtandſt :   374

366. *an*] *any* Q$_1$.   Steev. '85, Mal. '90.
370. *ſeaze*] *ſeize* Q$_1$.   371. *coffer*] *coſter* Q$_1$.
 one] *on* Q$_1$Q$_3$F$_4$, Rowe+, Cap.

---

and 'Tarry, Jew,' regarded as an interjectional line by itself, the metre is smooth enough.—ED.

364. ROLFE (*Shakespeariana*, p. 33, Jan., 1886) : It is a significant fact,—to me at least, for I believe that no commentator or critic has referred to it,—that the dramatist, after using the 'bad law' from the old tale, makes Portia go on to say, 'The law hath yet another hold on you'—namely, on account of his having *sought the life* of Antonio. Note at what length this is dwelt upon, and how much stress Portia lays on it. Note also that this is *not in the various forms of the old story*, but is Shakespeare's own addition thereto. I have no doubt that he added it solely because he knew that the original 'law' was 'bad' and was not willing to rest his case upon it, as a writer unfamiliar with legal matters would naturally have done. He kept the 'bad law' for stage effect, but added the 'good law' to satisfy his conscience or his sense of justice. REV. JOHN HUNTER : The charge now to be brought against the Jew is probably what Bellario's letter refers to in the words, 'he is furnished with my opinion;' the mode in which Shylock has been already defeated appears to be the suggestion of Portia's own ingenuity; Bellario stated that his opinion would be 'bettered with the young doctor's learning.'

368. **seeke**] See ABBOTT, § 368, for instances of the Subjunctive in subordinate clauses, denoting a purpose.

369. **contriue**] STAUNTON : In *Tam. of Sh.* I, ii, Shakespeare for once uses 'contrive' in its scholastic sense to *consume, spend,* and the like, from the Latin *contero, contrivi.* Here and elsewhere it means to *scheme,* to *devise,* to *plot,* and comes from the old French compound *controuver.* Thus *Jul. Cæs.* II, iii : 'If not, the fates with traitors do contrive;' and *Ham.* I, v : 'Nor let thy soul contrive Against thy mother aught.'

370. **seaze**] That is, take possession of. The usual law term. See *Oth.* V, ii, 443.

372. **in**] ABBOTT, § 163 : This example illustrates the apparently capricious change in the use of prepositions. We should now say '*at* the mercy.'

374. **predicament**] CLARENDON : Originally, a term in logic, the Latin equivalent for *category* Wilson, *Arte of Logike,* 1567, has a chapter, 'Of the Predicaments, called

15

For it appeares by manifeſt proceeding,   375
That indirectly, and directly to,
Thou haſt contriu'd againſt the very life
Of the defendant : and thou haſt incur'd
The danger formerly by me rehearſt.
Downe therefore, and beg mercy of the Duke.   380
   Gra. Beg that thou maiſt haue leaue to hang thy ſelfe,
And yet thy wealth being forfeit to the ſtate,
Thou haſt not left the value of a cord,
Therefore thou muſt be hang'd at the ſtates charge.
   Duk. That thou ſhalt ſee the difference of our ſpirit,   385
I pardon thee thy life before thou aske it :
For halfe thy wealth, it is *Anthonio*'s,   387

---

376. *to*] *too* F₂ et seq.
377. *haſt*] *had* Ff.
   contriu'd   againſt]   *contriued
gainſt* Q₁.   *contriued againſt* Q₂Q₃.
378. *incur'd*] *incurd* Q₁Q₂. *incurr'd*
Q₃.

379. *formerly*] *formorly* Q₂. *formally*
Warb. conj. Dyce iii, Huds.
385. *ſhalt*] *may'st* Pope+.
   difference] *diffrence* Q₁.
   ſpirit] *ſpirits* Q₁, Cam. Glo. Cla.
Rlfe, Wh. ii.

---

in English the most generall wordes.' The word must have become very common, as
it is put into the mouth of the Nurse in *Rom. and Jul.* III, iii, 86.

   379. **formerly**] WARBURTON : This danger was a judicial penalty, which the speaker
had just before recited, in the very terms and *formality* of the law itself; we should
therefore read *formally*. CLARENDON : 'Formerly' was used in legal documents for
above.

   380. **Downe**] ANONYMOUS (ap. Halliwell) : This latter part of Portia's address so
completely brings to mind the conclusion of every sentence of single felony pronounced
by the clerk of the arraigns, who concludes his address to each culprit with, 'Down
upon your knees, and crave the benefit of the statute,' that I cannot sometimes help
thinking but Shakespeare also must have borne it in mind when he wrote the passage.

   381. BOOTH : Shylock is about to kneel; Gratiano holds him by the shoulder while
he addresses him, and then drops him. When Shylock says, 'Nay, take my life,' and
so on, he is still kneeling, with head very low, and speaks with a trembling, tearful
voice. When Portia asks, 'What mercy can you render him, Anthonio?' Shylock
rises quickly, as if stung.

   383. **hast not left**] ALLEN : Not the negative of *hast-left*, but 'thou hast not,
remaining, the value,' &c. See III, v, 62.

   385. **shalt**] See ABBOTT, § 348, for instances of the future where we should use
the Subjunctive.

   385. **our spirit**] ECCLES : That is, my spirit, or the 'spirit' of us who profess Christianity as opposed to *thine*, requires that *our* should be pronounced with emphasis;
our spirits' (of the Qq) must signify *your spirit and mine*. HALLIWELL : The signification of the Qq reading suits less with the dignity and position of the speaker.

   386, 391. **pardon**] See SCHMIDT's *Lex.* for parallel passages where it means to
absolve, to release, to remit

The other halfe comes to the generall ſtate,   388
Which humbleneſſe may driue vnto a fine.
   Por.   I for the ſtate, not for *Anthonio.*   390
   Shy.   Nay, take my life and all, pardon not that,
You take my houſe, when you do take the prop
That doth ſuſtaine my houſe : you take my life
When you doe take the meanes whereby I liue.
   Por.   What mercy can you render him *Anthonio ?*   395
   Gra.   A halter *gratis*, nothing elſe for Gods ſake.
   Ant.   So pleaſe my Lord the Duke, and all the Court
To quit the fine for one halfe of his goods,   398

---

394. *whereby*] *wherby* Q₁.   398. *quit*] *quite* F₂.
396. *Gods ſake*] *Godſake* Q₂.   *for*] *from* Han.

---

390. MALONE: That is, the State's moiety may be commuted for a fine, but not
Anthonio's.

391. **Nay . . . all**] GOULD (*The Tragedian*, p. 74): Kean, after making the audience hate him, did, by one of his sudden turns of power, and by the pathos of his voice
in these words, produce an entire revulsion of feeling in the listener, so that pity took
the place of execration.

393. **you take my life**] HALLIWELL: ' He that taketh away his neighbour's living,
slayeth him.'—*Ecclesiasticus*, xxxiv, 22.

398–402. THEOBALD (Nichols's *Illust.* ii, 312): Dr Thirlby, by a change of these
lines, gives Anthonio a much more generous way of thinking. I will submit his read-
ing to you : ' To quit *their* fine *of* one-half of his goods; | I am content *to* let *him* have
the other | In use, to render it upon his death | Unto the gentleman that stole his daugh-
ter.' THEOBALD: The Jew had forfeited his whole substance; one moiety thereof to
go to the State, and the other to the Defendant. Anthonio proposes that the State
should be content with fining him only that moiety which was confiscated to them;
that, as to the other, which Anthonio might equally claim to himself, he only desires
to hold the benefit, paying interest for it to the Jew during his life; and, upon the
Jew's demise, to have it immediately vested in his Son and Daughter. JOHNSON:
The terms proposed have been misunderstood. Anthonio declares that, as the Duke
quits one-half of the forfeiture, he is likewise content to abate his claim, and desires
not the property but the *use* or produce only of the half, and that only for the Jew's
life, unless we read, as perhaps is right, ' upon *my* death.' RITSON (p. 55): Anthonio
tells the Duke that if he will abate the fine for the State's half, he (Anthonio) will be
contented to take the other, *in trust*, after Shylock's death, to render it to his daughter's husband. That is, it was, during Shylock's life, to remain *at interest* in Anthonio's hands, and Shylock was to enjoy the produce of it. MASON (p. 76): Anthonio's
offer is, that he will quit the fine for one-half of his fortune, provided that he will let
him have it at interest during the Jew's life, to render it at his death to Lorenzo. That
is the meaning of the words *to let me have in use.* LEWIN (*The Law of Trusts*, 6th
ed., 1875, chap. i, p. 13): That a trust was anciently known as a *use*, appears from the
Mer. of Ven. Thus, when Shylock had forfeited one-half of his goods to the State to
be commuted for a fine, and the other half of his goods to Antonio, the latter offered

I am content : ſo he will let me haue
The other halfe in vſe, to render it   400
Vpon his death, vnto the Gentleman
That lately ſtole his daughter.
Two things prouided more, that for this fauour
He preſently become a Chriſtian :   404

---

401. *Vpon*] *Until* Han.

---

that, if the Court, as representing the State, would forego the forfeiture of the one-half, he (Antonio) would be content himself to hold the other half in *use*, that is, in *trust* for Shylock for life, with remainder, after Shylock's death, for Jessica's husband. This interpretation clears Antonio's character from the charge of selfishness to which it would be exposed if he were to keep the half for his own use during his life. ANONYMOUS (cited by Halliwell) : That is, in trust for Shylock during his life, for the purpose of securing it at *his* (not *my*, as suggested by Johnson) death to Lorenzo. Some critics explain *in use*, upon interest, a sense which the phrase certainly sometimes bore, but that interpretation is altogether inconsistent, in the present passage, with the generosity of Anthonio's character. In conveyances of land, where it is intended to give the estate to any person after the death of another, it is necessary that a third person should be possessed of the estate, and the *use* be declared to the one after the death of the other ; or the estate to the future possessor would be rendered insecure. This is called a *conveyance to uses,* and the party is said to be possessed, or rather *seised,* to the *use* of such an one, or to the use that he render or convey the land to such an one, which is expressed in law French by the terms *seisie al use,* and in Latin, *seisitus in usum alicujus, viz. A. B. or C. D.* This latter phrase Shakespeare has rendered with all the strictness of a technical conveyancer, and has made Anthonio desire to have one-half of Shylock's goods in *use,* to render it upon his (Shylock's) death, to Lorenzo ; which is by no means an unfrequent mode of securing a future estate ; and in our author's time nothing was more common than for A to convey to B *in usum,* or to the *use* that he should on a certain day enfeoff C, or convey to C. Suppose a gift to A et heredibus suis, in usum, quod redderet B, and we have the exact words of Anthonio. CLARENDON : Bassanio was wealthy enough for both himself and Anthonio, and Shakespeare knew that Anthonio's argosies were 'richly come to harbour suddenly.'

402. BOOTH : Shylock shrinks at this ; and at the word 'Christian' utters a short, sharp groan, staggers backward, and raises his right hand with the palm upward—face also upraised, with a look of utter despair, until the Duke has spoken, then collapses.

404. **presently**] That is, at once. See line 295.

404. **Christian**] HALLIWELL : According to Coryat's *Crudities,* 1611, p. 234, 'all their goodes are confiscated as soone as they embrace Christianity ; and this I heard is the reason, because, whereas many of them doe raise their fortunes by usury, in so much that they doe sometimes not only sheare, but also flea many a poor Christian's estate by their griping extortion, it is therefore decreed by the Pope, and other free princes in whose territories they live, that they shall make a restitution of all their ill-gotten goods, and so disclogge their soules and consciences, when they are admitted by holy baptisme into the bosome of Christ's Church.' It is just possible there may be some connection between this regulation and the termination of the trial by Shylock's compelled recantation of his faith.

The other, that he doe record a gift   405
Heere in the Court of all he dies poſſeſt
Vnto his ſonne *Lorenzo*, and his daughter.
   Duk.   He ſhall doe this, or elſe I doe recant
The pardon that I late pronounced heere.
     Por.   Art thou contented I ew? what doſt thou ſay?   410
     Shy.   I am content.
     Por.   Clarke, draw a deed of gift.
     Shy.   I pray you giue me leaue to goe from hence,
I am not well, ſend the deed after me,   414

---

406. *poſſeſt*] *possess'd of* Cap. conj.   412. *Clarke*] *Clearke* Q₁.

---

407. François Victor Hugo (p. 48): The reconciliation decreed by the sentence of the Judge is consecrated by the lawful union of Lorenzo and Jessica. In marrying the daughter of Shylock to a Venetian gentleman, Shakespeare braved public opinion, which forbade as a sacrilege a misalliance between Jewish blood and Christian blood; in despite of furious prejudice he proclaimed the equality of the hostile races, and has, for all time, united and mingled them in the same love as in the same faith. Thanks to the brave inspiration of the poet, the terrible drama unfolds of itself into a delicious comedy. The immemorial animosity of the forefathers vanishes on the lips of infants in the lispings of tenderness. The oaths of hate, the shrieks of rage, the imprecations which have resounded through ages of bitter generations die away in a splendid night, amid the balmy shadows of tropical flowers and under intoxicating bowers of oranges and laurels in a duet of kisses.

410. say?] Booth: Shylock, thus addressed, raises both head and hands as if about to appeal to Portia, checks himself, and says very slowly, as head and hands drop, 'I am content.' His last words are uttered plaintively. As Shylock is leaving Gratiano seizes his left arm, and at the conclusion of the taunting speech with which he addresses him, casts Shylock's hand from him. Shylock bows low to the Duke, and slowly totters towards the door,—he meets Anthonio, and shrinks with abhorrence; raises his hand (as on previous occasions), which slowly descends upon the back of his head as it droops upon his breast,—falls against the door, which slowly opens. The Curtain should be 'timed' to Shylock's exit.

411. I am content] Rev. Dr Kohler (*Jewish Advance*, 13 Dec., 1878): These three words might have spared unto millions of Jews their lives and saved fearful, innumerable agonies. No, a thousand times no! Shylock has no Jewish blood in his veins; else with that very knife that was to pay Antonio's forfeited bond he would have spilled it to the very last drop.

411. Hawkins (*Life of Kean*, i, 152): The sudden change of Shylock's whole appearance when the cause turned against him; the happy pause in 'I am —— content,' as if it almost choked him to bring out the word; the partial bowing down of his inflexible will when he said, 'I pray you give me leave to go from hence, *I am not well*;' the horror of his countenance when told of his enforced conversion to Christianity, and, to crown all, the fine mixture of scorn and pity with which he turned and surveyed the ribald Gratiano,—all exhibited a succession of studies to which words fail to do justice. He retired, as Shakespeare intended he should retire, with the audience possessed in his favour.

And I will figne it.   415
   Duke.   Get thee gone, but doe it.
   Gra.   In chriftning thou fhalt haue two godfathers,   417

417. Gra.] Shy. Q₂.   Dyce, Cam. Glo. Cla. Wh. ii.
   thou fhalt] *fhalt thou* Qq, Cap.

---

414. GEORGE FLETCHER (*Fraser's Magazine*, p. 705, June, 1850): Shylock, then, instead of losing his life and all his property, keeps his life and one-half of his goods. But let us here consider a little of what value these can be to him in the moral position wherein he now finds himself. First, while seeking revenge for his baffled covetousness, he had received the additional and deeper wound inflicted on his Jewish love of offspring by the stealing of his daughter. And then, while pursuing vengeance for this latter injury above all, he finds himself subjected to the last and bitterest grief and humiliation, of consenting to abjure his faith and profess himself a Christian. Anthonio, indeed, with the same want of insight into Jewish character in general, and into that of Shylock in particular, which had made him exclaim on occasion of Shylock's pretended reconciliation: 'This Hebrew will turn Christian,—he grows kind,' now proposes, in sincere charity to his defeated enemy, and care for his salvation, 'that he presently Become a Christian;' believing in pure kindness and simplicity of heart that such a compulsory profession might bring with it a sincere conversion. For, otherwise, this demand of his, far from having anything of a merciful character, would have been the greatest refinement of malice on his part; since, as we see, its fulfilment must have inflicted on the hereditary religious pride and pertinacity of the Jew a refinement of moral torture more dreadful to him far than death itself. This part of Shylock's sentence, indeed, is clearly meant by the dramatist as his *death*-blow, and *therefore* the most merciful blow that could now be dealt him. For, what motive has even Shylock now to live and get money? His 'own flesh and blood' has 'rebelled;' and all the produce of his 'bargains' and his 'well-won thrift' is doomed, by this last judgement upon him, still to be inherited by this sole apostate daughter and her misbelieving husband,—by her whom he regards as faithless alike to her house, her nation, and her God,—and respecting whom he has exclaimed but a moment before, 'Would any of the stock of Barrabas Had been her husband, rather than a Christian!' The last and bitterest infliction, however, he can escape;—from apostasy in his own person he has an alternative,—to die;—and this is plainly what, at his final exit, he is going to do. His inflexibility is majestic to the last. He sues not for mercy,—he asks not his own life,—he says, on the contrary, 'Nay, take my life and all, since you do take The means whereby I live.' If, then, he would prefer death to beggary, yet more, as his whole behaviour through the piece has shown us, would he prefer it to apostasy. When he blankly utters the bare words, 'I am content,' and faintly adds, 'Let me go hence, I am not well,'—we feel that he is tottering to his death-bed,—his only remaining refuge,—and one of which no auditor can wish to deprive him. SOUTHESK (*Saskatchewan*, &c., 1875, p. 409): Are we to understand that Shylock, Judas-like, committed suicide when he left the Court? There is something peculiar in his exclamation, 'I am not well.' A man of his stern character would have scorned to acknowledge any feeling of illness at such a time, unless he intended to end illness and health alike by ending his life. Besides, he would never really have consented to become a Christian, and his ready acceptance of that condition showed that he meant to break it,—and for that there was but one way.

Had I been iudge, thou fhouldft haue had ten more,   418
To bring thee to the gallowes, not to the font.   *Exit.*

  Du.   Sir I intreat you with me home to dinner.   420

  Por.   I humbly doe defire your Grace of pardon,
I muft away this night toward Padua,
And it is meete I prefently fet forth.

  Duk.   I am forry that your leyfure ferues you not :   424

---

419. *not to*] Q₂ Ff Q₃, Rowe, Knt, Sing.
Ktly.   *not* Q₁ et cet.

420. *with me home*] Ff, Rowe, Knt,
Wh. i.   *home with me* Qq et cet.

    to] Om. Q₁.

421. *doe*] Om. Q₁.

    Grace of] *Graces* Q₃, Han. Johns.

424. *I am*] *I'm* Pope+, Dyce iii,
Huds.

---

418. **ten more**] THEOBALD : That is, a jury of twelve men.   STEEVENS : So in Jonson's *The Devil is an Ass*, V, iii, 'I will leave you To your godfathers in law.   Let twelve men work.'   MALONE : This appears to have been an old joke.   So in *A Dialogue both pleasaunt and pietifull*, &c., by Dr W. Bulleyne, 1564 : 'I did see him aske blessinge to xii godfathers at ones.'   CAPELL : This is an application of English usages to a state that did not observe them.

419. FRANÇOIS VICTOR HUGO (p. 46) : Shylock is defeated, but, ponder it well, he can be condemned only by a tribunal which is higher than all tribunals.   Verily, it is not Shylock that is 'tarried' by Portia ; it is the *lex talionis* that Portia's 'tarry a little' strikes, it is that rigorous justice which is only rigorous injustice, it is that vengeful legislation which promulgates all the edicts of princes, and which mercilessly sustains all established magistracies,—parliaments, absolutisms, inquisitions, star chambers, assizes, —it is that process of reprisal which tortures, mangles, breaks, quarters, hangs, beheads, assassinates the assassin, which washes blood with blood and punishes the fault in committing the crime.   It is not the Jew that is sentenced, it is Judaism.   Such is the true bearing of the halt that is called.   In point of fact, Shylock has gained what is far better than his own cause, he has gained the cause of a whole people ; he has reclaimed the ignored rights of his race, and established them by this condemnation of the code of extermination which weighed them down.

419. **bring**] CLARENDON : Used in a double sense.   The sentence [qu. verdict ?] of a jury brought a man to the gallows ; the godfathers brought, i. e. accompanied, a convert to the font.

  Exit] MACDONALD (*The Imagination*, p. 165) : I suspect Shakespeare sends the old villain off the stage at the last with more of the pity of the audience than any of the other dramatists of the time would have ventured to arouse, had they been capable of doing so.   I suspect he is the only human Jew of the English drama up to that time.

421. **of pardon**] See ABBOTT, § 174, for instances of a similar use of *of ;* or I, iii, 54.   ALLEN : Is not this use of the preposition a relic of the Norman French ?   Modern French has *de* with the Infinitive after a *verb* of asking : 'Je vous prie de me pardonner' (although not with a *noun*).   The *of* in these phrases is nearly equivalent to *for* (I ask *for* pardon).   Here, again, the French have *de*, and the Irish *of*.   'The boy wil be the better *of* a beating.'   (This Irish use of *of* may have arisen either from the English of the conquerors, or from the French idiom, imported by the Priests and Gentlemen who had received their education at St. Omer's.)

Anthonio, gratifie this gentleman.   425
For in my minde, you are much bound to him.
                    Exit Duke and his traine.
  Baſſ.   Moſt worthy gentleman, I and my friend
Haue by your wiſedome beene this day acquitted
Of greeuous penalties, in lieu whereof,   430
Three thouſand Ducats due vnto the Iew
We freely cope your curteous paines withall.
  An.   And ſtand indebted ouer and aboue
In loue and ſeruice to you euermore.
  Por.   He is well paid that is well ſatisfied,   435
And I deliuering you, am ſatisfied,
And therein doe account my ſelfe well paid,
My minde was neuer yet more mercinarie.
I pray you know me when we meete againe,
I wiſh you well, and ſo I take my leaue.   440
  Baſſ.   Deare ſir, of force I muſt attempt you further,
Take ſome remembrance of vs as a tribute,
Not as fee : grant me two things, I pray you
Not to denie me, and to pardon me.
  Por.   You preſſe mee farre, and therefore I will yeeld,   445
Giue me your gloues, Ile weare them for your ſake,

---

425. *gratifie*] *greatifie* F$_2$.
426. [Scene III. Pope+.
430. *lieu*] *lew* Q$_1$.   *lewe* Q$_2$.
432. *curteous*] *curtious* Q$_2$.   *courtious* Q$_3$.
438. *more*] *mere* Anon. (ap. Cam.).

443. *as*] Q$_2$Q$_3$, Sta.   *as a* Q$_1$, Ff et cet.
  things,] *things ;* Rowe, Pope.
446. [To Ant. Cam. Glo. Cla. Rlfe. Huds. Wh. ii.
  them] *'em* Theob. ii, Warb.

---

425. gratifie] ALLEN : Like χαρίζομαι, make a gratification, that is, a present, a reward.

432. cope] RICHARDSON (*Dict.* s. v.) : Junius thinks it is from the Anglosaxon *Ceap-an*, to traffic, to exchange ; to buy or sell (to pay—*Mer. of Ven.*), and that it may have been extended to any kind of exchange. HALLIWELL : The meaning is, evidently,—we freely offer the ducats in return for your 'courteous pains.' STAUNTON : *To cope* seems to be used here in the sense of *encounter* or *meet*, and not in that of *exchange*. DYCE (*Gloss.*) : To pay, to reward (see Richardson's *Dict.*). SCHMIDT (*Lex.*) : To meet, to have to do with, to encounter. [The present passage given in illustration.] CLARENDON : To requite, give an equivalent for.

432. withall] ABBOTT, § 196 : This emphatic form of *with* is used for *with* after the object at the end of a sentence.

446, 447. CLARENDON : We have inserted the Stage directions, '*To Ant.*,' '*To Bass.*' It seems natural that as Antonio had been requested to 'gratify' his deliverer, Portia shoul ̄ ̣ake something from him as well as from Bassanio, whose obligation was less ;

And for your loue Ile take this ring from you,   447
Doe not draw backe your hand, ile take no more,
And you in loue fhall not deny me this?

   Baſſ.   This ring good fir, alas it is a trifle,   450
I will not fhame my felfe to giue you this.

   Por.   I wil haue nothing elfe but onely this,
And now methinkes I haue a minde to it.

   Baſ.   There's more depends on this then on the valew,
The deareft ring in Venice will I giue you,   455
And finde it out by proclamation,
Onely for this I pray you pardon me.

   Por.   I fee fir you are liberall in offers,
You taught me firft to beg, and now me thinkes
You teach me how a beggar fhould be anfwer'd.   460

   Baſ.   Good fir, this ring was giuen me by my wife,
And when fhe put it on, fhe made me vow
That I fhould neither fell, nor giue, nor lofe it.

   Por.   That fcufe ferues many men to faue their gifts,   464

---

447. [To Bass. Cam. Glo. Cla. Rlfe,   *vpon* Q_1, Pope. *depends on this, than is*
Huds. Wh. ii.   Theob. *on this depends than is* Han.
   449. *this?*] $Q_2F_2F_3$. *this.* Q_1 et cet.   455. *will I*] *I will* Q_1.
   454. *depends...on*] *then this depends*   460. *beggar*] *begger* Qq.

---

and if she had already taken Bassanio's gloves there would have been less reason for
asking the ring. The emphatic 'you' closing line 447, seems also to bear out our interpretation. [An interpretation which carries instant conviction.—ED.]

   451. **to giue**] See I, i, 45, or ABBOTT, § 356.

   454. **then on the**] CAPELL (ii, 71): None will be at a loss for this line's meaning.
Might not the word 'on' rise out of some defect in the manuscript, or (rather) blot in
it, and the proper reading be this? 'There's more depends on this than the stone's
value;' the line is clearer this way, and without fault in the expression: the comma that
follows 'this' belongs to moderns, for old editions have none of it. [In Q_1 we have a
downright compositor's sophistication, unless we choose to make a blind defence of the
line, and imagine that its incoherence indicates Bassanio's stammering embarrassment.
—ED.]

   464. **scuse**] Both Abbott (§ 460) and Clarendon imply that the full form is *excuse.*
'Scuse,' which Shakespeare uses elsewhere only in *Oth.* IV, i, 93, Halliwell says is an
archaic, not a contracted form, and gives the two following instances: 'Ile devise some
scuse,'—*Famous Historye of Captaine Thomas Stukeley*, 1605 [in a prose speech by the
Page, line 214, ed. Simpson, where, in sooth, Simpson prints it ''scuse'], and 'Pharicles
.... therefore trickt up his talke with this cunning scuse,'—Greene's *Mamillia,* 1593
[p. 179, ed. Grosart, where, strangely enough, the text reads not 'scuse,' but *sense.* At
whose door, Halliwell's or Grosart's, lies the heinous charge of confounding *en* and *cu,*
is not of pressing moment, since, owing to Grosart's excellent Index to Greene's Works,

And if your wife be not a mad woman,   465
And know how well I haue deferu'd this ring,
Shee would not hold out enemy for euer
For giuing it to me : well, peace be with you.   *Exeunt.*
   Ant.   My L. *Baffanio,* let him haue the ring,
Let his deferuings and my loue withall   470
Be valued againft your wiues commandement.

465. *And*] *An* Cap. et seq.
466. *this*] *the* Q₁, Pope+, Cam. Glo. Cla. Rlfe, Wh. ii.
467. *enemy*] *enmity* Rowe+.
469. *My L.*] Q₂Q₃. *My Lord* Q₁ et cet.
471. *valued againft*] Ff, Rowe, Hal.

Wh. *valew'd gainft* Q₁, Pope+, Cap. Steev. '85, Dyce, Ktly. *valued gainft* Q₂. *valued 'gainft* Q₃ et cet.
471. *wiues*] *wife's* Rowe et seq.
   commandement] Q₁F₂Q₃F₃, Pope+, Cap. Steev. Mal. Coll. ii, Rlfe. *commaundement* Q₂. *commandment* F₄ et cet.

we can find two other examples of 'scuse.' On p. 210 of *Mamillia*, Pharicles, 'to cloake the cause of his care, coyned this pretie scuse;' and as this coyning of scuses appears to have been a foible of Pharicles, I am inclined to think that Halliwell is correct in the former instance and Grosart wrong. Again in Greene's *Defence of Conny-Catching*, 1592, ' He thought it good to visit some other of his wiues (for at that instant hee had sixteene aliue), and made a scuse to his wife . . . . to go into Yorkshire,' p. 89.—ED.].

465. **And if**] Needlessly changed, since the days of Capell, to *An if.* MURRAY, in the *New Eng. Dict.*, under *And*, as a Conditional Conjunction, says : ' This conditional use of *and* may have originated from ellipsis, as in the analogous use of *so*, e. g. " I'll cross the sea, *so* it please my lord " (Shaks.); cf. "and it please;" or it may be connected with the introductory *and* in, " And you are going ?" A direct development from the original prepositional sense, though *à priori* plausible, is on historical grounds improbable. Modern writers, chiefly since Horne Tooke, have treated this as a distinct word, writing it *an*, a spelling occasionally found *circa* 1600, especially in *an' 't = and it.'* Again, under *An = if*, the same excellent authority says : ' In this sense *an, an'*, is rare before 1600, when it appears occasionally in the dramatists, especially before *it*, as *an' 't please you, an' 't were*, &c. As the preceding sense was not at this time written *an*, modern writers have made a conventional distinction between the two forms, *an'* for *and*, Latin *et*, being dialectal or illiterate, but *an'* or *an* for *and*, Latin *si*, archaic, or even literary. Except in *an' 't, an* is found only once in F₁ of Shakespeare ['Nay then two treyes, an if you grow so nice,'—*Love's Lab. Lost*, V, ii, 232]; but modern editors substitute it for the full *and* usual in Shakespeare and his contemporaries. Dialectally, the two senses are alike *an'*; the intensified *and if, an if*, common in the 17th Century, remains in the South-western dialect as *nif.'*—ED.

467. **enemy**] STEEVENS : So in *Much Ado*, I, i, 91 : ' I will hold friends with you, lady.'

471. **commandement**] WALKER (*Vers.* p. 126) : In *commandment, payment, entertainment*, and some other words in *-ment*, the *e*, which, originally, in all such words, preceded the final syllable (and which was still in certain instances retained,) was sometimes pronounced, and sometimes omitted. In the Folio (and probably in all other books of that time) the word which we now write *commandment*, is, when used as a trisyllable, printed *command'ment;* [herein Walker is in error; see Dyce, *post*]

Baſſ.   Goe *Gratiano*, run and ouer-take him,   472
Giue him the ring, and bring him if thou canſt
Vnto *Anthonios* houſe, away, make haſte.   *Exit Grati.*
Come, you and I will thither preſently,   475
And in the morning early will we both
Flie toward *Belmont*, come *Anthonio.*   *Exeunt.*

[*Scene II.*]

Enter Portia and Nerriſſa.

Por.   Enquire the Iewes houſe out, giue him this deed,
And let him ſigne it, wee'll away to night,
And be a day before our husbands home: 4

474. Exit...] Exeunt... Q₁.
[Scene II. Street before the Court.
Cap. et seq.

1. Enter...] Enter Neriſſa. Qq.   Re-
enter... Theob.

---

the entire word being a quadrisyllable, *commandement.* So it was pronounced as late, apparently, as 1672. Wallis, the grammarian, lived 1616–1703; the first edition of his grammar was published in 1653; the third in 1672; from which latter I quote, p. 52: '—— non dubito fuisse quondam pronuntiatam [the *e* in *miles, finely, advancement,* &c.] non minus quam in voce *commandement* mandatum, ubi adhuc pronunciari solet.' A writer in *The Saturday Magazine,* Aug. 17, 1844, 'On the Language of Uneducated People,' says that many cockneys still pronounce it thus.   DYCE (ed. iii): Here 'commandment' is to be read as a quadrisyllable; and so again in a line in *1 Hen. VI:* I, iii, which the Folio gives thus, 'From him I haue expresse commandement,' &c.   (In all the other passages in Shakespeare where it occurs in his blank verse it is a trisyllable.)   But the *spelling* of this word in the old copies goes for nothing; e. g. in *King John,* IV, ii, the Folio has: 'Haue I commandement on the pulse of life?' *though* '*commandement*' *there is a trisyllable.*   And I cannot understand why several of the modern Editors should print '*commandement*' here and in the above-mentioned line of *Hen. VI,* while in a great number of other words, which, if the orthography is to be suited to the metre, require the addition of a syllable, they content themselves with the usual spelling; for instance, they print '*dazzled,*' '*children,*' '*England,*' '*remembrance,*' '*juggler,*' '*handling,*' '*enfeebled,*' &c. &c., when, to be consistent, they ought to have printed 'dazzeled,' 'childeren,' 'Engéland,' 'rememberance,' 'juggeler,' 'handeling,' 'enfeebeled,' &c. &c.

475. presently] At once.

2. COWDEN-CLARKE: It is worth noting how Shakespeare, in his short and apparently insignificant Scenes, makes them serve fullest dramatic purpose. Here, the very first thing, Portia fulfils in careful, practical, professional way, the duty of conveying the deed to Shylock for signature; and afterwards, by her desiring Gratiano to show her clerk the way to the Jew's house, the opportunity for Nerissa to obtain her husband's ring is naturally brought about.

This deed will be well welcome to *Lorenzo*.   5
Enter Gratiano.

Gra.   Faire ſir, you are well ore-tane :
My L. *Baſſanio* vpon more aduice,
Hath ſent you heere this ring, and doth intreat
Your company at dinner.   10

Por.   That cannot be ;
His ring I doe accept moſt thankfully ,
And ſo I pray you tell him : furthermore,
I pray you ſhew my youth old *Shylockes* houſe.

Gra.   That will I doe.   15

Ner.   Sir, I would ſpeake with you :
Ile ſee if I can get my husbands ring
Which I did make him ſweare to keepe for euer.

Por.   Thou maiſt I warrant, we ſhal haue old ſwearing
That they did giue the rings away to men ;   20
But weele out-face them, and out-ſweare them to :
Away, make haſte, thou know'ſt where I will tarry.

Ner.   Come good ſir, will you ſhew me to this houſe.
Exeunt.

---

12. *His*] *This* Q₁, Pope+, Steev. Mal. | 17. [To Portia. Pope et cet. Aside.
Sing. Ktly. | Cap.
   I doe] *do 1* Rowe. | 19. [Aside. Cap.
13. *him :*] *him.* Q₁. | 23. *houſe.*] *houſe ?* Q₁F₄.

---

8. aduice] STEEVENS : That is, upon more reflection or deliberation. [See I,
i, 152.]

19. old] DYCE (*Gloss.*) : Used as an augmentative in colloquial language, meaning
'plentiful, abundant, great.'   I believe I was the first to remark that the Italians use
(or at least formerly used) ' vecchio ' in the same sense : ' Perchè Corante abbandonava
il freno, E dette un *vecchio* colpo in sul terreno,'—Pulci, *Morg. Mag.*, C. xv, st. 54 ;
' E so ch'egli ebbe di *vecchie* paure.'—*Id.* C. xix, st. 30.   It is rather remarkable that
Florio, in his *Dict.*, has not given this meaning of ' vecchio.'   COLLIER : Shakespeare
is full of instances of this augmentative ' old ' applied to words of almost every description ; it is needless to cite instances.   ROLFE : Compare the slang phrase of our
day, ' a high old time.'

Aɕus Quintus.

[*Scene I.*]

Enter Lorenzo and Ieſſica.

Lor. The moone ſhines bright. In ſuch a night as this,
When the ſweet winde did gently kiſſe the trees,
And they did make no nnyſe, in ſuch a night   4

Actus Quintus] Om. Qq.   Avenue to Portia's House. Cap.
  [Belmont. Rowe. A Grove or Green   2. Two lines, Q₁.
place before Portia's House. Theob.   4. *nnyſe*] *noyſe* Q₁.

HAZLITT (p. 275): The graceful winding up of this play in the Fifth Act, after the tragic business is despatched, is one of the happiest instances of Shakespeare's knowledge of the principles of the drama.

OECHELHAEUSER, whose eminence among German critics as one who has given especial attention to Scenic arrangement entitles him to a respectful hearing, in the Fourth Vol. of the *Sh. Jahrbuch*, p. 348, reviews a work called *Das Burgtheater*, by Heinrich Laube. This work, written, as Oechelhaeuser says, by a well-known dramatist, with a thorough knowledge of stage management, of independent character, and of keen critical judgement, is of enduring value, and from it the reviewer quotes the following, to which, as he says, he gives his unreserved assent: The *Mer. of Ven.* was given with an entirely new arrangement of the Acts and Scenes. [Laube is speaking of the production of the play under his management on the Vienna stage in 1851.] The Scenes before Shylock's house constituted one Act, and the scattered wooing Scenes were likewise brought together. Thereby the progress of the whole was rendered smoother and more connected. The chief change, however, was in the last Act. The great Trial Scene evidently concludes the Fourth Act; and the Fifth Act merrily finishes, at Belmont, the love-affairs of the play, which have long been ripe. The commentators, making a virtue of necessity, even applaud this finale. The real need lies in the demand for a final Act wherewith to conclude the piece after the chief interest of the play is over. They pronounce a musical, lyric ending a virtue, because it sets on a bright piece a bright, beautiful crown. The public thinks differently. As soon as Shylock's fate is sealed in the Fourth Act, the public usually begins to arise and prepare to leave. To it Shylock's case is the main interest of the play. In vain do the commentators cry that the Shylock business is only a great episode. The public heeds them not, but follows its own impression. And this impression rests on indisputable, æsthetic laws. The discord between the tone of the comedy and the tragic tone of Shylock's fate cannot be denied. It cannot be denied that the deadly agony of that part of the play is not in accord with a Comedy; or that the Trial Scene, with its question of life or death, makes a far deeper impression than all the rest, and that a whole Act following thereon is, to the audience, intrusive and superfluous. In no æs-

[Scene I.   Enter Lorenzo and Iessica.]

thetic sense are last Acts to be used to clear up a play; the weaker cannot effectively follow the stronger.   In a drama the strict law of an ever-increasing interest is not to be ignored, and commentators had much better acknowledge it instead of making a virtue of necessity.   No one denies that this last Act, with its beautiful language, is valuable; but with all its value as a final Act, it is a fault in composition.   To render this defect as little conspicuous as possible is the work of Scenic arrangement.   We begin, therefore, on our stage, the last Act with the Trial Scene, which occupies three-quarters of it.   It is followed by the short Scene of the giving of the rings, and then, while music plays, the Scene changes to the Garden of Belmont.   Thus we are pre-pared to resign ourselves to the repose of the music and the sweet words of the lovers; we see,—after some free excisions of the text,—the whole company approach from Venice by torchlight; in a few minutes the jesting puzzle of the rings is solved, and the end is reached without our being conscious of any jarring influence from the weaker theme on the previous interest in the play.   Thus, without any intervals between Acts and by a quick evolution of the Scenes, we carry home the impression of a joyous play, and are not struck by any dissonance in the notes of the chord.   Whoever has seen the play as thus arranged at our *Burgtheater*,—and during sixteen years I have questioned, I know not how many,—has acknowledged that the awkwardness of the last Act is quite concealed, and that in spite of Shylock's tragic fate, the impression is that of a pleasant comedy.   The text is not changed, merely shortened, and the aim of our mode of representation is attained merely by a change of Scenes and Acts.

HUNTER (*New Ill.*, i, 309): The 'poet's pen' has nowhere given more striking proof of its power than in the Scene of the Garden of Belmont.   We find ourselves transported into the grounds of an Italian palazzo of the very first class, and we soon perceive them to be of surpassing beauty and of almost boundless extent.   It is not a garden of parterres and flowers, but more like Milton's 'Paradise,' full of tall shrubs and lofty trees,—the tulip tree, the poplar, and the cedar.   But it is not, like Milton's, a garden in which the hand of Nature is alone visible.   There are terraces and flights of steps, cascades and fountains, broad walks, avenues, and ridings, with alcoves and banqueting-houses in the rich architecture of Venice.   It is evening; a fine evening of summer, which tempts the masters of the scene to walk abroad and enjoy the breezes which ruffle gently the foliage.   The moon is in the heavens, full orbed and shining with a steady lustre; no light clouds disturbing the deep serene.   On the green sward fall the ever-changing shadows of the lofty trees, which may be mistaken for fairies sporting by the moonlight; where trees are not, the moonbeams sleep upon the bank. The distant horn is heard; and even sweeter music floats upon the breeze. . . . . For the four moonlights in classical or quasi-classical story the poet did not draw on his imagination, but his memory.   It is not that Troilus, Thisbe, Dido, and Medea *might* have done what they did when the moon was shining in full splendour, as on that night in the Garden of Belmont, but the poet had read that they did what they are described as having done, in the moonlight.   This, at least, is the fact in respect of three out of the four, and with respect to the fourth an explanation may be given which will bring it within the same category.   The first is Troilus.   [Steevens was the first, I believe, to note, which he did without further remark, that 'the image' of Troilus mounting the Trojan walls 'is from Chaucer's *Troilus and Cresseide*, Book v, 666.— ED.]   Though this is a classical name, and the story is a tale of Troy, yet cannot the story be traced to any of the ancient poets.   [See Clarendon's note, *post*.]   It seems to have been to Chaucer that Shakespeare was indebted for his knowledge of it.   The

[Scene I.   Enter Lorenzo and Iessica.]

next is Thisbe.   Every one remembers ' Quam procul ad lunæ radios Babylonia Thisbe
Vidit.'   [Ovid, *Metamorphoses*, iv, 99.]   But for the suggestion of this also, and even
of the two which follow, it seems that Shakespeare was indebted to Chaucer; that, in
fact, the old folio of Chaucer was lying open before him when he wrote this dialogue,
and that there he found Thisbe, Dido, and Medea, as well as Troilus.   It is at least
certain that Thisbe, Dido, and Medea do occur together in Chaucer's *Legend of Good
Women*, which in the folio immediately follows the *Troilus*.   Neither Vergil nor Ovid
represents Dido as standing by moonlight ' on the wild sea-bank,' as she is so pictur-
esquely depicted by Shakespeare, and the idea of placing a willow in her hand is modern,—' The willow worn of forlorn paramours;' but Chaucer, when he speaks of Dido,
says, ' It fell upon a nyght Whan that the moone upreysed had her light, This noble
Quene unto her reste y-wente; She sigheth sore,' &c.   But the truth seems to be that
Shakespeare has transferred to Dido what he found in Chaucer's *Legend* concerning
Ariadne :

> ' And to the stronde barefote faste she went,
> And cryed, " Theseus, myn herte swete !
> Where be ye, that I may not wyth yow mete ?
> And myghte thus with bestes ben yslayne."
> The holowe roches answerde her agayne.
> No man she sawe, and yet shone the moone,
> And hye upon a rokke she went soone
> And sawe hys barge saylynge in the see.
> Cold waxe hire herte, and ryghte thus sayde she :
> " Meker then ye fynde I the bestes wilde !"
> (Hath he not synne, that he hire thus begylde ?)
> She cried, " O turne agayne for routhe and synne,
> Thy barge hath not al thy meyny ynne."
> Hire kerchefe on a pole styked shee,
> Ascaunce that he shulde hyt wel ysee,
> And hym remembre that she was behynde,
> And turne agayne, and on the stronde hire fynde.'—
>
> [Lines 2187–2203, ed. Corson.]

There can be scarcely a doubt that this is the parent of the image of Dido; and the
merit of Shakespeare consists in a skilful adaptation, and in having produced in a few
strokes an effect superior to that which the older poet has produced with so much
labour, and with no mean success.   [Malone was the first to recall Chaucer's description of Ariadne.—ED.]   There remains only Medea.   In the Medea of Chaucer we have
no moon, nor even the going out at night to gather herbs.   What Shakespeare here
owes to Chaucer is the suggestion of the character.   Seeing Medea in *The Legend of
Good Women*, his mind was directed to Ovid, the Latin poet with whom he seems to
have been best acquainted, and he there found : ' As soone as that she shone Most full
of light, and did behold the earth with fulsome face, Medea with hir haire not trust so
much as in a lace, But flaring on hir shoulders twaine, and barefoote, with hir gowne
Ungirded, gate hir out of doores and wandred vp and downe Alone the dead time of
the night.'   [Golding's *Ouid*, p. 83, ed. 1567.]   I quote from Golding, because it is
evident that Shakespeare was accustomed to read Golding, without at all meaning to
insinuate that he might not have gone at once to the original, or that he might not have

Troylus me thinkes mounted the Troian walls,   5

5. *me thinkes*] *me-thinkes* Q$_1$. *methinks*   Cam. Cla.   *Trojan* Q$_3$.
F$_4$.   5. *walls*] *wall* Ff, Rowe+, Cap.
    Troian] *Troyan* Q$_1$F$_3$F$_4$, Rowe,   Steev. '85.

---

remembered in this and the other instances Vergil or Ovid themselves. [There is little doubt in my mind that Shakespeare remembered the translation and not the original, and that he was familiar with these pages of Golding. Only a few lines further on, in this very description, occurs that invocation which assuredly lingered in Shakespeare's memory. The original reads : ' Auræque, et venti, montesque, amnesque, lacusque, Dique omnes nemorum, dique omnes noctis adeste.' Thus Golding : ' Ye Ayres and windes : ye Elues of Hilles, of Brookes, of Woods alone, Of standing Lakes, and of the Night approche ye euerychone.' Who does not at once recall Prospero's invocation : ' Ye elves of hills, brooks, standing lakes and groves ' ?—ED.] I believe, however, that he was indebted in the first instance to Chaucer ; and that this is, perhaps, the best instance of the Chaucerisms which it is suspected lurk in greater abundance than is yet known in the writings of Shakespeare. It is pleasant thus to trace the pedigree of favourite passages, and to see one poet doing silent homage to the genius of another. STEEV-ENS notes that Gower, in his *Confessio Amantis,* has a description of Medea by ' sterre light.' VERPLANCK : The beauty and truth of this exquisite night-scene need not be pointed out to the American reader, who is familiar under his own skies with such moons pouring floods of liquid radiance, and such nights ' but little paler than the day,'—such as many an English traveller and many a poet have described with wonder and delight when seen in Italy or the East. It is the intense feeling of reality in this scene that, to my mind, gives strong confirmation of the opinion that Shakespeare had, at some period prior to this drama, wandered under the skies and moons of Italy. Still it is not conclusive. England has her own brighter nights, which the poet's fancy might light up to the golden star-paved heavens and the brilliant moonlight gazed upon by lovers' eyes from the gardens of Belmont. LLOYD (p. 554, Singer's ed.) : It is worth giving a note to the hints this Act contains of the stage management of what is apt to be tedious, a long darkened scene. In the first speech we have, ' The moon shines bright,' and again, ' How sweet the moonlight sleeps upon yon [sic] bank,' but by the time that Portia enters to converse for some time in front, unobserved by Lorenzo and his wife, the moon is overcast. ' When the moon shone,' says Nerissa, ' we did not see the candle,' and consistently Lorenzo had said just before, ' Come, ho, and wake Diana with a hymn ;' now Portia, with a parallelism that should have saved the line from a bad reading, exclaims, ' Peace, ho, the moon sleeps with Endymion, And would not be awakened.' When Bassanio approaches, however, the cloud again withdraws. '*Por.* This night, methinks, is but the daylight sick, It looks a little paler ; 'tis a day, Such as the day is when the sun is hid ;' and Bassanio accordingly, unlike Lorenzo shortly before, recognizes Portia by sight, and not by voice alone, and the stage remains fully moonlit to the end.

2. In] See II, iv, 2. WHALLEY refers to an imitation of this passage in the old Comedy of *Wily Beguiled.* See Appendix, ' The Date of Composition.'

5. Troylus] WALKER (*Vers.* p. 165) : ' Troilus ' in Shakespeare is always a dis-syllable. In the Folio *Tro. and Cress.* throughout, ... and to a great extent in the old English poetry, it is written *Troylus,* as if the name were formed immediately from Troy.

5. Troian walls] STEEVENS : This image is from Chaucer's *Troilus and Cresside :*

And figh'd his foule toward the Grecian tents   6
Where *Creffed* lay that night.
    Ief.   In fuch a night
Did *Thisbie* fearefully ore-trip the dewe,
And faw the Lyons fhadow ere hiuufelfe,   10
And ranne difmayed away.
    Loren.   In fuch a night
Stood *Dido* with a Willow in her hand
Vpon the wilde fea bankes, and waft her Loue   14

6. *foule*] soul out Allen.
  7. Creffed] Creffada Q₁. *Cresseid* Pope.
Cressid Theob. et seq.
  11. *dif nayed*] Qq Ff, Theob. Warb.
Johns. *dismay'd* Rowe et cet.

14. *wilde*] *wide* Rowe i.
  waft] *wav'd* Theob. Warb. Johns.
Steev. Var. Coll. Hal. Wh. i, Del. Dyce iii,
Huds.

'Upon the wallis fast eke would he walke,'—Bk v, 666. CLARENDON: The story of
Troilus and Cressida was probably already familiar to an English audience through a
play on the subject, which Shakespeare afterwards took for the groundwork of his
drama. Guido da Colonna, about 1260, worked up the old Latin tales, professedly
translations of Dares Phrygius and Dictys Cretensis, but really late forgeries, into his
romance called *Historia de Bello Trojano*, which became immensely popular, and was
the basis of Chaucer's poem of *Troilus and Cresseide*.

  13. **Willow**] STEEVENS: This passage contains a small instance out of many that
might be brought to prove that Shakespeare was no reader of the classics. 'And
why?' indignantly asks KNIGHT. 'Because the Dido of the classics is never represented
with a willow! Shakespeare was not, like many of Steevens's day who had made
great reputations with slender means, a mere transcriber of the thoughts of other men.
He has here given us a *picture* of the forsaken Dido, which was perfectly intelligible
to the popular mind. Those who remember Desdemona's Willow-song need no
laboured comment to show them that the willow was emblematic of the misery that
Dido had to bear.'

  14. **wilde sea bankes**] The Fourth Folio has 'wilde sea-banks,' and this hyphen
has retained its place in every edition, I think, since then, except Capell's, the Globe,
Clarendon, and White's Second Edition. I think it is wrong. If a hyphen be needed
at all, it should connect 'wilde' and 'sea;' it was the sea that was wild, not the banks.
Perhaps, it was this incongruity which led Rowe in his first edition to change 'wild'
into *wide*. In my copy of Capell there is a very dim mark between 'sea' and 'wild,'
which is possibly a hyphen, but I think not. Since writing this, I find that Allen has
noted in his MS a hyphen where I have suggested it. Now, I am sure it is right.—
ED.

  14. **waft**] WALKER (*Crit.* iii, 57) thinks that in all probability this is a corruption,
but gives another instance of it elsewhere than in Shakespeare, as well as the present
tense *wafts*, in *Ham.* I, iv, 61; and he also compares with this form, *saft* for *saved* in
several instances from Chapman. Abbott (§ 341), however, is much more likely to be
right, I think, in regarding it as an instance of the absorption in the final *t*, for the sake
of euphony, of the *-ed* of the past indicative; and in § 342 he gives another example
from *King John*, II, i, 73: 'A braver choice of dauntless spirits Than now the Eng-
16

To come againe to Carthage.   15
    Ief.   In fuch a night
Medea gathered the inchanted hearbs
That did renew old *Efon*.
    Loren.   In fuch a night
Did *Ieffica* fteale from the wealthy Iewe,   20
And with an Vnthrift Loue did runne from Venice,
As farre as Belmont.
    Ief.   In fuch a night
Did young *Lorenzo* fweare he lou'd her well,
Stealing her foule with many vowes of faith,   25

---

17. *gathered*] Qq Ff.   *gather'd* Rowe et seq. — 18. Efon] Æfon Rowe. — 23, 27. *In*] *And in* F$_2$, Pope+, Cap. — Steev. Sing. Walk. Coll. iii, Dyce iii, Huds. — 23, 24, 27, 28. *In...Did*] One line, Mal. '90. — 24. *lou'd*] *loued* Q$_1$Q$_2$.

---

lish bottoms have waft o'er.' As the textual notes show, Theobald is the first to print *wav'd.*—ED.

17. **Medea**] MINTO (p. 387): One of the pictures that the moonlight pours in upon these happy hearts is the sorceress Medea gathering her enchanted herbs,—a conception in the finest harmony with the soft mysterious light of the moon. But the other three are pictures of sighing, ill-starred, forlorn lovers, Troilus, Thisbe, and Dido. The moonlight hours are peculiarly sacred to lovers, and their placid influence tends to tranquillity and sadness. Happy successful love is akin to sadness; it is unsatisfied sighing that raises tempests in the soul, and confident hope or reckless despair that inspires to heroic deeds. In the moment of assured success the lover may be seated in the highest pinnacle of triumph, in rapture at having won the world's dearest possession; but triumph soon gives place to more tranquil joy, and falls naturally into the common pathetic key of love and soft diffused sadness. Shakespeare shows in many passages his deep feeling for the pathos and witchery of moonlight, and his delight in music under such circumstances appears to have been ecstatic.

20. **steale**] Could not Lorenzo have chosen a less suggestive word? But, after all, are there not two distinct, and utterly different, Jessicas? This Jessica, whose awakening soul can be saddened by sweet music, is not the Jessica of Venice, gilded with stolen ducats. In this growth of character is there one of Shakespeare's indications of Long Time lying perdue?—ED.

23. **In**] WHITE (ed. i): It must be confessed that the addition of *And* in F$_2$ helps the metre, and is not out of place in the concluding plea and rejoinder of the 'nighting;' but no addition is necessary, and, therefore, except upon authority, which F$_2$ lacks, none can be admitted. COLLIER (ed. ii) says, (and DYCE, ed. iii, repeats the assertion,) that it is only in some copies of F$_2$ that this *And* is found. 'If we are authorised,' he continues, 'in inserting words for any such reason, what is to be done with the lines in which Carthage and Æson are mentioned where there is a redundant syllable?' 'No alteration is necessary,' says BOSWELL; 'two hemistichs frequently occur at the end of one speech and the commencement of another.' [The 'And' is in my copy of F$_2$, and also, apparently, in that of the Cambridge Editors.—ED.]

And nere a true one.   26

   Loren.   In ſuch a night

Did pretty *Ieſſica* (like a little ſhrow)

Slander her Loue, and he forgaue it her.

   Ieſſi.   I would out-night you did no body come: 30

But harke, I heare the footing of a man.

Enter Meſſenger.

   Lor.   Who comes ſo faſt in ſilence of the night?

   Meſ.   A friend.   (friend?)

   Loren.   A friend, what friend *?* your name I pray you   35

   Meſ.   *Stephano* is my name, and I bring word

---

28. *ſhrow*] Q_2FfQ_3, Cap. *ſhrew* Q_1,   Stephano. Theob.
Rowe et cet.
                                  34. *friend ?*] Q_2. *friend.* Q_1.
30. *no body*] nobody Q_1, Sing.   35. *A friend,*] Om. Pope, Theob. Han.
32. Enter...] Enter a... Qq. Enter   Warb.

26. ABBOTT, § 510, would complete the metre by reading *never* for 'nere.' 'And
nev | er a | true óne | In súch | a night.' [But this sacrifices the emphasis, which, I
think, must fall on 'true.' I prefer to let the pause between the speeches complete
the metre.—ED.]

32. HUNTER (i, 315): The dramatic skill as well as the poetic power of Shakespeare
may be eminently illustrated from this Scene. Delightful as such discourse in such circumstances is, it must not be too long continued, as it conduces nothing to the business
of the drama. Yet the poet had not delivered his whole mind, and he meant still
longer to ravish the ears of young and old with this sweet and virtuous discourse. It
is that he might not seem inattentive to the business of the Scene, and that the audience might not grow impatient for the progress of the story, that he here introduces
the two servants with intelligence of the approach of Portia and Bassanio. This was
enough for the purpose. Orders are given for preparations to receive them, and for the
music. Then the dialogue proceeds.

33. **in silence**] ABBOTT, § 89: *The* was frequently omitted before a noun already
defined by another noun, especially in prepositional phrases. See I, i, 61; II, i, 17,
and 'In number of our friends,'—*Jul. Cæs.* III, i, 216; 'On most part of their fleet,'
Oth. II, i, 28.

36. **Stephano**] CLARENDON: Both here and in line 60 the accent is on the second
syllable. Shakespeare had learned the true pronunciation when he wrote *The Tempest*,
V, i, 277: 'Is not this Stéphano, my drunken butler?' TH. ELZE (*Sh. Jahrbuch*, xiii,
148): The reproach of a false accent in Stepháno, Rómeo, Desdemóna, Andrónicus
loses its force when we consider how very common it is in every language to change
proper names in form, in gender, and in accent. Livórno becomes Léghorn in English, Livourne in French; Miláno is in English Mílan, in German Mailand; Firénze is
turned into English Florence, and Venézia itself is in English Venice, French Veníse,
German Venedig. The Germanic races prefer an accent on the penult, and hence
Shakespeare has the same right to say Stepháno, as Schiller has to say Alcála. It is
common to hear English travellers speak of the 'Chiesa San Stepháno,' and Germans
scarcely understand the Italian Roméo and Desdémona.

My Miſtreſſe will before the breake of day   37
Be heere at Belmont, ſhe doth ſtray about
By holy croſſes where ſhe kneeles and prayes
For happy wedlocke houres.   40
 Loren. Who comes with her?
 Meſ. None but a holy Hermit and her maid:
I pray you it my Maſter yet rnturn'd?
 Loren. He is not, nor we haue not heard from **him**,
But goe we in I pray thee *Ieſſica*,   45
And ceremoniouſly let vs vs prepare
Some welcome for the Miſtreſſe of the houſe,

Enter Clowne.

Clo. Sola, ſola : wo ha ho, ſola, ſola.   49

37, 47, 75. *Miſtreſſe*] *miſtris* Q₁.	44. *we haue not*] *have we yet* Rowe+.
38. *Belmont,*] *Belmont;* Q₃.	46. *vs vs*] F₁.
40. *wedlocke*] *wedlockes* Q₁.	48. Enter...] Enter Launcelot. Rowe.
43. *it*] F₁. *is* Q₁ et cet.	49. *ha ho,*] *ha, ho* Qq. *ha, ho,* F₄.
rnturn'd] F₁.	

39. **crosses**] KNIGHT: These holy crosses still, as of old, bristle the land in Italy, and sanctify the sea. Besides those contained in churches, they mark the spot where heroes were born, where saints rested, where travellers died. They rise on the summits of hills, and at the intersections of roads; and there is now a shrine of Madonna del Mare in the midst of the sea between Mestre and Venice, and another between Venice and Palestrina, where the gondolier and the mariner cross themselves in passing, and whose lamp nightly gleams over the waters, in moonlight or storm. The days are past when pilgrims of all ranks, from the queen to the beggar-maid, might be seen kneeling and praying 'for happy wedlock hours,' or for whatever else lay nearest their hearts; and the reverence of the passing traveller is now nearly all the homage that is paid at these shrines.—M[artineau?]

42. **Hermit**] Dr Johnson, in his Edition, has here a needless note to the effect that he could not perceive the use of this hermit, of whom nothing is seen or heard afterwards. This was never repeated in any of the subsequent Editions which he issued in collaboration with Steevens; but it was the text for a coarse onslaught by Dr Kenrick, in which he called Dr Johnson 'a blockhead,' and was afterwards berated for it by Barclay. In thus becoming a part of the history of Shakespearian criticism, it has to be noted here.—ED.

46. **ceremoniously**] I cannot find that Schmidt, in his invaluable Appendix, has anywhere noted this kind of adverbial hypallage. Probably he thought that having collected many examples of a similar interchange of adjectives, the same observation would apply to adverbs; and so, in effect, it does. But it is well to note the instances when they occur, as ALLEN, in his MS, has done here, and afterwards in line 301, 'Your argosies Are richly come to harbour.' Of course the present line means, 'Let us prepare some ceremonious welcome,' &c.—ED.

49. STAUNTON: Launcelot is imitating the horn of the courier, or 'post,' as he **was**

Loren.   Who calls?   50
Clo.   Sola, did you fee M. *Lorenzo*, & M. *Lorenzo*, fola,
Lor.   Leaue hollowing man, heere.   (fola.
Clo.   Sola, where, where?
Lor.   Heere?
Clo.   Tel him ther's a Poft come from my Mafter, with   55
his horne full of good newes, my Mafter will be here ere
morning fweet foule.   57

---

51. *M...Lorenzo,*] *M.* Lorenzo, *& M.*
Lorenzo Q₂. *M.* Lorenzo, *M.* Lorenzo,
Q₁. *M.* Lorenzo, *M.* Lorenza, F₂.
M. Lorenzo, *and M.* Lorenzo, Q₃. *M.*
Lorenzo, *and Mrs.* Lorenza, F₃F₄. *Mr.*
Lorenzo and Mrs. Lorenzo? Rowe i. *Mr.*
Lorenzo and Mrs. Lorenza? Rowe ii.
master Lorenzo and mistress Lorenza
Pope+, Cap.   *Master Lorenzo? Master*
Lorenzo, Cam. Glo. Cla. Wh. ii. *Master*

Lorenzo and Mistress Lorenzo Steev. et
cet.
   52. *hollowing*] *hollaing* Mal. *hallooing*
Coll.
   57. *morning*] *morn* Ktly conj.
   [Exit Clo. Cap. et seq.
   fweet foule] Given to Loren. Rowe
et seq.
   foule] *love* Ff, Rowe+, Cap.

---

called, who always wore that appendage suspended from his neck.   HALLIWELL: The
postman's horn is often seen figured in the water-marks of paper of the 17th Century,
and would appear to have often been a real horn.

   51. **M. Lorenzo, & M. Lorenzo**] The Textual Notes will show the evolution of
these words, through a process of unnatural selection, into 'Master Lorenzo and Mistress Lorenzo,' as they now stand in the majority of modern Editions.   It has all along
been clear that F₁ was printed from Q₂; it seems to me not unlikely that in the faulty
composition of this Q₂, the ampersand is a misprint for an interrogation mark; this
ampersand was printed out in full in F₂ and a misprint added, 'Lorenza.'   This accidental feminine termination was accepted in full faith by the printer of F₃, and 'Mrs
Lorenza' stood forth confessed.   That the feeble joke is wholly the printer's, and not
Shakespeare's, and that Lorenzo alone is called, is shown, I think conclusively, by
Clarendon, who calls attention to the fact that in line 55 Launcelot says, 'Tell *him*,'
not 'Tell *them*.'—ED.

   51. All that Launcelot says in this Scene is clearly prose, and is so printed in all
editions except in White's ed. ii, where this line is divided after the first 'Lorenzo.'
But this division arose, I am sure, from a mere oversight.   That careful Editor printed
from the Globe Edition, where, for typographical reasons, the line had to be so divided,
and this fact escaped White's notice.—ED.

   57. CAPELL (ii, 72): That he ['the first modern,' i. e. Rowe] should not be bold
enough, nor any one after him, to put an *Exit* for the Clown [see Text. Notes] when
he has made his speech, is among the wonders of their Editions: but it rose, first, from
their not considering that his continuance on the stage were in the last degree faulty;
and, next, from their having no right conception of the odd, but proper, mode of his
entry: This, if rightly perform'd, should be--with a whip in his hand; with which
he runs slashing about, circling the two people he *hollows* for without once looking on
them; and having empty'd his budget, goes out slashing as he came in.

   57 **sweet soule**] As Walker, in his *Article* LXXXV (*Crit.* ii, 177), gives (accord-

Loren.   Let's in, and there expect their comming.   58
And yet no matter : why fhould we goe in?
My friend *Stephen,* fignifie pray you   60
Within the houfe, your Miftreffe is at hand,
And bring your mufique foorth into the ayre.
How fweet the moone-light fleepes vpon this banke,
Heere will we fit, and let the founds of muficke
Creepe in our eares foft ftilnes, and the night   65
Become the tutches of fweet harmonie :
Sit *Ieffica,* looke how the floore of heauen
Is thicke inlayed with pattens of bright gold,   68

60. *friend*] *good friend* Cap.
  Stephen] Stephano Q₁ Ff et seq.
  fignifie...you] *I pray you, fignify,*
Ktly.
  fignifie] F₂F₃. *fignifie,* F₄. *fignifie*
I Qq et cet.
  62. [Exit Stephano. Theob.

65. *eares*] *eares ;* Ff, Rowe et seq.
67. *floore*] *vault* as quoted by Hallam.
68. *inlayed*] *inlay'd* Rowe et seq.
  pattens] Q₂Q₃, Johns. Cap. *pattents*
Q₁. *patterns* Ff, Rowe, Pope, Theob. Han.
Coll. *patens* Warb. Hal. *patines* Mal. et
cet.

---

ing to my count) about seventy instances in the Folio of unquestionable errors in the
assignment of speeches, including cases in which two speeches have been confused or
the like, I think we need feel no hesitation in here following Rowe, and in giving
these two words to Lorenzo.—ED.

60. **signifie**] It is easy to see how the compositor, following his ear, came to omit
the *I.*—ED.

63. **sleepes**] KNIGHT : One characteristic of an Italian garden is that its trees and
shrubs are grown in avenues and gathered into thickets, while the grass-plots and turfy
banks are studded with parterres of roses and other flowers, which lie open to the sunshine and the dews.   The moonlight thus *sleeps* upon such lawns and banks, instead
of being disturbed by the flickering of overshadowing trees.—M[artineau?]

65. **in**] See ABBOTT, § 159, for instances of *in* used with verbs of motion; also II,
viii, 45.

66, 76. **tutches**] SCHMIDT (*Lex.*) : The act of the hand on a musical instrument.

68. **pattens**] WARBURTON : We should read *patens,* a round, broad plate of gold
borne in heraldry; ['This is a mistake,' says HUNTER (i, 318), 'such a plate of gold is
called a *bezant.*'] the cover of the sacramental cup.   MALONE : A *patine* (from *patina,*
Lat.) is the small flat dish or plate used with the chalice in the administration of the
Eucharist.   It was commonly made of gold.   DYCE (*Remarks,* p. 59) : By adopting
the gross misprint *patterns,* Mr Collier has done much to injure the picturesqueness of
a passage which an eminent writer has pronounced to be 'the most sublime, perhaps,
in Shakespeare.'   [See Hallam, *post.*]   What are 'patterns of gold'? and how could
the '*floor of heaven*' be 'INLAID' with 'patterns'?   The not uncommon word *patten,*
paten, patin, or *patine,* means a plate.   'The *Patine* of a Chalice, Calici operculum,
patina.'—Coles's *Dict.*   HUNTER (i, 318) : The formidable objection to 'patten' is
that nothing, at any period, so called, can be supposed to have been used to represent a
star.   To get quit of this difficulty the word was turned into *patine.*   There is no hap-

[68. **Is thicke inlayed with pattens of bright gold,**]

piness or propriety in likening stars to dishes, not even golden ones. I have no doubt that *pattern* was the word from the beginning, and that Lorenzo was speaking of the stars as in their constellations, not individually; and the constellations may not unsuitably be spoken of as *patterns*, just as we speak of the pattern of mosaic work, &c. [When Hunter printed the foregoing note, it is not likely that he had seen the *Remarks*, &c. of his friend Dyce, which must have been issued while his own *Illustrations*, &c. were going through the press. Though Dyce, therefore, did not influence Hunter, Hunter's opinion evidently impressed Dyce; when, nine years later, Dyce issued *A Few Notes*, &c., his tone is perceptibly less peremptory. On p. 66, after citing Hunter, he reiterates his belief] that *patterns* is 'a gross misprint,' and cites two passages from Sylvester's *Du Bartas :* 'Th' Almighties finger fixed many a million Of *golden scutchions* [the original has '*platines dorees*'—Dyce] in that rich pavillion,' —*The Fourth Day of the First Week*, p. 33, ed. 1641; and 'That sumptuous canapy, The which th' un-niggard hand of Majesty Poudred so *thick with shields* [the original has '*escussons*'—Dyce] so shining cleer,' &c.—*Id.*, p. 34. COLLIER (ed. ii) : The question here is between *patterns* and 'pattens :' the Rev. Mr Dyce prefers 'pattens,' but cites no older authority than Coles's *Dict. :* the *Promptorium Parvulorum* would have been better, and there he might have found, 'Patena, or pateyne of a chalys.'— p. 385, ed. Cam. Soc.   But the truth is, that Shakespeare had no such far-fetched allusion : he was thinking of the 'patterns of bright gold' which inlaid the floor of heaven. Mr Dyce asks, 'how could the floor of heaven be inlaid with patterns ?' Just like any other ornamental floor; ornamental floors are always inlaid with patterns, and generally of stars. DYCE (ed. iii) repeats that Shakespeare means that the floor of heaven is thickly inlaid with plates or circular ornaments of gold; adduces the two foregoing passages from Sylvester's *Du Bartas ;* and adds that Mr Lettsom observes, '*Patterns* seems to me rather a sophistication than a misprint.' VERPLANCK thinks that '*pattern*, in its modern sense, for the plan of a carpet or other similar work (which alone could give any sense here), is more modern than Shakespeare's text.' CLARENDON : The 'patine' is the plate used in the Eucharist, and the image is thus much finer and more suitable to 'the floor of heaven' than the common-place *patterns*. [I find a difficulty in accepting the usual interpretation of this passage. It certainly does seem that 'orb' refers to 'patines,' and that the 'patines' are the stars; and if this reference is not to be evaded, then I yield; but under the protest that to compare merely luminous points, always silvery, to golden objects of manifest dimension, thickly inlaying the floor of heaven like a tessellated pavement, is, to me, to say the least, strained. The planets at their brightest might look like silver patines, but then not enough of them are visible at any one time thickly to inlay the skies. The very first words of this Scene are, 'The moone shines bright,' and if any one impression of external nature is given to us up to this point deeper than another, it is that the landscape is flooded with brilliancy, so bright that Medea could have even selected from among other flowers her enchanted herbs. If the 'patines' are the stars, here my difficulty culminates. When the moon shines thus dazzlingly, as we all know, the stars are scarcely visible, and those that are the brightest on moonless nights are but as the 'smallest orbs' now; not only, moreover, would they be unlike patines of bright gold, but they could not thickly inlay the floor of heaven. Shakespeare knew, quite as well as Sir Henry Wotten, that when 'the Q een' rose the 'meaner beauties of the night' were dimmed. But may it not be that, after all, the patines are *not* the stars? We infer that they are because Lorenzo refers to the stars in he next line. But there may well be a full

There's not the fmalleft orbe which thou beholdft
But in his motion like an Angell fings,   70
Still quiring to the young eyed Cherubins;
Such harmonie is in immortall foules,
But whilft this muddy vefture of decay
Doth grofly clofe in it, we cannot heare it: 74

71. *young eyed*] *young-ey'd* Rowe et seq.

  Cherubins] *Cherubims* F₃F₄, Rowe +, Steev. Ktly.

72. *is in*] *listen* Bailey.

  immortall foules] *immortal sounds* Theob. Warb.

74. *in it*] Q₁ Ff. *us in it* Rowe i. *us in* Rowe ii+. *it in* Q₂Q₃ et cet. *in ours* Bailey. *on it* Spence.

[Enter Musick and Domesticks of Portia. Cap.

stop and a pause after 'pattens of bright gold,' before Lorenzo's thoughts expand into the music of the spheres. Are we not all familiar with summer nights, when, here and there, the skies are thick inlaid with broken clouds, like flaky disks of curdled gold which slowly drift across the heavens, and veil at times the brightness of the moon? Are not these resplendent tiles on heaven's floor 'the patines' through whose rifts faint stars gleam forth? When Lorenzo begins to speak, a mass of clouds with golden iridescent edges was rising heavenward and just touching the silvery circle of the moon; as he finished, the light of the moon was waning, half dimmed by the first thin edges of the fleecy clouds: 'Diana is drowsy and must be waked.' By the time that Portia had reached Belmont the patines had veiled the moon, the heavens were darkened; she was greeted by the beams of a candle, unseen 'when the moon shone;' slumber had succeeded drowsiness and the 'moon sleeps with Endymion.' The clouds float onward, the patines of bright gold glide past,—Bassanio arrives; the moon shines forth; the 'night is but a little paler than the day.' See Lloyd's note, line 1, *ante.*—ED.]

71. *quiring*] SCHMIDT (*Lex.*): To sing in concert, and be tuned accordingly. As a verb only here, and in *Cor.* III, ii, 113.

71. *Cherubins*] An English form of a Chaldee plural, which probably came to us through the French. See *Oth.* IV, ii, 73: 'Still' in this line is used, as it very commonly is, in the sense of *always, continually.*—ED.

74. JOHNSON: That this line is corrupt must be allowed, but it gives reason to suspect that the original was: 'Doth grossly close *it in.*' Yet I know not whether from this any thing better can be produced than the received reading. Perhaps 'harmony' is the *power of perceiving harmony*, as afterwards: *Music in the soul* is the quality of being 'moved with concord of sweet sounds.' This will somewhat explain the old copies, but the sentence is still imperfect; which might be completed by reading: Such harmony is in *th'* immortal *soul,* But while this muddy vesture of decay Doth grossly close *it in,* we cannot hear it. MALONE: 'Such harmony,' &c. is not an exclamation, but an illustration. The whole runs thus: 'There is not one of the heavenly orbs but sings as it moves, still quiring to the cherubin. Similar to the harmony they make is that of immortal souls;' or, in other words, 'each of us has as perfect harmony in our souls as the harmony of the spheres, inasmuch as we have the quality of being moved by sweet sounds (as he expresses it afterwards); but our gross terrestrial part, which environs us, deadens the sound, and prevents our hearing.' 'It' in 'Doth grossly close

[74. Doth grosly close in it, we cannot heare it :]

it in,' I apprehend, refers to 'harmony.' It may be objected that as this *internal* harmony is not an object of sense, it cannot be heard ;—but Shakespeare is not always exact in his language; he confounds it with that external and artificial harmony which *is* capable of being heard. This hath been imitated by Milton in his *Arcades*, 71 : 'the heavenly tune, which none can hear Of human mould, with gross unpurged ear.' [Had Malone looked into his Plato he would not have said that Milton had here imitated Shakespeare.—ED.] STEEVENS : The passage may be well explained by Hooker in his *Ecclesiastical Polity*, b. v. [published singly, in 1597,—Malone] : 'Touching musical harmony, whether by instrument or by voice, it being but of high and low sounds in a due proportionable disposition, such, notwithstanding is the force thereof, and so pleasing effects it hath in that very part of man which is most divine, that some have been thereby induced to think, that the soul itself by nature is or hath in it harmony.' For this quotation I am indebted to Dr Farmer. DU BOIS (*The Wreath*, p. 60) : The correspondent passage in Plato is in his tenth book *De Republica;* where he speaks of the harmony of the Spheres, and represents a Syren sitting on each of the eight orbs, and singing to each in its proper tone, while they are thus guided through the heavens, and consent in a diapason of perfect harmony, the Fates themselves chanting to this celestial music : ἐπὶ δὲ τῶν κύκλων αὐτοῦ ἄνωθεν ἐφ' ἑκάστου βεβηκέναι Σειρῆνα συμπεριφερομένην, φωνὴν μίαν ἱεῖσαν ἀνὰ τόνον· ἐκ πασῶν δὲ ὀκτὼ οὐσῶν μίαν ἁρμονίαν ξυμφωνεῖν. [chap. xiv, 617, ed. Hermann. 'Upon each of its circles stands a siren, who travels round with the circle, uttering one note in tone; and from all the eight notes there results a single harmony,'—Davies and Vaughan, p. 413. For the authorities concerning this doctrine of the harmony of the spheres, see Smith's *Dict.* s. v. Pythagoras.—ED.] KNIGHT quotes a passage from Coleridge's *Remorse*, III, i; and CLARENDON finds here reminiscences of *Job*, xxxviii, 7 : 'The morning stars sang together.' ELZE in his Essay on *The Tempest* (p. 7) thinks that this description of the music of the spheres is taken from Montaigne's Essay *On Custom* (book i, chap. xxii), which, as Elze confesses, would prove that Shakespeare read it in the original. Florio's translation was not put forth until 1603.

74. **close in it**] KNIGHT : The verb in this case is probably compound—*close-in it.* [Unquestionably. There is no need to change the Folio.—ED.] COLLIER and DYCE unite in referring 'it' to the soul, and not to 'harmony.' [Wherein the present Editor entirely agrees.] HALLAM (*Lit. of Europe*, vol. iii, chap. iii, 11) translates a passage from Campanella, *De Sensu Rerum* (1617 ?), which he says he 'can hardly read without recollecting the most sublime passage, perhaps, in Shakespeare,' and thereupon quotes the present lines 67–74. W. W. LLOYD, whose *Critical Essays* enrich Singer's Second Edition (in fact, these Essays constitute the best claim of that Edition to the student's consideration), sets forth at length, in a letter to *The Athenæum*, of 12th May, 1877, the Platonic mythus, and its modifications by Cicero in the *Somnium Scipionis*, and by Dante, and in the Timæus as far as they are all applicable in their associations to the elucidating of this present passage, and thus concludes : 'We must not press Shakespeare's grammar and construction too pedantically. Here, as in many an ancient writer, the reader, for delight, skips gaily along through passages which convey to him an unquestionable and perspicuous sense, and is surprised and vexed to be recalled by a grammarian who is caught in mid-thicket by thorns of syntactical irregularity, and struggles vainly to disentangle poetry and prose, and accommodate the words to the only meaning they can possibly have been intended to express. An interpretation like the following is, at least, intelligible, and forces nothing cruelly : "Such

Come hoe, and wake *Diana* with a hymne,   75
With fweeteft tutches pearce your Miftreffe eare,
And draw her home with muficke.
   Ieffi. I am neuer merry when I heare fweet mufique.
                  Play muficke.
   Lor. The reafon is, your fpirits are attentiue :   80
For doe but note a wilde and wanton heard
Or race of youthful and vnhandled colts,
Fetching mad bounds, bellowing and neighing loud,
Which is the hot condition of their bloud,
If they but heare perchance a trumpet found,   85
Or any ayre of muficke touch their eares,

75. *with a*] *with him a* Q₁.   78. *I am*] *I'm* Pope+, Dyce iii, Huds,
   hymne] *himne* Q₂Q₃.   79. Play...] Muficke playes. Q₁.
76. *tutches pearce*] Q₂. *touches pierce*   85. *but heare perchance*] *perchance but*
Q₁.   *heare* Q₁, Pope+, Steev. '85.

harmony is in the immortal souls of the planetary spheres, but this harmony we cannot hear while the earthly vesture of decay closes in our own souls." There is technical confusion, no doubt, unless the good wit and the familiar associations of the hearer can be relied on to catch the idea that is just sufficiently, in such case, intimated. That which cannot be heard is manifestly the harmony of the heavenly, immortal, animated starry spheres, and what is closed in is, as manifestly, the grammatical construction apart, the human soul, immortal also, and in virtue of identical and common participation in the divinely-given intelligence which is ascribed by Plato and Platonizers to the stars. But as harmony is here apprehended as resident in immortal souls, it is also resident in the "closed-in" human soul, and thus we justify the reading as no less consistent than the conception which the sympathetic reader adopts without inquiry, "while the earthly vesture of decay closes in" our soul with its natural harmony, we are incapacitated, so long as it is thus closed in, from benefit of sympathy, from hearing the external harmony of the immortal souls of the stars.'

77. **draw**] MALONE: Shakespeare was, I believe, here thinking of the custom of accompanying the last waggon-load, at the end of harvest, with rustic music. [Heaven save the mark! and, doubtless, in the preceding line 'pearce your Mistresse eare,' refers to the well-known operation for ear-rings!—ED.]

78. COWDEN-CLARKE: For the sake of this one line (a line that was an especial favourite with one of the profoundest musicians we ever knew), we feel inclined to forgive Jessica anything we may have charged her with elsewhere. Her avowal of the effect that music has upon her shows her to be capable of amelioration; and we may trust that this, her appreciation of a woman like Portia, and her husband's loving influence, may ultimately soften her into excellence. But thus it is that Shakespeare ever throws in redeeming points, making his characters illustrate 'the good and ill together' that exist in human nature.

82. **vnhandle . colts**] MALONE: We find the same thought, *Temp.* IV, i, 176:—
'Then I beat my tabor, At which, like unback'd colts, they prick'd their ears, Advanced their eye-lids, lifted up their noses, As they smelt music.'

You fhall perceiue them make a mutuall ftand,   87
Their fauage eyes turn'd to a modeft gaze,
By the fweet power of muficke : therefore the Poet
Did faine that *Orpheus* drew trees, ftones, and floods.   90
Since naught fo ftockifh, hard, and full of rage,
But muficke for time doth change his nature,
The man that hath no muficke in himfelfe,   93

89. *therefore*] *Thus* Pope, Han.   92. *for time*] F$_1$. *for the time* Q$_1$ et
90. *trees*] *teares* Ff.   cet.

87. **make**] See II, vii, 44, or Abbott, § 349, for the omission of *to*.

87. **mutuall**] CLARENDON: Common. This word is applied to signify what is common to more than two in *Tro. & Cress.* I, iii, 348 : 'And choice, being mutual act of all our souls.' Also, *Mid. N. D.* IV, i, 122 : 'Every region near seem'd all one mutual cry.'

89. **Poet**] KEIGHTLEY (p. 154) : I think we should read this in the plural, *poets*, as no particular poet was regarded as the author of this myth. [It is, nevertheless, told in Shakespeare's favorite Latin author, Ovid, books x and xi.—ED.]

92, 93. HUNTER (i, 321) : These lines might open the question of the effect of music on irrational animals, and the margins might overflow with the discordant opinions of critics. For the purpose of legitimate annotation it is sufficient to show that this was the opinion of Shakespeare's age, and of the persons for whose entertainment he wrote; and it happens that we have the testimony of a learned foreigner, who visited England a little before the time of Shakespeare, that a lion in the Tower, which is described as of extraordinary size, afforded a remarkable instance of brute susceptibility to the power of music. The traveler was Henry Stephens, [and the passage is to be found p. 65, *De Vitis Stephanorum*, Amst., 1683; in it Stephens describes how, on a visit to the Tower, he beheld with amazement the huge beast not only desist from devouring his food, but walk back and forth as though dancing (*tanquam tripudiantem*) when he heard by chance a young boy play on an organ].

93, &c. WARBURTON: The thought here is extremely fine; as if the being affected with music was only the harmony between the *internal* ('music in himself') and the *external music* ('concord of sweet sounds'), which were mutually affected like unison strings. The whole speech could not choose but please an English audience, whose great passion, as well then as now, was *love of music*. 'Jam vero video naturam,' says Erasmus, in *Praise of Folly*, 'ut singulis nationibus, ac pene civitatibus, communem quandam insevisse Philautiam : Atque hinc fieri, ut *Britanni*, præter alia, Formam, Musicam, & lautus Mensas propriè sibi vindicent.' STEEVENS : This present passage, which is neither pregnant with physical and moral truth, nor poetically beautiful in an eminent degree, has constantly enjoyed the good fortune to be repeated by those whose inhospitable memories would have refused to admit or retain any other sentiment or description of the same author, however exalted or just. The truth is, that it furnishes the vacant fiddler with something to say in defence of his profession, and supplies the coxcomb in music with an invective against such as do not pretend to discover all the various powers of language in inarticulate sounds. Our ancient statutes have often received the best comment by means of reference to the particular occasion on which they were framed. Dr Warburton has, therefore, properly accounted for Shakespeare's

[93. **The man that hath no musicke in himselfe,**]

seeming partiality to this amusement. He might have added that Peacham requires of his Gentleman *only* to be able 'to sing his part sure, and at first sight, and withal to play the same on a viol or lute.' Let not, however, this capricious sentiment of Shakespeare descend to posterity unattended by the opinion of the late Lord Chesterfield on the same subject. In his 148th Letter to his son, who was then in Venice, nis ordship, after having enumerated music among the *illiberal* pleasures, adds : ' If you love music, hear it ; go to operas, concerts, and pay fiddlers to play to you ; but I must insist upon your neither piping nor fiddling yourself. It puts a gentleman into a very frivolous and contemptible light ; brings him into a great deal of bad company, and takes up a great deal of time which might be much better employed. Few things would mortify me more, than to see you bearing a part in a concert, with a fiddle under your chin, or a pipe in your mouth.' Again, Letter 153 : 'A taste of sculpture and painting is, in my mind, as becoming, as a taste of fiddling and piping is unbecoming a man of fashion. The former is connected with history and poetry, the latter with nothing but *bad company.*' Again : ' Painting and sculpture are very justly called liberal arts ; a lively and strong imagination, together with a just observation, being absolutely necessary to excel in either ; which, in my opinion, is by no means the case with music, though called a liberal art, and now in Italy placed above the other two ; a proof of the decline of that country.' DOUCE (i, 269) : Had the sentiments in Mr Steevens's note been expressed by Dr Johnson, disorganized as he was for the enjoyment of music, it would not have been matter to wonder at ; but that such a man as Mr Steevens, whose ordinary speech was melody, and whose correct and elegant ear for poetical concord is so frequently manifested in the course of his Shakespearian labours, should have shown himself a very Timon in music, can only be accounted for by supposing that he regarded the speech in question as a libel on his great colleague's organization. He has here assumed a task which Dr Johnson would, for obvious reasons, have declined, and with the feeble aid of an illiberal passage from Lord Chesterfield's *Letters.* MONCK MASON : I doubt, indeed, whether there be any human being that is totally insensible to the powers of harmony ; but if there be any such, we may naturally suppose that the same sluggish motion of the blood, the same rigid texture of the nerves, the same hardened construction of body or mind, from whatever cause it may proceed, that makes them incapable of harmony, may also render them unsusceptible of the finer feelings of humanity, and, of course, more fit than the rest of mankind for rapine, premeditated murder, and such horrid crimes as require in the perpetrators a certain degree of hardness and insensibility. PYE (p. 76) : I confess even I, who would almost as soon stand up to my neck in water in winter as sit out a concert, should have no great opinion of that man who was dead to the effect of a pathetic song set to a simple melody. [It is difficult to decide, as we have had more than once to note, whether Steevens is in jest or in earnest. I am by no means sure that this attack on music was not a trap whereby to lure some honest Goodman Dull into a defence of it. If so, Steevens was certainly rewarded ; the foregoing notes are greatly abridged ; and I have omitted Eccles altogether,—but Pye, the Poet Laureate, alone would have repaid him. As Knight says, ' the interest of the dispute wholly consists in the solemn stupidity with which it is conducted.' The true light in which to view Lorenzo's exclamation is, I think, exactly put by COWDEN-CLARKE : ' That Shakespeare promulgated the axiom : " The man that hath no music," &c., as a solemnly delivered and deliberately uttered dogma, no one, we should think, would imagine ; but that it is in consonance with the poetical creed as to the weight of refining influence in music, held by men from the remotest ages, and that

Nor is not moued with concord of fweet founds,
Is fit for treafons, ftratagems, and fpoyles,　　　　　　95
The motions of his fpirit are dull as night,
And his affections darke as *Erobus*,
Let no fuch man be trufted : marke the muficke.

Enter Portia and Nerriffa.

Por. That light we fee is burning in my hall :　　　100
How farre that little candell throwes his beames,
So fhines a good deed in a naughty world.　　　　　(dle ?
Ner. When the moone fhone we did not fee the can　103

---

94. *moued*] Q₂. *moou'd* Q₁.　　　　　　tia. Q₁.
97. Erobus] Terebus Q₁Q₂. Tenebris　　　101. *candell*] Q₂. *candle* Q₁.
Q₃. Erebus Ff.　　　　　　　　　　　　103, 102. *candle ?*] Q₂F₂F₃. *candle.*
99. Enter...] Enter Nerriffa and Por-　　Q₁ et cet.

---

it is precisely one of those ardent expressions inspired by the immediate hearing of music, and by the impressions and emotions it produces, no one who has experienced those impressions and emotions will doubt.'—ED.]

96. **spirit**] See WALKER (*Crit.* i, 193), where he says that 'it may safely be laid down as a canon, that the word "spirit," in our old poets, whenever the metre does not compel us to pronounce it dissyllabically, is a monosyllable. And this is almost always the case.' After citing very many examples, of which the present line is one, he sums up : 'Perhaps it would be desirable, wherever the word occurs as a monosyllable, to write it *spright*, in order to ensure the proper pronunciation of the line. I prefer *spright* to *sprite ;* inasmuch as the latter invariably carries with it a spectral association ; although the old writers, in those passages where they write the word monosyllabically, use sometimes the one form, sometimes the other.' In citing the present line Walker, who trusted to his memory, writes *notions* for 'motions,' or it may be an oversight of Lettsom ; the recurrence here of the same sound *sprite* and *night* seems to have given him pause, and he thinks that they were not *exactly* the same ; in *The Historye of Romeus and Juliet* he finds instances where for the sake of euphony it must be pronounced, as it is there once spelled, *sprete.*—ED.

99. HUNTER (i, 320) : There is a dramatic purpose worthy of notice in the words which Portia utters when she first appears upon the scene. They were meant to connect the present with the past ; the defeated attempt of Shylock on the life of Anthonio with the scenes of Belmont ; and the spectators are thus led to look upon Portia returning to the house in which the scene of the caskets had been presented, crowned with the honours of the good deed she had done in freeing the merchant. There is also great dramatic skill shewn in the dialogue which now ensues between Portia and Nerissa. It is not quite unlike that to which we have been listening with such charmed ears between Lorenzo and Jessica ; yet it is less philosophical, and so leads gently to the change from those sweet discourses to the business of the story, to which it is now necessary to proceed.

102. HALLIWELL : Compare *Matthew*, v, 16 : 'Let your light so shine before men that they may see your good works,' &c.

Por.　So doth the greater glory dim the leſſe,
A ſubſtitute ſhines brightly as a King　　　　　　　　　105
Vntill a King be by, and then his ſtate
Empties it ſelfe, as doth an inland brooke
Into the maine of waters : muſique, harke.　　　*Muſicke.*
　　Ner.　It is your muſicke Madame of the houſe.
　　Por.　Nothing is good I ſee without reſpeƈt,　　　110
Methinkes it ſounds much ſweeter then by day?
　　Ner.　Silence beſtowes that vertue on it Madam.
　　Por.　The Crow doth ſing as ſweetly as the Larke
When neither is attended : and I thinke　　　　　　114

---

108. Muſicke.] Om. Qq.　　　　　　　　109. *Madame*] *Madam*, F₄.
109. *your ... the*] *the ... your* Rowe,　　112. *that*] *the* Rowe ii+.
Pope, Theob. Han. Warb.

---

102. **naughty**] COWDEN-CLARKE: Formerly used with greater force of meaning than at present. [See III, iii, 12.] Here it means 'evil,' 'wicked,' 'corrupt;' yet, somehow, its lighter form of expression harmonizes well with the light-hearted mood, the condition of internal happiness, that possesses Portia at this moment of her return from having successfully fulfilled a project for rescuing her husband's friend from peril. Her sweet cheerfulness, her readiness to find everything doubly bright, doubly melodious, has the exquisite charm of a spirit at ease with itself, from conscious rectitude.

105. **as**] For other instances of the omission of the first *as*, see ABBOTT, § 276.

110. **respect**] JOHNSON: Not absolutely good, but relatively good, as it is modified by circumstances. HALLIWELL: Portia is told by her attendant it is her own music, which she now finds sweeter than she ever noticed it before. Then she says nothing is good but by looking upon it through the circumstances in which it is placed, looking with a particular meaning, a reflection of mind. She proceeds to say that the crow and the lark sing equally sweet when not attended; that is, when the mind is not fixed particularly on them. It is the proper time, and state or preparation of mind, that gives the charm its full force. STAUNTON: By 'respect,' in this place, is meant *regard, attention, consideration*. When the mind is pre-engaged, it is influenced but little by the beautiful in Nature or in art : 'The crow doth sing as sweetly as the lark, *When neither is attended.*' CRAIK (*Jul. Cæs.* IV, iii, 69) : *Respect* in Shakespeare means, commonly, no more than what we now call *regard* or *view.* Thus, in *Mid. N. D.* I, i, Lysander says of his aunt, 'She respects me as her only son;' and in II, i, Helena says to Demetrius, 'You, in my respect, are all the world.' So, [in the present line,] Portia means merely that nothing is good without reference to circumstances, or that it is only when it is in accordance with the place and the time that any good thing can be really or fully enjoyed. So, afterwards, Nerissa to Gratiano : 'You should have been *respective ;*' that is, you should have been mindful (of your promise or oath).

114. **attended**] Abbott, § 200, regards this as an instance of the omission of the preposition *to ;* wherein Clarendon, Schmidt, and Rolfe agree; all hold it to be equivalent to *attended to, marked.* Clarendon says : 'The difference is in the hearer's mind, not in the songs themselves, and the nightingale is reputed the first of songsters, because

The Nightingale if fhe fhould fing by day   115
When euery Goofe is cackling, would be thought
No better a Mufitian then the Wren *?*
How many things by feafon, feafon'd are
To their right praife, and true perfection :
Peace, how the Moone fleepes with Endimion,   120

117. *Wren ?*] *Wren.* Q$_1$. *Renne ?* Q$_2$.   Coll. i.   *now* Coll. ii, iii (MS).   *hoa !* or
120. *how*] Qq Ff, Rowe+, Cap. Knt,   *ho !* Mal. et cet.

---

she sings at a time when she can best be heard, when the hearer's attention is not distracted.' The same view is held by Halliwell and Staunton, as is seen in the preceding notes. Nevertheless, I venture to think that a possible meaning of 'attended,' in this place, has been overlooked. To represent Portia as saying that the crow sings as sweetly as the lark if it is not attended to, is to impute to her a remark which, though perhaps profoundly true, is, I fear, not truly profound. Would it not be quite as true to say that they sing equally well if we do not hear them at all? It seems to me that the whole point of Portia's reflections is that nothing is good without respect, and of this law she had found an illustration in the moon and the little candle, when the less glory is dimmed if attended by a greater glory; or in a substitute who is nothing if attended by a king; and again it is the attendant circumstances alone which prevent the lark and the crow from being equally good; even the nightingale, if ill-attended, is no better musician than a wren. She sums up in saying, 'How many things *by season* season'd are.' It is by its fit 'season' that the lark and the nightingale must be attended' in order to receive 'right praise.' Wherefore, I think, 'attended' is not, perhaps, equivalent to *attended to*, but may be used absolutely.—ED.

115. **Nightingale**] MALONE: So in *Sonnet* 102: 'As Philomel in summer's front doth sing, And stops his pipe in growth of riper days; Not that the summer is less pleasant now, Than when her mournful hymns did hush the night; *But that wild music burdens every bough, And sweets grown common lose their dear delight.'*

120. **Peace, how**] MALONE: The oddness of the phrase: '*How* the moon would not be awak'd!' first made me suspect the passage to be corrupt; and the following line in *Rom. & Jul.* IV, v, 65: '*Peace, hoa*, for shame!' suggested the emendation, and appeared to me to put it beyond a doubt. Again, in *As You Like It*, V, iv, 131: 'Peace, hoa! I bar confusion.' Again, in *Meas. for Meas.* I, iv, 6: 'Hoa! peace be in this place!' Again, *Ibid.* III, i, 44: 'Hoa! peace here.' In *Ant. & Cleop.* the same mistake, I think, has happened. Portia first enjoins the music to cease: 'Peace, hoa!' and then subjoins the reason for her injunction: 'The moon,' &c. Tyrwhitt seems to be of opinion that the interjection *Ho* was formerly used to command a cessation of noise, as well as of fighting. See *Cant. Tales*, vol. iv, p, 230. BOSWELL: The old reading, I think, is right. *How*, as Johnson observes, is sometimes used as a mere affirmative. HUNTER (i. 319, foot-note): There is not a more inexcusable defeat committed on the text of Shakespeare by any Editor than is done by Malone in this exquisite passage. He not only would read, but actually prints, as his text: 'Peace, hoa!' And this because, as he says, of the oddness of the phrase: '*How* the moon,' &c. But can any one read the words as they stand in Shakespeare, and not recognize in a moment one of the commonest and most intelligible of English phrases by which we express admiration? All the beauty of the expression is lost by

[120. **Peace, how the Moone sleepes with Endimion,**]
the change : Portia looks upwards and observes the steady, still, settled, and almost
imperceptible motion of the fair planet of the night, and thus expresses her admiration
of the soft beauty of the scene.   KNIGHT : Malone thinks that Portia uses the words
as commanding the music to cease.   This would be a singularly unladylike act of Portia, in reality as well as in expression.   We apprehend that, having been talking somewhat loudly to Nerissa as she approached the house, she checks herself as she comes
close to it, with the interjection—'*Peace!*'—equivalent to *hush*, and then gives the poetical reason for being silent : How the moon sleeps,' &c.   ' The Stage-direction : *Music
ceases*, is a coincidence with Portia's *Peace!* but not a consequence of it.   HALLIWELL :
The exclamation *ho* is constantly thus printed in old plays.   The moon is not now
shining, as appears from what Nerissa had previously said, and from Lorenzo recognizing Portia by the voice ; she is sleeping with Endymion, and out of sight.   Portia is
merely giving a playful reason for desiring silence, and the moon being obscured, she
says that luminary is sleeping with Endymion and would not be disturbed.   COLLIER
(ed. ii) : *Now* seems to have been misprinted ' how ' in the old copies, and modern
Editors, not knowing what to do with it, have usually converted it into an interjection,
ho!   Portia is assigning a reason for the cessation of the music, viz. because it will
wake the moon, *now* sleeping with Endymion.   The emendation *now* is from the
(MS).   DYCE : I adopt Malone's alteration, and [after what Hunter has said] I am
forced, at the risk of being tedious, to state fully the grounds of my conviction that
Malone's is the true reading.   I. Shakespeare would hardly have employed such a
phrase as, ' How *the moon sleeps*,' &c. ; he would have interposed some adverb (or
adverbial adjective) between ' how ' and ' *the moon*,' &c. : so, previously, in this Scene
we have, ' How *sweet* the moonlight sleeps,' &c.   II. '*Ho*' was often written with the
spelling ' How;' and I may add, that previously in the present play [II, vi, 30], where
Lorenzo calls out, ' Ho! *who's within?*' Q₂ has, ' Howe *whose within?*'   (In like
manner examples are not wanting of ' Low ' being put for '*Lo;*' as in Hubert's *Edward the Second*, p. 32, ed. 1629, '*Low* now (quoth he) I haue my heart's desire.')
III. That Portia is enjoining the musicians to be silent, is proved by the Stage-directions of the old Eds.   So in *Jul. Cæs.* I, ii, Casca *silences the music* with '*Peace, ho!*
Cæsar speaks;' and again [as in the examples cited by Malone].   IV. It is quite natural that immediately after the command, '*Peace, ho!*' we should have the reason for
that command, viz. ' The moon sleeps,' &c. ; while, on the contrary, there is (as Malone
says) an ' oddness ' in ' Peace ' being followed by a mere exclamation, ' How *the moon
sleeps*,' &c.   [In answer to Knight] I see no impropriety in a lady ordering *her own
musicians, in her own domain*, to leave off playing ; and as to the ' expression,'—Mr
Knight seems to have forgotten both that on the next page we have ' *ho* ' from the
mouth of Portia, ' A quarrel, *ho*, already!' and that ' *ho*,' in our early writers, does not
necessarily convey the idea of bawling.   It is really difficult to believe that Mr Knight
can be serious when he goes on to say, ' Portia, having been talking somewhat loudly,
&c., *checks* HERSELF as she comes close to the house,' &c.   (If she speaks *piano*, how
happens it that Lorenzo immediately exclaims, ' That is the voice, Or I am much
deceiu'd of Portia' ?)—and that ' the Stage-direction is a COINCIDENCE with Portia's
Peace!'—a *coincidence* more surprising than any upon record.   [The Text. Notes
show how decided is the majority in favour of Malone's emendation.—ED.]

120. **Moone . . . Endimion**] PARRY (*Longman's Modern Series, Mer. of Ven.*
ad loc.) cites, ' In the ancient, poetical, and proverbial language of Elis, people said :
" Selene (the Moon) loves and watches Endymion," instead of " it is getting late;"

And would not be awak'd.   121
               Muficke ceafes.
  Lor.   That is the voice,
Or I am much deceiu'd of *Portia.*
  Por.   He knowes me as the blinde man knowes the   125
Cuckow by the bad voice?
  Lor.   Deere Lady welcome home?
  Por.   We haue bene praying for our husbands welfare
Which fpeed we hope the better for our words,
Are they return'd?   130
  Lor.   Madam, they are not yet:
But there is come a Meffenger before
To fignifie their comming.
  Por.   Go in *Nerriffa*,
Giue order to my feruants, that they take   135
No note at all of our being abfent hence,
Nor you *Lorenzo, Ieffica* nor you.
            A Tucket founds.
  Lor.   Your husband is at hand, I heare his Trumpet,
We are no tell-tales Madam, feare you not.   140
  Por.   This night methinkes is but the daylight ficke,
It lookes a little paler, 'tis a day,
Such as the day is, when the Sun is hid.   143

---

121. [Observing Lor. and Jess. Cap.
    Muficke...] Om. Qq.
125, 126. Prose, Ff, Rowe. Ending
lines, *knowes...voice* Q₁. Ending lines,
Cuckow...voice Q₂Q₃ et cet.
126. *Cuckow*] Cucko Q₁. cuckoe Q₂Q₃.
    voice ?] Q₂F₂. voice. Q₁.

128. *husbands welfare*] husband health
Q₁. husbands healths Pope+, Cam. Glo.
Cla. Ktly, Wh. ii.
134. *in*] Om. Pope+.
138. A Tucket founds] Om. Qq.
139. *his*] a Rowe i.

"Selene embraces Endymion," instead of "the sun is setting and the moon is rising;"
"Selene kisses Endymion into sleep," instead of "it is night." '—MAX MÜLLER [*Chips
from a German Workshop,* ii, p. 80, New York, 1872].

120. Capell's Stage-direction here is '*observing Lor. and Jes.,*' from which I infer
(for I can find no note on it) that he supposes the 'moon' and 'Endymion' to be applied
by Portia to the happy lovers. When Lorenzo speaks, line 123, Capell has the Stage-
direction '*rising.*'—ED.

125. blinde man] CLARENDON: This must refer to a proverb importing that there
are cases in which a blind man is at no disadvantage as compared with any other man.
[Moreover, the intimation is given us that the moon is now wholly obscured and that
the scene is quite dark.—ED.]

138. Tucket] STEEVENS: *Toccata,* Italian, a flourish of a trumpet.
  17

*Enter Baſſanio, Anthonio, Gratiano, and their
Followers.*   145

Baſ.   We ſhould hold day with the Antipodes,
If you would walke in abſence of the ſunne.

Por.   Let me giue light, but let me not be light,
For a light wife doth make a heauie husband,
And neuer be *Baſſanio* ſo for me,   150
But God ſort all: you are welcome home my Lord.

Baſſ.   I thanke you Madam, giue welcom to my friend
This is the man, this is *Anthonio*,
To whom I am ſo infinitely bound.

Por.   You ſhould in all ſence be much bound to him,   155
For as I heare he was much bound for you.

Anth.   No more then I am wel acquitted of.

Por.   Sir, you are verie welcome to our houſe:
It muſt appeare in other waies then words,
Therefore I ſcant this breathing curteſie.   160

Gra.   By yonder Moone I ſweare you do me wrong,
Infaith I gaue it to the Iudges Clearke,
Would he were gelt that had it for my part,
Since you do take it Loue ſo much at hart.   164

---

150. *ſo for*] *ſo from* Ff, Rowe, Pope,
Theob. Han. Warb.

151. *you are*] *y' are* Q₁. *you're* Pope+,
Dyce iii, Huds.

161. [To Nerissa. Rowe.

162, 176, &c. *Iudges*] *Judg's* F₄.
        Clearke] *Clarke* Qq.   *Clerk* F₃F₄.

144, &c. GUIZOT (*Notice*, &c., p. 5): In thus depicting the reunion of Portia and
Bassanio, Shakespeare has shown that he is almost the sole poet who has not feared to
pause over a picture of perfect happiness; he knew his own power to fill up the outlines.

146, 147. MALONE: If you would always walk in the night, it would be day with
us, as it now is on the other side of the globe.

148. light] JOHNSON: There is scarcely any word with which Shakespeare so much
delights to trifle as with *light*, in its various significations. STEEVENS: Most of the old
dramatic writers are guilty of the same quibble.

155. sence] WALKER (*Vers.* 248): Is 'sense' in this passage singular or plural?
CLARENDON: That is, in all reason. Compare, for this meaning of the word, *Meas.
for Meas.* V, i, 47: 'Poor soul, She speaks this in the infirmity of sense.'

158. our house] COWDEN-CLARKE: How delicate this little touch of generosity
and modesty; she has just endowed her husband with her property.

160. breathing curtesie] MALONE: This verbal, complimentary form, made up
only of *breath*, i. e. words. So, in *Timon.* III, v, 59: 'You breathe in vain.' So, in
Macb. V, iii, 27: 'mouth-honour, breath.'

Por.　A quarrel hoe alreadie, what's the matter?　　165
Gra.　About a hoope of Gold, a paltry Ring
That fhe did giue me, whofe Poefie was
For all the world like Cutlers Poetry
Vpon a knife ; *Loue mee, and leaue mee not.*
Ner.　What talke you of the Poefie or the valew :　　170
You fwore to me when I did giue it you,
That you would weare it til the houre of death,
And that it fhould lye with you in your graue,
Though not for me, yet for your vehement oaths,
You fhould haue beene refpectiue and haue kept it.　　175

167. *giue me*] *give to me* Steev. conj.
Coll. ii, iii, Dyce ii, iii, Huds.　*give me ;*
one Lettsom.

167, 170. *Poefie*] *pofie* Q₂Q₃. *posy* Cap.
Mal. '90, Steev. Sing. Hal. Dyce, Cam.

Glo. Cla. Del. Coll. iii, Wh. ii.
171. *it*] Om. Q₂.
172. *the houre*] Ff, Rowe, Knt, Wh. i.
your houre Qq et cet.

---

167. CAPELL (ii, 73) asserts that this verse is 'purposely incomplete, and of four feet only, "me" being redundant.' STEEVENS suggested the insertion of *to* after 'give;' it was also added by COLLIER'S (MS), and adopted by DYCE. KEIGHTLEY (*Expositor*, p. 154) would punctuate : ' That she did give me, whose—poësy was.' HALLIWELL says, and truly, ' the sense absolutely requires *posy ;* the spelling proves nothing.' ABBOTT, § 508, thus scans the line, as one where a foot is omitted after a marked pause : ' That shé | did gíve me, | ′ | whose pó | sy wás.'

167. **Poesie**] ROLFE : A motto inscribed on the inner side of a ring. The fashion of putting such 'posies' on rings prevailed from the middle of the 16th to the close of the 17th century. Inscriptions on the outside of rings have been common from the old Greek and Roman times. In 1624 a little book was published with the quaint title, *Love's Garland, or Posies for Rings, Handkerchiefs, and gloves ; and such pretty tokens that lovers send their loues.* [Arber, in his *English Garner*, vol. i, p. 611, has reprinted, from Harl. MS 6910, a collection of *Love Posies*, many hundred in number from a MS written about 1596.—ED.]

169. **knife**] REED : Knives, as Sir John Hawkins observes, were formerly inscribed, by means of *aqua fortis*, with short sentences in distich. In Dekker's *Satiromastix*, Sir Edward Vaughan says : ' You shall swear by Phœbus, who is your poets good lord and master, that hereafter you will not hire Horace to give you posies for rings, hand-kerchers, or *knives*, which you understand not.' [Halliwell gives several specimens of this 'cutler's poetry' with wood-cuts.]

169. **leaue**] STAUNTON : And *give* me not. So in *Two Gent.* IV, iv, 79: ' It seems you loved not her, to leave her token.' [See also 'leaue,' line 191, and 'left,' line 217.]

172. **the houre**] That there are so many *you*s and *your*s in this speech may be a reason against adding another one (which the Qq have here), or it may be a reason in favour of it. I rather prefer the Folio.—ED.

175. **respectiue**] That is, mindful. See CRAIK, s. v. 'respect,' line 110 above. ' Respective lenity,' in *Rom. & Jul.* III, i, 116, is paraphrased, by a majority of Editors, ' *considerate* gentleness.'—ED.

Gaue it a Iudges Clearke: but wel I know   176
The Clearke wil nere weare haire on's face that had it.

  Gra. He wil, and if he liue to be a man.

  Nerriʃʃa. I, if a Woman liue to be a man.

  Gra. Now by this hand I gaue it to a youth,   180
A kinde of boy, a little ʃcrubbed boy,
No higher then thy ʃelfe, the Iudges Clearke,
A prating boy that begg'd it as a Fee,
I could not for my heart deny it him.

  Por. You were too blame, I muʃt be plaine with you,   185

---

176. *but wel I know*] *no God's my*   178. *and*] *an* Pope et seq.
Iudge Qq, Coll. et seq. (except Rlfe).   179. *I,*] *If,* Ff, Rowe. *Ay,* Pope et
  177. *on's*] *on his* Cap. Steev. Mal. Ktly, seq.
Del.   185. *too*] *to* Q₂Q₃F₄ et seq.

---

176. **wel I know**] COLLIER: The Folio, perhaps in consequence of the statute of
James I, substituted this phrase for the Quarto's.

  178. **and if**] See IV, i, 465.

  181. **scrubbed**] WARTON: It is certain from the context and from the tenour of the
story, that Gratiano does not here speak contemptuously of the Judge's clerk. He only
means to describe the person and appearance of this supposed youth, which he does by
insinuating what seemed to be the precise time of his age, that of a young stripling. I
am therefore of opinion that Shakespeare wrote *stubbed*. In many counties it is a common provincialism to call young birds, not yet fledged, *stubbed young ones*. But, what
is more to our purpose, Hearne, a plain, unaffected writer, in the Preface to his *History
and Antiquities of Glastonbury*, ed. 1722, says that 'Saunders must be a stubbed boy,
if not a man, at the dissolution of Abbeys,' &c. It therefore seems to have been a common expression for *stripling*, the very idea which the speaker intends to convey. If
the emendation be correct here, we should also change it in Nerissa's speech, line 285.
STEEVENS: I believe 'scrubbed' and *stubbed* have a like meaning, and signify *stunted*
or *shrub-like*. So in Holland's *Pliny*: 'But such will never proue faire trees, but
skrubs only.' [Bk 13th, chap. iv, p. 386. That *scrub* and *shrub* were not exactly the
same, may be inferred, I think, from another passage in Holland's *Pliny*, where, in Bk
12th, chap. vii, p. 362, we find: 'Wee haue made means to haue the Pepper tree growing among vs; and verily a little scrubby plant it is, or shrub, rather.'—ED.] VER-
PLANCK: We retain the same use familiarly on this side of the Atlantic in 'scrub
oak,' a name given from the first settlement of the country to the dwarf or bush oak.
GRANT WHITE: But is not 'scrub oak' a corruption of *shrub* oak? and are not
'scrub' and 'shrub' originally the same word? HALLIWELL: 'Scrubbed' is used
here in contempt, the scornful way in which Gratiano talks of the disguised Nerissa
increasing the humour of the scene. It is unlikely the word should have been twice
printed *scrubbed* if that had not been the correct reading. DYCE (*Gloss.*): Here
'scrubbed' is generally explained *stunted;* but Cotgrave has 'Marpaut. An ill-fauoured
scrub, a little ouglie or swartie wretch;' and Coles, 'A Scrub (mean person), *Homo
misellus,*' and 'Scrubbed, *squalidus.*'

  185. **too blame**] ABBOTT, § 73: 'Too' is often used in the Folio, in the phrase, 'I
am *too* blame.' See *Oth.* III, iii, 244 and 328. This is so common in other Eliza-

To part fo flightly with your wiues firft gift, 186
A thing ftucke on with oathes vpon your finger,
And fo riueted with faith vnto your flefh.
I gaue my Loue a Ring, and made him fweare
Neuer to part with it, and heere he ftands : 190
I dare be fworne for him, he would not leaue it,
Nor plucke it from his finger, for the wealth
That the world mafters.   Now in faith *Gratiano*,
You giue your wife too vnkinde a caufe of greefe,
And 'twere to me I fhould be mad at it. 195

    Baff. Why I were beft to cut my left hand off,
And fweare I loft the Ring defending it.

    Gre. My Lord *Baffanio* gaue his Ring away
Vnto the Iudge that beg'd it, and indeede
Deferu'd it too : and then the Boy his Clearke 200
That tooke fome paines in writing, he begg'd mine,

---

188. *fo riueted*] *riveted* Pope+, Steev.
'85, Dyce iii. *riveted fo* Cap. Steev. '93,
Var. Sta. *fo rivetted* Ktly.
    195. *And*] *An* Theob. et seq.

196. [Aside. Theob. et seq.
198. Gre.] F$_1$.
200. *too*] *to* Qq.

---

bethan authors, that it seems to require more explanation than a simple confusion
between *to* and *too*. Perhaps 'blame' was considered an adjective, and *too* may have
been, as in Early English, used for *excessively*. [Even in a modernized text it is doubtful if this 'too' should not be retained.—ED.]

    188. **so riueted**] This line is cited by ABBOTT, § 472, as one of the examples, of
which we have had many, of the absorption of '-*ed* following *d* or *t*,' and it is thus
scanned by him : ' And só | rivet*ed* | with faíth | untó | your flésh.' DYCE (ed. iii) :
The 'so' in this line was evidently repeated by mistake from the 'so' just above it, in
the preceding line but one. [Wherefore Dyce returned, as he so often does in his last
Edition, to the reading of Pope. To me, as good a way as either Dyce's or Abbott's,
is to read *rivet* almost, if not quite, as a monosyllable. When *v* comes between two
vowels, its presence, as a general rule, was, I think, merely suggested, sometimes so
faintly as to be practically non-existent. This explains (I speak with diffidence) the
reason why the old printers, in such cases, always used *u* for *v*. See 'hauing,' III, ii,
131, and 'pouerty,' IV, i, 285.—ED.]

    194. **too vnkinde a**] ABBOTT, § 462 : Syllables ending in vowels are frequently
elided before vowels in reading, though not in writing. Thus : 'You gíve | your wífe
| *too* unkind | a cáuse | of grief.' [It is doubtful to me if this elision is permissible
here, where 'too' is an emphatic word. WALKER'S suggestion is preferable, and was
adopted by Dyce. In *Crit.* i, 87, the former says, '*Dele* "a" ; read too *únkind* cause ;'
as e. g., *Lear*, III, iv, '—nothing could have subdued nature To such a lowness, but
his únkind daughters.'—ED.]

    195. **And 'twere**] See IV, i, 465.

    196. **I were best**] See II, viii, 36.

And neyther man nor mafter would take ought   202
But the two Rings.
    Por. What Ring gaue you my Lord?
Not that I hope which you receiu'd of me.   205
    Baff. If I could adde a lie vnto a fault,
I would deny it : but you fee my finger
Hath not the Ring vpon it, it is gone.
    Por. Euen fo voide is your falfe heart of truth.
By heauen I wil nere come in your bed   21u
Vntil I fee the Ring.
    Ner. Nor I in yours, til I againe fee mine.
    Baff. Sweet *Portia*,
If you did know to whom I gaue the Ring,
If you did know for whom I gaue the Ring,   215
And would conceiue for what I gaue the Ring,
And how vnwillingly I left the Ring,
When nought would be accepted but the Ring,
You would abate the ftrength of your difpleafure?
    Por. If you had knowne the vertue of the Ring,   220
Or halfe her worthineffe that gaue the Ring,
Or your owne honour to containe the Ring,
You would not then haue parted with the Ring :   223

---

202. *neyther*] F$_1$. *neither* Qq Ff.
209. *Euen*] *And even* Ff, Rowe.
212. Two lines, Qq, Theob. et seq.

218. *nought*] *naught* Q$_2$Q$_3$, Steev. Var. Coll. Wh.
221. *Or halfe*] *Of halfe* Q$_1$.
222. *containe*] *retain* Pope+, Steev.

---

214. HALLIWELL: Jingling lines similar to those in this and the next speech, no fewer than nine ending with the same word, are met with in other dramatists. Compare *The Fayre Mayde of the Exchange*, 1607 : '*Ferd.* I have a brother, rival in my love; I have a brother hates me for my love; I have a brother vows to win my love; That brother, too, he hath incenst my love, To gain the beauty of my dearest love; What hope remains, then, to enjoy my love? *Anthony.* I am that brother rival in his love; I am that brother hates him for his love; Not his, but mine; and I will have that love, Or never live to see him kiss my love'—[p. 36, Ed. *Sh. Soc.*]. WALKER (*Crit.* iii, 58) adds the following: *King John*, III, i, 12–15; *Rich. III:* I, iii, 292–294; *Com. Err.* I, ii, 89, 90. HALES (quoted by Furnivall, *Introduction to Gervinus*, p. xxxvii, foot-note) cites *Edward III:* II, i, where 'the sun' ends eight consecutive lines.

222. **to containe**] COLLIER (ed. ii): This was used in Shakespeare's time for *to retain*, to which it was altered in the (MS). This was a change of language introduced between the date when the play was written and when the old corrector inserted his emendations,—an interval of about half a century. MALONE: See IV, i, 54.

What man is there fo much vnreafonable,
If you had pleas'd to haue defended it　　　　　　225
With any termes of Zeale : wanted the modeftie
To vrge the thing held as a ceremonie :
Nerriſſa teaches me what to beleeue,
Ile die for't, but fome Woman had the Ring?

　Baſſ.　No by mine honor Madam, by my foule　　230
No woman had it, but a ciuill Doctor,
Which did refufe three thoufand Ducates of me,
And beg'd the Ring; the which I did denie him,
And fuffer'd him to go difpleas'd away :
Euen he that had held vp the verie life　　　　　235
Of my deere friend.　What fhould I fay fweete **Lady ?**
I was inforc'd to fend it after him,
I was befet with fhame and curtefie,
My honor would not let ingratitude
So much befmeare it.　Pardon me good Lady,　　240

---

226. *Zeale :*] *zeale,* Q$_1$.
227. *ceremonie :*] *ceremony ?* Q$_1$.
230. *mine honor*] *my honor* Qq, Cap. Mal. Cam. Glo. Cla. Wh. ii.
232. *Which*] *Who* Pope+, Steev. '85.

234. *difpleas'd away*] *away difpleaſd* Q$_1$.
235. *had held vp*] *did vphold* Q$_1$, Pope +, Cam. Glo. Cla. Wh. ii.
237. *inforc'd*] *enforc'd* Q$_1$.

224. **much**] See ABBOTT, § 51, for examples of 'much' 'used as an ordinary adjective, like the Scotch *mickle*.'

225. **had pleas'd to have defended**] ABBOTT, § 360: It is now commonly asserted that such expressions as 'I hoped *to have seen* him yesterday' are ungrammatical. But in the Elizabethan, as in Early English authors, after verbs of *hoping, intending,* or verbs signifying that something *ought* to *have* been done, but was not, the Complete Present Infinitive is used. We still retain this idiom in the expression, 'I *would* (i. e. *wished to) have* done it.' 'I ought (i. e. was *bound) to have* done it.'

226. **wanted**] CLARENDON : That is, as to have wanted. This lax construction is due to the intervening parenthesis. The following words are grammatically faulty, though the general sense is clear. What man would have been so unreasonably wanting in modesty as to urge you to give up the thing you held as a sacred emblem ?

226. **modestie**] ALLEN : That is, moderation. Cf. II, ii, 183.

227. **ceremonie**] SCHMIDT (*Lex.*) finds three significations in which this word is used : First, external form, outward rite ; secondly, any thing or observance held sacred [as here] ; and thirdly, ritual and solemn performance of a sacred act. CLARENDON : In Hakluyt's *Voyages,* quoted by Richardson, a crucifix is called a ceremony.

231. **ciuill Doctor**] A Doctor of Civil Law.

235. **he**] CLARENDON : 'He' is used, not *him,* as if the words 'the which . . . . away' were merely parenthetical.

237. ALLEN : It indicates the gentleman and the soldier in Bassanio, that he does not expose Anthonio as the one that 'enforced' him to give the ring.

And by thefe bleffed Candles of the night,   241
Had you bene there, I thinke you would haue beg'd
The Ring of me, to giue the worthie Doctor?
 Por. Let not that Doctor ere come neere my houfe,
Since he hath got the iewell that I loued,   245
And that which you did fweare to keepe for me,
I will become as liberall as you,
Ile not deny him any thing I haue,
No, not my body, nor my husbands bed :
Know him I fhall, I am well fure of it.   250
Lie not a night from home. Watch me like Argos,
If you doe not, if I be left alone,
Now by mine honour which is yet mine owne,
Ile haue the Doctor for my bedfellow.
 Nerriffa. And I his Clarke: therefore be well aduis'd   255
How you doe leaue me to mine owne protection.
 Gra. Well, doe you fo : let not me take him then,
For if I doe, ile mar the yong Clarks pen.
 Ant. I am th'vnhappy fubiect of thefe quarrels.
 Por. Sir, grieue not you,   260
You are welcome notwithftanding.
 Baf. *Portia*, forgiue me this enforced wrong,
And in the hearing of thefe manie friends
I fweare to thee, euen by thine owne faire eyes   264

---

241. *And*] Ff, Rowe+, Wh. i. *For*
Qq et cet.
 242. *thinke*] think, Theob. et seq.(except Han. Wh. Cam. Glo. Cla. Rlfe).
 243. *the*] thee F$_2$F$_3$.
 251. *Argos*] Q$_1$Q$_2$F$_4$, Rowe. *Argus*
F$_2$ et cet.
 253. *mine owne*] *my own* Pope+,
Steev. Mal. Knt.

254. *the*] Ff, Rowe, Wh. i. *that* Qq
et cet.
 my] *mine* Q$_2$.
 257. *him*] him, Coll. Dyce, Cam. Glo.
[Non recte. *then* ad tempus refert, et 258
in sens. obsc. explicat.—ED.]
 260, 261. One line, Qq, Pope et seq.
 261. *You are*] *You're* Dyce iii, Huds.
 264. *euen*] *ev'n* Pope+.

---

241. **Candles**] MALONE: The same expression is to be found in the *Sonnets*, in
Macbeth, and in *Rom. & Jul.*
 242. **I thinke**] Theobald inserted an unhappy comma after 'think,' which has
retained its place in the majority of Editions to the present day. White was the first
to reject it and restore the original. 'The difference,' says WHITE (ed. i), 'though
slight in itself, is material in point of style; for, according to the Folio, "think" has
for its subject all the sentence that follows it; but in the text usually given, "I think"
is interjectional, and "you would have begged," &c., is the predication.' I also prefer
'And' at the beginning of line 241, to *For* of the Qq.—ED.

Wherein I fee my felfe.   265
   Por.   Marke you but that?
In both my eyes he doubly fees himfelfe:
In each eye one, fweare by your double felfe,
And there's an oath of credit.
   Baf.   Nay, but heare me.   270
Pardon this fault, and by my foule I fweare
I neuer more will breake an oath with thee.
   Anth.   I once did lend my bodie for thy wealth,
Which but for him that had your husbands ring
Had quite mifcarried.   I dare be bound againe,   275
My foule vpon the forfeit, that your Lord
Will neuer more breake faith aduifedlie.
   Por.   Then you fhall be his furetie: giue him this,
And bid him keepe it better then the other.
   Ant.   Heere Lord *Baffanio*, fwear to keep this ring.   280
   Baff.   By heauen it is the fame I gaue the Doctor.
   Por.   I had it of him: pardon *Baffanio*,
For by this ring the Doctor lay with me.
   Ner.   And pardon me my gentle *Gratiano*,   284

---

265. *my felfe.*] *myself*— Rowe et seq.   274. [To Por. Rowe et seq.
267. *my*] *mine* FfQ₃, Pope+.   *husbands ring*] *husband Ring*
273. [To Bass. Rowe.   Q₁.
    thy] Ff, Rowe. *his* Qq et cet.   282. *pardon*] Ff. *pardon me* Qq et
    wealth] *weal* Theob. Warb.   cet.

---

268. **double**] MALONE: Used in a bad sense for—*full of duplicity*.

273. **thy**] WHITE (ed. i): 'Thy' is plainly a corruption.   It is possible that it is a misprint for *the* or *that*, which had been underlined, and that Shakespeare meant Anthonio to say that he lent his body for that happiness (i. e. of both Bassanio and Portia), which else would have miscarried.   [This is a plausible suggestion; but I doubt if 'which' refers to 'wealth.'   Does it not refer to the lending, to the pledge, of which Antonio's *body* was the forfeit?   The happiness of Portia and Bassanio would not have been utterly and forever blasted by Anthonio's death.   It was not the wealth or happiness that might have miscarried, but the risk which Anthonio himself personally, ran for the sake of Bassanio.—ED.]

273. **wealth**] THEOBALD: I have ventured, against the Authority of the Copies, to substitute *weal* here; i. e. for his *welfare, benefit*.   'Wealth' has a more confined signification.   Though I must own that *weal* and 'wealth,' in our author's time, must be in some measure synonymous; as they are now in the words *Common-weal* and *Commonwealth*.   JOHNSON: 'For his wealth' is—for his advantage; to obtain his happiness.   'Wealth' was, at that time, the term opposite to *adversity* or *calamity*.   STEEVENS: So in *The Litany:* 'In all time of our tribulation; in all time of our wealth.'

276. **My soule**] ALLEN: A dearer pledge than 'my body.'

For that fame fcrubbed boy the Doctors Clarke   285
In lieu of this, laft night did lye with me.
   Gra.   Why this is like the mending of high waies
In Sommer, where the waies are faire enough :
What, are we Cuckolds ere we haue deferu'd it.
   Por.   Speake not fo groffely, you are all amaz'd ;   290
Heere is a letter, reade it at your leyfure,
It comes from Padua from *Bellario*,
There you fhall finde that *Portia* was the Doctor,
Nerriffa there her Clarke.   *Lorenzo* heere
Shall witneffe I fet forth as foone as you,   295
And but eu'n now return'd : I haue not yet
Entred my houfe.   *Anthonio* you are welcome,
And I haue better newes in ftore for you
Then you expect : vnfeale this letter foone,   299

---

286. *liew*] Q₂F₂.   *lieu* Q₁.
   this] *thee* Wh. i.
288. *where*] *when* Coll. ii, iii (MS),
Sing. Ktly, Dyce iii, Huds.

296. *but eu'n*] *euen but* Qq, Pope +,
Coll. Dyce, Wh. Cam. Glo. Cla. *but even*
Rowe, Cap. Steev. Mal. Sing. Ktly.
299. *Then*] *than* Q₂.

---

286. In . . . this] White, accepting 'in lieu' in its present use, changed 'this' to
thee. Halliwell considers the alteration 'plausible,' and also attributes the modern
meaning to 'in lieu.' But Dyce sets them both right by answering the former's question : 'What meaning has "in lieu of *this*" here' ? as follows : 'It means "in confid-
eration of this (ring)." Compare, earlier in this play, IV, i, 430, "in lieu (i. e. in consideration) whereof," &c.; and *The Tempest*, I, ii : "Which was, that he, in lieu o' (i. e.
in consideration of) the premises,—Of homage," &c.' And Schmidt (*Lex.* s. v.) adds
four or five more examples. White returned to the original text in his Second Edition.
—ED.

288. where] CAPELL (ii, 73) : *When* may appear a properer term in some eyes to
follow 'summer' than 'where :' but 'where' heightens the comparison ; for, with that,
this absurd summer-*mending* is said, too, to be of 'ways' that did not want it at any
time. [As White says, this change to *when* is 'very plausible, but not necessary.' The
aptness of Gratiano's simile is a little obscure. I suppose he means that his wife aimed
at the purification of his character before it was stained.—ED.]

296. eu'n now] See III, ii, 176. It is not impossible, for grammatical reasons, that
this line should be punctuated : 'And, but e'en now return'd, I have not yet,' &c.—ED.

298. ECCLES : There is not, perhaps, to be found in the dramatic writings of any poet
a more lame, awkard [*sic*], and inartificial expedient for suddenly bringing on a general satisfaction in the catastrophe, than that which is here had recourse to. How Portia should possess the means of acquiring intelligence respecting this happy reverse of
Anthonio's fortune earlier than himself, who is just arrived from the very same place,
is a matter wonderful to be conceived, and that she should desire to conceal from the
knowledge of the company, a circumstance, in its nature so singular and curious, is
little less extraordinary.

There you fhall finde three of your Argofies   300
Are richly come to harbour fo dainlie.
You fhall not know by what ftrange accident
I chanced on this letter.
   Antho.   I am dumbe.
   Baff. Were you the Doctor, and I knew you not?   305
   Gra. Were you the Clark that is to make me cuckold.
   Ner.   I, but the Clark that neuer meanes to doe it,
Vnleffe he liue vntill he be a man.
   Baff. (Sweet Doctor)you fhall be my bedfellow,
When I am abfent, then lie with my wife.   310
   An. (Sweet Ladie)you haue giuen me life & liuing;
For heere I reade for certaine that my fhips
Are fafelie come to Rode.
   Por.   How now *Lorenzo*?
My Clarke hath fome good comforts to for you.   315
   Ner.   I, and Ile giue them him without a fee.
There doe I giue to you and *Ieffica*
From the rich Iewe, a fpeciall deed of gift
After his death, of all he dies poffeff'd of.
   Loren.   Faire Ladies you drop Manna in the way   320
Of ftarued people.
   Por.   It is almoft morning,
And yet I am fure you are not fatisfied
Of thefe euents at full.   Let vs goe in,
And charge vs there vpon intergatories,   325

301. *fodainlie*] *suddenly* Rowe.
313. *Rode*] *Rodes* F$_2$.   Rhodes F$_3$F$_4$,
Rowe.   *road* Pope et seq.
315. *to*] Q$_2$.   *too* Q$_1$.
319. *of.*] *off.* Q$_1$.
323. *I am*] *Ime* Q$_1$.   *I'm* Pope+,
Dyce iii.

324. *Let vs*] *Let's* Q$_1$.
325. *vpon*] *on* Rowe, Pope, Han.
intergatories] F$_2$Q$_3$, Mal. Steev.
Hal. *intergotories* Q$_1$Q$_2$.   *interrogatories*
F$_3$F$_4$, Rowe, Han. Johns. *interr'gatories*
Theob. Warb. *inter'gatories* Cap. et cet.

301. **richly**] See line 46 of this scene.
311. **liuing**] STAUNTON: Riches, resources.   [See III, ii, 163.]
320. **Manna**] Warburton commended the use of this word, as peculiarly appropriate, by *Jessica*.   The unlucky slip did not escape Edwards (*Canons of Criticism*, p. 212), and he did not waste the chance.
324. **Of**] See 'I am provided of a Torch-bearer,' II, iv, 25; ABBOTT, § 171.
324. **at full**] ALLEN: Either, first, equivalent to 'fully satisfied;' or, secondly, a *confusio duarum locutionum :* 'You are not satisfied [but would like to know of thefe events] at full.   (I lean to the latter.)

And we will anfwer all things faithfully.   326
   Gra.   Let it be fo, the firft intergatory
That my *Nerriſſa* fhall be fworne on, is,
Whether till the next night fhe had rather ftay,
Or goe to bed, now being two houres to day,   330
But were the day come, I fhould wifh it darke,
Till I were couching with the Doctors Clarke.
Well, while I liue, Ile feare no other thing
So fore, as keeping fafe *Nerriſſas* ring.

                                        Exeunt.   335

FINIS.

---

327. *intergatory*] F$_2$Q$_3$, Mal. Steev. Hal. *intergotory* Q$_1$Q$_2$. *interrogotory* F$_3$F$_4$, Rowe, Han. Johns. *interr'gatory* Theob. Warb. *inter'gatory* Cap. et cet.

330. *bed, now*] *bed now* Q$_2$. *bed now,* Q$_1$Q$_3$, Theob. et seq.

332. *Till*] *That* Q$_1$, Cap. Steev. Mal. Sing. Dyce, Sta. Cam. Glo. Ktly, Wh. ii. *Doctors*] Om. Q$_1$.

334. In sens. obsc.

---

325. **intergatories**] CAMPBELL (p. 62): In the Court of Queen's Bench, when a complaint is made against a person for a 'contempt,' the practice is that before sentence is finally pronounced he is sent into the Crown Office, and being there 'charged upon interrogatories,' he is made to swear that he will 'answer all things faithfully.'

327. **intergatory**] In Praetorius's Facsimile of Q$_2$ taken from the Duke of Devonshire's copy, this word appears as *intergory*. Another instance, to be added to IV, i, 78, 79, in support of the assumption that this defective copy is an early impression.— ED.

329. **Whether**] Contracted to *whe'r*. See WALKER, *Vers.*, p. 103; or ABBOTT, § 466.

334. MRS JAMESON (i, 93): Shylock and his machinations being dismissed from our thoughts, and the rest of the *dramatis personæ* assembled together at Belmont, all our interest and all our attention are riveted on Portia, and the conclusion leaves the most delightful impression on the fancy. The playful equivoque of the rings, the sportive trick she puts on her husband, and her thorough enjoyment of the jest, which she checks just as it is proceeding beyond the bounds of propriety, show how little she was displeased by the sacrifice of her gift, and all are consistent with her bright and joyous spirit. In conclusion, when Portia invites her company to enter her palace to refresh themselves after their travels, and talk over 'these events at full,' the imagination, unwilling to lose sight of the brilliant group, follows them in gay procession from the lovely moonlit garden to marble halls and princely revels, to splendour and festive mirth, to love and happiness!

APPENDIX

APPENDIX

THE TEXT

THE TEXT of *The Merchant of Venice* is derived from two Quartos and the First Folio.

The earliest mention of the Play in the *Stationers' Registers* occurs in the following entry (Arber's *Transcript*, vol. iii, p. 122):

ꝶꝶii° Julii [1598, *Anno* 40ᵐᵒ
Regine Elizabeth]

James Robertes   Entred for his copie vnder the handes of bothe the wardens, a booke of *the Marchaunt of Venyce or otherwise called the Jewe of Venyce*. PROUIDED that yt bee not prynted by the said James Robertes or anye other whatsoeuer without lycence first had from the Right honorable the lord Chamberlen   . . . . . vjᵈ

The *proviso* in this entry is noteworthy. The company of actors to which Shakespeare belonged was known as 'the Lord Chamberlain's Servants.' This 'booke,' then, which Robertes entered, must have been a play which was acted by this company; only on this ground could the Lord Chamberlain have been interested in granting or withholding his license. There was no patent for the exclusive printing of 'plaie-bookes,' and it could have been only as the protector of 'his servants'' interests that the Lord Chamberlain could withhold the license. It may be that this caution on the part of the Wardens of the Stationers' Company is a tribute to the popularity of the play, since even the Wardens knew to what Company it belonged, or it may be that no play was entered without some kind of proof shown that it was done under authority; although this, I think, is doubtful. Some of the 'stolne and surreptitious copies' of which Heminge and Condell complained, appear to have been issued without any authority.

How James Robertes obtained this book, which aroused the suspicions of the Wardens, must remain a mystery. 'How he caught it, found it, or came by it, or whereof it was born, we are yet to learn.' Possibly through some friendly actor, or possibly James Robertes's reputation, in the estimation of the Wardens, was none of the fairest. Perhaps the cloud of a fine which had been imposed on him still hung over him. He was one of the older Printers and Stationers of the city, and ought to have been respectable. Ten years before this he had influence enough at Court to obtain from the Queen a patent for the exclusive printing of 'Almanackes and Pronostycacyons,' a remunerative branch of the trade, if we may judge by the size of the annual editions. And four years before, he had purchased Charlwood's estate in upwards of forty works, and he had been bold enough to poach upon even the Queen's Printer's manor and issue 'Catechismes,' but for this offence he had been fined by the Wardens of the Stationers' Company. After this he seems to have turned his attention to 'plaie-bookes;' for the next time

271

that his name appears in the Stationers' Registers, as far as I can discover, after the note of this fine, is in the foregoing entry of *The Merchant of Venice*, with its cautionary proviso. Two years later he entered two other pieces, which were played by the same Company; one was 'A morall *Clothe breches and veluet hose*,' and the other, '*The Allarum of London*,' and in both cases he was enjoined from printing 'without further and better Aucthoritie.' Wherefore, in view of all this, it looks much as though the solution of the mystery of the *proviso* in the foregoing entry of the *Merchant of Venice*, lies in mistrust of Robertes and of his lawful ownership.

The 'lycence from the Right honorable the lord Chamberlen' Robertes apparently failed for a while to obtain. That he did eventually obtain it is to be presumed from the publication of the book two years later; although when it appeared there was no reference on the title-page to the Lord Chamberlain's servants or to any others, an omission which occurs in only about half a dozen of all the Shakespearian Quartos, and which Robertes himself was careful to supply on the title-page of his Quarto of the *Midsummer Night's Dream*.

When Robertes at last published his Quarto, it had the following title-page: THE | EXCELLENT | Hiftory of the Mer- | *chant of Venice*. | With the extreme cruelty of *Shylocke* | the Iew towards the faide Merchant, in cut- | *ing a iuft pound of his flefh*. *And the obtaining* | of *Portia*, by the choyfe of | *three Caskets*. | Written by W. SHAKESPEARE. | (Vignette) | Printed by *J. Roberts*, 1600. |

This has been in recent times, by common consent, called THE FIRST QUARTO.

If we turn again to the Stationers' Registers, we find (vol. iii, p. 175, ed. Arber) the following entry:

28 octobris [1600, 42 Regine]

Thomas haies Entred for his copie under the handes of the Wardens and by Consent of master Robertes. A booke called *the booke of the merchant of Venyce* . . . . **vj**^d

An additional reason for the supposition that Robertes had at last obtained due authority from the Lord Chamberlain, is that the 'Consent of master Robertes' is deemed requisite for the validity of this entry. Without that authority Robertes's property in the book, based merely on his previous entry, would have been void, and the Wardens would have disregarded his claim in favour of Heyes, who evidently produced the permission of the Lord Chamberlain, since no allusion is made to the need of it. Heyes was a young 'master Stacioner,' and as this was only the second book he had ever entered, it is natural to suppose that he would select not only a popular book, but one in which his title would be secure as far as registering could make it

The book shortly appeared with the following title-page: The moft excellent | Hiftorie of the *Merchant* | *of Venice*. | VVith the extreame crueltie of *Shylocke* the Iewe | towards the fayd Merchant, in cutting a iuft pound | of his flefh: and the obtayning of *Portia* | by the choyfe of three | chefts. | *As it hath beene diuers times acted by the Lord* | *Chamberlaine his Seruants*. | Written by William Shakefpeare. (Vignette) | AT LONDON, | Printed by *I. R.* for Thomas Heyes, | and are to be fold in Paules Church-yard, at the | figne of the Greene Dragon. | 1600. |

This is THE SECOND QUARTO.

It is to be noted that reference is made to the company of actors; and also that it is printed by I. R., who has been generally assumed to be James Robertes, but Halliwell thinks that this 'supposition has been adopted without close examination,' and adds that 'some of the probabilities are in favour of another attribution of those initials, the 'types used in the two Editions belonging, at all events in part, to different fonts; and

'one positive coincidence only being to be traced in the materials employed, viz. a
'device, that might possibly have been obtained independently of the type.'

The difficulty that meets us, in supposing that 'I. R.' may stand for some other name
than James Robertes, is that there was no other printer in London at that time, as far
as I can find from Arber's lists, whose name these initials would represent. James
Robertes was the only 'I. R.' then, and for some years afterwards. Moreover, as we
learn from other entries in the Registers, it was not unusual for a printer who assigned
his claim, to stipulate that he should have the printing of the book.

Furthermore, the difference between the fonts of type is by no means conclusive that
both books were not printed by the same Master Printer. As Arber shows (vol. ii, p.
22), it was customary for Master Printers to give out work to Journeymen Compositors,
who, being for the most part householders, set up the copy at their own homes. Certainly we may assume that this would be done in cases where there was need of haste;
and I think it most likely that that need existed here. Haste assuredly goes far to
explain the carelessness with which this Heyes Quarto was set up and printed. Frag
mentary lines, which are utterly incomprehensible, such as 'the Ewe bleake for the
Lambe,' would not have been allowed to stand by any proof-reader or pressman unless
haste could have been pleaded in excuse.

No second impression of this Quarto did Thomas Heyes issue, and on the 8th of
July, 1619, his son, Laurence Hayes, entered it again on the Register, in order to
revive the claim in a book which had been his father's. Laurence Hayes did not, however, print it for many years, not until 1637. This is THE THIRD QUARTO, and has
no intrinsic value. It is merely a careless reprint of a careless book, to which we are
indebted for, I think, only one real emendation, and that is merely a change in spelling
on the part of the compositor; it is 'In measure *reine* thy joy,' III, ii, 118, which Singer, Collier, and the Cambridge Editors prefer to 'raine' of the Second Quarto. The
only other contribution which this Third Quarto makes is in the list of 'The Actors'
Names,' which here appeared for the first time.

In 1652 this play was issued for a FOURTH time as a Quarto, but the late Mr Bolton
Corney (*Notes and Queries*, 2d Series, vol. x, p. 21) asserted, from an examination of
his own copy, that this is merely the Third Quarto with a new title-page inserted.

It was reserved to Professor HALES to detect the one gleam of interest which ema-
nates from this Fourth Quarto. In a communication to *The Athenæum*, 15 December,
1877, and reprinted in his *Notes and Essays*, p. 215 (a book which should be in the
hands of every Shakespeare student), Prof. Hales calls attention to the date of this
Qto, 1652. 'It may have been,' he says, 'a mere coincidence,—it is undoubtedly a
'fact worth remarking,—that just at the time of this re-issue the Jews were beginning
'to ask for re-admission into England, and the consideration of their request to be seri-
'ously entertained. It was not till October, 1655, that Manasseh Ben Israel came over
'in person; not till the following December that the celebrated discussion at Whitehall
'took place; but for some years previously, that earnest and able patriot had been urging
'the claims of his people upon English consideration. He had petitioned "Barebone's
'Parliament," and still earlier the Long Parliament. . . . . And the cause he advocated
'was not without friends moved by motives far different from his. During the Dutch
'war, which began in May, 1652, both Blake and Monk recommended the re-admis-
'sion of the Jews "as a means of damaging the commerce of Holland, and Cromwell
'appeared favourable to it." Thus, just about the time of the republication of the
'famous portrait of Shylock, the question of the return of his race was "in the air,"—
'was a kindling question if not a burning one. . . . . The idea of a Jewish immigration

18

'was bitterly resented.   The clergy, the lawyers, the populace were all at one on the
'subject. . . . . The old clamour against the Jewerie was revived, especially in the city,
'where the merchants were jealous of the wealth of the Hebrews. . . . . Amongst the
'State Papers of the Restoration is a "remonstrance addressed to the King concerning
'"the English Jews, showing the mischiefs accomplished by them . . . . notwithstanding
'"their . . . . banishment by Edward the First at the desire of the whole Kingdom; yet
'"they have since returned, renewed their usurious and fraudulent practices, and flourish
'"so much, that they endeavored to buy St Paul's for a synagogue in the late usurper's
'"time." . . . . It must be allowed that the re-exhibition of Shylock in 1652 could
'scarcely have tended to soften this general disposition.   Whether William Leake had
'any sinister intentions when he had that Qto reprinted there would seem no means
'of knowing. . . . . There may or may not have been animus in the man; but he cer-
'tainly did the Jews no good turn when at such a time he reissued the *Merchant of*
'*Venice*.   For by "the general" little heed is paid to the profound skill and the Catho-
'lic humanity with which the Jew is treated in that play; . . . . it would see in Shylock
'only an atrocious monster, infamous for its greed, execrable for its spite.   And such a
'figure, seen at such a time, could scarcely have promoted the cause of the outcasts of
'Israel.'

This ends the series of Quartos, which, although four in number, furnish, in reality,
but two separate texts, the First, Robertes's, and the Second, Heyes's.

For a third text we turn to THE FOLIO of 1623, and, if we hope for novelty, are disappointed.   The text there given is not an independent one, but is a reprint of Heyes's
Quarto, and the inferior Quarto at that.

In their address 'To the great Variety of Readers,' Heminge and Condell lead us
to expect that in the First Folio we shall find Shakespeare's own text, direct from his
manuscript, which had 'scarce a blot;' and yet, here in this play, we know (as any
one can prove for himself by the Textual Notes of this Edition) that they have reproduced the printed page of the Second Quarto.

The explanation is not difficult if we do not hold Heminge and Condell to the very
strictest account, but grant them a certain latitude of expression.   A printed copy of a
play, which had been used at the theatre for twenty years, and had changes of the text
here and there, and Stage-directions added, might perhaps pass, in the opinion of Shakespeare's fellow-actors, as quite adequately making good their assertion.   Moreover, it
may well have been the custom, as it is now, for compositors to charge less for
setting up from printed copy than from MS.   Why they selected the poorer Quarto we
cannot possibly know for certain,—we can surmise that it was because Thomas Heyes
announced on his title-page that he had followed the acting of the Lord Chamberlain's
Servants.

The number of places where the Folio, in varying from the Second Quarto, shows
any genuine revision of the text, is not large.   The most noticeable is where 'the
Scottish lord' of Queen Elizabeth's time is changed 'to *other* lord' of King James's
(see notes on I, ii, 73); and where, out of deference to 3 Jac. I, c. 21, the name of
'God' is stricken out and the phrase varied, as in I, ii, 106, and V, i, 176.   Where,
in the Quartos, Shylock tells Gratiano (IV, i, 150) to repair his wit or it will fall to
'*cureless* ruin,' the change of the Folio to '*endless* ruin' is, perhaps, for the better, but
is scarcely likely to have been authorized by Shakespeare.   The most noticeable distinction, however, between the Quartos and the Folio, and which stamps the latter as a
Playhouse-copy, is in the Stage-directions throughout the play in reference to Music.
In the Folio a flourish of Cornets announces the arrival, each time that he appears, and

the departure, of the Prince of Morocco, and a flourish of Cornets heralds the Prince of Arragon. At all these entrances and exits the Quartos are silent. Whilst Bassanio comments on the Caskets, both Quartos and Folios have the same Stage-direction, but the Folio adds, in the imperative mood of a genuine Stage-copy, 'Here musicke.' Although these facts show, I think, conclusively that the First Folio is printed from a Stage-copy, they do not give any clew in discovering why its Editors preferred the Second Quarto as a text to print from. But the Stage-directions will, I think, again help us here. In the Fifth Act, where Diana has to be waked with a hymn, the Stage-direction in the First Quarto is 'Musicke playes;' in the Second Quarto and First Folio it is 'Play musick,' unquestionably the direction of a Stage-copy. Again, when Bassanio, after the choice of the Caskets, receives Anthonio's letter from Salerio, the Stage-direction (III, ii, 249) in the First Quarto is, 'He opens the Letter,' which is not the command or direction of a Stage-copy; nor is 'Opens the Letter' of the Folio; but in the Second Quarto it is a command to the actor—'Open the letter.'

Thus, then, in none of these instances do the Stage-directions indicate that the First Quarto was a Stage-copy; whereas, in two of them, they show that the Second Quarto was a Stage-copy, and hence, enable us to surmise, with some faint probability, the reason why Heyes's, and not Robertes's, Quarto, superior though the latter be in punctuation, in spelling, and in intelligent supervision, was selected by Heminge and Condell to be used in printing the Folio. Not that there are no indications in Robertes's Quarto that it was transcribed from a Stage-copy; but the indications we find in it are common to it and to Heyes's Quarto. Both Quartos and the Folio, in the insertion of *Exit*, anticipate by a line or two the actual *Exit* of the actor, as in II, ii, 166; but it is in the Stage-directions over and above these, that we can, I think, detect a longer use as a Stage-copy of the original of Heyes's Quarto.

I have spoken of the First Quarto, Robertes's, as better than the Second Quarto, Heyes's. The reasons therefor are to be found in the notes on the various passages as they occur in the text; they can be weighed to much better advantage there than if tabulated here. It is by no means to be supposed that Robertes's is uniformly better than Heyes's; there are many instances where it is inferior, much inferior, but these instances are counterbalanced, I think, by the number and character of the passages where it is superior. Roughly speaking, there are a dozen instances of inferiority to more than double that number of superiority; always thought, that I do not refer to mere typographical errors, though even on that score the First Quarto is far better composed than the Second Quarto.

In thus rating the First Quarto above the Second Quarto, I am countenanced by COLLIER, DELIUS, and the CAMBRIDGE EDITORS. The first says: 'The Edition of 'Robertes's is, on the whole, to be preferred to that of Heyes's;' the last: 'Q$_1$ seems 'to have been printed by a more accurate printer, or "overseen" by a more accurate 'corrector than Q$_2$, and therefore, *cæteris paribus*, we have preferred the authority of Q$_1$.' GRANT WHITE believes that Robertes's Quarto was a 'stolne and surreptitious' copy, and, therefore, on moral grounds, prefers Heyes's Quarto, which received the sanction of the Folio Editors. On the other hand, FLEAY and FURNIVALL prefer the Second Quarto.

In the following list are the lines which I have noted during my collation as giving indications more or less pronounced of the superiority of Q$_1$, Robertes, over Q$_2$, Heyes. To many of them I have called attention in the Commentary; for the rest reference must be had to the Textual Notes. It is not unlikely that to another student, in many of these instances, the superiority of one reading over another may seem not merely fanciful, but even wholly wanting, and second thoughts might show the same to me; but, nevertheless, I add the list for the benefit of any one who has time to waste after all the duties of life in 'teaching the orphan boy to read, and the orphan girl to sew' have been fulfilled.

Lines containing words or punctuation, wherein Q_1 is better than Q_2:

I, ii, 31, 32; I, iii, 65, 66; II, i, 32, 'out-stare'; II, i, 35, he *vs* a; II, i, 49, to *vs* unto; II, ii, 19; II, ii, 130, is———; II, ii, 160; II, ii, 172; III, i, 25 as verse; III, i, 102, in one night; III, ii, 65 (doubtful); III, ii, 107, 'then' of Q_2 superfluous; III, ii, 211, roof; III, iv, 23, misery *vs* cruelty; III, iv, 66, apparreld *vs* accoutered; III, v, 66, far'st *vs* cher'st; III, v, 73, 'then' for 'it'; IV, i, 79; IV, i, 362; V, i, 51.

Lines containing words or punctuation, wherein Q_1 is inferior to Q_2:

I, ii, 41; II, i, 8; II, vi, 75 (very bad); II, ix, 65; III, i, 38, 39; III, i, 121; III, ii, 64, 65; III, ii, 88; III, ii, 118, range *vs* raine; IV, i, 454.

In both lists some errors are noted which are purely typographical, and the lists make no sort of pretence to completeness.

To sum up—we have, theoretically, three texts, the two Quartos and the Folio; but the Folio followed Q_2; this leaves but two texts. The Quartos, though they were not set up from the same copy, are yet almost identical; it was only through a compositor's fault that a line was omitted in the First Quarto. Therefore, practically, there is but one text. How near this text came to Shakespeare's hand it is impossible to say. It is highly improbable that Robertes printed either his own or Heyes's Quarto direct from Shakespeare's manuscript; at best it could have been but a transcript from a Stage-copy, and had he used the same transcript for Heyes that he used for himself, there would have been a much closer resemblance than is observable, even making all allowances for careless journeyman-printing and for haste. I think it therefore likely that there were two transcripts, and that the transcriber of the copy for the Second Quarto was not only a more illiterate man, but also one with certain peculiarities of pronunciation or spelling, such as the persistent use of *au* for *a*, as in *graunt*, *aunswere*, *glauncing*, &c., and in the antiquated *ie* for *y*. This peculiarity was undoubtedly in the copy, and was not due to the compositor, who would not be likely to set up two types where one alone was called for.

DATE OF COMSITION

SINCE it is impossible to know, with unquestionable certainty, the year in which this play was written, it is pleasing to reflect that no single line of it depends on this knowledge for its wisdom or its wit.   Nevertheless, great stress is laid on the importance of the investigation, and much learning and time has been expended in its pursuit.   It is not easy, I think, to take interest in knowledge thus barren, for, granting that our calcu lations could be made with such nicety as that we could discover even the month and the day,—what would it avail us?   Would it add a charm to Portia's 'quality of mercy,' if we knew that it was written in 1594,—in August,—on the fifth day,—on Wednesday, —in the afternoon—at twenty minutes past three o'clock?   Would it not be quite as profitable to speculate on the quality of the paper on which it was written?   Is it any tribute to Shakespeare's genius that we should busy ourselves over what is not even the setting of the gem, but no more than the jeweller's case in which it is sent home?   It is not by such facts as these that we may hope to find out the man, Shakespeare. If he is not to be found in the plays themselves, he is not to be found in the dates when he wrote them.   And he *is* not in the Plays themselves,—if he were, the plays would fall to the level of Ben Jonson's or of Francis Beaumont's.   It is because Shakespeare is *not* there that his plays are heaven-high above the plays of all other dramatists. Shylock is Shylock; he is not Shakespeare behind a mask, dressed up as Shylock.   Could we at any instant catch a glimpse of Shakespeare himself peeping through the divinity that hedges his creations, that instant there will be revealed a flaw in that creation. Are there any such flaws?   From the highest to the lowest his characters are absolutely true to themselves, from fairest Portia, handing the leaden key to Bassanio, to the Carrier, better bitten with fleas than ne'er a king in Christendom; nowhere can we detect William Shakespeare.   His genius, his intellect, is everywhere, in all, and through all, from the first line to the last; but he, the man, the individuality, is nowhere.   He went out of himself and into his characters, leaving age, and sex, and idiosyncrasies behind.   Therefore in prefixing this or that date to any of these Plays, what else is it but re-arranging that Chronological Table, which, by courtesy, we now call a Life of Shakespeare, and which he who knows more about it than all the rest of us styles, as modestly as truthfully, merely 'Outlines'?   Of the real Life we know absolutely nothing, and I, for one, am genuinely thankful that it is so, and gladly note, as the years roll on, that the obscurity which envelops it is as utter and as impenetrable as ever.

At the same time, this subject of the Date of Composition has occupied, and profit ably occupied, the time and attention of eminent Shakespeare scholars.   It therefore behooves the Editor of an edition like the present faithfully and impartially to deal with the subject, unmindful of the lack of interest in it which he himself may feel.

Of positive *external* proof of the Date of Composition we have as the earliest date one solitary fact.

In the year 1598, when Shakespeare was thirty-four years old, Francis Meres, 'Mafter of Arts of both Vniuerfities,' published his *Palladis Tamia. Wits Treasury, Being the Second Part of Wits Common wealth*, and, in a chapter which he calls 'A com- paratiue difcourfe of our Englifh Poets, with the Greeke, Latine, and Italian Poets,' six times mentions Shakespeare in company with other poets, Sir Philip Sidney, and Mar- low, and Spenser, and others by whom 'the Englifh tongue is mightily enriched, and 'gorgeouslie inuefted in rare ornaments and refplendent habiliments;' and then men·

tions him thus particularly in a passage which has become threadbare and outworn in the memory of every student of Shakespeare, and which only necessity's sharp pinch compels me to repeat here : ' As the foule of *Euphorbus* was thought to liue in *Pythagoras :* fo the fweete wittie foule of *Ouid* liues in mellifluous and hony-tongued *Shake-* ' *fpeare,* witneffe his *Venus* and *Adonis,* his *Lucrece,* his fugred Sonnets among his pri-' uate friends, &c.

' As *Plautus* and *Seneca* are accounted the beft for Comedy and Tragedy among ' the Latines : fo *Shakefpeare* among the English is the moft excellent in both kinds for the ftage ; for Comedy, witneffe his *Gentlemen of Verona,* his *Errors,* his *Loue labors loft,* his *Loue labours wonne,* his *Midfummers night dreame,* and his *Merchant of* ' *Venice :* for Tragedy, his *Richard the fecond, Richard the third, Henry the fourth,* ' *King John, Titus Andronicus,* and his *Romeo and Iuliet.*

' As *Epius Stolo* faid, that the Mufes would fpeake with *Plautus* tongue, if they ' would fpeake Latine : fo I fay that the Mufes would fpeake with *Shakefpeares* fine ' filed phrase, if they would fpeake Englifh.'

To no other English poet does Meres give such high praise, and of no other dramatist does he enumerate so many plays.

This is, chronologically, the first instance where Shakespeare's name is connected with *The Merchant of Venice.* It is not the first allusion to the play itself. That allusion, as we have seen, is found in Robertes's entry in the *Stationers' Registers,* on the 22d of July of this year. Meres's *Wit's Treasury* was not there entered by Cuthbert Burbie until the 7th of September, and the actual appearance of the book from the press may have been much later. The date on any title-page may mean, according to Arber, any time between the 25th of March of one year, and the 24th of March of the next. At any rate, ' Master ' Francis Meres must have first composed and written his enthusiastic praise before the book was printed, and he probably did so early in 1598, long before Robertes tried to print his unauthorized copy.

Meres's allusion in 1598 may, therefore, stand as our earliest, positive, External Proof, bearing on the Date of Composition. It was Bishop Percy (*Reliques,* &c., i, 191) who, in 1765, first, I think, called attention to it.

Just as Malone was finishing his Edition of *Shakespeare* in 1790, an old folio account-book of Philip Henslowe was found at Dulwich College. The founder of Dulwich College was an actor, Edward Alleyn, a name to be held in reverence for all time ; not only did he found this College, which he called ' The College of God's Gift,' but he endowed besides thirty small almshouses in different London parishes. Alleyn had married the step-daughter of Philip Henslowe, and was a partner with his step-father-in-law in theatrical management during the latter's life, and at his death Alleyn succeeded to most of his property. Thus it happened that Henslowe's papers were found with Alleyn's at Dulwich College. Henslowe was evidently a shrewd, active man of business, and although bred to the trade, it is presumed, of a dyer, yet was, at one time, the servant of a well-to-do widow, and was doubtless of unusual personal attractions and good qualities, for the servant married the mistress. In what way Henslowe became concerned in theatrical matters is not known ; he appears to have had, in addition, several other business ventures, such as Iron Mines and Pawnbroking, and in 1592 he was the proprietor of the Rose Theatre. In this account-book, which Malone found, Henslowe has set down the various sums which he received from the performances of plays. Now, although at no time, I believe, did Henslowe have the management of the company of actors to which Shakespeare belonged, which was, from first to last, one and the same company, and at the time of Robertes's entry was called the Lord Chamberlain's

Company, ye', for some reason or other, possibly, as Collier suggests, while the Globe Theatre was building, the Lord Chamberlain's men did, for two years, from June, 1594, to July, 1596, unite, or at least occupy the same theatre at Newington Butts, with the Lord Admiral's men, Henslowe's Company.

Here, then, are the daily receipts of a man who had a pecuniary interest in every play which Shakespeare either wrote or acted in during two long years. At last, if we are young and ardent in Shakespeare-study, we may hope for some clear, well-defined fact concerning Shakespeare, but, if we are old and gray, we shall know beforehand that the impenetrable veil will descend; names of actors and of poets, even their handwriting, we have in abundance, but 'the greatest name in all literature' ' glares by its absence;' and, as though the more to tantalize us, in place of substance, which a few careless strokes of Henslowe's pen would have afforded, we have vague shadows, misty intimations which we must set our wits abroach to define. To add to our difficulties, Henslowe was, even for those times, a very illiterate man; his writing was crabbed and illegible, his spelling was phonetic (therein anticipating some later commentators), and his ear was not always of the nicest; thus, on 'the 6 of febery,' he records his receipts 'at tittus and ondronicus.'

Malone extracted from this account-book of Henslowe such items as he thought worthy of preservation, and printed them in Vol. I, Part ii, p. 288, ed. 1790, and they are repeated in the Variorum Editions down to and including 1821. They are, however, inaccurately reproduced, which may be, perhaps, attributed, as Collier suggests, to Malone's failing eyesight. When a new play was performed, Henslowe was wont to record the fact by inserting *ne*, the first two letters of the word *new*, somewhere in connection with the item; this *ne* Malone either overlooked or disregarded, and thereby impaired the value of his list; and instead of repeating the title of the play as often as it occurred, he simply appended to its first entry the number of times which it was subsequently to be found, and his counting was not always correct, or else mine is not.

However, the entire book was deciphered, and reprinted by 'The Shakespeare Society' in 1845, under the supervision of Collier.

With its value in regard to other plays of Shakespeare we are not here concerned. It is enough to note that during the two years above mentioned the titles occur of plays which are either the same as those of Shakespeare or very similar to his. All that is of present moment to us is, that in the Shakespeare's Society's Reprint, on p. 35, Henslowe begins a new leaf in his Ledger as follows:

'*In the name of God Amen, beginninge at Newington, my Lord Admeralle and my Lorde chamberlen men, as foloweth.* 1594.'

The first entry is ' 3 of June,' and records his receipts 'at Heaster and asheweros,' and so on, daily, until on p. 40 we find the following:

25 of aguste 1594 *ne* Rd at the Venesyon comodey . . . . 1s vj^d

'This,' says Malone, 'is probably *The Merchant of Venice.*'

Upon our acceptance or rejection of this supposition of Malone depends, as far as External Proof is concerned, the movable date of this play. If we accept it, we can push back the date four years earlier than the 1598 of Meres and Robertes.

In his note *ad loc.* in the Reprint, Collier is inclined to reject this supposition: 'Had it been,' he says, ' *The Merchant of Venice*, Henslowe would probably have called it by that name; we have already had *The Merchant of Emden.*'

In view of Henslowe's lawless spelling and pronunciation, it is almost rash to say what change a title might not receive in his accounts; but it seems to me noteworthy (and, as far as I know, it has not been noticed) that in the use of this title: 'The Venesyon comodey,' Henslowe, barring an occasional vagary in spelling, is uniformly faithful. It was acted eight times before the close of the year and three times in the early part of the next, and it is always recorded under the same title. It is not impossible that Henslowe wished to avoid any confusion with that popular play, *The Jew of Malta*, or with *The Merchant of Emden;* but then, on the other hand, he was liable to confound 'The Venesyon comodey' with what he was pleased to write 'The greasyon comodey,' or 'The frenshe comodey,' so that the uniformity of the title supports the belief that it was the genuine name of one of the many plays which have been lost, and in which there was no character of so pronounced a type as Shylock. At the same time it is to be remembered that during these two years, in Henslowe's diary, occur the names of several plays which at that date are supposed to be, in part at least, Shakespeare's,—for instance, *Titus Andronicus, Hamlet, Taming of a Shrew*, and *Henry V*.

Of *Internal* Proofs over and above those of style, and of maturity, there are very few.

Malone believed that he had discovered in the play an allusion to a contemporary event which was sufficiently pronounced, when coupled with other facts, to enable him to determine the Date of Composition. On the passage in III, ii, where Portia exclaims:—'He may win, And what is music then? then music is Even as the flourish when true subjects bow To a new crowned monarch,' Malone has the following:—
'Shakespeare is fond of alluding to events of the time he wrote, and the coronation of 'Henry the Fourth of France, who was crowned at Chartres in the midst of his *true* 'subjects in 1594, (Rheims, where that ceremony ought to have taken place, being 'possessed by the rebels,) seems to have excited great interest in England. The fol- 'lowing is an extract from a pamphlet published on that subject, entitled "The Order '"of Ceremonies observed in the Anointing and Coronation of the Most Christian '"French King of Navarre, Henry IIII of that Name, celebrated in our Lady Church '"in the Cittie of Chartres, uppon Sonday the 27 of February, 1594. Faithfully trans- '"lated out of the French Coppie, printed at Roan, by Commaundment of the said '"Lord. By E. A. London."
'After describing various parts of the Ceremonial, the writer proceeds thus:—"Then '"the said Archbishop, holding the King by the hand, caused him to sit down, saying, '"'In hoc regni solio,' &c. . . . . After him all the other peeres kissed him . . . . say- '"ing thus: 'Vivat Rex in æternum,' &c. Then the people gave a great shout, cry- '"ing, *God save the King,* and immediately the harquebuzes shot off, and after them '"the great ordinance, and *the trumpets, cornets, hautbois, drommes, and other instru- '"ments sounded;* and the said Lord Archbishop begun, Te Deum laudamus, &c. . . . . '"Here we are to note that so often as the King returned ever so little to the body of '"the church, the people being infinite in number, cryed God save the King; and the '"church rung with theyr cries, and with harquebuze shot. . . . . The people with '"great acclamation and signes of joy, cryed God save the King; the cannons and '"small shotte played their parts, the *trumpettes, drommes, and other instruments '"sounded and played.*"'

Whence MALONE'S date for this play is 1594, and, in order of composition, the ninth.

STEEVENS cites Meres and the *Stationers' Registers*, and dates it accordingly 1598, and places it the sixteenth in order of composition.

CHALMERS, accepting Farmer's suggestion in regard to Silvayn's *Orator*, published
in 1596 (this suggestion will be dealt with in discussing the Source of the Plot),
believed that proof was thus furnished that 'the *Merchant of Venice* may have been
'written either in 1597 or in 1596. From this state of uncertainty we may be relieved
'by attending to an allusion which did not catch the commentator's eyes: The mer-
'chant exclaims: "Nor is my whole estate Upon the fortune of *this* present year."
'The question, then, is, what year was it, which was a year of dread to traders? Mon-
'day, the chronicler, shall answer the question: After taking notice of the losses of
'Spain, from the capture of Hulst in 1596, he adds: Then did the "King of Spain
'"dispense with himself for payment of his debts, which made many merchants in
'"Spain, *Italy*, Antwerp, Amsterdam, and Middleburgh, to become *banquerouts*,"—
'*Monday's Briefe Chronicle*, 1611, p. 422. While the balance was thus vibrating,
'between the years 1596 and 1598, this curious fact fixes it for 1597.'

DOUCE is non-committal. If the author of an old Latin play, acted in 1597, took
the incident of a Jew's whetting his knife from Shakespeare, then Shakespeare's play
must have been acted before that date. If he took it from the ballad of *Gernutus*, then
Shakespeare borrowed from the same source, and we need a copy of the play to which
Gosson alludes (see *post*, Source of the Plot) to set all right.

In the opening of the Fifth Act, where Lorenzo and Jessica try to 'out-night' each
other, WHALLEY remarked that their speeches, beginning 'In such a night,' were imitated in the old comedy of *Wily Beguiled*. The passage in *Wily Beguiled* (p. 365,
ed. Hawkins) is as follows:

> *Sophos.* See how the twinkling stars do hide their borrow'd shine
> As half asham'd, their lustre is so stain'd
> By *Lelia's* beauteous eyes, that shine more bright
> Than twinkling stars do in a winter's night:
> In such a night did *Paris* win his love.
> *Lelia.* In such a night, *Æneas* prov'd unkind.
> *Sophos.* In such a night, did *Troilus* court his dear.
> *Lelia.* In such a night, fair *Phyllis* was betray'd.
> *Sophos.* I'll prove as true as ever *Troilus* was.
> *Lelia.* And I as constant as *Penelope*.

Although this imitation does not, as Whalley says, enable us to ascertain the date of
Wily Beguiled, yet 'it proves it to have been written after Shakespeare's *Merchant of
Venice*.' Whereupon Malone said that '*Wily Beguiled* was written before 1596, being
'mentioned by Nashe in one of his pamphlets published in that year.' If Malone is
right in this reference, the *Merchant of Venice* must have been written a year or two at
least before 1596. But HALES, a good authority, has shown (*Athenæum*, 4 Sept., 1875)
that Malone was mistaken; Nashe's words (in *Have with You to Saffron Walden*, p. 158,
ed. Grosart) do not refer to the play of *Wily Beguiled*, but, 'more probably, Nashe's phrase
'["Wily Beguily"] is one of those reduplications that are so common in English, and
'of which Nashe was particularly fond.' 'Dr Brinsley Nicholson' (another good
authority) 'concludes,' says Hales, 'that the play was written "in or after 1601."'
FLEAY, however, says (*Life and Work of Sh.*, p. 133, 1886): 'About this same time
'[July, 1597] the play of *Wily Beguiled* was acted.' For this assertion Fleay has,
doubtless, ample proof; but I have failed to find it, either in Henslowe's diary or in
Fleay's own book. Be that as it may, the agreement is general that, whatever the date,

Wily Beguiled imitated the *Merchant of Venice*, not only in this Scene, but in Shylock's outcries for his daughter and his ducats (see p. 368, cd Hawkins); and in still another place, detected by Hales (*Athenæum*, 17 July, 1875), where 'that venture harder to achieve Than that of Jason for the golden fleece' recalls Bassanio's speech in the First Scene.

DRAKE (vol. ii, p. 385) accepts Chalmers's chronology, and on Chalmers's grounds.

SKOTTOWE (vol. i, p. 360) places the date, 'without hesitation,' in 1597. Shakespeare's obligations to *The Orator* prove that this play was subsequent to 1596, and its mention by Meres that it was previous to 1598.

KNIGHT, without specifying any particular year, pleads for a much earlier date than any hitherto assigned, and where all is conjecture, one may be as liberal as the air. After enumerating all the plays which were written by Shakespeare before the 17th Century, Knight asks: 'What is the sum, then, of the work which we hold to have ' been produced by Shakspere before the close of the 16th Century? *Nine Comedies*, ' *eight Histories* (taking the Second and Third Parts of *Henry VI*, as remodelled by ' him), and *three Tragedies*. The common theory is that he began to write for the ' stage in 1591; he having been, as Mr Collier has unquestionably proved, a large pro- ' prietor in the Blackfriars' Theatre in 1589. We ask that the author of twenty plays, ' which completely changed the face of the dramatic literature in England, should be ' supposed to have begun to write a little earlier than the age of twenty-seven; that we ' should assign some few of these plays to a period antecedent to 1590. We have rea- ' son to believe that, up to the close of the 16th Century, Shakspere was busied as an ' actor as well as an author. It is something too much to expect, then, even from the ' fertility of his genius, occupied as he was, that he should have produced twenty plays ' in nine years; and it is still more unreasonable to believe that the consciousness of ' power, which he must have possessed, should not have prompted him to enter the lists ' with other dramatists (whose highest productions may, without exaggeration, be stated ' as every way inferior to his lowest) until he had gone through a probation of six or ' seven years' acquaintance with the stage as a humble actor. We cannot reconcile it ' to probability that he who ceased to be an actor when he was forty, should have been ' contented to have been only an actor until he was twenty-seven. Impelled by these ' convictions, we have somewhat pertinaciously clung to the belief that Shakspere, by ' commencing his career as a dramatic writer some four or five years earlier than is gen- ' erally maintained, may claim, in common with his less illustrious early contemporaries, ' the praise of being one of the great founders of our dramatic literature, instead of being ' the mere follower and improver of Marlowe, and Greene, and Peele, and Kyd. With- ' out sacrificing anything, we hope, to this theory we have endeavoured in balancing ' the evidence for the date of this play, not to be driven too easily into the belief that it ' *could not* have been produced before the ten last years of the 16th Century. But we ' have given all the evidence which we could find, [that is, the *Stationers' Registers* ' and Meres,] leaving the reader to decide for himself.'

COLLIER refers to Meres, and says that we have no means of knowing how long before Meres's time the play was written; and, in connection with Malone's conjecture that Henslowe's *Venyson comodey* was *The Merchant of Venice*, emphasizes the fact that Shakespeare's Company was playing with Henslowe's Company at that time,—a consideration which much influenced STAUNTON, who thinks that there is 'now very ' little doubt that the *Merchant of Venice* was written and acted some years before' 1598.

HALLIWELL, while acknowledging that there is no other certain information than that of the *Stationers' Registers* and Meres, suggests, on the strength of the imitation in *Wily Beguiled*, that 'it was probably written before the year 1596. And if, in ' addition to this, there is added the circumstance of several expressions which occur ' in the Trial Scene in Shakespeare being similar to others in *The Orator*, published ' in the same year, we may arrive not unreasonably at the conclusion that *The Mer-* ' *chant of Venice* was a new and favorite play in 1596. Another slight indication, ' tending towards a similar conclusion, may be found in the circumstance that the pro- ' nunciation of Stephano is erroneously given in this Comedy, but that after Shake- ' speare had taken a part in the representation of *Every Man in his Humour*, produced ' in 1598, where the same name occurs with its correct accent, he altered the cadence ' when he had occasion to write it in a subsequent composition.'

C. BATHURST (*Remarks on the Differences in Shakespeare's Versification*, &c., Lon- don, 1857, p. 57): 'The *Merchant of Venice* is very natural, sometimes excursive, not ' ratiocinative. The verse, generally, uniform and flowing. One weak ending. Some ' breaks. The speeches, where the speakers change, fit into the verse, but not always. ' It is remarkably one of those plays which were written when Shakespeare's mind was ' at ease, original, and independent. Neither disturbed by the rivalship of others, nor ' stimulated to take pains to write in a more active and dramatic style than naturally ' occurred to him in the course of his composition. He never, as I conceive, took pains, ' in the cool, deliberate way in which most writers of merit have done; but he certainly ' " lashed his sides with his tail," as Longinus says, out of Homer, as to Euripides, in ' such plays as *Macbeth*, and others of his highest class.

' This year 1598 is something like an epoch, I think; partly on account of Meres's ' list, however uncertain; partly, because, as appears to me, there is really a material ' change of style about this time; but also, because it was in this year that Ben Jonson ' came out, and with a play of great force and popularity, *Every Man in his Humour*, ' which was likely to have an effect on Shakespeare, both directly and indirectly, as ' influencing the public taste.'

GRANT WHITE, in his First Edition, finds warrant for the decided opinion that this play was new in 1594. ' The play itself bears evidence that it was written at a time ' when Shakespeare had obtained, by observation and experience, the highest use of ' his powers as a playwright, and when his faculties as a poet and philosopher were ' approaching their grand maturity, while it yet betrays in every line the ardor and ' hopefulness of youth. Judged, therefore, on its own evidence, *The Merchant of Ven-* ' *ice* is one of the earliest productions of Shakespeare's middle period, and this indica- ' tion agrees well with the external evidence which would assign it to his thirtieth year.' In his Second Edition, Grant White reaffirms his belief: ' At what particular time before ' 1598 Shakespeare did this beautiful piece of work we can only infer from the internal ' evidence of style and versification, and from Henslowe's diary. These confirm each ' other. The play, we may be sure, was written in 1594, when Shakespeare was thirty ' years old.'

The COWDEN-CLARKES come to the same conclusion, founded on Henslowe's diary. In 1594, Shakespeare was 'thirty years of age, in the very prime of intellectual vigour, ' and we can well imagine this fine play to have been the product of his pen at that period of his life. There is a strength of purpose in it as a drama, a tone of experi- ' ence in its views of men and life, a masterly treatment of character, and, withal, a ' wealth of romance about its story, that mark it for a composition on his arrival at ' manly maturity.'

DELIUS, on the faith of Henslowe's diary and the imitation in *Wily Beguiled*, and on the evidence of style and versification, sets it down in 1594.

DYCE, in his Third Edition, thinks that it may have been some years on the stage before Meres mentioned it, and that Malone's supposition about Henslowe's 'Venesyon comodey' is not improbable.

It is a little uncertain whether or not the CLARENDON Editors accept the item in Henslowe's diary as referring to *The Merchant of Venice*. They express a judicious doubt as to its identity with the 'Venesyon comodey,' and yet they speak of 'its first production in 1594' as though it were an established fact.

'The Venesyon comodey,' they say, 'may be Shakespeare's *Merchant*. But consider-
' ing that the dramatists of that time were fond of laying their scenes in Italy, this iden-
' tification is very uncertain. There are, however, in the play itself, indications which
' would lead us to suppose that its first composition was earlier than 1598, such as the
' many classical allusions, the frequent rhymes, and occasional doggerel verses. The
' " fooling " of Launcelot, too, has a strong resemblance to that of his almost namesake
' in *The Two Gentlemen of Verona*. On the other hand, the loftiness of thought and
' expression, the grace and freedom of the versification in general, point to a later time,
' and would lead us rather to class this play with *Twelfth Night*, *As You Like It*, and
' *Much Ado About Nothing*, than with the earlier plays, *Love's Labour's Lost* and *The
' Two Gentlemen of Verona*. On the whole, we incline to think that the play was in
' great part rewritten between the time of its first production in 1594 and its publication
' in 1600. The slight discrepancies may be due to this cause, particularly that in' [I,
ii, 120. See Hunter's note, *ad loc.*]

HUDSON inclines to 1598, the date of Meres's allusion. 'How long before that
' time,' he urges, 'the play was written we have no means of knowing; but, judging
' from the style, we cannot well assign the writing to a much earlier date.' As to
Henslowe's *Venesyon comodey*, Hudson is 'by no means certain that it refers to Shake-
' speare's play; while the workmanship here shows such maturity and variety of power
' as argue against that supposal. It evinces, in a considerable degree, the easy, unlabour-
' ing freedom of conscious mastery; the persons being so entirely under the author's
' control, and subdued to his hand, that he seems to let them act and talk just as they
' have a mind to. Therewithal, the style throughout is so even and sustained; the word
' and character are so fitted to each other; the laws of dramatic proportion are so well
' observed; and the work is so free from any jarring or falling out from the due course
' and order of art; as to justify the belief that the whole was written in the same stage
' of intellectual growth and furnishing.'

On the other hand, ROLFE relies on Henslowe's diary, and thinks 'there is good
' reason to believe that the play was written and acted as early as 1594.'

In FLEAY'S first published list (*New Shakspere Society's Trans.*, Series I, p. 10) of the Succession of Shakespeare's plays founded on metrical grounds, the date assigned to the *Merchant of Venice* is 1597. But in his *Shakespeare Manual* (p. 34), he says that he prefers 1596. 'Malone,' he there says, 'identifies this play with *The Venesyon
' comedy* acted at the Rose in 1594. But Shakespeare's plays were not at any time
' acted there.' Yet Fleay himself says, p. 82, that the Lord Chamberlain's men acted at the Rose in 1594; and Shakespeare belonged to that Company, and it acted his plays. Moreover, I cannot find that Malone says that the 'Venesyon comodey' was acted at the Rose; his conjecture merely is affixed to Henslowe's item, and there, as we have seen above, Henslowe expressly states that the performances were 'at New-ington,' where the Lord Chamberlain's men were playing with the Lord Admiral's

men. I am afraid that Fleay has given hardly enough weight to these facts, or else that there is an oversight in his statement, on p. 82, that the Lord Chamberlain's men acted at the Rose.

However, in his *Hist. of the Life and Work of Shakespeare*, 1886, Fleay returns to his former date, 1597. 'Early in this year,' he says, p. 30, 'was almost certainly ' produced *The Merchant of Venice*, founded on an old play of Dekker's called *Joseph* ' *the Jew of Venice*, written c. 1592, and acted in 1594 by the Admiral's men, but not ' now extant.' Again on p. 197 : '*The Merchant of Venice*, or *Jew of Venice*, was no ' doubt founded on an old play called *The Jew of Venice*, by Dekker. It seems from ' the title of the German version of this play that the Jew's name was Joseph. The ' name Fauconbridge in I, ii (where Portia's suitors are enumerated, compare *Two Gen-* ' *tlemen*, I, ii) points to a date soon after *John ;* and the "merry devil" of II, iii, 2, ' a phrase never elsewhere used in Shakespeare, indicates contemporaneity with *The* ' *Merry Devil of Edmonton*, produced in the winter of 1596. Again, the manifest ' imitations of this play in *Wily Beguiled*, which I show elsewhere to date in the sum- ' mer of 1597, give a posterior limit, which must be decisive. This play has no sign ' whatever of having been altered; the Clarendon Press guesses, founded on the dis- ' crepancy of the number of suitors (iv for vi) are as worthless as Mr Hales's proof, ' referred to by Mr Halliwell (*Outlines*, p. 251) of the date of *Wily Beguiled*. The ' conclusive evidence of imitation in this play is the conjunction of the "In such a ' "night" lines with the "My money, my daughter" iterations of Gripe.' I think that there is another indication of alteration besides the 'Clarendon Press guesses.' See *post*, in 'Source of the Plot,' p. 321.

It is to be regretted that Fleay does not give his authority for the assertion that Dek- ker's play of the *Jew of Venice*, which was not entered on the *Stationers' Registers* until 1653, was written about 1592, or, as he says on p. 310, 'about 1591.' That the comedy of *Josephus, a Jew of Venice*, twice played by the English Comedians in Dres- den in 1626, might possibly be a version of Dekker's *Jew of Venice* was first suggested by Cohn (*Shakespeare in Germany*, p. cxviii); but the assertion that it is the founda- tion of the *Merchant of Venice*, and that it was written in 1591 or 1592, is Fleay's own surmise. It is also to be regretted that Fleay does not cite the parallel passages in Dekker's *Jew* and Shakespeare's *Merchant* in proof that one was founded on the other. I believe, however, not an authentic line of Dekker's *Jew* has survived. Fleay's conjecture must therefore stand on its own merits. At present, as far as the Date of the Composition of the *Merchant of Venice* is concerned, nothing further need be said about the identity of Dekker's *Jew* and the German *Jud von Venedig*. The latter deserves notice when we come to consider the Source of the Plot, and will be there treated in full.

In enumerating the Internal Proofs mention should not be omitted of LEE's theory that a close connection exists between the date of the *Merchant of Venice* and the fate of Dr Lopez, who was hanged at Tyburn in May, 1594. The parallelism is certainly striking in some particulars, but the date, May, is very, very close to ' 25 aguste,' if we are to believe that the 'Venesyon comodey' and the *Merchant of Venice* are the same, which Lee assumes. See *post*, 'The Jews in England.'

In discussing the Date of the Composition of *Othello*, the Accounts of the Revels at Court in 1604 were of importance. The curious history of that forgery of what Hal- liwell-Phillipps believes to be a genuine record was given at length in *Othello*, pp. 347– 357, and need not be repeated here ; where, whether forged or not, the date 1604 can have no bearing on the Date of the Composition of the *Merchant of Venice*. However, merely as a matter of curiosity, it may be noted that in the forged pp. 204, 205 of the *Extracts from the Account of the Revels at Court*, published by the *Shakespeare Society*, 1842, occur the following entries:

[1606]

By his Ma^{tis} plaiers	On Shrousunday A play of the Marchant of Venis	Shaxberd.

*　　　*　　　*　　　*　　　*

By his Ma^{tis} players	On Shroutusday A play cauled The Martchant of Venis againe com̃auded by the Kings Matie.	Shaxberd.

According to a list of the Order of Succession, founded on the 'Numbers of Light and Weak Endings in the Several Plays,' by Prof. INGRAM (*New Shakspere Soc. Trans.*, Series I, p. 450), *The Merchant of Venice* stands ninth.

To recapitulate:

The Date of Composition of the *Merchant of Venice* is assigned by MALONE,
　　　STAUNTON, GRANT WHITE, COWDEN-CLARKE, DELIUS, ROLFE, LEE, to . 1594
By HALLIWELL to 'before'; by FURNIVALL 'about' 1596
By CHALMERS, DRAKE, SKOTTOWE, FLEAY 1597
By STEEVENS, BATHURST, HUDSON 1598
By KNIGHT to no precise date, but 'very early.'
By COLLIER, DYCE to 'some years before.' 1598
CLARK and WRIGHT (i. e. CLARENDON) think it 'was rewritten between 1594
　　　and 1600.'

SOURCE OF THE PLOT

It is lightly seen that in this play there are two stories intertwined, *The Pound of Flesh*, or, as it is frequently styled, *The Bond Story*, and *The Three Caskets;* some critics, indeed, add a third, that of *Jessica*, but this, I think, is an over-refinement of analysis; at all events, there are assuredly two, and each of them lends itself so readily to a symbolical interpretation, that it is not surprising to find them, more or less disguised, widely scattered and ascending even into the early literature of many nations. By the story of *The Three Caskets*, a pious monk enforces the moral of the deceitfulness of appearances and the temptations of the human soul, in the *Gesta Romanorum*, or we may find *the Pound of Flesh* set forth in the *Mahábhárata* as inculcating the beauty of self-sacrifice.

The task, however, now before us is to discover, if we may, the shape in which these materials lay to Shakespeare's hand; and in order to do this not only must our range be wide, but many a stray fragment must be examined for possible finger-marks, and many a dust-heap must be sifted.

From the records which have come down to us it is to be inferred that the audiences of Shakespeare's time constantly demanded novelty in the attractions of the stage. The playwrights were kept busy, and must have worked at a rate of speed which, though perhaps not without its parallel in Greece, is, I think, quite unknown among dramatists now-a-days. Collier has made the computation, by means of Henslowe's diary that the audiences of that day required a new play, upon an average, every seventeen or eighteen days, including Sundays. In addition to satisfying this demand for novelty, it follows as of course that the playwrights and poets had to keep touch with every gale and vary of the public, and this struggle for popularity, which meant daily bread, not unnaturally fomented intense rivalry between the different companies of actors. Into this scramble Shakespeare was ushered, it is generally agreed, in 1591, and in it he continued about twenty years, and wrote, in whole or in part, about forty plays—that is, on an average for the whole period, one every six months. Thus driven by the necessity of speed on the one hand, and by anxiety to catch the popular fancy on the other, is it any wonder that Shakespeare never stopped to devise a plot? What need was there that he should do so? The manager of the company had many an old play which, at one time or another, had been submitted to the test of public approval, and had been found not lacking in qualities more or less dramatic, or in points which had caught the fancy of the hour, even though it were by no greater charm than by the dismal repetition of the word 'Revenge!' To such plays, if selected for revision, a certain amount of popularity was thus assured in advance; and as for the plot,—the barest skeleton sufficed for Shakespeare. He knew that he could remodel it into fair proportions and relume it with life. Of all that goes to make up one of his dramas, the plot in itself, in its mere outlines, is of less importance than any other element in it. Of course, in the nature of things, it is not to be supposed that after he had selected the old play to be rejuvenated he either adhered to it closely, or refused hints from other sources. Old ballads, books of travels, histories, the gossip of the day,—all were put under contribution. As Emerson says: 'Every master has 'found his materials collected, and his power lay in his sympathy with his people, and 'in his love for the materials he wrought in.'

And we know the result.

I can find no trace of any attempt to identify the source of the plot of this play earlier than that of Warton, who, in his *Observations on the Fairy Queen*, 1754, in a foot-note

(p. 128, ed. 1762), says that, 'in all probability,' the story of The Merchant of Venice 'is founded upon the following antient ballad,' which he 'met with in *Mus. Ashmol.* 'Oxon. cod. impress. A. Wood.' Warton did not give the whole ballad, but merely the first stanza and some of the concluding stanzas. The whole of it was printed by Bishop Percy in *The Connoisseur* for 16 May, 1754; this text he did not follow subsequently, in his *Reliques,* 1765, vol. i, p. 191, but there printed from an ancient black-letter copy in the Pepys Collection. There is really no difference in the texts; the few variations here and there might readily have arisen from mere transcription. Percy's text, as in his *Reliques,* is here given; it has been reprinted by Editors more frequently than the other :

A new Song, shewing the crueltie of GERNUTUS, *a* JEWE, *who lending to a merchant an hundred crownes, would have a pound of his fleshe, because he could not pay him at the time appointed. To the tune of Black and yellow.*

THE FIRST PART.

IN Venice towne not long agoe
   A cruel Jew did dwell,
Which lived all on ufurie
   As Italian writers tell.

Gernutus called was the Jew,
   Which never thought to dye,
Nor never yet did any good
   To them in ftreets that lie.

His life was like a barrow hogge,
   That liveth many a day,
Yet never once doth any good,
   Until men will him flay.

Or like a filthy heap of dung,
   That lyeth in a whoard
Which never can do any good,
   Till it be fpread abroad.

So fares it with the ufurer.
   He cannot fleep in reft,
For feare the thiefe will him purfue
   To plucke him from his neft.

His heart doth thinke on many a wile,
   How to deceive the poore ;
His mouth is almoft ful of mucke,
   Yet ftill he gapes for more.

His wife muft lend a fhilling,
   For every weeke a penny,
Yet bring a pledge, that is double worth,
   If that you will have any.

And fee, likewife, you keepe your day,
  Or elfe you loofe it all :
This was the living of the wife,
  Her cow fhe did it call.

Within that citie dwelt that time
  A marchant of great fame,
Which being diftreffed in his need,
  Unto Gernutus came :   .

Defiring him to ftand his friend
  For twelve month and a day,
To lend to him an hundred crownes ;
  And he for it would pay

Whatfoever he would demand of him,
  And pledges he fhould have,
No (quoth the Jew with flearing lookes)
  Sir, afke what you will have.

No penny for the loane of it
  For one yeare you fhall pay ;
You may doe me as goode a turne,
  Before my dying day.

But we will have a merry jeaft
  For to be talked long ;
You fhall make me a bond, quoth he,
  That fhall be large and ftrong :

And this fhall be the forfeyture ;
  Of your owne flefhe a pound.
If you agree, make you the bond,
  And here is a hundred crownes.

With right good will ! the marchant fays :
  And fo the bond was made.
When twelve month and a day drew on
  That backe it fhould be payd,

The marchant's fhips were all at fea,
  And money came not in ;
Which way to take, or what to doe
  To thinke he doth begin :

And to Gernutus ftrait he comes
  With cap and bended knee,
And fayde to him, Of curtefie
  I pray you beare with mee.

My day is come, and I have not
  The money for to pay :
And little good the forfeyture
  Will doe you, I dare fay.

19

With all my heart, Gernutus fayd,
    Commaund it to your minde :
In thinges of bigger waight then this
    You fhall me ready finde.

He goes his way ; the day once paft
    Gernutus doth not flacke
To get a fergiant prefently ;
    And clapt him on the backe :

And layd him into prifon ftrong,
    And fued his bond withall ;
And when the judgement day was come,
    For judgement he did call.

The marchants friends came thither faft,
    With many a weeping eye,
For other meanes they could not find,
    But he that day muft dye.

THE SECOND PART.

Of the Jews crueltie ; fetting foorth the mercifulneffe of the Judge towards the Marchant.   To the tune of Blacke and yellow.

Some offered for his hundred crownes
    Five hundred for to pay ;
And fome a thoufand, two or three,
    Yet ftill he did denay.

And at the laft ten thoufand crownes
    They offered him to fave,
Gernutus fayd, I will no gold,
    My forfeite I will have.

A pound of flefhe is my demand,
    And that fhall be my hire,
Then fayd the judge, Yet my good friend,
    Let me of you defire

To take the flefh from fuch a place,
    As yet you let him live ;
Do fo, and lo ! an hundred crownes
    To thee here will I give.

No : no : quoth he, no : judgement here :
    For this it fhall be tride,
For I will have my pound of flefhe
    From under his right fide.

It grieved all the companie
    His crueltie to fee
For neither friend nor foe could helpe
    But he muft fpoyled bee.

The bloudie Jew now ready is
　With whetted blade in hand,
To ſpoyle the bloud of innocent,
　By forfeit of his bond.

And as he was about to ſtrike
　In him the deadly blow:
Stay (quoth the judge) thy crueltie;
　I charge thee to do ſo.

Sith needs thou wilt thy forfeit have,
　Which is of fleſh a pound:
See that you ſhed no drop of bloud,
　Nor yet the man confound.

For if thou doe, like murderer,
　Thou here ſhalt hanged be:
Likewiſe of fleſh ſee that thou cut
　No more than longes to thee;

For if thou take either more or leſſe
　To the value of a mite,
Thou ſhalt be hanged preſently
　As is both law and right.

Gernutus now waxt franticke mad,
　And wotes not what to ſay;
Quoth he at laſt, Ten thouſand crownes,
　I will that he ſhall pay;

And ſo I graunt to ſet him free.
　The judge doth anſwere make;
You ſhall not have a penny given;
　Your forfeyture now take.

At the laſt he doth demaund
　But for to have his owne.
No, quoth the judge, doe as you liſt
　Thy judgement ſhall be ſhowne.

Either take your pound of fleſh, quoth he,
　Or cancell me your bond.
O cruel judge, then quoth the Jew,
　That doth againſt me ſtand!

And ſo with griping grieved mind
　He biddeth them fare-well,
'Then' all the people prays'd the Lord,
　That ever this heard tell.

Good people, that do heare this ſong,
　For trueth I dare well ſay,
That many a wretch as ill as hee
　Doth live now at this day;

> That feeketh nothing but the ſpoyle
> Of many a wealthey man,
> And for to trap the innocent
> Deviſeth what they can.
>
> From whome the Lord deliver me,
> And every Chriſtian too,
> And ſend to them like ſentence eke
> That meaneth ſo to do.

'It may be objected,' says Warton, 'that this ballad may have been written aftei, and copied from Shakespeare's play. But if that had been the case, it is most likely that the author would have preserved Shakespeare's name of Shylock for the Jew; and nothing is more likely than that Shakespeare in copying from this ballad, should alter the name from Gernutus to one more Jewish; and by alteration of the name his imitation was the better disguised. Another argument is, that the ballad has the air of a narrative written before Shakespeare's play; I mean that if it had been written after the play, it would have been much more full and circumstantial. At present, it has too much the nakedness of an original. Besides, the first stanza ' informs us that the story was taken from some Italian novel. Thus much, therefore, ' is certain, that is, that Shakespeare either copied from that Italian novel, or from this ' ballad. Now we have no translation, I presume, of such a novel into English; if ' then it be granted, that Shakespeare generally took his Italian stories from their Eng-' lish translations, and that the arguments above concerning the prior antiquity of this ' ballad are true, it will follow that Shakespeare copied from this ballad.'

It is strange that Warton did not see that there was another source from which Shakespeare could have drawn his plot, for he goes on to refer to an extract from Gosson's *Schoole of Abuse*, apparently quite unconscious of its important bearing on the question, which critics since his time, and following his lead, have found in it. This extract will be duly set forth further on.

As I have said, Bishop Percy reprinted the whole of this ballad, of which Warton had given but a few stanzas, in *The Connoisseur* for May 16, 1754; at least it is to be inferred that the anonymous contributor was Bishop Percy; in the remarks on the ballad in his *Reliques*, Bishop Percy repeated substantially the arguments in *The Connoisseur*, which he would not have done had they not been his own.

It seems to be pretty generally conceded, and for the reasons adduced by Warton, that Gernutus preceded Shylock; and DYCE and the CLARENDON EDITORS go so far as to say that perhaps Shakespeare derived some hints from the ballad,—which I think doubtful. The points wherein there is an agreement, such as whetting the knife, &c., are commonplace enough, and were probably found in the original story or play which was the common source of both ballad and comedy. KNIGHT agrees with Warton that Gernutus preceded Shylock, but not because it would otherwise have been 'more full and circumstantial,' and points in proof of this to Jordan's *Ballad* (see Appendix, *post*), which was unquestionably written *after* the play, in 1664, and yet is much *less* full and circumstantial than the old ballad of *Gernutus*. But it is in the omission of Portia from the old ballad that Knight finds the strongest confirmation that *Gernutus preceded* the comedy. HALLIWELL, on the other hand, inclines to the belief that the comedy preceded the ballad, no copy of which, he says, 'of the time of Shakespeare is known to exist; but as it was the common practice to continue the republication of such pieces during several generations, it is possible, notwithstanding the epithet

'*new* in the title to one copy of it, that it may be a reprint of a composition belonging
' to the Elizabethan era.   The simplicity of the ballad story, however, is no proof of
' its antiquity; for several writers of the 17th Century were accustomed to adopt the
' merest outline incidents of a novel or play, and construct with them, often with altered
' names, those doggerel songs which were so popular amongst the lower classes up to a
' comparatively recent period.   On the whole, unless some evidence could be adduced
' of the existence of the ballad of *Gernutus* in the 16th Century, the probability seems
' in favour of its having been constructed either on Shakespeare's play, or on the more
' ancient drama of the Jew, mentioned by Gosson.   The incident of the Jew whetting
' his knife is one very likely to have been remembered by a writer who was forming a
' ballad from his recollections of the performance of the comedy; and it is the only
' very remarkable coincidence to be traced in the two productions.   It may, however,
' be worth mentioning that the Jew, in the ballad, grants the loan without pecuniary
' interest, and speaks of the bond as a "merrie jest."   The name Gernutus might
' either have been borrowed from the older play, or have been suggested by that of a
' personage introduced in the comedy of the *Three Ladies of London,* 1584, where a
' Jew, of a very different character from Shylock, is introduced, whose name is Geron-
' tus.   The writer of the ballad, indeed, professes to derive his tale from an Italian
' source; but little reliance can be placed upon a statement of this kind in a compo-
' sition belonging to a class in which deceptive assertions of origin and antiquity are
' of continual occurrence.'

There is one expression in the ballad which seems to me to indicate the antiquity
either of the ballad itself or of the source whence it was derived, and that is where
' the wife' calls her usurious means of living ' her cow.'   Hunter (i, 306) says that the
application of the word is not peculiar to this ballad, but that a salt-pit, in the salt districts, in the reign of Henry the Second, was known by the name *Vacca.*   Still, from
internal evidence and after what has been said above, I think we may dismiss all
thoughts that this ballad, whatever its date, in any wise contributed to the *Merchant
of Venice.*

Before we leave the region of Ballads, it is proper to mention another whose claims
are put forward by HUNTER (i, 301), as follows :

' It has occurred to no one to observe that, besides the ballad of *Gernutus,* we have
' in the popular literature of England another ballad containing incidents which bear a
' close resemblance to the part of this play which relates to the bond, as it contains also
' other incidents which are very like the part of *Cymbeline* which relates to Posthumus,
' Iachimo, and Imogen.   This ballad continued to be occasionally printed, even till
' within the present century.   The copy which I possess is entitled *The Northern
' Lord.*   The verse is exceedingly low and groveling, but the story is full of romantic
' incidents.   This ballad is little, if at all, known within the range of Shakespearian
' criticism, so that an abstract of it may be acceptable.   Of its age I can pronounce no
' opinion which would be of any value; but it appears to me not of modern date, that
' is, there are expressions which seem to belong to the earlier ages of the existing
' ballad-poetry, and that the incidents are too numerous, and of too romantic a cast, to
' allow of its being considered a modern invention.

' A certain lord has two daughters, the one "brown," the other "fair."   A knight
who presents himself to the father as a suitor is informed that with the brown he
' will give as a portion her weight in gold, and that he expects to receive her weight
' in gold from the person to whom he gives the fairer daughter.   The knight, of
course, selects the beauty, and to raise the money has recourse to a Jew usurer, who

supplies him with it, taking his bond for the repayment at a certain day, and in de-
‘ fault he is to lose several ounces of his flesh. They marry; in due time a son is born,
‘ and time also brings round the day when the money is to be repaid, or the forfeit taken.
‘ The knight, as the time of repayment drew near, is not prepared with the money, and
‘ the lady urges upon him, as the only resource, that they should fly beyond sea.   They
‘ go to Germany, where the Emperor, having learned the circumstances under which
‘ they had come into his dominions, built for them a “ court,” and showed them great
‘ respect, and the rather because they came from Britain, “ That blest land of fame.” ’

‘ Here they lived for some time in great felicity, till a “ Dutch lord,” who was in the
‘ Emperor’s court, wagered with the knight a ton of gold that he would “ enjoy his lady
‘ “ gay,” and that he would produce a diamond ring from her finger in proof.   The
‘ Dutch lord has recourse to what is the approved stratagem on such occasions; he
‘ bribes a waiting-maid of the lady, who steals the ring and gives it to him.   When
‘ the English knight sees the ring in the stranger’s possession he almost swoons; and
‘ then, in a state of distraction, flies to his house, and, meeting the lady, who had come
to the gate to welcome him, he throws her at once headlong into the moat.

‘ So cruel a murder shocks every one, and the knight is brought to trial, convicted,
‘ and sentenced to death.   While he is awaiting the execution of his sentence, there
‘ suddenly appears in the Emperor’s court another English knight attired in green, who
‘ easily prevails upon the Emperor to grant a second hearing of the case.   At this hear-
‘ ing the maid is brought to make confession of her guilt, and the court become struck
‘ with the possibility that the crime of murder may not have been committed, as the
‘ evidence went no further than to prove that the lady was thrown into the moat.   The
‘ life of the knight is thus saved, and he claims and receives from the Dutch lord the
‘ ton of gold which he had justly won.

‘ His mind bent on revenge, the Dutch lord sends information to the Jew where his
‘ debtor was living.   The exasperated Jew instantly repairs to the Emperor, and claims
‘ in his court, not the money due him, but the penalty of the bond.   While this claim
‘ is under consideration, the green knight again appears; mean as the verse is, a short
‘ specimen need not be withheld :

> ‘ Said the noble knight in green,
> ‘ “ Sir, may not your articles be seen ?”
> ‘ “ Yes, that they may,” replied the Jew,
> ‘ “ And I resolve to have my due.”
>
> ‘ Lo, then, the knight began to read :
> ‘ At length he said, “ I find, indeed,
> ‘ “ Nothing but flesh you are to have :”
> ‘ Answers the Jew, “ That’s all I crave.”
>
> ‘ The poor distressed knight was brought :
> ‘ The bloody-minded Jew, he thought
> ‘ That day to be revenged on him,
> ‘ And part his flesh from limb to limb.
>
> ‘ The knight in green said, “ Mr Jew,
> ‘ “ There’s nothing else but flesh your due,
> ‘ “ Then see no drop of blood you shed,
> ‘ “ For if you do, off goes your head ” ’

‘ The Jew hereupon acts as Shylock in the play.

'The father now appears. The report has reached him that his daughter has been
'drowned by her husband. He brings with him "many brave horses," one of which
'is purchased of him immediately by the green knight. The father is clamorous for
'justice, insisting that his child must have been murdered, and finally the knight is
'brought out to execution on his former sentence. At this juncture the knight in
'green again appears with the steed which he had purchased, and, to the surprise of
'every one, but most of all of the father, he runs his sword through the body of the
'noble animal, and lays it dead upon the place. The father expressing his astonish-
'ment at such an act, the knight in green argues with him that, as he had purchased
'the horse, he surely might do with it what he pleased; and then presses home upon
'him that he, having sold his daughter, the purchaser had an equally entire proprie-
'torship in her. Now comes the dénouement. The green knight retires, and re-
'appears in splendid female habiliments, when the father and husband recognize the
'lady who had been supposed to be drowned, and the Emperor "proclaims a universal
'"joy."

'Whether it may ultimately turn out that this ballad is earlier than the date of
'this play as an English ballad, and as it is evidently in some way connected with
'two of Shakespeare's plays, and has hitherto remained unnoticed, or at least not
'publicly noticed, either by the commentators on Shakespeare or the collectors
'of the ballad poetry of England, the preceding notice of it will not be thought
'misplaced.'

To return once more to Bishop PERCY. His note in the *Reliques* (vol. i, p. 189,
1765) is as follows:

'In the *Life of Pope Sixtus V, translated from the Italian of Greg. Leti, by the
'Rev. Mr. Farneworth* [p. 401, ed. 1779], is a remarkable passage to the following
'effect: It was reported in Rome that Drake had taken and plundered St. Domingo
'in Hispaniola, and carried off an immense booty. This account came in a private
'letter to Paul Secchi, a very considerable merchant in the city, who had large con-
'cerns in those parts, which he had insured. Upon receiving this news, he sent for
'the insurer, Sampson Ceneda, a Jew, and acquainted him with it. The Jew, whose
'interest it was to have such a report thought false, gave many reasons why it could
'not possibly be true, and, at last, worked himself into such a passion, that he said,
'"I'll lay you a pound of my flesh it is a lye." Such sort of wagers, it is well known,
'are often proposed by people of strong passions, to convince others that are incredu-
'lous or obstinate. Nothing is more common than to say, "I'll lay my life on it;"
'"I'll forfeit my right hand, if it is not true," &c. Secchi, who was of a fiery, hot
'temper, replied, "If you like it, I'll lay you a thousand crowns against a pound of
'"your flesh, that it is true." The Jew accepted the wager, and articles were imme-
'diately executed betwixt them, the substance of which was, That if Secchi won, he
'should himself cut the flesh, with a sharp knife, from whatever part of the Jew's
'body he pleased. Unfortunately for the Jew, the truth of the account was soon
'confirmed; and the Jew was almost distracted when he was informed that Secchi
'had solemnly sworn he would compel him to the exact performance of his contract,
'and was determined to cut a pound of flesh from that part of his body which it is
'not necessary to mention. A report of this transaction was brought to the Pope,
'who sent for the parties, and being informed of the whole affair, said, "When con-
'"tracts are made, it is just they should be fulfilled, as we intend this shall. Take a
'"knife, therefore, Secchi, and cut a pound of flesh from any part you please of the

' " Jew's body. We would advise you, however, to be very careful; for if you cut but
' " a scruple, or a grain, more or less than your due, you shall certainly be hanged; go,
' " and bring thither a knife, and a pair of scales, and let it be done in our presence."
' The merchant, at these words, began to tremble like an aspen leaf, and throwing him-
' self at his Holiness's feet, with tears in his eyes, protested, " It was far from his
' " thoughts to insist upon the performance of the contract." And being asked by the
' Pope what he demanded, answered, " Nothing, holy father, but your benediction, and
' " that the articles may be torn in pieces." Then, turning to the Jew, he asked him,
' " What he had to say, and whether he was content?" The Jew answered, " He
' " thought himself extremely happy to come off at so easy a rate, and that he was per-
' " fectly content." " But we are not content," replied Sixtus, " nor is there sufficient
' " satisfaction made to our laws; we desire to know what authority you have to lay
' " such wagers? The subjects of princes are the property of the state, and have no
' " right to dispose of their bodies, nor any part of them, without the express consent
' " of their sovereigns." They were both immediately sent to prison, and the governor
' ordered to proceed against them with the utmost severity of the law, that others
' might be deterred, by their example, from laying any more such wagers. The Gov-
' ernor, thinking to please Sixtus, and willing to know what sort of punishment he had
' a mind should be inflicted upon them, said, " Without doubt, they had been guilty of
' " a very great crime, and he thought they deserved each of them to be fined 1000
' " crowns." " To be fined, each of them, 1000 crowns!" answered Sixtus. " Do you
' " think that sufficient? What! shall any of our subjects presume to dispose of his
' " life without our permission? Is it not evident that the Jew has actually sold his
' " life, by consenting to have a pound of flesh cut from his body? Is not this a direct
' " suicide? And is it not likewise true that the merchant is guilty of downright, pre-
' " meditated murder, in making a contract with the other, that he knew must be the
' " occasion of his death if he insisted upon its being performed, as it is said he did?
' " Shall two such villains be excused for a simple fine?" The Governor alleging,
' " That Secchi protested he had not the least design of insisting upon the performance
' " of the contract, and that the Jew did not at all imagine he would when he laid the
' " wager," Sixtus replied, " These protestations were only made out of fear of pun-
' " ishment, and because they were in our presence, and therefore no regard ought to
' " be had to them; let them both be hanged; do you pass that sentence on them, and
' " we shall take care of the rest." In a word, they were both condemned to death, to
' the great terror and amazement of everybody, though no one durst open his mouth, or
' call it an unjust sentence. As Secchi was of a very good family, having many great
' friends and relations, and the Jew one of the most leading men of the synagogue,
' they both had recourse to petitions; strong application was made to Cardinal Mon-
' talto, to intercede with his Holiness, at least to spare their lives. Sixtus, who did not
' really design to put them to death, but to deter others from such practices, at last con-
' sented to change the sentence into that of the galleys, with liberty to buy off that too
' by paying each of them 2000 crowns, to be applied to the use of the hospital (which
' he had lately founded), before they were released.'

I have here given a much fuller extract from Leti than is given by Percy, who thus
continues in reference to Farneworth's translation:

' The Editor of that book is of opinion, That the scene between Shylock and Anto-
' nio is taken from this incident. But Mr Warton has, with more probability, referred it
to the [ballad of *Gernutus*], which would seem to have taken its rise from some such
' story. After all, we should be glad to know what authority Leti, who wrote in the

'time of Charles II, had for the foregoing fact, or, at least, for connecting it with the
'taking of St. Domingo by Drake; for this expedition did not happen till 1585, and it
'is very certain that a play of the *Jew* was mentioned by Gosson in 1579.'

As far as this story of Secchi and Ceneda is concerned, no one, I think, who has
read that very entertaining farrago of improbable gossip which Leti wrote as a *Life
of Pope Sixtus V*, will consider it as veracious history, or as any othei than one of those
pleasing little stories with which Leti lightened his pages. DOUCE considers it 'a mere
'fabrication, grafted on one of those that Leti had met with on the same subject;' and
HALLIWELL echoes the same opinion, adding that, 'Leti refers the narrative to the
'time of Elizabeth, but it was neither written nor printed till some time after the death
'of Shakespeare.'

To CAPELL belongs the credit of having discovered a story whose main features so
strongly resemble the story of The Bond that it has been widely accepted as the basis
of Shakespeare's play. 'The *Jew of Venice*,' says Capell (vol. i, p. 63), 'was a story
'exceedingly well known in Shakespeare's time; célebrated in ballads: and taken
'(perhaps) originally from an *Italian* book, intitl'd—"Il Pecorone:" the author of
'which calls himself,—*Ser Giovanni Fiorentino;* and writ his book, as he tells you
'in some humorous verses at the beginning of it, in 1378, three years after the death
'of Boccace: it is divided into *giornata's,* and the story we are speaking of, is in the
'first novel of the *giornata quarta;* Edit. 1565, octavo, *in Vinejia.* This novel
'Shakespeare certainly read; either in the original, or (which I rather think) in some
'translation that is not now to be met with, and form'd his play upon it. It was trans-
'lated anew, and made publick in 1755, in a small octavo pamphlet, printed for *M.
'Cooper:* and at the end of it, a novel of Boccace (the first of day the tenth) which,
'as the translator rightly judges, might possibly produce the scene of the caskets, sub-
'stituted by the Poet in place of one in the other novel, that was not proper for the
'stage.'

Although we of these latter days do not agree with the earlier Editors in our estimate of Shakespeare's learning, and cannot think with Steevens that if Shakespeare
was indebted to an Italian novelist, 'it *must* have been through the medium of a translation,' yet there is no difficulty in supposing that a translation of *Il Pecorone* existed
and was widely read, albeit no single copy has survived. Apparently, England was
flooded at that time with translations of Italian stories, if we may judge by the hot
indignation which their popularity and profusion excited in the breast of admirable
Roger Ascham, who, in his *Scholemaster*, 1570, inveighs most bitterly against the
introduction into England of 'the Religion, the learning, the policie, the experience,
the maners of *Italie*,' and then continues (p. 78, ed. Arber): 'These be the inchante-
mentes of *Circes*, brought out of *Italie*, to marre men's maners in England; much, by
example of ill life, but more by preceptes of fonde bookes, of late translated out of
Italian into English, sold in euery shop in London, commended by honest titles the
soner to corrupt honest maners; dedicated ouer boldlie to vertuous and honourable
personages, the easielier to begile simple and innocent wittes.' Again (on p. 81),
'There be moe of these vngratious bookes set out in Printe within these fewe
monethes, than haue bene sene in England many score yeare before.'

We need have no compunction, therefore, in supposing that Shakespeare was familiar with Ser Giovanni in English. The first translation, however, which is known to
us is that referred to by Capell, and of which Dr Johnson, in his Edition, gives the
following epitome, which, with some few changes, I much prefer to the original literal

translation, which they who list can find in Collier's *Shakespeare Library*, vol. ii, p. 65, &c., or in Hazlitt's reprint of the same:

There lived at Florence a merchant, whose name was Bindo. He was rich and had three sons. Being near his end, he called for the two eldest, and left them heirs; to the youngest he left nothing. This youngest, whose name was Giannetto, went to his father and said: What has my Father done? The father replied, Dear Giannetto, there is none to whom I wish better than to you. Go to Venice to your godfather, whose name is Ansaldo; he has no child, and has wrote to me often to send you thither to him. He is the richest merchant amongst the Christians; if you behave well, you will certainly be a rich man. The son answered, I am ready to do whatever my dear father shall command; upon which he gave him his benediction, and in a few days died.

Giannetto went to Ansaldo, and presented the letter given by his father before his death. Ansaldo reading the letter, cried out, My dearest godson is welcome to my arms. He then asked news of his father. Giannetto replied, He is dead. I am much grieved, replied Ansaldo, to hear of the death of Bindo; but the joy I feel in seeing you mitigates my sorrow. He conducted him to his house, and gave orders to his servants that Giannetto should be obeyed, and served with more attention than had been paid to himself. He then delivered him the keys of his ready money; and told him, Son, spend this money, keep a table, and make yourself known; remember that the more you gain the good will of everybody, the more you will be dear to me.

Giannetto now began to give entertainments. He was more obedient and courteous to Ansaldo, than if he had been an hundred times his father. Everybody in Venice was fond of him. Ansaldo could think of nothing but him: so much was he pleased with his good manners and behaviour.

It happened that two of his most intimate acquaintances designed to go with two ships to Alexandria, and told Giannetto he would do well to take a voyage and see the world. I would go willingly, said he, if my father Ansaldo will give leave. His companions go to Ansaldo, and beg his permission for Giannetto to go in the spring with them to Alexandria; and desire him to provide him a ship. Ansaldo immediately procured a very fine ship, loaded it with merchandise, adorned it with streamers and furnished it with arms; and, as soon as it was ready, he gave orders to the Captain and sailors to do everything that Giannetto commanded. It happened one morning early that Giannetto saw a gulph, with a fine port, and asked the Captain how the port was called? He replied, That place belongs to a widow lady, who has ruined many gentlemen. In what manner? says Giannetto. He answered, This Lady is a fine and beautiful woman, and has made a law that whoever arrives here must be her wooer, and if he can win her he must take her for his wife, and be lord of all the country; but if he cannot win her, he loses everything he has brought with him. Giannetto, after a little reflection, tells the Captain to get into the port. He was obeyed; and in an instant they slide into the port so easily that the other ships perceived nothing.

The lady was soon informed of it, and sent for Giannetto, who waited on her immediately. She, taking him by the hand, asked him who he was? whence he came? and if he knew the custom of the country? He answered, That the knowledge of that custom was his only reason for coming. The lady paid him great honours, and sent for barons, counts, and knights in great number, who were her subjects, to keep Giannetto company. These nobles were highly delighted with the good breeding and manners of Giannetto; and all would have rejoiced to have him for their lord.

The night being come, the lady said, It seems to be time to go to bed; and immediately two damsels enter with wine and sweetmeats. The lady entreats him to taste the wine; he takes the sweetmeats, and drinks some of the wine, which was prepared with ingredients to cause sleep. He then goes into the bed, where he instantly falls asleep and never wakes till late in the morning; but the lady rose with the sun and gave orders to unload the vessel, which she found full of rich merchandize. After nine o'clock the women servants go to the bedside, order Giannetto to rise and be gone, for he had lost the ship. The lady gave him a horse and money, and he leaves the place very melancholy, and goes to Venice. When he arrives, he dares not return home for shame; but at night goes to the house of a friend, who is surprised to see him, and inquires of him the cause of his return? He answers, his ship had struck on a rock in the night, and was broke in pieces.

This friend going one day to make visit to Ansaldo, found him very disconsolate. I fear, says Ansaldo, so much, that this son of mine is dead, that I have no rest. His friend told him that he had been shipwrecked, and has lost his all, but that he himself was safe. Ansaldo instantly gets up and runs to find him. My dear son, says he, you need not fear my displeasure; it is a common accident; trouble yourself no further. He takes him home, all the way telling him to be cheerful and easy.

The news was soon known all over Venice, and every one was concerned for Giannetto. Some time after, his companions arriving from Alexandria very rich, demanded what was become of their friend, and having heard the story ran to see him, and rejoiced with him for his safety; telling him next spring he might gain as much as he had lost the last. But Giannetto had no other thoughts than of his return to the lady; and was resolved to marry her, or die. Ansaldo told him frequently not to be cast down. Giannetto said he should never be happy till he was at liberty to make another voyage. Ansaldo provided another ship of more value than the first. He again entered the port of Belmonte, and the lady looking on the port from her bed-chamber, and seeing the ship, asked her maid if she knew the streamers? The maid said, it was the ship of the young man who arrived last year. You are in the right, answered the lady; he must surely have a great regard for me, for never any one came a second time; the maid said, she had never seen a more agreeable man. He went to the castle, and presented himself to the lady; who, as soon as she saw him, embraced him, and the day was passed in joy and revels. Bed-time being come, the lady entreated him to go to rest; when they were seated in the chamber, the two damsels enter with wine and sweetmeats; and having eaten and drunk of them, they retire, and immediately Giannetto falls asleep, and the lady lay down by his side; but he waked not the whole night. In the morning the lady rises, and gives orders to strip the ship. He has a horse and money given to him and away he goes, and never stops till he gets to Venice; and at night goes to the same friend, who with astonishment asked him, what was the matter? I am undone, says Giannetto. His friend answered, You are the cause of the ruin of Ansaldo, and your shame ought to be greater than the loss you have suffered. Giannetto lived privately many days. At last he took a resolution of seeing Ansaldo, who rose from his chair, and running to embrace him, told him he was welcome: Giannetto with tears returned his embraces. Ansaldo heard his tale: Do not grieve, my dear son, says he, we have still enough; the sea enriches some men, others it ruins.

Poor Giannetto's head was day and night full of the thoughts of his bad success. When Ansaldo inquired what was the matter, he confessed he could never be contented till he should be in a condition to regain all that he had lost. When Ansaldo found him resolved, he began to sell everything he had to furnish this other fine ship with merchandise; but as he wanted still ten thousand ducats, he applied himself to a Jew at Mestri, and borrowed them on condition that if they were not paid on the feast of St John in the next month of June, the Jew might take a pound of flesh from any part of his body he pleased. Ansaldo agreed, and the Jew had an obligation drawn, and witnessed, with all the form and ceremony necessary; and then counted him the ten thousand ducats of gold; with which Ansaldo bought what was still wanting for the vessel. This last ship was finer and better freighted than the other two, and his companions made ready for the voyage, with a design that whatever they gained should be for their friend. When it was time to depart Ansaldo told Giannetto, that since he well knew of the obligation to the Jew, he entreated that if any misfortune happened he would return to Venice, that he might see him before he died; and then he could leave the world with satisfaction; Giannetto promised to do everything that he conceived might give him pleasure. Ansaldo gave him his blessing, they took their leave, and the ships set out.

Giannetto had nothing in his head but to steal into Belmonte; and he prevailed with one of the sailors in the night to sail the vessel into the port. It was told the lady that Giannetto was arrived in port. She saw from the window the vessel, and immediately sent for him. Giannetto goes to the castle, the day is spent in joy and feasting; and to honour him a tournament is ordered, and many barons and knights tilted that day. Giannetto did wonders, so well did he understand the lance, and was so graceful a figure on horseback; he pleased so much, that all were desirous of having him for their lord.

The lady, when it was the usual time, catching him by the hand, begged him to take his rest. When he passed the door of the chamber, one of the damsels in a whisper said to him, Make a pretence to drink the liquor, but touch not one drop. The lady said, I know you must be thirsty, I must have you drink before you go to bed; immediately two damsels entered the room and presented the wine. Who can refuse wine from such beautiful hands? cries Giannetto: at which the lady smiled. Giannetto takes the cup, and making as if he had drank, pours the wine into his bosom. The lady thinking he had drank, says aside to herself with great joy, You must go, young man, and bring another ship, for this is condemned. Giannetto went to bed and began to snore as if he slept soundly. The lady perceiving this, laid herself down by his side. Giannetto at once exclaimed, Now I have gained the trial, and you must marry me. When Giannetto came out of his chamber he was knighted, and placed in the chair of state; had the sceptre put into his hand, and was proclaimed sovereign of the country, with great pomp and splendour; and when the lords and ladies were come to the castle, he married the lady in great ceremony.

Giannetto governed excellently, and caused justice to be administered impartially. He continued some time in this happy state, and never entertained a thought of poor Ansaldo, who had given his bond to the Jew for ten thousand ducats. But one day, as he stood at the window of the palace with his bride, he saw a number of people pass along the piazza, with lighted torches in their hands. What is the meaning of this? said he. The lady answered, They are artificers going to make their offerings at the Church of St John, this day being his festival. Giannetto instantly recollected Ansaldo, gave a great sigh, and turned pale. His lady enquired the cause of his sudden change. He said he felt nothing. She continued to press with great earnestness, till he was obliged to confess the cause of his uneasiness, that Ansaldo was engaged for the money, that the term was expired; and the grief he was in was lest his father should lose his life for him; that if the ten thousand ducats were not paid that day, he must lose a pound of his flesh. The lady told him to mount on horseback, and go by land the nearest way, to take some attendants, and an hundred thousand ducats; and not to stop until he arrived at Venice; and if he was not dead to bring Ansaldo to her. Giannetto takes horse, with twenty attendants, and makes the best of his way to Venice.

The time being expired, the Jew had seized Ansaldo, and insisted on having a pound of his flesh. He entreated him only to wait some days, that if his dear Giannetto arrived, he might have the pleasure of embracing him; the Jew replied he was willing to wait, but, says he, I will cut off the pound of flesh according to the words of the obligation; Ansaldo answered, that he was content.

Several merchants would have jointly paid the money; the Jew would not harken to the proposal, but insisted that he might have the satisfaction of saying, that he had put to death the greatest of the Christian merchants. Giannetto making all possible haste to Venice, his lady soon followed him in a lawyer's habit, with two servants attending her. Giannetto, when he came to Venice, goes to the Jew, and (after embracing Ansaldo) tells him he is ready to pay the money, and as much more as he should demand. The Jew said he would take no money, since it was not paid at the time due, but that he would have the pound of flesh. Every one blamed the Jew; but as Venice was a place where justice was strictly administered, and the Jew had his pretensions grounded on publick and received forms, their only resource was entreaty; and when the merchants of Venice applied to him he was inflexible. Giannetto offered him twenty thousand, then thirty thousand, afterwards, forty, fifty, and at last, an hundred thousand ducats. The Jew told him if he would give him as much gold as Venice was worth, he would not accept it; and, says he, you know little of me, if you think I will desist from my demand.

The lady now arrives in Venice, in her lawyer's dress; and alighting at an inn, the landlord asks of one of the servants who his master was? The servant answered, that he was a young lawyer who had finished his studies at Bologna. The landlord upon this shows his guest great civility; and when he attended at dinner, the lawyer inquiring how justice was administered in that city; he answered, justice in this place is too severe, and related the case of Ansaldo. Says the lawyer, this question may be easily answered. If you can answer it, says the landlord, and save this worthy man from death, you will get the love and esteem of all the best men of this city. The lawyer caused a proclamation to be made, that whosoever had any law matters to determine, they should have recourse to him: so it was told to Giannetto that a famous lawyer was come from Bologna, who could decide all cases in law. Giannetto proposed to the Jew to apply to this lawyer. With all my heart, says the Jew; but let who will come, I will stick to my bond. They came to this judge and saluted him. Giannetto did not remember him; for he had disguised his face with the juice of certain herbs. Giannetto and the Jew each told the merits of the cause to the judge; who, when he had taken the bond and read it, said to the Jew, I must have you take the hundred thousand ducats, and release this honest man, who will always have a grateful sense of the favour done to him. The Jew replied, I will do no such thing. The judge answered, it will be better for you. The Jew was positive to yield nothing. Upon this they go to the tribunal appointed for such judgements; and our judge says to the Jew, Do you cut a pound of this man's flesh where you choose. The Jew ordered him to be stripped naked; and takes in his hand a razor, which had been made on purpose. Giannetto seeing this, turning to the judge, this, says he, is not the favour I asked of you. Be quiet, says he, the pound of flesh is not yet cut off. As soon as the Jew was going to begin, Take care what you do, says the judge, if you take more or less than a pound, I will order your head to be struck off; and beside, if you shed one drop of blood you shall be put to death. Your paper makes no mention of the shedding of blood, but says expressly that you may take a pound of flesh, neither more nor less. He immediately sent for the executioner to bring the block and axe; and now, says he, if I see one drop of blood, off goes your head. At length the Jew, after much wrangling, told him, Give me the hundred thousand ducats, and I am content. No, says the judge, cut off your pound of flesh according to your bond; why did you not take the money when it was offered? The Jew came down to ninety, then to eighty thousand; but the judge was still resolute. Giannetto told the judge to give what he required, that Ansaldo might have his liberty; but he replied, let me manage him. Then the Jew would have taken fifty thousand; he said, I will not give you a penny. Give me at least, says the Jew, my own ten thousand ducats, and a curse confound you all. The judge replies, I will give you nothing; if you will have the pound of flesh, take it; if not, I will order your bond to be protested and annulled. The Jew seeing he could gain nothing, tore in pieces the bond in a great rage; Ansaldo was released, and conducted home with great joy by Giannetto, who carried the hundred thousand ducats to the inn to the lawyer. The lawyer said, I do not want money; carry it back to your lady, that she may not say that you have squandered it away idly. Says Giannetto, my lady is so kind, that I might spend four times as much without incurring her displeasure. How are you pleased with the lady? says the lawyer. I love her better than any earthly thing, answers Giannetto. Nature seems to have done her utmost in forming her. If you will come and see her, you will be surprised at the honours she will shew you. I cannot go with you, says the lawyer; but since you speak so much good of her, I must desire you to present my respects to her. I will not fail, Giannetto answered; and now let me entreat you to accept of some of the money. While he was speaking, the lawyer observed a ring on his finger, and said, if you will give me this ring, I shall seek no other reward. Willingly, says Giannetto; but as it is a ring given me by my lady, to wear for her sake, I have some reluctance to part with it, and she, not seeing it on my finger, will believe that I have given it to a woman. Says the lawyer, she esteems you sufficiently to credit what you tell her, and you may say you made a present of it to me; but I rather think you want to give it to some former mistress here in Venice. So great, says Giannetto, is the love and reverence I bear to her, that I would not change her for any woman in the world. After this he takes the ring from his finger, and presents it to him. I have still a favour to ask, says the lawyer. It shall be granted, says Giannetto. It is, replied he, that you do not stay any time here, but go as soon as possible to your lady. It appears to me a thousand years till I see her, answered Giannetto; and immediately they take leave of each other. The lawyer embarked and left Venice. Giannetto took leave of his Venetian friends, and carried Ansaldo with him, and some of his old acquaintance accompanied them.

The lady arrived some days before; and having resumed her female habit, pretended to have spent the time at the baths; and now gave orders to have the streets lined with tapestry; and when Giannetto and Ansaldo were landed, all the court went out to meet them. When they arrived at the palace, the lady ran to embrace Ansaldo, but feigned anger against Giannetto, tho' she loved him excessively: yet the feastings, tilts, and diversions, went on as usual, at which all the lords and ladies were present. Giannetto seeing that his wife did not receive him with her accustomed good countenance, called her and would have saluted her. She told him she wanted not his caresses; I am sure, says she, you have been lavish of them to some of your former mistresses. Giannetto began to make excuses. She asked him where was the ring she had given him? It is no more than what I expected, cries Giannetto, and I was in the right to say you would be angry with me; but I swear by all that is sacred, and by your dear self, that I gave the ring to the lawyer who gained our cause. And I can swear, says the lady, with as much solemnity, that you gave the ring to a woman; therefore, swear no more. Giannetto protested that what he had told her was true, and that he said all this to the lawyer when he asked for the ring. The lady replied, you would have done much better to stay at Venice with your mistresses, for I fear they all wept when you came away. Giannetto's tears began to fall, and in great sorrow he assured her that what she supposed could not be true. The lady seeing his tears, which were dag-gers in her bosom, ran to embrace him, and in a fit of laughter showed the ring, and told him that she was herself the lawyer, and how she obtained the ring. Giannetto was greatly astonished, finding it all true, and told the story to the nobles and to his companions; and this heightened greatly the love between him and his lady. He then called the damsel, who had given him the good advice in the evening not to drink the liquor, and gave her to Ansaldo for a wife; and they spent the rest of their lives in great felicity and contentment.

DOUCE says (i, 280): 'A part of the novel in the *Pecorone* is most likely of Oriental 'origin, and might have been transmitted to Ser Giovanni from the same source that 'supplied Boccaccio and many of the French minstrels with their stories, viz. the 'Crusades.'

SKOTTOWE (i, 321): 'The similarity between the novel and the play is striking. In 'both the money engaged for by the bond is borrowed, not for the use of the borrower, 'but to enable a young man to obtain the hand of a wealthy lady resident at Belmont. 'The forfeiture of the same portion of flesh is stipulated on failure of payment, and the 'flesh, in both instances, is to be taken from what part of the merchant's body pleased 'the Jew; who, in each case, is offered ten times the amount of his debt by the person 'for whom it was contracted. The bride, in both cases, arrives at Venice disguised as 'a lawyer, and interposes the same insurmountable obstacles to the exaction of the 'bloody penalty. Both the fair judges refuse pecuniary recompense; both request from 'the fingers of their husbands rings which they themselves had given to them, and the 'same species of *badinage* is the consequence of compliance when the ladies resume 'their own characters at Belmont.'

SPEDDING (*Cornhill Maga.*, March, 1880, p. 282): 'I suppose nobody who reads 'this story and knows the play,—two conditions which do not seem to have been 'generally united,—will doubt that Shakespeare had either read or heard it, and that 'it was from this . . . . that he derived his idea, not only of the forfeiture of the pound 'of flesh, but of the entire train of incidents, and the characters and relations of the 'persons of the drama. . . . . The changes which he introduced were only such as the 'conversion of a narrative into an actable play required. The action had to be brought 'within compass; the stage to be peopled; the persons to speak and act, instead of 'being described; new incidents to be invented or imported for entertainment and 'variety. But all this he did in careful conformity with the fundamental conception 'of the several characters as indicated in the old story. Giannetto's first two voyages 'being ignored, the play begins at once with the preparations for the third, which 'involves the bargain with the Jew; whereby, without sacrificing anything material,

'the action is considerably shortened. The original condition of the marriage, being
'at once unpresentable to a Shakespearian audience and irreconcilable with the lady's
'character as shown in the sequel, is rejected altogether; but, in substituting for it the
'device of the three caskets, care is taken to preserve all the essential features of the
'situation. Bassanio, having run in debt by living beyond his income, resolves to try
'his chance with a great heiress,—a lady for whom in her father's time he had con-
'ceived an affection, which he had reason to believe was mutual,—but who could only
'be sought in marriage upon the perilous condition of losing all if a riddle were not
'rightly read. To furnish himself for the adventure he has to borrow money from his
'kinsman and dearest friend and benefactor, Antonio; who, in order to supply him
'without delay, borrows it from Shylock on the security of the pound of flesh. Thus
'we have Bassanio and Antonio essentially in the same condition towards each other
'as Giannetto and Ansaldo when parting for the final voyage; while Bassanio, as soon
'as he has chosen the right casket, is in exactly the same position as Giannetto after
'the successful performance of his appointed task; and in all the scenes that follow
'we have only to imagine Giannetto in Bassanio's place, and we feel that he would
'have both spoken and acted in the same way,—that the characters are, in fact, iden-
'tical. So, again, the Ansaldo of the story and the Antonio of the play are only two
'portraits of the same man by different artists, one of whom sees further into him than
the other. We are not told by the novelist that Ansaldo suffered from a constitutional
'depression of spirits, but it probably occurred to Shakespeare as necessary to account
'for that extraordinary indifference to all mortal accidents (the happiness of his adopted
'son excepted), which, in the degree to which it is carried in the novel, he appears to
'have thought impossible in nature after all, and has, therefore, shown in Antonio
'much mitigated; for whereas, Ansaldo, knowing himself to be ruined, signs the bond
'with a clear presentiment of the consequence, and yet asks Giannetto for nothing
'more than a promise that he will see him before he dies, Antonio when he signs,
'though short of ready money for the moment, is still in the full flow of his fortunes,
'and laughs at the idea of being called on to pay the forfeit. It is true that when the
'danger fronts him, and cannot be escaped, he meets it as patiently, and with as much
'apparent indifference, as Ansaldo,—making no vain remonstrance, not complaining of
'the rigour of the law, but justifying its execution, and content to die, provided only
'that he may see Bassanio again before he is put to death. But there is a great differ-
'ence between accepting such a fate with equanimity when it is inevitable, and delibe-
'rately incurring it when it is foreseen and may be declined.

'Then, again, the absolute inoffensiveness of Ansaldo, who does not seem to have
'uttered a harsh word, or entertained an unkind thought against anybody,—with whom
'the very man who is avowing his determination to take his life, though all Venice were
'offered him to spare it, does not pretend any cause except his being the greatest of the
'Christian merchants,—seemed to make the Jew's proceeding too monstrous to be endur-
'able by an English audience. Such malice needed some provocation to make it cred-
'ible enough for the human imagination, and a probable cause of provocation readily
'offered itself in the disputes which must have occurred on the Rialto between two
'such men. A man who would enforce his contract for a pound of flesh in such a
'case was sure in all his transactions to take advantages of the helpless, which a lib-
'eral and beneficent merchant would be sure to be disgusted with and interfere to
'thwart. On such occasions feelings would be expressed and words uttered which
would not sting the less for being just and well deserved. And that this was the
real history of the revengeful hatred on one side, and the contemptuous dislike on

'the other, we are made to understand at once, as soon as they meet, by the irritating
'and sarcastic speech of Shylock (finding himself for the first time at an advantage)
'and the angry retort which it provokes from Antonio. This revelation of their
'respective feelings towards each other shows ground enough for Shylock's malice to
'bring it within the range, not indeed of human *sympathy*, which was not intended, but
'of possibility in human nature. We can imagine nature so diseased and perverted as
'to be capable of it without ceasing to be human. . . . . If the characters of Bassanio,
'Antonio, and Shylock are manifestly and directly derived from Ser Giovanni's story,
'it need hardly be said that the lady of Belmonte suggested the idea of Portia, every
'one of whose qualities, as we see them brought out in the play by Shakespeare's own
'hand,—the generosity, the affection, the spirit, the intellect, the gayety, and playful-
'ness,—he found hints of in the novelist's account of the lady's proceedings between
'her discovery of Ansaldo's position and her reception of him and her husband at
'Belmonte. What need, then, have we to seek further, either for the source of the
'plot, or the choice of the subject, or the manner of its treatment?'

Thus far we have examined the *Ballad* source started by Warton, the *Leti* source by
Farneworth, and the *Pecorone* source by Capell, and all of them dealing with the Pound
of Flesh or the Bond Story. Still harping on that, we must now go back to Tyrwhitt,
who, in the Variorum of 1773, suggested that a 'common *remote* origin' might be found
for both the Bond and the Casket Stories in the *Gesta Romanorum*, a collection of
stories presumably compiled towards the end of the 13th Century in England.* 'The
Gesta Romanorum, in its original form,' says its admirable Editor, Mr Herrtage, in the
Early English Text Society's Series, 'is a collection of fictitious narratives in Latin,
'compiled from Oriental apologues, monkish legends, classical stories, tales of chron-
'iclers, popular traditions, and other sources, which it would be now difficult and per-
'haps impossible to discover.'
Tyrwhitt was obliged to say 'remote' origin, because 'the completest copy' he had
ever seen (Harl. 2270) was not only a MS, but in Latin, and, in Tyrwhitt's days, it
was not to be supposed that, in that form and in that language, it was either accessible
or intelligible to Shakespeare.
An English translation, however, did exist, and was popular in Shakespeare's time.
Originally it was printed by Wynkyn de Worde, presumably, according to Herrtage, in
1510–15, and of this issue but one single copy survives; Dr Farmer cites it, and Tyrwhitt may have seen it, and it is now one of the treasures of St John's College, Cambridge.
The editions that were popular in Queen Elizabeth's reign were brought out by one
Richard Robinson, and to the number of no less than six between 1577 and 1601.
Although Robinson speaks of having 'translated' the *Gesta Romanorum*, and that it
was 'by mee perused, corrected, and bettered,' yet it is known from the very few copies
(only two) that survive of all these six editions, that he retained the same number and
the same order of the stories as in Wynkyn de Worde. Now, in Wynkyn de Worde,
and in Robinson's re-issue, the Bond Story is not to be found. The Casket Story is
there, but the Bond Story is not.† I think, therefore, we may hold Tyrwhitt justified
in thinking that the *Gesta Romanorum* was only a 'remote' source of the Bond Story.

---

* Oesterley, as quoted by Herrtage, p. xvii.

† My authorities for all that I say about the *Gesta Romanorum* are Warton's *Hist. of Eng. Poetry*,
1781, iii, xlix; Douce, i, 272, and the admirable exhaustive *Introduction* by S. J. Herrtage, of the
Early Eng. Text Society.

Nevertheless, an early English version of the *Gesta Romanorum* containing this Story does exist, but it is a Manuscript (Harl. 7333) of the time of Henry the Sixth, about 1440. This version Douce printed for the first time, I think; and he did so, not because he believed it to be the direct source of Shakespeare's plot, but as 'an interesting specimen of ancient English.'

It is scarcely worth while to reprint it word for word here; it is readily accessible in Douce, in the *Early English Text Society's* Series, and it is also given entire in Halliwell. Substantially it is the same story as in the *Pecorone*, but instead of the drugged wine there was 'bi-tweene the shete and the couerlyte of the bed a letter of swiche vertu, 'that who so euer gothe to bed he shall anon falle in to a dede slepe.' This secret was told to the knight by Virgile, 'the philesofere,' whom he consulted, and the knight exorcised the spell by removing the letter. The bribe of 'an c. marke of florens,' which 'the mayde' demanded, the knight had been obliged to borrow of a marchaunt 'in conducion, that yf thowe kepe not thi day of payment, hit shalle be lefulle to me 'for to draw awey alle the flesh of thi body froo the bone, with a sharp swerde.' In the charms of his love's society the knight 'for-gate the marchaunt; and the day of 'payment was passid by the space of xiiij dayes.' The knight offered his creditor double payment, in vain. The merchant refused, even for the wealth of the whole city, to forgo the penalty, and 'anon he made the knighte to be I-take, and lad to the 'castell, and sette him in a safe warde, abydinge the Iustice.' On the trial the Judge decides that as the contract was made with the knight's full consent, and by his own act, 'he shal Resseyve as he servithe; and therefore this merchaunt shalle haue cove-'naunt, as lawe wolle.' But the 'damysell' was not idle; through spies she learned that the knight had fallen under the law, and thereupon 'she kytte of al the longe her 'of hir hede, and cladde hir in precious clothing like to a man;' and went to the palace and announced to the Judge that she had come to deliver the knight from the merchant. After the Judge had again expounded the law, the 'damisell turnid to the 'marchaunt and saide, "der frend, what profite is it to the that this knighte that '"stondithe her redy to the dome, be slayne? it wer better to the to have monye, than '"to have him slayne." "Thou spekist al in veyne," quod the merchant, "for with '"oute dowte I wolle have the lawe, sithe he bonde him so frely; and therefor he '"shalle have noon other grace than lawe wolle; for he come to me, and I not to '"him; I desirid him not thereto a-yenste his wille." To the offer of his "monye '"double," or of any amount that he chose to demand, the merchant replied, "thow '"harde me neuer seye, but that I wolde have my covenaunt kepte." "Sothely," 'seyde she, "and thou shalt, trowe me," whereupon she calls all to witness how much 'she had offered and how the merchant steadily refused and demanded the lawe, "and '"that likithe me moche. And therefor, lordinges, that bethe her, herithe me what I '"shalle seye." She acknowledges that the knight had bound himself that the "mar-'"chaunt shulde have power to kitte his fleshe fro the boons, but there was no coue-'"naunt made of sheding of blode; there of was nothing I-spoke. And therefor late '"him set hond on him anoon; and yf he shede ony bloode with his shavinge of the '"fleshe, for sothe then shalle the kynge have good lawe vpon him." And when the 'marchaunt harde this, he said, "yef me my monye, and I foryeve my accion." "For '"sothe," quod she, "thowe shalt not have oo penye; for a-for al this companye I "proferid to the al that I myght, and thou forsoke hit, and saydist withe a lowde "voyse, I shalle have my covenaunte; and therfor do thi beste withe him, but loke '"that thow shede no blode, I charge the, for it is not thin, ne no covenaunt was there '"of." Thenne the marchaunt seynge this, yede awey confus, and so was the knightes lyf sauid, & no penye I-payde. And she yede home ayene, and dude of that clothinge, & clothid hir as she was afor, like to a woman. And the knighte yede home a-yene; and the damisell turnid, and met him, and askid howe he had I-spedde, as thowhe she had not knowen ther of. "A! lady," quod he, "this day was I in poynt to be "dede for thy love, but as I was in point to be dampnid, there came in sodeynlye a '"knite, a fair and wel I-shape, the whiche I sawe neuer afor; and he deliuerid me '"by his Excellent wisdam, bothe from dethe and eke from payment of moneye." '"Thenne were thow," quod she, "vnkynde, that woldest nat bidde that knighte to '"mete, that so faire had savid the." He aunswerde there to, & saide, that he come 'sodenly, and sodenly yede. Thenne seide she, "knowiste thow him, if thou seye '"him?" "yee," quod he, "Right wele." She yede vp, and cladde hir as she dide 'afore; and then she yede forthe, and the knighte knewe her thenne wele, and for Ioye 'fel dovne vpon hire, and saide, "blessid be thow, & the houre in the whiche I fyrste '"knew the!" And he wepte; and aftir he weddid hir, and livid & deyde in the 'service of god; and yelde to god goode sowlis.'

In the Variorum of 1793, Malone brought forward 'a Persian manuscript in the pos 'session of Ensign Thomas Munro,' at Tanjore. The age of the MS could not be determined; several leaves at the beginning and the end were lacking. It contained the following story, translated by Mr Munro :
'It is related that in the town of Syria a poor Mussulman lived in the neighbour- 'hood of a rich Jew. One day he went to the Jew, and said, "Lend me 100 dinars, '"that I may trade with it, and I will give thee a share of the gain." This Mussul- 'man had a beautiful wife, and the Jew had seen and fallen in love with her, and 'thinking this a lucky opportunity, he said, "I will not do thus, but I will give thee a '"hundred dinars, with this condition, that after six months thou shalt restore it to '"me. But give me a bond in this form, that if the term of the agreement shall be '"exceeded one day, I shall cut a pound of flesh from thy body, from whatever part I '"choose." The Jew thought that by this means he might perhaps come to enjoy the 'Mussulman's wife. The Mussulman was dejected, and said, "How can this be?" 'But as his distress was extreme, he took the money on that condition, and gave the 'bond, and set on a journey; and in that journey he acquired much gain, and he was 'every day saying to himself, "God forbid that the term of the agreement should pass '"away, and the Jew bring vexation upon me." He therefore gave a hundred gold 'dinars into the hand of a trusty person, and sent him home to give it to the Jew. But 'the people of his own house, being without money, spent it in maintaining themselves. 'When he returned from his journey, the Jew required payment of the money, and the 'pound of flesh. The Mussulman said, "I sent thy money a long time ago." The 'Jew said, "Thy money came not to me." When this, on examination, appeared to 'be true, the Jew carried the Mussulman before the Cazi, and represented the affair. 'The Cazi said to the Mussulman, "Either satisfy the Jew, or give the pound of flesh." 'The Mussulman not agreeing to this, said, "Let us go to another Cazi." When they 'went, he also spoke in the same manner. The Mussulman asked the advice of an 'ingenious friend. He said, "Say to him, Let us go to the Cazi of Hems. Go there, '"for thy business will be well." Then the Mussulman went to the Jew, and said, '"I shall be satisfied with the decree of the Cazi of Hems;" the Jew said, "I also '"shall be satisfied." Then both departed for the city of Hems. When they pre- 'sented themselves before the judgement-seat, the Jew said, "O my Lord Judge, this '"man borrowed an hundred dinars of me, and pledged a pound of flesh from his own

' "body. Command that he give the money and the flesh." It happened that the
' Cazi was the friend of the father of the Mussulman, and for this respect, he said to
' the Jew, " Thou sayest true, it is the purport of the bond;" and he desired that they
' should bring a sharp knife. The Mussulman, on hearing this, became speechless.
' The knife being brought, the Cazi turned his face to the Jew, and said, " Arise, and
' " cut one pound of flesh from the body of him, in such a manner, that there may not
' " be one grain more or less, and if more or less thou shalt cut, I shall order thee to
' " be killed." The Jew said, " I cannot. I shall leave this business and depart."
' The Cazi said, " Thou mayest not leave it." He said, " O Judge, I have released
' " him." The Judge said, " It cannot be; either cut the flesh or pay the expense of
' " his journey." It was settled at two hundred dinars : the Jew paid another hundred,
' and departed.

STEEVENS : ' To the collection of novels, &c., wherein the plot of the foregoing play
' occurs, may be added another, viz. from *Roger Bontemps en Belle Humeur*. In the
' story here related of the Jew and the Christian, the Judge is made to be Solyman,
' Emperor of the Turks. See the Edition of 1731, tom. ii, p. 105.

' Perhaps this Tale (like that of Parnell's Hermit) may have found its way into every
' language.'

DOUCE (i, 278) says that a similar story is related in Gladwin's *Persian Moonshee*,
story 13 (which Halliwell gives, and which appears to have been copied in a translation of ' Tales told in the Deccan,' as pointed out by Mr G. L. Gomme in *The Athenæum*, 18 Oct., 1880) : ' And another, likewise from an Oriental source, in the *British
' Magazine* for 1800, p. 159. In Tyron, *Recueil de plusieures plaisantes nouvelles*, &c.,
' Anvers, 1590, a Christian borrows 500 ducats of a Jew at Constantinople on condition
' of paying two ounces of flesh for usury. At the expiration of the term the Christian
' refuses to pay more than the principal. The matter is brought before the Emperor
' Solyman, who orders a razor to be brought, and admonishes the Jew not to cut off
' more or less than the two ounces, on pain of death. The Jew gives up the point.
' The same story occurs in the *Tresor des récreations*, Douay, 1625, p. 27 ; in *Doctæ
' nugæ Gaudensij, Jocosi*, 1713, p. 23 ; in the *Courier facetieux*, Lyon, 1650, p. 109 ;
in the *Chasse ennuy*, Paris, 1645, p. 49 ; in Corrozet's *Divers propos mémorables*, 1577,
' p. 77.' [Of this, also, Halliwell gives a translation, which was published in London,
1602. It is merely the same old story.] ' It has been imitated by Antony Munday
' in his *Astræpho*, &c., 1580. Instead of the cutting off a pound of flesh, it is agreed
' that one of the party's eyes shall be pulled out.'

It is over eighty years ago that Douce collected these various versions, and since
then here and there others have been added. SIMROCK thinks that the conclusion
that the story is of ' Oriental origin is too hasty ; the East has, in many forms, received
' reflex impressions from the West, and has taken back, for the fictions which it lent, a
' rich return of others transplanted thence. The internal form of the story must decide
' its origin.'

SIMROCK, again, thinks that the real meaning of the story is to represent the triumph
of the *æquitas* over the *jus strictum*. By the severe Roman law of The Twelve Tables
creditors could cut to pieces their debtors upon proof of their debt, and without any
express provision when the loan was made, and they need be under no restriction as
to the exact amount of their slice. [See Muirhead, *post.*—ED.] When, therefore,
this old law has to be revived by express agreement, and is further restricted to absolute
exactness, then Simrock thinks we have the meaning of the Bond Story. ' Our opin-
' ion,' says Simrock (p. 56), ' that the story contains an old law anecdote, and one, too,

full of the most meaning and incident that can exist, is supported by the form of the
'fable in the old *Meistergesang of Kaiser Karls Recht*, printed at Bamberg in 1493,
'the contents of which are thus given in the *Old German Museum*, ii, 279 : "A rich
'" merchant left his whole possession to his son, which he squandered in the first year.
'" He then borrows a thousand guilders of a Jew, to try his fortune abroad.   The con-
'" dition is the one already known.   He returns with great gain, but does not find the
'" Jew at home, and so overstays the time ; at least, the Jew maintains that he has not
'" fulfilled the contract, because the time has elapsed.   They conclude to travel to the
'" Emperor Charles (this must be Charlemagne) that he may decide the dispute.   On
'" the road the merchant falls asleep on his horse, and runs over and kills a child who
'" was in the way.   The child's father proclaims him for a murderer, and follows him,
'" to make good his accusation, to the Emperor's court.   Here the merchant is taken
'" into custody, but by a new misfortune falls out of the window, and kills an old
'" knight who was sitting below on a bench.   The son of this knight now comes for-
'" ward as plaintiff against the merchant, so that the Emperor has three causes to
'" decide.   The dispute with the Jew is settled in the well-known manner ; the claim
'" as to the child he settles in a less satisfactory way.   ' Let him beget thee another.'
'" ' Nay,' said the man, ' I will rather say nothing more of my loss.'   He advises the
'" son of the old knight, as the most satisfactory manner of avenging his father, to go
'" up into the chamber, have the merchant placed upon the bench, and the young man
'" may then fall upon him and kill him.   But the young knight fears he may miss him,
'" and so gives up his claim to vengeance." '

M. D. CONWAY (*The Wandering Jew*, 1881, p. 128) maintains that the chief features
of the story have a deep meaning and lie at the very foundations of our moral nature.
' Side by side, in all ages and races, have struggled with each other the principle of
' Retaliation and that of Forgiveness.'   The following legend was related to him by a
Hindu as one he had been told in his childhood : ' The chief of the Indian triad, Indra,
' pursued the god Agni.   Agni changed himself into a dove in order to escape ; but
' Indra changed himself to a hawk, to continue the pursuit.   The dove took refuge
' with Vishnu, second person of the triad, the Hindu Saviour.   Indra, flying up, de-
' manded the dove ; Vishnu, concealing it in his bosom, refused to give up the dove.
' Indra then took an oath, that if the dove were not surrendered he would tear from
' Vishnu's breast an amount of flesh equal to the body of the dove.   Vishnu still
refused to surrender the bird, but bared his breast.   The divine hawk tore from it the
' exact quantity, and the drops of blood,—the blood of a Saviour,—as they fell to the
' ground wrote the Scriptures of the Vedas.   The earliest version, probably B. C. 300,
' is the story in the Mahábhárata (*Vana parva*) of the trial of the best of mankind,
' King Usinára.   Indra and Agni, wishing to test his fidelity to the laws of righteous-
' ness, assume the forms of falcon and pigeon.   The latter (Agni), pursued by the for-
' mer (Indra), seeks and receives the king's protection.   The falcon demands the
' pigeon, and is refused on the ground that it is written that, to kill a twice-born man,
' to kill a cow, and to abandon a being that has taken refuge with one, are equal sins.
' This is a quotation from the laws of Manu.   The falcon argues that it is the law of
' nature that it shall feed on pigeons, and a statute against nature is no law.   He (the
' falcon) will be starved, consequently his mate and little ones must perish, and thus, in
' preserving one, the king will slay many.   The falcon is offered by Usinára other food,
' —a boar, bull, gazelle,—but the falcon declares that it is not the law of its nature to
eat such things.   The king then declares that he will not give up the pigeon, but he
will give anything else in his power which the falcon may demand.   The falcon

'replies that he can only accept a quantity of the king's own flesh equal in weight to
'the pigeon's body. Usinára gladly accedes to this substitution. Balances are pro-
'duced, and the pigeon is placed in one scale. The king cuts off a piece of his flesh
'that appears large enough, but is insufficient; he cuts again and again, but still the
'pigeon outweighs his piled-up flesh. Finally, all his flesh gone, the king gets into the
scale himself. The two gods then resume their divine shape, announce to Usinára
'that for the sacrifice he has made he will be glorified in all worlds throughout eter-
'nity, and the king ascends transfigured into heaven.' [Many variations of this legend
have been collected by the learned author, and are duly set forth in the highly interesting volume from which the foregoing extract is taken, but lack of space forbids more
than this reference to them here.]

But however interesting all these stories, and their geographical distribution, may
be in an archæological view, surely their connection with Shakespeare's Shylock and
Anthonio is the thinnest gossamer. I have, nevertheless, thought it my duty, in an
edition like the present, to give them all, or allusions to them, seeing that various editors, commentators, and critics have at times laid stress on one or other of them, or at
least alluded to them with approbation, as possible sources of the Plot.

There remains one other book to which reference has been made several times, and
in which two or three points of resemblance have been detected, which are so emphatic
that, as we have seen by the allusions in the preceding pages, the date of this volume
has much influenced several editors in fixing the date of Shakespeare's comedy.

It was Dr FARMER who first called attention to this book, whereof the long title
runs thus: *The Orator: Handling a hundred feuerall Difcourfes, in forme of Declamations: Some of the Arguments being drawne from* Titus Liuius *and other ancient
Writers, the reft of the Authors owne inuention: Part of which are of matters happened in our Age. Written in French by Alexander Siluayn, and Englifhed by L. P.*
London. Printed by Adam Islip, 1596. The initials L. P. stand, as the Dedication
shows, for Lazarus Piot, which again, according to Ritson, stands for Anthony Munday.

This volume is of more than usual attractiveness, whereof but little intimation
is given in the title. It consists of a number of incidents, historical and imaginary,
involving in the mere statement questions of morality on which much can be said
for both sides; the questions are not of that chop-logic nature which at one time was
the delight of Schoolmen, and which Rabelais ridiculed in his books at St Victor:
utrum Chimæra in vacuo bombinans poffit comedere secundas intentiones, but many
of them are questions which have an interest even at the present day, such as, for
instance, 'Declamation 81, Of a Chirurgion, who murthered a man to see the mouing
of a quicke heart,' wherein some of the arguments of the advocates of vivisection are
duly set up and overthrown. Other 'Declamations' are referred to at III, ii, 34, and
again in the account of the *Jud von Venedig, post.* The Declamation, however, which
in many particulars bears a striking resemblance to Shylock's speech in the Trial Scene,
is the Ninety-fifth, and is as follows:

DECLAMATION. 95.

Of a Jew, who would for his debt haue a pound of the flefh of a Chriftian.

*A Iew vnto whom a Chriftian Marchant ought nine hundred crownes, would haue
fummoned him for the fame in Turckie: the Merchant, becaufe he would not be dij-*

credited, promiſed to pay the ſaid ſumme within the tearme of three months, and if he
paied it not, he was bound to giue him a pound of the fleſh of his bodie.　The tearme
being paſt ſome fifteene daies, the Iew refuſed to take his money, and demaunded the
pound of fleſh : the ordinarie Iudge of that place appointed him to cut a iuſt pound
of the Chriſtian's fleſh, and if he cut either more or leſſe, then his owne head ſhould be
ſmitten off : the Iew appealed from this ſentence, vnto the chiefe iudge, ſaying :

Impoſſible is it to breake the credite of trafficke amongſt men without great detriment
vnto the Commonwealth : wherefore no man ought to bind himſelfe vnto ſuch coue-
nants which hee cannot or wil not accompliſh, for by that means ſhould no man feare
to be deceaued, and credit being maintained, euery man might be aſſured of his owne;
but ſince deceit hath taken place, neuer wonder if obligations are made more rigorous
& ſtrict then they were wont, ſeeing that although the bonds are made neuer ſo ſtrong,
yet can no man be very certaine that he ſhal not be a loſer.　It ſeemeth at the firſt
ſight, that it is a thing no leſſe ſtrange then cruel, to bind a man to pay a pound of the
fleſh of his bodie, for want of money : Surely, in that it is a thing not vſuall, it appeareth to be ſomewhat the more admirable, but there are diuers others that are more
cruell, which becauſe they are in vſe ſeeme nothing terrible at all : as to binde al the
bodie vnto a moſt lothſome priſon, or vnto an intollerable ſlauerie, where not only the
whole bodie but alſo al the ſences and ſpirits are tormented, the which is commonly
practiſed, not only betwixt thoſe which are either in ſect or Nation contrary, but alſo
euen amongſt thoſe that are all of one ſect and nation, yea amongſt neighbours and
kindred, & euen amongſt Chriſtians it hath ben ſeene, that the ſon hath impriſoned the
father for monie.　Likewiſe in the Roman Commonwealth, ſo famous for laws and
armes, it was lawfull for debt, to impriſon, beat, and afflict with torments the free Citti-
zens : How manie of them (do you thinke) would haue thought themſelues happie, if
for a ſmall debt they might haue ben excuſed with the paiment of a pound of their
fleſh ?　Who ought then to maruile if a Iew requireth ſo ſmall a thing of a Chriſtian,
to diſcharge him of a good round ſumme ?　A man may aske why I would not rather
take ſiluer of this man, then his fleſh : I might alleage many reaſons, for I might ſay
that none but my ſelfe can tell what the breach of his promiſe hath coſt me, and what
I haue thereby paied for want of money vnto my creditors, of that which I haue loſt
in my credit : for the miſerie of thoſe men which eſteeme their reputation, is ſo great,
that oftentimes they had rather indure anything ſecretlie then to haue their diſcredit
blazed abroad, becauſe they would not be both ſhamed and harmed.　Neuertheleſſe, I
doe freely confeſſe, that I had rather loſe a pound of my fleſh, then my credit ſhould
be in any ſort cracked : I might alſo ſay that I haue need of this fleſh to cure a friend
of mine of a certaine maladie, which is otherwiſe incurable, or that I would haue it to
terriffie thereby the Chriſtians for euer abuſing the Iewes anie more hereafter : but I
will onelie ſay, that by his obligation he oweth it me.　It is lawfull to kill a ſouldior if
he come vnto the warres but an houre too late, and alſo to hang a theefe though he
ſteale neuer ſo little : is it then ſuch a great matter to cauſe ſuch a one to pay a pound
of his fleſh, that hath broken his promiſe manie times, or that putteth another in danger
to loſe both credit & reputation, yea and it may be life and al for greife ? were it not
better for him to loſe that which I demand, then his ſoule, alreadie bound by his
faith ?　Neither am I to take that which he oweth me, but he is to deliuer it me : And
eſpeciallie becauſe no man knoweth better then he where the ſame may be ſpared to
the leaſt hurt of his perſon, for I might take it in ſuch a place as hee might thereby
happen to loſe his life : what a matter were it then, if I ſhould cut of his [head], ſup-

poſing that the ſame would weigh a iuſt pound, although it were with the danger of mine owne life? I beleeue I ſhould not; becauſe there were as little reaſon therein, as there could be in the amends wherevnto I ſhould be bound: or els if I would cut off his noſe, his lips, his eares, and pull out his eies, to make of them altogether a pound, ſhould I be ſuffered? Surely I thinke not, becauſe the obligation dooth not ſpecifie that I ought either to chuſe, cut, or take the ſame, but that he ought to giue me a pound of his fleſh. Of euery thing that is ſold, he which deliuereth the ſame is to make waight, and he which receiueth, taketh heed that it be iuſt: ſeeing then that neither the obligation, cuſtome, nor law doth bind me to cut, or weigh, much leſſe vnto the aboue mentioned ſatisfaction, I refuſe it all, and require that the ſame which is due ſhould bee deliuered vnto me.

The Chriſtians Anſwere.

It is no ſtrange matter to here thoſe diſpute of equitie which are themſelues moſt vniuſt; and ſuch as haue no faith at all, deſirous that others ſhould obſerue the ſame inuiolable, the which were yet the more tollerable, if ſuch men would bee contented with reaſonable things, or at the leaſt not altogether vnreaſonable: but what reaſon is there that one man ſhould vnto his own preiudice deſire the hurt of another? as this Iew is content to loſe nine hundred crownes to haue a pound of my fleſh, whereby is manifeſtly ſeene the antient and cruell hate which he beareth not only vnto Chriſtians, but vnto all others which are not of his ſect: yea, euen vnto the Turkes, who ouer-kindly doe ſuffer ſuch vermine to dwell amongſt them, ſeeing that this preſumptuous wretch dare not onely doubt, but appeale from the iudgement of a good and iuſt Iudge, & afterwards he would by ſophiſticall reaſons prooue that his abhomination is equitie: trulie I confeſſe that I haue ſuffered fifteene daies of the tearme to paſſe, yet who can tell whether he or I is the cauſe thereof, as for me I thinke that by ſecret meanes he hath cauſed the money to bee delaied, which from ſundry places ought to haue come vnto me before the term which I promiſed vnto him; Otherwiſe, I would neuer haue been ſo raſh as to bind my ſelfe ſo ſtrictly; but although he were not the cauſe of the fault, is it therefore ſaid, that he ought to bee ſo impudent as to goe about to prooue it no ſtrange matter that he ſhould be willing to be paied with mans fleſh, which is a thing more natural for Tigres, then men, the which alſo was neuer heard of; but this diuell in ſhape of a man, ſeeing me oppreſſed with neceſſitie propounded this accurſed obligation vnto me. Whereas hee alleageth the Romanes for an example, why doth he not as well tell on how for that crueltie in afflicting debtors ouer greeuouſly, the Common-wealth was almoſt ouerthrowne, and that ſhortly after it was forbidden to impriſon men any more for debt. To breake promiſe is, when a man ſweareth or promiſeth a thing, the which he hath no deſire to performe, which yet vpon an extreame neceſſitie is ſomewhat excuſable; as for me, I haue promiſed, and accompliſhed my promiſe, yet not ſo ſoone as I would; and although I knew the danger wherein I was to ſatisfie the crueltie of this miſcheeuous man with the price of my fleſh and blood, yet did I not flie away, but ſubmitted my ſelfe vnto the diſcretion of the Iudge who hath iuſtly repreſſed his beaſtlineſſe. Wherein then haue I falſefied my promiſe, is it in that I would not, (like him) diſobey the iudgement of the Iudge? Behold I will preſent a part of my bodie vnto him, that he may pay himſelfe, according to the contents of the iudgement, where is then my promiſe broken? But it is no maruaile if this race be ſo obſtinat and cruell againſt vs, for they doe it of ſet purpoſe to offend our God whom they haue crucified; and wherefore? Becauſe he was holie, as he is yet ſo reputed of this worthy Turkiſh nation: but what ſhall I ſay? Their own bible is full of their rebellion againſt God, againſt their Prieſts, Iudges, & leaders.   What did not the verie Patriarks themſelues, from whom they haue their beginning?   They ſold their brother, and had it not been for one amongſt them, they had ſlaine him euen for verie enuie.   How manie adulteries and abhominations were committed amongſt them?   How manie mur-thers?   *Abſalon* did not he cauſe his brother to be murthered?   Did he not perſecute his father?   Is it not for their iniquitie that God hath diſperſed them, without leauing them one onlie foot of ground?   If then, when they had newlie receiued their law from God, when they ſaw his wonderous works with their eies, and had yet their Iudges amongſt them, they were ſo wicked, What may one hope of them now, when they haue neither faith nor law, but their rapines and vſuries?   And that they beleeue they do a charitable work, when they do ſome great wrong vnto anie that is not a Jew?   It may pleaſe you then moſt righteous Iudge to conſider all theſe circumſtances, hauing pittie of him who doth wholly ſubmit himſelfe vnto your iuſt clemencie; hoping thereby to be deliuered from this monſters crueltie.

The reader will readily recognize the parallels to the Jew's argument: 'It is impos-sible to break the credit of trafick amongst men without great detriment to the Com-monwealth;' to his reference to 'binding the body vnto an intollerable slavery,' and to the passage: 'A man may ask why I would not rather take silver of this man,' &c.

In his Preface to *The Legends of the Holy Rood* (*Early Eng. Text Soc.*, 1871), Dr MORRIS calls attention to the fact that in one of the legends 'we get the story, so well known to us all, in the *Merchant of Venice*, of the merchant and the pound of flesh.' The Legend thus referred to is from the *Cursor Mundi*, which Dr Morris subse-quently printed *in extenso*.

Miss L. TOULMIN SMITH, in an admirable note read at a meeting of the *New Shak-spere Society* in April, 1875, shows that this story in the *Cursor Mundi*, dating as it does from about the end of the 13th Century, is the very earliest reference to the Bond Story in English.   Miss Smith gives the following paraphrase of it:

'A Christian goldsmith in the service of Queen Eline (mother of Constantine)
'owed a sum of money to a Jew; if he could not pay it by a certain term he was
'to render the weight of the money wanting in his own flesh.   The day came, the
'money was unpaid, the Jew would have his judgement, and came to the court of
'Queen Eline, where Benciras and Ansiers, two messengers who had been sent by
'Constantine to beg his mother to seek for the Holy Cross, were sitting as judges.
'The Jew bore a sharp knife in his hand, the Christian stood naked before them, but
'the Jew would not hear of ransom,—no more than a rush!   Benciras and Ansiers
'promise the Jew he shall have right judgement, and ask how he will treat the man if
'he be adjudged to him.   "How?" said the Jew, "the worst that I can or may by my
'"law.   I shall first put out his eyes, then have his hands that he works with, tongue,
'"and nose, and so on till I have my covenant."   The judges answer, "It seems you
'"will not spare him, take his flesh, he grants you that, so that you save his blood; if
'"he lose a drop of blood the wrong is on you; though his flesh were bought or sold,
'"he never thought to sell his blood."   The Jew swore at this;

> 'Then said the Jew, "by Saint Drightin
> '"Me think the worse part is mine,
> '"To take the flesh if I assay
> '"Then the blood will run away;
> '"Fordon ye have me with your dome
> '"That ye Romans brought from Rome

    ' " Curses therefore may they have
    ' " All that such a dome me gave !''

'Then said Benciras, "All has heard you abuse us in your ire, the queen has sent us
' " her₂ tɔ do righteousness, and we have told you truth." The Queen, being sure
'that the Christian was safe, bade them adjudge the Jew to give up to her all his
'goods and that he should lose his abusive tongue. The Jew found this so keen a
'judgement that he cried out, "I would rather tell you where your Lord's rood-tree lies
' " than be thus condemned," and Queen Eline forgives him on condition of his show-
'ing where the cross is hid, which he does.'

    Chronologically, the next appearance, as it seems, of the Bond Story is in a MS
(Harl. 7322), in Latin indeed, but written in England, for the benefit of preachers. It
was discovered by T. Wright after he had published his Latin Stories for the Percy
Society, and is given by Halliwell at the end of the translation of Simrock's notice of
the present play : 'The scene of the tale is laid in Denmark :—In Dacia erat quidam
'homo habens duos filios, quorum senior est maliciosus et parcus, junior autem non
'tantum liberalis sed prodigus. Cum autem junior hospitalitati omnia quæ habuit
'expendisset, accidit ut duos homines peterent ab eo hospitium. Ille autem, quan-
'quam nihil haberet unde honeste eos reciperet, propter tamen verecundiam eos
'recepit. Cum autem nihil haberet unde cibaria eis pararet præter unam vaccam,
'eam occidit. Deficiente igitur pane et potu, fratrem seniorem adivit, subsidium ab
'eo requirens; qui respondit se sibi nihil penitus daturum, nisi emeret. Contestante
'autem juniori se nihil habere, respondit senior, 'Immo,' inquit, 'carnem tuam habes,
'vende mihi ad latitudinem manus meæ de carna tua in quibus et in quadruplum
ubicunque voluero recipere.' Junior parvipendens pepigit cum eo, testibus adhibi-
'tis. Modus autem et istius patriæ est sic vel alibi sub quavis falsitate scripti vel
'chirographi ita nisi sub teste licet emere vel vendere. Recedentibus igitur hospiti-
'bus et consumptis cibariis, pactum poposcit senior frater. Negat junior, et adductus
'est coram rege, et sententiatus coram juniore ut ad locum suppliciorum deducatur,
'et accipiat senior tantum de carne quantum pactum est vel in capite vel circa cor.
'Misertus autem sui populus eo quod liberalis erat, nunciaverunt filio regis quæ et
'quare hæc facta fuerant, qui statim misericordia motus, induit se, et palefridum
'ascendens secutus est miserum illum sic dampnatum; et cum venisset ad locum
'supplicii, videns eum populus qui ad spectaculum confluxerant, cessit sibi. Et allo-
'quens filius regis fratrem illum seniorem crudelem, et dixit ei : 'Quid juris habes in
'isto?' Respondit : 'Sic,' inquit, 'pacti sumus, ut pro cibariis tantundem de carne
'sua mihi daret, et condempnatus est ad solutionem per patrem tuum regem.' Cui
'filius regis, 'Nihil,' inquit, 'aliud petis nisi carnem?' Respondit, 'Nihil.' Cui
'filius, 'Ergo sanguis suus in carne sua est;' et ait filius isti condempnato, 'Da mihi
'sanguinem tuum,' et statim pepigerunt, insuper fecit sibi condempnatus homagium.
'Tunc dixit filius regis fratri seniori, 'Modo cape ubicunque volueris carnem tuum;
sed si sanguis meus est, si ex eo minimam guttam effunderis, morieris.' Quo viso,
recessit senior confusus, et liberatus est junior per regem.'

    Concerning the source of the second story, *The Choice of Three Caskets*, there is less
diversity of opinion than in regard to *The Bond Story*.

    Dr FARMER was the first to show its similarity to a tale in the *Gesta Romanorum*,
and asserted that Shakespeare had 'closely copied some of the language' in the latter;
the copying, I think, can be applied only to the mottoes on the caskets, which would

be likely to retain much of their phraseology wheresoever found, and even of these Shakespeare did not 'copy' all three.

In what was stated above in regard to the *Gesta Romanorum* in connection with the Bond Story, it will be remembered that an English translation was printed, *circa* 1510–15, by Wynkyn de Worde. This translation contained only forty-three stories out of the hundred and more found in other MSS; among them, though the Bond Story was lacking, this of the Three Caskets was given. As it was this translation which Richard Robinson issued in six editions between 1577 and 1601, 'by mee perused, corrected, and bettered,' it is likely that it was in one of Robinson's re-issues that Shakespeare read the story, if he used it at all as the source of his Plot.*

Robinson's version is reprinted in Collier's *Shakespeare's Library*, ii, 102. It is *The Thirty-second Historie.* There is small interest for us in the beginning of it, wherein it is told that there was 'a mightie Emperor, named Anselme,' who dwelt in Rome, and how, for the sake of confirming peace and good-will, it was decided that the Emperor's son should marry the daughter of the 'King of Ampluy.' It then proceeds as follows: 'Therefore when the letters of covenant and compact were sealed, the king 'furnished a faire ship, wherein he might send his daughter with many noble knights, 'ladyes, and great riches, unto the emperour, for to have his sonne in marriage.

'Now when they were sayling in the sea toward Rome, a storme arose so extremee-'lye and so horribly, that the ship all to brast against a rock of stone, and they were 'all drowned, save onely that yong lady, which fixt her hope and heart so firmly on 'God, that she was saved. And about three of clocke the tempest ceased, and the 'lady drave foorth over the waves in the broken ship, which was cast up againe, but 'an huge whale followed after, readie to devoure both the ship and her; wherefore 'this faire yong lady when night came, smote fire with a stone, wherewith the ship 'was greatly lightened, and then the whale durst not adventure toward the ship, for 'feare of the light. At the cock-crowing, this yong lady was so weary of the great 'tempest and trouble of the sea, that she slept, and within a little while after the fire 'surceased, and with that came the whale and devoured this virgin. But when she 'wakened and found her selfe swallowed up in the whale's belly, shee smote fire, and 'within a little while shee wounded the whale with a knife in many places, and when 'the whale felt himselfe wounded, according to his nature, he began to swim to land.

'There was at that time dwelling in that country an earle that was a noble man, 'named Parris, the which for his recreation walked by the sea shore, and as he was 'walking thus, he saw where the whale was comming towards the land, wherefore he 'turned home againe, and gathered many strong men and came thither againe, and 'caught the whale, and wounded him very sore, and as they smote, the mayden that 'was in his belly cried with an high voice and said, O gentle friends have mercie 'and compassion on me, for I am a kings daughter and a true virgin from the houre 'of my birth unto this day. When the earle heard this he wondred greatly and 'opened the side of the whale and tooke her out. And when she was thus delivered, 'shee told him forthwith whose daughter she was, and how shee had lost all her goods 'in the sea, and how shee should have beene married unto the emperour's sonne. And

---

* According to a 'Table of the Stories' in the *Gesta Romanorum*, given in Herrtage's edition for the *Early English Text Society*, p. xxix, this story is the Ninety-ninth in the Anglo-latin Text, MS, Harl. 2270; the Sixty-sixth in the English Version, MS, Harl. 7333; the Thirty-second in W. de Worde's edition; and the Hundred and Ninth in Latin Printed Editions. I think it well to note this, because different Editors cite different editions. Tyrwhitt quoted from Harl. 2270, Warton from the Latin Printed Edition, as did, likewise, Douce, and it was from Harl. 7333 that the Bond Story was given above.—ED.

' when the earle heard this hee was right glad, wherefore hee comforted her the more,
' and kept her still with him till she was well refreshed. And in the meane time he
' sent messengers to the emperour, giving him to know how the kings daughter was
' saved.

' Then was the emperour right glad of her safety and comming, and had great com-
' passion on her, saying : Ah faire lady, for the love of my sonne thou hast suffered
' much woe, neverthelesse if thou be worthie to be his wife, soone shall I prove.

' And when he had thus said, he commanded to bring forth three vessels, the first
' was made of pure gold, beset with precious stones without, and within full of dead
' mens bones, and thereupon was ingraven this posey : Whoso chooseth me shall finde
' that he deserveth.

' The second vessel was made of fine silver, filled with earth and wormes, and the
' superscription was thus : Whoso chooseth me shall finde that his nature desireth.

' The third vessel was made of lead, full within of precious stones, and the super-
' scription, Who so chooseth me shall finde that God hath disposed to him.

' These three vessels the emperour shewed to the maiden and said, Lo, here daugh-
' ter, there be faire vessels, if thou choose one of these, wherein is profit to thee and to
' other, then shalt thou have my sonne : but if thou choose that wherein is no profit to
' thee nor to none other, soothly thou shalt not marrie him.

' When the mayden saw this, she lift up her hands to God and said : Thou, Lord,
' that knowest all things, grant me grace this houre so to choose, that I may receive
' the emperours sonne. And with that she beheld the first vessell of gold, which was
' engraven, and read the superscription, Who so chooseth me, &c., saying thus : Though
' this vessel be full precious and made of pure gold, neverthelesse I know not what is
' within, therefore my deare lord, this vessel will I not choose.

' And then she beheld the second vessel that was of pure silver, and read the super-
' scription, Who so chooseth me shall finde that his nature desireth. Thinking thus
' within her selfe, If I choose this vessel, what is within it I know not, but well I wot
' there shall I finde that nature desireth, and my nature desireth the lust of the flesh,
' therefore this vessel will I not choose. When she had seene these two vessels, and
' given an answere as touching them, shee beheld the third vessell of lead, and read the
' superscription, Who so chooseth me, shall finde that God hath disposed. Thincking
' within her selfe this vessel is not passing rich, nor throughly precious : neverthelesse,
' the superscription saith : Who so chooseth mee, shall finde that God hath disposed :
' and without doubt God never disposeth any harme, therefore now I will choose this
' vessell, by the leave of God.

' When the emperour saw this, hee said, O faire mayden open thy vessell, and see
' if thou hast well chosen or no. And when this yong lady had opened it, shee found
' it full of fine gold and precious stones, like as the emperour had told her before.

' And then said the emperour, O my deere daughter, because thou hast wisely
chosen, therefore shalt thou marry my sonne. And when he had so said, he ordained
' a marriage, and married them together with great solempnitie and much honour, and
' they lived peaceably a long time together.'

In the Latin Printed Editions, one of which Warton used, *pasties* or *loaves* are substituted for the ' vessels.'

According to Warton (iii, xlix, ed. 1781), the ' remote but original source' of this
story is one which is told by the hermit Barlaam to King Avenamore (in which the
' vessels' or ' pasties' are called *arcellæ*), written in Greek about the year 800 by
Joannes Damascenus, a Greek monk of St Saba in Syria, and translated into Latin

before the 13th Century, entitled *Barlaam and Josaphat*. The Greek text, according to Clarendon is published in the *Jahrbücher der Literatur*, vol. xxvi, p. 42. The principal story of Barlaam and Josaphat is told with no little dry humour by Dunlop (pp. 35–40, ed. 1845), who says that its 'many beautiful parables and apologues bear evident marks of an Oriental origin.' They were incorporated, according to Warton, in the *Speculum Historiale* of Vincent of Beauvais, who wrote about the year 1290. Thence they trickled, with more or less purity, into the *Cento Novelle Antiche* (Nov. lxv), thence into the somewhat turbid pool of Boccaccio's *Decameron*, into the *Golden Legend*, and finally into the *Gesta*.

Warton gives a translation, from the original Greek of *Barlaam and Josaphat*, of the conclusion of the story. For the beginning we are indebted to Clarendon, as follows : 'A certain rich and glorious king, attended by the officers of his court, is riding ' with regal pomp in a gilt chariot, when he is met by two men of mean appearance in ' squalid and threadbare garments. The king descends from his chariot and salutes ' them. His courtiers are disgusted, and remonstrate with him through the medium ' of the king's brother. They are then taught a lesson of the folly of judging by ' external appearances.' [Warton thus concludes :] 'The king commanded four chests ' to be made; two of which were covered with gold, and secured by golden locks, but ' filled with the rotten bones of human carcasses. The other two were overlaid with ' pitch, and bound with rough cords; but replenished with precious stones and the ' most exquisite gems, and with ointments of the richest odour. He called his nobles ' together, and, placing these chests before them, asked which they thought the most ' valuable. They pronounced those with the golden coverings to be the most precious, ' supposing they were made to contain the crowns and girdles of the king. The two chests covered with pitch they viewed with contempt. Then said the king, I pre- ' sumed what would be your determination; for ye look with the eyes of sense. But ' to discern baseness or value, which are hid within, we must look with the eyes of the ' mind. He then ordered the golden chests to be opened, which exhaled an intolerable ' stench, and filled the beholders with horror.' 'In the *Metrical Lives of the Saints*,' adds Warton, 'written about the year 1300, these chests are called *four fates*, that is, ' four *vats*, or vessels.'

Warton says that 'a like story' is in the *Confessio Amantis*, and believes that Gower copied it from the foregoing; and Gower's beginning the story (liber v, p. 203, ed. Pauli) : 'In a cronique this I rede,' gives colour to the belief. But Clarendon suggests (wherein, I think, all will fully agree) that this cannot be; 'for,' as they say, 'not only ' are the details different, there being two caskets instead of four, and both of the same ' external appearance, but the moral lesson sought to be conveyed is entirely dissimilar. ' It is told of a king whose officers complained that their promotion was not in propor- ' tion to their service. To prove to them that it was all of fortune, the king adopted ' the device of making his coffers so exactly alike that no one could tell one from the ' other. The one was filled with fine gold and precious stones, the other with straw ' and rubbish. The courtiers were asked to choose, and of course their choice fell ' upon the latter. The contents of the other were then d'splayed, and the moral ' follows :

> 'Lo, saith the king, now may ye se,
> 'That there is no defaulte in me ;
> 'Forthy my self I woll acquit
> 'And bereth ye your owne wit
> 'Of that fortune hath you refusel.'

After finishing this story Gower goes on to tell another, of which the moral is about the same, or, as he expresses it, 'Somdele to this matere like,' concerning 'Frederike, of Rome, that time emperour,' who put to the test the faith of two 'beggers' (one of whom trusted in God, and the other in the king) by means of 'two pastees,' in one of which was a capon, and in the other a 'great richesse of floreins.' This version, Sir Frederic Madden says, according to Clarendon, came from the Chronicle of Laner-cost, compiled about the year 1346, wherein the beggars are blind.

A form, in which this version of the story, in its essential features, viz. where fortune or the will of God is the arbiter, is to be found also in the *Gesta*, Chapter 109, of the Latin Printed Editions, and is thus given by Douce (i, 277): 'A smith had lost a ' chest of money, which being carried by the sea to the shores of a distant country, ' was taken up by an inn-keeper, who, not suspecting that it contained anything, threw ' it carelessly aside. Having occasion one day for some fuel to warm his guests, he ' broke up the chest, and finding the money, laid it by safely, till some one should ' arrive to claim it. The smith soon afterwards appeared; and having publicly ' declared his loss, the inn-keeper resolved to ascertain if it were the will of Provi-' dence that he should make restitution. He therefore caused three pasties to be ' made; the first he filled with earth, the second with dead men's bones, and the third ' with money. He then invited the smith to dinner, and gave him the choice of the ' pasties. The smith fixed on those with the earth and bones, and relinquished the ' others. The host now concluded that it was not the will of Heaven that he should ' restore the money; he therefore called in the blind and the lame, opened the other ' pasty in their presence, and divided the treasure between them.' (I can find no such story in Herrtage's edition of the *Gesta*, wherein Chap. 109 of the Latin Editions is tabulated as the same as Robinson's *Thirty-second Historie*, given above from Collier's Reprint.)

The source of these versions is evidently the same as of that version which Boccaccio gives in The First Story of the Tenth Day. Boccaccio, Gower, and the Chronicle of Lanercost are all so nearly contemporaneous that it is not easy to decide from whose hands we receive the earliest version.

Dr Johnson gives Boccaccio's story at full length. Dunlop (p. 239, ed. 1845) gives an abbreviation, which is amply sufficient: 'A noble Italian, called Ruggieri, entered ' into the service of Alphonso, King of Spain. He soon perceives that his majesty is ' extremely liberal to others, but thinking his own merits not sufficiently rewarded, he ' asks leave to return to his own country. This the king grants after presenting him ' with a fine mule for his journey. Alphonso directs one of his attendants to join him ' on the road, to note if he make any complaint of the treatment he had received, and, ' if he should, to command his return. The mule having stopped in a river and refus-' ing to go on, Ruggieri said she was like the person who gave her. Ruggieri being ' in consequence brought back to the capital, and his words reported to the king, he is ' introduced into the presence of his majesty and asked why he had compared him to ' the mule. "Because," replied Ruggieri, "the mule would not stop where it ought, ' "but stood still when it should have gone on; in like manner you give where it is ' "not suitable, and withhold where you ought to bestow." On hearing this, the king ' carries him into a hall, and shows him two shut coffers' [the rest I give from Payne's admirable translation for *The Villon Society*] 'and said to him in presence of many, ' "Messer Ruggieri, in one of these coffers is my crown, the royal sceptre and orb, ' "together with many goodly girdles and ouches and rings of mine, and, in fine, every "precious jewel I have; and the other is full of earth. Take, then, one, and be that

‘ “which you shall take yours; and you may thus see whether of the twain hath been
‘ “ungrateful of your worth, myself or your ill-fortune.” Messer Ruggieri, seeing that
‘ it was the king’s pleasure, took one of the coffers, which, being opened by Alphonso’s
‘ commandment, was found to be that which was full of earth; whereupon, quoth the
‘ king laughing, “ Now can you see, Messer Ruggieri, that that I tell you of your for-
‘ “tune is true; but certes your worth meriteth that I should oppose myself to her
‘ “might. I know you have no mind to turn Spaniard, and therefore I will bestow
‘ “upon you neither castle nor city in these parts; but this coffer, of which fortune
‘ “deprived you, I will in her despite shall be yours, so you may carry it off to your
‘ “own country, and justly glorify yourself of your worth in the sight of your country-
‘ “men by the witness of my gifts.” Messer Ruggieri accordingly took the coffer, and
‘ having rendered the king those thanks which sorted with such a gift, joyfully returned
‘ therewith to Tuscany.’

‘ Quære,’ says Douce as a final word (ii, 276), ‘if the general construction of all
‘ these stories have not been borrowed from the trick related to have been put by Pro
‘ metheus on Jupiter with the two bull-skins filled with flesh and bones ?’

The elopement of Jessica and her theft of jewels has been construed into a third
subsidiary plot, and its origin traced by Dunlop (p. 254) to the Fourteenth Tale of
Massuccio di Salerno, who flourished about 1470: ‘It is the story of a young gentle-
‘ man of Messina, who becomes enamoured of the daughter of a rich Neapolitan
‘ miser. As the father kept his child perpetually shut up, the lover has recourse to
‘ stratagem. Pretending to set out on a long journey, he deposits with the miser a
‘ number of valuable effects, leaving, among other things, a female slave, who prepos-
‘ sesses the mind of the girl in favour of her master, and finally assists in the elope-
‘ ment of the young lady, and the robbery of her father’s jewels, which she carries
‘ along with her. . . . . It is not improbable that the avaricious father in this tale, the
‘ daughter so carefully shut up, the elopement of the lovers managed by the interven-
‘ tion of a servant, the robbery of the father, and his grief on the discovery, which is
‘ represented as divided between the loss of his daughter and ducats, may have sug-
‘ gested the third plot in Shakespeare’s drama,—the love and elopement of Jessica and
‘ Lorenzo.’

Thus far we have been dealing with the plot of this play as if it were a mosaic,
which Shakespeare had combined into one group by gathering its diverse elements
from diverse sources, and he has been greatly praised for showing so much dramatic
and artistic skill in the combination. But Warton in the last century supplied us with
a hint, which admits the possibility that Shakespeare was indebted for the framework
at least of this drama to an older play, in which the Bond Story and the Casket Story
were already combined.

The note in which Warton calls attention to the Ballad of *Gernutus* concludes
with: ‘I shall only add that it appears from Gosson’s *Schoole of Abuse*, printed in
‘ 1579, that the character *of a cruel and covetous Jew* had been exhibited with good
‘ applause before Shakespeare’s Shylock appeared.’ (See p. 292, *ante*.)

Gosson, who had been himself a writer of plays, and even an actor, was evidently
serious-minded young man: the ‘disorder in every playhouse’ greatly offended him
and before his twenty-sixth year he published, in 1579, ‘*The Schoole of Abufe*, contein-
‘ ing a plesaunt inuectiue against Poets, Pipers, Plaiers, Iesters and such like Cater-
‘ pillers of a Commonwelth, Setting vp the Flagge of Defiance to their mischieuous

exercise, and ouerthrowing their Bulwarkes, by Prophane Writers, Naturall **reason,**
'and common experience: A discourse as pleasaunt for Gentlemen that fauour learn-
'ing, as profitable for all that wyll follow vertue. By Stephan Gosson, Stud. Oxon.'
It was dedicated, but without permission, 'To the right noble Gentleman, Master
'Philip Sidney Esquier,' but Master Sidney was thereat by no means pleased, and,
according to a letter of Spenser's to Gabriel Harvey, Gosson 'was for hys labor
'scorned; if at leaste it be in the goodnesse of that nature to scorne.' We, at least,
should be grateful for this dedication, in that to the indignation stirred up by it and by
the book itself we probably owe Sidney's *Apologie for Poetrie.* As is to be expected
from the title of his book, Gosson's hand falls heavily on the 'Caterpillers;' 'Cookes,' he
says, 'did neuer shewe more crafte in their iunckets to vanquish the taste, nor Painter·
'in shadowes to allure the eye, then Poets in Theaters to wounde the conscience,' and
as for the Players, they 'are the Basiliskes of the world, that poyson, as well with the
'beame of their sighte, as with the breath of their mouth.' After many pages of this
lashing he relents, and acknowledges that there are some players that are 'sober, dis-
'creete, properly learned honest householders,' and so also he confesses (p. 40, ed.
Arber) that 'some of their Playes are without rebuke: which are as easily remembered
'as quickly reckoned. The twoo prose Bookes plaied at the Belsauage, where you
'shall finde neuer a woorde without wit, neuer a line without pith, neuer a letter
'placed in vaine. The *Iew* and *Ptolome,* showne at the Bull, the one representing the
'greedinesse of worldly chusers, and bloody mindes of Usurers: The other very liuely
'discrybing howe seditious estates, with their owne deuises, false friendes, with their
'own swoordes, and rebellious commons in their owne snares are ouerthrowne: neither
'with Amorous gesture wounding the eye: nor with slouenly talke hurting the eares
'of the chast hearers.'

At last we seem to have encountered something substantial. Here is a play, in which
first, the chief character is a Jew; secondly, in which the choice of the caskets is
adumbrated in the 'greedinesse of worldly chusers,' and thirdly, where the 'bloody
mindes of Usurers' may be typified in Shylock; small wonder, indeed, that so many
critics and editors have set up their rest on 'the *Jew,* mentioned by Gosson' as the
immediate Source of the Plot of the *Merchant of Venice.*

DOUCE refers to the 'mistake that has been committed by those who speak of
'Shakespeare's *imitations* of the sources of this play, and who forget that one on the
'same subject had already appeared, and which might have furnished him with the
'*whole* of the plot.' Again, in referring to Tyrwhitt's conjectures concerning the
Gesta Romanorum, Douce says: 'He also had forgotten the elder drama mentioned
'by Gosson.'

STEEVENS: 'It is therefore not improbable that Shakespeare new-wrote his piece,
'on the model [of Gosson's *Iew*], and that the elder performance, being inferior, was
'permitted to drop silently into oblivion.'

SKOTTOWE (i, 330) thinks the loss of Gosson's *Iew* is 'justly a subject of regret, for
'as it combined within its plot the two incidents of the bond and the caskets, it would,
'in all probability, have thrown much additional light on Shakespeare's progress in the
'composition of his highly-finished comedy.'

But KNIGHT holds back; he thinks that Skottowe 'somewhat leaps to a conclusion'
that Gosson's *Jew* was the original of Shylock. 'As all we know of this play,' he
continues, 'is told us by Gosson, it is rather bold to assume that it combined the two
'incidents of the bond and the caskets. The combination of these incidents is per-
'haps one of the most remarkable examples of Shakespeare's dramatic skill. . . . . The

' rude dramatists of 1579 were not remarkable for the combination of incidents. It
' was probably reserved for the skill of Shakespeare to bring the caskets and the bond
' in juxtaposition. We cannot absolutely deny that Gosson's play *might* have furnished
' our poet with the whole of the plot; but it is certainly an abuse of language to say
' that it *did* furnish him, because the Jew shown at the Bull deals with " worldly
' " chusers " and the " bloody mindes of Usurers." '

SINGER (2d ed., 1856): ' It cannot be doubted that Shakespeare, as in other instances,
' availed himself of this ancient piece.'

COLLIER, after quoting Gosson, says: ' It is possible, therefore, that a theatrical performance should have existed, anterior to the time of Shakespeare, in which the sep-
' arate plots were united; and it is not unlikely that some novel had been published
' which gave the same incidents in a narrative form.'

HALLIWELL refers to the fact, derived from the *Stationers' Registers*, that the *Merchant of Venice* was originally also entitled the *Jew of Venice*, and then, after quoting
Gosson's reference to *the Jew*, continues: ' The coincidence of this description with
' the subject of the *Merchant of Venice* is so remarkable, that when we add to it the
' identity of title, little doubt can fairly remain that the play mentioned by Gosson in
' 1579 contained similar incidents to those in Shakespeare's play, and that it was, in
' all probability, the rude original of the *Merchant of Venice*. . . . . That Shakespeare
' adopted any of the dialogue of this ancient composition is highly improbable, but that
' he may have been indebted to it for the general outline of the structure of his plot,
' and that the title also was originally adopted from it, may be admitted without much
' fear of incurring a serious error.'

STAUNTON: ' The expression *worldly chusers* is so appropriate to the choosers of the
caskets, and the *bloody mindes of usurers* so applicable to the vindictive cruelty of
Shylock, that it is very probable Shakespeare in this play, as in other plays, worked
upon some rough model already prepared for him.'

CLARENDON: ' It is clear the plot of a play [as described by Gosson] must have
' been essentially the same as that of the *Merchant of Venice*, and that we have here
' combined, if not for the first time, the two stories of the caskets and the pound of
' flesh, which had previously a separate existence in many forms.'

DELIUS is inclined to think with Knight that the description in Gosson is too vague
to authorize so bold an assumption as that the *Merchant of Venice* was founded on the
Jew.

ROLFE thinks it probable that the plots of the two dramas were ' essentially the
' same,' and that Shakespeare ' worked upon some rough model already prepared for
' him.'

GRANT WHITE (2d ed.): ' This play [Gosson's *Jew*], manifestly, Shakespeare worked
' over into the *Merchant of Venice*, as we have it.'

In this general agreement I beg to be included, and, while accepting fully the
improbability of Shakespeare's having adopted any of his predecessor's dialogue, I
think it not unlikely that here and there, in two places at least, we may discern in
the dialogue traces of the old play. One of these is noted by Hunter. The Serving-
man in the second scene tells Portia that ' the *four* strangers ' wish to take leave of
her, whereas *six* strangers have been enumerated; and Hunter suggests that in the
first draught of the play there were, perhaps, but four. See I, ii, 120.

Again, I think we have an outcropping of the old play in Lorenzo's unpleasant
banter with Launcelot. Lorenzo's allusion is not explained by anything whatsoever
in the course of the story; it serves no purpose (albeit Daniel does allude to it in his

21

computation of time); it has 'neither wit, manners, nor modesty,' but is an unsightly excrescence which, I trust, is to be thus accounted for.

Finally, EDWARD SCOTT (*Athenæum*, 2 July, 1881) has discovered, in an unpublished letter of Spenser, an allusion which corroborates the supposition that Gosson's *Jew* is the prototype of *The Merchant of Venice*. The letter is from Spenser to his friend Gabriel Harvey, wherein ' he signs himself thus : " He that is fast bownde vnto ' " the in more obligations then any marchant in Italy to any Jewe there." This letter ' was a reply to one from Harvey, dated 1579, and enclosed a whimsical bond between ' the two friends in allusion to the bond of the Jew. . . . . It is evident, I think, that ' Spenser and Harvey had lately together paid a visit to the Bull, had enjoyed the ' representation of this piece, *the Jew*, and it had made such an impression on their ' minds that their correspondence at this time is full of allusions to it.'

Although in the foregoing pages nearly everything is given that has been supposed to have contributed to Shakespeare's Plot, there yet remains a Tragedy which, it has been claimed, influenced him more or less in the composition of the play.

This tragedy, which naturally occurs to every one, is Marlowe's *Jew of Malta;* the mere similarity of the titles suggests some parallelisms at least. It was probably written about 1589 or 1590, according to COLLIER, whom DYCE quotes without dissent; and was very popular, to judge from the frequency with which it occurs in Henslowe's diary. The part of the Jew, named Barabas, was 'presented by so unimitable an actor as Master Alleyn,' as we learn from the Dedication by Heywood, who, in 1633, put forth the first edition. From the play itself we learn that the actor wore an artificial nose, presumably of extraordinary proportions. Of the character itself, CHARLES LAMB says (*Specimens of Dram. Poet.*), ' Marlowe's Jew does not approach so near to Shake- ' speare's as his Edward the Second does to Richard the Second. Shylock, in the ' midst of his savage purpose, is a man. His motives, feelings, resentments, have ' something human in them. " If you wrong us, shall we not revenge ?" Barabas ' is a mere monster, brought in with a large painted nose to please the rabble. He ' kills in sport, poisons whole nunneries, invents infernal machines. He is just such ' an exhibition as, a century or two earlier, might have been played before the Lon- ' doners *by the Royal Command*, when a general pillage and massacre of the Hebrews ' had been resolved on in the cabinet.'

' Marlowe,' says DYCE (*Works*, i, xxi), ' violated the truth of nature, not so much ' from his love of exaggeration, as in consequence of having borrowed all the atro- ' cities of the play from some now-unknown novel, whose author was willing to flatter ' the prejudices of his readers by attributing almost impossible wickedness to a son of ' Israel. . . . . That Shakespeare was well acquainted with this tragedy cannot be ' doubted ; but that he caught from it more than a few trifling hints for the *Merchant* ' *of Venice* will be allowed by no one who has carefully compared the character of ' Barabas with that of Shylock.'

ELZE, whose opinions are always entitled to a respectful hearing, maintains with earnestness (*Sh. Jahrbuch*, vi, 133, 1871) that ' the prototype of Shylock, beyond all ' conjecture, is to be found in Marlowe's *Jew of Malta*, without which, in all probabil- ' ity, the *Merchant of Venice* would never have been written.' Elze is not to be under- stood as asserting that Shakespeare copied Marlowe; on the contrary, Shakespeare observed Barabas in order to know what to avoid in Shylock. After giving an epitome of Marlowe's play, Elze continues (p. 137): ' Can there be any doubt, after all this, that we have here, if not the prototype, at least the germ and suggestion of Shylock ?

To such a master of the human heart as Shakespeare the temptation was irresistible
'to transform this Barabas into a genuine Jewish usurer, and out of this mouthing and
'impossible criminal to create a real, live man, with human motives, passions, and
'actions. Barabas, of all men, was the one best suited to be the claimant in a lawsuit
'over a pound of flesh; in his avarice and in his thirst for revenge for the long series
'of wrongs he stood forth not only as the inexorable enemy of the Christians, but also
'through his daughter supplied the opportunity of bringing him into relationship of a
'different kind with the Christian world. Accordingly, we cannot doubt but that Mar-
'lowe's Barabas and his daughter are to be regarded as the true starting-point of Shake-
'speare's play. The novel in the *Pecorone* not only leaves the character of the Jew
'wholly undeveloped, but also makes no allusion to any daughter.'

WARD (*Hist. Eng. Dram. Lit.*, 1875, i, 188) is inclined to go farther than Elze:
'Between Shylock and Barabas there is doubtless a very marked difference; but that
'the two plays are, so far as their main subject is concerned, essentially written in the
'same spirit, I cannot hesitate in affirming. It is, I am convinced, only modern read-
'ers and modern actors who suppose that Shakespeare consciously intended to arouse
'the sympathy of his audience on behalf of the Jew. The sympathy which, notwith-
'standing, is aroused, is in truth merely the adventitious result of the unconscious tact
'with which the poet humanized the character. In both Shakespeare's and Marlowe's
'plays the view inculcated is, that on the part of a Jew fraud is the sign of his tribe,
'whereas on the part of Christians counter-fraud, though accompanied by violence, is
'worthy of commendation. This I cannot but regard as the primary effect of the
'whole of either play; but just as Shakespeare, in working out character and action,
'could not fail incidentally to indicate his consciousness of a counter-argument *ad*
'*Christianos*, so Marlowe puts into the mouth of Barabas the following plea in defence
'of his conduct: "It's no sin to deceive a Christian. For they themselves hold it a
'"principle: Faith is not to be kept with heretics; But all are heretics that are not
'"Jews; This follows well." Apart, however, from the much grosser developement of
'the evil tendencies of the Jew in Marlowe, the caricature (for such it is) of Barabas
'is, in general, far more coarsely drawn than the character of Shylock in Shakespeare.
'As to other resemblances, I will not dwell on the similarity of the situation between
'father and daughter in the two plays, which is essential to the conception of either.
'But it seems worth while to enumerate certain passages too closely approaching one
'another to have done so by accident, which have occurred to me in reading Marlowe's
'play:

Jew of Malta, I, i: First appearance of Bar. He enumerates his argosies.
Mer. of Ven. I. iii: First appearance of Shyl. He enumerates the argosies of Ant.

Jew of Malta, I, i: 'These are blessings promised to the Jews,
          And herein was old Abraham's happiness,' &c.
Mer. of Ven. I, iii: Passage about Jacob, with a reference to Abraham, ending:
          'This was a way to thrive, and he was bless'd;
          And *thrift* is blessing, if men steal it not.'

Jew of Malta, I, ii: 'You have my goods, my money and my wealth, &c.
          . . . . You can request no more'
          (Unless you wish to take my life).
Mer. of Ven. IV, i: Greatly improved in Shylock's speech:
          'Nay, take my life and a l,' &c.

Jew of Malta, Ib. :   'What, bring you Scripture to confirm your wrongs?'
Mer. of Ven. I, iii :   'The devil can cite Scripture for his purposes.'

Jew of Malta, II, i :   'Oh my girl,
                    My gold, my fortune, my felicity . . . .
                    Oh, girl, oh, gold, oh, beauty, oh, my bliss.'
Mer. of Ven. II, viii : ' My daughter!—O my ducats!—O my daughter! . . . .
                    Justice! the law! my ducats, and my daughter!' *

Jew of Malta, II, ii : Barabas and Slave (against hearty feeders in general).
Mer. of Ven. II, v: Shylock and Launcelot Gobbo.

'There are several other parallel passages (some not very striking) in Waldron's
'edition of Ben Jonson's *Sad Shepherd*, p. 209 *seq.*; among them the following speech
'of Barabas, to which I need not apply the Shakespearian parallel: " I learned in Flor-
' " ence how to kiss my hand, Heave up my shoulders when they call me dog, And
' " duck as low as any barefoot friar." . . . . The number of these parallel passages
'might be perhaps increased.   They prove, as it seems to me, conclusively that Mar-
'lowe's *Jew of Malta* was present to Shakespeare's mind when he wrote his *Merchant*
'*of Venice*.' [Ward then proceeds to show the immeasurable superiority of the *Jew*
of Shakespeare to that of Marlowe.]

SWINBURNE (p. 151): In the *Merchant of Venice* there is hardly a single character
from Portia to old Gobbo, a single incident from the exaction of Shylock's bond to the
computation of hairs in Launcelot's beard and Dobbin's tail, which has not been more
plentifully beprosed than ever Rosalind was berhymed.   Much wordy wind has also
been wasted on comparison of Shakespeare's Jew with Marlowe's; that is, of a living
subject for terror and pity with a mere mouthpiece for the utterance of poetry as magnificent as any but the best of Shakespeare's.

In the preceding pages, in 'The Date of Composition,' mention was made of the
record in Henslowe's Diary of a 'new' play, called by that illiterate manager 'the
Venesyon comodey,' acted on the 25 August, 1594.

This Venetian comedy, Fleay assumes to be a lost play of Dekker's, which he calls
Joseph the Jew of Venice; on this play Fleay asserts (*Life and Work of Sh.*, pp. 30,
197) that the *Merchant of Venice* was founded.   (It was not entered in the Stationers'
Registers until 9 Sept., 1653, as given by Fleay, p. 360, and there the title is simply
The Jew of Venice).   I cannot find that Fleay anywhere supplies the proof of this
identity of 'the Venesyon comodey' with Dekker's *Jew of Venice*, or any proof, other
than in the similarity of the title as given in Robertes's entry, that the *Merchant of
Venice* was founded upon either.

In an old German Almanac, published in 1626, there is a MS list of performances by
'the English Comedians' at the Dresden Court.   This list was printed for the first
time, I think, by COHN in his valuable *Shakespeare in Germany*, 1864, p. cxv; it
appears from it that on the 13th of July and on the 5th of November of that year, 1626,
a comedy was given called *Josephus, a Jew of Venice*, which Cohn surmised to be the
same as that contained in a MS in the Imperial Library in Vienna, and, from a description which he received from the Librarian in that city, he inferred it to be a 'mix-

---

* There is a strong resemblance to both these passages in Ben Jonson's *The Case is Altered*, V,
ii.—*Ward*.

'ture of Shakespeare's *Merchant of Venice* and Marlowe's *Jew of Malta.*' 'It is also 'possible,' adds Cohn, 'that this play is a version of Thomas Dekker's *Jew of Venice*, 'which appears to be irrecoverably lost.' In 1611, 'A German comedy, *The Jew of Venice*, from the English,' was acted in Halle by the English Comedians (*Cohn*, p. lxxxix), and as this is the very title of Shakespeare's play given in Robertes's entry on the Stationers' Registers, Cohn, with praiseworthy zeal, claims for this performance, and for Halle, the honour of 'the earliest authentic evidence that one of Shakespeare's 'masterpieces had been performed during the poet's lifetime in Germany;' but by the time Cohn had reached, in his history, the records of 1626 and of '*Josephus* the Jew of Venice,' he had grown more cautious, and his faith that the German and the English *Jews* were twins, or even cater-cousins, was somewhat shaken; and he circumspectly surmises, as we have seen, that Joseph may have been Shakespeare's Shylock and Marlowe's Barabas rolled into one, or even Dekker's lost wanderer; at any rate he wisely refrained, where all is vague, from any positive assertion.

In 1884, JOHANNES MEISSNER, in Vienna, printed the MS, alluded to by Cohn, of *Josephus, the Jew of Venice*, from the Imperial Library, and prefaced it with a highly interesting account of the English Comedians in Germany in those early times. This MS dates from the 17th Century, 'probably from the second half of the century;' but Meissner traces it back, under slight variations in title, or rather 'under the various descriptions given of it by spectators,' to 1674, in Dresden; to 1651, by the Dresden Comedians, in Prague; to 1626, by Green's troupe, in Dresden; to 1611, in Halle, and, finally, in 1608, to Green's troupe, in Graz. The whole story presents an exceedingly valuable chapter in Dramatic History, but naturally it is much more interesting to Germans than to us. It is to the presence in Germany of these English strolling players, with their garbled versions of plays of which they retained the whiff and wind from the London stage, that Germany owes the first germ of its Drama of to-day. In accepting from Germany the fine volumes of the German *Shakespeare Society*, let us quench our blushes in the thought that they are but the repayment to us of a debt.

What is with Cohn a bare surmise, viz. that in *Josephus, the Jew of Venice*, we may have Dekker's lost play, becomes, if I understand him aright, a conviction to Fleay, and hence, as we have seen above, his assertion that *Josephus* was Dekker's play, and that Dekker's play was the 'Venesyon comodey' of 1594, and that the Venetian comedy was the foundation of the *Merchant of Venice*. It therefore behooves us to examine well this German play, which, thanks to Meissner, can now be satisfactorily done.*

Thus runs the title: *Comoedia Genandt Dass Wohl Gesprochene Uhrtheil Eynes Weiblichen Studenten oder Der Jud Von Venedig;* or, in English, A Comedy called *The Righteous Judgement of a Girl Graduate, or the Jew of Venice*. The Dramatis Personæ are: King of Cyprus; Prince of Cyprus, in love with Ancilletta; Duke of Venice; Barrabas, a Jew, afterwards Joseph; Florello, a Counsellor of Venice; Ancilletta, his daughter, beloved of the Prince; Grimaldi, Santinelli, Ancilletta's lovers; Pickleherring, servant to the Prince; Franciscina, maid to Ancilletta and beloved by Pickleherring; the Prince's Steward, Counsellors, &c.

The play opens at the palace in Cyprus, where the young Prince begs his father to banish the Jews, who have by their tricks and usury gained enormous wealth and beggared the Cypriotes of all classes, both rich and poor, high and low; moreover, worse things are to be feared from them than beggary,—'we know what they lately did at 'Malta. It may well happen that they betray this kingdom to the Turks.' (It is not

---

* GENÉE (*Geschichte der Sh'n Dramen in Deutschland*, 1870, p. 409) gives a short synopsis of it, which is good as far as it goes.

worth while to emphasize by comments the various parallelisms as they arise, which recall either Marlowe's *Jew of Malta* or *The Merchant of Venice*. A parallelism is supposed to be indicated by quotation marks.)   The old King grants his son's request, and orders are issued for the banishment of the Jews and the confiscation of their goods, which evil stroke is due to the Prince, and supplies the motive for the hatred of him by Barrabas.   Pickleherring enters.   This character is, perhaps, the most prominent in the play, and presents a study of the manners and refinement of the times, which may be curious, but is certainly repulsive.   It is inconceivable that such language and actions could ever have been tolerated in public.   What this favorite character says is not fun but filth.   There is nothing in the whole range of the old English drama with which I am acquainted, and I will confess to many a quagmire, that is not sweet and wholesome beside this Pickleherring's disgusting vileness.   Towards the end of the play he is somewhat less outrageous, partly perhaps because there is an end to all things, and that end was reached in the earlier Scenes; and partly because whatever similarity is to be noted between this play and Shakespeare's *Merchant* is more pronounced towards the conclusion.

Pickleherring enters and presents certain petitions to the King, of which only one is translateable.   It is 'from a dead fellow who was standing before a door, and another fell from the roof and killed him, and now the dead fellow petitions that the other be put to death too.'   The petition was granted by commanding 'the fellow who fell from the roof to stand underneath and the dead man's friend to go up and fall down on him and kill him.'   In Silvayn's *Orator*, which, as we have seen, p. 310, is supposed to have influenced the speech of Shylock before the Court, the 27th 'Declamation' is: 'Of him that falling downe from the top of his house slew another 'man, against whom the sonne of the slaine man demandeth iustice;' the Judge decides 'that the said plaintife should ascend vp to the top of the same house, and throwing 'himselfe downe vpon the defendant should kill him if he could.'   *The date of the 'Venesyon comodey' is 1594; the date of the Orator is 1596;* if the subject of the foregoing petition be taken from *The Orator*, can the *Venesyon comodey* and the *Jud von Venedig* be the same?

The Prince decides to go to Venice, not only to see that city in the lovely spring weather, but to form an alliance with it against the Turks, although there is not much danger to be apprehended from them, because they had been '*lately*' so terribly defeated by 'Sefi of Persia' (Meissner notes that *this battle took place in August, 1605*). The King parts reluctantly with his son, and hesitates to expose the heir of the throne to the raging sea in a few 'boards' nailed together.

The Jew is sent for, and the decree of confiscation and banishment announced to him by the Prince.   He pleads in vain for permission to remain, but the Prince is inexorable; he must depart penniless on the morrow with his wife and children.

In the last Scene of this Act the Jew returns disguised as an old soldier, with a patch over one eye, and requests, and obtains, permission to go to Venice in the same ship with the Prince.   In a soliloquy the Jew vows vengeance on the tyrannical Christian, and if he can find no other means of killing the Prince, he has secreted enough gold and jewels about his person to bribe some banditti to assassinate him.   Though not printed as verse, the Act closes with a rhymed couplet: I'll find some means to regain my pelf, The Prince shall die, I'll kill him myself.

In the next Act we are in Florello's house in Venice, and Santinelli and Grimaldi are wooing Ancilletta.   Florello insists upon his daughter's making choice of one or other, but she protests that she cannot choose, they are both so excellent, and 'rehearses their admirable qualities;' the one is noble and the other of good family, the one is handsome and the other finely formed, the one is rich and the other not poor; one is friendly, the other magnanimous, &c. &c.; where qualities are so evenly divided she cannot decide; they must wait a year, and whichever during that time makes himself more agreeable, him she will espouse. The lovers must perforce acquiesce, and after Ancilletta has gone decide that, to kill time, they will make merry during the Carnival.

The Prince, Pickleherring, and the disguised Jew reach Venice in safety, and while they are talking over the adventures of the voyage they see Ancilletta and her maid, Franciscina, approach on their way to church, and the Prince falls at once in love with the mistress, and Pickleherring with the maid. The Prince orders Pickleherring to follow them and find out where they live and who is the Father of the lady; when the clown returns he tells the Prince that the Father lives 'in the Broad street, on the 'right hand, on the left side.'

The Second Act also closes with a rhyming couplet, but as Pickleherring utters one of the lines, it is untranslateable.

In the Third Act, Ancilletta reveals to Franciscina how deeply she is enamoured with the Prince, and Franciscina acknowledges that she is just as deeply in love with Pickleherring; all four contrive to meet in the street, and mutual vows are exchanged all round, in the course of which we discover from the style of Franciscina's conversation that she and Pickleherring are well matched. The plot, whereby future interviews are to be had, is devised by Ancilletta, who is to tell her Father on her return that she has had a fainting fit in the street; thereupon she will take to her bed, and grow worse and worse, and Franciscina is to bring her a newspaper wherein there is the advertisement (which the Prince is to insert) of a celebrated French Doctor. This Doctor, she will tell her Father, that she must see, and will keep on telling him until the Prince, disguised as a Doctor, is sent for, and her continued illness will afford continued opportunities for interviews, and for becoming better acquainted with her Father. The Scene closes in rhyme, but it is Franciscina who this time has the last word, and, like Pickleherring's, it is equally untranslateable.

The Jew now appears in fine array; he has made a good use of his time and talents, and is already richer than he was in Cyprus. He exults in his advantage over the Prince, in that he has thrown off his disguise, but the Prince must still remain incognito until the arrival of his credentials, which were to follow him. Of old he was called Barabas; he has now assumed the name of Joseph. It is true, he says, I am not Joseph of Arimathea, but just wait, my Prince; let me only get you in my clutches, and I'll be the Joseph who will help you into your grave.

The Doctor's cap and gown, which the Prince must don, together with his false beard, Pickleherring hires from the Jew Joseph, and is so peremptory in his demand that the Jew has no time to sprinkle poison in them as it occurred to him to do. The Third Act closes in prose.

Ancilletta's plot succeeds. The Prince is called in, and appears disguised as a French Doctor and talks broken German in the presence of the Father, but when the latter is called away the lovers renew their vows of fidelity.

In the mean time the Prince's remittances from Cyprus have not yet arrived. Pickleherring is therefore dispatched to the Jew to borrow two thousand ducats. When the Jew is apprised of the request, he utters, according to the Stage direction, 'very slowly' (*langsahm aussgesprochen*) 'two thousand ducats is a great sum.' Whereupon Pickleherring replies: Who said anything about two thousand ducats? he doesn't want two thousand ducats, but only 2000 ducats (*spoken very fast*).

When the Prince meets Joseph at the appointed hour to receive the money, the latter is already prepared with the bond, whereby the Prince is to bind himself to repay to the pious Jew Joseph, within one month at the farthest, the aforesaid two thousand ducats without defalcation, but if otherwise, then the pious Jew Joseph is hereby empowered to cut a 'just pound of flesh' from whatsoever part of the Prince's body it pleaseth him. That is a remarkable bond, says the Prince, who would ever let his body be maimed for the sake of money? what do you mean, with your pound of flesh? and why don't you exact the customary interest? I am, replies the Jew, everywhere known as the pious Jew Joseph. That name I wish to keep, and to that end I take no interest from any one, least of all from a stranger, and for so short a term; but in order that the bond may not fail through insufficiency, I have inserted, instead of interest, this pound of flesh, seeing that I need the one as little as the other.

Prince. Why didn't you exact some other penalty than flesh, if there is no trickery here?

Jew. The thought just occurred to me, upon my word. Sir, you are very suspicious. You won't trust me, and yet I, on your mere name, must trust you for two thousand ducats.

Prince. But to cut a pound of flesh out of one's body—that requires circumspection.

Jew. Oh, very well sir; if you won't trust me, I'll keep both the money and the bond. 'But just think, what could I do with a pound of flesh.' We are forbid by our laws to eat flesh of any kind, and should I undertake to eat human flesh?

Prince. Then I have no treachery to fear?

Jew. I swear by the God of my fathers that the pound of flesh is mere verbiage.

The Prince signs the bond, and after his exit the Jew says he has signed this bond, and 'Venice is a state where strangers are well received and can collect their debts;' at any rate, should he fail to get the pound of flesh, he will give the Prince such a slash with a poisoned knife that he'll not want anything more. There is no rhyming couplet at the end of the Fourth Act.

The Fifth Act opens with an interview between Florello and Ancilletta, in which the Father objects to any further employment of the French Doctor, on account of the mystery which hangs round him, and forbids Ancilletta to leave the house during his absence at the Council. No sooner, however, had he gone than Ancilletta determines to seek her lover through the streets, and for that purpose dispatches Franciscina to the Jew for two students' costumes, in which she and her maid can wander everywhere unrecognized.

In the next Scene the Prince's two thousand ducats are all gone, mostly lost at play, and Pickleherring has to apply to the Jew for a thousand more. The Jew says that what he has already lent comprises almost his whole fortune, but 'I will go to my neighbour and get enough to help your master.' Ay, do so, replies Pickleherring, 'you are, my Jew, the quintessence of all Hebrews;' you are only a Jew, but better than a Christian, especially than one who is not so good as you are. The Jew departs, and returns, not with the money, but with bailiffs, who arrest the Prince and carry him off. Pickleherring storms at the Jew, and while words are high the Scene at the back opens and discloses the Duke in council with Florello, Santinelli, and Grimaldi. The Duke learns the cause of the uproar, and commands the Jew to produce the Prince. As the Prince enters the Duke is much struck with his noble bearing, and Florello feels for him a strange compassion. The Prince acknowledges his signature to the bond, and the Jew demands the penalty. But, says the Duke, addressing the Jew, 'do you feel no compassion' for this comely youth? you call yourself the pious Jew; you show no piety now.

Look you, Jew, the two thousand ducats which he owes you, I will lend him. But I am not content therewith, the Jew replies, I will prove my right to be called the pious Jew Joseph by living up to strict justice, and will not yield one hair's breadth from it. The time is up, he has not paid me, and ' I will have nothing but my judgement.'

Florello. The Jew is stiff-necked and immoveable, we must find a way to help this young man without violating justice. Harkye, Jew, you'll be content if I give you a thousand ducats in lieu of your judgment, just to help out this young nobleman?

Jew. No, not for one second. It is my duty to give taxes and money to my gracious masters, and not they to me. I hold myself fast and immoveable by my promised pledge, and will in no wise let myself be diverted from it.

Prince. Look to it, Jew, lest you be punished for your cruelty.

Duke. Who are those people that are coming in?

Florello. It appears to be a young gentleman with his servant.

Duke. Inquire out, who he is and what he wants; it seems as though he had some business here.

Enter Ancilletta and Franciscina disguised.

Pickleherring. I say, stubbed [*Kurtzer*] Sir, who are you?

Ancilletta. I am a student [*Studiosus*] from Badua. I pray you pardon me, my lords, if I disturb this trial. Doctor Camillo sends me hither, and begs to be excused for being incapacitated to appear, but since he has understood that an extraordinary lawsuit was pending, he instructed me as to what I should say in the matter in his behalf.

Duke. You are welcome, young man, assume the duties of your Master. You will achieve the greatest honour if you can devise any relief for this defendant, and he himself will be indebted to you for all time.

Ancilletta. Are not two thousand ducats in controversy?

Jew. Yes, he owes them to me.

Ancilletta. And what is the pledge? a pound of flesh to be cut from his body.

Jew. That is all I ask.

Ancilletta. Let me hear the bond. [*The Jew reads it.*] Do you confess it all?

Prince. Yes, my signature proves it.

Ancilletta. The affair is all right.

Pickleherring. How about the pound of flesh?

Duke. Camillo is a wise man, he must direct us to a judgment whereby we can at once clear up this tangled business.

Ancilletta. I do not see how we can get at the Jew; wherefore, Jew, cut the guarantied pound of flesh out of his body.

Jew. Sacra Justia, Sancta Justitia! a second [*anderer*] Daniel, a second Daniel!

Pickleherring. Rascally Jew, thievish coward! Master, let them know that you're a Prince, perhaps they'll let you off.

Prince. Rather will I die than disobey my Father.

Pickleherring. Then say you're a hog, Jews can't eat that.

Jew. Hold on, Christian, now I will pay you an old debt, which perhaps you have forgotten. [*Draws a sharp knife, and is about to cut.*

Pickleherring. If you spoil my Master's side, I'll take a bigger piece out of you. [*Makes a lunge at the Jew*

Jew. What are you about, Pickleherring? Let me alone.

Ancilletta. Hold!

Pickleherring. Jew, you must hold up!

Ancilletta. Be quiet, both of you! Jew, the bond expressly states a pound of flesh; if you cut more or less by a single grain, and shed only one drop of blood, you are guilty of death and have lost your life.

Jew. How, gracious Sir; how is it possible to cut living flesh without shedding blood, and how can I do it?

Duke. You have heard the decision, conform to it or await your punishment.

Pickleherring. Sacra Justitia, Sancta Justitia! a second Daniel!

Jew. Why, gracious Sir, it was all mere banter. Do you suppose that I would give away so much money for a pound of flesh? what should I do with it? I was not in earnest; I only wanted to scare him. If I am paid my two thousand loaned and my thousand besides, which you promised me, I am content, and will willingly release him.

Duke. Just a little while ago you would take nothing but the pound of flesh; but because you did not at once accede, you shall now have neither flesh nor money.

Jew. You cannot thus deprive me of my two thousand ducats, therefore let them be paid to me so that I can go home to my house.

Florello. Neither from us nor from the stranger shall you receive a stiver.

Duke. If you won't go home without your money, you shall be hurried to prison to teach you to take such bonds from people.

Pickleherring. Sacra Justitia, Sacra Justitia! a second Daniel, a second Daniel! You mouse-head!   [*He gives him the finishing stroke* (Dat ipsi colaphum).

Jew. O ye Christians, ye unrighteous Judges, you help only each other, and rob the poor Jews of their own!

Duke. What does the rascal say? Quick there, thrash him and thrust him forth.

[*He is beaten off the stage.*

Duke. Now you are clear of your debt and your pledge, but this young man you have greatly to thank, through his cleverness the Jew was paid and you were set free. Such friendship can be repaid only by unending gratitude.

The Prince expresses his willingness to testify his gratitude with his life, and hopes that the Studiosus will some day come to Cyprus, which the Studiosus promises to do; and in order that the bond of friendship may be strengthened, she begs Florello to act the part of a Father and to recommend her to the Prince's safekeeping in the strongest possible terms. Florello joins their hands and tells the Prince to receive the Student from him as though from a Father, and to love the Student with all his heart, for he has done you such a service that if you desert him let heavenly grace desert you; but if you live fast-bound and united to him, let all heavenly blessings hover over you. Ancilletta throws off her disguise, confesses that she did not come from Dr Camillo, and thanks her Father for having betrothed her to her lover. Florello repudiates the betrothal, but at last consents, just as the Prince's Steward arrives and the Prince's incognito is at an end. The Prince takes Ancilletta, and Pickleherring Franciscina. The Duke welcomes the Prince, and on the spot concludes an offensive and defensive alliance with Cyprus, and bursts into rhyme as the curtain falls:

> In ties of friendship close is noble Cyprus bound,
> The Prince a lovely bride has here in Venice found,
> We keep our peace at home and all our foes can scare.
> The smiles of Heaven are ours, so let the Turk beware!

Whether or not this wretched, wretched stuff is the 'Venesyon comodey,' or an adaptation of it, cannot, of course, with our present information be decided. To say that it is the *Jew of Venice* by Dekker shows not the least possible respect to Dekker's memory. Meissner suggests that if it really be Dekker's play, a reason may be found for the long delay in publishing it in England (it was not entered on the *Stationers' Registers* till 1653), in the fact that the MS was travelling around in Germany. It cannot have been Gosson's play; there is not a trace of the 'greediness of worldly choosers.' Can it possibly have been the play on which Shakespeare modelled the *Merchant of Venice?* I cannot imagine that any one will seriously maintain it. The solitary striking resemblance to be found is in the exclamation: 'a Daniel, a second Daniel;' but this is far more likely to have been copied from Shakespeare than that Shakespeare copied it. If the dates of Silvayn's *Orator*, 1596, and of the 'late' battle with the Turks, 1605 (p. 326) be accepted as Internal Proofs of the date of the Play, the whole question is settled at once; but, however desirable it might be to settle it thus decisively, we must remember that such allusions might have been added or inserted at any time. They prove, however, conclusively that this particular version of the play, *and the only version we possess,* is over ten years subsequent to the date of the Venesyon comodey, and over five years later than the Quartos of the *Merchant of Venice.* I find it impossible to believe that Fleay would ever have asserted that it was the foundation of Shakespeare's play had he ever read it. It is the positiveness of Fleay's assertion, and the high position which Fleay holds among Shakespeare scholars, that have made it seem at all worth while to devote so much space to it.

The conclusion, therefore, of the whole subject of the Source of the Plot is, that *The Merchant of Venice* was founded on the play mentioned by Gosson, and that on the one or the other the Italian novel of *Il Pecorone* exercised decided influence, with a possible reading by Shakespeare of Silvayn's *Orator.*

DURATION OF THE ACTION

THERE have been at least three attempts to calculate the days and hours during which the events of this play occur. The first is by ECCLES, in 1805, who makes certain changes in the arrangement of the Scenes and n. 'he division into Acts in the first half of the play; his computation of time will, therefore, to that extent differ from any other. He does not end his First Act with the interview between Anthonio, Bassanio, and Shylock, but extends it into Act II, so as to include the arrival of the Prince of Morocco. The First Scene of our Act II is, therefore, the Fourth Scene of Eccles's Act I, and then, having Morocco in hand, he thinks that the Prince should proceed to his choice of the caskets without delay, and therefore he transposes what is our Seventh Scene of that Second Act (containing Morocco's failure) to follow this Fourth Scene. Eccles's First Act, therefore, has five Scenes, the two additional Scenes being respectively II, i, and II, vii. His Act II begins with Gobbo's soliloquy, and all the subsequent Acts and Scenes follow as in other editions. The reasons he gives for these changes are twofold: First, in no other way can he harmonize the indications of time, and, secondly, for dramatic effect; each Act of the first three contains a trial scene of the Caskets.

His computation of time is, then, as follows:

The FIRST DAY is consumed in the first three Scenes of Act I. It begins in the forenoon before dinner, to which meal frequent reference is made; and as a messenger brings word that the Prince of Morocco 'will be here *to-night*,' the day is supposed to close with his arrival, and the SECOND DAY begins with his interview with Portia. This interview cannot be on the night of his arrival, because Portia tells him that his hazard shall be made after dinner.' It therefore begins a new day, whose close sees Morocco's discomfiture.

Eccles now encounters the difficulty of disposing of the long pause in the action which apparently has to take place while Anthonio's bond to Shylock is running its three months' course. These months Bassanio must spend somewhere, either at Venice or at Belmont. Eccles compromises. Obstacles to Bassanio's departure may have arisen which keep him at Venice long beyond his original intention, and when he does at last reach Belmont 'it will be highly proper to imagine that, won by the charms of 'his mistress's society, he may be induced to defer, for a considerable time after his 'arrival there, the determination of his fate.' Eccles recognizes the fact that by hastening Bassanio's departure before nine o'clock, 'when the wind had come about,' as Anthonio said, a day might be saved and Bassanio start for Belmont just as Morocco was leaving, but this would involve a three months' state of suspense at Belmont; and Eccles wisely relinquished it, as 'fraught with no little degree of improbability.'

Wherefore Eccles supposes a considerable time to have elapsed before he begins a new day, the THIRD, with the Second Act, and Launcelot Gobbo's soliloquy. 'The 'time of the day is undetermined; Bassanio, however, upon his entrance desires that '"supper may be ready by five of the clock."' And this day continues until Bassanio sets sail at nine o'clock at night for Belmont.

The next morning, the FOURTH DAY, Salarino and Salanio meet and describe Shylock's frenzy over the loss of his ducats and his daughter (II, viii).

As Belmont 'lay at no very great distance from Venice,' 'it may well be considered' that Bassanio reaches there on this same day.

How much time certainly elapses after Bassanio's arrival and the Scene between Salanio, Salarino, and Shylock (III, i) Eccles cannot decide, but as, before its close,

Shylock asks Tubal to 'bespeak an officer a *fortnight before*,' he supposes that this, the FIFTH DAY, is about that length of time before the Scene where Bassanio makes choice of the caskets (III, ii).

That choice is made on the SIXTH DAY, in the forenoon. The marriage ceremony takes place; Bassanio leaves for Venice; Portia commits the charge of her house to Lorenzo and Jessica, and follows Bassanio to Venice; and Lorenzo and Jessica pass their merry jests with Launcelot—all, according to Eccles, before dinner-time, which we know was about noon. In the afternoon of this day the Scene shifts to Venice, and Shylock refuses Anthonio's appeals. This must be the day before the trial, because Anthonio says that ' his griefs and losses have so bated him that he shall hardly spare a pound of flesh *to-morrow* to his bloody creditor.'

The SEVENTH and last day opens in the Court of Justice in Venice; and, after the trial, very late at night, Portia reaches Belmont, followed by Bassanio.

As will be seen by the foregoing Journal, the greatest obstacle encountered by Eccles, and, indeed, by all who examine the subject critically, is to account for the term of three months during which the Jew's bond runs. By his transposition of Scenes Eccles gains somewhat in ease in the general computation of time, but no mere shifting of Scenes will obliterate the three long months, and Eccles, with evident reluctance, is forced to suppose that Bassanio remains in Venice until that term has nearly expired.

Professor Wilson's theory, or, as he calls it, his 'great discovery,' that Shakespeare makes use of two different computations of time, by one of which time is protracted and by the other contracted, was set forth at length in *Othello* (p. 358 *et seq.*), and need not be repeated here. Unfortunately, Wilson did not apply his theory to this play, and we therefore can have no such brilliant exposition of its application as we had in the tragedy last mentioned.

No sooner had Wilson announced his discovery than the Rev. N. J. HALPIN asserted that he had independently made the same discovery, and by way of proof at once issued a small volume entitled *The Dramatic Unities of Shakespeare*, Dublin, 1849; in it he pronounced his theory identical with Wilson's, and proceeded to apply it to *The Merchant of Venice*. His application, however, does not, I think, substantiate the claim to identity of theory; indeed, a careful examination of his book leads me to believe that, so far from lighting upon the same discovery, Halpin did not even clearly comprehend what Wilson's discovery really was. The mere title of his book shows his bias; he seems anxious to prove that Shakespeare duly observed the Three Unities, and that, when dealing with the Unity of Time, Shakespeare rightly adhered to a limit, longer, it is true, than Aristotle's twenty-four hours, but logically, and naturally, better. What the duration of this limit is, Halpin thinks that Shakespeare has himself told us where Iago says of Cassio, that ' He'll watch the horologe a *double set*,' that is, according to Italian computation, *forty-eight* hours. Therefore, Shakespeare's Unity of Time, according to Halpin, is within *forty-eight* or *fifty-six* consecutive hours. ' By this lim-
' itation, transactions which, according to our experience in life, would *naturally* occupy
' weeks or months, nay years, are *dramatically* drawn within the compass of a few con-
' secutive hours; just as the almost interminable views of the landscape are represented,
' in all verisimilitude, on the uniform plane surface of canvas. Indeed, Shakespeare
' appears to have done for *time* what the painter has done for *space*,—thrown it into
' PERSPECTIVE, and given to the *remote* and to the *near* its proper and distinctive place,
' colouring, and character.'

It is one thing to undertake to harmonize what Wilson calls Shakespeare's 'Long Time and Short Time,' but it is a much harder task to have to prove that the Long Time is, dramatically, no longer than forty-eight hours, which is what Halpin now undertakes; and it is not surprising that thus heavily handicapped, with this additional weight, he should stagger and succumb.

Halpin asserts that the dramatic time of this play is compressed to within less than the forty-eight hours, viz., within thirty-nine consecutive hours.

The proof is as follows, as much as possible in his own language:

'The transaction naturally divides itself into *two distinct periods*,—and *the interval* 'between them.

'1. The first period ranges from the opening of the action and the borrowing of 'Shylock's money to the embarkation of Bassanio for Belmont.

'2. The second includes the time between *his arrival at Belmont* and *his return* to 'it, with Anthonio, after the trial.

'3. And the interval between these two periods is *concurrent with the time of the* 'bond, whatever that may be. Let us now examine *each period* of visible action by 'the dates exactly laid down in the text; and then fix the *interval* by the same rule.'

We all agree that the play opens before dinner, 'say at eleven o'clock in the fore-noon,' and since Halpin assumes that Bassanio, as soon as he has 'touched the ducats,' begins to make rapid preparations for his journey, there is no difficulty in computing the time up to the hour of embarkation at nine P. M., which period is 'exactly limited 'to ten consecutive hours, viz:

'From the opening of the action to dinner-time . . . . . 1 hour
'From dinner-time (12 o'clock) to supper (5 o'clock) . . . 5 hours
'From supper to the embarkation (9 o'clock) . . . . . . 4 hours
'First Period . . . . 10 hours

'The Second Period of action *begins* with Bassanio's arrival at Belmont, and *end.* 'with his return to it, with Antonio, after the trial.'

In the Second Scene of Act Third, Halpin assumes that Bassanio has his first inter-view, in the capacity of a suitor, with Portia; and 'the dialogue shows there has been 'no delay between the announcement of his arrival and his waiting on the lady. She 'prays him to pause, to tarry,—but he is too impatient to let a moment interpose be-'tween his arrival and the decision of his fortune.'

'Considering the very early hours which our forefathers, from the highest rank to the 'lowest, were used to keep in Shakespeare's time, it is not too early,' says Halpin, 'to 'assign this Scene and the departure of Bassanio for Venice to about eight o'clock in 'the morning.'

From what Portia says to Nerissa in regard to their journey, that 'we must measure 'twenty miles to-day,' Halpin infers that Venice and Belmont are 'but ten miles apart,' 'and that the distance might be easily traversed, with a pair of horses to her coach, in 'a couple of hours. Taking, then, *eight* o'clock A. M. for the time of the Casket scene, 'and allotting *four* hours for the marriage ceremony, the preparations for the journey, 'and the journey itself, Portia may have arrived at Venice by *noon*, and taken her place 'in court after the trial had been begun.'

As soon as the trial is over, which takes only the time of its representation, Portia sets out on her return to Belmont, and the whole party reassemble in Portia's garden 'at the final close of the dramatic action, at no later hour than about *two o'clock* of the 'morning after the trial; that is to say, the Second Portion of the visible action cannot

have occupied more time than between eight o'clock A. M. of one day, and two o'clock in the forenoon of the succeeding, that is to say, in *eighteen consecutive hours.'*

Thus Halpin disposes his two periods, and, for the sake of argument, we may grant his arrangement, though not without much lifting of eyebrows, and shrugging of shoulders, here and there.

Now comes the Third Period, the interval between the two, the interval within which lies the term of the three months' bond. This interval, so Halpin expresses it as his 'conviction,' is 'really but *a single night;* that night, to wit, which intervenes 'between Bassanio's embarkation and his arrival at Belmont.' 'And that, conse- 'quently, the received period of the bond is an *illusory* period.'

Halpin then proceeds to prove that, as Jessica's flight from Venice was contempora- neous with Bassanio's embarkation, and as, furthermore, she arrived at Belmont shortly after Bassanio had reached there, the interval between the two periods was from nine in the evening of one day to eight in the morning of the next, the day on which the bond expires, and was, therefore, *eleven* hours.

Thus we have *ten hours* for the First Period; *eighteen hours* for the Second, and *eleven* for the Interval between the two. In all, *thirty-nine* hours.

But how about the bond? We seem to get no light on the solution of that three months' puzzle. If only we can ignore that, our path is plain as way to parish church. But, unfortunately, Halpin does not ignore it. I say 'unfortunately' because, in solv- ing it, he betrays, I fear, that he has failed to comprehend Shakespeare's art in deal- ing with time, and that instead of detecting, with Wilson, Shakespeare's legerdemain, he has, no less than Eccles, fallen a victim to it. Instead of accepting the drama as it stands and endeavoring to reconcile its apparent discrepancies, Halpin introduces a device which, while it certainly helps out Halpin, not only throws a deeper shade on Shylock, but, in my opinion, I am sorry to say, degrades the whole play; and for which I cannot see that he has a tittle of evidence.

'The bond,' says Halpin (p. 35), 'upon which *ostensibly* the money is lent is a bond 'for "three thousand ducats at three months;" that upon which it is *really* advanced 'is a bond substituted for the former, through the affected good nature and kindliness 'of Shylock. The first was, of course, the ordinary mercantile bond of the country, 'bearing the usual interest, payable at a certain specified date, and, doubtless, subject 'to the usual penalty of double the amount on forfeiture. Of the second, we know 'little or nothing beyond the penalty on forfeiture,—"a pound of flesh," &c. It is a '"merry bond" drawn, signed, and sealed in "a merry sport." It bears no interest, 'indeed, but we are left in ignorance of the sum really advanced, or of the time and 'place when and where it should become payable. The Jew's own description of the 'instrument is in the following ambiguous terms:—seal me there Your *single* bond; 'and in a merry sport If you repay me not on *such a day*, In *such a place, such sum* '*or sums* as are express'd in the condition, *let the forfeit* Be nominated, for, &c. To 'lure the merchant more effectually into his snare, the Jew represents this proffer as an 'act of disinterested kindliness. And further, to disarm Antonio and Bassanio of all 'suspicion, he sneers at the absurdity of their supposing that, in any case, he would 'think of exacting the forfeiture. A penalty like this was not, with due time for 'preparation, likely to be incurred; still less, under such professions, to be enforced. 'The terms are agreed to, and Shylock *proceeds alone* [Italics are mine. This over- 'sight on the part of Halpin is inexplicable] to give the notary "directions for this '"merry bond." Antonio, in his reliance on the Jew's reasoning and assurances, signs 'and seals the instrument, perhaps without examination; and the deed being legally 'drawn up, and the penalty not unprecedented, he must abide the consequences of his own rash act.

'Correct, however, in its technical forms, as this "merry bond" may have been, we ' yet know that in some respects it was *fraudulent* in its substance; for, at the trial, ' Shylock is charged with having "*Indirectly* and *directly* too Contrived against the ' "very life of the defendant." *Directly*, by proceeding with knife, scales, and weights ' to exact the fatal forfeiture; and *indirectly*, no doubt by some *fraudulent* contrivance ' in the deed. What could this fraud have been? Comparing the date of the exe- ' cution of the bond with the date of its expiring, we are led to the irresistible conclu- ' sion, that the fraud lay either in the omission of any date or period at all, or the sub- ' stitution of a false one; and, in the latter case, we must suppose it was payable, ' according to a very usual practice among merchants, *at sight* or *on demand*. This ' view entirely reconciles the apparent discrepancy between the actual time of Bas- sanio's journey to Belmont and the time of the bond's arrival at maturity.' Halpin hen goes on to prove that Anthonio never was a bankrupt at all. He learns at Bel- mont, within twenty-four hours after signing the bond, that his ships have come in. ' Nothing but surprise could have reduced him to a state of forfeiture; and nothing ' could have reduced him to such a surprise, except the fact that the bond was *uncon* ' *ditionally payable on demand or at sight.*'

Although this pure invention of a second, fraudulent bond to which Anthonio tamely and silently submits is fanciful enough and wide enough of the mark of revealing Shake- speare's art, yet in dealing with the 'protractive allusions,' Halpin shows even more clearly that he failed to appreciate Wilson's 'discovery.' Instead of accepting these allusions as intentional blinds, creating a false show of time, Halpin goes to work to show that they are all mistakes, not on Shakespeare's part, but on ours, for supposing them to be what in reality they are not; we think that they refer to the three months' bond, whereas, says Halpin, they refer to the substituted bond, payable in a day. In the conference between Shylock and Tubal, Halpin acknowledges that Tubal has been to Genoa, 'but it does not appear that he went thither in quest of Shylock's daughter.' ' Tubal is a manifest liar,' continues Halpin; 'he reports the loss of one of Anthonio's ' argosies, ... but we know (at the last) that Anthonio has sustained no loss at all,— ' no wreck,—and that Tubal's story is a falsehood invented for the nonce. Again, if by ' his speech, as given in all the editions, Tubal means to say that Jessica had "spent in ' "Genoa, as he heard, one night, fourscore ducats," we know also he must be a liar; ' for Jessica was not in Genoa at all. In fact, she had not reached many miles from ' Venice when, between that city and Belmont, she and her lover were overtaken by ' Salerio, who was hastening to acquaint Bassanio with the news of Anthonio's misfor- ' tune.' But, rightly regarded, Tubal is not the liar that he seems; he is more sinned against than sinning; he is a victim of punctuation, so it appears from Halpin, who says that in Tubal's speech: 'Your daughter spent in Genoa, as I heard, one night,' &c., the words 'in Genoa' should be in parentheses, as they were in answer to Shy- lock's 'where?—in Genoa?' and were just added, 'in order to answer, ere he forgot.' ' Your daughter spent—(in Genoa)—as I heard,' &c. Shylock's instruction to Tubal to ' bespeak him an officer a *fortnight* before,' suggests to Halpin 'nothing more than ' the extreme impatience of the cruel creditor to glut his revengeful animosity with the ' utmost certainty and with the shortest delay.'

Jessica's report of what she had heard her Father swear to Tubal and to Chus about his eagerness for Anthonio's flesh, Halpin explains by saying that Jessica is referring to ' conversations *prior to the bond*..... Since the day on which the bond was con-

'tracted she has *never been at home* so as to overhear any of her Father's conver-
'sations with his countrymen on the subject. In fact she has had but a single inter-
'view with him between that day and her elopement, and having ourselves been ear
'and eye witnesses to that interview, we know that no such conversation took place
'between her Father and his countrymen on that occasion.'

Anthonio's speech that he should 'hardly spare a pound of flesh *To-morrow*' to his
bloody creditor, Halpin pronounces a 'miscalculation of the Merchant, not the poet;'
Anthonio may have thought that he would not have been brought to trial *until* 'to-
morrow,' &c.

Unless a theory which we believe to be erroneous bids fair to become popular, and
we fear the spread of contagion, it seems to be a sad waste of time or labour to refute
it. No such fear need be anticipated from this theory of Halpin. There is no likelihood that a convert will be found to this thimblerigging device of a substituted bond,
which its author never would have started, I think, had he had an inkling of Professor
Wilson's 'dual time.' It is well to note it as an inexplicable vagary of a clever scholar,
and there an end.

In 1879, Mr P. A. DANIEL contributed to *The New Shakspere Society* a *Time-
Analysis of the Plots of Shakspere's Plays,* and, of course, therein, a 'time-analysis'
of the present play. He followed the usual arrangement of Acts and Scenes, and,
therefore, does not go step by step with Eccles. The latter, as we have seen, allotted
Seven Days to the action; the Seventh and last day he devoted to the trial and to the
return to Belmont. Of this day Daniel makes two,—one for the trial, and one for the
return to Belmont,—on the ground that when Nerissa returns her ring to Gratiano she
says that the Doctor's clerk was with her 'last night.' Otherwise, Daniel's computation, as far as the number of days is concerned, is the same as Eccles's. In regard
to the disposition of the three months, however, there is this difference: Eccles supposes that Bassanio remains chiefly at Venice; and Daniel, that Bassanio sojourns at
Belmont.

Daniel's computation is as follows:

Day 1. Act I. *Interval*—say a week.

Day 2. Act II, i–vii. *Interval*—one day.

Day 3. Act II, viii and ix. *Interval*—bringing the time to within a fortnight or
the maturity of the bond.

Day 4. Act III, i. *Interval*—rather more than a fortnight.

Day 5. Act III, ii–iv.

Day 6. Act III, v–Act IV.

Days 7 and 8. Act V.

It is needless to remark that Daniel does not believe in Shakespeare's art of dealing
with time as set forth by Wilson.

Daniel's disposition of the three months' term must be told in his own words:

'In Act III, Sc. i (Day No. 4) we arrived at the conclusion that all but a fortnight of
'the three months of the bond had expired. [Shylock had told Tubal to bespeak him
'an officer "a *fortnight* before."] More than a fortnight's interval, therefore (allowing
for Salerio's journey, and the time passed by him in Venice after the arrest, during
'which the chief citizens interceded with Shylock on behalf of Anthonio), must be
'supposed between Sc. i and Sc. ii–iv of this Act. So far all is clear; the difficulty is
'to account for Bassanio's proceedings since his arrival at Belmont. We cannot fix
'the time of his arrival with precision; but granting the first week's interval, spent in

22

'Venice in preparing for his journey, and his arrival at Belmont on the second day
'after his embarkation, we still are but nine days from the signing of the bond, and
'now, when he makes his choice of the caskets, more than three full months of the
'bond have expired. We allowed Morocco a week in which to make his suit to Por-
'tia; to Arragon we could only afford one day; but Bassanio has taken the uncon-
'scionable time of some twelve weeks! And yet when he at last determines to risk
'his fortunes in the choice of the caskets, Portia addresses him with, "I pray you
'"tarry; pause a day or two. . . . . I would detain you here some month or two Before
'"you venture for me," &c. This speech apart, however, we need not find much diffi-
'culty in allowing for a somewhat lengthy sojourn at Belmont of Bassanio and his
'suite. The dialogue between him and Portia is that of two persons who, by long
'intercourse, are mutually certain of each other's love, and tremble lest fate should
'divide them. It is certain, also, that Bassanio is no new-comer, for he refers to the
'time—"When I did first impart my love to you," &c., and the mere sound of this
'line carries us back a long way into time past. We must suppose—and the poet
'intended we should suppose—that Bassanio has been following Antonio's advice,
'and staying "the very riping of the time" (II, viii, 43). And Portia and he have
'not been alone in their wooing; Gratiano has been hard at it too, wooing till he sweat
'again, and "at last" Nerissa has promised him her hand if Bassanio achieve her
'mistress.'

Daniel's computation bears the mark of conscientious fidelity; his weakest point, I
think, is where, for the sake of proving Bassanio's prolonged stay at Belmont before
choosing the casket, he is forced to disregard, or to obliterate, Portia's entreaty to Bas
sanio to 'pause a day or two,' and that she would 'detain him some month or two
before he ventured;' which, considering that, according to Daniel, Bassanio had been
there already two full months, betokens in Portia a kindly, hospitable nature, to say the
least. As Daniel most truly says, 'there is not much difficulty, *this speech apart,*'—
a dangerous, although a very convenient, freedom to take in nice calculations. For
the rest, if Wilson's theory of Shakespeare's Double Time be correct, it would seem as
if with Daniel every illusion of Shakespeare's legerdemain had succeeded, except, perhaps, Daniel's failure to note that Bellario said in his letter to the Duke, that he had
'turned o'er many books' with the young Doctor. Still, as so much of that letter was
fabricated, Daniel may have thought that this was a fabrication also; albeit, it is not
without importance if considered as an intentional indication of prolonged time.

The COWDEN-CLARKES are the only Editors who have adopted Wilson's Double
Time. Not only have they noted indications of it in this present play, but in their
extremely valuable *Shakespeare Key* (which every Shakespeare student should own)
they have collected the instances, which they consider proofs of it, in all of Shakespeare's Plays.

It seems to me that whatever Professor Wilson says of the Double Time in *Othello*
is applicable to the Double Time in the *Merchant of Venice*, and that Shakespeare's
consummate art is shown here no less than there. Wilson claimed for Shakespeare
originality in the use, or in the invention, of this art. Original it unquestionably was,
as far as Shakespeare's knowledge of it was concerned, but I think it can be shown
that the same art was employed in *The Agamemnon*, by Shakespeare's greatest predecessor in Tragedy.

In *Othello*, through this art, we accept as perfectly natural the gradual change of intense love to a murderous frenzy of jealousy, all within the space of thirty-six hours. Days and weeks are compressed into minutes and hours, not only without our detecting any improbability, but with a full faith that events have followed their natural, orderly course.

Here in the *Merchant of Venice*, by the same thaumaturgy, three months are to be compressed into as many days, a harder task than in *Othello*, in so far as the limit is fixed. At the very outset we are told that the bond is to be for so much money '*and for three months.*' There is no attempt to weaken the impression. As soon as it is firmly fixed, then Shakespeare begins at once to 'hurl his dazzling spells into the spongy air.' He knew, none better, that just as soon as the ducats were pursed, Bassanio, swift as the thoughts of love, must fly to Portia. Did not Bassanio know, had he not himself told Anthonio, that the wide world knew Portia's worth, and the four winds blew in from every coast renowned suitors? Could he afford to risk an hour's delay? In that longing sigh, 'Oh, my Anthonio,' did he not breathe his soul out for the means to hold a rival place with the many Jasons? As soon, therefore, as he has received the means from Shylock, he comes before us full of eager, bustling haste,—supper must be ready, at the very farthest, by five of the clock,—letters must be delivered,—his servant must make purchases and stow them aboard,—he must return in haste,—he must go for Gratiano to come at once to his lodging,—and then after all the commissions, full of feverish impatience, he bids his servant,—'hie thee,— go.' But—and here we catch the first glimpse of Shakespeare's spell—the three months have begun to run, and against the swift current of Bassanio's haste there must be some check. Bassanio tells his servant to 'put the liveries to making.' This takes time. Liveries are not made in a day. Next, Bassanio tells Launcelot that Shylock had spoken with him that very day about Launcelot's change of masters. This sounds as though Bassanio and Shylock had met casually in the street; surely they would not mingle the business of signing such a bond and of handing over so large a sum of money with discussing the qualities of servants. But these two checks will serve well enough for the thin edge of the wedge; and Bassanio's eager haste returns again, and he excuses himself to Gratiano on the plea that he has 'business.' In this bustling, feverish, hurrying mood we leave him, and do not see him or hear him again until he has reached Belmont, and is entreating Portia to let him choose, to let him to his fortune and the caskets, for, as he is, he '*lives upon the rack.*' What man is there, whose blood is not snow-broth, but knows that Bassanio has sped to Belmont with all speed of wind and tide.

But Shakespeare's magic will be busy with us before we see Bassanio again. Nearly a fourth of the play is carried on (herein revealing Shakespeare's art in the mere construction of his dramas), and days and weeks and months must pass before us, consuming the time of the Bond.

A new interest is excited. Jessica and her fortunes are introduced. Time obliterates Shylock's antipathy to eating with Christians. We are taken to Belmont to see the Prince of Morocco and watch his choice of the casket. We are brought back to Venice to find Shylock so publicly furious over the loss of his ducats and his daughter that 'all the boys in Venice follow him.' Rumours, too, are in the air of the loss of Anthonio's ships. Salarino talked with a Frenchman about it 'yesterday.' Again we are taken to Belmont; by this mere shifting of scenes, back and forth, from Belmont to Venice, and from Venice to Belmont, is conveyed an impression of the flight of time. The deliberate fool, the Prince of Arragon, fails in his choice, and departs. Lest we should be too much absorbed in all this by-play and lose our interest in Bassanio, we are told immediately after Arragon has left that a young Venetian has alighted at the gate. We are not told outright that it is Bassanio, yet we know that he is on the way, and it must be he. But before we actually see him, fresh from Venice as we know he is, although it is so long since we saw him and so much has happened, more spells must be woven round us; there must be the very riping of the time.

One is always conscious that between the Acts of a play a certain space of time elapses. To convey this impression is one of the purposes for which a drama is divided into Acts. Thus here, after merely intimating that Bassanio has reached Belmont, an entr'acte artfully intervenes, and when the curtain again rises we are all the more ready to accept any intimations of the flight of time which may be thrown out. Accordingly, when the Third Act opens with Salanio's question: 'What news on the Rialto?' Salarino replies that '*it yet lives there unchecked*' that Anthonio has lost a ship. Furthermore, the wreck has taken place not on any sea-coast near at hand, from which communication could be speedy, but on the remote Goodwins, almost as far off as it could be, within the limits of Europe; even for rumour to reach Venice from so remote a quarter implies much time; it could be brought only by slow argosies or heavy carracks, and days and weeks might elapse before any arrived direct from the scene of the disaster, and for many a long day the rumour might live unchecked. Much more time was implied to an Elizabethan audience, in this distance between the Goodwins and Venice, than it is to us.

Then Shylock enters, still so deeply cut by his daughter's flight that his first words are reproaches to Salarino and Salanio for being privy to it; but evidently his first ebullition has cooled, and time has brought some self-control. It must have been days, nay, weeks. Have not Anthonio's bearing and deportment undergone a gradual change that only time can bring about? Shylock says, that Anthonio scarce dare show his head on the Rialto; this is not the work of hours, but of days, perhaps weeks. Anthonio's smug air upon the mart is spoken of as a thing long past: 'he *that was used* to come so smug upon the mart.' Then comes in with startling effect, '*let him look to his bond.*' By this one allusion the three months shrink; we feel the first cold chill of Anthonio's fast-approaching peril, and this impression is deepened with every repetition of the allusion by Shylock: 'let him look to his bond! He was wont [again, how long ago that seems!] to call me usurer. Let him look to his bond! *he was wont* to lend money for a Christian courtesy. Let him look to his bond!' This is one of the masterstrokes of art in the play. Except one fleeting allusion to it by Salarino, we have heard nothing of the bond. We have watched Jessica elope with her lover, and gilded with ducats glide out of sight in a gondola, the Prince of Morocco has come and gone, the Prince of Arragon has strutted forth and back, the Rialto, with its busy life and whispered rumours of Anthonio's losses, has passed before us day after day, week after week, the smug merchant has broken down, and now all of a sudden looms up the fateful bond, and its term is shrivelling as a scroll. To deepen this impression of the Long Time that has elapsed, Tubal returns from his weary quest after Jessica; he tells Shylock that he *often* came where he heard of her; he must have kept moving from place to place, because Shylock groans over the money that was spent in the search. Then, too, another of Anthonio's ships has been cast away coming from Tripolis, much nearer home than the Goodwins; and some of the ship-wrecked sailors have reached Genoa, nay, have even talked with Tubal. There is no hope for Anthonio now, his bankruptcy is sure; and so close has the limit come that Tubal must go, and go at once, to secure an officer for Anthonio's arrest; within a fort-night the term will have expired and the bond be forfeit.

The minute-hand that has recorded for us so many varied events is fast catching up with the hour-hand.

There is no entr'acte now. We are taken at once to Belmont, at last to meet Bassanio in happy torment, full of eagerness and haste, fresh from Venice, unwilling to piece the time or stay one minute from his election. With the success of Bassanio's hazard and with the winning of his prize, the only obstacle to the completion of the full term of the bond disappears. There is no longer need of further delay. Time's steeds may now be fiery-footed and gallop apace. Yet even at this last minute two more spells from the past are to be cast around the present, and our imaginations must untread again the long weeks that have passed since the bond was signed. Salerio brings word from Venice that *morning and night* Shylock is plying the Duke for justice, and that twenty merchants, the Duke himself, and the magnificoes, have been pleading with the Jew for mercy. And Jessica, too, who left Venice when Bassanio left it, has reached Belmont after her merry junketings at Genoa, (which we accept without questioning their possibility,) and adds a masterstroke of legerdemain by saying that she had heard her Father swear to Tubal and to Chus that he would rather have Anthonio's flesh than twenty times the value of the bond. We never stop to think that she left Venice within a few hours after the signing of the bond, and had seen her Father but once, and then for only a few minutes. Her words summon up pictures of many a discussion between the three old usurers in the seclusion of Shylock's house, and tell plainly enough of the gradual hardening of Shylock's heart. Thus the mighty magician ' winds him into us easy-hearted men, and hugs us into snares;' and so completely entangled are we that there is no jar now when Anthonio's letter says that his ships have all miscarried, his creditors grow cruel, his estate is very low, and *his bond to the Jew forfeit!*

The minute-hand is on the stroke of the hour. But one more fleeting impression and the hammer falls. Anthonio says that his griefs and losses have so bated him that he will hardly have a pound of flesh to spare for his ' bloody creditor *to-morrow.*' The royal Merchant's gaunt and haggard looks tell of many a weary week, and the bond expires to-morrow!

Although it was necessary that Portia should hasten to Venice as rapidly as Bassanio, yet some time must be given to her to master her brief; she might have done it while on the ferry, after receiving Bellario's notes and garments from Balthasar at the Traject, and probably did do so; but Bellario's letter to the Duke supplies the requisite time, if any be needed, in our imagination, by saying that he and the young Doctor ' had turned over many books together,' evidently a faithful and prolonged consultation, ending in an ' opinion,' the result of laborious and learned research.

How long the home journey from Venice to Belmont lasted, whether it took one day or two days, is a matter of small moment. Nothing was at stake, no art is demanded, nothing has to be smoothed away; we need neither Long Time nor Short Time. For aught that concerns the dramatic action, it might have taken a month. All that is needed is that Portia should reach home first, and that Bassanio should follow hard after. When Nerissa tells Gratiano that the Doctor's Clerk had been in her company ' last night,' she had already given Gratiano the ring, or was in the act of handing it to him; the jest was revealed, her eyes were dancing with merriment, and he would know in a flash that what was true of *last night*, be it in Belmont or Venice, was equally true of every night since she had been born.

It is to Dr W. W. Goodwin, of Harvard College, that I owe the suggestion that in

The Agamemnon an illustration might be possibly found of a treatment of Dramatic Time similar to Shakespeare's Double Time. In representing the arrival of Agamemnon at Argos within a few hours of the fall of Troy, Æschylus has been charged by many an Editor with a violation of the Unity of Time. Dr Goodwin suggested that a solution of the difficulty might be traced in the Herald's speech to the Chorus. It is greatly to be regretted that a pressure of many duties has kept these pages from being enriched with Dr Goodwin's promised investigation of the question, and that the task has therefore fallen, instead, to my unskilful hands.

In the first place, if there be in *The Agamemnon* a violation of the Unity of Time, Æschylus committed it either wittingly or unwittingly. To say that he committed it unwittingly is almost unthinkable. From the very structure of a Greek tragedy, a downright violation of the Unity of Time, during the continued presence of the Chorus, would be a defect glaring alike to auditors and author; if to our eyes there appears to be such a violation, the presumption is strong, so strong as to amount almost to a cer tainty, that the defect lies in our vision, not in the play itself.

This apparent violation, then, Æschylus must have committed wittingly; and if so, an analysis of the tragedy will show, I think, that in dealing with time he waved ovei his audience, with a master's art, the same magician's wand that Shakespeare wields, and that by subtle, fleeting impressions of the flight of time a false show of time is created, which is accepted by us for the real. We must remember that in listening to Shakespeare or to Æschylus we are subject to their omnipotent sway, and that when they come to us 'with fair enchanted cup, and warbling charms,' we are powerless to 'fence our ears against their sorceries.'

The opening Scene of *The Agamemnon* reveals the tired Watchman on the Palace top at Argos. Of a sudden he sees on the distant horizon the flash of the fire on Mt Arachnæum, the signal that Troy is taken.

The Chorus enters, and the Watchman hastens to tell Clytemnestra.

When the Queen enters, and is asked by the Chorus to tell how long it is since the city had fallen, she replies that 'it was this night, the mother of this very day' ($T\tilde{\eta}\varsigma$ $\nu\tilde{\nu}\nu$ $\tau\varepsilon\kappa o\acute{\nu}\sigma\eta\varsigma$ $\phi\tilde{\omega}\varsigma$ $\tau\acute{o}\delta$' $\varepsilon\dot{\nu}\phi\rho\acute{o}\nu\eta\varsigma$, $\lambda\acute{\varepsilon}\gamma\omega$, line 279).

The Chorus, knowing how far it is from Troy, and how many days and nights must pass in journeying thither, expresses surprise that the news could travel so fast; whereupon Clytemnestra explains that it was through the aid of Hephaistos; a fire was lit on Ida, then on the Hermæan crag of Lemnos, then on Mount Athos, and so on, till the great beard of flame' flashed on the roof of the Atreidæ, and 'this very day the Achæans hold Troy' ($T\rho o\acute{\iota}a\nu$ '$A\chi a\iota o\grave{\iota}$ $\tau\tilde{\eta}\delta$' $\check{\varepsilon}\chi o\upsilon\sigma$' $\dot{\varepsilon}\nu$ $\dot{\eta}\mu\acute{\varepsilon}\rho\alpha$, line 320).

The opening hour of the Tragedy has struck. It is the morning after the night dur ing which Troy was taken. The release of the weary Watchman from his sleepless years, Clytemnestra's description of the speed, the speed of light, with which the beacon-fires had brought the news, her rejoicings over the end of the warriors' hardships, all emphasize it. No impression with regard to Anthonio's three months' bond is conveyed more clearly than that here, in Argos, it is but a few hours since Troy had fallen.

'The voyage from Troy to the bay of Argos,' says Dr Goodwin, in a letter, 'would ' now be a good day's journey for a fast steamship. So I think we are entitled to at ' least a week of good weather for the mere voyage, leaving out the storm and the ' delays.' That much time, then, will it take Agamemnon to reach his home, if he starts within an hour after he has conquered Troy. But the drama has begun, the Chorus is on the stage, and before it leaves the stage Agamemnon must arrive, here in Argos, and yet all traces of improbability must, if possible, be concealed.

The time during which the Chorus is on the stage is Æschylus's Short Time, and corresponds to Bassanio's journey from Venice to Belmont. Æschylus's Long Time is Agamemnon's week's voyage from Troy to Argos, corresponding to Anthonio's three months' bond. The same power that can compress three months at Venice into one day at Belmont, must expand a few hours at Argos into a se'en nights' voyage from Troy.

The task in *The Agamemnon* is the reverse of the task in *The Merchant of Venice*. Shakespeare must compress a long term into a short one, while Æschylus must dilate a short time into a long one. Shakespeare presents to us the spy-glass, and bids us see what is distant close at hand; while Æschylus reverses the glass, and what is but an arm's length from us recedes to the verge of the horizon.

To a certain extent and for many purposes, what Shakespeare can effect by Acts and the shifting of Scenes, Æschylus can bring about by means of the Chorus. Yet here it is not easy to see how the Chorus can help him; nothing that the Chorus could say would lessen the shock to our sense of the fitness of things if Agamemnon himself were to be brought at once upon the scene. Old Argive citizens compose this Chorus; they have remained here quietly in Argos; of Agamemnon, or of his journey, they can tell us nothing.

Of a sudden Clytemnestra sees a Herald hastening from the shore. In thus introducing a Herald, art is shown. Heralds always travel in advance of their lords, and this Herald, as far as we know, may possibly have left Troy before its fall. That it is a Herald from the Argive king we feel sure, and having accepted the fact of his presence, we sink into a receptive mood for any impression which his story can impart. But while he is yet at a distance, Clytemnestra sees that he is travel-stained with dust and grime.* Thus is the spell begun, the magician is at work. We accept the Herald without a shade of suspicion; what can be more natural than that he should have travelled with extreme haste? The thrill of joy at the sight of one who can bring us news is heightened by waving olive branches, the pledges of peace and victory, which he bears aloft. Thus artfully is the Herald announced before he enters on the stage; when at last he does enter and breaks out into a thrilling greeting of his home, criticism is forgotten in joy and sympathy.

We must remember, and we cannot too deeply remember, that both *The Agamemnon* and *The Merchant of Venice* were written, not to be studied and pored over, line by line, and analyzed sentence by sentence, but to be acted; to be communicated by the speaking voice to the hearing ear and interpreted by the quick thought. It is by a repetition of faint, fleeting, subtle impressions, felt but scarcely heeded at the time, that a deep, abiding effect may be at last produced. The 'snowflake on the river' may be but 'a moment there, then gone for ever;' yet let but enough fall and the stream is locked in frost.

What need to hurry with our questionings how the Herald came hither; he stands before us, and his story will tell us all.

In order to appreciate the delicacy with which Æschylus smooths away the objections to this speedy appearance of the Herald, we must bear in mind that every allusion to the flight of time since the hour that Troy has fallen, however light and evan-

---

* Thus I prefer to paraphrase the κάσις πηλοῦ ξύνουρος διψία κόνις; although it may, and perhaps ought to, refer to the dust raised by the Herald as he hurries forward. I think it no disgrace to confess that I know of no harder Greek to master, with every aid that Notes and Translations can yield, than *The Agamemnon*, and those who know it best will be most tolerant, I am sure, of my version or perversion.

escent the allusion may be, helps to make that hour recede into the past; and, for my purpose, I think I may be permitted to claim every possible impression which I can detect, of this nature, however fleeting, and then to multiply its effect on Grecian ears many times over. How clearly must it not have spoken to those ears, when it can penetrate even my adder's sense!

Thus, when the Herald in his first speech (lines 523 *et seq*) says that Agamemnon must be welcomed back, who has, with the crowbars of the just gods, levelled Troy to the ground, with all its towers and fanes, and that all earth's seed lies scattered on the ground, is not Time's thievish progress intimated here? Can walls, and towers, and temples be toppled over in a minute? Can harvests be burnt, and acres ploughed up, for leagues around, in an hour? Lost in the thought of these great tasks and of the mighty victory, we never stop to count the days; but the succession of pictures creates the flight of time, and the hour of Troy's fall begins to recede.

Too much, however, is not demanded of us at once; the Chorus here speaks; and then Clytemnestra exults in the assurance that the beacon-fires are true, and we are gently prepared for Agamemnon's approach by the message which the Chorus is to deliver when he arrives, telling him of her fidelity during his absence. Hereupon the Chorus asks after Menelaus, and the Herald reluctantly confesses that his fate is unknown. The Chorus presses for a more exact reply, and asks whether *he set sail with all the rest of the fleet* and then left them, or whether a storm snatched him away, but the Herald only ambiguously replies that it was even so. The Chorus returns to the point, and asks *what rumours* there were about him in the fleet, among the sailors. ' No one knows anything about him,' replies the Herald; 'the sun, the nourisher of the ' earth, alone can tell his fate.'

It seems needless to point out how insidiously, up to this point, the passage of time has been worked in by a succession of pictures, every one of which is suggested by a word or phrase which could not have fallen unheeded on Grecian ears. Troy has been conquered; and burnt; and razed to the ground; and reduced to a desolate ruin; the Greeks have divided the spoils; and allotted the trophies to be hung up in temples (577); the armies have been gathered together; and embarked in their fleet; and have advanced on their voyage; and been overtaken by a storm; and after the storm sufficient time has elapsed for the fleet to be collected; their losses counted; and ' rumours to live unchecked ' as to the fate of their companions.

(*And Troy fell only last night !*)

Trusting to the effect already produced, the Poet advances more boldly. Moreover, on the emotion, the uncritical emotion, excited in his auditors by the absorbing interest of the Tragedy he has a right to count.

Urged by the Chorus, the Herald hereupon describes this frightful storm which fell upon the fleet '*by night*' (line 653 *et seq*.), when fire and sea combined against it, and Thracian blasts dashed all the ships together; and 'when *the fair light of the sun arose,* we saw the Ægean Sea enamelled like a meadow (ἀνθοῦν) with the drowned corpses of sailors and of Greeks.'

To all the previous indications of the flight of time, which were but delicate, artful hints, there must be now added the explicit description of a *night* of storm, when the fleet was well on its way (the blasts came down from Thrace), and the next *morning afterwards* when the sun shone bright and clear.

Is not the goal won? The days of gloom, the night of storm, the smiling morrow, have passed before us; we have lived through them all, and the journey from Troy to Argos is accomplished. To Grecian eyes has not every league been measured?

Not to disturb this impression, but to deepen it by repose, the Chorus breaks in with four Strophes and four Antistrophes, wherein no allusion to the journey is found,—that is left as something fixed and settled; but it anathematizes Helen, and at the close, so far away have our thoughts been carried that any allusion to the journey from Troy to Argos seems like a thrice-told tale; that journey has become a fact around which no shadow of mistrust can cling.

Thus heralded, thus prepared for, Agamemnon enters, and the task is done. After the spells that have been woven around us, we find no more violation of probability in Agamemnon's appearance, from Troy, at that minute than in the expiration of the three months' Bond within the hour after Bassanio has chosen the leaden casket; and is there a man, who, when sitting at the play, can say with truth that, on that score, he ever felt a jar?

I do not think it is claiming too much thus to urge that the two greatest dramatic poets of the world used a kindred skill in producing kindred dramatic effects. If we find those effects in their dramas, their hands put them there, and to imagine that we can see them and that the mighty poets themselves did not, is to usurp a position which I can scarcely conceive of any one as willing to occupy.

LANSDOWNE'S VERSION

THERE have been in the history of this play two noteworthy Revivals; the first by MACKLIN and the second by KEAN. Although on the score of genius no comparison between the two actors can be made, yet the revival by Kean did not imply, perhaps, as great a revolution of popular feeling as the revival by Macklin. It is one thing to elevate and refine, to convert 'snarling malignity' into the 'depositary of the vengeance of a race,' but it is another and a bolder flight, I suggest, to transform a character, as Macklin transformed Shylock, from the grimacings of low Comedy to the solemn sweep of Tragedy. This was Macklin's achievement, and the best way to estimate its proportions is to examine the Thing which had supplanted Shakespeare. To turn back and read the page in the history of the Drama is a depressing duty. Our cheeks grow hot enough with shame over Dryden, or Shadwell, or Otway, or when 'Tate put his hook into the nostrils of the Leviathan;' but all is as nothing to the sight of Shylock drinking to his 'Mistress, Money,' and shouting a toast to 'Interest upon Interest,' or to the desecration of Portia's refined mouth by the objections put into it, to her German suitor.

In estimating this *Version*, which held sway for more than a generation, two facts, at least, we should remember.

First, that it was written in 'the teacup times of hood and hoop, while yet the patch was worn,' and that in those Dark Ages of the Drama, as in all ages, 'the drama's laws, the drama's patrons give,' and the men and women behind the footlights merely respond to the men and women before the footlights; and, Secondly, that it is scarcely to be called a modern version. Let us, at least, push the odium as far back as possible. The Fourth Folio was only fifteen years old when George Granville wrote this *Jew of Venice;* and Rowe, the first real Editor of Shakespeare, did not issue his edition until eight years afterwards. If due weight be given to these two considerations, I think we shall be inclined to leniency, and even wonder, perhaps, that as much of Shakespeare as we find here was left untouched.

Although it may fairly be called an uncommon book, it would be a waste of space to reprint the whole of its forty-seven quarto pages here; extracts erring on the side of fulness, and containing all the passages where Shakespeare is improved, must suffice.

This Version by GEORGE GRANVILLE, VISCOUNT LANSDOWNE (he was only thirty-three years old when he wrote it), appeared in 1701, and held the stage for exactly forty years. It bore the following title: *The Jew of Venice. A Comedy. As it is Acted at the Theatre in Little-Lincolns-Inn-Fields, by His Majesty's Servants.* London, Printed for Ber. Lintott at the Post-House in the Middle Temple-Gate, Fleetstreet, 1701.

Hereupon follows: 'Advertisement to the Reader. The Foundation of the following Comedy being liable to some objections, it may be wonder'd that any one should make Choice of it to bestow so much labour upon; But the judicious Reader will observe so many Manly and Moral Graces in the Characters and Sentiments, that he may excuse the Story for the sake of the Ornamental parts. Undertakings of this kind are justified by the Examples of those Great Men who have employ'd their Endeavours the same Way. The only dramatique attempt of Mr. Waller was of this Nature, in his alterations of *The Maid's Tragedy;* To the Earl of Rochester we owe *Valentinian;* To the Duke of Buckingham, *The Chance;* Sir William Davenant and Mr Dryden united in restoring *The Tempest; Troilus and Cresida, Timon,* and *King Lear* were the works of three succeeding Laureats. Besides many others too numerous to mention,' &c.

Then we have :—

PROLOGUE.

The Ghosts of Shakespear *and* Dryden *arise Crown'd with Lawrel.*
Written by Bevill Higgons, Esq;

   Dry. This radiant Circle, reverend *Shakespear*, view;
An Audience only to thy Buskin due.
   Shakes. A Scene so noble, antient *Greece* ne'er saw,
Nor *Pompey's* Dome, when *Rome* the World gave law.
I feel at once both Wonder and Delight,
By Beauty warm'd, transcendently so bright,
Well, *Dryden*, might'st thou sing; well may these Hero's fight.
   Dry. With all the outward lustre which you find,
They want the nobler Beauties of the Mind.
Their sickly Judgments, what is just, refuse,
And French Grimace, Buffoons, and Mimicks choose;
Our Scenes desert, some wretched Farce to see;
They know not Nature, for they tast not Thee.
   Shakes. Whose stupid Souls thy Passion cannot move,
Are deaf indeed to Nature and to Love.
When thy *Ægyptian* weeps, what eyes are dry !
Or who can live to see thy *Roman* dye.
   Dryd. Thro' Perspectives revers'd they Nature **view**,
Which give the Passions images, not true.
Strephon for *Strephon* sighs; and *Sapho* dies,
Shot to the soul by brighter *Sapho's* Eyes;
No Wonder then their wand'ring Passions roam,
And feel not Nature, whom th' have overcome.
For shame let genial Love prevail agen,
You Beaux Love Ladies, and you Ladies Men.
   Shakes. These crimes unknown, in our less polisht **Age,**
Now seem above Correction of the Stage;
Less Heinous Faults our Justice does pursue,
To day we punish a Stock-jobbing Jew.
A Piece of Justice, terrible and strange;
Which, if pursued, would make a thin Exchange.
The Laws Defect the juster Muse supplies,
Tis only we, can make you Good or Wise,
Whom Heav'n spares the Poet will chastise.
These Scenes in their rough Native Dress were mine;
But now improv'd with nobler Lustre shine;
The first rude Sketches *Shakespear's* Pencil drew,
But all the shining Master-stroaks are new.
This Play, ye Criticks, shall your Fury stand,
Adorn'd and rescu'd by a faultless Hand.
   Dryd. I long endeavour'd to support thy Stage
With the faint Copies of thy Nobler Rage,
But toyl'd in vain for an Ungenerous Age.
They starv'd me living; nay, deny'd me Fame,
And scarce now dead, do Justice to my Name.

Wou'd you Repent?   Be to my Ashes kind,
Indulge the Pledges I have left behind.

[A foot-note in the Second Edition, 1713, referring to the last two lines, says that 'the Profits of this Play were given to Mr Dryden's Son.']

DRAMATIS PERSONÆ.—MEN: *Bassanio*, Mr Betterton; *Antonio*, Mr Verbruggen; *Gratiano*, Mr Booth; *Lorenzo*, Mr Baily; *Shylock*, Mr Dogget; *Duke of Venice*, Mr Harris.

WOMEN: *Portia*, Mrs Bracegirdle; *Nerissa*, Mrs Bowman; *Jessica*, Mrs Porter.

ACT I.   SCENE I.

Anto.   I hold the World but as a Stage, *Gratiano*,
Where every Man must play some certain Part,
And mines a serious one.
    Grat.   Laughter and Mirth be mine,
Why should a Man, whose blood is warm and young,
Sit like his Grandsire, cut in Alablaster!
Sleep, when he wakes, and creep into the Jaundice,
By being peevish!   I tell thee what, *Antonio!*
I love thee, and it is my Love that speaks;
There are a sort of Men, whose Visages
Do cream and mantle, like a standing Pond;
And do a willful Stillness entertain,
Screwing their Faces in a politick Form,
To cheat Observers with a false Opinion
Of Wisdom, Gravity, profound Conceit;
As who should say, I am, Sir, an Oracle,
Oh my *Antonio!* I do know of these,
Who therefore only are reputed Wise,
For saying nothing; But more of this
Another time.   Let you and I, *Lorenzo*,
Take a short turn: Once more, my Friends, be merry,
All have their Follies; merry Fools are best.
Lorenzo, come, Sir Gravities, farewell,
I'll end my Exhortation after Dinner.   [*Exeunt* Grat. *and* Lorenz.
    Bass.   *Gratiano* speaks an infinite deal of nothing, &c.
                    [*And so on, without change, down to line 140.*]
    Bass.   To you, *Antonio*,
I owe the most in Money and in Love,
    Anto.   My Friend can owe me nothing; we are one.
The Treasures I possess, are but in trust,
For him I love.   Speak freely your Demand,
And if it stand, as you your self still do,
Within the Eye of Honour, be assur'd
My Purse, my Person, my extreamest Means,
Are all my Friend's.
                    [*Here follow lines 150–162.*]
    Anto.   You know me well, and herein spend but time,
To wind about my Love with Circumstance.

Believe me my *Bassanio*, 'tis more wrong
Thus to delay the Service of your Friend
Than if you had made waste of all I have;
Is this to be a Friend? With blushing Cheek,
With down-cast Eyes, and with a faltring Tongue
We sue to those we doubt: Friendship is plain,
Artless, familiar, confident, and free,
Ask then as you would grant, were yours the Power,
Were yours the Power, so would I ask of you;
No longer hesitate. Give me to know
What you would have me do, and think it done.

    Bass. Then briefly thus. In *Belmont* is a Lady
Immensely rich, and yet more fair than rich,
And vertuous as she's fair; sometimes from her Eyes
I have receiv'd kind speechless Messages.
Her Name is *Portia*; You have heard her Fame,
From the four Corners of the World; the Winds
Blow in, from every Coast, adoring Crowds;
The watry Kingdom, whose ambitious Head
Spets in the Face of Heaven, is no Bar
To æmulous Love, as o'er a Brook they come
To Anchor at her Heart; Her sunny Locks
Hang on her Temples, like a golden Fleece,
For which these many *Jason's* sail in Quest.
O my *Antonio*, had I but the Means
To hold a Rival-Place with one of 'em.

    Anto. The Means be thine, if I can find the Means,
My present Fortunes are, thou know'st, at Sea.
No Money, nor Commodity is left me
To raise immediate Sums. Therefore go forth,
Try what my Credit can in *Venice* do,
It shall be rack'd even to the uttermost
To furnish thy Desires: Nay, no set Speech
Of formal Thanks, which I must blush to hear.
Go, presently enquire. And so will I,
Where money is; In Friendship, who receives,
Obliges, by Acceptance, him that gives. *Exeunt.*

        Scene changes to Belmont. *Enter Portia and Nerissa.*

    Port. In short, *Nerissa*, my little Body is weary of this
Great World.

    Neriss. It might indeed, if your Wants were as great as your
Plenty.
For aught I see, they are as sick, who surfeit
With too much, as those who starve with too little;
From whence I conclude, that Happiness is seated in
The Mean: Superfluity brings Care, Care both
Robs us of our Time, and shortens our Days,
But Competency is the easiest and the longest Liver.

    Port. Good Sentences, and well pronounc'd.

Neriss. They would be better, if well follow'd.

Port. It is a good Divine, who follows his own Teaching;
I could easier instruct Twenty, what were good to do,
Than be one of the Twenty, to follow my own Instruction.
The Brain may devise Laws for the Blood; but the hot
Part will be sure to get the better of the cold; but what
Is all this to my choosing a Husband?

[*And so on, as in the original, down to line 30,* 'chooses you,

Neriss.   I have Superstition
Enough to believe the Benefit Lot is destin'd for
The best Deserver.
Love is at best, but a Lottery to all,
Your Case looks different, but is in Effect the same
With the rest of the World; For it is Fortune that
Always decides——
And now pray discover to whom of this Retinue of Suitors
Stand your Affections most inclined.
Never was Woman so surrounded as you are.

Port. *Penelope* was but a poor Princess to *Portia*,
But come, out with your List; Read me the Names,
And according as I describe, guess at my Inclinations.

Neriss. What a long List is here! Alas for poor Men, that
Among so many, but one can be happy!

Port. Alas! for poor Woman! that when she might have so
Many, she must have but one; but come, a Truce
To moral Reflections: Read, read.

Neriss. *Imprimis*, here in the Front, stands Monsieur *le Compte*
Your French Lover.

Port. Of himself, thou mean'st; He has more Tricks than
A Baboon: If my Bird sings, he strait falls into a capering;
He will fence with his own Shadow; nor is his Tongue
Less nimble than his Heels; I would as soon marry
My Squirrel, or my Monkey.

Neriss. What think you then of your Englishman, he comes next.

Port. The Frenchman's Ape: No, give me an Original,
Whatever it be. The Ape of an Ape must needs be a strange Monster.

Neriss. *Myn Heer van Gutts*, the Dutchman, how like you him?

Port. Very vilely in the Morning, when he is sober, and
More vilely in the Afternoon, when he is drunk;
At best, he is worse than a Man; and at worst, no better
Than a Beast: I will do anything, *Nerissa*, e're I'll
Be marry'd to a Sponge.

Neriss. For anything I find, this Lottery is not likely to be
Fair drawn: For if he should choose the right Casket,
You'll refuse to perform your Father's Will.

Port. Therefore, I prithee, set a Bumper of Rhenish
On the contrary Casket, for if the Devil be within,
And the Temptation without, I know he will
Choose it.

La Seignora Gutts! oh hideous! what
A Sound would there be in the Mouth of an
Italian?

Enter Servant.

Serv. Some of the Strangers, Madam, desire to take
Their Leaves: And there are others just arriv'd, and
Alighting at the Gate.

Port. Would some one would come, to whom I could bid
Welcome, as heartily, as I can bid all these Farewel.
There is a Man, *Nerissa*, such a Man; But what we wish,
Either never arrives, or is always longest in coming:
Fellow, go before: *Nerissa*, come! Whilst we shut
Out one Lover, another knocks at the Gate.

Neriss. This Lottery will certainly be drawn full. *Exeunt.*

[*The next Scene adheres to the original with but trifling changes down to line 145.
Shylock repels any imputation of Anthonio's honesty:* 'When a man is rich, we say
He is a good man, As on the contrary, when he has nothing we say a Poor Rascal;
'tis the Phrase, 'tis the Phrase.' *He omits the pun on* 'Pyrats,' *and closes his refusal
to eat or drink or pray with Christians by the assertion:* 'that's flat.' *He passes over
the account of Jacob and Laban with* 'You know the Story.' *Anthonio omits line 105*
'A goodly apple rotten at the heart.']

Shyl. And you'll
Not hear me,—were this offer kind?

Bassa. This were Kindness.

Shyl. This Kindness will I show; nay, more, I'll take
Antonio's single Bond: And that we may henceforth
Be Friends, no Penalty will I exact
But this, meerly for Mirth——
If you repay me not on such a Day, in such a Place,
Such Sum or Sums as are express'd— Be this
The Forfeiture.
Let me see, What think you of your Nose,
Or of an Eye— or of— a pound of Flesh
To be cut off, and taken from what Part
Of your Body— I shall think fit to name,
Thou art too portly, Christian!
Too much pamper'd— What say you then
To such a merry Bond?

Anto. The Jew grows witty; I'll seal to such a Bond,
And say there is much Kindness in the Jew.

Bassa. You shall not seal to such a Bond—
There is some Trick, some farther Fetch in this;
You shall not seal to such a Bond for me.

Anto. Fear not, my Friend, within two months, that is
A month before the Bond expires, I expect Returns
Of thrice three times the value of this Bond.

Shyl. O Father *Abraham*, what these Christians are!
Whose own hard Dealings teaches 'em to suspect
The Truth of others Pray tell me, should he fail

His Day— what should I get by the Exaction
Of the Penalty? A Pound of Man's Flesh?
Not to be sold nor eaten——
To buy his Favour I propos'd these Terms,
Such as I thought could bear no wrong
Construction; but since you're so suspicious
Fare you well.   [*going.*

   Anto. Stay, *Shylock*, I will seal as you propose.

   Shyl. Then meet me at the Notary's,
Give him Directions to prepare the Bond,
In the meantime, I'll fetch the Duccats,
See to my House, least some unthrifty Knave
Be on the Guard! Christian, thy Hand
I'll presently be with you.   *Exit Jew.*

   Anto. Thou'rt now a very gentle Jews.
This Hebrew will turn Christian, he grows kind.

   Bassa. I like not yet the Terms,
A Villain, when he most seems kind,
Is most to be suspected.

   Anto. There is not the least Danger, nor can be,
Or if there were, what is a pound of Flesh?
What my whole Body, every Drop of Blood,
To purchase my Friend's Quiet! Heav'n still is good
To those who seek the Good of others: Come, *Bassanio,*
Be chearful, for 'tis lucky Gold we borrow.
Of all the Joys that generous Minds receive,
The noblest is, the God-like Power to give.   *Exeunt.*

[*This closes Act I. As will be seen by the Dramatis Personæ, Morocco, Arragon, Gobbo, Salarino, Salanio, and Tubal are all omitted. With* II, v, 14, '*I am bid forth to supper, Jessica,' Lansdowne begins his Act II, and, omitting Gobbo, adheres to the original down to line 57, when, with* 'Fast bind, fast find,' *Shylock exit. Jessica then says:*]

   Jess. Alas! what Sin is it in me
To be asham'd to be my Father's Child?
But how can he be said to have given me Life,
Who never suffer'd me to know,
What 'tis to live. O *Lorenzo!*
Keep but thy Word to Night, and thou shalt be
A Father, and a Husband both to me.   *Exit.*

[*Enter* Lorenzo *and* Gratiano. *The former repeats, substantially, his words in* II, iv, 32–40: '*She hath directed How I shall take her,' &c., whereto Gratiano replies:*]

Young, handsome, willing, with Gold and Jewels to Boot!
Plague on't, when shall I have such Luck?

           Enter Jessica, *in the Balcony.*

   Jess. Who are you? Tell me for more Certainty,
Albeit I swear that I do know your Voice,
I love the Repetition of thy Name.

     [*With trifling verbal alterations to line 58.*]

Grat. Now, by my Soul, a Gentile, and no Jew,
She robs her Father with a Christian's Grace.

Lor. Beshrew me, but I love her from my Soul!
For she is Fair, or else my Eyes are false;
And true she is. What Proofs could she give more?
And Oh she's kind; she loves me, and I love,
A greater Bliss, scarce Heav'n it self can boast
Than mutual Love.

Enter Jessica *shutting the Door after her.*

Jess. Shut Doors after you; fast bind, fast find,
These were his last Words; Thus I avoid the
Curse of Disobedience! Be thou shut till I
Open thee.

Lor. So whilst old *Laban* snor'd in Bed,
Jacob with sprightly *Rachel* fled.

Jess. His Gold, and Gems of Price they took,
And eke the Flower of every Flock. [*Holds up a Bag.*

Lor. But not one precious thing was there
That could with *Jessica* compare.

Enter Antonio.

Ant. Fy, Fy, my Friends, why do you loyter thus?
Gratiano and *Lorenzo*, for Shame make haste:
Bassanio frets, that you are wanting,
He has sent twenty times to look you out.

Grat. Matters of State, *Antonio*, Matters of State,
A Rape and a Robbery: Matters of State,
Matters of State, *Antonio*.

Ant. Away, away, for Shame. [*Exit.*

Lor. Farewel, *Gratiano:* Excuse me to *Bassanio.*
Come *Jessica*, this must be your way and mine. [*Exeunt*

Grat. Jew, Turk and Christian differ but in Creed;
In ways of Wickedness, they're all agreed:
None upwards clears the Road. They part and cavil,
But all jog on—unerring to the Devil. [*Exeunt.*

Scene opens, and discovers Bassanio, Antonio, Shylock, *and others, sitting, as at an Entertainment. Musick playing: During the Musick,* Gratiano *enters, and takes his Place.*

Anto. This to immortal Friendship; fill it up—
Be thou to me, and I to my *Bassanio*,
Like *Venice* and her *Adriatick* Bride,
For ever link'd in Love.

Bassa. Thou joyn'st us well: And rightly hast compared;
Like *Venice* on a Rock, my Friendship stands
Constant and fix'd; but 'tis a barren Spot;
Whilst like the liberal *Adriatick*, thou
With Plenty bath'st my Shoars—
My Fortunes are the Bounty of my Friend.

Anto. My Friend's the noblest Bounty of my Fortune
Sound every Instrument of Musick there,

23

To our immortal Friendship.   [*All drink.   Loud Musick.*

  Bassa.   Let Love be next, what else should

Follow Friendship?

To Love, and to Love's Queen; my charming *Portia,*

Fill; till the rosy Brim reflects her Lips;

Then Kiss the Symbol round:

Oh, in this Lottery of Love, where Chance

Not Choice presides: Give, give, ye Powers, the Lot,

Where she her self would place it: Crown her Wish,

Tho' Ruin and Perdition catch *Bassanio;*

Let me be wretched, but let her be blest.   [*Drink, and Musick again.*

  Grat.   Mine's a short Health: Here's to the Sex in general;

To Woman; be she Black, or Brown, or Fair;

Plump, Slender, Tall, or Middle-statur'd—

Let it be Woman; and 'tis all I ask.   [*Drink again, Musick as before.*

  Shyl.   I have a Mistress, that out-shines 'em all—

Commanding yours—and yours tho' the whole Sex:

O may her Charms encrease and multiply;

My Money is my Mistress! Here's to

Interest upon Interest.   [*Drinks.*

  Anto.   Let Birds and Beasts of Prey howl to such Vows,

All generous Notes be hush'd; Pledge thy self, Jew:

None here will stir the Glass—   [*All Rise.*

Nor shall the Musick sound: O *Bassanio!*

There sits a Heaviness upon my Heart

Which Wine cannot remove; I know not

But Musick ever makes me that.

  Bassa.   The Reason is your Spirits are attentive, &c.

[*Hereupon follows what Lorenzo says to Jessica about music in* V, i, 80–98, *and ends with the words:* '*Mark the Music,*' *and this* '*Music*' *which Bassanio requested his friends to mark, turns out to be a Masque composed by Lord Lansdowne, called* PELEUS AND THETIS, *and consists of about a hundred and fifty lines of dreary inanities, wherein certain stanzas appear to have been special favorites of his lordship, thus:*

        Thetis.   Accursed Jealousy!

        Thou Jaundice in the Lover's Eye

        Thro' which all objects false we see;

           Accursed Jealousy!

Again:

        But see! the mighty Thund'rer's here,

          Tremble, Peleus, tremble, fly.

        The Thunderer! the mighty Thunderer!

          Tremble, Peleus, tremble, fly.

These are so good that his lordship thought they would bear repeating, and after serving their turn from the mouth of Thetis they are repeated as a Chorus.   If Antonio knew that Bassanio had this Masque in preparation, we need find no difficulty in accounting for that '*Heaviness*' *which sat upon Antonio's heart, beyond the power of* '*wine to remove.*' *The last we see of Peleus and Thetis they are warbling a duet, whereof the refrain cannot be judiciously gainsaid:*

Be true, all ye Lovers, whate're you endure,
Tho' cruel the Pain is, how sweet is the cure!'
Hereupon the play is resumed by Antonio's exclaiming :]
With such an Air of true Magnificence,
My noble minded Brother treats his Friends ·
As hardly has been known to *Italy*.
Since *Pompey* and *Lucullus* entertain'd ;
To frame thy Fortunes ample as thy Mind,
New Worlds should be created.

Enter Servant.

Serv. The Master of the Ship sends word the Wind is
Come about : And he desires you would haste Aboard.

Bassa., turning to Anto.] Oh my lov'd Friend! till now I never knew
The Pangs of parting Friendship.
At distance I have tasted of the Pain,
When the rude Morn has sunder'd us away,
To our Repose : But, by my Soul, I swear
Even then my Eyes would drop a silent Tear,
Repugnant still, to close, and shut out thee.

Anto. You go for your advantage, and that Thought
Shall keep *Antonio* comforted.

Bassa. The Traject is from hence to *Belmont* short,
And Letters may come daily : Such Intercourse
Is all the Cordial absent Friends enjoy :
Fail not in that. Your trouble shall be short,
I will return with the best speed I can.

Anto. Be not too hasty, my *Bassanio* neither ;
Slubber not Business for my sake, my Friend,
But stay the very ripening of thy Love.
Be gay, assiduous, and employ such Arts,
As best incline the Fair : Love is not seiz'd, but won :
Hard is the Labour ; You must plant and prune,
And watch occasion just : This Fruit is nice,
'Twill promise Wonders, and grow fairly up ;
Seem hopeful to the Eye, look ripe, and then
A sudden Blast spoils all.

Enter another Servant.

Serv. The Master of the Ship has sent agen.

Bassa. One more Embrace : To those who know not Friendship
This may appear unmanly Tenderness ;
But 'tis the Frailty of the bravest Minds.

Anto. I ask but this, *Bassanio ;*
Give not your Heart so far away,
As to forget your Friend.
Come, is all ready ? I must hasten you.

Grat. If you were ready to part,
'Tis all we stay for now.

Bassa. *Shylock*, thy Hand, be gentle to my Friend,
Fear not thy Bond, it shall be justly paid,

We soon shall meet again,
Always, I hope, good Friends.
Oh my *Antonio!* 'tis hard, tho' for a Moment,
To lose the Sight of what we love.
   Shyl. aside.] These two Christian Fools put me in mind
Of my Money: Just so loath am I to part with that.
   Bassa. *Gratiano*, lead the way: *Shylock*, once more farewel.
We must not part, but at the Ship, *Antonio:*
Lovers and Friends, should they for Ages stay,
Would still find something left, that they would say.   [*Exeunt.*

ACT III. SCENE I.

Enter Portia, Bassanio, Nerissa, Gratiano, *and their Train.* Nerissa *ana* Gratiano
discourse apart.

   Bass. Why if two Gods should play some Heavenly match
And on the Wager lay two earthly Beauties,
And Portia, one, there must be something more
Pawn'd with the other; for the poor rude World
Has not her Equal: But alas, the while
Should *Hercules* and *Lychas* play at Dice
Who were the better Man? The greater throw
Might turn by Fortune from the weaker Hand;
So were a Gyant worsted by a Dwarf
And so may I, having no Guide but Chance,
Miss that, which one unworthier may obtain,
And dye with the Despair.
   Port. Therefore forbeare to chuse, pause for a while
Before you hazard; for in chusing wrong
You lose for ever; Therefore, I pray forbear
For something tells me, but it is not Love,
I would not lose you; I could teach you
How to chuse right: But then I am forsworn,
So will I never be
Yet should you miss me
I should repent that I was not forsworn;
For oh, what heavier Curse for Perjury
Could Heav'n provide, than losing all my Hope?
I speak too much; tho' Thought will have no bound,
A Virgin's Tongue should shame to hint a Thought,
At which a Virgin's Cheek should blush.
Think it not Love, yet think it what you please,
So you defer a Month or two,
For fain I would detain you as a Friend,
Whom as a Lover I might lose,
Should you persist to venture the rash throw.
'Tis better still to doubt, and still to hope,
Than knowing of our Fates, to know
That we have lost for ever.
   Bassa. Doubt is the worst Estate: 'Tis better once

To die, than still to live in Pain.
Desire is fierce, nor brooks the least delay.
Fortune and Love befriend me : I'm resolv'd;
My Life, and all my Earthly Happiness
Sits on the Chance : Where may I find the Casket !
 Port. Yet, let me persuade you : If for your self
You cannot fear, tremble for her——
For her, to whom you have so often sworn,
More than your self, you love her. Think ! oh Think !
On *Portia's* Fate : Who may not only lose
The Man, by whom she wishes to be won,
But being lost to him, remain expos'd
To some new Choice; another must possess
What Chance denies to you. O fatal Law !
Lost to each other were a cruel Doom,
But 'tis our least Misfortune; I may live
To be enjoyed by one I hate. And you
May live to see it.
 Bassa. To love, and to be lov'd, yet not possess
No greater Curse could be, but what thou fear'st,
Yet I will on : With double Flames I burn,
Knowing that *Portia* loves me; all my fear
Was for her Love : Secure of that I go
Secure of the Reward : Lead me to the Caskets.
 Port. Away then, and find out where *Portia's* lock'd.
Thy Courage is an Omen of Success
If Love be just, he'll teach thee where to chuse.
Nerissa, show him, since he is resolv'd,
The rest all stand aloft, while Musick plays
That if he lose, like Swans we may expire,
In softest Harmony; but if he win
Ah what is Musick then
 [*And so on to line 63,* ' The issue of the Exploit. Goe Hercules.']
Love that inflames thy Heart inspire thy Eyes,
To chuse aught where *Portia* is the Prize.
   [Portia *and the rest stand at a distance observing soft*
  Musick. Till re-enter Bassanio *in each Hand a Casket.*
 Bassa. Who chuses me, shall get what he deserves,
The like Inscription bears this Silver Casket.
Shall get what he deserves; who chuse by outward show,
Entic'd by gilded Baits and flattering Forms,
Who look not to th' Interiour : But like the Martlet,
Build in the Weather on the outward Wall,
Even in the force and Road of Casualty,
What may their Merit be ? agen let me consider.
     [*Walks about thinking.*
 Grat. Take the Gold, Man, or the Silver : plague on't
Would I were to chuse for him.
 Bass. Shall get what he deserves : Let none presume

Without the Stamp of Merit to obtain.
Oh that Estates, Degrees and Offices,
Were not deriv'd Corruptly: and that clear Honour
Were purchas'd by the Merit of the Wearer,
How many then would cover who stand bare!
How many be commanded, who command!
How much low Peasantry would then be glean'd
From the true seed of Honour! And how much Honour
Pickt from the Chaff and ruine of the Times,
To be new varnisht: Let me not be rash,
There yet remains a Third: well will I weigh
E'er I resolve.   [*Exi.*

  Grat. Take the Gold, I say; pox on Lead; what is it good
For, but to make Bullets, 'tis the image of
Death and Destruction.

                Re-enter Bassanio *with a Casket of Lead*

  Bass. The World is still deceiv'd with Ornament;
In Law what Plea so tainted or corrupt,
But being season'd with a gracious voice,
And cover'd with fair specious Subtleties
Obscures the show of Reason. In Religion
What dam'd Error, but some sober brow
Will bless it, and approve it with a Text.
There is no Vice so artless, but assumes
Some Mark of Vertue on its outward Parts
Hiding the Grossness with fair Ornament.
How many Cowards with Livers white as Milk
Have Backs of Brawn, and wear upon their Chins
The Beards of *Hercules* and frowning *Mars,*
Look even on Beauty; what are those crisped Locks
That make such wanton Gambols with the Wind?
What, but the Dowry of a Second Head:
The Skull that bred 'em in the Sepulcher.
Thus Ornament is as a beauteous Scarf
Veiling Deformity. Therefore thou gawdy Gold
Hard Food for Midas, I will none of thee.
Nor none of thee, Silver, thou Common Drudge
'Twixt Man and Man. But thou, thou meager Lead,
Which rather threaten'st, than do'st promise ought,
Thy sullenness moves more than Eloquence.
And here I fix: Joy be the Consequence.

  Grat. Undone, undone: I'll not stand to't, *Nerissa,* I'l
Chuse for myself.

  Port. [*Aside.*] How all the other Passions fleet to Air
As doubtful Thoughts, and rash, embraced Despair,
Tormenting Fears, and Green-ey'd Jealousy.
O! Love! be moderate; allay this Extacy.
In measure pour thy Joy, stint this excess:
I feel too much thy Blessing, make it less,

For fear I surfeit.
    Bass. What find I here?   [*Opening the casket.*
The Portraiture of Portia.
What Demi-God has come so near Creation, move these Eyes!
Or whether riding on the Balls of mine,
Seem they in Motion? Here are sever'd Lips
Parted with sweetest Breath: The very odour
Seems there express'd, and thus invites the Taste!   [*Kissing the Picture*
And here agen, here in her lovely Hair,
The Painter plays the Spider, and has woven
A golden Snare, to catch the Hearts of Men:
But then her Eyes!
How could he gaze undazled upon them,
And see to imitate: Let me peruse the Motto.
Reads.] Who chuses me; let him whose Fate it is,
Turn to the Fair, and claim her with a Kiss.
A gentle Schrole; fair Lady, by your Leave,
I come by note, to give and to receive,
Like one of two contending for a Prize,
Who thinks he has done well, looks round to mark
(Hearing applause and universal Shout)
Whether those Peals of Praise are meant to him
So stands *Bassanio;* full of Hopes and Fears,
Still anxious what to trust, and what believe,
Till you confirm his hopes.
    Port. Had Choice decided, and not only Chance:
As Fortune has dispos'd me, so had I.
Myself, and what is mine, to you and yours
Is now converted. But now I was the Lady
Of this fair Mansion, Mistress of these Servants,
Queen o'er my self, even now, and in a Moment
This House, these Servants, and my self their Queen,
Are yours, my Lord. I plight 'em with this Ring,
Which when you part from, lose or give away,
Let it presage the Ruin of your Love
And stand, as a Record, that you were false,
A follower of my Fortunes not of me,
And never meant me fair.
    Bassa. Dye first, *Bassanio*, My Mistress, and my Queen,
As absolute as ever shall you reign,
Not as the Lord, but Vassal of your Charms,
Not as a Conqueror, but Acquisition.
Not one to lessen, but enlarge your Power;
No more but this, the Creature of your Pleasure,
As such receive the passionate *Bassanio*,
Oh there is that Confusion in my Powers,
As Words cannot express: But when this Ring
Parts from this Finger, then part Life from thence;
Then say, and be assured, *Bassanio*'s dead.

[Gratiano *and* Nerissa *seem in earnest dispute.*

Grat.   I say, a Bargain's a Bargain, and I will have Justice.

Neriss.   I say, we drew Stakes.

Grat.   That was only in Case I had lost, Child.

Port.   A Dispute between our Friends! What's the matter, Cozen?

Grat.   I'll tell you, Madam, the Matter in short, and you shall be Judge;
I happen'd to say to this Lady, that it was her Destiny to
Have me; she consented to put it to Tryal, and agreed
To be determined by the Choice, my Friend should make
If he had you— I should have her; and here
Stand I to claim her Promise.

Port.   Is this true, *Nerissa?*

Nerissa.   Ay! but he recanted; and said afterwards, he
Would chuse for himself.

Grat.   Why sure so I can, now I know the right Casket.
What sort of a Tramontane, do you take me to
Be? You are gone that way too, as I take it.

Neriss.   Then Madam, all my Hope is, that you won't let
Me keep my Word.

Grat.   'Tis false, to my certain Knowledge she hopes
Otherwise—*Nerissa!* we'll play with 'em the first
Boy for 1000 Ducats.

Neriss.   Methinks this looks like the last Act of a Play.
All Parties are agreed; there remains nothing but
To draw the Curtain, and put out the Lights.

Grat.   A good hint, my Love: Let you and I make our *Exit*
About that same last Act, as you call it.

Bassa.   I rejoice, *Gratiano*, that my good Fortune
Thus included yours.
Oh that *Antonio* knew of our Success,
It would o're-joy him. Prithee *Gratiano*,
Send a special Messenger to *Venice*,
To inform him of our Fortunes—
Shylock shall now be paid, my Friend is safe,
And Happiness, on every side surrounds us.

[Gratiano *going out, meets* Lorenzo, Jessica, *and a*
Servant from Antonio *entring.*

Grat.   *Lorenzo*, and his pretty Infidel,
Salerio too, *Antonio's* Servant; If I mistake him not,
Look here, *Bassanio;* here is News from *Venice.*

Bassa.   *Lorenzo*, Welcome! *Salerio* too! what News
From my *Antonio?* Oh, 'tis the best of Friends!
Y'are welcome hither. By your Leave, my Love,
Tho' my interest here be yet but young, I
Take upon myself to bid my Friends most welcome

Port.   So do I my Lord.

[*And so on, with a few verbal changes, and omissions, among the latter* Jessica's *speech about her father, and Tubal and Chus, down to line 328.*]

Port. Will live as Maids and Widows. Let none reply
For I will have it thus.

Bassa. O Love! O Friendship!
Was ever Man thus tortured!

Grat. What, not one quarter of an hour to pack up
My Baggage?

Ner. Whereabouts is the last Act now *Gratiano?*

Grat. Faith Child, I have the Part ready
If I might have leave to play it.

Port. Away ye Triflers.
Nay then *Bassanio* I must thrust you from me:
'Tis hard for both to be divided thus
Upon our Wedding-day. But Honour calls,
And Love must wait. Honour, that still delights
To tyrannize o'er Love. Farewel, my Lord,
Be chearful in this Tryal: As you prove,
Your Faith in Friendship, I shall trust your Love.

> [*She conducts him to the Door. Exit* Bass., **Grat.**

Loren. Madam, if you knew to whom you show this Honor,
How true a Lover of your Lord!

Port. I never did repent of doing good;
Nor shall I now; But we have much to do
In other things; Therefore to you, *Lorenzo,*
And to this Lady, whose pardon I should crave,
For having stood so much unnoted by me,
I will commit as to my Lord's best Friends,
The Husbandry, and Conduct of my House
Until my Lord's Return: For my own part
I have to Heav'n breath'd a secret Vow,
To live in Prayer and Contemplation,
Only attended by *Nerissa* here,
Until her Husband and my Lord come back.
There is a Monastery two miles off
And there we will abide. I do desire you
Not to deny this Imposition, which
My Love and some Necessity
Now lays upon me.

Loren. Madam with all our Hearts;
We will observe your Pleasure.

Port. Come on, *Nerissa ;* I have Work in hand
That thou yet know'st not of. *Balthazar,*
Thou art honest; so let me find thee still.
Follow me in; I have some short Directions
For you all.   [*Exeunt.*

[*The next Scene is a combination of the Third and First Scenes of Act III. It is
laid in* 'a Prison in Venice,' *and opens with Shylock's command to the Jailer :* 'Jailer,
'looke to him, Tell not me,' &c., *and so on, for about twenty lines of the original. Shylock says he'll not be made a* 'soft relenting Fool,' *instead of* 'dull-eyed,' *and instead
of leaving, after saying in line 20,* 'I will have my Bond,' *he remains, and Anthonio*

asks: 'Thou wilt not take my Flesh; what's that good for?' *Shylock replies in the familiar passage* in III, i, 'To bait fish withal,' *and continues to the end of it with scarcely a variation; instead of saying Anthonio* 'mocked at his gains,' *he says,* 'repin'd at his gains,' *and at the close:* 'The Charity you practise I will Imitate: And t shall go hard, but I will improve By the instruction.' *Whereupon:*]

  Anto. Thou art the most impenetrable Curr
That ever kept with Men.
  Shyl. My Daughter too! None knew so well as you of my
Daughters flight. Why there, there, there is a
Diamond gone, cost me 2000 Ducats in *Frankfort.*
A Ring too, it was my Turkis; I had it of *Leah*
When I was a Batchelour; besides Gold, and many other
Precious Jewels. Would my Daughter were dead
At my Foot, so the Jewels were in her Ears.
Would she were Hears'd, so the Ducats were in the
Coffin. No News, and I know not how much
Spent in the Search: Loss upon Loss. The Theif [*sic*] gone
With so much, and so much to find the Theif;
And no Satisfaction, no Revenge: But thou art
Caught, and thou shalt pay the whole Theif's bill.
Thou who wast wont to lend out money for a Christian
Curtesy; Thou Christian Fool, pay thy Debts:
Jaylor, I say, look to him. [*Thrusts him after the Jailor and Exeunt.*

[*The Fourth Act opens with the Trial Scene. The variation in the first 146 lines is wholly in omissions. Anthonio's speech (ll. 9–16) is omitted, as also is Shylock's answer to the Duke (ll. 51–66); also Shylock's discomfiture of Bassanio (ll. 68–74) At line 75 Anthonio says:*]

  I pray you think you question with a Jew
You may as well expostulate with Wolves;
You may as well go stand upon the Beach,
And bid the Waves be still, and Winds be husht;
You may as well forbid the Mountain Pines
To wag their Tops and dance about their Leaves,
When the rude Gusts of Heav'n are whistling round
As seek, &c.

[*When Shylock, at line 108, asks:* 'Shall I have it?' *the Duke replies.*]

  The Court will first advise. Here is a Letter
From fam'd *Bellario*, which does much commend
A young and learned Doctor in our Court,
Whose Wisdom shall direct us. Where is he?
Call in the Council.

[*Anthonio's speech,* 'I am a tainted wether of the flock,' &c., *is omitted. At line 148, Shylock says:*]

  Thou but offends thy Lungs to speak so loud.
Thy Curses fall on thy own Head, for thus
Ensnaring thy best Friend, thou didst it, and not I.
I stand for Law. Thy Prodigality brought him
To this.
  Bass. Inhumane Dog!

Offic. Room for the Council there.
     Enter Portia *disguis'd like a Lawyer,* Nerissa
     like her Clerk, with Bagg and Papers.
Duke. Take your Place.
Are you acquainted with the Difference
Which holds the present Question in the Court?
 Port. I am instructed fully in the Case, &c.
 [*To line 185, Portia's speech is improved, as follows :*]
The Quality of Mercy is not strain'd;
It drops as does the gentle Dew from Heav'n
Upon the Place beneath : It is twice blest,
It blesses him that gives and him that takes
Tis mightiest in the mightiest : It becomes
The Crown'd Monarch, better than his Crown
It is the first of sacred Attributes,
And Earthly Power does then seem most Divine,
When Mercy seasons Justice. I have spoke thus much
To mitigate the Rigour of thy Plea;
For if thou followest this strict Course of Law
Then must *Antonio* stand condemn'd.

[*From this line to line 271 the improvements are trifling. Shylock exclaims:* 'A
Daniel, a *Daniel:* So ripe in Wisdom And so young in years! A second Solomon.'
*But in Antonio's dying speech the opportunity is too good to be thrown away, and
Shakespeare's* 'rough native dress' *is made by his lordship to* 'shine with nobler lustre,'
as follows :]

  An Age of Poverty, from which lingering Penance
She kindly cuts me off: Once more farewell:
Grieve not my Friend, that you thus lose a Friend,
For I repent not thus to pay your Debt
Even with my Blood and Life: Now do your Office,
Cut deep enough be sure, and whet thy Knife
With Keenest Malice; for I would have my Heart seen by
My Friend.
 Shyl. Doubt it not, Christian; thus far I will be Courteous.
 Duke. Antonio, is this all thou hast to say?
 Anto. 'Tis all.
 Bassa. Stand off, I have a word in his behalf,
Since even more than in his Avarice,
In Cruelty, this Jew's insatiable;
Here stand I for my Friend. Body for Body,
To endure the Torture. But one pound of Flesh
Is due from him; Take every piece of mine,
And tear it off with Pincers. Whatever way
Invention can contrive to torture Man,
Practice on me: Let but my Friend go safe,
Thy Cruelty is limited on him;
Unbounded let it loose on me: Say, Jew,
Here's Interest upon Interest in Flesh;
Will that content you?

Anto. It may him, not me.

Bassa. Cruel *Antonio.*

Anto. Unjust *Bassanio.*   [*Jew laughs.*

Bassa. Why grins the Dog?

Shyl. To hear a Fool propose: Thou shallow **Christian**!
To think that I'd consent: I know thee well,
When he has paid the Forfeit of his Bond,
Thou canst not chuse but hang thy self for being
The Cause: and so my Ends are serv'd on both.
Proceed to Execution.

   Bassa. Then thus I interpose.
            [*Draws and stands before* Antonio: *The Jew starts back.*
                        Antonio *interposes.*]

   Anto. Forbear *Bassanio*, this is certain Death
To both.

   Bassa. In one, both die: Since it must be,
No matter how.

   Duke. Before our Face this Insolence! And in a Court
Of Justice. Disarm and seize him.

   Port. Spare him, my Lord; I have a way to tame him.
Hear me one word.

   Shyl. Hear, hear the Doctor: Now for a Sentence
To sweep these Christian Vermin, coupled
To the Shambles. O 'tis a Solomon!

   Port. Hark you, Shylock, I have view'd this Bond,
And find it gives thee not one drop of Blood;
The Words expressly are—*A Pound of Flesh*,
No more. Take thou that Flesh,
But in the cutting it, if thou dost shed
One drop of Christian Blood, thy Lands and Goods
Are, by the Laws of *Venice*, mark you me,
Confiscate to the State.   [Shylock *starts surprized.*

   Shyl. Humph.

   Bassa. O, upright Judge! Mark, Jew. O learned Judge!
Forgive, most potent Duke, and Reverend Seigniors,
That thus enforc'd by my Despair——

   Duke. We do forgive thee, and admire thy Virtue
More than we blame thy Passion. But proceed.

   Port. *Shylock*, thy self shall see the Act,
And Letter of the Law: For as thou urgest Justice.

[*From this line 330, for the rest of the Act, the original is followed, with here and
there the change of a word, or an omission of a line or two; of improvements, the following are the most noticeable:*]

   Duke. Get thee gone; but do it.   [*Exit Shylock.*

   Port. Clerk, draw a deed of gift.   [*The Duke and Court rise.*

   Duke. *Antonio*, I rejoice at this Conclusion;
And I congratulate with you *Bassanio*,
Your Friends escape: You will do well
To gratify that learned Councellor

For in my Mind you both are in his Debt.

     [*Exit Duke with his Train, the Court breaking up.*

  Bassa. Let me embrace the Man, by whom my Friend
Has Life : For in that Life I live—
3000 Ducats due on *Shylock's* Bond
I freely offer to requite your Pain.

[*Portia refuses them and asks for the ring, which Bassanio withholds, but makes no
allusion to its being the gift of his wife, presumably because reference to the marriage
ceremony was omitted after the Casket Scene. After Portia and Nerissa have left,
Antonio says :*]

  My Lord *Bassanio*, let him have the Ring;
Let his Deservings, and my Love withal,
Be valu'd against every other Scruple.

  Bassa. Prithee *Gratiano*, run and overtake him :
Give him the Ring; and bring him, if thou can'st,
To my *Antonio's* House——away, make haste.   [*Exit* Gratiano.
Once more, let me embrace my Friend, welcome to Life,
And welcome to my Arms, thou best of Men :
Thus of my Love and of my Friend possess'd
With such a double Shield upon my Breast,
Fate cannot pierce me now, securely blest.

[*As they go off, Portia and Nerissa re-enter; Gratiano follows, and presents the
Ring; he then undertakes to show Shylock's house to Nerissa, and the Act closes as
follows :*]

  Grat. Come on, Sir; The first Cause I have to split,
You shall have all my Practice.

  Neriss. That may be sooner than you dream of,
Sir, I follow you.
So many Shapes have Women for Deceipt,
That every Man's a Fool, when we think fit.

               [*Exeunt.*

[*Act V opens with Lorenzo and Jessica.*]

  Loren. The moon shines bright. In such a Night as this
Did pensive *Troilus* mount the *Trojan* Wall,
Sighing his Soul towards the *Grecian* Tents,
Where beauteous Cressid lay——

[*The allusion to Thisbe is omitted, and Jessica refers to Dido. Lorenzo replies with
Medea, and, the reference to Jessica's stealing from Venice being omitted, Jessica refers
to Lorenzo. At line 40 Jessica says she hears a footing, and Portia enters with
Nerissa.*]

  Port. That light we see is burning in my Hall.

  Loren. 'Tis sure the voice of *Portia.*

  Port. He knows me as the Blind Man does the Cuckow,
By the bad Voice. *Lorenzo*, is it you?

  Loren. Madam, you are most welcome.

  Port. We have been praying for my Lords Success,
Who fares we hope the better for our Pray'rs :
Is he return'd?

  Loren. Madam, not yet. But here are Letters from him,

Will give a good Account of his Proceeding,
And that he will be here to night;
We were walk't out to wait his Coming.

Port. Give Order to my Servants, that they take
No Note at all of our being absent hence;
And let our Musick play, and every thing
So direct as we were here in formal Expectation
Of his return——
This Night methinks is but the Day-light sick;
It looks a little paler. 'Tis a Day,
Such as the Day is when the Sun is hid.

> *Enter* Bassanio, Antonio, Gratiano, *and Followers.*

Bass. We should hold day with the *Antipodes,*
If you would walk in Absence of the Sun?
My *Portia,* this was kind to meet me thus.

Port. O never more let any Cause of Grief
Divide my Lord and me.

> [Gratiano *runs to* Nerissa, *who discourse apart.*

Bass. Nothing can: Here, Madam, is my Friend,
Let me present him to you: This is *Antonio*
Whom, if you love *Bassanio,* you must love.

Port. I should behold him with a jealous Eye,
Who has so large a Share in my Lord's Heart.

To Ant.] Having his Leave, you'll not deny me yours,
To make a third in Friendship: I doubly joy
That you are safe and here.

Anto. I thank you, Madam.

Port. Play all our Instruments of Musick there,
Let nothing now be heard but sounds of Joy,
And let those glorious Orbs that we behold,
Who in their Motions, all like Angels sing,
Still Quiring to the blew-ey'd Cherubims,
Join the Chorus; that in Heav'n and Earth
One universal Tune may celebrate
This Harmony of Hearts. Soft Stilness, and the Night
Become the Touches of Sweet Harmony.   [*Music.*

Grat. By yonder Moon and Stars, I swear you wrong me,
By Heav'n, I gave it to the Lawyer's Clerk.

Port. A quarrel! what, already?

[*As in the original, substantially, the variations chiefly omissions, down to line 266.*]

Port. Let not that Man, whoe'er he is, come near me:
Since he has got the Jewel that I priz'd,
I shall become as liberal as you,
And nothing can deny the Man that has it.
A Ring it was of wondrous Mystery,
And Sanctify'd by Charms to rivet Love:
Whoever has it, has the sure Command
Of me, my Person, and of all that's mine:
The dire Enchantment was so strongly wrought;

One Mind directs us, and one Bed must hold **us:**
Know him I shall, I must; nay, I will know **him**
I feel the Effects already,   Watch me like *Argos,*
If you do not, if I be left alone,
Now by my Honour, which is yet entire,
That Man and I are one.

 Neriss.   Just such a Ring was mine:
Methinks I love that Lawyer's Clerk already,
Just as I love myself.

 Bassa.   Forgive me this first Fault;
I'll trust thy Honour above any Charms:
My Love is built upon Esteem so strong,
As cannot doubt your Virtue.

 Grat.   I am not quite so liberal of good Thoughts;
But this I'll say, if I can catch this Clerk,
His Pen shall split for't.

 Anto.   I am the unhappy Subject of this Quarrel
By my Perswasion——

 Port.   Sir, grieve not you;
You're welcome notwithstanding.

        [Walks about as in a Passion.

 Bassa.   But hear me, *Portia;*
Pardon this Error; by my Soul, I swear,
By what is dearer to me than my Soul,
Your precious self——

 Anto.   I dare be bound for him;
My Life upon the Forfeit, that your Lord
Shall never more break Faith.

 Port.   You have been oft his Surety, and
Have paid for't dearly.

 Anto.   No more than I am well acquitted of.

 Port.   Then be his Surety still: Here is a Ring,
Of the same Virtue, and so qualify'd
With equal Spells.   This only can retrieve
With Counter-Magick what the other lost.
Antonio, give him this: But make him swear
To keep it better.

 Anto.   Here, Lord *Bassanio:* Swear to keep this Ring.

 Bassa.   By Heav'n!   *[Starts.*
This is the same I gave the Lawyer.

 Port.   Why so it is; I had it from him: You see
How quick an Operation is in Magick,
We have met already.

 Bassa.   Met! how have you met!

 Neriss.   Met— why by Art Magick, to lie together;
Ask that same scrubbed Boy, the Lawyer's Clerk.

 Grat.   Why this is worse and worse.

 Bassa.   *Antonio!* this was your doing.   *[Angrily.*

 Anto.   Take your Revenge, and kill me.

Bassa. I am answer'd—— Is it then true?
And can it be? That by the secret Workings
Of Mystick Words, and Spells, and dire Compounds,
Potions and Invocations horrible,
Nature can be so led? What then is Virtue?
And what Security has Love or Reason,
Thus subjected to every Hell-born Hagg
Who, by such Conjurations can dis-join
United Hearts? Uniting the Averse!
How, wretched Man! how can'st thou boast free Will?
If this in very deed be true. I'll not suppos't——
But then that Ring! How could she have it: 'Tis Witchcraft!
Damn'd, damn'd Witchcraft; And I will fathom Hell,
But I will find a Fiend shall Counter-work
The Devil that has done this.   [Portia *and* Nerissa *laugh.*

Port. ⎫
Neriss. ⎬ Ha, ha, ha.

Grat. Is this true, Nerissa! are we then two Scurvy
Cuckcolds by Art Magick!

Port. Ha, ha, ha; Well; since you grow so serious,
I will be serious too: Read this *Bassanio,*
The Adventures writ at large: Look not so sullen; Lord,
But read it. *Lorenzo* here and *Jessica*
Can witness for me: I set out almost
As soon as you. And am but even now return'd,
I have not yet enter'd my House: But
For farther Proof, Clerk, give *Lorenzo*
The Writings sign'd by *Shylock.*

Neriss. I'll give 'em without Fee; Here *Lorenzo,*
Here is a Deed of Gift to you and *Jessica,*
Of all the Jew, your Father, dies possess'd of.

Loren. See Jessica, is this his hand?

Jess. 'Tis his own signing.

Loren. What Prodigy is this?

Bassa. I am struck dumb with wonder.

Grat. Was *Portia* then the little Smerking Lawyer,
And *Nerissa* the Clerk? I'll never forgive such a
Trick. Art-Magick do you call it?

Neriss. Nay, but *Gratiano.*

Grat. Away, away.   [*Dispute aside.*

Port. Antonio! Here are Letters too for you;
Ask me not yet, by what strange Accident
They fell into my Hands— but read 'em.

Bass. Amazement has bereft me of all Words.

Ant. Why here I read, for certain, that my scatter'd Ships,
Are safely all arriv'd at *Rhodes,*
With their whole Cargo.

Port. Doubt it not, *Antonio.* 'Tis most true,
Virtue like yours; such Patience in Adversity,

And in Prosperity such Goodness,
Is still the Care of Providence.

    Ant.   My Life and Fortunes have been all your Gift;
Dispose 'em, and command 'em, Madam,
As you please.   [Gratiano *and* Nerissa *advance*

    Neriss.   What can you bear no Jests, but of your own
Making?

    Grat.   You have so scar'd me with your Art Magick,
That I shall scarce be a true Man these two Days;
But therein lies my Revenge: And so shake
Hands from this Day forwards.
As the most precious of all Gems, I swear!
Nerissa's Ring shall be *Gratiano's* Care.

    Port.   All look amaz'd, in every Face I see
A thousand Questions: 'Tis time we should go in,
There will I answer all: Cease your Astonishment,
My Lord; by these small Services to you
And to your Friends, I hope I may secure
Your Love; which, built upon meer Fancy,
Had else been subjected to Alteration.
With Age and Use the Rose grown Sick and Faint,
Thus mixt with friendly Sweets, secures its Scent.

    Bassa.   The Sweets of Love shall here forever blow:
I needs must Love, rememb'ring what I owe.
Love, like a Meteor, shows a short-liv'd Blaze,
Or treads thro' various Skies a wandring Maze,
Begot by Fancy; and by Fancy led;
Here in a Moment, in a Moment fled;
But fixt by Obligations, it will last;
For Gratitude's the Charm that binds it fast.   [*Exeunt omnes*

24

ACTORS

WHEN Collier published his *History of English Dramatic Poetry* in 1831, he mentioned (vol. i, p. 430) a MS *Elegy on the Death of Richard Burbadge,* consisting of eighty-six lines, wherein allusion was made to the performance by BURBADGE of certain characters in the plays of Shakespeare and of others. The Shakespearian characters thus specified were Hamlet, Lear, and Othello. This MS then belonged to Haslewood, and is now in the Huth Library.

When, five years later, Collier printed his *New Particulars regarding the Works of Shakespeare,* he mentioned (p. 27) a second MS, belonging to Heber, and then went on to say : ' I have since met with a third copy of the same Elegy, in which the list ' of characters is enlarged . . . . to no fewer than twenty, of which twelve are in plays ' of Shakespeare.'

This third copy Collier afterwards printed in full, in his *Memoirs of Actors* (Shakespeare Society, 1846, p. 52), and also in the Second Edition of his *History of English Dramatic Poetry* (1879, vol. iii, p. 299). The lines are increased from eighty-six to one hundred and twenty-four, and the number of Shakespearian characters from three to twelve. To account for this enlargement, Collier suggests that perhaps ' the author ' had not intended in the first instance to give Burbadge's characters, because they ' were matters of notoriety at the time, although he afterwards thought fit to introduce ' them, in order to render his tribute more complete.'

These lines Ingleby has not admitted to his *Centurie of Prayse,* and Miss TOULMIN SMITH (p. 132, 2d ed.) says that the original of them has ' not yet come to light.' The inference, therefore, is that doubts attach to their genuineness. It is proper that this fact should be stated ; the *Elegy,* as given by Collier, is our sole authority for the tradition that Burbadge was not only the original actor of Shylock, but that he wore a *red-haired* wig.

It is thus entitled : ' A FUNERAL ELEGY, ON THE DEATH OF THE FAMOUS ACTOR, RICHARD BURBADGE, *who died on Saturday in Lent, the 13th of March, 1618 ;'* and the lines which relate to Shylock, all that concern us here, are as follows :

> ' Heart-broke Philaster, and Amintas too,
> ' Are lost forever; with the red-hair'd Jew,
> ' Which sought the bankrupt merchant's pound of flesh,
> ' By woman-lawyer caught in his own mesh,
> ' What a wide world was in that little space,
> ' Thyself a world—the Globe thy fittest place !' &c.

The next actor whose name is associated with Shylock is THOMAS DOGGET. He appears in the Dramatis Personæ prefixed to Lansdowne's *Version.* Of his interpretation of the part I can find no details whatever; we can infer that it was comic from the fact that Dogget was a comic actor, and it is difficult to imagine, considering the text that was used, how it could have received any other interpretation. We frequently hear it asserted that ' Shylock ' was at one time acted as a comic part, an assertion which should not be made without qualification; it was not Shylock, but a thing called ' Shylock ' in Lansdowne's *Version.* There is no ground for the belief that Shylock was ever presented on the stage in a comic light. To assert it is to imply that Lansdowne's ' Shylock ' and Shakespeare's Shylock are identical.

Downes, the Prompter at the Theatre in Lincoln's-Inn-Fields for over forty years, gives us, in his *Roscius Anglicanus* (p. 52, ed. Knight), the earliest description of Dogget. Downes was fond of high-sounding words : to say that an actress left off acting when she was married is far too homespun for Downes; from him we learn that 'by force of Love she was erept the stage;' in an Opera called *The British Enchanters* (Lord Lansdowne's, by the way), 'making Love,' says Downes, 'the *Acme* of all Terrestrial Bliss, infinitely arrided both sexes and pleas'd the Town;' wherefore we may be puzzled, but not startled, by learning that ' Mr Dogget, On the Stage, he's very Aspect-' abund, wearing a Farce in his Face; his Thoughts deliberately framing his Utterance ' Congruous to his Looks : He is the only Comick Original now Extant : Witness, *Ben,* ' *Solon, Nikin,* The *Jew* of *Venice,* &c.'

Colley Cibber was the personal friend, and at one time partner, of Dogget, and gives (*Apology,* &c., p. 287) an account of his acting, to which high praise is accorded. ' In ' dressing a character to the greatest exactness, he was remarkably skilful; the least ' article of whatever habit he wore seem'd in some degree to speak and mark the dif-' ferent humour he presented. . . . . His greatest success was in characters of lower ' life. . . . . In songs, and particular dances too, of humour, he had no competitor.'

Lansdowne's *Version* continued on the stage forty years, but to the credit of the public taste, be it noted, it does not appear to have been popular.

At the end of that time there happened to be in London an actor of some eminence who had discernment enough to perceive the dramatic capabilities of Shylock, and who determined to try the verdict of the public. He was an Irishman named McLaughlin, but this name had been dropped, with his brogue, on coming to London, and converted into the less guttural MACKLIN. Macklin was attached to the Drury Lane Company, and in 1741 persuaded Fleetwood, the manager, to revive Shakespeare's *Merchant of Venice.*

Of this important event in the stage history of the Play we have accounts by Kirkman and by Cooke, both substantially the same. The former better describes the opposition encountered by Macklin before the performance; the latter the performance itself.

KIRKMAN (*Memoirs of Charles Macklin,* 1799, vol. i, p. 256) : During the rehearsal of the play Mr Macklin did not let any person, not even the players, see how he intended to act the part. He merely repeated the lines of the character, and did not, by so much as one single look, tone, gesture, or attitude, disclose his manner of personating this cruel Israelite. The actors declared that Macklin would spoil the performance; and Mr Quin went so far as to say that he would be hissed off the stage for his arrogance and presumption. Nay, even the manager himself expostulated with him concerning the propriety of his persevering in his intention of having *The Merchant of Venice* represented in opposition to the judgement of so eminent a personage as Lord Lansdowne; to the opinion of Mr Quin and the rest of the actors; and, indeed, to the voice of the public, who had so often testified their approbation of the noble Lord's play. Thus did Mr Fleetwood argue with Macklin, and strenuously urge him to abandon his resolution. His character as an actor might (he said) be materially injured by a perseverance in his determination, and ultimately by a failure in the performance of the part; but Mr Macklin, supported throughout by his sound sense and acute discrimination, continued firm to his purpose, and had *The Merchant of Venice* announced for representation on the 14th of February.

On the first night of the representation, no sooner were the doors of the theatre opened than the house was crowded in every part. Some came from motives of pleasure, some to express their disapprobation; some to support the actor, and a great number appeared merely to gratify their curiosity.

Before the curtain rose the manager appeared in the green-room in great distress. The actors were anticipating the reception that awaited them, and indulging themselves in malicious remarks upon the headstrong conduct of Macklin. It is impossible for us to describe the feelings of poor Shylock at this precise juncture.

[The rest is better told by Cooke, who professes to give it in Macklin's own words :—]

COOKE (*Life of Macklin*, 1806, p. 92, 2d ed.): The long-expected night at last arrived, and the house was crowded from top to bottom with the first company in town. The two front rows of the pit, as usual, full of critics, 'who, sir' (said the veteran), 'I eyed through the slit in the curtain, and was glad to see there, as I wished, in such a cause, to be tried by a *special jury*. When I made my appearance in the green-room, dressed for the part, with my red hat on my head, my piqued beard, loose black gown, &c., and with a confidence I never before assumed, the performers all stared at one another, and evidently with a stare of disappointment. Well, sir, hitherto all was right,—till the last bell rung; then, I confess, my heart began to beat a little; however, I mustered up all the courage I could, and, recommending my cause to Providence, threw myself boldly on the stage, and was received by one of the loudest thunders of applause I ever before experienced.

'The opening Scenes being rather tame and level, I could not expect much applause; but I found myself well listened to,—I could hear distinctly in the pit the words, "Very well,—very well, indeed!—This man seems to know what he is about," &c. &c. These encomiums warmed me, but did not overset me,—I knew where I should have the pull, which was in the Third Act, and reserved myself accordingly. At this period I threw out all my fire; and, as the contrasted passions of joy for the Merchant's losses, and grief for the elopement of Jessica, open a fine field for an actor's powers, I had the good fortune to please beyond my warmest expectations. The whole house was in an uproar of applause, and I was obliged to pause between the speeches, to give it vent, so as to be heard. When I went behind the scenes after this Act, the manager met me and complimented me very highly on my performance, and significantly added: "Macklin, you was right at last." My brethren in the green-room joined in his eulogium, but with different views. He was thinking of the increase of his treasury; they only for saving appearances, wishing at the same time I had broke my neck in the attempt. The Trial Scene wound up the fulness of my reputation: here I was well listened to; and here I made such a silent, yet forcible, impression on my audience, that I retired from this great attempt most perfectly satisfied.

'On my return to the green-room, after the play was over, it was crowded with nobility and critics, who all complimented me in the warmest and most unbounded manner; and the situation I felt myself in, I must confess, was one of the most flattering and intoxicating of my whole life. No money, no title could purchase what I felt; and let no man tell me after this what Fame will not inspire a man to do, and how far the attainment of it will not remunerate his greatest labours. By G—, sir, though I was not worth fifty pounds in the world at that time, yet, let me tell you, I was *Charles the Great* for that night.'

A few days afterwards Macklin received an invitation from Lord Bolingbroke to dine with him at Battersea. He attended the rendezvous, and there found Pope and a select party, who complimented him very highly on the part of Shylock, and questioned him about many little particulars relative to his getting up the play, &c. Pope particularly asked him why he wore a *red hat?* and he answered, because he had read that Jews in Italy, particularly in Venice, wore hats of that colour. 'And pray, Mr Macklin,' said Pope, ' do players in general take such pains?' ' I do not know, sir, that they do; but as I had staked my reputation on the character, I was determined to spare no trouble in getting at the best information.' Pope nodded, and said, ' It was very laudable.'

Macklin took this play for his benefit on the nineteenth night, and had an overflowing audience; several noblemen of the first distinction took what is commonly called *gold* tickets; and Lord Bolingbroke made him a present of twenty guineas. The play had a successful run through the whole of the season, and for many seasons afterwards; it established his reputation as an actor, and not a little added to his discernment as a critic in reviving a piece which, perhaps, except for his research, might have been lost to the stage for ever.

KIRKMAN (vol. ii, p. 427): Several years before his death, Mr Macklin happened to be in a large company of ladies and gentlemen, among whom was the celebrated Mr Pope. The conversation having turned upon Mr Macklin's age, one of the ladies addressed herself to Mr Pope, in words to the following effect: ' Mr Pope, when Macklin dies, you must write his epitaph.' ' That I will, madam,' said Pope; ' nay, I will give it now:'

> ' Here lies the Jew
> That Shakespeare drew.'

The whole company highly approved of this epitaph, and Mr Macklin has often related this anecdote in our hearing with great glee; and a more just, comprehensive, and concise inscription never was written.

GENTLEMAN (*Dramatic Censor*, 1770, i, 291): There is no doubt but Mr Macklin looks the part of Shylock as much better than any other person as he plays it; in the level scenes his voice is most happily suited to that sententious gloominess of expression the author intended; which, with a sullen solemnity of deportment, marks the character strongly; in his malevolence there is a forcible and terrifying ferocity; in the Third Act scene, where alternate passions reign, he breaks the tones of utterance and varies his countenance admirably; in the dumb action of the Trial Scene, he is amazingly descriptive.

[Macklin is supposed to have been born in May, 1690. If this were so, he was nigh his hundredth year when, in May, 1789, he undertook to play Shylock once more. Although his exact age cannot be determined, it is undeniable that at this time he was extremely old, and that the thread of life was stretched beyond the limit when it is pleasant either to hold it, or to behold it. Of this attempt Cooke gives the following account:]

His last appearance on the Stage was on the 7th of May, 1789, in Shylock for his own benefit. The Manager, Fleetwood, had Mr Ryder under-study the part, ready dressed to supply Macklin's deficiencies if necessary.

When Macklin had dressed himself for the part, which he did with his usual accuracy, he went into the Green-Room, but with such ' lack-lustre' eyes, as plainly indicated his inability to perform, and coming up to Mrs Pope said, ' My dear, are you to play to-night?'—' Good God! to be sure I am, Sir. Why, don't you see I am dressed for Portia?'—' Ah! very true; I had forgot. But who is to play Shylock?' The imbecile tone and the inane look, with which this last question was asked, caused a melancholy sensation in all who heard it. At last Mrs Pope, rousing herself, said, ' Why you, to be sure; are not you dressed for the part?' He then seemed to recollect himself, and, putting his hand to his forehead pathetically exclaimed, ' God help me—my memory, I am afraid, has left me.'

He, however, went upon the Stage and delivered two or three speeches of Shy-lock in a manner that evidently proved he did not understand what he was repeating. After a while, he recovered himself a little and seemed to make an effort to rouse himself; but in vain— Nature could assist him no further; and, after pausing some time, as if considering what to do, he came forward, and told the audience, 'That he now found he was unable to proceed in the part, and hoped they would accept Mr Ryder, as a substitute, who was already prepared to finish it.' The audience accepted his apology with mingled applause of indulgence and commiseration—and he retired from the stage for ever. [He lived eight years longer, until 1797.]

[P. 405]: All the succeeding Shylocks, though just and pleasing portraits of the character, wanted the original firmness and colouring of Macklin's pencil. There was, besides his judgment which went to the study of every line of it, such an iron-visaged look, such a relentless, savage cast of manners, that the audience seemed to shrink from the character, nor could they recover the true tone of their feelings till the merchant was liberated from the fangs of such a merciless creditor. Cooke seems to be nearest the original of any we have seen.

LICHTENBERG, whose notices of the actors and actresses whom he saw in London are all too short, gives us in a few sentences a vivid description of Macklin. His letter is dated the 2d of December, 1775 (*Vermischte Schriften*, iii, 266, Göttingen, 1867):—

I have seen the Shylock of Macklin, so well known for his high deserts, his law-suit, and his physiognomy. [This lawsuit was brought by Macklin against certain citi-zens, who, in their opposition to him as an actor, behaved so riotously one evening that they obliged the manager to discharge Macklin before they would allow the play to proceed. Macklin gained his suit, and was awarded exemplary damages. In this lawsuit the public took extraordinary interest, involving, as it did, the right to hiss an actor, on which point Lord Mansfield decided that, 'Every man that is at the play-house has a right to express his approbation or disapprobation instantaneously, accord-ing as he likes either the acting or the piece. That is a right due to the theatre,—an unalterable right,—they must have that.'—ED.] You know that the announcement of Macklin as Shylock sounds as attractively on the play-bill as Garrick in Hamlet. It was the evening on which he appeared for the first time after his suit was decided. When he appeared he was received with great applause, thrice given, each time lasting a quarter of a minute. It is not to be denied that the sight of this Jew suffices to awaken at once, in the best-regulated mind, all the prejudices of childhood against this people. Shylock is none of your petty cheaters, who can talk for an hour over the excellence of a pinchbeck watch-chain. He is slow, calm in his impenetrable cun-ning, and when he has the law on his side he is unflinching, even to the extreme of malice. Picture to yourself a somewhat strong man, with a sallow, harsh face and a nose which is by no means lacking in any one of the three dimensions, a long double chin or dewlap; and in making his mouth, Nature's knife seems to have slipped and gone all the way to his ears, at least on one side, so it seemed to me. His cloak is black and long, his pantaloons also are long and broad, and his hat three-cornered and red, probably in accordance with the style of the Italian Jews. The first words which he utters are spoken slowly and deliberately: '*Three thousand ducats*.' The *th* and the *s* twice occurring and the last *s* after the *t* have a lickerish sound from Macklin's lips, as if he were tasting the ducats and all that they can buy; this speech creates for the man, upon his first appearance, a prepossession which is sustained throughout. Three such words, thus spoken and at the very first, reveal a whole character. In the Scene in which he first misses his daughter he appears hatless, with hair all flying, some of it standing up straight, a hand's breadth high, just as if it had been lifted up by a breeze from the gallows. Both hands are doubled up, and his gestures are quick and convulsive. To see a man thus moved, who had been hitherto a calm, determined villain, is fearful.

BOADEN (*Life of Kemble*, i, 440): As I paid much attention to Macklin's performances, and personally knew him, I shall endeavor to characterize his acting and discriminate it from that of others. If Macklin really was of the old school, that school taught what was truth and nature. His acting was essentially manly,—there was nothing of trick about it. His delivery was more level than modern speaking, but certainly more weighty, direct, and emphatic. His features were rigid, his eye cold and colourless; yet the earnestness of his manner, and the sterling sense of his address, produced an effect in Shylock that has remained to the present hour unrivalled. Macklin, for instance, in the Trial Scene, 'stood like a TOWER,' as Milton has it. He was 'not bound to *please*' any body by his pleading; he claimed a right, grounded upon LAW, and thought himself as firm as the Rialto. To this remark it may be said, 'You are here describing Shylock.' True; I am describing Macklin. [This was written eleven years after Kean's first appearance as Shylock, but Boaden makes no allusion to him. Boaden was an enthusiastic admirer of Kemble, whose school of acting differed widely from that of Kean.]

Macklin's interpretation of Shylock appears to have been the standard until the appearance of Edmund Kean in 1814; of this appearance I shall give the accounts both of Dr Doran, and of Kean's biographer, Hawkins. If there is repetition, it can do no harm. The story is in itself so dramatic that custom cannot stale it.

DORAN (*Their Majesties' Servants*, 2d ed., 1865, p. 428): Howard died [Kean's elder son, to whom he was passionately attached, and who lived but five years] and Kean played, danced, sorrowed, and hoped,—for the time at which he was to go up to London was at hand; and thither they went, at the close of the year 1813. When that season of 1813–14 opened, Drury was in a condition from which it could be relieved only by a genius;—and there he stood in that cold hall, a little, pale, restless, dark-eyed man, in a coat with two or three capes, and nobody noticed him! In Cecil Street his family were living on little more than air; and he was daily growing sick, as he stood, waiting in that hall, for an audience with the manager, and subject to the sneers of passing actors. Even Rae, handsome and a fool, affected not to know him, though they had played together, when Rae's mother was matron at St George's Hospital; and they had acted together at the Haymarket in 1806, when Rae led the business and Kean was but a supernumerary! Arnold treated him superciliously, with a '*young man!*' as he condescended to speak and put him off. Other new actors obtained trial parts, but there was none for that chafed, hungry little man in the capes. Even drunken Tokely, like himself, from Exeter, could obtain a 'first appearance,' but Kean was put off. Stephen Kemble played Shylock, and failed! why not try a new actor? The Committee did so, and Mr Huddart, from Dublin, went on as Shylock, and was never heard of more. And the poor stroller looked through the darkness of that miserable passage the while, and murmured, 'Let me but get my foot before the floats, and *I'll* show them—!'

The permission came. Would he,—no he *must* play Richard. 'Shylock, or nothing!' was his bold reply. He was afraid of the littleness of his figure (which he had heard scoffed at) being exposed in the 'trunks' of Glo'ster. He hoped to hi'e it under the gown of Shylock. The Jew, or nothing! The young fellow, he was but six-and-twenty, was allowed to have his way. At the one morning rehearsal, he fluttered his fellow-actors, and scared the manager, by his independence and originality. 'Sir, this will never do!' cried Raymond, the acting manager. 'It is quite an innovation; it cannot be permitted.' 'Sir,' said the poor, proud man; 'I wish it to be so;' and the players smiled, and Kean went home, that is, to his lodgings, in Cecil Street, on that snowy, foggy 26th of January, 1814, calm, hopeful, and hungry. 'To-day,' said he, 'I must *dine*.'

Having accomplished that rare feat, he went forth alone and on foot. 'I wish,' he remarked 'I was going to be shot!' He had with him a few properties which he was bound to procure for himself, tied up in a poor handkerchief, under his arm. His wife remained with their child at home. Kean tramped on beneath the falling snow, and over that which thickly encumbered the ground—solid here, there in slush—and bye and bye, pale, quiet, but fearless, he dressed in a room shared by two or three others, and went down to the wing by which he was to enter. Hitherto no one had spoken to him, save Jack Bannister, who said a cheering word; and Oxberry, who had tendered him a glass and wished him good fortune. 'By Jove!' exclaimed a first-rater, looking at him, 'Shylock in a black wig! Well!!' In the good old times the wig was of a *Judas colour*.

The house could hold, as it is called, £600; there was not more than a sixth of that sum in front. Winter without, his comrades within, all was against him. At length he went on, with Rae as Bassanio, in ill-humour, and groups of actors at the wings to witness the first scene of a new candidate. All that Edmund Kean ever did was gracefully done; and the bow which he made in return to the welcoming applause was eminently graceful. Dr Drury, the head-master of Harrow, who took great interest in him, looked fixedly at him as he came forward. Shylock leant over his crutched stick with both hands; and, looking askance at Bassanio, said, 'Three thousand ducats?' paused, bethought himself, and then added, 'Well?' *He is safe!* said Dr Drury.

The groups of actors soon after dispersed to the green-room. As they reached it, there reached there, too, an echo of the loud applause given to Shylock's reply to Bassanio's assurance that he may take the bond,—'I *will be* assured I may!' Later came the sounds of the increased approbation bestowed on the delivery of the passage ending with, 'and for these courtesies, I'll lend you thus much moneys.' The Act came to an end gloriously; and the players in the green-room looked for the coming among them of the new Shylock. He proudly kept aloof; knew he was friendless; but felt that he was, in himself, sufficient.

He wandered about the back of the stage, thinking, perhaps, of the mother and child at home; and sure, now, of having at least made a step towards triumph. He wanted no congratulations; and he walked cheerfully down to the wing where the scene was about to take place between him and his daughter, Jessica, in his very calling to whom, 'Why Jessica! I say'—there was, as some of us may remember, from an after-night's experience, a charm, as of music. The whole Scene was played with rare merit; but the absolute triumph was not won till the Scene (which was marvellous in his hands) in the Third Act between Shylock, Solanio, and Salarino, ending with the dialogue between the first and Tubal. Shylock's anguish at his daughter's flight; his wrath at the two Christians who make sport of his anguish; his hatred of all Christians, generally, and of Antonio in particular; and then his alternations of rage, grief, and ecstasy, as Tubal relates the losses incurred in the search of that naughty Jessica, her extravagances, and then the ill-luck that had fallen on Antonio,—in all this there was such originality, such terrible force, such assurance of a new and mighty master, that the house burst forth into a very whirlwind of approbation. 'What now?' was the cry in the green-room. The answer was, that the presence and the power of the genius were acknowledged with an enthusiasm which shook the very roof. How so select an audience contrived to raise such a roar of exultation, was a permanent perplexity to Billy Oxberry.

Those who had seen Stephen Kemble's Shylock, and that of Huddart, this season, must have by this time confessed that the new actor had superseded both. He must himself have felt that, if he had not yet surpassed Cooke, and Henderson, and Macklin, he was tending that way; and was already their equal. Whatever he felt, he remained reserved and solitary; but he was now sought after. Raymond, the acting manager, who had haughtily told him his innovations 'would not do,' came to offer him oranges. Arnold, the stage-manager, who had *young-manned* him, came to present him, 'sir!' with some negus. Kean cared for nothing more now than for his Fourth and last Act; and in that his triumph culminated. His calm demeanour at first; his confident appeal to justice; his deafness when appeal is made to him for mercy; his steady joyousness when the young lawyer recognizes the validity of his bond; his burst of exultation when his right is confessed; his fiendish eagerness when whetting the knife;—and then the sudden collapse of disappointment and terror, with the words,—'Is *that*—the Law?'—in all, was made manifest that a noble successor to the noblest of the actors of old had arisen. Then, his trembling anxiety to recover what he had before refused; his sordid abjectness, as he finds himself foiled at every turn; his subdued fury; and, at the last (and it was always the crowning glory of his acting in this play), the withering sneer, hardly concealing the crushed heart, with which he replied to the jibes of Gratiano, as he left the court;—all raised a new sensation in an audience, who acknowledged it in a perfect tumult of acclamation. As he passed to his dressing-room, Raymond saluted him with the confession that he had made a hit; Pope, more generous, avowed that he had saved the house from ruin.

And then, while Bannister was dashing through Dick, in *The Apprentice*, I seem to see the hero of the night staggering home through the snow, drunk with delicious ecstasy, all his brightest dreams realized, and all his good impulses surging within him. He may be in a sort of frenzy as he tells of his proud achievement; but, at its very wildest, he exclaims: 'Mary, you shall ride in your carriage, yet!' and taking his son, Charles, from the cradle, swears he 'shall go to Eton;' but therewith something over-shadows his joy, and he murmurs, 'If Howard had but lived to see it!' . . . .

His audiences rose from one of £100 to audiences of £600; and £20 a week rewarded efforts, for far less than which, he subsequently received £50 a night. He was advanced to the dignity of having a dressing-room to himself. Legislators, poets, nobles, thronged his tiring-room, where Arnold took as much care of him as if on his life hung more than the well-being of the theatre. . . . . And old Nance Carey turned up, to exact £50 a year from her not too delighted son. . . . . He played, in this first season, Shylock fifteen times, Richard twenty-five, Hamlet eight, Othello ten, Iago eigh., and Luke four; and in those seventy nights the delighted treasurer of Drury Lane struck a balance of profit to the theatre amounting in round numbers to £17,000.

F. W. HAWKINS (*Life of Kean*, 1869, vol. i, p. 124): The 26th of January at length arrived. Morning dawned upon a miserable, dreary aspect; a heavy fall of snow which had taken place a few days previous was melting away before a sudden and unexpected thaw; a drizzling rain kept falling the whole day; and a cloudy atmosphere, hiding the sun from view, projected a melancholy gloom over the whole metropolis. The *one* morning rehearsal of *The Merchant of Venice* had been fixed for 12 o'clock, and precisely at the appointed time Kean made his appearance at the theatre. The rehearsal was proceeded with. A bombshell exploding in the midst of the slender company could not have startled them more than the thoroughly original interpretation which Kean gave to each line of his part. Raymond, the acting manager, protested against the 'innovation,' as he termed it. 'Sir,' returned Kean, proudly, 'I wish it to be an innovation.'—'It will never do, depend upon it,' remarked the stage manager, with a patronizing air that was excessively galling.—'Well, sir,' rejoined Kean, 'perhaps I may be wrong; but if so, the public will set me right.' Notwithstanding the bold originality in question, his rehearsal was remarkably ineffective; and the performers, taking his intentional tameness as a criterion of what the public performance would be, predicted his failure with energetic liberality. The rehearsal concluded, Kean returned home to enjoy with his wife the unusual luxury of a dinner. He remained at home until six o'clock, when the striking of the church clocks warned him that it was time to depart. Snatching up a small bundle containing the few necessaries with which he was bound to provide himself, he kissed his wife and infant son, and hurriedly left the house. 'I wish,' he muttered, 'I was going to be shot.' With his well-worn boots soaked with the slush, he slunk in at the stage door, and proceeded to a small, dilapidated dressing-room in the remotest part of the house, occupying it in common with three or four of the secondary actors. He quickly exchanged his dripping threadbare apparel for the more comfortable gaberdine of Shylock, slipped his feet into the traditional Venetian slippers, and taking a little *black* wig from his little bundle, adjusted it to his head, heedless of or inattentive to the astonishment depicted on the faces of his companions. Nevertheless, they did not attempt to expostulate with him; the reserved manner he had invariably maintained rendered *that* out of the question; but the news spread like wildfire, that the little man in the capes had rejected the conventional red wig. Arnold lamented such extraordinary conduct; Raymond tapped his forehead significantly when he heard of 'the black wig.' Both kept aloof. Not so Bannister and Oxberry. The former, with his characteristic good nature, came to give him an encouraging word; Oxberry, with a closer eye to business, to give him a glass of brandy and water. Gratefully accepting both, he issued from the dressing-room, and, proud in the consciousness of the approaching triumph, walked slowly to the wings, where he was heartily greeted by Dr Drury. Peeping through the eyelet-hole in the curtain, he surveyed a dreary, hopeless aspect. The announcement of 'Mr Kean, from Exeter,' carried with it no charm; another addition to the list of failures, for which the public were indebted to the discrimination of the managers, was anticipated; and 'there was that sense of previous damnation which a thin house inspires.' The boxes were empty; there were about fifty people in the pit, 'some quantity of barren spectators and idle renters being thinly scattered to make up a show.' Undaunted by the discouraging aspect of affairs, he awaited the decisive moment.

The cherished hope of twenty years is realized. He is before the floats of Drury-Lane, and is going to show them what an obscure strolling player can do. His fine Italian countenance, the lightness of his step, the piercing brilliancy of his eye, the expressiveness of his gesture, and the buoyancy and perfect self-possession of his manner, impress the scanty audience in his favour. His personal disadvantages are so great that it is at once evident that a success can only be achieved by sheer excellence, exposed to the discriminating test of the understanding. But there can be no doubt that he will pass triumphantly through the rigid severity of the ordeal. There is an

animating soul in all he says and does, which at once gives a high interest to his acting, and excites those emotions which are always felt in the presence of genius—a
union of power with a fine sensibility. It is giving fire to his eye, energy to his tones,
such a variety and expressiveness to all his gestures that you might have said, 'his
body thinks '

The Scene begins. The manner in which he acknowledges the applause usually
accorded to a stranger is a study for a painter. There is nothing of the sullen gaol
delivery common to the traditional Shylocks of the stage; a vague expectation is
excited. He takes up his position, leans across his cane, and looks askance at Bassanio as he refers to the three thousand ducats. ' He is safe,' cried Dr Drury. The
Scene goes on. ' I will be assured I may ' is given with such truth, such significance,
such beauty, that the audience bursts into a shower of applause; then !—as he himself
expressed it, 'then, indeed, I felt, I knew, I had them with me.'

In that part where, leaning on his stick, he told the tale of Jacob and his flock with
the garrulous ease of old age and animation of spirit that seems borne back to the olden
time, and the privileged example in which he exults, he shows them that a man of
genius has lighted on the stage. His acting here is all a study. There is one present
who notes with delight ' the flexibility and indefiniteness of outline about it, like a figure with a landscape background; Shylock is in Venice with his money-bags, his
daughter, and his injuries; but his thoughts take wing to the East; his voice swells
and deepens at the mention of his sacred tribe and ancient law, and he dwells with
joy on any digression to distant times and places, as a relief to his rooted and vindictive purposes.' The audience is then stirred to enthusiasm by the epigrammatic point
and distinctness with which he gives the lines: ' Hath a *dog* money ? Is it possible A
cur can lend three thousand ducats ?' &c.

The Act drop falls; all doubts as to a splendid success have been removed. In the
interval between this and his appearance in the Fifth Scene of the Second Act, there
was an obvious disposition on the part of those who had previously contemned him to
offer their congratulations; but, as if divining their intentions, he shrank from observation, and only emerged from his concealment as the scene came on between Shylock
and Jessica, in his very calling to whom, ' Why, Jessica, I say,' there was a charm as
of music. [Hawkins here quotes much of the foregoing extract from Dr Doran, and
thus concludes:]

With every limb trembling from excitement, the hero of the night returned to his
damp and threadbare apparel; and, having received with a hurried carelessness the
congratulations offered to him, he waited on Arnold in the manager's room. He was
formally informed that their expectations had been exceeded. To Kean, the announcement was quite superfluous. In an almost frenzied ecstasy he rushed through the wet
to his humble lodging, sprang up the stairs and threw open the door. His wife ran to
meet him; no words were required, his radiant countenance told all; and they mingled
together the first tears of true happiness they had as yet experienced. He told her of
his proud achievement, and in a burst of exultation exclaimed, ' Mary, you shall ride
in your carriage, and Charley, my boy,' taking the child from the cradle and kissing
him, 'you shall go to Eton, and '—a sad remembrance crossed his mind, his joy was
overshadowed, and he murmured in broken accents,—' Oh, that Howard had lived to
see it !—but he is better where he is.'

HAZLITT (*Characters of Shakespeare's Plays*, 1817, p. 276): When we first went
to see Mr Kean in Shylock, we expected to see what we had been used to see, a de-
crepid old man, bent with age and ugly with mental deformity, grinning with deadly

malice, with the venom of his heart congealed in the expression of his countenance, sullen, morose, gloomy, inflexible, brooding over one idea, that of his hatred, and fixed on one unalterable purpose, that of his revenge. We were disappointed, because we had taken our ideas from other actors, not from the play. There is no proof there that Shylock is old, but a single line, 'Bassanio and *old* Shylock, both stand forth,'— which does not imply that he is infirm with age,—and the circumstance that he has a daughter marriageable, which does not imply that he is old at all. It would be too much to say that his body should be made crooked and deformed to answer to his mind, which is bowed down and warped with prejudices and passion. That he has but one idea, is not true; he has more ideas than any other person in the piece; and if he is intense and inveterate in the pursuit of his purpose, he shows the utmost elasticity, vigour, and presence of mind in the means of attaining it. But so rooted was our habitual impression of the part from seeing it caricatured in the representation, that it was only from a careful perusal of the play itself that we saw our error. The stage is not, in general, the best place to study our author's characters in. It is too often filled with traditional common-place conceptions of the part, handed down from sire to son, and suited to the taste of *the great vulgar and the small*. ''Tis an unweeded garden; things rank and gross do merely gender in it!' If a man of genius comes once in an age to clear away the rubbish, to make it fruitful and wholesome, they cry, ''Tis a bad school; it may be like nature, it may be like Shakespeare, but it is not like us.' Admirable critics! [Hazlitt is here apparently making amends for his earlier opposition to Kean. I doubt if in a more deliberate mood he would have rated the stage thus low as an interpreter of Shakespeare. Clearly he was vexed that Macklin's interpretation had held possession of him so long, and his vexation is a sufficient excuse for his mixing up quotations from *Hamlet* and *Othello*, and for mistaking Bassanio for Anthonio.

In *The Music of Nature*, by William Gardiner, is the following valuable record of the quality of Edmund Kean's voice. It is much to be regretted that the record is so brief and that more passages are not noted. Such a record as this transmits to posterity a more vivid sense of an actor's power, and of one of the secrets thereof, than pages of praise as vague as it is lavish can convey :—

[P. 57]. Musically speaking, he is the best orator, who, to his natural speaking voice, unites the upper and lower voices, that is, the *voce de testa* and the *voce de petto*. Mr Kean possesses these qualifications in the highest degree. He has at his command the greatest number of effects, having a range of tones from F below the line to F above it—

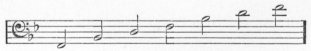

the natural key of his voice being that of B♭, a note lower than Talma's. His hard guttural tone upon G is as piercing as the third string of a violoncello; whilst his mezzo and pianissimo expressions are as soft as from the voice of a woman. He has three distinct sets of tones; as if he occasionally played upon a flute, clarionet, and bassoon, which he uses as the passion dictates. In the Scene with Lady Anne [*Rich. III.* I, ii] his notes are of the most touching and persuasive kind, often springing from the harmonies of his natural voice, which he elicits with exquisite delicacy. We instance the peculiar softness of the following expressions :

You mock me, mo - ther.

Re - mem - ber.

But the same voice, when moved with a ruder stroke, gave the yell and choked utterance of a savage [*Shylock*, I, iii, 46]:

Oh! if I can catch him once up - on the hip.

His tones of furious passion are deep-seated in the chest, like those of the lion and tiger; and it is his mastery over these instinctive tones by which he so powerfully moves his audience. At times he vomits a torrent of words in a breath, yet avails himself of all the advantages of deliberation. His pauses give a grandeur to his performance, and speak more than words themselves [*Shylock*, IV, i, 240]:

Oh . . . . no, not for Ven-ice.

HAWKINS (*Life of Kean*, i, 342): [When DOWTON acted Shylock] the great point of novelty consisted in the introduction of some Jewish friends into the court, and when, on being told that one of the conditions of his release was his becoming a Christian, Shylock fell fainting in their arms, and in this state was carried off, the tittering which had been excited from the Scene with Tubal was exchanged for roars of laughter. Dowton was deeply mortified, and anathematized Kean, Shylock, and the audience with all the vigour of a 'good hater.' He never boasted of his Shylock again!

The Theatre (December, 1879, p. 292): IRVING evidently believes that Shakespeare intended to enlist our sympathies on the side of the Jew, and the conception is embodied in a manner altogether new to the stage. The fierceness associated with the character since Macklin appeared in it is not absent. Except in the scene with Tubal, where passion will out, the bearing of this Shylock is distinguished by a comparatively quiet and tranquil dignity,—perhaps we ought rather to say the superb dignity of the Arabian race. The whole force of an 'old, untainted religious aristocracy' is made manifest in his person. He feels and acts as one of a noble but long-oppressed nation, as a representative of Judaism against the apostate Galilean, as an instrument of vengeance in the hands of an offended God. In point of intelligence and culture he is far above the Christians with whom he comes into contact, and the fact that as a Jew he is deemed far below them in the social scale is gall and wormwood to his proud and sensitive spirit. . . . . Exhibited in this light, not so much as a man grievously wronged in his own person as a representative of a great but oppressed tribe, Shylock acquires on the stage what Shakespeare evidently intended to impart to the character,— a sad and romantic interest, an almost tragic elevation and grace.

In Mr Irving's performance, as in the play, Shylock appears under three different aspects. First of all he is the usurer, then the outraged father, and finally the vengeful creditor. Mr Irving's appearance is in harmony with this view of the part. He comes forward as a man between fifty and sixty years of age, infirm enough to need the support of a stick, with an iron-gray wisp of beard, and wearing a sober brown gaberdine, an Oriental shawl girdle, and a close-fitting black cap with a yellow line across it. The law of Venice, it may be remembered, required Jews living in that city to wear a red hat as a distinctive sign of their tribe, but in this instance an actor may well be pardoned for dispensing with historical accuracy. A picturesque background is at the outset provided for this striking figure by a view of the Palace of St Mark, with a quay on which porters are landing bales of merchandise. Mr Irving's acting here is studiously quiet in tone, but full expression is given to the religious fervour of the Jew, the sense of wrong which rankles in his bosom, the undercurrent of sarcasm in his affected humility, and the cynical humour which breaks forth in, 'I will be assured I may,' and other passages. It is as he utters the words,—'Antonio shall become bound,—well?' that the idea of vengeance crosses his mind. In the Scene where the loan is agreed upon we have a fine illustration of the text; the Jew touches Antonio on the heart, and, seeing the merchant recoil from him, apologizes for his error by a bow in which we can perceive all the bitterness induced by the hard distinction drawn between Christian and Jew. The background of the Scene of Jessica's elopement is formed of Shylock's house at night, with a bridge over the canal which flows by it, and with a votive lamp to the Virgin on the wall. There a barcarolle is sung by some Venetians in a gondola, and a number of masqueraders rush merrily past. The noise having subsided, the curtain drops, to be raised again a few moments afterwards, —a pleasing innovation,—to exhibit Shylock returning without any suspicion of Jessica's treachery to his plundered and deserted home. The Scene which follows the discovery of Jessica's flight is sustained by Mr Irving with great power. His reason seems to reel under the heavy blow it has received, and the brief allusion to his dead wife is full of pathos and tenderness. The father is here more visible than the usurer. Then comes the fierce thirst for revenge which follows the news of Antonio's ill-fortune. By the time of the Trial, however, the storm has subsided into a dead calm. Bidden to appear in the Duke's Court,—a fine mediæval chamber, with portraits of Venetian dignitaries of times gone by on the walls, and with a crowd of deeply-interested spectators, including Tubal and other Jews, at the back,—he slowly and gravely comes in. The tone in which he replies to the appeals for mercy is even more significant than are his words. He stands there like a figure of Fate,—pitiless, majestic, implacable. The hour of vengeance has at length struck, and he will not be balked of his prey. There is no necessity for deference now; the law is on his side. His face wears a hard, set expression, relieved at long intervals by a glance of bitter hate towards Antonio, or a faint smile of triumph. Nor is this superb calm less conspicuous when the cause turns against him. The scales drop from his hands, but that is all. For a time he seems to be turned to stone, to be as immovable as a statue. The Christian, as might have been expected, has again conquered. Eventually, crushed by the conditions on which his life is spared, he stalks with a heavy sigh from the Court, only stopping to cast a look of deep pity at the ribald youth who is barking like a cur at his heels.

[The only introduction that the following letter needs is the statement that it was written to the Editor with no thought of publication, but was merely the continuance of a verbal discussion and the vindication of a position then maintained. It seems, however, to supplement so well the suggestions, from the same hand, in the Commentary on the foregoing pages, that at the request of the Editor, it is here printed, with the permission of—]

EDWIN BOOTH : My notion of Shylock is of the traditional type, which I firmly believe to be 'the Jew which Shakespeare drew.' Not the buffoon that Dogget gave according to Lord Lansdowne's Version, but the strongly marked and somewhat grotesque character which Macklin restored to the stage, and in which he was followed by Cooke, by Edmund Kean, and by my Father. 'Tis nonsense to suppose that Shylock was represented in other than a serious vein by Burbadge, merely because he 'made up,' doubtless after some representation of Judas, with red hair to emphasize the vicious expression of his features. Is there any authority for the assertion which some make that he also wore a long nose? What if he did? A clever actor once played the part of Tubal with me, and wore red hair and a hook'd nose. He did not make the audience laugh; 'twas not his purpose; but he looked the very creature that could sympathize with Shylock. His make up was admirable. He's the son of the famous John Drew, and is an excellent actor, now a leading member of Daly's Company. Let Burbadge have the long nose, if you will, but I am sure that he never under Shakespeare's nose made the character ridiculous. No, not till Lansdowne's bastard came did the Jew make the unskilful laugh and the judicious grieve. From that time, perhaps, until Macklin restored the original method of representing the character, it was treated as a 'low comedy' part. I doubt if Macklin or Cooke wore red wigs for Shylock,—but no matter, Burbadge did, and neither was he nor were they funny. If Edmund Kean was the first to wear black hair when red was the usual color worn at that time, 'tis easily accounted for, when you reflect that he was very poor and probably had a very limited stock of stage 'props'—he doubtless had no other old man's wig (except a white one for Lear) and the 'black bald' did service for Sir Giles Overreach, and several other elderly gentlemen besides Shylock. I know that such was my Father's case, and also mine in my strolling days. I believe that Burbadge, Macklin, Cooke, and Kean (as did my Father) made Shylock what is technically termed a 'character-part,'—grotesque in 'make up,' and general treatment, not so pronounced, perhaps, as my personation has been sometimes censured for. I think Macready was the first to lift the uncanny Jew out of the darkness of his native element of revengeful selfishness into the light of the venerable Hebrew, the Martyr, the Avenger. He has had several followers, and I once tried to view him in that light, but he doesn't cast a shadow sufficiently strong to contrast with the sunshine of the comedy,—to do which he must, to a certain extent, be repulsive, a sort of party that one doesn't care to see among the dainty revellers of Venice in her prime. Antonio's liver-trouble is gloom enough for them, but to heighten the brilliancy for us a heavier cloud is necessary, and it takes the form of Shylock,—'an inhuman wretch, uncapable of pity, void and empty From any dram of mercy.' It has been said that he is an affectionate father and a faithful friend. When, where, and how does he manifest the least claim to such commendation? Tell me that, and unyoke! 'Twas the money value of Leah's ring that he grieved over, not its associations with her, else he would have shown some affection for her daughter, which he did not, or she would not have called her home 'a hell, robbed and left him. Shakespeare makes her do these un-Hebrew things to intensify the baseness of Shylock's nature. If we side with him in his self-defence, 'tis because we have charity, which he had not; if we pity him under the burthen of his merited punishment 'tis because we are human, which he is not,—except in shape, and even that, I think, should indicate the crookedness of his nature. His refusal to accept thrice the amount he loaned seems to have given some critics the idea that as a great Avenger of his wronged people he rises above all selfish considerations, but had he accepted, what a lame and impotent conclusion it would have been! No, this other un-Jewlike action was necessary for stage-effect.

Do not forget, while you read the poet's plays, that he was a player, and, mark you! a theatrical manager with a keen eye to stage-effects; witness the 'gag' of Shylock's sharpening the knife,—a most dangerous 'bit of business,' and apt to cause a laugh; be careful of that 'point.' Would the heroic Hebrew have stooped to such a paltry action? No, never, in the very white-heat of his pursuit of vengeance! But vengeance is foreign to Shylock's thought; 'tis revenge he seeks, and he gets just what all who seek it get,—'sooner or later,' as the saying is. Had his motive been the higher one, Shakespeare would have somehow contrived his success without doubt; but Shylock had grown too strong for him. 'Tis said, you know, that he had to kill Mercutio, else the merry fellow would have killed the tragedy; so Shylock would have killed the comedy had he been intended to typify Vengeance. The storm-cloud of his evil passions having burst, he is forgotten in the moonlight of fair Portia's gardens.

GENTLEMAN (*Dram. Censor*, i, 296): Mrs WOFFINGTON, whose deportment in a male character was so free and elegant, whose figure was so proportionate and delicate, notwithstanding a voice unfavourable for declamation, must, in our opinion, stand foremost as Portia; her first Scene was supported with an uncommon degree of spirited archness; her behaviour during Bassanio's choice of the caskets conveyed a strong picture of unstudied anxiety; the trial scene she sustained with amiable dignity, the speech upon mercy she marked as well as anybody else; and, in the Fifth Act, she carried on the sham quarrel in a very laughable manner; to sum up all: while in petticoats she showed the woman of solid sense and real fashion; when in breeches, the man of education, judgement, and gentility.

Mrs CLIVE was a ludicrous burlesque on the character; every feature and limb contrasted the idea Shakespeare gives us of Portia; in the spirited scene she was clumsy, and spoke in the same strain of chambermaid delicacy she did Lappet or Flippanta; in the grave part, she was awkwardly dissonant; and, as if conscious she could not get through without the aid of trick, flew to the pitiful resource of taking off the peculiarity of some judge or noted lawyer; from which wise stroke she created laughter in a scene where the deepest attention should be preserved, till Gratiano's retorts upon the Jew work a contrary effect.

BOADEN (*Life of J. P. Kemble*, i, 326): It was compensation rich, and rich enough, to hear from the lips of Mrs SIDDONS the triumphant delirium of joy when Bassanio had chosen the right casket.

According to the *Jahrbuch*, xii, p. 212, it appears that about 1780 Shylock was given as a serious character by REINECKE for the first time on the German stage, and, to judge from a contemporary account, his interpretation must have been much the same as Macklin's. In a notice of a later performance in Mannheim by Reinecke, I find a curious contemporary criticism referred to by Genée (p. 272), to the effect that the public were not satisfied with the scarcely perceptible Jewish accent with which Reinecke spoke the part, and the partial failure of the play was attributed to this cause. The public demanded that the Jewish accent should be very decided and sustained throughout. Genée agrees with the public of that day, if I understand him aright.

The prevalence of this practice of imparting a foreign accent to Shylock's words, I find confirmed in the caution against its extreme use which Oechelhäuser (*Einleitung*, p. 22) deems it proper to give; 'especially,' as he says, 'since Shakespeare and his 'translator, Schlegel, have adequately indicated, by the turn of expression, phraseology, '&c., the Jewish mode of speech. It is only in moments of extreme excitement, as 'Rötscher explains, that a more emphatic dialectic, and, in especial, a Jewish, colour- 'ing is permissible. Charles Kean pronounced Shylock's words wholly free from any 'trace of dialect; this is carrying it too far.'

The passage in Rötscher, to which Oechelhäuser refers, is evidently to be found in his *Charactergebilde* (Dresden, 1864, p. 53), where, it is said, that 'the actor who per- 'sonates Shylock must keep in view the intimation of the Poet and show the stamp 'of Shylock's nationality, particularly in the pronunciation, but the actor must never 'deviate into an absolute copy or counterfeit of the Jewish speech. A delicate shade 'must be shown between a stamp of nationality and the Jewish tone and style of the 'lower classes. If the actor fails to indicate any Jewish element at all, the character 'will lose its deepest basis. Shylock will then stand on a plane above his national 'characteristics. . . . . It is natural, however, that when he is deeply moved, in moments 'of wild wrath, the national peculiarities will be more unrestrained and ring out more 'clearly than in moments of brooding cunning or calculating deliberation. In the for- 'mer the natural man is revealed involuntarily, in the latter he is under the restraints 'induced by Christian intercourse.'

Can it be that it is the use of the word 'monies' which has induced the belief among our German brothers that Shylock 'talks Jewish'? It is impossible to recall any other word or phrase which can hint at such a supposition; and even the use of this word by Shylock fails to help us when we hear his 'monies' spoken of by a Grecian Senator in *Timon of Athens*. The knot is too intrinse for me to unloose. If it were not for its antiquity, as indicated in the criticism on Reinecke, we might infer that the adoption of this Jewish accent was due to the suggestions of Schlegel (see Extract from Schlegel, *post*), wherein Rötscher is anticipated. But evidently Schlegel merely followed the public opinion of his day and the practice of the stage.

As was quoted in regard to Lansdowne's *Version*, 'the drama's laws the drama's patrons give;' and German actors must bow to the decision of the German public; but I cannot forbear remarking that any such practice on our stage would be abhorrent. Undoubtedly, it would mark the Jew, but it would mark a Jew of the lowest class, socially and intellectually, to which class Shylock does not belong; its befitting accom- paniments would be three old hats and a spasmodic cry of 'Old Clo'.' The smallest hint of a Jewish accent would be monstrous and revolting here, where, between native Jews and Christians of the educated classes, there is no difference whatever in language or pronunciation to be detected.

25

COSTUME

SHYLOCK

DOUCE (i, 251): Shylock's dress should be a *scarlet hat lined with black taffeta*. This is the manner in which the Jews of Venice were formerly distinguished. See Saint Didier, *Histoire de Venise*. In the year 1581 they wore *red caps* for distinction's sake, as appears from Hakluyt's *Voyages*, p. 179, ed. 1589; and also from Lord Verulam, in his Essay on *Usury*. [See note on 'usance,' I, iii, 45.]

COLLIER (*New Particulars*, &c., 1836, p. 38. Foot-note to Jordan's *Ballad*, where reference is made to Shylock's nose. See p. 462 of this Appendix): I have little doubt that the part of Shylock was originally played in a false nose as well as a false beard. Of old, it was the custom so to dress Jews and usurers on the stage; we know that such was the case with Barrabas, in Marlowe's *Jew of Malta*, before 1593, in which Ithamore exclaims: 'Oh, brave master, I worship your nose for this;' and Rowley, in his *Search for Money*, 1609, speaks in express terms of 'the artificial Jew of Malta's nose.'

HUNTER (i, 307): Shylock was a Levantine Jew [see Hunter's grounds for this assertion, p. ix, Actors' Names, *ante*], and, therefore, on the stage, if it is intended that strict regard shall be paid to propriety in matters of costume, he ought, according to Coryat, to appear in a yellow turban. [See Halliwell, *post*.]

KNIGHT: Vecellio expressly informs us that the Jews differed in nothing, as far as regarded dress, from Venetians of the same professions, whether merchants, artisans, &c., with the exception of a *yellow bonnet*, which they were *compelled to wear by order of the government*. In confirmation of the assertion in Hakluyt's *Voyages* [mentioned by Douce] that Jews wore *red caps* for distinction's sake, we remember to have met somewhere with a story that the colour was changed from *red* to *yellow*, in consequence of a Jew having been accidentally taken for a cardinal! Yellow has always been in Europe a mark of disgrace. Tenne (i. e. orange) was considered by many heralds as *stainant*. The Jews in England wore yellow caps of a peculiar shape as early as the reign of Richard I. As late, also, as the year 1825 an order was issued by the Pope that 'the Jews should wear a *yellow* covering on their hats, and the women a *yellow* riband on the breast, under the pain of severe penalties.'—Vide *Examiner*, Sunday newspaper, Nov. 20th, 1825.

HALLIWELL (p. 321): Coryat, in his *Crudities*, ed. 1611, p. 230, says: 'I was at the place where the whole fraternity of the Jews dwelleth together, which is called the Ghetto, being an iland; for it is inclosed round about with water. It is thought there are of them in all betwixt five and sixe thousand. They are distinguished and discerned from the Christians by their habites on their heads; for some of them doe weare hats and those redde, onely those Jews that are borne in the Westerne parts of the world, as in Italy, &c., but the Easterne Jewes, being otherwise called the Levantine Jewes, which are borne in Hierusalem, Alexandria, Constantinople, &c., weare turbents upon their heads, as the Turkes doe; but the difference is this: the Turkes weare white, the Jewes yellow. By that word turbent I understand a rowle of fine linnen wrapped together upon their heads, which serveth them instead of hats whereof many have bin often worne by the Turkes in London.' On p. 232, speaking of the Jews when at the synagogue, Coryat observes that 'every one of them, whatsoever he be, man or childe, weareth a kinde of light yellowish vaile, made of linsie woolsie (as I take it) over his shoulders, something worse than our coarser Holland, which reacheth a little beneath the middle of their backes.'

EDWIN BOOTH (MS): My costume for Shylock was suggested by one of a group of Oriental figures in a picture by Gérôme ('The Nautch Girl,' I think it was called). It consists of a long, dark-green gown, trimmed at the edge of the skirt with an irregular device of brown colour. A dark-brown gaberdine, with flowing sleeves and hood, lined with green and trimmed as the gown. A variegated scarf about the waist, from which depends a leather pouch. Red leather pointed shoes, and hat of orange-tawny colour, shaped somewhat like the Phrygian cap, but with a rim of about two inches, turned up.

Head grey and pretty bald; beard of same colour and quite long. Ear-rings and several finger-rings, one on the thumb and one on forefinger; a long knotted staff. Complexion swarthy; age about sixty, I judge, from what is said of it by one of the young gallants when he is bemoaning the loss of his daughter, but 'tis difficult to determine the years of such natures.

[IRVING'S costume is somewhat described on p. 382.]

ANTHONIO

E. W. GODWIN (*The Architect*, 3 April, 1875, p. 196): Antonio, with whom we may class Shylock and Tubal, for the difference between them was only in the colour of their caps, would be attired like any other merchant, i. e. in doublet, trunk hose, stockings and shoes, old men wearing over all a gown reaching to the heels, with sleeves tight in lower arm and loose above. The gown was fastened in front, from top to bottom, with buttons and buttonholes sewn in braids, and the skirt was open at the sides, fastened by four or five buttons at the bottom, likewise on braids. It was girded at the waist with a silk sash, having small tassels depending in front. Over the dress, gowned or not, was worn a large cape or short cloak of silk or brocade, light or heavy according to the season, with a collar as before mentioned. Round the neck the merchant wore a ruff, and ruffs again appear at the wrists. The cap was sometimes high and hat-shaped, with a narrow brim, and sometimes flat and largely projecting, like the modern Scotch cap. Like the nobles and gentlemen, they indulged in the luxury of gloves. [Portia asks Anthonio for his gloves.—ED.] The Jew was distinguished from the Christian by being compelled to have his cap made of a tawny-yellow material, sometimes so tawny as to appear almost like a faded red.

PORTIA

GODWIN: Portia would do her shopping probably at Padua, and would therefore follow the fashions of the mainland. The chief difference we have to note is the absence of the square-cut body. High-necked bodies, with fine cambric ruffs, was the every-day attire usually worn by Paduan ladies of noble birth. On state occasions, on festivals, and at receptions, the dress, though still high on the shoulders, was open in front, terminating at a point a little above the waist. There is also a marked difference to be observed between the dress of a maiden and that of a married woman, and there is no question that the Paduan ladies (wives or not) indulged in a considerably extensive wardrobe. So, too, there was more than one mode of dressing the hair (false hair was by no means unusual). In some cases it was crimped, parted in the middle, brought round to the back over the ears, and rolled up *à la grec;* in others it fell loosely down the back *au naturel*, confined, however, at the poll by a delicately-wrought band or tiara of goldsmith's work; but the more usual plan was to arrange the front hair in massive curls, assuming somewhat the form of a couple of low horns, and carried down each side in smaller curls to the ears, the hair behind being strained (sometimes crimped) and fastened up into a plait, with strings of pearls interwoven. From this plait depended the veil, which sometimes also appears to have covered the head up to a point between the horned curls or rolls, over which it could be raised like a double hood. The veil itself was also worn in various ways, and as it was often arranged with the utmost grace and made of the finest material,—a sort of silken gauze, enriched with gold, interwoven and even sometimes embroidered and decorated further with pearls and gems,—its lovely film-like effect, like an iridescent mist over the rich materials of the gown, can be better imagined than described. The gown, with the exception already noted, was cut like the Venetian dress, and was made of silk, brocade, gold cloth, or costly velvet. Over the shoulders was worn a chain, usually of gold set with jewels, and suspending a large jewel or cross. The pouch or gipciere worn at the girdle was not quite yet abandoned, and Portia may wear one or not as she pleases. Gowns with the skirt open up the front and with loose hanging sleeves were also used by the 'Sposa di Padoua.' Rings were worn on the first, third, and fourth fingers. Earrings of pearls and jewels appear, and sometimes we see a string of pearls, one end attached to the ear and the other looped up to the back hair. The veil is occasionally omitted, and a stiff semi-circular collar of lace is seen standing up behind the neck and reaching as high as the poll. Portia's stockings would be of silk or the finest thread worked with clocks and even open seams. Her shoes, of slipper form, would be of morocco, or of velvet embroidered with gold, cork being used for the soles. On her journey to Venice she would use a velvet mask or visor, and gloves highly perfumed and embroidered with gold or silver. A pocket looking-glass, with ladies of rank, was not an uncommon possession, and was sometimes set in the back of the fan, which was usually made of nine or more ostrich feathers, the handle set with pearls and jewels and fastened to the end of the girdle-chain, if the lady was married. The pocket handkerchief was of large size and of fine cambric, having an embroidered border, and a tassel at each corner. Finally, on going abroad ladies wore, in the winter and later autumn, a mantle or pelisse over the gown, reaching to below the knee, open in front to the neck, and with long, loose, open, hanging sleeves. Over this came the veil, and a round velvet hat, with a broad brim, completed the costume, whose chief glory consisted in its richly embroidered or woven or cut patterns.

CIVIL DOCTOR

KNIGHT: Vecellio also furnishes us with the dress of a Doctor of Laws, the habit in which Portia defends Antonio. The upper robe was of black damask cloth, velvet, or silk, according to the weather. The under one of black silk, with a black sash, the ends of which hang down to the middle of the leg; the stockings of black cloth or velvet; the cap of rich velvet or silk.

GODWIN: The D. C. L. of Padua wore a tight doublet, silk belt, trunk hose, and stockings, all of black; velvet in winter, silk in summer. Over these he put on his official robe or gown, ungirdled, having an upright collar and long, capacious open sleeves reaching nearly to the ground. This was made of velvet, silk, or damask, covered with rich pattern, cut, embroidered, or woven, according to the nature of the material. (All the patterns cut on velvet or in brocade and damask were large. I have seen none which could be drawn within less compass than twelve inches square.) On his head he wore a tolerably high cap, made with a narrow brim and a flat top, and on his feet were seen the usual slipper-shoes. His clerk would wear a black cloth doublet, trunks, stockings, and ruffs, but no robe or gown.

NERRISSA

GODWIN: Nerissa, 'the waiting-maid,'—or as we should now call her, *the lady's maid,*—·must be dressed as the confidential servant of a noble and wealthy lady, neither too rich nor yet too poor. There will still be the ruffs at neck and wrists, but of less delicate material than those on Portia; the skirt of her gown will be shorter than her ladyship's, and there will be an absence of ornament, except, perhaps, as a border to the dress. She must wear a ring or two, and from her girdle would hang a pouch and huswife. She would also have a short veil of plain lawn or cambric, which she might use as a hood, pinned under the chin.

JESSICA

KNIGHT: Jewish females, Vecellio says, were distinguished from Christian women by their being 'highly *painted*' and wearing *yellow* veils, but that in other respects their dresses were perfectly similar.

EDWIN BOOTH (MS): Jessica should wear a yellow sash or veil of the same colour as Shylock's cap.

GODWIN: As the daughter of a rich merchant of Venice, Jessica would be dressed in the ordinary costume of a Venetian gentlewoman. A tightly-fitting body, square-cut neck before and behind, waist high at the sides and coming down low to a point both before and behind; the body laced across a stomacher; frilled shoulder-pieces; sleeves loose above, and tightly fitting to lower arm; lawn or cambric ruffs at the wrist; flowing skirt; a necklet of pearls; slipper-shaped shoes, raised on sloping chopines; front hair arranged in short massive curls on forehead, the rest strained back and done up in plait, from which depended the veil, that in the costume of a Jewess would be yellow. The dress was of no particular colour, and the skirt underneath was open in front, and tied together at intervals.

DOGE

KNIGHT: Cæsar Vecellio describes at some length the alterations made in the Ducal dress by several princes, from the close of the twelfth century down to that of the sixteenth, the period of the action of the play before us; at which time the materials of which it was usually composed were cloth of silver, cloth of gold, and crimson velvet, the cap always corresponding in colour with the robe and mantle. Coryat, in his *Crudities*, says: 'The fifth day of August being Friday . . . . I saw the Duke in some of his richest ornaments. . . . . He himself then wore two very rich robes, or long garments, whereof the uppermost was white cloth of silver, with great massy buttons of gold; the other cloth of silver also, but adorned with many curious works made in colours with needlework.' Howell, in his *Survey of the Signorie of Venice*, London, 1651, after telling us that the Duke 'always goes clad in silk and purple,' observes, that 'sometimes he shows himself to the public in a robe of cloth of gold and a white mantle; he hath his head covered with a thin coif, and on his forehead he wears a crimson kind of mitre, with a gold border, and, behind, it turns up in the form of a horn; on his shoulders he carries ermine skins to the middle, which is still a badge of the Consul's habit; on his feet he wears embroidered sandals [Vecellio, a much better authority, says 'slippers'—KNIGHT], tied with gold buttons, and, about his middle, a most rich belt, embroidered with costly jewels, in so much, that the habit of a Duke, when at festivals he shews himself in the highest state, is valued at about 100,000 crowns.

GODWIN (*The Architect*, London, 3 April, 1875): The Doge's dress consists of an ermine cape or tippet reaching to the elbow, shaped with a slight upright collar, entirely open from the throat downwards, and having six large buttons on the left edge. These buttons were sometimes very costly, and always important features. Under the cape appears a robe or cloak with a train, which is borne by one of the Doge's esquires.

The robe is covered with a large rich pattern of conventional branch and leaf, and a similar pattern is seen on the gown, which nearly touches the ground, and has large open sleeves reaching below the knee, is trimmed with fur, is open down the front and gathered in at the waist by a belt. On the head was worn the curious horn-shaped biretta, and beneath this a closely-fitting white cap, coming down under it so as to cover the ears and the back of the head. Strings were attached to the front edges of this cap, sometimes tied under the chin, but often allowed to hang loose. The every-day biretta was of red velvet, with a deep border of gold embroidery. The state one had jewelled borders, and crests of gold knobs or jewels on the top of the border, and edging the central line or seam from the front to the back. Whatever the colour of the robe, the biretta must be of the same colour and material, except only its deep gold border or band.

BASSANIO, SOLANIO, &c.

KNIGHT: 'Young lovers,' says Vecellio, 'wear generally a doublet and breeches of satin, tabby, or other silk, cut or slashed in the form of crosses or stars, through which slashes is seen the lining of coloured taffeta; gold buttons, a lace ruff, a bonnet of rich velvet or silk with an ornamental band, a silk cloak, and silk stockings, Spanish mo-rocco shoes, a flower in one hand and their gloves and handkerchief in the other.' This habit, he tells us, was worn by many of the nobility, as well of Venice as of other Italian cities, especially by the young men before they put on the gown with the sleeves, 'a comito,' which was generally in their eighteenth or twentieth year.

GODWIN: Bassanio, as a noble of Venice, would be dressed in doublet, trunk hose to below the knee, stockings and shoes, and over all, in the house, a houpelande, with hanging sleeves of much the same shape as that worn in the 15th century. But abroad he would change the over-garment for the large-sleeved gown or toga. The cream of the aristocracy—that is, the chiefs or heads of the leading families—adopt, commonly, crimson for the colour of the underdress, and black for the gown. Gloves, having stiff wrist-bands attached, are worn or carried in the hand, and the cap is a plain, round, flat-topped, limp sort of pork-pie hat. The gown was shaped at the neck so as to produce a stand-up collar, and over one shoulder was worn the long, narrow strip which distinguished nobles and magistrates—altogether not a very picturesque costume. Solanio, Salarino, Gratiano, and Lorenzo may be attired in eminently pic-turesque dresses. The long gown reaching to the feet, with its ugly baggy sleeves, forms no part of the ordinary Venetian habit. The scholars and young gentlemen wore short cloaks with collars, slashed doublets thick set with buttons down the front, slashed sleeves, rather easy in the upper part, but tight on the forearm, slashed trunk hose, with three or four buttons at the side of the knee, stockings, and light, slipper-like shoes. Round the neck they wore ruffs like those adopted by all Western Europe in the last quarter of the 16th century. The hat or cap was a tall bag-like structure with a stiff narrow rim. They wore ruffs at the wrist, and carried swords.

MOROCCO. ARRAGON

GODWIN: The Prince of Morocco would wear a loose and full white cotton gown with capacious sleeves and high neck, girded with a sash of delicate crape-like mate-rial full of coloured stripes and gold, the ends of which were deeply fringed and hung as low as the knee. On his head he would wear a spotlessly white turban, shaped like a small pillow, bound round the centre with a broad band. The skirt of his dress would be tucked through his girdle, hanging therefrom in irregular and graceful folds nearly to the ground. On his legs red morocco buskins, and his shoes of leather of another colour, both often richly embroidered with gold and silver. Large rings of gold depend from his ears, and across his breast glitters his leathern sword-belt, loaded, I might almost say, clogged, with precious stones. The Prince of Arragon would be dressed like a noble in the Court of the King of Spain. The most important points to be noticed is the shortness of the trunks, which are only just visible below the doublet, the short cloak, and the increased length of the skirt of the doublet. Ruffs appear round the neck and wrists, and on the head a tall bag-like hat with very narrow brim. The cloak was usually of 'purple' (crimson) silk or velvet, lined with costly material, sometimes richly embroidered with gold. It was worn occasionally with a hood, and was often wrapped round the breast in a careless-looking, but eminently artistic, manner.

MAGNIFICOES, &c.

KNIGHT: The Chiefs of the Council of Ten, who were three in number, wore 'red gowns with long sleeves, either of cloth, camlet, or damask, according to the weather, with a flap of the same colour over the left shoulder, red stockings, and slippers.' The rest of the Ten, according to Coryat, wore black camlet gowns with marvellous long sleeves, that reach almost down to the ground.

The 'Clarissimoes' generally wore gowns of black cloth faced with black taffeta, with a flap of black cloth edged with taffeta, over the left shoulder; and 'all these gowned men,' says the same author, 'do wear marvellous little black caps of felt, without any brims at all, and very diminutive falling bands, no ruffs at all, which are so shallow, that I have seen many of them not above a little inch deep.' The colour of their under-garments was also generally black, and consisted of 'a slender doublet made close to the body, without much quilting or bombast, and long hose plain, without those new-fangled curiosities and ridiculous superfluities of panes, pleats, and other light toys used with us Englishmen. Yet,' he continues, 'they make it of costly stuff, well beseeming gentlemen and eminent persons of their places, as of the best taffetas and satins that Christendom doth yield, which are fairly garnished also with lace of the best sort.'

GOBBO

GODWIN: Launcelot Gobbo, as the Jew's servant, would not be a servant in livery, but would have a plain doublet, not unlike a Norfolk shirt in general outline, trunks, stockings, shoes, and a high cap with a narrow brim. As Bassanio's servant, he would be in livery like Leonardo, or Balthazar and Stephano, servants to Portia, whose doublets would be covered with guards, or braids and buttons set very closely together.

Old Gobbo would wear a kind of blouse with turn-over collar, cut down to the waist in front and tied together with two or three bows. The skirt would be open at the sides, belted round the waist with a leathern strap, and beneath it would appear the ends of loose breeches, bare knees, turn-over coarse stockings, and tied shoes. The neck and throat were bare.

RICHARD GRANT WHITE (*Introduction*, p. 144): *The Merchant of Venice* has never been put on the stage in the costume of the time at which it was written; and gorgeous as that costume was, it is by no means certain that much would be gained by absolute correctness in this particular. Should the Duke and Magnificoes enter in their cumbrous and all-enveloping mantles, with their queer little bird's nests of caps perched upon gray and bearded heads, the grave Antonio with a bonnet like an inverted porringer shadowing his melancholy countenance, Bassanio with one half a yard high, taller before than behind, and puffed out like a pillow with bombast, which also swelled his fantastically decorated breeches to an enormous size, Portia in the stiff and clumsy skirt and stomacher of a Venetian lady of rank of that day, formidable with bristling ruffs, and with her hair engineered into two little conical turrets of curls upon her forehead, one over each eye,—it is to be feared that the splendour and faithfulness of the scene would be forgotten in its absurdity, and that the audience would explode in fits of uncontrollable laughter as the various personages came upon the stage. Any Italian costume, rich, beautiful, and sufficiently antique to remove the action out of the range of present probabilities, will meet the dramatic requirements of this play; but the orange-tawny bonnet, that mark of an outcast race, ought not to be missed from the brow of Shylock.

GODWIN: We must remember that the officials in a Venetian Court kept their hats on in presence of the Doge, that the manners of the period were characterized by courtesy combined with a stately, dignified action, and that what we call stiffness of manner was then regarded as quite the correct thing. But modern actors and actresses rarely hold the mirror high enough to reflect the mien, deportment, or bearing of the men and women of a past age. The air or look of gentlemen and ladies during the great period of the Renaissance can be ascertained from the documents and the pictures of the time, and if an actor fails to reproduce it he is not fitted to play in the comedies of the great dramatist of that period. Correctness of costume, and scenery, and properties, and furniture is all very well, but if through it all we see 19th-century action, modern style, the mode of Robertsonian society, or the special graces and charms which are the delight of our own time, but which would have been looked upon as antics, or at the least as bad form, in the Courts of Philip or Elizabeth, then the picture must be discordant, and the dramatic representation woefully incomplete. [It is difficult to avoid the conclusion that there is one requisite which Godwin has overlooked, and that is, that the characters should all talk in Italian.—ED.]

SCENERY

EDWARD W. GODWIN (*The Architect*, London, 27 March, 1875): The architectural scenery, divided between Venice and Belmont, may be said to consist at most of five Scenes, viz.: VENICE: *1, A street or public place. 2, The street before Shylock's house. 3, A court of justice.* BELMONT: *4, A grand hall. 5, A garden.* The short Third Scene of the Second Act contains nothing but what might just as well be said on the doorstep of Shylock's house as inside a room; so that this may be included in the Scene numbered 2 in the above list.

So, too, I see scarcely any reason why the talk between Portia and Nerissa in I, ii, or in III, iv, should not have happened in the grand hall or apartment where the caskets are placed. If there were choice flowering shrubs placed in this room, so that the lady and her maid might busy themselves about them while they are conversing, and if a corridor at the back of this hall led from some other part of the house into the garden, so that one might pass the hall of the caskets without necessarily entering it, there is nothing in the text inconsistent with these two Scenes being located in the same room as the more important Casket Scenes. . . . . If we wish still further to abridge our stock of scenery, the Scenes Nos. 1 and 2 may be easily made one, and we shall thus have brought the play into the compass of four set Scenes. . . . . It is essential first of all that the Scene-painter should bear well in mind that in 1590 Venice was neither a city of palaces nor a city of ruins, and that along her canals and streets two great styles of art, broadly speaking, prevailed, and a third was gradually usurping the place of both; these three styles were the Byzantine, the Gothic, and the

Renaissance. . . . . Photographs of the old houses of Venice are so common and so readily to be had, that the only difficulty left to a Scene-painter is the archæological one—that of recognizing any deductions or additions in detail that may have been made to any mediæval house *since* 1590. Moreover, the red brick of Venice is full of such charming colour, and the weather stains upon the stone and marble give such delicious tone to these materials, that one hesitates to write a word that would tend to dispel the vision. But yet, if we desire to realize the Venice of Shakespeare, we shall have to cover most of the brick with veneer of marble, either plain or in coloured diaper, or with stucco decorated with painted diapers, and the few exceptions to this rule would be the very smallest and poorest houses and the earliest of the Byzantine works. . . . . Another point for the Scene-painter to bear in mind is, that the streets and open places were usually paved with red brick arranged in simple patterns, and most commonly in that known as herring-bone. A third very important thing to remember in connection with the Venice of the merchant Antonio is the universality of *applied* colour as distinguished from the parti-coloured *construction* adopted by the rest of Western Europe. The coloured marble pattern on the Ducal Palace was by no means a solitary example. . . . . In houses of less pretension the stucco was painted in two or three simple earth colours, with small diapers. [Godwin gives diagrams of the setting of these several Scenes, and also a list of Venetian buildings which might be used as guides in depicting the architecture. For the Trial Scene he selects the *Sala dello Scrutinio* in the Ducal Palace, and refers the Scene-painter to photographs; the setting of this Scene he pronounces] one of the most difficult problems among the scenic questions of Shakespeare's plays. We have to maintain the dignity of the strict Court of Venice, to find room not only for the Doge and the Magnificoes, but for officials who might attend as senators, magistrates, doctors of law, &c.; we have to provide for a crowd of lawyers, —some of them young men,—so that Portia may not appear *too* singular; we must not forget the question, 'Which is the merchant here and which the Jew?' showing that both plaintiff and defendant were absorbed in the two opposing crowds of Christians and Israelites, and we must remember that, although the secret tribunal of the Council of Ten had its fearful power somewhat curtailed in 1582, its servants were still to be seen watching and listening wherever two or three were gathered together. Under these circumstances I again propose a diagonal set for this Scene [where the left side of the angle is taken up with the raised platform for the Doge and Magnificoes; in front of it the lawyers' table, at which, in the very centre of the stage, stands Portia; to her left and in front of her stands Antonio; on her right, at the end of the lawyers' table, in advance of Antonio, and the nearest character to the footlights, stands Shylock. Bassanio's position is on the platform, among the nobles around the Doge.] The fittings should be of sumptuous carved wood almost covered with gilding. . . . . The table for the lawyers might have a rich cover of crimson velvet reaching to the floor, but cut up at the angles and fastened by a number of long loops of gold lace or braid, as may be seen in pictures of the time. On the table we might see the folios of the statutes of Venice with their magnificent binding and gilded clasps; inkstands of bronze, chased and moulded of circular form and of about the size of the common lead office-inkstand of the present day; the portfolios of the lawyers and learned doctors, 12 to 18 inches square, beautifully worked in leather. The deed or bond would be on a small strip of vellum, well creased and tearable at the creases; the scales were just the same as we have now. Shylock, being a merchant in jewels and precious metals, would have probably brought his own private scales; [He says that he has them ready, —ED.] the knife was doubtless the glaive-shaped instrument then common; the letter was folded longwise, with the direction in one corner, tied with silk and sealed. [For the Casket Scene Godwin also recommends a diagonal set, with an arcade on both sides; on one side is an ascending staircase, and a corridor leading to the garden on the other, near the back a platform for the caskets; from the arches are hung curtains having large patterns in broad stripes, like those preserved in the Kensington Museum.] In looking at the furniture of the time we shall find that the candles or lights were held in sconces of *repoussé* metal, brackets and lamps suspended from the ceiling. Chinese porcelain vases for flowers, some carved and gilded chests, a table and chair of the same description, cabinets, Limoges enamels, mirrors, majolica, lapis lazuli cups, crystals, Eastern rugs, a movable clock, Murano glasses, antique statues, and a parrot or some love-birds in a cage or on a stand may be brought in to help the Scene. Among the musical instruments we may have the violin, tambourine, harp, and theorbo, all illustrated in Poliphilus, and some specimens to be seen at South Kensington. . . . . But whether a theatrical manager does or does not attend to these things; whether he wishes to do right, or whether, owing to profound ignorance respecting the manners, customs, and general surroundings of any past time which distinguishes the modern stage and its ' patrons,' he thinks it a matter of very small moment, one thing he must do, and that is provide three caskets. Now for these things, the style which was the most costly and the most sumptuous in the lifetime of Lady Portia's father was that introduced from Damascus, and which has always gone under the name of *damascened work*. Iron or steel caskets, most elaborately wrought with sharp mouldings and carvings, were covered on the plain surfaces with rich ornament pressed in of gold or silver, and in the examples before us the sides of the caskets might be panelled, and in each panel *repoussé* work of gold and silver for two of them, and cast work of lead for the third. . . . . Portia's counterfeit would be probably enclosed in a flat, wide frame of the same style of art, or of walnut inlaid with rich patterns of ivory, mother-of-pearl, lapis lazuli, &c.

The Fifth Act, and indeed the whole episode of the rings, might be very well omitted in modern stage representation.

[In Collier's *English Dramatic Poetry* (vol. iii, p. 170, second edition) there is a sentence which is to me profoundly true :—' We decidedly concur with Malone in the general conclusion, that painted moveable scenery was unknown on our early stage; and it is a fortunate circumstance for the poetry of our old plays, that it was so; the imagination of the auditor only was appealed to, and we owe to the absence of painted canvas many of the finest descriptive passages in Shakespeare, his contemporaries, and immediate followers. *The introduction of scenery*, we apprehend, *gives the date to the commencement of the decline of our dramatic poetry.*'—Ed.]

JEWS IN ENGLAND

FROM the fact that the Jews were expelled from England by Edward the First in 1290, and were not permitted to return until 1650, under Cromwell, it has been inferred that Shakespeare could have acquired no personal knowledge of them unless he had obtained it abroad. That, however, he might have had opportunities of seeing them in London has been for a long time suspected; not only does Bacon refer to them familiarly, but in Coryat's *Crudities* (vol. iii, p. 303, ed. 1776) we have one clear assurance that Jews in his day were born and bred in England. When in Constantinople, in 1608, Coryat narrates at length his visit to 'the house of a certaine English ' Iew, called *Amis*, borne in *Crootched* Friers in *London,* who hath two sisters more ' of his owne Iewish Religion, commorant in *Galata,* who were likewise borne in the ' same place.'

Furthermore, that a certain Dr Lopez, a Jewish resident of London, had been executed in 1594 for treasonable practices, was known from Stowe's *Annals;* but the first to call attention to a possible connection between the notoriety of this execution and the appearance of *The Merchant of Venice* was, I think, FREDERICK HAWKINS, in an article on *Shylock and other Stage Jews,* which appeared in *The Theatre,* November, 1879. As an investigation of Dr Lopez's case did not come within the scope of his article, Mr Hawkins restricted himself to the simple statement that 'it was amidst the excitement induced by the supposed iniquities of Dr Lopez . . . . that *The Merchant of Venice* appeared,' and briefly rehearsed the most prominent incidents connected with the trial.

In the following February, 1880, S. L. LEE, in the *Gentleman's Magazine,* set forth the result of an examination, apparently thorough, of the State Papers at the time of Lopez's trial, in an article called *The Original Shylock,* whereof a condensation is here given:

S. L. LEE: On the evidence of contemporary records we can safely assert that Jews were residing in England throughout Shakespeare's life-time, and that opportunities of more or less intimate intercourse with them were for many years open to him.

We need not go very far to find two important pieces of evidence to show that at the beginning and at the end of the sixteenth century the presence of Jews in this country was acknowledged by the highest authorities. In the State Papers relating to the marriage of Katharine of Arragon with Arthur, Prince of Wales, we are told that Henry VII had a long interview with a Spanish envoy to discuss the presence of Jews in England. [The foot-notes wherein the author cites his authorities are not here reprinted, through lack of space.—ED.] Similarly, in a very rare tract descriptive of English society, and evidently written within the first quarter of the seventeenth century, we are informed that 'a store of Jewes we have in England; a few in Court; many i' th' Citty, more in the Countrey.' These witnesses can leave little doubt of the fact that Jews were known here before their formal re-admission under Cromwell, and many disconnected notices in addition can be produced to prove it in fuller detail. Indeed, from a great mass of private correspondence we are enabled to trace the fortunes of a Jewish family, named Lopez, living in England near the beginning of the second quarter of the sixteenth century.

This discovery promises to throw light on contemporary stage history. It is certainly significant that, rarely as the Jew has made his appearance on the English stage, he was the hero of no less than three plays [Gosson's 'Jew showne at the Bull,' Marlowe's Barrabas, and Shakespeare's Shylock], all written and produced within the same fifteen years, and that during these very years a Jewish doctor—Roderigo Lopez by name (the head of the family to which we have referred)—held a very prominent position in London and at Court, and shared with actors an intimacy with those noblemen who were the warmest patrons of the drama. It is, perhaps, a more remarkable circumstance that in the same year, and just before the earliest form of *The Merchant of Venice* was first produced, this Jew became the victim of what bears all the appearance of a Court intrigue, and through his trial and execution brought his family and faith into such notoriety that one theatrical manager at least found it to his advantage to utilize it. In a more minute examination of this man's public and private relations than has yet been attempted, we intend to inquire if any grounds exist on which we may (within the limits of historical probability) establish a connection between his career and the creation and development of Shakespeare's Jew.

[The early history of Lopez is hidden in obscurity. All authorities, however, are agreed that he was descended from a Spanish Jewish family. There are records of two of that name, one in 1515, and the other in 1550, and both doctors; the latter was known to be a 'Jewe borne.' The supposition is reasonable that they were of the same family; it is not unlikely, then, that Roderigo was born in England;] and as in the year 1594 he is represented in a contemporary engraving and in written documents as being well advanced in years, we may place the date of his birth between 1520 and 1530. He probably obtained his medical education (as was the usual custom) at some Southern university. But he returned to England comparatively early in life, and joined the recently formed College of Physicians. He rapidly gained reputation in 'his faculty.' In 1569 he was selected to read the Anatomy Lectures of the year and in 1575 his name appears almost at the head of the list of the chief doctors of London, quoted by Stowe. Some years before he had married a Jewess named Sarah who apparently had wealthy relations in Antwerp, and he soon became the father of a large family of daughters.

Lopez, who numbered among his patients the chief statesmen of the day, was for a long time attached to the household of Lord Leicester. With the Earl he lived on terms of great intimacy, 'being withal a man very observant and officious, and of a pleasing and appliable behaviour.' But the connection is noticeable on other grounds. While Lopez was attending him professionally, Leicester frequently summoned to Kenilworth a number of actors, many of whom came from the neighbouring town of Stratford, and he subsequently incorporated the chief of them by special license as 'the Earl of Leicester's company of servants and players.' [To this company, under its various titles, Shakespeare belonged throughout his career.—ED.] At the head of them stood James Burbadge, a fellow-townsman of Shakespeare, whose son Richard became the dramatist's most intimate friend. The invention of the kind of beard that has been for centuries a stage-tradition with Shylock is attributed to him, and in this detail he seems to have imitated, to judge from a portrait of the day, the Jewish physician, to whom his father doubtless had previously introduced him on one of the occasions when all three were enjoying Leicester's hospitality.

In 1586, Lopez became sworn physician to Queen Elizabeth. The promotion gave him new prominence in political society.

In 1590, Lopez obtained an additional claim to public attention. A foreigner, fleeing from the wrath of King Philip of Spain, sought protection at the Court of St James. An illegitimate connection of the royal family of Portugal, he had, on the death of the king in 1580, laid claim to the throne, and gathered round him a large body of adherents. . . . . The Duke of Alva was despatched to put an end to him, but the pretender was fortunate enough to escape, about 1588, to England.

In London he was received with wild enthusiasm. The Spanish fever was at its height, and so long as it lasted the refugee was sure to be the popular idol. His real name was the ordinary Portuguese one of Antonio Perez, but he was known popularly as King Antonio, and references to him as to a royal personage abound in contemporary records. . . . . Antonio, in spite of his extravagant pretensions, was a person of singularly small intelligence. Portuguese was the only language he could speak or in which he could correspond. An interpreter was therefore required before he could maintain any regular intercourse with his new friends. Among the courtiers Lopez was famed for a more or less intimate knowledge of five European languages, and he was accordingly invited by the Queen and Essex to come to Antonio's assistance. The doctor complied with the invitation, and from that date he was closely associated in the public mind with their hero Antonio. . . . . At first all went well, ... but before two years had passed the intercourse [between Essex and Lopez and Antonio] showed itself to be wanting in harmony. Lopez was old, and his health had begun to fail. He grew irritable, and endured with impatience Essex's impetuosity. His enthusiasm for Antonio was cooling, whose conduct was characterized by intense arrogance and by an incapacity to show gratitude. Sharp words, therefore, occasionally passed between Antonio and his chief adviser. The young courtiers took the part of their foreign *protégé*, and seized the opportunity of taunting the doctor with his religious profession, the number of his daughters, and his anxiety to see them matched to wealthy suitors. [In 1592, Essex endeavoured to make Lopez a political tool in a Spanish intrigue, and Lopez revealed the plan to the Queen, who told Essex that she regarded it 'as a mean expedient.'] Essex, angry at this betrayal of his confidence, retaliated by advising Antonio to treat with less forbearance the doctor's uncertain temper, and to complain of his irritability to the Queen. [Lopez, not to be outdone, divulged to Antonio some professional secrets 'which did disparage to Essex's honour;' this led to an open rupture, and Antonio sided with the Earl.] This gross act of ingratitude so enraged Lopez that it is said he swore an oath that he would have his revenge.

With Antonio's followers Lopez had always been on very good terms. Some were of Jewish descent, and had often stayed with him at his house in London. Their master's temperament had proved as little agreeable to them as to the doctor. [Of this discontent the Spanish emissaries of King Philip took advantage, and secretly offered large rewards to have Antonio assassinated. Lopez was drawn into the plot, and 50,000 crowns were guaranteed to him if he would undertake to be the instrument, whereupon Lopez incautiously declared that 'Don Antonio should die the first illness that befel him.'] But another plot was hatching of still greater importance. If Don Antonio, the impostor, was Philip's enemy, much more so was Queen Elizabeth, the heretic. . . . . As soon as Lopez had been inveigled into the minor plot, the conspirators revealed to him the greater. . . . . Lopez declared that he had received too many favours from Elizabeth to allow him to listen to the villanous proposal, and returned no further answer. But aware that any disclosure on his part would balk him of his revenge on Antonio, he made no open communication of the conspiracy, and contented himself with letting drop vague hints of the Spanish king's designs in Elizabeth's presence, who so little understood them that she charged Lopez with breach of courtesy in speaking of such matters before her. [A letter addressed to one of the conspirators fell into the hands of Essex, and as the offender was staying at the time with Lopez, suspicion fell on the doctor; whereupon] Essex obtained permission to examine his papers, but with so unsatisfactory a result that Elizabeth told Essex that 'he was a rash and temerarious youth to enter into a matter against the poor man which he could not prove.' But the rumour ran among the courtiers that 'like a Jew he had burned all his papers a little before.'

The rebuff Essex had received roused him to more vigorous exertions. Those already accused were further examined, and they were threatened with the 'manacles' unless they returned the answers their questioners were seeking to obtain. So plausible a story was thus concocted that Lopez was implicated beyond all chance of extrication, and Essex declared to his friends that he could make the whole business 'as clear as the noon-day.' Little more than a week, therefore, after Lopez's first accusation, London was startled by the news that 'old Dr Lopez is in the Tower for intelligence with the King of Spain.'

Four weeks later the trial took place. In the interval, Lopez, to avoid the rack, had, after many vehement denials, confessed that he was aware of the twofold plot. Shortly after, Essex obtained a commission from the Queen to preside at the trial, in conjunction with the Lord Mayor and others of Her Majesty's advisers. The case for the Crown was confided to Solicitor-general Coke, and the Guildhall was prepared for the scene of the proceedings.

From the first, feeling in the City rose high against the Doctor. He was, the report went, of a religious profession that fitted him for any 'execrable undertaking.' The preservation of the two lives that had seemed so nearly threatened was attributed to a miraculous intervention of Providence. Antonio received every mark of sympathy from the citizens. The law-officers pressed to the full the advantage that these sentiments gave them. Coke laid especial stress on the fact that Lopez was a Jew. This 'perjured and murdering traitor and Jewish doctor,' he said, 'is worse than Judas himself.' His judges spoke of him as 'that vile Jew;' and 'wily and covetous,' 'mercenary' and 'corrupt,' were the mildest of the epithets that assailed him.

Lopez saw the futility of a long defence. He merely asserted that he had much belied himself in his confession 'to save himself from racking.' But the statement had no weight with his judges: 'a most substantial jury found him guilty of all the treasons, and judgment was passed with the applause of the world.' Even Sir Robert Cecil, Lopez's former friend, acquiesced in the justice of the verdict.

But the result of the trial does not seem to have been universally satisfactory. The Queen refused to sign the death-warrant, and the judges who had been excluded from the case did not advise in the matter. For more than seven weeks after the trial Lopez remained in the Tower, and it was not till one of Essex's partisans had been raised to the Bench as Lord Chief Justice that the Queen was induced to proceed with the execution of the sentence. On his representation that 'much scandal and dishonour would ensue' from further delay, she signed the necessary orders for the hanging of Lopez at Tyburn.

At the gallows the Doctor made an endeavour to address the vast mob that had collected to see him die, but his first utterances were interrupted with the cruelest jeers. Exasperated by the treatment he received from the unruly crowd, he contented himself with crying out, before the hangman adjusted the noose, that he loved the Queen and Antonio as well as he loved Jesus Christ. The irony called forth loud peals of laughter, and as the bolt fell the people shouted, 'He is a Jew!' The excitement that his death created was not allowed by the Government to subside immediately. No less than five official accounts of Lopez's treason, with many semi-official pamphlets, were prepared for publication, to keep the facts of this important case well before the public mind.

No one living in London at the time could have been ignorant of Lopez's history and fate, and it cannot surprise us that the caterers for public amusements gave expression to the popular sentiments respecting him. . . . . The entries in Henslowe's diary inform us that *The Jew* formed the subject of no less than twenty representations between May, 1594, and the end of that year. . . . . Barrabas, in Marlowe's *Jew of Malta*, renders with great faithfulness the bitter hate that the Hebrew had for the Christian, but even a greater fidelity to Jewish customs is expressed in another characteristic of Barrabas. He is fond of quoting foreign languages. His French is passable, but the jargon he more frequently indulges is a mixture of Spanish and Italian. . . . . To whom Marlowe was specially indebted for this knowledge cannot be determined, but, as he never travelled, we may, with great probability, attribute it to some Jew residing in London at the time, perhaps to some member of Lopez's family, if not to Lopez himself.

But however that may have been, there can be no doubt at all that circumstances connected with the Jewish doctor's career reached the ears of Shakespeare. Throughout the year of the execution the dramatist was living in London, and opportunities were open to him of hearing fuller details than those in the popular reports. He was on terms of considerable intimacy with Essex's friend Southampton, and it is not impossible that he formed some acquaintance at the same time with the Earl himself. In their company he may not unfrequently have met the Doctor.

[In conclusion, Lee refers to certain important points connected with the story of Lopez and *The Merchant of Venice* which he finds : first, in the name Antonio ; secondly, in the date of Henslowe's 'Venesyon comodey,' which Lee supposes to be the first rough draft, whose existence was surmised by Hunter, brought out hastily in August, within three months of Lopez's execution in May. Thirdly, 'in their devotion to their family,' says Lee, 'the two Jews closely resemble each other. Neither Lopez nor Shylock, in good fortune or in bad, fail to exemplify the Jewish virtue of domesticity.' Perhaps the less emphasis that is laid on this point in Shylock's case the better, and for alluding to it at all Mr Lee is responsible, not the Editor. Fourthly and lastly, the reference to the rack, which is noteworthy ; Gratiano's reference to the twelve jurymen to send Shylock to the gallows ; and in the allusion also by Gratiano to the wolf who was hanged for human slaughter, to which attention was called *ad loc.*]

That we have succeeded in discovering the actual original of Shylock we are not presumptuous enough to imagine. Our knowledge of Lopez is only fragmentary, and it is quite possible that had we the means of learning their characters and lives, Lopez's cousin, his Jewish friend Geronimo, and any of the 'other divers kinsmen here,' to whom Coke referred at the Doctor's trial, would present as striking a likeness to Shylock as Roderigo himself. What we may fairly claim to have proved is that Jews were residing in England in Shakespeare's day, and that the Jew of Venice bears evidence of having had a contemporary prototype. We have placed, at least beyond all reasonable doubt, the fact that one Jew of England came into considerable prominence while the dramatist was growing up to manhood, and that he was treated with great indignity because of his religious belief towards the end of his remarkable career, which closed only a few months before *The Merchant of Venice* appeared ; and we have shown what grounds there are for believing that Shakespeare and Burbadge came into contact with this famous Jew.

A DRAMATIC REVERIE

In *The Monthly Chronicle*, November, 1838, there is to be found an article called *Shylock, A Critical Fancy.* This 'Fancy' had been suggested, so said the writer, by an article which had appeared some time previously in another magazine, entitled 'A Lawyer's Criticism on Shakespeare,' in which the assertion was made, half in jest, half in earnest, that the distress in *The Merchant of Venice* 'turns chiefly upon an embarrassment with which no *lawyer* can seriously sympathize,' and that Anthonio's difficulties 'arise entirely from his gross oversight in not effecting an insurance upon his various argosies. He should have opened a set of policies at once upon the Rialto, where *marine assurance* was perfectly well understood.' The writer in *The Monthly Chronicle* then goes on to fancy what Shylock might have said had he been better prepared with physiological knowledge to meet the quibble in regard to flesh without blood, &c.

The writer, anonymous in the *Chronicle*, now turns out to have been the late Richard Hengist Horne. The 'Fancy,' much amplified, has been kindly lent to the Editor, in the original MS, by the present owner, Mr Harry Edwards, of New York. The additions to Shakespeare's Scene are in blank verse, and show great vigour. It appears that this 'Fancy' was submitted to a public test in 1850, at Sadler's Wells, when that theatre was under the management of Mr Phelps. On the 16th of May a performance was given in 'aid of the Grand Exhibition of 1851,' and a portion of *Henry VIII* was acted; it was followed by 'Shylock, A Scene from *The Merchant of Venice*,' wherein the part of Shylock was undertaken by Mr R. H. Horne himself, and Portia by Miss Glynn.

On the first page of the MS is the following note by the author:

'It is not for a moment intended, in the present alteration of a Scene from *The Merchant of Venice*, either to follow the example of those who so grossly mangled the 'Acting Copies of Shakespeare some years ago, nor to suggest that presumption to 'others. It is simply attempted to embody in action, *on a special occasion*, a dramatic 'speculation as to what might have passed through *Shylock's* mind on listening to certain parts of *Portia's* line of defence, supposing the same trial (granting all other 'circumstances) had occurred in Venice in the present century.

'The idea of this Scene was first put forth in an early number of a monthly journal 'conducted some years ago by Sir E. Bulwer Lytton and Sir David Brewster.'

Then follows: SHYLOCK IN 1850. *A Dramatic Reverie.* By R. H. Horne. *Act IV. Scene—The Court of Justice.* [*The Fourth Act opens as usual, and continues as acted down to the following speech*, line 319:]

> *Portia.* Tarry a little—*there is something else.*
> This bond doth give thee here no jot of blood.
> The words expressly are 'a pound of flesh.'
> Take then thy bond!—take thou thy pound of flesh;
> But, in the cutting it, if thou dost shed
> One drop of Christian blood, thy lands and goods
> Are by the laws of Venice confiscate
> Unto the State of Venice.
> *Shylock.* Peace, false Judge!
> There's no such thing as flesh devoid of blood!
> Flesh is made up of vessels, and they're filled
> With blood alone,—nay, blood is liquid flesh.
> Oh, thou false Judge! Most treacherous, wicked Judge!

Send to your butcher for your daily meal—
What will you say if he do sell a pound
Of skin and empty veins? Till you can show me
Flesh that is bloodless, be't what kind it may,
My claim is good; one flesh alone exists,
And that hath blood, for each includes the other.
Doth all your wisdom in a quibble end
Like bubbles, blown by Law?
　　　　　[*The Duke and the Magnificoes look confounded.*
　　　　　Portia stands troubled and perplexed.

Portia.　Yet——fear the Law!
Shylock.　This bond holds blood!—out on your cullender wits!
If Laws be folly, all are fooled by them.
I am your fool in suffering these delays.
But *he* is mine, by wisdom and by law.
A Jew may be the dog
That's hated by a Christian's charity,
But not the dupe of *words!*
Bassanio.　O Jew, forbear!
Shylock.　Forbear!—I came here to be paid a debt.
Bassanio.　Lash not thyself to fury, like a beast!
Shylock.　'Tis ye who have lashed me thus: I'll have my bond!
Trifle no more—there is no power in Venice
To alter a decree established;
Said not the Doctor so?—then was he wise,
But afterwards he spake as doth a fool;
Nay worse; he damned his soul with lies, to save
That Christian beast who spat upon my beard.
　　　　　[*The Court is thrown into utter perplexity, and remain silent.*
Portia. [*After a troubled pause*] The Jew shall have all justice;
Therefore prepare thee to cut off the flesh;
Yet, Shylock, see thou cut not less nor more
But just a pound of flesh; if thou tak'st more
Or less, than just a pound, be it so much
As makes it light or heavy in the substance
Or the division of the twentieth part
Of one poor scruple;—nay, if the scale do turn
But in the estimation of a hair,
Thou diest, and all thy goods are confiscate.
Shylock. [*With deadly bitterness*] I'll not take more; I'll take it *by degrees*
Therefore not more,—since thou'd'st be so exact;
Be not thou hasty, treacherous young Judge;
I am not bound to take it all, at once.
Bassanio.　O villanous Jew! thou'd'st torture him to death!
Shylock [*calmly*] If in some days after the half be paid,
He chance to die—that is no fault of mine;
My bond doth say a pound; but doth not say
That I must take the whole immediately.
We're not compell'd to ruin thus our debtors.
　26

I'll take it *by instalments*—would you jeer **me?**
Old Shylock hath his jest!
   Portia.   But since the whole
Is offered and not taken, thou canst **have**
No claim hereafter.
   Shylock.   I do claim all, now.
   Portia.   Take then the pound of flesh and blood, fierce **Jew!**
But see you spill not aught that is *not yours.*
   Shylock.   Why must I have this care—look *ye* to that;
It is the very nature of all flesh
When cut to bleed; and here my bond declares
That—from the Christian breast of one who scoffs
At me, my tribe, and ever used to mock
My prosperous dealings, I shall forthwith cut
A pound in forfeit! No more words,—prepare!
   Portia.   His wasted blood shall yet bring ruin on thee.
   Shylock.   Let ruin come!—so I can once behold
That streaming breast, I care not if his blood
Swell to a second Galilean Sea,
And with its humming and abhorrent surge
Sweep away Venice! Now! now! stand aside!
   Duke [*rising*].   Restrain him!—sure some devil speaks in him! [*A'l rise.*
Keep back the bearded vulture!
   Portia [*as by a sudden thought*].   The ruin thou defiest shall fall upon thee!
Thy vengeance be thy sentence, e'en by the bond
Which thou so fiercely urgest! By its terms,
Purport, and stratagem, thou seek'st the life
Of a Venetian citizen; for which *crime*
The Law unwinds itself from that man's neck
And with a terrible and just recoil
Springs back on thee! Shylock! one half thy goods
Are forfeit to Antonio! The other half
Comes to the privy coffer of the State,
And thine offending life lies in the mercy
Of the Duke only.
   Gratiano.   O upright Judge! mark, Jew!—O learned Judge!
   Shylock.   Is that the law?
   Portia.   Thyself shalt see the act.
For, as thou urgest justice be assured
Thou shalt have justice more than thou desirest.
                             [*Shylock drops the scales and knife.*
   Gratiano.   O learned Judge! Mark, Jew;—a learned Judge!
   Shylock.   I take his offer then,—pay the bond thrice
And let the Christian go.
   Bassanio.   Here is the money.
   Portia.   Soft.
The Jew shall have all justice,—soft!—no haste.
   Shylock.   Give me my principal, and let me go.
   Bassanio.   I have it ready for thee; here it is.

Portia.   He hath refused it in the open Court;
He shall have merely justice.
   Shylock [*drawing out his bond*] Shall I not barely have my principal?
   Portia.   Thou shalt have nothing.
   Shylock.   Why then the devil give him good of it.
I'll stay no longer question.
   Portia.   Tarry, Jew.
The law hath yet another hold on you.
   Duke.   That thou shalt see the difference of our spirit,
I pardon thee thy life before thou ask it;
For half thy wealth, it is Antonio's;
The other half comes to the general state,
Which humbleness may drive into a fine.
   Portia.   Ay, for the State; not for Antonio.
   Shylock [*dropping his bond*].   Nay take my life and all, pardon not that,
You take my house, when you do take the prop
That doth sustain my house; you take my life
When you do take the means whereby I live.
[The rest of the Scene adheres to the original text, except that the Stage-direction
      reads, *Exit Shylock wildly*].

LAW IN THE TRIAL SCENE

IT is only within recent times that special attention has been bestowed upon the
Legal Principles involved in the Trial Scene, or in Shakespeare's dealing with the
forms of Legal Procedure.   As long as Shylock was held to be a wolfish, bloody,
inexorable dog, it made but little difference how he was defeated or his victim saved;
a Jew had no rights which a Christian was bound to respect.   Even charming, gentle Mrs Inchbald believed that Shakespeare's purpose in writing the play was to
'hold up the Jew to detestation,' and such undoubtedly was the general impression
created by the 'snarling malignity' of Macklin's Shylock.   But when Edmund Kean,
in 1814, revealed a Jew almost more sinned against than sinning, and one who simply
bettered the instruction of Christian example, the 'pit rose at him' and a revulsion of
feeling began.   From that hour a reaction in favour of Shylock set in, until now it is
generally agreed that up to a certain point he was the victim of a downright quibble,
and that even on the third point, that of conspiracy, his conviction was, perhaps, of
doubtful propriety.

Chronologically, the earliest voice, as far as I know, which was raised in defence of
Shylock and in denunciation of the illegality of his defeat is that of an Anonymous
Contributor to a volume of *Essays by a Society of Gentlemen at Exeter*, printed in
1792.   The Essay is called 'An Apology for the Character and Conduct of Shylock,'
and is signed 'T. O.'   The Essayist's plea for Shylock is, that if his character is cruel
it was made so by ill-treatment; that the derision with which his daughter's flight was
treated was calculated to embitter the sweetest nature, let alone that of an outcast of
society; that his Mosaic law authorized him to exact 'an eye for an eye, a tooth for a
tooth;' that money-making was the sole occupation the laws suffered him to follow;
that he knowingly violated no divine or human law; and, finally, the Essayist depicts
an imaginary performance of the play by Hebrews in a future so far ahead that Shake-

speare is but a traditionary 'old British bard,' and reproduces a criticism of the acting which appeared the following morning in the columns of *The Jebusite Morning Post*, or *The Jerusalem Daily Advertiser*. The criticism begins thus : 'On the fourth day of the first week in the month of Nisan was represented the tragedy of " Shylock," written by Nathan Ben Boaz. The plot is borrowed from an old British bard, who flourished about the beginning of the 17th century of their æra; and who composed it under the influence of the spirit of inveterate malice against our nation for which, in that and many preceding ages, the Europeans were notorious. . . . . Shylock, the hero of the drama, is represented as an exemplary follower of the law, and as having acquired a considerable property by adhering to that precept, which *enjoins lending to the stranger upon usury*.' The critic then proceeds to relate the various indignities which are heaped on Shylock, under which he 'would have sunk but for the consolation he received from Antonio's having forfeited his bond.' . . . . 'Shylock expects to show the world an example that a son of Abraham is not to be wronged and trampled on with impunity. His firmness and patriotic sentiments on the Trial deserve the highest commendation. His resentment though severe is just ; he had endured irreparable wrongs, and had a right to expect the most exemplary vengeance for their atonement. The law, however, on which he founds his claim, is evaded by shameful sophistry. Shylock is permitted to take the pound of flesh, but is warned at the same time that if he sheds " one drop of Christian blood his lands and goods are confiscate to the State, by the laws of Venice." But how can we suppose its legislators could have foreseen and obviated the fulfilling of so singular a contract as that between the Merchant and Shylock ? that, in their great wisdom, they could enact a decree by which a man is allowed to take his debtor's forfeiture, yet is punished for not performing an impossibility in taking it ? Can we imagine that Shylock's notary could have drawn, or himself have signed, such a bond that *fairly* admitted such an interpretation or incurred such a penalty ? Yet on this absurd, perverted construction of a plain contract is Shylock condemned.

'Another quibble of equal weight is urged against him ; that having a right to cut from the Merchant's breast a pound of flesh, and a pound *only*, if he took more or less than that,—even the minutest particle,—he should suffer death ; as if the spirit of the bond did not clearly imply that he was limited to take no more than a pound ! Shylock is found guilty of death by this curious exposition of the Venetian laws.' . . . . The condition that he become a Christian he complies with, 'but at the inhuman proposal not an eye was to be seen unmoistened with tears in our theatre.' . . . . 'On examining Shakespeare's numerous commentators, and other records of the times, it appears that no censure was ever cast, no unfavourable sentiment entertained of the unjust judge, the injurious merchant, the undutiful daughter, and prodigal lover. . . . . What an idea does this give of the English nation when such sentiments could be applauded ! What a striking instance does it afford of the lax state of morality !' . . . . 'The sudden yet natural death of the benevolent Merchant is well imagined. The turbulent frenzy of the judge, brought on by the recollection of his corrupt decision, and the tender melancholy of the daughter, who bewails her misconduct too late, are equally affecting, and demonstrate the author's perfect knowledge of the human heart. The moral sense may be a while suppressed or perverted, but conscience, some time or other, will resume its dominion and severely punish the violators of her laws.'

Twenty-five years later, HAZLITT spoke a good word for Shylock, but so far from seeing 'hat he was the victim of a legal quibble, Hazlitt expressly referred to the sound 'maxims of jurisprudence' which characterized the trial.

Mrs JAMESON, with a vision clearer than Hazlitt's, speaks of Portia's eagerness to save Antonio by any appeal rather than by 'the legal quibble with which her cousin Bellario has armed her.'

CAMPBELL, in 1838, was the first among Editors to maintain openly that Shylock was an ill-used man, with nothing unnatural in his character, and that he was overcome 'only by a legal quibble.'

In the same year, 1838, C. A. BROWN espoused Shylock's cause, and discerned in the play a plea for toleration not alone of the Jews, but of all others; yet l e failed to notice any legal ill-treatment of Shylock.

CHARLES KNIGHT, too, speaks bravely for him, but makes no allusion to the quibble other than in quoting, without comment, the paragraph by Mrs Jameson, wherein she refers to it.

HORNE'S *Dramatic Reverie*, which immediately precedes the present topic, should not be overlooked in tracing the developement of the belief that Shylock was the victim of illegality, although in that striking modification of the Trial Scene, Shylock appeals not so much to a law of the land as to a law of language, and it is there tacitly conceded that on the last point, that of indirectly conspiring against the life of a Venetian citizen, he was justly condemned.

In chronological order, HAYNES (from whose *Lectures*, under the title of *Outlines of Equity*, an extract is given at IV, i, 319) must here follow; the exact date I cannot give. The American Reprint of his volume, published in 1858, affords no clue whatsoever as to the date of the English original, but, for the present purpose, 1852–58 is near enough. Lord Cranworth is mentioned by Haynes as the Chancellor of the day, and his tenure of the great seal was during these years.

In order to account for the knowledge of law as shown in these plays, Malone, nigh a hundred years ago, conjectured (ed. 1790, i, 104) that Shakespeare, on leaving the Grammar School, had been placed in the office of some country attorney or the seneschal of some manor court. In the process of time this suggestion became more and more widely accepted, until, in 1859, at the request of Collier, LORD CAMPBELL examined the plays throughout for the purpose of arriving at some decision, and his final admission is that such a view as conjectured by Malone may be right, and that while there is weighty evidence for it, there is nothing conclusive against it. Although Lord Campbell professes to have read all the plays with some care for the purpose of detecting the legal references in them, and has made several notes on *The Merchant of Venice*, the legal principles involved in the Trial Scene do not seem to have attracted his serious attention; he says explicitly that 'the trial is duly conducted according to the strict forms of legal procedure.'

In 1872, there appeared in *The Albany Law Journal* the Report of a decision of the Supreme Court of New York, on Appeal, of the case of *Shylock* v. *Antonio*. The bare statement of the title indicates plainly enough that this 'Report' is a travestie, and as such, pure and simple, it cannot yield sufficient interest to justify its reproduction here. But it is more than a mere travestie: the statement of the points of law involved is lucid and the law controlling them is well taken; it ought not, therefore, to be overlooked because of the form in which its wisdom is presented. Anthonio could pun in his dying farewell to Bassanio, and he has read his Shakespeare to little purpose who does not know that in the channels fretted in the cheeks the tears of sorrow and of mirth find alternate course. Moreover, this 'Report' is of importance historically, inasmuch as it anticipates some of the points which were afterwards brought forward by one of the most eminent of German Professors of Jurisprudence in a pamphlet which has had, and is still having, wide-spread popularity throughout Europe, and in which the treatment of Shylock in the Trial Scene is used as an illustration.

In the following abstract of the 'Report' I have omitted many local and temporary allusions; the date of the number of the *Law Journal* in which it appeared is the Thirtieth of March, p. 193; and it may be added that in a later number of this same Journal (27 December, 1879, p. 502) the author is stated to be ESEK COWEN, Esq., of Troy, New York.

The case is set forth with due formality, and the opinion by the Court is thus given:

In order fully to understand this case, it will be necessary to refer to certain facts, not very material, perhaps, to its final determination. The defendant, Antonio, is an Italian merchant, doing an extensive business in the city of New York as an importer. Prior to the transactions which resulted in this suit he had been remarkably successful, had made much money, which he spent in a princely manner, and stood well in society, in spite of a tendency to mental unsoundness. We say 'mental unsoundness,' though there is no direct proof on the subject, because it seems to be conceded that he lent money to his friends without interest, which would, in most business circles, be considered evidence to warrant a commission *de lunatico*. He had a sporting friend of the same nationality, by the name of Bassanio, who, having been completely 'cleaned out' (as the vile phrase is) by a season at Saratoga, conceived a novel method of restoring his fortunes. It seems that an eccentric resident of Venango county, Pennsylvania, having made a large fortune by speculations in oil lands, left the whole of it to his daughter on condition that she should take for her husband the suitor who should prove most proficient in the ancient and noble game of 'Thimble Rig.' As Bassanio had been accustomed to witness this game at horse-races, he felt confident that if he had an opportunity he could tell in which box the 'little joker' was. But he had no money to take him to Venango county, and no acquaintance with railroad officials sufficiently intimate to justify him in asking for a pass. In this extremity he applied to the defendant for a loan. Antonio would gladly have complied, but just before he had invested every dollar he could raise in contraband goods and vessels for running the Southern blockade. . . . . The two friends then applied to the plaintiff, a gentleman of the Hebrew persuasion, for a loan of 3000 dollars upon Antonio's credit. For several reasons the plaintiff was little inclined to look upon the defendant with favour. Besides, his unjustifiable habit of lending money without interest, which, as Shylock very properly observed, had a tendency to 'lower the rate of usance,' Antonio chewed tobacco freely, and expectorated with great carelessness upon all objects in his vicinity. Indeed, it appeared in evidence, without objection, that the defendant had frequently spit upon Shylock's 'Jewish gaberdine.' The Court is not exactly certain as to what a 'gaberdine' is; no definition was attempted by either counsel upon the argument; but we may safely assume that it is a garment which is not improved by contact with tobacco, and such incidents will go far to excuse, if they do not justify, the somewhat vindictive manner in which the suit was prosecuted. The plaintiff, however, at the time of this application, concealed his feelings and told Antonio that he would charge him no interest, but would merely take a bond conditioned to the effect that, if the loan was not paid when due, the borrower would forfeit a pound of flesh nearest his heart. Bassanio pretended to demur, but Antonio was confident that the loan would be paid when due; and this somewhat singular business transaction was concluded as above stated. Bassanio went to Venango county, guessed the right box, and married the heiress. Antonio's fate was far different. . . . . His ships were sunk by the blockading-squadron. And when Bassanio returned from his wedding-tour, he found all Antonio's effects sold out by the sheriff and numerous executions returned unsatisfied. He found, too, that the plaintiff had already commenced this action to enforce the forfeiture on the bond. As soon as the cause was at issue, ... all parties agreed to accept as referee a young and unknown lawyer by the name of Balthazar, which arrangement was the more singular, as he does not appear to have been a relative of any of the judges.

And just here arises one of the most curious questions of the case. It is asserted by the counsel for the appellant that this referee was in fact a *woman;* that her maiden name was Mary Jane Portia, and that she was the same oleaginous heiress whom Bassanio had just married; and the decision itself furnishes the strongest internal evidence that it is the work of one of that pernicious sex which 'brought sin into the world and all our woe,' and has been bringing sinners into the world ever since with a similar disregard of consequences.

In this case the facts were conceded by all the parties, and after a tender, in open court, of three times the amount of the debt had been made and refused, this referee of uncertain sex proceeded to pronounce judgement. His (or her) conclusions of law were as follows:

1st. That the bond was valid, and that the plaintiff was entitled to his pound of flesh.

2d. That he was entitled to *exactly* a pound of flesh, neither more nor less, and not to a drop of blood; and that if he drew blood, or took a grain of flesh more or less than a pound, he would be guilty of murder.

3d. That under an ancient and obsolete ordinance of the city of New York, passed in the time of Peter Stuyvesant, the plaintiff was liable to capital punishment 'for practising against the life of a Christian.'

4th. That he could only escape this punishment by giving half his fortune to his daughter (who had just married a Christian) and by turning Christian himself.

On hearing the latter portion of this decision, the plaintiff felt a considerable abatement of his enthusiasm and inquired in a tremulous tone, 'if that was the law.' On being assured that it was, he offered to take the amount of his bond and discontinue without costs; to which proposition this astonishing referee replied that the plaintiff had forfeited all claim to his money by refusing it in open court! The plaintiff being without counsel, no stay of proceedings was obtained; and the decree of the referee was carried into effect, the plaintiff being baptized, we presume, by the sheriff of the city and county of New York. Upon a subsequent appeal the judgement was affirmed by the General Term, and the plaintiff appealed to this Court.

Upon hearing the first conclusion of law announced by the referee, the plaintiff exclaimed in his delight, 'O! wise young judge! A Daniel come to judgment!' and during the remainder of the decision, one Gratiano, a sort of 'next friend' of the defendant, made the court-house ring with cries of 'A Daniel! A Daniel come to judgment!' It is the unanimous opinion of this court that these allusions to the lamented Webster, from whichever side they proceeded, were most unfortunate. Nothing could be more unlike the calm, clear judgement of that lawyer and statesman than this truly feminine decision, half-civil decree, half-criminal sentence, and the other half commutation of punishment. No part of it bears the slightest semblance to any principle of law or equity ever recognized in a civilized country.

The first conclusion of law, though apparently in favor of the plaintiff, was utterly erroneous for two reasons: 1st, It is well settled that, when a bond contains a condition that is unreasonable and absurd, it will be considered as good only for the sum actually secured or lent on the faith of it. As in the familiar case where a party, in consideration of a sum of money, agreed to give the price of the twenty-fourth nail in a horse's shoe, at the rate of a penny for the first nail, two for the second, and so on in geometrical progression. This bond was not only unreasonable, but provided for the commission of a capital crime, and was clearly void under the principle to which I have adverted. 2d, The bond was extinguished by the tender of the amount of the loan which it was given to secure. This Court has explicitly decided that a tender of the debt, even after it is due, extinguishes all collateral securities. *Kortright* v. *Cady*, 21 N. Y. 343, and the tender at the trial was sufficient to cancel the bond if it ever possessed any validity.

But, if the referee's first proposition of law is sound, the second becomes a stupendous absurdity. It is a familiar rule of construction that the right to do a certain act confers the right to the necessary incidents of that act. The referee holds that the plaintiff had a right to cut off a pound of the defendant's flesh. Now as no one can cut an exact pound of flesh to a grain, as no one can do it without drawing blood, it seems too plain for argument that the parties could have intended no such restrictions, and the Court had no right to supply them. If the bond was valid, the plaintiff could have subjected himself to no penalty by simply taking what it gave him.

We have not before us the statute referred to in the third conclusion of the referee, but we have great doubts whether the plaintiff, upon any reasonable construction of its terms, could be held liable for taking a bond voluntarily signed by the defendant. It does not seem to us that this was 'practising against the life' of the defendant, within the meaning of the law. . . . .

The pretence that the plaintiff had forfeited his debt by the refusal of the tender was extremely shallow. Nothing is better settled than that a tender does not extinguish the *debt*, but only things collateral thereto, such as interest. . . . . But the climax of usurpation and cruelty was to come. The plaintiff was not only required to despoil himself for his daughter's benefit, but to embrace Christianity for his own. . . . . It is certainly difficult for us to see how any benefit could arise to the Christian Church if all the criminals in the land were compelled to adopt that religion at—if the expression is admissible—the point of the halter. We do not mean to deny the power to the legislature to prescribe the union of the criminal with some religious body as a penalty for crime. If coupled with the obligation of hearing two average sermons a week, we are not prepared to say that the punishment would not be exemplary. . . . . And here we pause to set ourselves right before the public. Absorbed in our arduous duties, we can pay but little attention to general literature, but we read the public prints, and we cannot ignore the fact that this case has created much interest in the minds of the community. If we are rightly informed, the facts have formed the basis of a powerful drama, which has lately been placed upon the stage, and the conduct of the referee has been loudly applauded by audiences unlearned in the law, who doubtless saw in her the embodiment of the classical idea of justice—namely, a woman with her eyes completely blinded.

To prevent any misunderstanding, therefore, we assert most positively that our decision upon this point is not influenced by the feeling which seems to have actuated one of the witnesses, who objected to the conversion of the daughter of the plaintiff, Miss Jessica Shylock, upon the ground that 'the making of so many new Christians would raise the price of pork.' The Court is of the opinion that, in moderation, a pork diet is both healthful and invigorating, and that sausages, when their origin is not involved in too much obscurity, are a 'dish fit for a judge.'

But, if we know our own hearts, we would not allow a slight advance in the price of a favourite esculent to stand in the way of the genuine conversion of the humblest Hebrew in the land. And in this, we believe that we speak the sentiment of the American people, even outside of Chicago and Cincinnati; while in those two cities, the fact that such a fulfilment of Scripture would tend to raise the price of pork would doubtless be considered the strongest possible reason for the conversion of the whole world. To their citizens no two events could appear more desirable than that 'the knowledge of the Lord should cover the earth as the waters cover the sea,' and that 'prime mess' should go up a dollar a barrel. Personal motives, therefore, have nothing whatever to do with our decision. It is the law of the land and our own feelings of duty that call upon us to relieve the plaintiff from his unfortunate position. We have thus disposed of the questions raised by this appeal, but we cannot close without a word of warning to Mrs Bassanio. . . . . The result of the whole matter is that . . . . the entire decree of the referee must be reversed . . . . All the judges concurring, ordered accordingly.

The question of the Law of the Trial Scene was again brought forward in this same *Journal* (16 January, 1875, p. 45) in a communication from Emporia, Kansas, signed 'W. A. R.,' wherein it was maintained that the downright unsoundness of the law which ruled against Shylock's Bond rendered the claim that Bacon wrote the play 'most pretentious and unfounded.' Whereupon, in reference to Shakespeare's share of responsibility for the unsound law, the Editor of *The Albany Law Journal* thus judiciously comments : ' Many considerations must here be taken into account. For ' instance, the Scene is laid in Venice, and we are not to assume without positive proof ' that the Venetian Law was similar to the Common Law of England. . . . . It is evi-' dent from the spirit of the play that the judge regarded the contract as void, even ' civilly, and he doubtless adopted the legal fiction of so strictly construing the con-' tract as that, without nominally declaring it void, he practically nullified it. This ' case may then be an evidence of Shakespeare's legal ingenuity. . . . . In considering ' Shakespeare's law, we must always take into account the conditions of time, place, ' and circumstance, and how much is intended for dramatic effect.'

In 1872, there appeared in Germany a remarkable book by Dr IHERING, called *The Struggle for Law*, which, before two years had elapsed, had been translated nineteen times, and into sixteen different languages. With the subject of the book itself we are not here concerned; it suffices to say that its central idea may be tersely expressed in a saying of Kant, which the learned author quotes in the Preface to his Eighth Edition, and which, as he says, he had not seen when he wrote the book : ' Whosoever prefers to be a worm must not complain if he is trodden under foot.' But what is of moment to us is, that in the course of his treatise, Prof. Ihering strongly condemns the treatment of Shylock. Although in the substance of his remarks the learned professor had been anticipated (all unconsciously by him), yet the prominence of his position and the great popularity of his book gave an emphasis to Shylock's ill-treatment which it had not hitherto received. Two opponents to Ihering appeared; the first, A. PIETSCHER, Landsgericht-Präsident, in a brochure entitled *Jurist and Poet ;* in which, in a bold, dashing way, it is acknowledged that Portia treated the Jew unfairly, but the meeting of trickery with trickery is justified; a second, who, it would be, perhaps, more correct to say followed Ihering, rather than was called forth by him, is Prof Dr KOHLER, whose book bears the title, *Shakespeare before the Forum of Juris prudence;* wherein there is no attempt to show that, by the use of legal phraseology, it is to be inferred that Shakespeare had spent some years of his life in a lawyer's office, but it is maintained that in Shakespeare's works, as in no other poet's, there live and stir the grand ideas of abstract justice, the elemental principles of law, coeval with man's nature, and which the history of the world, in all nations, reveals as in a process of evolution. *The Merchant of Venice,* as disclosing the evolution of the Law of Debtor and Creditor, was selected as an example by the learned jurist, who, in opposition to Ihering, believes that, viewed from loftier ground, the treatment of Shylock is in harmony with the growth or development of the truest justice. The book is especially interesting in its history of the realistic interpretation of the law of the XII Tables, to which appeal is frequently made by critics, in justification of Shylock's attempt to regard human flesh as an equivalent for a debt; but I am forced to select only those extracts from all three authors, Ihering, Pietscher, and Kohler, which have impressed me as best illustrating the legal treatment of Shylock on the Trial.

The extracts are as follows, beginning with Dr RUDOLF VON IHERING (Professor at Göttingen: *Der Kampf um's Recht,* Wien, 1886, 8te Aufl., p. 58):

It is hatred and revenge that take Shylock to court to get his pound of flesh from the body of Anthonio, but the words the poet puts into Shylock's mouth are just as true as from the mouth of any other. It is the language which an injured sense of right always speaks in all times and in all places; the force, not to be shaken, of the conviction that law must for ever remain law; the lofty strain and pathos of a man, conscious that he pleads not merely for his own person, but for the enacted law.

'I crave the law.' In these four words Shakespeare has marked the true relation of law in its subjective sense to law in its objective sense, and the significance of the struggle for law, in a way that no philosopher learned in the law could have done more strikingly. With these words the case is at once changed, and it is not the claim of Shylock which is on trial, but the law of Venice. To what mighty, gigantic proportions does not the figure of Shylock dilate as he utters these words! It is no longer the Jew demanding a pound of flesh; it is Venice herself that knocks at the door of the court,—*his* rights and the rights of *Venice* are one; with *his* rights, the rights of *Venice* are struck down. And when, under the weight of the decision of a Judge who nullifies law by a miserable quibble, Shylock succumbs, and, the butt of bitter scorn and jeers, totters away with trembling knees, who can help feeling that in his person the law of Venice also is broken down, that it is not Shylock the Jew who staggers off, but the typical figure of the Jew of the Middle Ages, that pariah of society, who cried for law in vain? The mighty tragedy of his fate lies not in the denial of his right, but in that he, a Jew of the Middle Ages, has faith in the law,—we might say, just as if he were a Christian!—a faith firm as a rock which nothing can shake, and which the Judge himself sustains; until the catastrophe strikes him like a thunderbolt, shivering his delusion to atoms, and teaching him that he is nothing but the despised mediæval Jew, whose rights are in the same breath acknowledged, and, by fraud, denied.

[In the foregoing, where reference is made to the nullification of the law by a 'miserable quibble' of the Judge, Ihering has the following foot-note:] It is just here that in my opinion the deep tragic interest lies which Shylock wrings from us. He is indeed cheated out of his rights. So at least must a jurist regard the case. The Poet of course is free to make his own jurisprudence, and we do not regret that Shakespeare has done it here, or rather that he has kept the old story unchanged. But when the jurist undertakes to criticise it, he cannot say otherwise than that the bond was in 'tself null and void, in that its provisions were contrary to good morals; the Judge, therefore, on this very ground should from the very first have denied it. But since he did not so deny it, since the 'second Daniel' acknowledged its validity, it was a wretched quibble, a disgraceful, pettifogging trick, to withhold from the plaintiff the right to draw blood after the right had been granted to take the flesh. Just as well might a Judge acknowledge the right of entry on land, but forbid the right to make footprints, because this was not expressly stipulated. One might almost believe that this drama of Shylock had been played in the most ancient days of Rome; for the authors of the Twelve Tables held it necessary, in reference to the maiming (*in partes secare*) of a debtor by his creditors, to declare expressly that the creditors should be unrestricted as to the size of the piece to be taken. (*Si plus minusve secuerint, sine fraude esto!*)

[The extract which follows is from the Preface to the Eighth edition of the *Kampf um's Recht*, wherein the strictures of Pietscher and Kohler are discussed. Chronologically, therefore, it should follow instead of precede these strictures, but as what I have selected is merely explanatory of Dr Ihering's own view, it is better inserted here.]

(P. xi.) What I maintained in my first edition is not, that the Judge was bound to acknowledge the validity of Shylock's bond, but that after that validity had been acknowledged, he had no right afterwards, in the enunciation of the judgement, to nullify it by a contemptible quibble. The Judge was free to pronounce Shylock's bond valid or invalid. He pronounced it valid, and Shakespeare represents the case as if, according to the law, he could not have decided otherwise. No one in Venice doubted the validity of the bond; the friends of Anthonio, Anthonio himself, the Doge, the Court, all were unanimous that the Jew had the law on his side. And in absolute trust in his right, acknowledged by all, Shylock appeals to the Court for aid, and the 'wise Daniel,' after in vain attempting to induce the vindictive creditor to renounce his claim, recognizes that claim as valid. And now after the decree of the Court has been pronounced, after every doubt of the right of the Jew has been overruled by the Judge himself, and not a word of dissent is uttered, after the whole assembly, the Doge included, have admitted that inevitable claim of the law,—then, when the successful suitor, in full assurance of his cause, is about to take what the sentence of the Court has authorized, he is balked by that very same Judge, who had solemnly recognized his right, by an objection, a quibble too wretched and worthless to merit any serious refutation. Is there ever flesh without blood? The Judge who admitted Shylock's right to cut a pound of flesh from the body of Anthonio, by that very admission recognized Shylock's right to the blood inseparable from the flesh; and he who has a right to cut a pound, may, if he pleases, take less. Both rights are denied to the Jew; he must take the flesh without blood, and he must take a just pound, neither more nor less. Have I said too much in affirming that the Jew is cheated out of his right? To be sure it is done in the interest of Humanity, but does wrong, committed in the interest of Humanity, cease to be wrong? And if ever the end sanctifies the means, why was not the wrong committed betimes in the sentence,—why, not until *after* the sentence, was it first revealed?

A. PIETSCHER (Landgerichts-Präsident: *Jurist und Dichter*, Dessau, 1881, p. 13): In truth there is nothing genuinely tragic about Shylock. Hence the poet called the piece, not *The Jew*, but *The Merchant*, of Venice, and termed it a *Comedy*, not a *Tragedy*. He knew nothing of the modern sympathy with a 'persecuted race,' and surely Shylock was not regarded by him as typical of one. He needed for his drama a *usurer*, not a *Jew*, —confessions of faith or nationalities have nothing to do with the central idea of the piece,—and in accordance with the views of his day he took him very naturally from the race of Jews. Then, to be sure, Shylock became for him *not merely* the 'usurer,' but a mortal and a Jew with human passions and the characteristics of his race.

(P. 16.) When the Jew has demanded 'What judgement shall I dread, doing no wrong?' he must be driven from this pharasaical pretext. It is doing him an unmerited honour to impute to him the will, at any dictate of mercy, to put an end to the contest between his legal rights and the baseness of his claim. For once this flinty heart must be made to feel that he himself may need mercy, and all other means must be exhausted before proceeding to use his own weapons against him. If Ihering finds Shylock typical, let us, too, find him typical. He typifies all who mercilessly insist upon their rights. All such are admonished that there are other and higher duties than maintaining one's rights, and our jurists are herein instructed who call a legal contest for justice, a duty. . . . . Even Shylock demands the law, he 'stands for judgement,'—we have seen how this imposes upon Ihering,—but we know well enough how hollow these high-sounding words are, and that the man cares nothing for the law, but only that by means of it he may feed his hatred, and above all his greed. . . . . It is the wretched envy of a business rival that instigates him. And when this 'man of law' invokes 'his deeds upon his head,' and his bold invocation is answered, it is brought home to every one that whoever pursues his own rights in violation of the dictates of 'mercy,' is himself crushed by merciless Right.

(P. 19.) I am much afraid that Anthonio would have had to succumb, if Ihering had been of his counsel. His only plea was *turpis causa*; if that would not carry him through, he would have given up his client. But his chance of making this plea good, before the Doge and the Senate, was small; they had probably from the first noticed that in this case an abominable design lay concealed under legal forms, but they could not have known how these latter were to be evaded. I believe that I dare assert that at that time in Venice the consideration that 'a contract against morals was void' was not yet recognized or regarded as a valid plea. For this consideration, or more properly its recognition in law, belongs only to the higher grades of culture, and always even then depends on the prevailing estimate of what is immoral, and its *full* significance and worth will have to remain, I suppose, a pious wish.

(P. 21.) Ihering is particularly hostile to the way in which Portia deals with Shylock, which he terms quibbling and pettifogging.

For my part, commend me to our Portia, who, in true woman's fashion, does not allow herself to be in the least disconcerted by the pathetic appeal: 'If you deny me, fie upon your law! There is no force in the decrees of Venice;' but steadily regarding the present case alone, takes no thought whatever of any dangerous consequences. [Portia never heard this appeal; it was made before she entered the Court.—ED.] If the law of Venice is so bad that it will help a scoundrel to ruin an honest man, it is worthless and does not deserve the least consideration. When a man stands in peril of his life he does not stop to choose his weapon,—the first is the best,—and just so in the present case, it may be permissible to meet chicanery with chicanery, pettifogging with pettifogging. Did it really escape our learned jurist, what the poet with sovereign humour has scourged with joyous jest, that a legal contest, if it is a fight, is subject to all the chances of a fight, and that in it often enough cunning must be overcome by cunning? To observe it may be unwelcome, but it may be observed, nevertheless, every day in courts of justice. A lawsuit is therein like a duel or a fight, and the talk is of 'winners' and 'losers.' When Portia's plea that flesh and not blood is in the bargain, is met by Ihering with the replication that blood is implied, and that the plea is frivolous, he may be met with the rejoinder that bargains of this nature are to be strictly interpreted, and in doubtful points *against* him in whom the power lay of making the terms of the agreement more explicit. And so it could go on with surrejoinders and rebutters for a good long while. But is it really 'a wretched quibble' which is here used against Shylock? What was the Jew after? The life of Anthonio. There is not the least doubt of that. For the pound of flesh in itself he cared not a jot. Well, then, why did he not have that stated clearly in his bond? He dared not; and hence he used the ambiguous phrase, 'a pound of flesh.' And to his own words he is now kept. Is that unjust?

The discomfiture of the Jew is not the lamentable downfall of a hero; it is the victory of cunning by greater cunning; the rogue is caught in his own snare. No tears need fall; there can be here only the smiling satisfaction of a genuine comedy. But why did not the prudent man anticipate the possibility of the objection which Portia afterwards actually made? Or else why did he not consult a jurist who could have told him that the Twelve Tables of Rome had contemplated exactly that possibility (*si plus minusve secuerint sine fraude esto*), and that, since the laws of Venice had not yet attained to that wise prevision in the interest of revengeful creditors, it would be necessary to stipulate expressly for it in the bond? The clever man was not clever enough, and a cleverer overcame him.

Nevertheless, it is to be unhesitatingly admitted that the wound which law and right received in the victory over Shylock is not healed,—a wound received at the hands of Shylock, not Portia; it is only skinned over. To overcome cunning with cunning, to take advantage of an opponent's weakness, cannot be termed executing justice. *If* the Jew had been more careful, the Merchant would have been lost. But even this point Shakespeare did not overlook. Through the mouth of Portia he shows [that 'the law hath yet another hold' on Shylock]. Here, then, at last comes forth the violated majesty of abstract law, punishing, crushing him who dared presume to make law aid wrong. The violation of private rights yields place to the deeply outraged State of Venice that now demands atonement for itself. And so the Jew, because he stood upon his law, gets more law than he desired, a different law from that for which he hoped.

Dr JOSEPH KOHLER (Professor in Würzburg: *Shakespeare vor dem Forum der Jurisprudenz*, Würzburg, 1883, p. 6): In point of fact, the Trial Scene is no Jurisprudence unto itself, it is no ideal imaginary farce, inserted merely to serve poetic purposes; it is rather a typical representation of the developement of Law, in all ages; it bears within it the Quintessence of the Present and Future of Law, it contains a Jurisprudence profounder than ten Pandects, and opens to us a deeper insight into the history of Law than all the legal histories from Savigny to Ihering.

Dr Kohler enters at once on the discussion of the validity of Shylock's bond, which, he maintains, is to be regarded not in the light of the jurisprudence of to-day, but of that period when debtors could be forced to pay with their flesh. *Qui non habet in aere, luat in cute.* He then proceeds, by a review of the comparative jurisprudence of all nations, to prove that the cruel law of the Twelve Tables, which gave to creditors the right to cut up debtors, and whereof Shylock's bond was the legitimate descendant, has received from the earliest times a realistic interpretation; and thus concludes [p. 19]: Hence we see that the holding of the body of the debtor as security for the debt is an institution of universal application, and where by chance it is modified and assumes a milder type, we are not to ascribe it to superior culture, but to an inferior estimate of the rights of property.

(P. 71.) This developement from the barbarous practices of ancient times to milder forms was gradual, it did not take place all at once, there were many intermediate steps before the idea of right was fully recognized. Before the law reached the point of rendering null and void such contracts as that of Shylock, there had to be a reaction against them in the popular mind, not on the score of legality, but on the score of morality and social decency. Long before the law branded as illegal the execution of such practices against insolvent debtors, popular opinion regarded such practices, even when countenanced by the law, as disgraceful and inimical to the interests of society. There is many a practice even now interdicted in good society of which the law takes no cognizance. Literary thieving, long before the idea of an author's rights was legally acknowledged, was held to be disgraceful, and at this very day, plagiarism, that infringes no author's rights, is nevertheless utterly condemned throughout the literary world; and when, in the course of legislation, the successful attack against usury had not been effected, the usurer was none the less excluded from respectable society, and usury was regarded as degrading.

(P. 78.) He is a hero who, for the sake of a high ideal, disinterestedly challenges society; but he who tramples under foot the dictates of society, only in order to drain the cup of law for his own selfish interests, is a pariah, who outrages himself because he rates his own interests higher than decency and honesty, and thereby opposes those conditions whereunder alone a well-ordered society can exist. This is Shylock's position.

(P. 79.) When Shylock says that he 'can give no reason, nor he will not, more than a lodged hate and a certain loathing that he bears Anthonio,' he utters the most shameless profanation which the sanctity of justice can experience, far more disgraceful than any violation of the law; it is an abuse of law by means of law, an abuse which paralyzes law; it is a degradation of law, and a degradation of a court of justice into a tool of the lowest aims. Must the court yield the law to Shylock? What a tragic situation! Almost the most tragic of all situations, I think, is that of a judge who sees himself the tool of an infamous scoundrel, an aider and abettor in an act of atrocious infamy, and with no loophole of escape.

(P. 80.) In this tragic situation the play reaches its highest point, the dramatic tension has reached that strain to which some solution must immediately succeed. May not justice, we ask anxiously, just for this one time yield a little, and give his dues to the hard-hearted creditor? Shakespeare has answered us through Portia. Even the ancient Celtic law-book, the *Senchus Mor*, announced that 'there are three periods at which the world is worthless; the time of a plague; of a general war; and of the *dissolution of express contracts.*' Hence there is no escape: judgement must be given against Anthonio. There is the valid deed, a right pushed *à l'outrance* by a creature who knows no remorse, no human ruth,—like Junius Brutus, the judge must veil his face and sacrifice Anthonio. We all know the way in which the second Daniel solved it; we all feel light-hearted at the sunny ray which pierced that deadly gloom, just as when the Devil, to whom a soul has been covenanted, loses his game and is bilked of his prey. But can the solution be justified at the Forum of Jurisprudence, where we must deal not with an ideal metaphysical justice, but with actual, human justice? It seems that this must be answered in the negative. [Kohler then proceeds to apply the tests of the law, such as *omne majus in se continet minus*, &c., and also condemns Pietscher's expedient of meeting cunning with cunning, and concludes that, apparently, Ihering's position is irrefragable, and yet asks how is it possible that our feelings so deceive us that, when we see the play on the stage, our legal conscience receives no pricks? The answer to this he finds in that inner consciousness of what is right and just in the breast of the judge], that instinct for the right in the soul of the judge which has not fully worked itself out into open acknowledgement, and is still lying perdu in the ostensible reasons of the wise Daniel.

The age in which the time of the play is cast is when, in the course of the developement of law and right, such a bond as Shylock's was opposed not merely to public sentiments of morality and decency, but to law and equity. Personal mutilation of insolvent debtors was already beginning to be repugnant to the judicial mind as something rude, and as beyond the pale of civilized law, and no longer to be granted as of unquestionable right. Thus it was that a process was in operation which belongs to the growth of legal life,—that process, namely, whereby the lawyer accepts the principles which obtained at former times, and moulds them anew. [Kohler then traces the growth of various legal ideas, now everywhere accepted, by means of this process of absorption, whereby the public sentiment of what is right finds expression through the judges, whose hearts are quickened by the pulses of the people, and a judicial conscience is created which judges are bound not only to obey, but also to interpret.]

(P. 88.) At last we can see the springs which set in motion the sentence of the wise Daniel; the sentence is good, but its premises are bad; which is, after all, much to be preferred to a bad sentence with good premises; let us only have good sentences, and good reasons will soon follow. Such has been the way of the world from the earliest times. Long before the rights of an inventor were formulated into laws, the sentiment prevailed of a right of property in what is immaterial, and at this day in England and in France [and in America—Ed.] we hear of property in names, and signs, and trademarks. It is not difficult to demonstrate that such judicial construction is untenable; but is it sound policy, at the dictates of German pedantry, to throw overboard precious goods which do not happen to have been secured in befitting cases? Are we justified in spilling the precious contents because the cask is ugly and offensive to the eye of a jurist? Irregular judicial premises are often, although, of course, not always, the ladder on which the consciousness of legal right mounts ever higher. Such irregular premises urge themselves on the judge most especially when some rigid inflexible legal dictum has survived from ancient times, and like a ruin of the past no longer harmonizes with to-day. Such a dictum no jurisprudence in the world would dare openly oppose, but the comedy is eminently respectable whereby it is evaded in a thousand byways. I will not express an opinion as to the justification of this proceeding. I neither praise it nor blame it; I maintain it only as a fact in the universal history of evolution, which proves through all ages the developement of law and right, in the Orient as well as in the Occident.

(P. 90.) It is a trial of world-wide fame which the Poet unfolds before us; it bears the victory of a refined consciousness of law and right over the dark night which weighed heavily from of old on the courts,—a victory concealed behind pretexts, which assumes the mask of false springs of action, because it is necessary; but it is a victory, a great, a powerful victory, a victory not alone in this particular case, but a victory in the history of law and right; it is the sun of progress which once more casts its quickening beams on the judicial bench, and the kingdom of Sarastro triumphs over the powers of night. And when Shylock succumbs, it is not, as Ihering supposes, under the weight of a false sentence, but it is because the voice of the second Daniel has reached the inmost recesses of the heart of the usurer, who is after all a man, and crumbles to ruin a whole laborious structure of logic. If he felt that his rights were violated, why did he not, with all the keenness of his analytic intellect, dissipate into thin air the false pretexts of the wise and righteous Daniel? We forsooth can do it, albeit we are jurists far less skilled and formal than Shylock. But from the very first in his inmost heart he knew that his aim was through and through unrighteous, but he believed it to be concealed and assured by the legislation of the day; he believed that he had a charm against every possible legal or logical attempt to evade his plea. He knew that he had ventured on a slippery path, where right and wrong join hands, and where it needed but the least jar to bring him to grief; he foresaw that the judge would use every possible, conceivable evasion to avoid the execution of the Law, and what he foresaw was verified.

(P. 95.) As a lawyer there is yet one thing lying heavy on my heart. Was no injustice done to Shylock in not only denying his bond, but in condemning him, and in condemning him almost to the destruction of his means of life? Grant that Shylock had sought the life of Anthonio, he had at least sought it by legal forms, by judicial procedure; and he sought it under an appeal to law that was still formally recognized as law, albeit that the popular conscience of law and right had already superseded it. Such a one can, with as little propriety, be deemed punishable for an attempt to kill as a creditor could be pronounced guilty of an attempt at false imprisonment who should bring suit after the cause of action had ceased to exist, or at least had ceased to exist in the opinion of many, but not of all, lawyers. In this regard, there has been an injustice; but such an injustice is founded on universal history, it is a universal necessity; and in the admission of this element, Shakespeare, as an historian of law and right, has surpassed even himself. No progress in the world, although it be the progress of law and right, is possible without injustice to the individual; every great advance taken by society is made over corpses, just as every health-giving walk costs the lives of many an innocent little creature. Shylock's non-suit and subsequent punishment are needed to crown the victory gained by the new conception of law and right.

(P. 99.) And just as we hail the conclusion of *Faust* with joyful huzzas, and exult in the defeat of the Devil for all his contract sealed with blood, so we greet with huzzas the bond of Shylock torn to shreds; and when he totters off bent, bowed, and with knocking knees, we know of a surety that Justice has shed abroad its beams, and the goblins of night, that have hitherto fluttered round a wretched tallow candle, henceforth will hide in their gloomy recesses. The victory over Shylock reveals the higher potency of human law, just as the victory over the Devil reveals the higher potency of divine law; the Devil remains black even when he steps before the court with his paper and blood, and Shylock remains a foe to Law even when he boasts of his parchment and seal.*

---

* The Law of the XII Tables, which is supposed to permit the mutilation of insolvent debtors, has been so frequently cited in connection with Shylock's claim, that it is perhaps as well to note that doubts have been cast on the correctness of this interpretation of the ancient Roman Law. Dr JAMES MUIRHEAD, of Edinburgh, shows (*Historical Introduction to the Private Law of Rome*, 1886, pp. 202 *et seq.*) that the phrase in that Law, *capite poenas dato*, does not refer to death or slavery, but was used in opposition to *bona ;* and that the debtor paid the penalty with his person, in his services, in contradistinction to his means. 'But for the mistaken notion,' says Dr Muirhead, 'that a creditor was entitled after the expiry of the three months to put his debtor to death,—of which there is not a single instance on record,—it is unlikely that so many would have thought of imputing to the *partis secanto* such an inhuman meaning as that a plurality of creditors might cut the body of their *addictus* in pieces, and each take a share.' The whole difficulty lies, so thinks Dr Muirhead, in the arrangement of the provisions of the XII Tables, and he, therefore, with great ingenuity, solves it by a slight re-arrangement, whereby the plurality of creditors, referred to by Aulus Gellius (from whom we derive our fullest account of this Law), is made to apply only to the special case where 'co-heirs take proceedings against a debtor of their predecessor's ;' and the explanation of the whole question is, that 'where there was but one creditor . . . . the debtor definitely became his creditor's

In *The Overland Monthly* for July, 1886, there appeared, as a letter addressed to Mr LAWRENCE BARRETT, an article by Mr JOHN T. DOYLE, entitled 'Shakespeare's Law—The Case of Shylock.' It supplies information in regard to the legal procedure of the Trial Scene which I have searched for in vain elsewhere, and presents Portia's conduct of the Trial in a light certainly novel. The substance of it is as follows :

JOHN T. DOYLE : The Trial Scene has always seemed inconsistent with Shakespeare's supposed legal learning, for the proceedings in it are such as never could have occurred in any court administering English law. Save in the fact that the Scene presents a plaintiff, a defendant, and a judge—characters essential to litigation under any system of procedure—there is no resemblance in the proceedings on the stage to anything that could possibly occur in an English court or any court administering English law. No jury is impanelled to determine the facts, no witnesses called by either side; on the contrary, when the court opens, the Duke who presides is already fully informed of the facts, and has even communicated them in writing to Bellario, a learned judge of Padua, and invited him to come and render judgement in the case; and the extent of his power was to adjourn the court unless the Doctor arrived in season. Such an occurrence as this, we all know, could never take place in a court proceeding according to English methods. . . . . From my boyhood I regarded it as an instance of the failure of the cleverest men (not themselves lawyers) to introduce a lawsuit into fiction without violating the common rules of procedure. To make the situation dramatic they invariably make it impossible. I concluded that the failure of others might be excused, when even Shakespeare missed it. Subsequent experience convinced me, however, that he did not miss it, after all. This is how it happened.

In 1851–52, I passed several months in the neighbouring Republic of Nicaragua. It was at that time, perhaps, the least known and least frequented of the Spanish-American States. Originally explored and colonized by an expedition from Panama, its communications with Europe and all the outer world were maintained almost wholly from the Pacific side of the continent; its commerce was insignificant, travel never reached it, and it had probably kept up the customs and practices in vogue under the Spanish rule with less variation than any of the colonies. The affairs of the company I represented having become considerably entangled by the transactions and omissions of the former agent, I found myself, ere long, involved in half a dozen lawsuits, the proceedings of which gave me a new light on the Shylock case. To explain this, I will briefly relate what occurred in the first of them. The course of the others was similar.

' free-bondman, ... but where co-heirs were concerned, as bondage and service to all of them ' would have been inconvenient, if not impossible, when they were not to continue to possess the ' inheritance in common, the debtor was sent over Tiber and sold as a slave, and the price got for ' him divided amongst them. If one or other got more than his fair share, no harm was done, for ' the disproportion would eventually be redressed by an action of partition.' Dr Muirhead's rearrangement, is as follows :—' Tertiis nundinis addicitor. Capite poenas dato. Si plures sunt, trans Tiberim peregre venum danto : partis secanto. Si plus minusve secuerint, se fraude esto.' ' On the third market-day there shall be a decree of addiction. The *addictus* shall then pay the penalty with his person. If there be several creditors to whom he is awarded, let them sell him beyond Tiber and divide the price. If any of them have got more or less than his fair share, this shall not prejudice them.' Dr Kohler advocates the old orthodox interpretation of this law, and alleges in support of his view an imposing array of comparative jurisprudence in which he is, as Dr Muirhead says, ' profoundly versed ;' it is, therefore, only just to add that Dr Kohler refers (p. 8) to the attempts which have been made to give a milder interpretation to this Law, and that he believes them to be utterly wrong. Of course his remark does not apply to Dr Muirhead, whose volume had not then been published. It is to Mr J. FOSTER KIRK that I am indebted for having my attention called to this interesting and learned book by Dr Muirhead.—ED.

27

Business having brought me to the city of Grenada, i was one day accosted on the street by a dapper little man, carrying an ivory-headed cane, who, calling me by name, said, '*El alcalde le llama*'— 'The alcalde sends for you.' I thought the invitation rather wanting in courtesy, and, to pay like with like, intimated that I was busy then, without saying whether I would wait on His Honor or not. The little man simply repeated his message and left. A person present, seeing that I showed no disposition to move, then informed me that the dapper little man with the cane was an *alguazil*, and that, by his verbal notice, I had been legally summoned to the alcalde's court, to which I was recommended to go without unnecessary delay. I accordingly repaired at once to the court-room in the *juzgado*, as directed.

Proceedings of some sort were going on at the moment, but the alcalde suspended them, received me very courteously, and directed some one present to go and call Don Dolores Bermudez, the plaintiff, into court. The substance of Mr Bermudez's complaint against the company was then stated to me, and I was asked for my answer to it. I sent for my counsel, and the company's defence was stated orally. The contract out of which the controversy arose was produced, and perhaps a witness or two were examined, and some oral discussion followed; those details I forget, for there was nothing in them that struck me as strange. There was, in fact, little if any dispute about the facts of the case, the real controversy being as to the company's liability and its extent. We were finally informed that on a given day we should be expected to attend again, when the Judge would be prepared with his decision.

At the appointed time we attended accordingly, and the Judge read a paper in which all the facts were stated, at the conclusion of which he announced to us that he proposed to submit the question of law involved to Don Buenaventura Selva, a practising lawyer of Grenada, as a 'jurisconsult,' unless some competent objections were made to him. I learned then that I could challenge the proposed jurisconsult for consanguinity, affinity, or favor, just as we challenge a juror. I knew of no cause of challenge against him; my counsel said he was an unexceptionable person; and so he was chosen, and the case was referred to him. Some days after, he returned the papers to the alcalde with his opinion, which was in my favour, and the plaintiff's case was dismissed.

In the course of the same afternoon, or the next day, I received an intimation that Don Buenaventura expected from me a gratification—the name in that country for what we call a gratuity—and I think the sum of two hundred dollars was named. This did not harmonize with my crude notions of the administration of justice, and I asked for explanations. They were given in the stereotyped form used to explain every other anomaly in that queer country, '*Costumbre del pais*.' I thought it a custom more honoured in the breach than in the observance, and declined to pay. I found out afterwards that this was a mistake; that under their system of administration the Judge merely ascertains the facts, and as to the law and its application to the case reference is had to a jurisconsult, or doctor of the law; and that he, after pronouncing his decision, is entitled to accept from either party—in practice always from the successful one—a '*quiddam honorarium*,' or gratification, his service to the court being gratuitous, just as that of an *amicus curiæ* is with us.

With this experience, I read the case of Shylock over again, and understood it better. It was plain that the sort of procedure Shakespeare had in view, and attributed to the Venetian court, was exactly that of my recent experience. The Trial Scene opens on the day appointed for hearing judgement; the facts had been ascertained at a previous session, and Bellario had been selected as the jurist to determine the law applicable to them. The case had been submitted to him in writing, and the Court was awaiting his decision. The defendant, when the case is called, answers as is done daily in our own courts : 'Ready, so please your Grace.' Shylock is not present. In a common law court his absence would have resulted in a nonsuit, but not so here; he is sent for, just as my adversary was, and comes. After an ineffectual attempt to move him to mercy, the Duke intimates an adjournment unless Bellario comes, and it is then announced that a messenger from him is in attendance; his letter is read, and Portia is introduced. Bellario's letter excuses his non-attendance on the plea of illness, and proposes her, under the name of Balthazar, as a substitute. 'I acquainted him with the cause of the controversy,' &c., and ending, '*I leave him to your gracious acceptance*, whose trial shall better publish his commendation.' The Duke, of course, had the right, so far as concerned himself, to accept the substitution of Balthazar for Bellario; but Shylock, I take it, would have had the right to challenge the substitute; and perhaps it is to avoid this, by disarming his suspicions, that all Portia's utterances in the case, until she has secured his express consent to her acting, are favourable to him. Thus: 'Of a strange nature is the suit you follow, Yet in such rule that the Venetian law Cannot impugn you as you do proceed;' and again, after her splendid appeal for mercy: 'I have spoken thus much, To mitigate the justice of thy plea, Which, if thou follow, this strict court of Venice Must needs give sentence 'gainst the merchant here.'

Shylock would have been mad to object to a judge whose intimations were so clearly in his favour. He first pronounces her 'A Daniel come to judgement! yea, a Daniel!' This does not, however, amount to an express acceptance of her as a substitute; it is but an expression of high respect, consistent, however, with a refusal to consent to the proposed substitution. She carries the deception still further, pronounces the bond forfeit, and that 'Lawfully, by this the Jew may claim A pound of flesh, to be by him cut off Nearest the merchant's heart;' and again pleads for mercy.

The poor Jew, completely entrapped, then '*charges her by the law to proceed to judgement.*' Antonio does the same, and both parties having thus in open court accepted her as such, she is fairly installed as the *Judex substitutus* for Bellario, and almost immediately afterwards suggests the quibble over the drop of blood and the just one pound of flesh, on which Antonio escapes.

To complete the parallel to my Nicaragua experience above recounted, we find, after the trial is over and the poor discomfited Jew has retired from the court, the Duke says to the defendant, whose life has been saved by Portia's subtlety, 'Antonio, *gratify* this gentleman,' &c.; and Bassanio offers her the three thousand ducats which were the condition of the bond.

One difficulty yet remained in the case, which the above explanation did not touch, and which to me was still a stumbling-block, viz.: In the play the action is promoted by Shylock to enforce against Antonio the penalty of his bond; it concludes with a judgement against the plaintiff that his estate be forfeited, one-half to the commonwealth, the other to the defendant, and that his life lie at the mercy of the Duke. Justice, perhaps, but excessively raw justice, such as we would think could only be meted out in the court of a Turkish cadi, who fines the plaintiff, imprisons the defendant, and bastinadoes the witnesses. Yet a few years since I met with a case in a Mexican court involving just as marked a departure from all our notions of the proper course of justice as this. A question arose in this city as to the disposition of the estate of a gentleman who died at Mazatlan, where he had been slain in an encounter with his partner, while discussing in anger the state of their accounts. There had been a trial over the case in Mexico. The surviving partner put forward claims before our court, which caused me, in behalf of the next of kin of the deceased, to send to Mexico for a complete transcript of the judgement-record there. [Mr Doyle here gives an account of the official inquiry as to the cause of death before the alcalde, who] conducted the trial with pretty evident partiality to the survivor, whom, at the conclusion of it, he acquitted. [Thereupon, after some intermediate proceedings], the Fiscal, on behalf of the State, intervenes, and appeals to the Supreme Court. There the witnesses are re-examined; they contradict each other badly, and break down. . . . . The judgement below is then reversed, the defendant sentenced to death, and the alcalde, before whom the trial had been had below, is sentenced to a fine of $100 for his partiality and misconduct.

After reading this record it occurred to me that, in a court proceeding according to such methods as these, a judgement against the plaintiff of forfeiture of life and goods might be supposed, even in an action on a bond, without grossly violating probability; and it seems to me that Shakespeare was acquainted (however he acquired the knowledge) with the modes of procedure in tribunals administering the law of Spain, as well as with those of his own country; if like practice did not obtain in Venice, or if he knew nothing of Venetian law, there was no great improbability in assuming it to resemble that of Spain, considering that both were inherited from a common source, and that the Spanish monarchs had so long exercised dominion in Italy.

ENGLISH CRITICISMS

ROWE (*Some Account of the Life, &c., of Mr. William Shakespear*, 1709, p. xix): To these I might add that incomparable Character, *Shylock* the *Jew*, in *The Merchant of Venice;* but tho' we have seen that Play Receiv'd and Acted as a Comedy, and the Part of the *Jew* perform'd by an excellent Comedian, yet I cannot but think it was de-sign'd Tragically by the Author. There appears in it such a deadly Spirit of Revenge, such a savage Fierceness and Fellness, and such a bloody designation of Cruelty and Mischief, as cannot agree either with the Stile or Characters of Comedy. The Play it self, take it all together, seems to me to be one of the most finish'd of any of *Shake-spear's*. The Tale indeed, in that Part relating to the Caskets, and the extravagant and unusual kind of Bond given by *Antonio*, is a little too much remov'd from the Rules of Probability: But taking the Fact for granted, we must allow it to be very beautifully written. There is something in the Friendship of *Antonio* to *Bassanio* very Great, Generous, and Tender.

CHARLES GILDON (*Remarks on the Plays of Shakespeare*, Rowe's edition, vol. vii, p. 321, 1710): The Ignorance that *Shakespear* had of the *Greek Drama* threw him on such odd Stories as the Novels and Romances of his time cou'd afford, and which were so far from being natural that they wanted that Probability and Verisimilitude, which is absolutely necessary to all Representations of the Stage. The Plot of this Play is of that Number. But the Errors of the Fable and the Conduct are too visible to need Discovery. This Play has receiv'd considerable Advantages from the Pen of the honorable *George Granville*, Esq.

The Character of the *Jew* is very well distinguish'd by Avarice, Malice, implacable Revenge, &c. But the Incidents that necessarily show those Qualities are so very Romantic, so vastly out of Nature, that our Reason, our Understanding is everywhere shock'd; which abates extremely of the Pleasure the Pen of *Shakespear* might give us. This is visible in *Shylock's* speech to the Doge, for all the while that Distinction of Character, which is beautiful and otherwise pleases you, the Incredibility of such a Discourse to such a Prince, and before such a Court of Judicature, has so little of Nature in it, that it is impossible to escape the Censure of a Man of Common Sense. The Character of *Portia* is not everywhere very well kept, that is, the Manners are not always *agreeable* or *convenient* to her Sex and Quality; particularly where she scarce preserves her Modesty in the Expression. . . . . Tho' there are a great many Beauties in what our modern Gentlemen call the *Writing* in this Play, yet it is almost every-where calm, and touches not the Soul, there are no sinewy Passions, which ought everywhere to shine in a serious Dramatic Performance, such as most of this is.

Dr JOHNSON: Of *The Merchant of Venice* the style is even and easy, with few peculiarities of diction, or anomalies of construction. The comic part raises laughter, and the serious fixes expectation. The probability of either the one or the other story cannot be maintained. The union of two actions in one event is, in this drama, emi-nently happy. Dryden was much pleased with his own address in connecting the two plots of his *Spanish Friar*, which yet, I believe, the critic will find excelled by this play.

HALLAM (*Introduction to the Literature of Europe*, 1837, vol. ii, chap. vi): *The Merchant of Venice* is generally esteemed the best of Shakespeare's comedies. . . . .

In the management of the plot, which is sufficiently complex without the slightest confusion or incoherence, I do not conceive that it has been surpassed in the annals of any theatre. Yet there are those who still affect to speak of Shakespeare as a barbarian; and others who, giving what they think due credit to his genius, deny him all judgement and dramatic taste. A comparison of his works with those of his contemporaries, —and it is surely to them that we should look,—will prove that his judgement is by no means the least of his rare qualities. This is not so remarkable in the mere construction of his fable, though the present comedy is absolutely perfect in that point of view; and several others are excellently managed, as in the general keeping of the characters and the choice of incidents. If Shakespeare is sometimes extravagant, the Marstons and Middletons are seldom otherwise. The variety of characters in *The Merchant of Venice,* and the powerful delineation of those upon whom the interest chiefly depends; the effectiveness of many scenes in representation; the copiousness of the wit, and the beauty of the language, it would be superfluous to extol; nor is it our office to repeat a tale so often told as the praise of Shakespeare. In the language there is the commencement of a metaphysical obscurity which soon became characteristic; but it is, perhaps, less observable than in any later play. The sweet and sportive temper of Shakespeare, though it never deserted him, gave way to advancing years, and to the mastering force of serious thought. What he read we know but very imperfectly; yet, in the last years of the century, when five and thirty summers had ripened his genius, it seems that he must have transfused much of the wisdom of past ages into his own all-combining mind. In several of the historical plays, in *The Merchant of Venice,* and especially in *As You Like It,* the philosophic eye, turned inward on the mysteries of human nature, is more and more characteristic.

THOMAS CAMPBELL (*Remarks,* &c., 1838, p. xxxv) : In the picture of the Jew there is not the tragic grandeur of Richard III; but there is a similar force of mind, and the same subtlety of intellect, though it is less selfish. In point of courage I would give the palm to Shylock, for he was an ill-used man and the champion of an oppressed race; nor is he a hypocrite, like Richard. In fact, Shakespeare, whilst he lends himself to the prejudices of Christians against Jews, draws so philosophical a picture of the energetic Jewish character, that he traces the blame of its faults to the iniquity of the Christian world. Shylock's arguments are more logical than those of his opponents, and the latter overcome him only by a legal quibble. But he is a usurer and lives on the interest of lent moneys; and what but Christian persecution forced him to live by these means? But he is also inhuman and revengeful. Why? because they called him dog, and spat upon his Jewish gaberdine. They voided their rheum upon him, and he in return wished to void his revenge upon them. All this is natural, and Shylock has nothing unnatural about him. His daughter Jessica is a very faithful picture of a love-inclined young woman; betraying the Oriental warmth of her race, together with their craftiness. But she is not to be taken as a true sample of a Jewish daughter, for among no people are the ties of domestic life held more sacred than among the Hebrews.

Throughout this whole piece there is a flow of incident and richly-imagined language that bears us, on a spring-tide of interest, to the settlement of the plot in the Trial Scene, which is a drama in itself. Yet there Shakespeare does not forsake us, as a vulgar writer would have done. On the contrary, he prolongs our voluptuous sympathy, in the union of the happy characters, by a little pleasantry about the rings and by a moonlight serenade of music. Our imaginations retire from the play soothed and gratified, and perhaps with more hints to our understanding respecting the charity which we owe to the Jews than Shakespeare has ventured to insinuate.

EDINBURGH REVIEW (1840, vol. lxxi, p. 481): In *The Merchant of Venice* the poetical elevation is obtained by a migration into a foreign and southern region; the tideless bosom of the Adriatic reflects the Venetian palaces, the pine trees and fountains and terraces of Portia's villa, and the deep-blue sky of the Italian clime. But everywhere, in the garden or the Doge's hall, on the little 'campo' of the Rialto, or beneath the penthouse that projects from the Jew's den, we feel that we are still in the world, among men jostling one another on the crowded highway of life and hurrying towards the common goal. Here action is in its appropriate place; and here, therefore, adventure and surprise are accumulated upon each other; the drama invades the domain of the romantic novel, but, unlike most usurpers, ameliorates the region into which it has intruded. During four acts of the play we are hurried from one crisis to another, each of the two leading plots is in itself improbable and even revolting; but the harshness of each balances and conceals that of the other. Poetical fancy, likewise, wedded to the charm of love, disguises the story of the caskets; while that of the pound of flesh is ennobled at once by variety and unsurpassed truth of character, by the most vigorous strokes of passion, and by a temperate judgement which is the most admirable feature of the piece. At length the perplexities and dangers are overcome; love and hatred have both received their reward, and most poets would have dropped the curtain on their characters. But Shakespeare saw that something was still wanting. If the play had closed there, it would have deserved to be called a tragi-comedy in a reproachful sense of the term; it would have been a play, in which it was impossible either by reflection or by the surer test of feeling, to determine which of the two opposed aspects of life was intended to be exhibited as the prominent one. The main action of the piece in both its branches had touched the very frontier of that region within which it was designed to move. The scenes at Belmont had been prevented from becoming tragic by mere accident; the judgement-scene is really and sublimely tragic, in everything except the artifice which gives the turn to its catastrophe. The feeling which genuine comedy should leave on the mind, the perception of those relations of man to higher powers which make his very weakness the fountain of happiness and reconciliation, is assuredly not that which rests on the mind as we retire slowly from the piazza of St Mark, still agitated by the perils of the trial, and perhaps not less moved by the blow which has smitten down into broken-hearted abasement Shylock's whole soul, his intellectual strength, his bitterly pregnant humour, his Hebrew devotion, and his hatred for those who have oppressed and insulted his nation and his name. The Fifth Act, forming what Coleridge in similar instances calls 'a lyrical movement,' gradually and gently relieves the heart from its oppression. A sportive love-trick, introduced purposely in the preceding scene, furnishes its materials; the tragic ideas, removed to a distance, serve but to heighten the new impression by contrast, and thus justify for themselves the place they hold; and the drama closes in music by moonlight, amidst the placid gladness of rescued innocence and united love.

D. J. SNIDER (*System of Shakespeare's Dramas*, St Louis, 1877, vol. i, p. 305): The general movement of the play lies in the conflict between the Right of Property and the Existence of the Individual, and in the Mediation of this conflict through the Family, which owes its origin in the present case to that same individual whom it rescues. That is, the Family, represented by Portia, the wife, returns and saves the man who

aided, by his friendship and generosity, to bring it into being. All the characters of
the play, though possessing peculiarities of their own, must be seen in their relation to
this fundamental theme of the work.

There are three central movements, which may be named in order: The Conflict,
the Mediation, the Return. Of the first movement there are two threads, showing,
respectively, the Property-conflict and the Love-conflict, though the former is raised to
the highest spiritual significance by the underlying religious element. These two
threads, moreover, are interwoven in the subtlest manner; still, an analysis has to tear
them apart temporarily. In the first thread the antagonists are Antonio, the Christian,
and Shylock, the Jew. Antonio is the centre of a group of five friends, who, in a variety of ways, ingraft themselves upon the action; around Shylock also are to be placed
his daughter, Jessica, his clownish servant Gobbo,—both of whom are leaving him and
going over to his opponents,—and his friend Tubal. The contrast between the two
men in their personal relations is this : Antonio is the object of the warmest friendship,
while Shylock is disrupting his own family,—driving away daughter and servant. The
second thread unfolds the Love-conflict, which has here three phases, represented by
Portia, Jessica, and Nerissa. The second Movement,—the Mediation,—has the same
two threads : the Property-conflict is brought to a successful conclusion by Portia, disguised as a lawyer; the Love-conflict has ended in all three cases with a happy solution, namely, marriage. But both friends and lovers have been torn asunder in the
performance of their various functions; hence the Third Movement will be the Return,
which brings all to Belmont,—the blissful abode of harmony.

(P. 307.) The Collision which supplies the nerve of the play may be stated, in a
general form, to be between Christianity and Judaism. But mark! it is not between
these religions as dogmatic systems of Theology, but as realized in the practical life of
men. . . . . We desire to lay stress upon an important fact. Shakespeare has nowhere,
in any of his dramas, made religion, *as such*, the principal motive. This was no doubt
intentional on his part, for no man understood the concrete nature of religion—religion
as determining the conduct of mankind—better than he. In this form he uses it continually. But to make men die for an abstract principle of Theology, Shakespeare
utterly refused,—and he was right.

(P. 313.) Put a man in the world with this notion : ' I am the favorite of the Al-
mighty; the rest of mankind is only so much material to make money out of, which I
can use as I please,' and you have Shylock. It is curious to observe how the Poet
paints him as penetrated with the morality of the Old Testament. He tells the story
of Jacob's deceiving Laban, as Scriptural proof that his end was justifiable : ' This was
the way to thrive, and he was blest; And thrift is blessing, if men steal it not.' Note
that only one exception is made,—no stealing; everything else is allowable. The reason
is manifest. Theft would annihilate property, and, with the destruction of it, his end
also must perish, for that end itself is Property. Hence his motto is : Thrift, but no
Theft.

(P. 316.) Let us now take up the second thread,—the Love-conflict,—in which
Portia is the main figure, supported, however, by Nerissa and Jessica. Portia is the
third great character of the play, and in importance stands quite on a par with Antonio
and Shylock. Her function is mediatorial; in fact, she may be called the grand
mediatrix of the entire drama. In her we see the instrumentality by which the main
results of the drama are brought about. Through her courtship by Bassanio, Antonio
comes into the power of the Jew by means of the loan. At her house all the personages of the play assemble, and the wooing is done. Moreover, she accomplishes the

rescue of Antonio, which is the main mediation of the poem. The great principle of which she is the bearer may be termed the Right of Subjectivity. She asserts the validity of the Internal and Spiritual against the crushing might of externality; but she does not deny the Right of the Objective in its true limitation. Only when this Objective becomes destructive of its end and self-contradictory, as in the case when the Law was about to murder Antonio, does she place a limit to it and invoke a higher principle. Her struggle is with legality and prescription asserting themselves in spheres where they do not belong; but, in relations where this contradiction no longer appears, she is the most ethical of women. In the Family her subordination is complete,—indeed, devout. We shall see that all her acts have one end and one impelling motive,—devotion to her husband, an absolute unity with his feelings and interests; in other words, subordination to the Family. She vindicates the Right of Subjectivity for herself, in order that she may obtain the one whom she really loves,—without which principle, it need hardly be said, the true existence of the Family is impossible.

(P. 325.) Shylock ranks as one of the most perfect characterizations in Shakespeare. How complete in every respect! How vividly does he rise up before us! Not merely his physical appearance, but his entire spiritual nature stands forth in the plainest lineaments. In fact, we feel as if we knew him better than we could possibly have done in real life. The Poet has laid open the most hidden recesses of character, has portrayed him in the most diverse relations, with a truth and fulness unapproached and unapproachable. We ask ourselves, Whence this completeness, this richness, this concreteness, of characterization? If we wish to see the infinite difference upon the same subjects, compare Shylock with the best efforts of other dramatists. Take *L'Avare*, by Molière. Placed by the side of Shylock, how meagre and unsatisfactory! Can we get at the ground of this extraordinary superiority? First, we should say that Shylock is something more than mere avarice; he has a deeper motive in his nature, and his greed for gain is only one of its manifestations. It is true that his end in life is Thrift, as before stated, but that end is the offspring of his moral and spiritual being, —of his religion. Everything goes back to this centre. Shylock is a Jew,—one of the 'peculiar people.' In all his actions this deepest principle of his faith and his consciousness wells out; given the motive, he marches logically to its consequences. Thus we have arrived at an absolute spiritual unity in the man. The second reason for the transcendent excellence of this characterization is the breadth which it exhibits. The activities of Shylock embrace quite the totality of Life. We see him in his family, in business, in civil relations, in social relations, in morality, in religion. We behold him brought into contact with every essential form of society; and he acts in them, brings his principle to the test through them. Nor is he plunged into them from the outside, but is brought into living relation with them. Hence the concreteness, the perfection, the complete individualization of character. But it is different with *L'Avare*. How limited is the range of the piece in this respect! Harpagon almost descends to the common miser,—cut off from the world in obscurity, dirt, and rags,—holding fast to his money-bags. His niggardliness in his household, his tyranny in his family, and an example of his extortionate usury express quite all that we see of him. This is not Shylock, who is exhibited in many more, and also far more important, relations,— who sees the world and grapples with it in all its essential forms; this is what gives content and concreteness to his character. Hence the Harpagon of Molière is empty, —almost like an abstract personification of avarice; in fact, it is a meagre caricature compared with the Shylock of Shakespeare. But it gives occasion to many laughable ıncidents and situations; this was what Molière wanted; he sought for predicaments more than for characters.

(P. 328.) But does Portia really give any hint to Bassanio which of the caskets to choose? It will be recollected that it was forbidden her in her father's will to tell this secret. A suspicious circumstance is the introduction of a song during the choice of Bassanio, which the previous choosers did not have the benefit of. Hence one is inclined to scrutinize closely the meaning of the song. It is somewhat enigmatic, yet its general purport may be stated to be: 'Do not choose by the eye,—by the glittering outside,—for it is the source of all delusion.' Hence Portia, after observing with the greatest care all the formalities of her father's will, breaks it just at the point of its conflict with her subjective right. This is done so delicately by her that it is scarcely perceived; still, it is none the less real. Thus she stands here as the grand bearer of the Right of Subjectivity, in its special form of Love versus Obedience, to the will of the parent.

(P. 338.) To aid the readers who may desire to grasp these results in the more difficult, yet more precise, forms of philosophical statement, the following summary is given: The collision is between Antonio and Shylock, and is mediated by Portia. Its logical basis is the contradiction between the Objective as realized in the institutions of Reason, and the Subjective as the individual side of man. The former undertakes to crush the latter, through which alone it had existence, for it is posited by the Subjective; hence it becomes contradictory of itself, and is negated. The Subjective, since it is not universal, is, in its turn, a new self-contradiction, and, hence, a negation of itself,—which results in its subsuming itself under the Objective. So Portia asserts the Right of Subjectivity only to end in subordinating herself to one of the forms of objective reality,—the Family.

HUDSON (*Introduction to The Merchant of Venice*, Boston, 1879, p. 54): Critics have too often entertained themselves with speculations as to the Poet's specific moral purpose in this play or that. Wherein their great mistake is the not bearing in mind that the special purposing of this or that moral lesson is quite from or beside the purpose of Art. Nevertheless a work of Art, to be really deserving the name, must needs be moral, because it must be proportionable and true to Nature; thus attuning our inward forces to the voice of external order and law; otherwise it is at strife with the compact of things; a piece of dissonance; a jarring, unbalanced, crazy thing, that will die of its own internal disorder. . . . . As to the moral temper of *The Merchant of Venice*, critics have differed widely, some regarding the play as teaching the most comprehensive humanity, others as caressing the narrowest bigotries of the age. This difference may be fairly taken as an argument of the Poet's candour and even-handedness. A special pleader is not apt to leave the hearers in doubt on which side of the question he stands. In this play, as in others, the Poet, I think, ordered things mainly with a view to dramatic effect; though to such effect in the largest and noblest sense. And the highest praise compatible with the nature of the work is justly his, inasmuch as he did not allow himself to be swayed either way from the right measures and proportions of Art. For Art is, from its very nature, obliged to be 'without respect of persons.' Impartiality is its essential law, the constituent of its being. And of Shakespeare could it least of all be said :—' he narrow'd his mind, And to party gave up what was meant for mankind.' He represented men as he had seen them. And he could neither repeal nor ignore the old law of human nature, in virtue of which the wisest and kindest of men are more or less warped by social customs and prejudices, so that they come to do, and even to make a merit of doing, some things that are very unwise and unkind; while the wrongs and insults which they are thus led to practise have the effect of goading the sufferers into savage malignity and revenge. Had he so clothed the latter with gentle and amiable qualities as to enlist the feelings all in their behalf, he would have given a false view of human nature, and his work would have lost much of its instructiveness on the score of practical morality. For good morals can never be reached by departures from truth. A rule that may be profitably remembered by all who are moved to act as advocates and special pleaders in what they think a good cause.

[For the sake of convenience I have attempted to classify the following Extracts under their several subjects.—ED.]

SHYLOCK

HAZLITT (*Characters of Shakespeare's Plays*, 1817, p. 269): In proportion as Shylock has ceased to be a popular bugbear 'baited with the rabble's curse,' he becomes a half-favourite with the philosophical part of the audience, who are disposed to think that Jewish revenge is at least as good as Christian injuries. Shylock is *a good hater;* 'a man no less sinned against than sinning.' If he carries his revenge too far, yet he has strong grounds for 'the lodged hate he bears Anthonio,' which he explains with equal force of eloquence and reason. He seems the depository of the vengeance of his race; and though the long habit of brooding over daily insults and injuries has crusted over his temper with inveterate misanthropy, and hardened him against the contempt of mankind, this adds but little to the triumphant pretensions of his enemies. There is a strong, quick, and deep sense of justice mixed up with the gall and bitterness of his resentment. The constant apprehension of being burnt alive, plundered, banished, reviled, and trampled on might be supposed to sour the most forbearing nature, and to take something from that 'milk of human kindness' with which his persecutors contemplated his indignities. The desire of revenge is almost inseparable from the sense of wrong; and we can hardly help sympathizing with the proud spirit hid beneath his Jewish gaberdine, stung to madness by repeated undeserved provocations, and labouring to throw off the load of obloquy and oppression heaped upon him and all his tribe by one desperate act of 'lawful' revenge, till the ferociousness of the means by which he is to execute his purpose, and the pertinacity with which he adheres to it, turn us against him; but even at last, when disappointed of the sanguinary revenge with which he had glutted his hopes, and exposed to beggary and contempt by the letter of the law on which he had insisted with so little remorse, we pity him, and think him hardly dealt with by his judges. In all his answers and retorts upon his adversaries he has the best, not only of the argument, but of the question, reasoning on their own principles and practice. They are so far from allowing any measure of equal dealing, of common justice or humanity between themselves and the Jew, that even when they come to ask a favour of him, and Shylock reminds them [of their treatment of him], Anthonio, his old enemy, instead of any acknowledgement of the shrewdness and justice of the remonstrance, which would have been preposterous in a respectable Catholic merchant in those times, threatens him with a repetition of the same treatment. After this, the appeal to the Jew's mercy, as if there were any common principle of right and wrong between them, is the rankest hypocrisy or the blindest prejudice.

SKOTTOWE (*Life of Shakespeare*, etc., 1824, vol. i, p. 325): Shylock is abhorred and execrated; but the skill of the poet has endued him with qualities which preserve him from contempt. His fierceness, cruelty, and relentlessness are dignified by intellectual vigour. His actions are deliberate, they are the emanations of his bold and masculine understanding. Let the art with which he negotiates his bond be contemplated; consider his coolness, his plausible exaggeration of the dangers to which Antonio's property is subjected; his bitter sarcasms and insulting gibes; all efforts of the mind to induce a belief of his indifference and to disguise his real design; follow him into court, behold him maintaining his superiority in argument, unmoved by insult and unawed by power, till disappointment leaves him nothing to contend for and anguish stops his speech, and then let his claims to intellectual distinction be decided on.

C. A. BROWN (*Shakespeare's Autobiographical Poems*, 1838, p. 276): Toleration is an intolerable word, never used by our poet, unless, possibly, in a disapproving manner, under cover of Dogberry's ignorance,—'most tolerable, and not to be endured.' To call it therefore in kindlier words,—respect for another's sincere opinions,—has hitherto made but slow progress in the world; though, bereaved of *The Merchant of Venice*, it might have been slower. No argument in its favour could be more complete, or put in a stronger light, than that which we find here. Shylock, a usurer, a suspicious father, and altogether a bad man, compels us to grant him a portion of our involuntary good-will, solely on account of his being persecuted for constancy in his creed; and, thwarted in his hopes of a hateful revenge, we look at his ominous scales, balance his injuries against his rancour, and cannot forbear granting him our pity when he is defeated. How careful the author has been to maintain our fellow-feeling, and to make Shylock's religion meet persecution at every step! Not only Antonio is his reviler,—he runs the gauntlet of abuse through Venice; his daughter forsakes and robs him because of his religion; wherever he turns, his misfortunes are a subject of exultation; and his fall is hailed with insulting open triumph. His claim to be enrolled among his fellow-beings, in that powerful language, 'Hath not a Jew eyes?' &c. has nothing urged against it, nor could a word be said in denial, yet his claim is allowed by none, and he is never treated with a show of respect until he is feared. We acknowledge his right, and we are glad to see him at last, by any resource, treated with respect; we only recoil at his appalling vengeance. On the other hand, Antonio is a man justly honoured for every virtue, with one exception,—a want of charity, a good feeling, a decent behaviour towards a fellow-creature, purely because he is an unbeliever. The religious animosity of Shylock was no more than retaliation. Antonio, indeed, may have had reason to accuse Shylock of extortion; but his calling him 'misbeliever' and 'dog,' spitting on him, and spurning him, force us instantly to side with the usurer against the christian of unblemished fame. When reminded of these injuries, the virtuous merchant is ready to repeat them, so unconscious is he of acting with injustice. Representing the persecutor, on all other points truly estimable, and the persecuted in no degree estimable, yet entirely unanswerable in his defence, puts personal merit out of the question, and places the argument on the broadest principle, including the worst as well as the best among believers and infidels. Shakespeare strove to alleviate the bitter persecutions, not only towards the Jews, but towards all others. Catholics and Protestants, though the burnings in Smithfield existed no more in his day, were fearfully hateful to each other, when good men were contaminated by evil, and worse men by revenge, rendering the persecutor blind to his want of charity, and giving all the truth of reasoning to the persecuted, however unreasonable might be the creed to the more powerful party. For the benefit of those who could apply, or might hereafter apply, Antonio and Shylock to themselves, Shakespeare portrayed them. Should any one think the application was unthought of and accidental, let him contend that wheat grows into nourishment by chance, or try what philosophic works he can write by chance.

W. W. LLOYD (p. 550): In the case of Bassanio the mind glides pretty easily over extravagance by confidence in his nature and motives, but many have been staggered by what is only another enunciation of the same principle, in the flight of Jessica with her father's ducats and jewels. A chief difficulty has arisen from the maudlin sentimentality that has been bestowed on the murderous Jew. . . . . Shylock is ready to impute his disgraces to antipathy to his race and envy of his gains, but the poet leaves us in no uncertainty that his gains were those of a usurer, in the sense which, under any dispensation of political economy, involves at least dishonesty, dishonour, cruelty, and fraud. The arts by which a victim is enmeshed and ruined by a usurer are even now not obsolete; and, under defective laws, might have flourished tenfold. . . . . The Jew is the very impersonation of avarice, meanness, and cruelty, as Antonio of generous and sympathetic liberality, and the hellish intention of his treacherous bond is already patent.

(P. 551.) The plea of the Jew, in exacting forfeiture of the bond, is the epitome of the very history and genius of Judaism regarded from its most unfavourable side, bigoted reliance in the fulfilment of precept by the letter, and disregard of spirit and purpose, and obstinate claim of privilege by interpretation of terms in covenant or bond, to the neglect of the foregone intention of the bond, in subjection to which alone it can be reasonably valid. All are familiar with the spirit of Pharisaism to claim privilege by natural descent from the favoured Abraham, and to disallow in others the value of the very qualities to which the favour of Abraham was ascribed; to cleanse the outside of the platter and to be scrupulous of days and meats, but take little thought of the impurities of the heart. Those only, however, can have full conception of the degradation of the human mind by slavery to written text, who have had some glimpses of the Rabbinical literature that is a monument of a tyranny in comparison with which Egyptian bondage was enfranchisement. The iron of this slavery has entered into the very soul of Shylock, and his appeal to his bond, as identified with justice, embodies the very soul and being of ceremonialism. The bond is signed, is sealed, is admitted, and he rests upon it as on a rock; borne out by this, he fears no judgement, as doing no wrong. The word of law is to him sanctity, and he has no sense of the ends for which law was framed. So he has an oath in heaven, he has sworn by the sacred Sabbath; bonds and obligations again invalid, by incongruity of purport, with all the ends for which oaths are sacred. Such oaths are air, such bonds are waste paper; even the very rights of nature and paternity are dissolved by cruelty and malice, and no amount of wealth can purchase the happiness or power of which the moral conditions are forfeit; the ark of his trust and veneration is, like the gilded casket, but a painted sepulchre, and within are dead men's bones.

GILES (*Human Life in Shakespeare*, 1868, p. 124): But when the sense of loss and the sense of wrong arise in harder natures [than in Lear and Othello]; when the heart does not bleed out of wounded affection, but is bitter with the gall of vindictive pride; when the sense of loss and the sense of wrong merge, but do not lose their personal, their individual consciousness in an abstract fierceness which gathers into the embrace of its detestation whole centuries of loss and wrong inflicted on millions of a race, and this detestation is concentrated into an impassioned antipathy such as hereditary persecution can excite and the most energetic inheritor of enmity can feel; or when the loss and wrong experienced are not traced to the weakness of the victim himself and to the vices of his injurers, but are made the crime of the human species, —when *such* conditions of hatred are embodied and expressed we have the characters of Shylock and of Timon. These men do not move pity, but awaken terror. Shylock is inwardly a dark nature; also he is inwardly a strong nature. In purpose, will, and passion he is a man of energy; and, by the bigotry of society, his energy is restricted to one mode of power,—the power of money. Money engages his activity, but does not exhaust his being. To have potency, he must have money. Having any amount of money, he may still be trodden on as a reptile; but wanting money, he is a reptile without a sting. Contempt is around him, as the light of day; he breathes, as he walks, an atmosphere of odium; but the light does not shame him; the atmosphere does not sicken him; he has the stout vitality of a proud constitution, and though he cringes, and bows, and smiles, and seems as servile as a dog, mean as his scorners think him, their lowest idea of *him* is reverence itself, compared with his highest idea of *them*. The lords of Venice may call the Jew a slave, but he is an aristocrat in every drop of his blood; and more value does he set on any drop that trickles in a Hebrew beggar's veins than the richest streams they can boast of from their upstart sires. They may use foul words to him, but that is their *own* discredit; they may spit on him, but that is *their* infamy, and not *his;* he cannot give them blow for blow, but he can give them bigotry for bigotry; he refuses their doctrine, he willingly accepts their example. . . . . Christians represent all who have done the worst to his people in any age, on any soil; his personal foes stand before him for all that is worst even in Christians; and one man he has in the fangs of his power whom he deems the worst of his foes. Here is a wrath, which might fill the hollow globe that holds the stars, conveyed into a single point,—the anger of many generations condensed into one heated bolt, against one devoted head. The evil done to his people and to himself he cannot here repay; but he will prove that he has the disposition to repay it with more of usury than the most greedy miser ever craved, dreamed, or imagined. Shylock's law with the Christians is the law of enmity; he is zealous to obey it, to make it perfect in revenge; for him revenge is sanctity; and to immolate Antonio, as the fulfilment of it, assumes the merit and the glory of solemn and sacrificial righteousness. But as the hating passions, however provoked, react ever with misery on the individual who indulges them, so the contrivances of Shylock for the torture of others accomplish only the destruction of himself.

Rev. John Hunter (p. xv): Shakespeare, the interpreter of nature and humanity, felt that the prejudices against the Jews were cruelly immoderate. He could not, indeed, represent the Jew of Venice as magnanimous or in any respect amiable, for this would have been inconsistent with the general character of the Jews, and would have been so opposed to popular prejudice that the public representation of the play would not have been tolerated; but while he had prepared avarice, malignity, and cruelty, as the colours with which he meant to portray the Jew of Venice, he saw that Shylock's moral deformity might be in great measure justly attributed to the influence of social circumstances, and he felt that the Jew, even in a temper of malignity, might convincingly show to Christians that their persecuting spirit impressed on his tribe the character which the Jews bore in society. Shylock, accordingly, is a man whose intellectual power is not to be despised, a man who can deeply feel, and powerfully expostulate against, the indignity to which he is subjected. He cannot be allowed any Christian advocate among the *dramatis personæ*, but he himself can forcibly demonstrate that it is far more reasonable in him to act according to what was said 'by them of old time '—'an eye for an eye and a tooth for a tooth'—than it is for Christians to boast of the excellence of that gospel charity which their conduct habitually violates. And herein was the dramatist a faithful and skilful monitor to professing Christians. Had the Jew been enabled to resent in proper time, and with proper impunity, any wrongs that might have been inflicted upon him, his resentment would have had vent, and might have left his heart capable of charity; but he had to endure, without retaliation, injury and insult, time after time, until his heart became hardened as a stone that would whet keenly the knife of vengeance should legal justice ever give him an oppor‐ tunity of obtaining redress.

J. W. HALES (*The Athenæum*, 15 Dec., 1877): By 'the general' little heed is paid to the profound skill and the catholic humanity with which the Jew is interpreted. 'The general' sees only a monster, and hisses and hates. A more careful eye observes that this monster is accounted for,—that the great poet is considering the problem how such ossifications come to be. He is 'anatomizing' Shylock, seeing 'what breeds about' his 'heart.' 'Is there any cause in nature that makes these hard hearts?' The Christian who looks frankly and faithfully at this work will not find matter for exulta‐ tion or for ridicule, but only for shame and sadness. Shylock had been made the hard, savage, relentless creature we see him by long and cruel oppression. He inherited a nature embittered by centuries of insult and outrage, and his own wretched experience had only aggravated its bitterness. 'Sufferance' had been, and was, the badge of all his tribe; it was his badge. As fetters corrode the flesh, so persecution corrodes the heart. Shakespeare, truly detesting this dreadful being, yet bethinks him, we say, how he became so. He was once a man,—at least, his breed was once human; and Shake‐ speare, no less than the supreme creative genius of our own age, recognized in the Jew splendid capacities and powers, however, so far as he knew the race, misapplied and debased; was no less fascinated by a character of such singular force and ineradicable nationality.

HUDSON (p. 72): As avarice was the passion in which Shylock mainly lived, the Christian virtues which thwarted this naturally seemed to him the greatest of wrongs.

With these strong national traits are interwoven personal traits equally strong. Thoroughly and intensely Jewish, he is not more a Jew than he is Shylock. In his hard, icy intellectuality and his dry, mummy-like tenacity of purpose, with a dash, now and then, of biting, sarcastic humour, we see the remains of a great and noble nature, out of which all the genial sap of humanity has been pressed by accumulated injuries. With as much elasticity of mind as stiffness of neck, every step he takes but the last is as firm as the earth he treads on. Nothing can daunt, nothing disconcert him; remonstrance cannot move, ridicule cannot touch, obloquy cannot exasperate him; when he has not provoked them, he has been forced to bear them; and now that he does provoke them, he is hardened against them. In a word, he may be broken; he cannot be bent.

(P. 74.) Thus his religion, his patriotism, his avarice, his affection, all concur to stimulate his enmity; and his personal hate thus reinforced overcomes for once his greed, and he grows generous in the prosecution of his aim. The only reason he will vouchsafe for taking the pound of flesh is, 'if it will feed nothing else, it will feed my revenge;' a reason all the more satisfactory to him, forasmuch as those to whom he gives it can neither allow it nor refute it; and until they can rail the seal from off his bond, all their railings are but a foretaste of the revenge he seeks. In his eagerness to taste that morsel sweeter to him than all the luxuries of Italy, his recent afflictions—the loss of his daughter, his ducats, his jewels, and even the precious ring given him by his departed wife—all fade from his mind. In his inexorable and imperturbable hard-ness at the trial there is something that makes the blood to tingle. It is the sublimity of malice. We feel that the yearnings of revenge have silenced all other cares and all other thoughts. In his rapture of hate the man has grown superhuman, and his eyes seem all aglow with preternatural malignity. Fearful, however, as is his passion, he comes not off without moving our pity. In the very act whereby he thinks to avenge his own and his brethren's wrongs, the national curse overtakes him. In standing up for the letter of the law against all pleadings of mercy, he has strength-ened his enemies' hands, and sharpened their weapons, against himself; and the terrible Jew sinks at last into the poor, pitiable, heart-broken Shylock.

Early in the play, when Shylock is bid forth to Bassanio's supper, and Launcelot urges him to go, because 'my young master doth expect your reproach,' Shylock replies, 'So do I his.' Of course he expects that reproach through the bankruptcy of Antonio. This would seem to infer that Shylock has some hand in getting up the reports of Antonio's 'losses at sea;' which reports, at least some of them, turn out false in the end. Further than this, the Poet leaves us in the dark as to how those reports grew into being and gained belief. Did he mean to have it understood that the Jew exercised his cunning and malice in plotting and preparing them? It appears, at all events, that Shylock knew they were coming before they came. Yet I suppose the natural impression from the play is, that he lent the ducats and took the bond on a mere chance of coming at his wish. But he would h⸱ ⸱y grasp so eagerly at a bare possibility of revenge, without using means to turn it into something more. This would mark him with much deeper lines of guilt. Why, then, did not Shakespeare bring the matter forward more prominently? Perhaps it was because the doing so would have made Shylock appear too deep a criminal for the degree of interest which his part was meant to carry in the play. In other words, the health of the drama as a work of *comic* art required his criminality to be kept in the background. He comes very near overshadowing the other characters too much, as it is. And Shy-lock's character is *essentially tragic;* there is none of the proper timber of comedy in him.

FREDERICK HAWKINS (*The Theatre*, Nov., 1879, p. 194): The sympathy enjoyed by Shylock is designedly aroused in the interest of the great but downtrodden race he represents. The man who exhausted worlds and then imagined new, whose mind was such that at times he seemed to touch some awful secret of the Cosmos, whose works are lighted up by wisdom, generosity, and tenderness,—such a man could have had no share in an outburst of vulgar envy and fanaticism. He saw the Jews as they were, and so seeing them wrote *The Merchant of Venice* in order to exhibit one of their number at a disadvantage as a direct result of the unreasoning prejudice against them. He more than counteracted with one hand what he seemed to do with the other. In availing himself of the greatest popular madness of his time he sought to appease it. His play might have been regarded as an attack upon the Jews, but in reality it defended them. Much of the true significance of the play is to be appreciated only by those who read between the lines, for even if Elizabethan audiences and readers had been well-disposed towards the Jews, the dramatist was too great a master of his art to preach his moral. No pains appear to have been spared to dignify the character of Shylock. The whole force of an old untainted religious aristocracy is breathed in some of his speeches. He is filled with a generous enthusiasm for his sacred tribe and ancient law. His avarice, a vice forced on him by circumstances, is relieved by gleams of an originally noble nature. He has so deep a veneration for the memory of his dead wife that ' a wilderness of monkeys' would not compensate for the loss of the ring she had given him in youth. He is tenderly attached to his daughter, whom he leaves in charge of his house and his keys. Many of the graces of intellect, too, are engrafted upon him, as may be seen from his wealth of ideas and the felicitous language in which they are expressed.

(P. 195.) In the Trial Scene Shylock's reason seems to have been shaken by the flight of his daughter; and the knowledge that Antonio has assisted her to get away, a circumstance often overlooked, may account in some measure for the increased malignity he here displays towards the Merchant.

[The foregoing view, that in *The Merchant of Venice* we have a 'plea for toleration,' evoked a discussion in the next number of *The Theatre* (December, 1879), which I should like to transfer to these pages, but lack of space restricts me merely to a para graph here and there. Mr Spedding's contribution I give in full, not only for the sake of the *clarum et venerabile nomen*, but for the sound, wholesome truths which, as I think, it sets forth.]

THEODORE MARTIN: I can find no trace of any 'plea for toleration.' Nobody in the play urges anything in the nature of such a plea. Jew and Christian are alike intolerant. . . . . Even after the discipline of suffering and peril which had brought him face to face with death, Antonio seeks to force upon Shylock a renunciation of his faith, not from any belief that this could operate a change in his convictions or in his cruel nature, but in the very harshest spirit of intolerance. Everybody in the court, the Duke himself, indeed, seems to think this a most proper and reasonable demand. . . . . While I cannot think that a plea for religious liberty was in Shakespeare's thoughts in writing this play, I frankly admit that it indirectly inculcates the un-wisdom of religious persecution in the mischief it works upon the persecutors as well as upon the perse-cuted. . . . . Only in Portia is the sweet and humble spirit of Christianity illustrated. . . . . Save in the words which fell from Portia, there is not in the play, to my mind, a trace of any recognition of the great doctrine of religious toleration. That Shakespeare held by that doctrine as stoutly as man ever did, I can have no doubt, but I see no symptom of an intention to expound, or even to illustrate it. 'I cannot find it in the bond.'

AN ACTOR: The tendency of the play is undoubtedly to show that 'the worst pas-sions of human nature are nurtured by undeserved persecution and obloquy.' How far this tendency was a matter of deliberate design we shall never know, but Mr Haw-kins's arguments are hardly overthrown by the fact that the principle of religious tole-ration is not expressly enforced in the text.

F. J. FURNIVALL: Had a plea for toleration been Shakespeare's object, would he have clinched the argument that Shylock uses with that 'shall we not revenge?' the claim that Jews had a right to turn devils as freely as Christians had? Was there no nob e Jew in history, no suffering one, specially no woman, in romance, through whom he could have put forth his plea more effectively than through Shylock? Assuredly there were many.

28

FRANK MARSHALL: It is not necessary to suppose that Shakespeare had any especial views with regard to the removal of Jewish disabilities in his portrayal of the character of Shylock. Shakespeare was not a *doctrinnaire ;* he was essentially a dramatist, and possessed in a greater degree than any other author the faculty of entering into the feelings of the characters which he introduced into his plays.

ISRAEL DAVIS: Shakespeare was too thoroughly an artist to write a play with a moral purpose. In regard to the essence of a drama, he was guided irresistibly by a keen appreciation of the real nature of men's thoughts and feelings. Shylock is an interesting character, not evil by nature, but made evil by the treatment to which he has been subjected. The moral suggests itself, that if the Jew had been treated in a better way he would have been a better man; and Shakespeare cannot have been unconscious that he preached that moral, although the purpose of his play was to preach no lesson, but to describe human life. . . . . It was a greater step for Shakespeare, in the sixteenth century, to create the Shylock of *The Merchant of Venice* than for George Eliot, in our own times, to imagine the Mordecai of *Daniel Deronda*.

DAVID ANDERSON: I see no reason why the Jewish race should be ashamed of Shylock; and I venture to suggest that at the period of the play there may have been hundreds of such characters in the cities and towns of Italy. Save for his revengeful spirit, the Jew compares favourably with the other principal characters of the play.

JAMES SPEDDING: The best contribution I can offer to this discussion is the expression of an old man's difficulty in accepting these new discoveries of profound moral and political designs underlying Shakespeare's choice and treatment of his subjects. I believe that he was a man of business,—that his principal business was to produce plays which would draw. I believe that he took the story of the caskets and of the pound of flesh because he thought he could combine them (I forget whether he found them together or put them together) into a good romantic comedy that was likely to succeed; and I think he managed it very well. But if, instead of looking about for a story to ' please ' the Globe audience, he had been in search of a subject under cover of which he might steal into their minds ' a more tolerant feeling towards the Hebrew race,' I cannot think he would have selected for his hero a rich Jewish merchant plotting the murder of a Christian rival by means of a fraudulent contract, which made death the penalty of non-payment at the day, and insisting on the exaction of it. In a modern Christian audience it seems to be possible for a skilful actor to work on the feelings of an audience so far as to make a man engaged in such a business an object of respectful sympathy. But can anybody believe that, in times when this would have been much more difficult, Shakespeare would have *chosen* such a case as a favourable one to suggest toleration to a public prejudiced against Jews? A lawyer retained to defend a man who has kicked his wife to death will try to prove that his client was an injured husband, and had served her right, and this may succeed with a jury that have had experience of conjugal provocations. But if his business were to plead for a mitigation of the severity of the law *against husbands,* he would surely keep his injured friend's case as far out of sight as he could. I do not believe, in fact, that Shakespeare, either in choosing the subject or treating it, was thinking about Jewish grievances or disabilities at all either way. What he had to think about was, how he could introduce into a *comedy*, without putting everything out of tune, an incident so shocking, and a project so savage, that ' the imagination almost refuses to approach

it.' And I think he managed this also very skilfully, by first depriving Shylock of all pretence of grievance or excuse, which was done by the offer of all the money due him upon his bond, with twice as much more to compensate him for the very short time he had had to wait for it beyond the appointed day,—an offer which leaves him without any conceivable motive for preferring the pound of flesh except the worst,— and then dismissing him with a punishment very much lighter than he deserved.

MACDONALD (*The Imagination*, 1883, p. 125): There is for every one of Shake- speare's characters the firm ground of humanity, upon which the weeds, as well as the flowers, glorious or fantastic, as the case may be, show themselves. His more heroic persons are the most profoundly human. Nor are his villains unhuman, though inhu man enough. Compared with Marlowe's Jew, Shylock is a terrible *man* beside a dreary *monster*, and, as far as logic and the *lex talionis* go, has the best of the argu- ment. It is the strength of human nature itself that makes crime strong. Wicked- ness could have no power of itself; it lives by the perverted powers of good. And so great is Shakespeare's sympathy with Shylock even, in the hard and unjust doom that overtakes him, that he dismisses him with some of the spare sympathies of the more tender-hearted of his spectators. Nowhere is the justice of genius more plain than in Shakespeare's utter freedom from party-spirit, even with regard to his own creations. Each character shall set itself forth from its own point of view, and only in the choice and scope of the whole shall the judgement of the poet be beheld. He never allows his opinion to come out to the damaging of the individual's own self-presentation. He knows well that for the worst something can be said, and that a feeling of justice and his own right will be strong in the mind of a man who is yet swayed by perfect selfish- ness. Therefore the false man is not discoverable in his speech, not merely because the villain will talk as like a true man as he may, but because seldom is the villainy clear to the villain's own mind.

PORTIA

HAZLITT (*Characters of Shakespeare's Plays*, 1817, p. 273): Portia is not a very great favourite with us; neither are we in love with her maid, Nerissa. Portia has a certain degree of affectation and pedantry about her, which is very unusual in Shakespeare's women, but which, perhaps, was a proper qualification for the office of a 'civil doctor,' which she undertakes and executes so successfully. The speech about Mercy is very well; but there are a thousand finer ones in Shakespeare. We do not admire the scene of the caskets, and object entirely to the black Prince Morochius. We should like Jessica better if she had not deceived and robbed her father; and Lorenzo, if he had not married a Jewess, though he thinks he has a right to wrong a Jew. The dia- logue between the newly-married couple by moonlight in Act V is a collection of classical elegancies.*

---

* CHARLES COWDEN-CLARKE (*Shakespeare-Characters*, London, 1863, p. 393): I have always regretted that Hazlitt set down that passage. It has been often quoted; and, as his staid opinion, it has awakened a natural opposition to him on the part of those critics who could better perceive the true beauties of Portia's character than they knew of, or could discern, the variable moods of Hazlitt's temperament. Every one who knew him would feel convinced that he penned these words under some temporary fit of spleen, some wayward, momentary feeling of petulance against *high- bred* women. Hazlitt was very sensitive—personally sensitive—on the score of women's liking toward himself; and he occasionally made some curious mistakes, such as many men who are at once self-diffident and self-confident, intellectually proud and constitutionally shy (for all the quali- ties are perfectly compatible), often do make about women and women's preferences. Even in his writings these peculiarities are plainly perceptible. Turn to his Essay ' On Great and Little Things,' where he professes his admiration for ' humble beauties, servant-maids and shepherd-girls ;' his own

MRS JAMESON (*Characteristics of Women*, 2d ed., 1833, vol. i, p. 66): Portia, Isa
bella, Beatrice, and Rosalind may be classed together, as characters of intellect,
because, when compared with others, they are at once distinguished by their mental
superiority.   In Portia it is intellect kindled into romance by a poetical imagination.
. . . . The wit of Portia is like attar of roses, rich and concentrated. . . . . As women
and individuals, as breathing realities, clothed in flesh and blood, I believe we must
assign the first rank to Portia, as uniting in herself in a more eminent degree than the
others, all the noblest and most lovable qualities that ever met together in woman.

Portia is endued with her own share of those delightful qualities which Shakespeare
has lavished on many of his female characters; but, besides the dignity, the sweetness,
and tenderness which should distinguish her sex generally, she is individualized by
qualities peculiar to herself; by her high mental powers, her enthusiasm of temperament, her decision of purpose, and her buoyancy of spirit.   These are innate; she has
other distinguishing qualities more external, and which are the result of the circumstances in which she is placed.   Thus she is the heiress of a princely name and count-
less wealth; a train of obedient pleasures have ever waited round her; and from
infancy she has breathed an atmosphere redolent of perfume and blandishment.
Accordingly, there is a commanding grace, a high-bred, airy elegance, a spirit of magnificence in all that she says and does, as one to whom splendour had been familiar
from her very birth.   She treads as though her footsteps had been among marble palaces, beneath roofs of fretted gold, o'er cedar floors and pavements of jasper and por-
phyry—amid gardens full of statues, and flowers, and fountains, and haunting music.
She is full of penetrative wisdom, and genuine tenderness, and lively wit; but as she
has never known want, or grief, [not when her father died?—ED.] or fear, or disappointment, her wisdom is without a touch of the sombre or the sad; her affections are
all mixed up with faith, hope, and joy; and her wit has not a particle of malevolence
or causticity.

(P. 72.)   We are not told expressly where Belmont is situated; but as Bassanio takes
ship to go thither from Venice, and as we find [Portia] afterwards ordering horses from
Belmont to Padua, we will imagine Portia's hereditary palace as standing on some
lovely promontory between Venice and Trieste, overlooking the blue Adriatic, with the
Friuli Mountains or the Euganean hills for its background, such as we often see in one
of Claude's or Poussin's elysian landscapes.   In a scene, in a home like this, Shakespeare, having first exorcised the original possessor, has placed Portia; and so endowed
her that all the wild, strange, and moving circumstances of the story become natural,
probable, and necessary in connection with her.   That such a woman should be chosen
by the solving of an enigma is not surprising; herself and all around her, the scene,

---

words, declaring, too, that he 'admires the Clementinas and Clarissas at a distance,' while the
Pamelas and Fannys of Richardson and Fielding *make the blood tingle.*'   But at the very time
that he tries to exalt the ignorant charmers, he permits the reader to perceive that they provoke
him with their inapprehensiveness.   And in another Essay, entitled 'On the Disadvantages of Intellectual Superiority,' he, with much bitterness, takes up the opposite side of the question, saying,
where he is speaking of the wooing of men of letters, 'Women of education may have a glimpse of
their meaning, may get a clue to their characters; but to all others they are thick darkness.   If the
mistress smile at their *ideal* advances, the maid will laugh outright.'   Here we find that the pretty
ignorants had lost their fascination for him; that he saw through their insufficiency to form the solid
and permanent delight of a man of intelligence; whereas, when he wrote that line, 'Portia is not a
very great favourite with us,' the Fannys and the Pamelas chanced to be in the ascendant.   His
imagination was beguiling him with some image of captivating *simpletonism;* frequently and oddly
confounded with *simplicity,* when he asserted that 'Portia has a certain degree of affectation and
pedantry about her.'

the country, the age in which she is placed, breathe of poetry, romance, and enchantment.

(P. 74.) But all the finest parts of Portia's character are brought to bear in the Trial Scene. There she shines forth all her divine self. Her intellectual powers, her elevated sense of religion, her high honorable principles, her best feelings as a woman, are all displayed. She maintains at first a calm self-command, as one sure of carrying her point 'n the end; yet the painful, heart-thrilling uncertainty in which she keeps the whole court, until suspense verges upon agony, is not contrived for effect merely; it is necessary and inevitable. She has two objects in view: to deliver her husband's friend, and to maintain her husband's honour by the discharge of his just debt, though paid out of her own wealth ten times over. It is evident that she would owe the safety of Antonio to anything rather than to the legal quibble with which her cousin Bellario has armed her, and which she reserves as a last resource. Thus all the speeches addressed to Shylock in the first instance are either direct or indirect experiments on his temper and feelings. She must be understood from the beginning to the end as examining with intense anxiety the effect of her own words on his mind and countenance; as watching for that relenting spirit which she hopes to awaken either by reason or persuasion. She begins by an appeal to his mercy, in that matchless piece of eloquence which falls upon the heart like "gentle dew [*sic*] from heaven,"—but in vain. She next attacks his avarice. Then she appeals in the same breath both to his avarice and his pity.

All that she says afterwards—her strong expressions, which are calculated to strike a shuddering horror through the nerves—the reflections she interposes—her delays and circumlocution to give time for any latent feeling of commiseration to display itself,—all, all are premeditated and tend in the same manner to the object she has in view. Thus: 'You must prepare your bosom for his knife,' 'Therefore lay bare your bosom.' These two speeches, though addressed apparently to Antonio, are spoken *at* Shylock, and are evidently intended to penetrate *his* bosom. In the same spirit she asks for the balance to weigh the pound of flesh, and entreats of Shylock to have a surgeon ready.

So unwilling is her sanguine and generous spirit to resign all hope, or to believe that humanity is absolutely extinct in the bosom of the Jew, that she calls on Antonio, as a last resource, to speak for himself. His gentle, yet manly resignation—the deep pathos of his farewell, and the affectionate allusion to herself in his last address to Bassanio—are well calculated to swell that emotion which, through the whole scene, must have been labouring suppressed within her heart.

At length the crisis arrives, for patience and womanhood can endure no longer, and when Shylock, carrying his savage bent 'to the last hour of act,' springs on his victim —'A sentence! come, prepare!' then the smothered scorn, indignation, and disgust burst forth with an impetuosity which interferes with the judicial solemnity she had at first affected; particularly in the speech: 'Therefore prepare thee to cut off the flesh,' &c. But she afterwards recovers her propriety, and triumphs with a cooler scorn and a more self-possessed exultation.

It is clear that, to feel the full force and dramatic beauty of this marvellous scene, we must go along with Portia as well as with Shylock; we must understand her concealed purpose, keep in mind her noble motives, and pursue in our fancy the undercurrent of feeling working in her mind throughout. The terror and the power of Shylock's character,—his deadly and inexorable malice,—would be too oppressive; the pain and the pity too intolerable, and the horror of the possible issue too overwhelming, but for the intellectual relief afforded by this double source of interest and contemplation.

I come now to that capacity for warm and generous affection, that tenderness of heart, which render Portia not less lovable as a woman than admirable for her mental endowments. The affections are to the intellect what the forge is to the metal; it is they which temper and shape it to all good purposes, and soften, strengthen, and purify it. What an exquisite stroke of judgement in the poet, to make the mutual passion of Portia and Bassanio, though unacknowledged to each other, anterior to the opening of the play! Bassanio's confession very properly comes first, and prepares us for Portia's half-betrayed, unconscious election of this most graceful and chivalrous admirer. Our interest is thus awakened for the lovers from the very first; and what shall be said of the Casket Scene with Bassanio, where every line which Portia speaks is so worthy of herself, so full of sentiment and beauty, and poetry, and passion? Too naturally frank for disguise, too modest to confess her depth of love while the issue of the trial remains in suspense, the conflict between love and fear and maidenly dignity causes the most delicious confusion that ever tinged a woman's cheek, or dropped in broken utterance from her lips.

(P. 83.) A prominent feature in Portia's character is that confiding, buoyant spirit which mingles with all her thoughts and affections. And here let me observe, that I never yet met in real life, nor ever read in tale or history, of any woman, distinguished for intellect of the highest order, who was not also remarkable for this trusting spirit, this hopefulness and cheerfulness of temper. . . . . In the Casket Scene she fears indeed the issue of the trial, but while she trembles, her hope is stronger than her fear.

(P. 86.) Her subsequent surrender of herself in heart and soul, of her maiden freedom, and her vast possessions, can never be read without deep emotion; for not only all the tenderness and delicacy of a devoted woman is here blended with all the dignity which becomes the princely heiress of Belmont, but the serious, measured self-possession of her address to her lover, when all suspense is over and all concealment superfluous, is most beautifully consistent with the character. It is, in truth, an awful moment, that in which a gifted woman first discovers that, besides talents and powers, she has also passions and affections; when she first begins to suspect their vast importance in the sum of her existence; when she first confesses that her happiness is no longer in her own keeping, but is surrendered for ever and for ever into the dominion of another! The possession of uncommon powers of mind are so far from affording relief or resource in the first intoxicating surprise—I had almost said terror—of such a revelation, that they render it more intense. The sources of thought multiply beyond calculation the sources of feeling; and, mingled, they rush together, a torrent deep as strong. Because Portia is endued with that enlarged comprehension which looks before and after, she does not feel the less, but the more: because from the height of her commanding intellect she can contemplate the force, the tendency, the consequences of her own sentiments,—because she is fully sensible of her own situation, and the value of all she concedes,—the concession is not made with less entireness and devotion of heart, less confidence in the truth and worth of her lover, than when Juliet, in a similar moment, but without any such intrusive reflections,—any check but the instinctive delicacy of her sex,—flings herself and her fortunes at the feet of her lover: 'And all my fortunes at thy foot I'll lay, And follow thee, my lord, through all the world.' In Portia's confession, which is not breathed from a moonlit balcony, but spoken openly in the presence of her attendants and vassals, there is nothing of the passionate self-abandonment of Juliet nor of the artless simplicity of Miranda, but a consciousness and a tender seriousness approaching to solemnity, which are not less touching.

(P. 92.) And in the description of her various suitors in the first scene with Nerrissa, what infinite power, wit, and vivacity! She half checks herself as she is about to give the reins to her sportive humour: 'In truth, I know it is a sin to be a mocker.' But if it carries her away, it is so perfectly good-natured, so temperately bright, so lady-like, it is ever without offence; and so far, most unlike the satirical poignant, unsparing wit of Beatrice, 'misprising what she looks on.' In fact, I can scarcely conceive a greater contrast than between the vivacity of Portia and the vivacity of Beatrice. Portia, with all her airy brilliance, is supremely soft and dignified; everything she says or does displays her capability for profound thought and feeling as well as her lively and romantic disposition; and as I have seen in an Italian garden a fountain flinging round its wreaths of showery light, while the many-coloured Iris hung brooding above it, in its calm and soul-felt glory; so in Portia the wit is ever kept subordinate to the poetry, and we still feel the tender, the intellectual, and the imaginative part of the character as superior to, and presiding over, its spirit and vivacity.

C. A. BROWN (p. 279): Portia is a greater favourite with me than with Hazlitt; but I do not think her quite so amiable as she is described by Mrs Jameson. Laying down the law, in which Portia seems to rejoice, cannot be perfectly amiable, though it were in a male counsel; for then we could feel no more than admiration at his professional talents. It is true, circumstances forced her into that situation; and, feudal lady as she was, she executes her task thoroughly. All she does is consistent; yet I much question if she does not experience a triumphant delight while she detains the Court in suspense. Shakespeare has done much in softening the objection; but, somehow, it could not be entirely overcome.

W. W. LLOYD (p. 552): In some respects Portia has always appeared to me the most wonderful of all Shakespeare's feminine creations. The part she was to play in the Scene of the Trial gave the leading condition of her character, the possession of the highest intellectual endowments that are compatible in woman, with the age and the susceptibilities for tender and romantic love. The power of the poet, however, is less wonderful, even in the wondrous Trial Scene, than in the exhibition of the blending of the logical and intellectual element in the very web of rapture and passion when Bassanio stands before the caskets. A spirit of inference, a sequence of deduction, run through the very confusion of her agitated hopes, and govern and correct by apprehensive standards the comparisons that crowd upon her imagination. In her, meet and adjust themselves all the perfections of all the other less perfect characters of the play. She is as sympathetic as Anthonio, but, with equal abhorrence of cruelty, she avoids an outbreak of vituperation against the Jew, and zealously gives him every chance of retiring, appealing first to the finer chords of humanity, and, when these fail to respond, to the coarser motives of lucre; and when the Duke, with precipitateness which he has afterwards to qualify, remits part of the fine, she reserves the rights of Anthonio, 'Ay, for the State, not for Anthonio,' not merely by way of sustaining her assumed character of legal accuracy, but to allow him the opportunity, which he only employs when she still more directly furnishes him the cue, to render some proportion of mercy. Nay, I may here add, in her first declaration of the consequences of shedding a drop of Christian blood, she names only the forfeiture of lands and goods. Whenever again the play is worthily represented, I believe that, during the intermediate speeches, the changing demeanour of Shylock would give reason to apprehend that, as he had already subjected avarice to revenge, he would even have risked all

to glut his cruel purpose, and that it is therefore that Portia now adds other consequences, 'Thou diest, and all thy goods are confiscate,' and so pursues his sentence to
the end.　In the novel the Jew's defeat turns entirely on the matter of the blood-shed-
ding, which, in itself, is little better than a quibble; Shakespeare wisely retained and
put this first to degrade the literal principle of the Jew to the uttermost, by exhibiting
him foiled at the weapons of his own cunning, when wielded with simplicity and
straightforwardness; but the dignity of the moral, which is that of Portia's character,
required and supplied the more substantial reference to criminality of murderous intent.

REV. JOHN HUNTER (p. xviii): There is, indeed, a methodical style in the expression even of Portia's most impassioned thoughts, which has induced some critics to
impute to her a degree of affectation unusual in Shakespeare's delineations of female
character; but we believe that the dramatist has herein observed a most judicious consistency, and that the language in which Portia describes her emotions is not less indicative of genuine feeling for containing some reflex of that peculiar aptitude of mind
which she displays in the Trial Scene.　There she is methodical amidst all her excitement of anxiety for the honour of her husband. . . . . Though the appeals by which she
endeavours to make the Jew relent are characterized by an observance of formal argument, we should remember that she is all the while actuated by intense solicitude in the
utterance of these appeals.

MRS F. A. KEMBLE (*Atlantic Monthly*, June, 1876): I chose Portia, then as now
my ideal of a perfect woman,—

> ' The noble woman nobly planned,
> ' To warn, to comfort, and command;
> ' The creature not too bright or good
> ' For human nature's daily food ;
> ' For transient sorrows, simple wiles,
> ' Praise, blame, love, kisses, tears, and smiles ;'

the wise, witty woman, loving with all her soul, and submitting with all her heart to a
man whom everybody but herself (who was the best judge) would have judged her
inferior; the laughter-loving, light-hearted, true-hearted, deep-hearted woman, full of
keen perception, of active efficiency, of wisdom prompted by love, of tenderest unselfishness, of generous magnanimity; noble, simple, humble, pure; true, dutiful, religious,
and full of fun; delightful above all others, the woman of women.

HUDSON (p. 65): Being to act for once the part of a man, it would seem hardly possible for her to go through the undertaking without more of self-confidence than were
becoming in a woman; and the student may find plenty of matter for thought in the
Poet's so managing as to prevent such an impression.　For there is nothing like osten-
tation or conceit of intellect in Portia.　Though knowing enough for any station, still
it never once enters her head that she is too wise for the station which Providence or
the settled order of society has assigned her. . . . . Portia's consciousness of power does
indeed render her cool, collected, and firm, but never a whit unfeminine; her smooth
command both of herself and of the matter she goes about rather heightens our sense
of her modesty than otherwise; so that the impression we take from her is, that these
high mental prerogatives are of no sex; that they properly belong to the common free-

hold of woman and man. Some of her speeches, especially at the trial, are evidently premeditated; for, as any good lawyer would do, she of course prepares herself in the case beforehand; but I should like to see the masculine lawyer that could premeditate anything equal to them.

(P. 68.) How nicely Shakespeare discriminates things that really differ, so as to present in all cases the soul of womanhood, without a particle of effeminacy! and how perfectly he reconciles things that seem most diverse, pouring into his women all the intellectual forces of the other sex, without in the least impairing or obscuring their womanliness!—all this is not more rare in poetry than it is characteristic of his workmanship. Thus Portia is as much superior to her husband in intellect, in learning, and accomplishment, as she is in wealth; but she is none the less womanly for all that. Nor, which is more, does she ever on that account take the least thought of inverting the relation between them. In short, her mental superiority breeds no kind of social displacement, nor any desire of it. Very few of the Poet's men are more highly charged with intellectual power. While she is acting the lawyer in disguise, her speech and bearing seem to those about her in the noblest style of manliness. . . . . Yet to us, who are in the secret of her sex, all the proprieties, all the inward harmonies of her character, are exquisitely preserved.

LADY MARTIN (*Shakespeare's Female Characters*, 1885, p. 30 *et seq.*): To know how Portia has been able to accomplish [the rescue of Bassanio's friend] we must go back to her youth. I think of her as the cherished child of a noble father,—a father proud of his child's beauty, and of the promise which he sees in her of rare gifts, both of mind and heart. These gifts he spares no pains to foster. He is himself no ordinary man. He anticipates the danger to which the beautiful and wealthy heiress may be exposed; and it was by one of those 'good inspirations' which, as Nerissa says, 'holy men have at their death,' that he fixed upon the device of the three caskets, 'whereof who chooses his meaning chooses' his beloved daughter. From the first his aim has been to train her to succeed him in his high position. With this view he has surrounded her with all that is beautiful in art and ennobling in study, and placed her in the society of scholars, poets, soldiers, statesmen, the picked and noblest minds of her own and other lands. Amid this throng of honoured guests, not the least honoured, we may be sure, was the learned 'cousin, Dr Bellario.' This cousin of hers we may suppose to have been a constant visitor at princely Belmont, and, indeed, to have been her instructor in jurisprudence, a not unfitting branch of the future heiress of Belmont's education. One can imagine how the girl Portia would rush to him for help in her youthful perplexities. Perhaps they have, even in these early days, 'turned over many books together.' Her father may have seen with pleased surprise the bias of her mind toward such studies; and this, as well as her affection for her learned teacher, may have led him to take her to some of the famous trials of the day, so that when her own hour of trial comes, when heart and head must alike be strong, and her self-possession is taxed to the uttermost, she knows at least the forms of the court, and through no technical ignorance would be likely to betray herself. If this were not so, how could she, however assured of her power to overcome the Jew, have dared to venture into the presence of such an assembly as that 'great court of Venice,' where any failure would have been disastrous, not merely to herself, but to Bellario?

. . . . During the time, brief as it can be made, of the preparations for the marriage ceremony, Portia will have heard all the particulars of the 'merry bond;' she will have discovered that money alone, however squandered, cannot shake the obdurate Jew's determination. Accustomed by her peculiar training to look with a judicial mind upon serious matters, she, after many questionings about its terms, hits by a happy instinct, as I believe, upon the flaw in the bond. She will say nothing of this to Bassanio, but hurries him away with her wealth to use as his own; and then herself hastens towards Venice, after despatching a messenger to Bellario with a letter informing him of her approach, as well as of her belief that she has found a flaw in the bond, and requesting his presence at the trial. We find her before her departure in the brightest spirits, feeling virtually assured of success, and even jesting in her new happiness with Nerissa. This state of mind, it appears to me, could not have been possible had Portia known what was before her. She is at ease, because she is sure of the full sympathy of her friend and cousin, Bellario, and counts with confidence on his presence in Venice to take the lead in court.

In the play we see that Portia sends Balthazar to Dr Bellario, and bids him wait for her at 'the traject.' But either her mind must have changed, or she must have met messengers from Bellario on the road, who tell her of his illness and inability to help her in person. Consequently she hurries on to Padua; but when they meet—for that they do meet is certain—all her first joyful anticipations receive a woeful shock. She finds her dear old friend grievously sick. What is to be done? There is no help near; no time to be lost! The Jew 'plies the Duke at morning and at night.' Bellario's aid, she learns, has been summoned already by the Duke as a last resource. In this extremity, with no other help at hand, Bellario no doubt proposes that Portia shall go in his stead, recommended by him as a 'young Doctor of Rome,' then visiting him. This must be done or all is lost. Bellario confirms her belief as to a flaw in the bond, and furnishes her with his 'own opinion' upon all the points of law most vital to the question. They 'turn o'er many books together,' and Portia proceeds to Venice furnished, as Bellario writes to the Duke, with the Doctor's opinion, 'which, bettered with his own learning (the greatness whereof I cannot enough commend), goes with him, at my importunity, to fill up your Grace's request in my stead.' All this suggests to me that Portia's eye had been the first to see the flaw in the bond, and that her own impression had been confirmed by the great lawyer.

Grave and anxious must have been her thoughts as she crossed the lagoons by 'the common ferry that trades to Venice.' Hers was not a mind, however, to shrink before difficulty; and, confirmed as she had been by the opinion of the great Doctor of Laws, she feels sure of success, if she can but be true to herself and 'forget she is a woman.' All the gay light-heartedness with which she started from Belmont has vanished under this unexpected aspect of affairs. With what trepidation, with what anxious sense of responsibility must she find herself engaged in such a task, the mark for every eye! Nothing but her deep love and grateful happy heart could sustain her through such a trial. To cease to be a woman for the time is not so hard, perhaps, to one who has all her life been accustomed to a position of command and importance; but, in the peculiar circumstances of this case, the effort must have been one of extreme difficulty.

[If the desire assail us to knit up the ravell'd sleave of Portia's early life, we must not forget the gay and pretty web that MRS COWDEN-CLARKE has woven in her *Girlhood of Shakespeare's Heroines.*—ED.]

NERISSA

MRS JAMESON (p. 104): Nerissa is a good specimen of a common genus of characters; she is a clever, confidential waiting-woman, who has caught a little of her lady's elegance and romance; she affects to be lively and sententious, falls in love, and makes her favour conditional on the fortune of the caskets, and, in short, mimics her mistress with good emphasis and discretion. Nerissa and the gay, talkative Gratiano are as well matched as the incomparable Portia and her magnificent and captivating lover.

JESSICA

C. A. BROWN (p. 280): I cannot see that Jessica is intellectual or kind-hearted. Her eulogy on Portia, appropriately dashed with her new-fledged piety, is elegantly cold, like a dedication; and her classical moonlight talk with Lorenzo, though very elegant, has nothing to do with the affections, and is more a proof of ready wit and a good education than of intellect.

Jessica, the pretty Jewess,—I beg pardon, 'Mistress Lorenzo,' the Christian, —has her character, such as it is, hit off by a few masterly strokes. Beauty is her best recommendation. I imagine she is small of stature; a little plump, with a delicate hand and foot, and remarkable for a well-turned ankle. Her eye is full and lustrous; there is great richness in her lips, especially when she smiles; she has a profusion of glossy black ringlets; and there is a touch of slyness in addition to her native expression of countenance. To these charms, she possesses, we know, an arch and pleasant style of chatting, well suited to the hours of dalliance. Here she is at home; even more than when she talks with her 'merry devil' Launcelot. But when she has to speak as a lady, which she seldom attempts, we perceive a constraint, arising from her former recluse life, and perhaps from a poorness in her ideas where her inclinations are not her prompters. . . . . When at Belmont she speaks of her father as of a person in whose company she once happened to be; the first words, 'When I was with him,' are painfully unfeeling to those inclined to sympathize for a father whom she has robbed; but there were none such in the company, because the man was a Jew, and she knew that opinion was in her favour. With one of firmer intellect, even in those days, fashion would not have confounded wrong with right; but Jessica was born to be cajoled by fashion. She could lose 'fourscore ducats at a sitting,' and exchange a turquoise ring for a monkey, as unconcernedly as she stole them from a Jew, because she could reconcile them all to the fashion of the day.

GILES (p. 147): Shakespeare has done the grandest justice to this elemental force of affection in woman's nature. He presents it to us in every mode of beauty and truth. In his less serious plays, all the characters whom he intends for lovable have not only graces and charms, but natural femininely sensibilities. One exception there is,—which not even Shakespeare can make me like,—and that is the pert, disobedient hussy Jessica. Her conduct I regard as in a high degree reprehensible; and those who have the care of families must, I think, feel as I do. She was a worthless minx, and I have no good word to say of her. If the fellow who ran away with her had, like old Pepys, left a diary behind him, I am quite sure that we should learn that his wife turned out an intolerable vixen. She selfishly forgot the duty of a daughter when she should have most remembered it. Why should she, a maiden of Israel, leave her poor old father, Shylock, alone in the midst of his Christian enemies? What if he was wrong? The more need he had of *her*. What if most wrong? Even then, even in the madness of defeated vengeance, in the misery of humbled pride, when regarded as most guilty, when there was nothing in the world for him but contempt without pity, the child of his home—his only child—should have had in her woman's heart a shelter for her scorned father. But was she not a good girl? Did she not turn Christian? Well, as to her turning Christian, I view the matter as honest Gobbo did; it merely increased the number of pork-eaters. Besides, she turned Christian for a husband. Changes of religion *for* husbands, or *with* them, may do for the children of kings; it is not to be commended in the children of the people.

HUDSON (p. 62): Jessica's elopement, in itself and its circumstances, puts us to the alternative that either she is a bad child or Shylock is a bad father. And there is enough to persuade us of the latter; though not in such sort but that some share of the reproach falls to her. For if a young woman have so bad a home as to justify her in thus deserting and robbing it, the atmosphere of the place can hardly fail to leave *some* traces in her temper and character.

ANTONIO

REV. JOHN HUNTER (*Introductory Remarks*, Longmans' Series, London, 1872, p. xiv): Antonio is a good man,—a man whom we love for his high integrity, his disinterested liberality, his devoted friendship; but his rashness in signing the bond suggested to the dramatist the propriety of characterizing him as deficient in worldly prudence, and too easy and unwary in his dealings with mankind. It was certainly through simplicity, though not what Shylock calls 'low simplicity,' that Antonio condemned interest; it was through simplicity that he thought lightly of the condition stipulated in the bond; he was imprudent in allowing himself to forget, or in failing to exert himself that he might be prepared for, the day of payment; he was incautious in venturing the whole of his wealth in argosies upon the ocean. That he was a rich merchant we may suppose to have been owing more to patrimonial inheritance than to his own mercantile sagacity and success. That he should be found unable, though a wealthy man, to lend three thousand ducats, was necessary to give occasion for the bond; and the inability is made to arise out of that incautiousness by which Shakespeare has so consistently characterized him.

BASSANIO

W. W. LLOYD (*Critical Essay*, Singer's 2d ed., 1856, p. 546): In coarser terms, from a less favourable point of view, Bassanio has lived like a prodigal, run in debt with his friends, and now coolly proposes to his chief creditor to make a serious addition to his debt, on the speculation that it will give him a chance to pay all by that very precarious, as well as undignified, resort of making up to an heiress. How is it that in reading the play we never withdraw our sympathies from the hero of transactions that affect us in common life with the unpleasant associations of dissipation, imprudence, impudence, and meanness? The reason, I apprehend, is partly because we are reading a romance, and we accept the compatibility of whatever phenomena the poet chooses to group in the moral as in the material world. Portia has faith that the lottery of the caskets will give her infallibly the husband who deserves her, and we are not disposed to check agreeable sympathy with the generous liberality, in mind and purse, of the Merchant of Venice by any mistrust, shabby it would seem to us, of the desert of his friends or the co-operation of natural chances with his free intentions. Character gives confidence; truth is bondsman for troth. We believe Bassanio on the same ground that Antonio does; we approve of the consent of Antonio on the same grounds that made Bassanio think it not wrong to ask it. The character of an act or a proceeding is founded at last on the motive, and the motive is the man, and poetry and romance are allowed to invent perfections of humanity that may yet be unattainable; and thus in a poetic drama we admire and sympathize with a debt-burdened suitor to a wealthy lady, because there is no moral impossibility in the nature of things, of such a suit, even when the contingencies of dowry are recognized, being in truth unsordid,—though, practically speaking, it will usually be a fool who allows himself, or herself, to think it can be otherwise. In brief, we look on with unhesitating, unalarmed confidence in the power of a pure spirit of unselfishness to pass untainted through the very dens and haunts of selfishness, and to vindicate its purity in a transaction which only selfishness makes wrong. Soundness at heart in a recipient makes imprudence prudent, and our faith is made happy when Bassanio, who has nothing either to give or hazard, chooses the casket of least promising exterior. . . . . Even in setting forth his project to Antonio, the leading tone of his description makes her wealth but one accessory of her attractions, and, as a lover should, he passes on with more fervour to observe—' and she is fair,' and yet again to the crowning praise which no lover of Portia could overlook and be worthy,—' and fairer than that word, of wondrous virtues.' Hence we confide most absolutely in the ingenuousness of Bassanio, and if he appears to engage his friend somewhat inconsiderately to a bond, or even to the merest transaction with Shylock, we are prepared to ascribe this to the eagerness of a lover who has such cause to love as encouragement from Portia.

GRATIANO

CHARLES COWDEN-CLARKE (*Shakespeare-Characters; Chiefly those Subordinate,* 1863, p. 402): Gratiano is a most delightful and most natural character. He is one of those useful men in society who will keep up the ball of mirth and good-humour, simply by his own mercurial temperament and agreeable rattle; for he is like a babbling woodside brook, seen through at once, and presenting every ripple of its surface to the sunbeams of good-fellowship. If a picnic were proposed, Gratiano would be the man for the commissariat department; and the wines shall be unimpeachable in quantity as well as quality; the ladies shall lack no squire of dames, and the men no stimulus to keep their gallantry from rusting. And, what is better than all, if a friend be in adversity, Gratiano will champion him with good words and deeds, if not with the most sagacious counsel. He would no doubt talk a man off his legs; and, therefore, Shakespeare brings him as a relief against the grave men, Antonio and Bassanio, who, being both anxious on account of worldly cares, resent his vivacity, and they are at all events as peevish as he is flippant and inconsiderate. Bassanio says of Gratiano, that he 'speaks an infinite deal of nothing.' The best of it is, that Bassanio himself advances no claim to be the censor of his lively companion; for, in comparison with him, he is dull in capacity; and the very observation just quoted follows one of the most agreeable and sensible speeches in the play, made by 'the infinite-deal-of-nothing' Gratiano. Shakespeare has made the best apology for the Merchant and his friend; but his own love of cheerfulness with good temper could not fail to throw liberally into Gratiano's scale, and he has nowhere produced a better defence of natural vivacity. Moreover, he has not made Gratiano selfishly boisterous, indulging his own feelings only; he first manifests a solicitude for Antonio's lowness of spirits, and then he rallies him. These are the small and delicate lights thrown into his characters that render them exhaustless as studies, and give us that indefinable, rather, perhaps, that unrecognized and unconscious, interest in all they say and do, and which, to the same extent, appears to be the almost undivided prerogative of Shakespeare alone.

LAUNCELOT

C. A. BROWN (p. 281): My notion of Launcelot, as I have seen him, has not been reflected from the stage. 'The patch is kind enough;' yet he is amazingly wrapped up in himself, and his soliloquies are intense on that darling subject. An obtrusive fea‧ture in his character is the conceit in his skull that he is better than he should be. Having been called by one who did not see him 'master' and 'young gentleman,' he insists, over and over again, on his being 'young master Launcelot,' and at last styles himself 'the young gentleman.' All this, like everything he says, is a mixture of vanity and drollery,—on the latter he stakes his fame as a wit. Nature never formed a more egregious coxcomb,—he is Lord Foppington in low life, as far as his imbecility can reach. In the same strain he talks of his 'manly spirits' and of the Jew's having 'done him wrong,' as if he and his master were on an equality. No doubt his solace as a servant was, that he must, sooner or later, owing to his intrinsic merit, come to excellent fortune. He spells his fate on his palm; where, though neither coronet nor mastership offers itself to his imagination, there is something of equal value to the young animal,—'eleven widows, and nine maids, is a simple coming-in for one man.' His jokes are generally failures, but, coming from him, they are laughable. . . . . [The banter between him and Lorenzo gives the latter occasion to observe], 'How every fool can play upon a word!' which, together with what follows, may be mistaken for a self-condemnation, made at hazard, on the part of Shakespeare. By no means; the difficulty is to play well upon a word; besides, as Launcelot then and afterwards proves, the poverty of a jest may be enriched in a fool's mouth, owing to the complacency with which he deals it out; and because there are few things which provoke laughter more than feebleness in a great attempt at a small matter.

GERMAN CRITICISMS

A. W. SCHLEGEL (vol. ii, p. 169): *The Merchant of Venice* is one of Shakespeare's most perfect works: popular to an extraordinary degree, and calculated to produce the most powerful effect on the stage, and at the same time a wonder of ingenuity and art for the reflecting critic. Shylock the Jew is one of the inconceivable master-pieces of characterization of which Shakespeare alone furnishes us with examples. It is easy for the poet and the player to exhibit a caricature of national sentiments, modes of speaking, and gestures. Shylock, however, is everything but a common Jew; he possesses a very determinate and original individuality, and yet we perceive a light touch of Judaism in everything which he says and does. We imagine we hear a sprinkling of the Jewish pronunciation in the mere written words, as we sometimes still find it in the higher classes, notwithstanding their social refinement. In tranquil situations what is foreign to the European blood and Christian sentiments is less perceivable, but in passion the national stamp appears more strongly marked. All these inimitable niceties the finished art of a great actor can alone properly express. . . . . The letter of the law is Shylock's idol; he refuses to lend an ear to the voice of mercy, which speaks to him from the mouth of Portia with heavenly eloquence; he insists on severe and inflexible justice, and it at last recoils on his own head. Here he becomes a symbol of the general history of his unfortunate nation. . . . . The danger that hangs over Antonio till towards the conclusion of the Fourth Act, and which the imagination is almost afraid to approach, would fill us with too painful an anxiety if the poet did not also provide for our entertainment and dissipation. This is particularly effected by the Scenes at the country-seat of Portia, which transport the spectator into quite another sphere. And yet they are closely connected, by the concatenation of causes and effects, with the main business: the preparations of Bassanio for his courtship are the cause of Antonio's subscribing the dangerous bond; and Portia again, by means of the advice of her cousin, a celebrated counsel, effects the safety of the friend of her lover. But the relations of the dramatic composition are still here admirably observed in another manner. The trial between Shylock and Antonio, though it proceeds like a real event, still remains an unheard-of and particular case. Shakespeare has, consequently, associated with it a love-intrigue not less extraordinary; the one becomes natural and probable by means of the other. A rich, beautiful, and clever heiress, who can only be won by the solving of a riddle; the locked caskets; the foreign princes who come to try the adventure; with all this wonderful splendour the imagination is powerfully excited. The two Scenes in which the Prince of Morocco, in the language of Eastern hyperbole, and the self-conceited Prince of Arragon, make their choice of the caskets, merely raise our curiosity and give employment to our wits; in the Third Act, where the two lovers stand trembling before the inevitable choice, which in one moment must unite or separate them for ever, Shakespeare has lavished all the seductions of feeling, all the magic of poetry. We share in the rapture of Portia and Bassanio at the fortunate choice; we easily conceive why they are fond of each other, for they are both deserving of love. The Trial Scene, with which the Fourth Act is occupied, is alone a perfect drama, concentrating in itself the interest of the whole. The knot is now untied, and according to the common ideas of theatrical satisfaction, the curtain might drop. But the poet was unwilling to dismiss his audience with the gloomy impressions which the delivery of Antonio, accomplished with so much difficulty, contrary to all expectation, and the punishment of Shylock, were calculated to leave behind; he has, therefore, added the Fifth Act by way of a musical after-piece in the piece itself.

ULRICI (*Shakespeare's Dramatic Art*, ii, p. 121, Bohn's Ed. 1876, trans. by L. Dora Schmitz): As regards the lawsuit between Antonio and the Jew, there can, as I think, be scarcely any doubt that its meaning and significance coincide with the old legal maxim: *Summum jus summa injuria*. Every one who knows the maxim and its legal significance will unconsciously, when witnessing the celebrated Trial Scene, be struck with its applicability here. For the maxim merely maintains that an acknowledged and positive law turns into its opposite and becomes a wrong when carried to the extreme point of its limited nature and one-sided conception, and when driven to its extreme consequence. Shylock holds fast to the law: forbearance, gentleness, kindliness, and all the lovely names which greet the happy on the threshold of life and accompany them on their paths, he has never known; injustice, harshness, and contempt stood around his cradle, hate and persecution obstructed every step of his career. With convulsive vehemence, therefore, he clutches hold of the law, the small morsel of justice which cannot be withheld even from the Jew. This legal, formal, external justice Shylock obviously has on his side, but by taking and following it to the letter, in absolute one-sidedness, he falls into the deepest, foulest wrong, which then necessarily recoils ruinously upon his own head. The same view of the dialectic and double-edged nature of justice, which is here set forth in its utmost subtilty, is, however, I think, also exhibited in manifold lights and shades throughout the other parts of the play. The determination of Portia's father, which deprives her of all participation in the choice of a husband, is indeed based upon paternal right, but this very right —even though justified by the best intentions of anxious affection—is again, at the same time a decided wrong, and Portia has good reason for complaining: 'O, these naughty times Put bars between the owners and their rights.' Who would have cast a stone at her had she broken her vow, and guided her well-beloved, amiable, and worthy lover by hints and intimations in making the right choice? The wrong, which is here again contained within what is in itself right, would have fallen with tragic force, had not accident—in the form of a happy thought, as in the lawsuit—led to a happy result. Jessica's flight and her marriage in opposition to her father's will is, according to generally recognized principles, a flagrant wrong. And yet, who would condemn her for withdrawing herself from the power and rights of such a father, of whom she is justly ashamed, and to obey whom truly is a matter of impossibility to her conscience and to her innocent heart? Here, again, therefore, we find a point of right at strife with the demands of morality and asserting itself emphatically; Shakespeare himself brings it forward clearly enough in Act II, Sc. iii, and still more so in Act III, Sc. v, in the conversations between Launcelot and Jessica. The penalty which the Court imposes upon the Jew, and by which he is compelled to sanction the marriage of his daughter with Lorenzo, also neutralizes the conflicting elements more in an external and accidental manner than by true and internal adjustment. Lastly, right and wrong are no less carried to their extreme points, and consequently placed in a balancing state of uncertainty, in the quarrel between the two loving couples about the rings which they had parted with, in violation of their sworn promises—a scene with which the play closes. Here, again, we have a sufficiently distinct reflex of the maxim, *Summum jus summa injuria ;* here again right and wrong are brought to such straits, are driven to such extremes, that the two are no longer distinct, but pass over directly one into the other. Thus we see that the meaning and significance of the many, apparently, heterogeneous elements are united in one point: they are but variations of the same theme.

(P. 126.) Shakespeare, as I think, has clearly enough intimated that he does not in any way consider Shylock a tragic character. Shylock's conduct, in general, makes rather a decidedly comic impression, and particularly in the scene of the outburst of his sorrow and rage at the elopement of his daughter and the loss of his ducats, which alternates in the sharpest contrast with his diabolical expressions of joy at the losses experienced by Antonio. His very behaviour at the Trial Scene has somewhat the flavour of comedy, because his whole being, his appearance, his manner of expressing himself in word and gesture, are obviously described intentionally in such a way as always to verge upon caricature. And if the punishment which overtakes him is, nevertheless, offensive to our finer feelings, we must bear in mind that the scene of the play is laid in the sixteenth century, and that Shylock forfeits our pity owing to his inhuman, almost devilish, wickedness and hardness of heart, and has lost all claim to humane treatment. Moreover, owing to the desultory, irregular manner in which the sentence is pronounced, we feel that it is doubtful whether all the points will be strictly adhered to.

GERVINUS (*Commentaries,* vol. i, p. 326; trans. by Miss F. E. Bunnett, 1863): We could after our own fashion say in a more abstract and pretentious form, that the intention of the poet in *The Merchant of Venice* was to depict the relation of man to property. The more commonplace this might appear, the more worthy of admiration is that which Shakespeare, in his embodiment of this subject, has accomplished with extraordinary, profound, and poetic power.

(P. 329.) Thus has Shakespeare, in the poem before us, represented a genuine brotherhood between the pictures he sets forth of avarice and prodigality, of hard usury and inconsiderate extravagance, so that the piece may just as well be called a song of true friendship.

(P. 333.) Portia is superior to all circumstances; that is her highest praise: she would have accommodated herself to any husband, for this reason her father might have felt himself justified in prescribing the lottery.

(P. 334.) Between both, Portia and Antonio, stands Bassanio, the friend of one, the lover of the other, utterly poor between two boundlessly rich, ruined in his circumstances, inconsiderate, extravagant at the expense of his friend. He seems quite to belong to the parasitical class of Antonio's friends. In disposition he is more inclined to the merry Gratiano than to Antonio's severe gravity; he appears on the stage with the question: 'When shall we laugh?' and he joins with his frivolous companions in all cheerful and careless folly. This time he borrows once more three thousand ducats, to make a strange Argonautic expedition for the Golden Fleece, staking them on a blind adventure, the doubtful wooing of a rich heiress. His friend breaks his habit of never borrowing on credit; he enters into an agreement with the Jew upon the bloody condition, and the adventurer accepts the loan with the sacrifice. And before he sets forth, even on the same day and evening, he purchases fine livery for his servants with this money, and gives a merry feast as a farewell, during which the daughter of the invited Jew is to be carried off by one of the free-thinking fellows. Is not the whole, as if he were only the seeming friend of this rich man, that he might borrow his money, and only the seeming lover of this rich lady, that he might pay his debts with her money?

(P. 336.) When Bassanio perceives the portrait he divines indeed his happiness, but he ventures not yet to hope it, and, in spite of his agitation, he seems absorbed only with the work of art.

(P. 339.) Shylock is the contrast, which we hardly need explain; although indeed, in this age of degeneration of art and morals, lowness and madness could go so far as to make a martyr on the stage of this outcast of humanity. The poet has certainly given to this character, in order that he may not sink quite below our interest, a perception of his pariah condition, and has imputed his outbursts of hatred against Christians and aristocrats partly to genuine grounds of annoyance. Moreover, he has not delineated the usurer from the hatred of the Christians of that time against all that was Jewish, else he would not have imparted to Jessica her lovely character.

(P. 342.) Thus delicately feminine, Jessica has no scruples of conscience to steal herself the ducats and the jewels of her father. A new relation to possession it brought to view in this nature; it is that of the inexperienced child, who is quite unacquainted with the value of money, who innocently throws it away in trifles, having learned in her paternal home neither domestic habits nor economy. In this, Lorenzo is only too congenial with her, although he would have her believe that he was as a man what Portia is as a woman; Antonio, who knows them better, takes both under his guardianship, and manages their inheritance for them.

HEINE (*Sämmtliche Werke*, Philadelphia, 1856, vol. v, p. 324): When I saw this Play at Drury Lane, there stood behind me in the box a pale, fair Briton, who at the end of the Fourth Act, fell to weeping passionately, several times exclaiming, 'The poor man is wronged!' It was a face of the noblest Grecian style, and the eyes were large and black. I have never been able to forget those large and black eyes that wept for Shylock!

When I think of those tears I have to rank *The Merchant of Venice* with the Trag-

29

edies, although the frame of the Piece is decorated with the merriest figures of Masks, of Satyrs, and of Cupids, and the Poet meant the Play for a Comedy. Shakespeare intended perhaps, for the amusement of 'the general,' to represent a tormented Were-wolf, a hateful, fabulous creature that thirsts for blood, and of course loses his daughter and his ducats, and is ridiculed into the bargain. But the genius of the Poet, the Genius of Humanity that reigned in him, stood ever above his private will; and so it happened that in Shylock, in spite of all his uncouth grimacings, the Poet vindicates an unfortunate sect, which, for mysterious purposes, has been burdened by Providence with the hate of the rabble both high and low, and has reciprocated this hate—not always by love.

But what do I say? The genius of Shakespeare rises above the little squabble of two religious sects, and the Drama shows us neither Jew nor Christian exclusively, but oppressor and oppressed, and the mad, bitter exultation of the latter when they can pay back to their haughty tormentors with interest the shames they have suffered. There is not the slightest trace in this Play of a religious difference, and Shakespeare shows us in Shylock only a man whom Nature bids to hate his enemy, as in Antonio and his friends the Poet by no means describes the followers of that Divine teaching which commands us to love our enemies. When Shylock says to the man who wants to bor-row money of him, 'Still have I borne it with a patient shrug,' &c., Antonio replies, 'I am as like to call thee so again, to spet on thee again, to spurn thee too.'

Where here is the love of a Christian? Verily, it would have been a satire on Christianity had Shakespeare meant to represent it in the persons who are enemies to Shylock, and who are hardly worthy to unloose the latchets of his shoes. The bank-rupt, Antonio, is a poor-spirited creature, without energy, without strength enough to hate, or, of course, to love, with the heart of a worm, whose flesh is really worth nothing else but 'to bait fish withal.' He never pays back the three thousand ducats to the cheated Jew. Bassanio, too, never returns him his money, and the fellow is a down-right 'fortune-hunter,' as an English critic calls him; he borrows money to 'show a more swelling port' with, and to capture a rich heiress and a fat marriage-portion.

As for Lorenzo, he is an accomplice in a most infamous burglary, and under Prussian laws he would have been condemned to fifteen years in the penitentiary, and to be branded, and to stand in the pillory, for all his sensibility to the alluring charms, not only of stolen ducats and jewels, but of moonlit landscapes and of music. As to the other noble Venetians who appear on the scene as the comrades of Antonio, they do not seem to hate money very much, and for their poor friend, when he is in ill luck, they have nothing but words, coined air. Our good pietist, Franz Horn, here makes the very watery, but very correct, remark : 'The question very reasonably occurs : How was it possible that Antonio could be reduced to such a condition? All Venice knew and esteemed him; his good acquaintance knew all about the terrible bond, and that the Jew would not remit a tittle of it. Nevertheless, they let day after day pass, until at last the three months are over, and with them all hope of deliverance.' It would have been easy enough for those good friends, whole troops of whom the princely mer chant appears to have had around him, to contribute the sum of three thousand ducats to save a human life—and such a life! but anything of that sort would have been rather inconvenient, and so nothing, nothing whatever, is done by these dear, good friends, just because they are only so-called friends, or, if you please, only half or three-quarters friends. They pity the excellent merchant who gave them such fine dinners, uncommonly, but with due regard to their own ease they denounce Shylock, as only heart and tongue can when no danger is involved, and then probably think they have fulfilled the duty of friendship. Much as we must hate Shylock, we can hardly blame him if he has, as he well may have, a little contempt for these people. . . . .

In truth, with the exception of Portia, Shylock is the most respectable person in the whole Play. He loves money, he does not hide this love—he cries it out aloud in the marketplace, but there is something that he prizes above money; satisfaction for a tortured heart—righteous retribution for unutterable shames; and although they offer him the borrowed sum tenfold, he rejects it, and the three thousand, ay and ten times three thousand, ducats he would not regret if he can but buy a pound of his enemy's flesh therewith.

Ay, Shylock does indeed love money, but there are things which he loves still more, among them his daughter, 'Jessica, my girl.' Although he curses her in his rage, and would see her dead at his feet with the jewels in her ears and the ducats in the coffin, he loves her more than ducats and jewels. Debarred from public intercourse, out cast from Christian society, and thrust back upon a narrow domestic life, to the poor Jew there remains only devotion to his home, and this is manifested in him with the most touching intensity. When in the Trial Scene, Bassanio and Gratiano declare their readiness to sacrifice their wives for their friend, Shylock says to himself, not aloud, but aside : 'These be the Christian husbands; I have a daughter; Would any of the stock of Barrabas Had been her husband, rather than a Christian!'

Upon this passage, upon these few words spoken aside, we base the sentence of condemnation that we must pass on the fair Jessica. It was no unloving father whom she forsook, whom she robbed, whom she betrayed.—Shameful treachery! She even makes common cause with the enemies of Shylock, and when at Belmont they say all manner of evil things about him, Jessica never casts down her eyes, her lips never lose colour, but she says the worst of her father.—Horrible fault! She has no heart, but only a light mind. She wearies of the secluded, 'sober' house of the embittered Jew, that seems to her at last a hell. She has an ear only for the stirring drum and wry-necked fife. Did Shakespeare intend here to pourtray a Jewess? In sooth, no. He paints only a daughter of Eve, one of those pretty birds who, as soon as they are fledged, flutter away to their dear little husbands. So Desdemona follows the Moor, so Imogen follows Posthumus. It is the way with woman. In Jessica there is observable a certain hesitating modesty, which she cannot overcome, at putting on boy's clothes. In this particular we may perhaps recognize a trait peculiar to her race, and which lends to its daughters so wonderful a charm. . . . .

(P. 332.) What Mrs Jameson says of Portia, contrasted with Shylock, is not only beautiful, it is true. If we regard the latter in the usual light as the representative of the stern Jew, hostile to all Art, Portia, on the contrary, represents that after-bloom of Greek Art which, in the 16th century, impregnated the world, from Italy out, with its delightful fragrance, and which we at the present day love and treasure under the name of 'the Renaissance.' Portia is at the same time the representative of the serene good fortune which is the opposite of the gloomy lot that Shylock represents. What a rosy bloom, what a ring of purity, is there in all her thoughts and speeches! How warm with joy are her words, how beautiful all her images, mostly borrowed from mythology! How sad, on the contrary, how incisive and repulsive, are the thoughts and speeches of Shylock, who uses only Old Testament similitudes! His wit is spasmodic, caustic; his metaphors he seeks among the most repulsive objects, and even his words are discords crashed together, shrill, hissing, acrid. As are the persons, so are their abodes. As we see how the servant of Jehovah, who will suffer in his 'sober house' the likeness neither of God nor of man, the created image of God, even stopping up the ears thereof, the casements, that into it the sounds of shallow foppery may not enter,—so we see, on the other hand, the costly, tasteful villeggiatura life in the beautiful palace at Belmont, where all is light and music, where, among pictures, marble statues, and lofty laurel trees, the suitors in their brilliant array wander, meditating on the love-riddle, and from amid all this splendour Signora Portia shines forth like a goddess, ' Her sunny locks Hanging on her temples.'

By such a contrast the two chief persons of the drama are so individualized that one might swear they are not the work of a poet's fancy, but real human beings, born of woman. Indeed, as neither time nor death can touch them, they are more alive than the ordinary creatures that Nature makes. The immortal blood, eternal poesy, pulsates in their veins. When thou comest to Venice and wanderest through the Doge's palace, thou knowest very well that neither in the Senate Chamber nor upon the Giant Stairs wilt thou meet Marino Faliero;—in the Arsenal thou wilt, 'tis true, be reminded of old Dandolo, but in none of the gilded galliots wilt thou seek the blind hero;—if thou seest at one corner of the street Santa a serpent hewn in stone, and at another corner the winged lion with the head of the serpent in his claws, there comes, perhaps, the remembrance of the proud Carmagnole, yet only for a moment; but, far more than of all such historical persons, thou thinkest in Venice of Shakespeare's Shylock, who is still alive, while those others have long mouldered away in the grave; and on the Rialto thine eye looks for him everywhere, and thou thinkest he must be found there, behind some pillar, in his Jewish gaberdine, with his cautious, calculating face, and every now and then thou fanciest that thou hearest his grating tones : ' Three thousand ducats,—well.'

At least I, wandering hunter after dreams that I am, I looked round everywhere on the Rialto to see if I could not find Shylock. I could have told him something that would have pleased him—namely, that his cousin, Herr von Shylock in Paris, had become the mightiest baron in Christendom, invested by her Catholic Majesty with that Order of Isabella which was founded to celebrate the expulsion of the Jews and Moors from Spain. But I found him nowhere on the Rialto, and I determined to seek my old acquaintance in the Synagogue. The Jews were just then celebrating their Day of Atonement, and they stood enveloped in their white talars, with uncanny motions of the head, looking almost like an assemblage of ghosts. There the poor Jews had stood, fasting and praying, from earliest morning;—since the evening before they had taken neither food nor drink, and had previously begged pardon of all their acquaintances for any wrong they might have done them in the course of the year, that God might thereby also forgive them their wrongs—a beautiful custom, which, curiously enough, is found among this people, strangers though they be to the teaching of Christ.

Although I looked all round the Synagogue, I nowhere discovered the face of Shylock. And yet I felt he must be hidden under one of those white talars, praying more fervently than his fellow-believers, looking up with stormy, nay frantic wildness, to the throne of Jehovah, the hard God-King! I saw him not. But towards evening, when, according to the Jewish faith, the gates of Heaven are shut, and no prayer can then obtain admittance, I heard a voice, with a ripple of tears that were never wept by eyes. It was a sob that could come only from a breast that held in it all the martyrdom which, for eighteen centuries, had been borne by a whole tortured people. It was the death-rattle of a soul sinking down dead tired at heaven's gates. And I seemed to know the voice, and I felt that I had heard it long ago, when, in utter despair, it moaned out, then as now, ' Jessica, my girl !'

HEBLER (*Shakespeare's Kaufmann von Venedig*, 1854, p. 66) cites the following words of Luther, which have been frequently quoted by subsequent German commentators (and they may be well cited again as an illustration of the intense prejudice against the Jews): 'Know, then, thou dear Christian, that, next to the Devil, thou canst have no bitterer, fiercer foe than a genuine Jew, one who is a Jew in earnest. The true counsel I give thee, is that fire be put to their synagogues, and that, over what will not burn up, the earth be heaped and piled, so that no stone or trace of them be seen for evermore.'

F. KREYSSIG (*Vorlesungen über Shakespeare*, Berlin, 1862, vol. iii, p. 358): To these two bizarre fables Shakespeare joins the principal incidents of a wanton tale of abduction from Masuccio di Salerno. He moulds into one the stories of the daughter of the King of Apulia and the bride of Gianetto, lets the suitors choose the caskets, devotes himself to the noble character of the merchant who sacrifices himself for his friend, takes the light, hot blood of Lorenzo and Jessica into the service of poetic justice,—and then lets the sun of his genius rise upon this chaos of odd entanglements and incredible fictions. Under its beams the sharp outlines of the Piece are softened into lines of beauty, contradictions are reconciled, the little poetic world gains its due proportions, its own perspective and colouring. The Actual is nowhere copied, and yet its inner, essential laws are not violated. The facts indeed belong to the fabulous; all the firmer and the more real is the soil out of which the motives and characters spring; and in applying ourselves to work through the ever-involved details to a point of view commanding the whole, we are compensated at every step for the difficulty of the journey by an abundance of single beauties. It is as if we were seeking the spot where we may see the whole, in some charming, thickly-overgrown park. The path leads us, by artificial windings, through green, fragrant woods. Lovely pictures open on the right and on the left, side-paths are lost in the shrubberies; flowers and fruits tempt us to linger and enjoy them. We have no fatigue, no weariness to fear, but we must take care to mark the way, lest in the beautiful labyrinth we miss our goal. But, metaphor aside, in few of his Pieces does Shakespeare play hide-and-seek with his readers and commentators as happily as here. The wisdom everywhere introduced, cropping out in the action and in the scenes, allures us, in a peculiar degree, to seek ever more curiously for a 'moral' in the Play.

(P. 367.) At the conclusion of Bassanio's choice the finely balanced character of Portia is fully shown in her exquisite address to her lover. Shakespeare here pourtrays the ideal woman, made for practical life, for lasting happiness, material and spiritual. She is neither the ethereal original of a higher, lost humanity, nor the alluring, deceitful form behind which a malignant fate lurks for its victim. Equally removed from the lofty beauty of a Urania and from the treacherous charm of a Pandora, Portia dwells in the happy medium, where spiritual and sensuous life unite in health, strength, and beauty. Juliet's enthusiastic heroism would be foreign to her. We may imagine that she would have cut short the Balcony Scene with some sharp witticism, unless, perhaps, she would have declined altogether to enjoy the night air except in congenial company. Wherein an Othello was lacking she would very soon have discovered, and Cassio might have relied upon a calm hearing. Even Shakespeare's choice heroes, Henry and Percy, would have had to mend their manners somewhat to stand before her refined taste. She is the personification of the fact that the finest ornament of social and domestic life, and its nobler moral well-being, are in the hands of woman, as it is hers, when she is not equal to that office, to destroy its bloom irrevocably. Portia tells the secret of woman's true, happy influence in the marriage state when she, the prudent, the cultivated, the much-wooed, gives herself up to the fortunate suitor with these words: '—— but the full sum of me Is sum of nothing, which to term in gross, Is an unlessoned girl,' &c. (III, ii.). And these words immediately find their full confirmation. Far removed from the false demand for exclusive devotion, her love keeps open eye and ear for duty, even though its summons should come at the most unseasonable hour. Her whole behaviour is a protest againt that comfortless idea of domestic virtue which sacrifices the respectability of husband and father, according to the degree of selfishness with which it postpones the claims of friendship and fatherland to the only business of increasing the *res familiaris*. Not for a moment does she hold back the husband she has just won from the duty he owes to his friend. She does even more. Exalted above all trivial considerations by the gravity of the occasion, she ventures to test her woman's wit in this deadly crisis. In her noble speech upon the blessedness of mercy the earnestness and tenderness of her woman's nature are profoundly impressive. But with her sound, practical sense she does not expect, by this poesy, to gain the victory in the hard world. As wise and keen as she is tender-hearted, she does not hesitate to fight the foe with his own weapons. And then,— surest sign of a sound understanding,—in the jubilee of success all excitement is toned down to the quiet grace of a genial, arch humour. A due sense of proportion is the groundwork of her character. This appears most emphatically in the conversation with Nerissa, in which, without any apparent necessity for it, Shakespeare engages her as she returns home from her successful enterprise: 'Nothing is good, I see, without respect.' And again: 'How many things by season season'd are To their right praise and true perfection!' This is a way of thinking essential to a healthy view of practical life. It completes here one of the most beautiful pictures of womanhood which the Poet has created, not exactly for its poetical and ideal charm, but for its true and harmonious development.

(P. 374.) In Lorenzo and Jessica we descend a step still lower. Here the humour breaks out into reckless excess. The whole relation between them could not but have appeared immoral and repulsive, if the Poet had not reconciled us to it æsthetically by two equally effective means which justify to our feelings the happy ending. First of all, this hot love, athirst only for pleasure, certainly violates the law. But it violates it by disregarding a blood-relationship which stands out in sharp contrast to the majesty of the law: Jessica has good reasons for feeling ashamed of being her father's child, and for calling herself a daughter of his blood, not of his heart. Her father's house has been a hell to her; later on, it becomes evident enough that she was a mere addition to the old man's money and wealth, perhaps only a burdensome addition. So, without scruple, she takes from that hell the stones with which to pave the way to her heaven. Only one trait has she inherited from her forefather, Jacob—practical sense. She knows excellently well that one cannot live on love alone, and she has evidently not been brought up to practise any extraordinary generosity. It is not without significance that Shakespeare puts into the mouth of Lorenzo, the bold child of fortune and pleasure, that fine praise of music, that sweet language of the heart, the mysterious tie binding together the world of thought and the world of feeling. Thus the haughty levity of the cavalier receives the consecration of Beauty, and the success which circumstances accord to his bold adventure is made poetically possible, although it is strictly without moral grounds.

(P. 381.) *The Merchant of Venice*, in our opinion, was written neither to glorify friendship, nor to condemn the usurer, nor, finally, to represent any moral idea, rich

and manifold as are the moral allusions which the thoughtful reader carries away with him, together with the æsthetic enjoyment of this work of Art. The essential and definite aspect of life here illustrated admonishes us that lasting success, sure, practical results can be secured only by a just estimate of things, by prudent use and calm endurance of given circumstances, equally far removed from violent resistance and cowardly concession. Strong feeling and clear, good sense hold the scales in the pervading character of the whole Drama; fortune helps the honest in so far as they boldly and wisely woo its favour; but rigid Idealism, although infinitely more amiable and estimable, shows itself as scarcely less dangerous than hard-hearted selfishness.

KARL ELZE (*Essays*, 1871; translated by Miss L. Dora Schmitz, London, 1874, p. 90): Shylock's relation to his daughter is a point where least can be said in his excuse. The ossification of his mind and feelings, his selfishness and bitterness, have also entered his family life, and, like corrosive acids, have eaten and destroyed it. While his co-religionists are wont to hold family ties in high estimation, and to keep their domestic life in a certain patriarchal holiness, so as to escape from the pressure of the outer world, Shylock, according to Jessica, makes his home a hell. He does not succeed in leaving harshness, avarice, hatred, and revenge out of doors, and in being gentle, kind, and generous within the bosom of his family; it is, indeed, an almost impossible task. Can the early death of his wife have contributed to this? But the remembrance of her attaches only to the turquoise which she has given him. If we may infer Shylock's conjugal love from his paternal love, there can be as little said of the one as of the other, and, consequently, we can scarcely suppose that had Leah lived longer she would have exercised a softening and ennobling influence upon her husband's character. His ducats, and his jewels, and the feeling of revenge against his Christian oppressors have so completely taken possession of his heart, that there is not even the smallest space left for conjugal or paternal love. Jessica is nothing to him but the keeper of his house and the guardian of his treasures. She leads the life of a prisoner; she is to shut the ears of the house, and, according to Oriental custom, is not allowed to put her head out of the window to gape at 'varnished' Christian fools, who are an abomination to her father. That she should possess any claim to the enjoyment of life Shylock never dreams; his withered soul never supposes that hers is expanding in youthful excitement and desire. Why does he not surround her life with at least such ornaments and finery as young girls are accustomed to regard as a great part of their happiness? Why does he not place her under the motherly care of a companion, instead of leaving her completely to herself at home while he goes about his money transactions? Why? From greed, selfishness, and hard-heartedness. The want of fatherly feeling on his part necessarily produces a want of filial feeling on hers. She indemnifies herself by a confidential relation with the servant, who is a kind-hearted creature and a merry devil ('the patch is kind enough,' says Shylock), and thus makes the domestic hell somewhat endurable; besides, he serves her as *postillon d'amour*.

(P. 105.) From the beginning Antonio has abused and ill-treated the Jew, but this is the only stain on his character. Otherwise he is distinguished by gentleness, benevolence, and kind-heartedness, and it cannot be conceived that his hatred of the Jew would amount to such cruelty, and this at the very moment when, in regard to the confiscation of the Jew's property, he gives an unmistakable proof of his generosity. His demand for the conversion arises, in all probability, from an entirely different motive, and we shall hardly err in seeking it in the general religious conviction of the Middle Ages, according to which none but believers in Christianity could partake of salvation and eternal blessedness. That the Jews are eternally lost is known even to Marlowe's Barabas, who says: 'I am a Jew, and therefore am I lost.' It is well known that this conviction rose to the belief that it was a meritorious work to assist the non-Christians to the blessings of Christianity, even against their own wish, by forcing them to become converts. From this point of view Antonio's demand and the Doge's action appear in a different light, and it is easily understood that they should regard the proposed conversion as a proof of mercy as well. They intended to save Shylock's soul from eternal perdition. There is no need of further discussion to show how this doctrine of the Romish Church contained the germ of the most terrible fanaticism, and how it went hand in hand with the fiercest hatred of Jews and heretics; proofs of this may be found in almost every page of the history of the Middle Ages. 'At the time of the great European persecution of the Jews, in the year 1349,' says Menzel in his *History of the Germans*, 'all the Jews in Strasburg who refused to kiss the crucifix, nine hundred in number, were burned on one huge pile of wood: the *Brandgasse* or *Rue Brû-lée* still bears its name in memory of this terrible scene. Only children were spared, and they were baptized before the eyes of their parents. Eleven hundred Jews escaped death by kissing the cross and becoming Christians.' The Jews, therefore, had only the choice between conversion and death, exactly as Shakespeare has shown in his play. The public of that day saw no objection to the enforced conversion, but rather found it quite correct, and considered it a merciful punishment. Those who found pleasure in Marlowe's *Jew of Malta* must have revelled in Shylock's despair and Gratiano's mockery. 'To undo a Jew is charity and not sin,' says Ithamore in Marlowe, at the end of the Fourth Act.

(P. 111.) If Shakespeare, from his broader and more tolerant religious standpoint, disapproved of the enforced conversion of Jews, why did he make it a condition in Shylock's case? The Jew might, of course, have come off with the fine only, even had it been heavier. The contrasts in the play, designed as a comedy, would then have been less harsh, and the stage effect would scarcely have been less. However, as has been said, Shakespeare considered a dramatic poem as a mirror, not a kaleidoscope; it is nowhere his custom to embellish or to suppress; he gives us the world and history as they are, even at the risk of every now and then resembling a naturalistic landscape-painter; nay, he possesses an undeniable predilection for sharp and definite outlines, even although they are not always within the confines of the beautiful. Moreover, his public wished above all things to see Shylock crushed, just as in Lessing's *Nathan* the Patriarch insists upon having the Jew burned. Nay, it seems questionable whether we ourselves would approve of a representation of the play in which the condition of baptism were omitted for once, by way of trial.

IBID. (*Shakespeare Jahrbuch*, 1873, vol. viii, p. 59): This drama is impregnated, in an inimitable manner, with a thoroughly Italian air, with an aroma of Italy, more readily felt than analyzed and defined. All is fresh and true to nature to a degree that cannot be surpassed. Byron, who considered it essential that the Poet should write from his own observation and experience, and could not himself write but upon this condition, although he lived several years in Venice never succeeded in attaining to this perfect truth to nature. Shakespeare, with incomparable art gives us slight allusions and hints, apparently insignificant particulars, which suggest trains of thought leading our sympathies in a certain way and giving the imagination a direction to a determined aim. By these means ·ve are transported, without being aware of it, completely into an Italian atmosphere, and in the Fifth Act into the enjoyment of an Italian night, which could not be more vivid were we actually there on the spot. We are led into the bustle of the Bourse on the Rialto, and we see in the distance the gondola which is bearing Jessica away with her lover. To appreciate the art and beauty of Shakespeare in this respect we have only to compare *The Merchant of Venice* and Ben Jonson's *Volpone*, the scene of which is also laid in Venice. Jonson shows a thorough knowledge of the Italian tongue and of Italian, and especially Venetian, manners and localities. He lays on the local colouring as thick as one's hand, but it is everywhere the work of a book-learned student aiming with evident self-satisfaction to display the learning patched up from books *ad hoc.* One sees the design throughout, and is put out of tune. Jonson imagines he is making his personages genuine Italians by making them speak a great deal, and wherever possible, in Italian phrases, about the institutions, manners, and localities of their native land. Thus we hear them tell, in a motley medley, of *Avocatori, Mercatori, Commendatori, Notario,* of the *Piazza San Mark, Zan Fritada, sforzato, ciarlitani, scartoccios,* the *mal caduco; vertigine* in the head, *moscadelli, unguento, osteria, Pantalone di Besogniosi, ragion del Stato, Procuratia,* the *Scrutineo, canaglia, tremorcordia, Signiory* of the *Sanita, saffi,* the *Forty,* the *Ten,* the *Lazaretto, Bolognian sausages, Piscaria,* the monastery of *San Spirito,* the grand *Canale,* &c.; all the Italian poets are introduced by name: *Petrarca, Tasso, Dante, Guarini, Ariosto, Aretin,* and *Cieco di Hadria*—'I have read them all,' says (in the name of the poet?) Lady Politick Would-be. Had Ben Jonson wished to be thoroughly logical, he should have gone a step further, and made his Italians speak Italian, as Chapman does in his *Alphonsus* with the German princess Hedwig. But, instead of this, they are often not true to their parts, betraying by their speech their acquaintance with the Cock-pit, with Smithfield Fair and Fleetstreet; the native sixpence is found (II, i) in one and the same line with the Italian *moccinigo* and *Bagatine,* which is a blunder from Jonson's own point of view; he should at least have avoided English local colour. It is, so to speak, the negative side of local colouring when the Poet uses nothing that in respect of the locality disturbs the illusion of the hearer or reader. Jonson's whole treatment is purely from the outside, wherein the Poet is lost in the Philologist, and it is remarkable that he could have reckoned upon the knowledge and intelligence of his Public; his hearers must have listened with open mouths; he ought to have furnished *Volpone,* as well as his *Masques,* with explanatory annotations. How utterly different is Shakespeare's way! Here and there he lets his characters still be English, although this is hardly observable in *The Merchant of Venice,* but he breathes into them Italian souls, Italian passion, Southern glow and enjoyment of life. While Shakespeare treats costume and scenery only incidentally, Jonson, especially in the scenes where English travellers are introduced, actually enlarges our knowledge of travelling as it was in his day. We learn that an English traveller had to have a 'license,' that he presented himself, as at this day, to my lord the Ambassador, that, above all things, he must 'have the languages,' such is the standing phrase; Sir Politick gives as the reason of his travelling to Venice that he wanted 'to learn the language' (II, i); we learn further that in Venice one must go about with a silver fork, and finally that Lady Would-be in Venice learned '*tires, fashions, and behaviour*' from the courtesans, just as at the present day the ugliest fashions are set by the Parisian demi-monde.

Such is Jonson's local colouring compared with Shakespeare's. One may safely say, that it would have been better in this respect, as in all else, for Jonson's poetry if he had had no more Greek and Latin—Italian included—than his friend Shakespeare.

Dr Bellario

TH. ELZE (*Shakespeare Jahrbuch*, 1878, xiii, 149): When in the *Pecorone* the much-married mistress of Belmonte, after the celebration of the marriage festivities, appears like a *Dea ex machinâ* in the disguise of a young judge fresh from his studies in Bologna, and saves poor Ansaldo from his mortal peril, we acquiesce in the old fairy tale, as it might almost be termed, without any demur. In *The Merchant of Venice*, on the contrary, according to our present ideas, a similar dénouement appears at first sight fantastic, unsatisfactory, nay, childish. The charming Portia, who becomes even before her wedding-night a 'grass widow,' suddenly conceives the girlish, romantic plan of saving, under the disguise of a judge, the life of the noble friend of her newly-wedded lord, and—Shakespeare here avails himself of the convenient vicinity of Belmont to Padua—she deems it all-sufficient to provide herself with the counsel and the garments of her cousin, Bellario, a highly-respected lawyer in Padua. She has not withal the slightest knowledge of Dr Bellario's having been summoned by the Duke to Venice for this very case. This unexplained, lucky accident comes to her aid, and so she suddenly appears as his substitute and deputy before the Supreme Court of the Republic in the Doge's palace, over which the Doge himself presides. Here she appears, not with the legal opinion of her cousin as a kind of Crown lawyer, or of the Law Faculty in Padua, but as a veritable and downright judge. Such a proceeding in a State having a clearly-defined system of legal procedure—which was emphatically true of Venice at that period—seems, at least to the reader of the present day, almost, if not quite, incomprehensible. But if we accept this too as an echo of earlier mediæval law (as in the story of the *Pecorone*), there remains only this alternative: Either Portia's whole plan, with its accidental coincidence with Bellario's being summoned by the Doge, is a poorly-contrived, improbable fable, and therefore scarcely worthy of a great dramatist,—or an expedient of this kind must have appeared to the poet and to his contemporaries as not at all out of the way, nay, quite natural and customary, at least in Venice. This latter is possible only in case there were at that time in Padua men whose position, reputation, and public weight in the Venetian State were of such a nature that they could furnish an original for Dr Bellario. Then, assuredly, this character in *The Merchant* will present nothing remarkable or incredible to any one.

Shakespeare brings this Dr Bellario plainly and distinctly before us, without introducing him personally, by a few allusions and by the appearance of his substitute, even Portia herself disguised as Dr Balthazar. He is an elderly man ('old Bellario,' as he is called), 'a learned Doctor' of Laws, erudite, famous everywhere, highly respected by the Doge and Signorie, and often called on to counsel and to decide; in complicated civil cases an experienced, sharp-witted barrister; in criminal cases (for parties 'standing in danger') an eloquent advocate, and in all respects, by everybody, held in highest confidence and esteem.

Now, since Shakespeare laid the time of the action of this play in his own days, he had this advantage: That at that very time there was living in Padua a professor in the University there whose characteristics fully and entirely corresponded to all these qualifications and requisites in the play. OTTONELLO DISCALZIO, born in 1536 of a distinguished patrician family, which at an earlier period had produced a celebrated jurist of the same name, was at that time the most eminent Professor of Law, especially of Civil Law, in the University of Padua. Profound knowledge, acuteness, and eloquence pre-eminently distinguished him. The Government of the Republic continually consulted him, and heaped him with honours, commissions, and embassies. For the extraordinary services which he thus rendered to the State he received the conspicuous distinction of the

Order of San Marco. The Emperor of Germany also made him a Knight und a Pfalzgraf, and other Princes their counsellor. Various invitations to take up his residence at foreign courts he declined. Many a defendant in civil cases he rescued from the perils of legal procedure; for more than twenty years he was the kindly protector and friend of the German law-students in Padua. In the seventy-first year of his age, in 1607, he died in Padua. Upon the monuments erected to his memory by his widow in the Church of the Eremites, and by the law-students in the Church of St Anthony, he is termed: 'Primarius juris civilis interpres;'—'eximia juris utriusque scientia et admirabili disputandi ac dicendi acumine et copia excellens, patriae in honoribus, legationibus consilliisque utilissimus, privatorum in judiciis pericula singulari eloquentia propulsans.' We need not indicate how admirably the words of these inscriptions fit Dr Bellario, and even Shakespeare's very words. Let the name Bellario be substituted for Discalzio, and even to scholars the actual existence of the former is rendered credible. And no one can justly argue that Shakespeare could not have had as thorough a knowledge of this distinguished contemporary of his, this Discalzio, as of the country on the Brenta between Padua and Venice.

We do not desire to ascribe to the personality which has just been depicted more influence on Shakespeare's work than it really has. It may well be that in all times and among all peoples there have been Jurists of like wisdom, character, and repute to Ottonello Discalzio, but only one, occupying in Venice such a position as his, can be regarded and accepted as the prototype of Bellario. If we imagine Bellario as filling a position like Discalzio's, then it is easily conceivable that Portia, knowing her cousin's reputation and high position with the Doge and Signorie, could presume that in a case of such importance and notoriety as that of Shylock *versus* Antonio, he would be called on for an opinion, and perhaps even be summoned to Venice. Her surmise proves correct, and thereby her plan succeeds. Thus, by a side-light from Discalzio, Bellario emerges from the twilight of romantic invention into the clear, bright light of real life, and Portia's adventure, from a novelistic freak of a girl, becomes an intelligible and sensible act.

[In his concluding section Th. Elze describes the University of Padua at the close of the sixteenth century, when so great was the University's reputation everywhere that there were at that time representatives of twenty-three nations among its students. From the lists of these students it appears 'that not a few Englishmen took up their abode in Padua for a longer or shorter time for the purpose of study, and all of whom assuredly must have visited Venice also; and it is also to be inferred that the number of English travellers who visited the city of the Doges must have been much larger than is commonly supposed. Hereby is disclosed another source, not hitherto noticed, whence a knowledge of Venetian manners and customs reached England. And if it has been hitherto impossible to prove that Shakespeare drew his knowledge of Venice and Padua and the region around from personal observation, it is quite possible to suppose that he obtained it by word of mouth, either from Italians living in England, or from Englishmen who had pursued their studies in Padua.'

Among the names that Th. Elze gives may be noticed two Danes—one, Rosenkranz, in 1587–89, and another, Güldenstern, in 1603. A list is given from the Records at Padua, extending from September, 1591, to October, 1594, during which time twenty-five English students were matriculated. Thus in:

1591, on 29 Nov., D. Thomas Sackavillus, nobilis, Anglus—cum naevo sub dextra aure. [A birthmark or scar is always itemized. This is, as Th. Elze notes, the son of the author of the *Mirror for Magistrates*.]

1592.   22 Jan., D. Franc. Tusser, Anglus—cum cicatrice in suprema parte pellicis sinistri.

15 Sept., D. Ricard. Sands, Anglus—cum parva cicatrice in facie.

1593.   21 Nov., D. Fynes Morison, Anglus—cum cicatrice sub oculo dextro; and others; but the foregoing are names which become afterwards familiar to all Shakespeare students.]

W. Oechelhäuser * (*Shakespeare's Dramatische Werke*, Weimar, 1877, p. 14): Passive, inactive rôles like Antonio's generally require less attention to by-play. But the great Trial Scene is an exception; here by-play in the circle of his friends is indispensable on the part of Antonio. And furthermore, as the Poet has given Antonio but few words to say, he must in dumb show fully, and warmly, express his gratitude to Portia, which is unfortunately much neglected by Actors. Portia, too, must emphasize this by-play, lest at the conclusion of the Trial, Antonio, on whose fate the whole plot turns, should become too completely overshadowed.

(P. 16.) Bassanio's situation in the exciting Trial Scene must not be forgotten by the actor for a moment; morally regarded, he suffers greater torture than Antonio, who suffers only for himself. On this account, at every step of the Trial, Bassanio must pourtray in all possible ways through by-play his distress and anxiety, as well as his boundless joy over the deliverance of his friend, hard as it may be in a scene which fills an entire long Act. The highest expression of his sympathy for Antonio (the full significance whereof is rarely appreciated) lies in the words, 'Antonio, I am married to a wife,' &c. Here, at the moment when every hope for Antonio's relief appears to have vanished, expression must be given in the most impressive way to the intensest anguish, but most actors regard this passage only as the occasion for the roguish remarks of Portia which follow. Generally too little is made of Bassanio's thanks, and Antonio's also, to Portia, so that an almost cold, frosty sound is imparted to Bassanio's graceful words. In the final scene at Belmont, where he again enters the realm of love and happiness, Bassanio's earnest and dignified vindication in regard to the ring gives us the pleasing and distinct idea of a pure and noble character, deserving of his good fortune.

(P. 21.) Shakespeare in his Shylock did not cater to the blind hatred of the Jews prevalent in his time, but stood forth with large-hearted boldness for the oppressed, and threw upon the persecutors of the Jews their well-merited share in producing the extreme degeneracy of the people to which Shylock belongs.

The conclusion of the Trial Scene is a special confirmation of my idea that in the characterization the typical Jew, as such, should by no means predominate over the typical miser. When the Doge announces the confiscation of half of Shylock's property, Shylock breaks out into passionate complaints, declaring his money to be his life; but when his becoming a Christian is made the condition of his retaining the other half, he simply says: 'I am content.' Money is more to him than his faith, the miser is stronger than the Jew. But this trait belongs to the individual, not to the race, for in the world's history no people but just the Jews have with greater decision and energy subordinated every earthly consideration to their devotion to their faith, notwithstanding centuries of terrible persecution and their innate thirst for gold. The miser in Shylock has sprung up on common human soil; only his cunning, his hatred, his thirst for revenge on his Christian oppressors reflect the representative of degenerate Judaism.

---

* Especial attention is bestowed by Oechelhäuser in the Introduction of each play in his translation (which is an adaptation of Schlegel and Tieck's) on the costume, on the scenery, or stage-setting, and particularly on directions to actors.

Greed for gold and hatred of Christians are the springs of his actions, and upon their working the character of Shylock is formed.

(P. 23.) In his brief appearance in the Second Act with Jessica and Launcelot, where he puts no restraint upon himself, Shylock shows himself as the dirty miser, always the cross domestic tyrant who has made the house 'a hell' to his daughter. No word of love or kindness to his child, only the command to keep the doors fastened and not go to the window to see the maskers pass. The tender farewell of his daughter that many actors represent him as taking is in obvious opposition to the design of the Poet, and not only do the subsequent outbreaks of heartless rage give the lie to it, but it would cast a sad reflection upon Jessica's character. On the contrary, Shylock should be represented as turning his back on Jessica at his departure without any leave-taking. Jessica says expressly she is not the daughter of his heart. She loves him not, because she is not loved.

JORDAN'S BALLAD

As this Ballad has been frequently cited by Editors and Commentators, it must find a place in this volume. Its chief interest lies in the proof which it yields that an argument for age cannot be judiciously founded merely on the extreme simplicity of the ballad style—the ground, it will be remembered, on which several critics claimed a high antiquity for the ballad of *Gernutus*. Incidentally, it gives us a glimpse of Shylock, with red hair and a hooked nose, in the days halfway between Burbadge and Dogget. It was first reprinted by Collier (*New Particulars*, p. 38), who prefaced it as follows:

'After the death of Burbadge in 1619–20, I do not recollect any trace of the per-
'formance of *The Merchant of Venice* until Lord Lansdowne revived the play in
'1701, with alterations. So much does Shakespeare's production seem to have been
'forgotten in 1664, that Thomas Jordan made a ballad of it, and printed it as an orig-
'inal story (at least without any acknowledgement) in his *Royal Arbor of Loyal*
'*Poesie* in that year. . . . . Jordan felt authorized to take such liberties with the story
'that he has represented the Jew's daughter, instead of Portia, as assuming the office
'of Assessor to the Duke of Venice in the Trial Scene, for the sake of saving the life
'of the Merchant, with whom she was in love. Here, also, he describes Shylock as
'having a red beard, and mentions some other particulars of his dress and appearance,
'regarding which he doubtless spoke from the custom of the stage, Jordan having himself
'been an actor before the temporary suppression of theatres by the Puritans, though he
'could hardly have seen Burbadge.' [I have followed the text given by HALLIWELL (p. 321), which bears evidence of being reprinted with closer fidelity than that by Collier.]

THE FORFEITURE, a Romance; tune—Dear, let me now this evening dye.

1. You that do look with Christian hue,
    Attend unto my sonnet,
I'le tell you of as vilde a Jew,
    As ever wore a bonnet.
No Jew of Scotland I intend,
    My story not so mean is:
This Jew in wealth did much transcend
    Under the States of Venice.
2. Where he by usury and trade,
    Did much exceed in riches;
His beard was red; his face was made
    Not much unlike a witches.

His habit was a Jewish gown,
  That would defend all weather;
His chin turn'd up, his nose hung **down**
  And both ends met together.
3. Yet this deformed father had
  A daughter and a wise one,
So sweet a virgin never lad
  Did ever set his eyes on.
He that could call this lady foul
  Must be a purblinde noddy;
But yet she had a Christian soul
  Lodg'd in a Jewish body.
4. Within the city there did live,
  If you the truth will search on't,
One whose ill fate will make you **grieve,**
  A gallant Christian Merchant;
Who did abound in wealth and wit,
  In youth and comely feature,
Whose love unto a friend was knit
  As strong as bonds of nature.
5. A gentleman of good renown,
  But of a sinking fortune,
Who having no estate of 's own,
  Doth thus his friend importune:
Friend, lend me but one thousand **pound**
  It shall again be paid ye,
For I have very lately found
  A fair and wealthy lady.
6. The Merchant then makes this **reply:**
  Friend, I am out of treasure,
But I will make my credit flye,
  To do my friend a pleasure.
There is a Jew in town (quoth he),
  Who, though he deadly hate me,
Yet cause my wealth is strong at sea,
  This favour will not bate me.
7. When they were come unto the Jew,
  He did demand their pleasure:
The Merchant answers, I of you
  Would borrow so much treasure.
The Jew replies, you shall not ha't,
  If such a summe would save ye,
Unless in three moneths you will **pay't,**
  Or forfeit what I'de have you (*sic*).
8. If at the three moneths end you do,
  As you shall sign and seal to't,
Not pay the money which is due,
  Whereere I have a minde to't,——
Ile cut a pound out of your flesh.
  The Merchant is contented,
Because he knew in half that time,
  His shipping would prevent it.
9. Ill news by every ship comes in,
  His ships are drown'd and fired;
The Jew his forfeiture doth win,
  For three moneths are expired.
He is arrested for the debt;
  The Court must now decide it:
The flesh is due, and now the **Jew**
  Is ready to divide it.

10. The Merchant's friend that had the gold,
    Now being richly married,
    Offer'd the summe down three times told,
    To have his friend's life spared.
    'T would not be took, but strait steps in
    One in Doctor's apparel,
    Who, though but young, doth now begin
    Thus to decide the quarrel.

11. Jew, we do grant that by the law,
    A pound of flesh your due is,
    But if one drop of blood you draw,
    We'l show you what a Jew is:
    Take but a pound, as 'twas agreed,
    Be sure you cut no further,
    And cut no less, lest for the deed
    You be arraign'd for murther.

12. The Jew inrag'd doth tear the bond,
    And dares not do the slaughter.
    He quits the Court, and then 'twas found
    The Doctor proves his daughter,
    Who for the love she long time bore,
    From a true heart derived,
    To be his wife, and save his life,
    This subtle slight contrived.

13. The Court consent and they are wed;
    For hatching of this slaughter
    The Jew's estate is forfeited,
    And given to his daughter.
    She is baptiz'd in Christendome,
    The Jew cryes out he's undone;
    I wish such Jews may never come
    To England, nor to London.

MUSIC

All that glisters is not gold, &c.

Act II, Scene vii, Lines 67–75.

ALFRED ROFFE (*Handbook of Shakespeare Music*, London, 1878, p. 45): A duet taken from this scroll was composed by Mr Charles Horn, and sung in the *Merry Wives* when that play was *musically* performed many years ago.

Tell me where is fancy bred, &c.

Act III, Scene ii, Lines 69–78.

ROFFE: Besides the well-known setting of this song, in the duet form, by SIR JOHN STEVENSON, it has at least four other settings. The earliest I have as yet become aware of is a solo by Dr ARNE, which was sung in *Twelfth Night* by the celebrated Mrs Clive. I am informed that the play was revived at Drury Lane Theatre, on January 17, 1741, when Olivia was personated by Mrs Clive. Dr Arne's setting of this song for Olivia is in the key of D minor, and is elegant and pensive in its character. It is reprinted in Mrs Caulfield's collection, and only there, that I am aware of. The burden, 'Let us all ring fancy's knell,' has here been omitted by the Doctor; it could not have been felt to be in any sort of harmony with such a person as the love-lorn lady of *Twelfth Night*.

Another of the settings is by Mr *R. J. S. STEVENS*, and is for the comparatively very

unusual combination of three sopranos and a tenor. The composition is decidedly out
of the *strict glee* category, inasmuch as it possesses an *instrumental* bass. In the second movement the effect of the 'knell' is assigned to this instrumental bass, so that Mr
Stevens's work, in this case, is rather to be considered as an accompanied quartet than
as a glee. Mr *WILLIAM LINLEY* has set these words as a dialogue duet for first and
second attendant, with a chorus in three parts for sopranos and base. Then there is a
setting by Mr *JOHN HATTON,* concerning which it may interest amateur ladies to be told
that it was sung by Miss Poole, with *a chorus of female voices only,* in *The Merchant
of Venice.* The composition is in two movements, the first an *andante con moto* up to
the word 'reply.' ' Let us all ring fancy's knell' forms an *allegro* movement. The
chorus is written in three parts, for soprano, mezzo-soprano, and contralto voices. The
whole together would, as I conceive, form a very pleasing addition to the somewhat
limited repertory of ladies' music.

THE NEW SHAKSPERE SOCIETY (*List of Songs,* &c., Series VIII, Miscellanies, No.
3, p. 28) adds the following :—

REV. L. RICHMOND, about 1810 or 1820.   Round.

M. BARTHOLOMEW (Mrs Mounsey), Part Song.   Soprano, Alto, Tenor, Bass.
Novello.

G. A. MACFARREN, 1869.   Part Song.   S., A., T., B.   Novello.

B. LUETZEN, 1877.   Duettino.   Brighton.

C. PINSUTI, about 1880.   Part Song.   A., T., T., B.   Novello.

C. PINSUTI.   The same arranged for S., C., T., B.

J. G. CALCOTT, 1883.   Part Song. S., S., C.   Novello.

In such a night as this, &c.

Act V, Scene i, Lines 2–29.

NEW SHAKSPERE SOCIETY :—

SIR A. S. SULLIVAN, 1865.   Duet for Soprano and Tenor, introduced in the Cantata
of *Kenilworth.*

How sweet the moonlight sleeps upon this bank, &c.

Act I, Scene v, Lines 63–77.

ROFFE (p. 47) : There have been at least six pieces of music connected with these
parts of Lorenzo's beautiful address to Jessica. One of these is a setting for three
voices, with a distinct pianoforte accompaniment, constituting it rather a trio than a glee.
It is the composition of Mr *M. P. KING.* A second setting, in the form of a little duet
for soprano voices, was by Mr *CHARLES DIGNUM.* This duet is to be found in a volume of Mr Dignum's miscellaneous vocal compositions, the date about 1800 (?). Both
these settings are confined to the four lines 63–66. There is also a pleasing duet to
these lines, set by Mr *THOMAS HUTCHINSON,* in or about 1807. It is written for a
soprano and a tenor.

Mr *JOHN PERCY* (the composer of 'Wapping Old Stairs') has set these words in the
solo form. Mr Percy's composition, if without any very marked character, has a certain degree of elegance, but it is not easy to see the expediency of some peculiar dealings with the words. For instance, stopping at the first two lines and a half, ' How
sweet the moonlight sleeps upon this bank ! Here will we sit, and let the sounds of
music Creep in our ears,' the composer proceeds with the following lines from *Twelfth
Night (with alterations)* :—' Oh ! it comes o'er me like the gentle south, That o'er the
violet breathes, and charms the soul.' After this the other line and a half of Loren-

zo's speech are admitted, with two additional syllables, thus :—'Soft stillness and the night *Do well* become the touches of sweet harmony.'

Again, not many years ago, appeared a setting from Lorenzo's speech by Miss *E. Naylor*, as an accompanied duet. This composition has two movements, the first closing at the words 'Become the touches of sweet harmony,' while the second is an *allegro*, written to the last three lines of Lorenzo's same speech, specially addressed to the musicians when they enter—'Come, ho, and wake Diana,' &c.

Finally, in 1866, in the notice of a performance by Mr Henry Leslie's choir, we are told of a part-song, composed by Mr *Leslie* himself, to Shakespeare's lines—'How sweet the moonlight sleeps upon this bank!' It appears that the choir gained an encore in this part-song.

New Shakspere Society adds the following :—

Sir *A. S. Sullivan*, 1865. Recitative for Tenor before the Duet for Soprano and Tenor, introduced into the Cantata of *Kenilworth*.

T. Blanchard. Song.

J. G. Calcott, 1883. Part Song. S., C., T., B., B. First sung by Leslie's choir, Feb. 2, 1883.

J. G. Calcott, 1883. The same arranged as a Trio. S., S., C.

For do but note a wild and wanton herd, &c.

Act V, Scene i, Lines 81–98.

Roffe: There is a song on these words composed by Mr *T. Cooke*, and sung by Mr Braham in the operatized *Taming of the Shrew*. The opening is in recitative, and there is an air of varied movements. The close is made upon the words—'Let no such man be trusted.'

New Shakspere Society: See Geneste's *English Stage*, ix, 418.

Miss Helen A. Clarke (*Shakespeariana*, January, 1888, p. 17) : *The Merchant of Venice* has been turned into an Opera by a modern Italian, *Signor Petrella*, and is said to possess merit. This play, however, as far back as 1787, fell into the clutches of one of the insatiable army of mediocre German composers, *J. A. Just*, and was performed at Amsterdam, let us hope for the first and last time.

[When this play was produced in Philadelphia in 1878 with extraordinary magnificence, under the management of W. D. Gemmill, the Song in Oxberry's Edition 'My bliss too long my bride denies,' II, vi, 30, was set to music by Mr *Simon Hassler*, and published as a *Serenade-Barcarole, with Solo and Chorus*.]

30

PLAN OF THE WORK, &c.

IN this Edition the attempt is made, to give, in the shape of TEXTUAL NOTES, on the same page with the Text, all the Various Readings of *The Merchant of Venice*, from the First Quarto to the latest critical Edition of the play; then, as COMMENTARY, follow the Notes which the Editor has thought worthy of insertion, not only for the purpose of elucidating the Text, but as illustrations of the history of Shakespearian criticism. In the APPENDIX will be found discussions of subjects, which on the score of length could not be conveniently included in the Commentary.

The LIST OF EDITIONS COLLATED IN THE TEXTUAL NOTES, is as follows:

THE FIRST QUARTO (*Roberts*)	[Q₁]	.. 1600
THE SECOND QUARTO (*Heyes.* Ash-bee's Facsimile)	[Q₂]	.. 1600
THE FIRST FOLIO	[F₁]	.. 1623
THE SECOND FOLIO	[F₂]	.. 1632
THE THIRD QUARTO	[Q₃]	.. 1637
THE THIRD FOLIO	[F₃]	.. 1664
THE FOURTH FOLIO	[F₄]	.. 1685
ROWE (First Edition)	[Rowe i]	.. 1709
ROWE (Second Edition)	[Rowe ii]	.. 1714
POPE (First Edition)	[Pope i]	.. 1723
POPE (Second Edition)	[Pope ii]	.. 1728
THEOBALD (First Edition)	[Theob. i]	.. 1733
THEOBALD (Second Edition)	[Theob. ii]	.. 1740
HANMER	[Han.]	.. 1744
WARBURTON	[Warb.]	.. 1747
JOHNSON	[Johns.]	.. 1765
CAPELL	[Cap.]	(?) 1766
JOHNSON and STEEVENS	[Steev. '73]	.. 1773
JOHNSON and STEEVENS	[Steev. '78]	.. 1778
JOHNSON and STEEVENS	[Steev. '85]	.. 1785
MALONE	[Mal.]	.. 1790
STEEVENS	[Steev.]	.. 1793
RANN	[Rann]	(?) 1794
REED'S STEEVENS	[Var. '03]	.. 1803
ECCLES	[Ec.]	.. 1805
REED'S STEEVENS	[Var. '13]	.. 1813
BOSWELL'S MALONE	[Var.]	.. 1821
KNIGHT	[Knt]	.. 1841
COLLIER (First Edition)	[Coll. i]	.. 1842
HALLIWELL (Folio Edition)	[Hal.]	.. 1856
SINGER (Second Edition)	[Sing. ii]	.. 1856
DYCE (First Edition)	[Dyce i]	.. 1857
COLLIER (Second Edition)	[Coll. ii]	.. 1858

466

STAUNTON	..	..	..	..	[Sta.]	..	..	..	..	1858
R. GRANT WHITE (First Edition)		..		[Wh. i]	..	..	..	..	1861
CAMBRIDGE (CLARK and WRIGHT)		..		[Cam.]	..	..	..	..	1863
GLOBE (CLARK and WRIGHT) ..		..		[Glo.]	..	..	..	..	1864
KEIGHTLEY	..	..	..	..	[Ktly]	..	..	..	..	1864
CHARLES and MARY COWDEN-CLARKE			[Clarke]	..	..	..	(?)	1864
DYCE (Second Edition) ..	..		..	[Dyce ii]	..	..	..	..	1866
CLARENDON (CLARK and WRIGHT)		..		[Cla.]	..	..	..	..	1869
DELIUS (Third Edition) ..		..		[Del.]	..	..	..	..	1872
DYCE (Third Edition) ..		..		[Dyce iii]	..	..	..	..	1875
COLLIER (Third Edition)		..		[Coll. iii]	..	..	..	..	1877
HUDSON ..	..	..	..	..	[Huds.]	..	..	..	..	1879
ROLFE	..	..	..	..	[Rlfe]	..	..	..	..	1883
R. GRANT WHITE (Second Edition)		..		[Wh. ii]	..	..	..	..	1883

In the TEXTUAL NOTES the symbol Ff indicates the agreement of the Second, Third, and Fourth Folios. The agreement of the three Quartos is indicated by Qq.

The omission of the apostrophe in the Second Folio, a peculiarity of that edition, is not generally noted.

The sign + indicates the agreement of ROWE, POPE, THEOBALD, HANMER, WARBURTON, and JOHNSON.

When WARBURTON precedes HANMER in the Textual Notes, it indicates that HANMER has adopted a suggestion of WARBURTON'S.

The words *et cet.* after any reading indicate that it is the reading of *all other* editions. The words *et seq.* indicate the agreement of all subsequent editions.

The abbreviation (*subs.*) indicates that the reading is *substantially* given, and that immaterial variations in spelling, punctuation, or stage directions are disregarded.

COLL. (MS) refers to COLLIER'S annotated Second Folio.

An Emendation or Conjecture which is given in the Commentary is not repeated in the Textual Notes; nor is *conj.* added to any name in the Textual Notes unless it happens to be that of an editor, in which case its omission would be misleading.

The colon is used as equivalent to 'namely.'

All citations of Acts, Scenes, and Lines in *Romeo and Juliet, Macbeth, Hamlet, Lear,* and *Othello* refer to this edition of those plays; in citations from other plays the GLOBE EDITION is followed.

I have not called attention to every misprint in the Folio. The Textual Notes will show, if need be, that they are misprints by the agreement of all the Editors in their correction.

Nor is notice taken of the first Editor who adopted the modern spelling, or who substituted commas for parentheses, or changed ? to !.

Otherwise, even insignificant variations in spelling and punctuation in the Quartos and Folios are recorded, that every aid may be supplied not alone for comparing the Texts in general, but for deciding from which text the Folio was printed.

Hitherto, before going to press, I have verified the collation, in the Textual Notes, of all the Editions. In the present volume this verification has been restricted to the collation of the Quartos and Folios.

Again be it urged in palliation of the obtrusive First Person Singular, that the monarchical 'we' implies the semblance of an authority which it is the farthest removed from the Editor's wish, to claim; moreover, the impression in him is ineradicable, that the Editorial ' we ' when it stands for only one wee editor smacks ineffaceably of the Three Tailors of Tooley Street. As long as the notes of other editors are given on the same page with his, the greater glory will dim the less, and his inland brook will be lost in the main of waters.

I cannot but think that some of the most valuable notes in the foregoing pages are to be found under the name of Allen. They are the *marginalia* of the late Professor GEORGE ALLEN, from whose daughters I lately received several plays thus annotated,— a precious gift. It scarcely need be added that they were written with no view to publication, but are, what their fragmentary style reveals, the jottings, for his own use merely, of a keen critic, accustomed by a life-long study of Greek to the close analysis of thought and language. How much these brief notes have lost through the lack of their author's revision cannot but be sadly apparent to all who recall the wide range of Professor Allen's learning.

Again for this Play, as for *Othello*, Mr EDWIN BOOTH kindly furnished me with a Prompt-book, wherein he had noted his interpretations; they are to be found duly recorded in the Commentary.

A work in six volumes, called *Discoveries in Hieroglyphics*, &c. by ROBERT DEVER-ELL was published in London in 1813, and again, a second edition in 1816. In this work *Hamlet, Lear, Othello*, and the present play are reprinted with explanatory notes and wood-cuts. But, as was mentioned in *Othello*, the interpretations are the witless, almost incoherent, ravings of a pure lunatic; to have cited them only to raise a laugh, and they could be cited for no other purpose, would have been simply heartless.

The LIST OF BOOKS, from which citations have been made at first hand, is here given, chiefly for the purpose of setting them forth in chronological order, and as a means of identification. To save space in the Commentary the volumes are generally cited with extreme brevity. It may be added that it is not to be supposed that the List represents all the volumes that have been fruitlessly examined for stray notes of value; were all included the List would be twice, if not thrice, as large. A list of Dictionaries is added, for the sake of convenient chronological reference:

ASCHAM: *Scholemaster* (Arber)	1570
GOSSON: *Schole of Abuse* (Arber)	1579
SILVAYN: *The Orator*	1596
MERES: *Palladis Tamia*	1598
GOULART: *Admirable Histoires*	1620
HOLLAND: *Translation of Plinie's Natural History*	1635
ASCHAM: *Toxophilus* (Arber)	1640
HOWELL: *Instructions for Forraine Travel* (Arber)	1642
LANSDOWNE: *The Jew of Venice* (2d ed., 1713)	1701
GILDON: *Remarks, &c.*	1710
THEOBALD: *Shakespeare Restored*	1726
PECK: *New Memoirs of Milton*	1740
COLLEY CIBBER: *Apology*	1740
UPTON: *Observations, &c.*	1746

COLLIER: *New Particulars, &c.* 1836
GARDINER: *Music of Nature* (Boston Reprint) 1837
HALLAM: *Introduction to the Literature of Europe* (New York, 1866) .. 1837
THOMAS CAMPBELL: *Dramatic Works of Shakespeare* 1838
C. A. BROWN: *Shakespeare's Autobiographical Poems* 1838
COLLIER: *Further Particulars, &c.* 1839
SHAKESPEARE SOCIETY: *Revels Book* 1842
LEWIN: *Law of Trusts* 1842
COLLIER: *Shakespeare Library* (Hazlitt's ed., 1875) 1843
DYCE: *Remarks, &c.* 1844
DUNLOP: *History of Fiction* (ed. ii) 1845
SHAKESPEARE SOCIETY: *Henslowe's Diary* 1845
HUNTER: *New Illustrations, &c.* 1845
SHAKESPEARE SOCIETY: *Memoirs of Actors* 1846
VERPLANCK: *Shakespeare's Works,* New York 1847
HALPIN: *Dramatic Unities* 1849
REV. SYDNEY SMITH: *Lectures on Moral Philosophy* (New York) 1850
MARLOWE: *Jew of Malta* (ed. Dyce) 1850
COLLIER: *Notes and Emendations* 1852
SINGER: *Shakespeare's Text Vindicated* 1853
DYCE: *Few Notes, &c.* 1853
HEBLER: *Kaufmann von Venedig,* Bern 1854
LAMB: *Specimens of Dramatic Poetry* (Bohn's ed.) 1854
W. S. WALKER: *Shakespeare's Versification* 1854
R. G. WHITE: *Shakespeare Scholar* 1854
HEINE: *Sämmtliche Werke,* Philadelphia 1856
COLLIER: *Seven Lectures of Coleridge, &c.* 1856
BATHURST: *Remarks on the Differences in Shakespeare's Poetry, &c.* .. 1857
HAYNES: *Outlines of Equity* 1858
CHARLES KEAN: Acting Edition 1858
G. L. CRAIK: *English of Shakespeare* (ed. ii), London 1859
DYCE: *Strictures, &c.* 1859
WALKER: *Critical Examination of the Text, &c.* 1859
LORD CAMPBELL: *Shakespeare's Legal Acquirements,* New York 1859
S. JERVIS: *Proposed Emendations* 1860
DR J. C. BUCKNELL: *Shakespeare's Medical Knowledge* 1860
ANON: *Alter Ego. Eine Studie zu Shakespeare's Kaufmann,* Hamburg .. 1862
F. KREYSSIG: *Vorlesungen über Shakespeare,* Berlin 1862
S. BAILEY: *The Received Text* 1862
C. COWDEN-CLARKE: *Shakespeare Characters, &c.* 1863
GERVINUS: *Commentaries,* trans. by F. E. Bunnett 1863
W. BELL: *Shakespeare's Puck* 1864
H. THEO. ROETSCHER: *Charactergebilde* 1864
A. COHN: *Shakespeare in Germany* 1864
BISHOP WORDSWORTH: *Shakespeare and the Bible* 1864
W. R. ARROWSMITH: *Shakespeare's Editors, &c.* 1865
DR DORAN: *Their Majesties Servants* 1865
R. CARTWRIGHT: *New Readings* 1866
W. W. SKEAT: *William of Palerne* (E. E. T. Soc.) 1867

G. C. LICHTENBERG: *Vermischte Schriften*, Göttingen 1867
THOS. KEIGHTLEY: *Shakespeare Expositor* 1867
GUIZOT: *Œuvres Complètes de Shakespeare*, Paris 1868
H. GILES: *Human Life in Shakespeare* 1868
T. R. GOULD: *The Tragedian* 1868
W. L. RUSHTON: *Shakespeare's Testamentary Language* 1869
E. MONTÉGUT: *Œuvres Complètes de Shakespeare*, Paris 1869
ELLIS: *Early English Pronunciation* (E. E. T. Soc.) 1869
F. W. HAWKINS: *Life of Edmund Kean* 1869
R. GENÉE: *Geschichte der Shakespeare'schen Dramen, &c.,* Leipzig 1870
E. A. ABBOTT: *Shakespearian Grammar* 1870
P. A. DANIEL: *Notes and Emendations* 1870
JAMES GAIRDNER: *The Paston Letters* 1872
FR. V. HUGO: *Œuvres Complètes de Shakespeare*, Paris 1872
REV. JOHN HUNTER: *Merchant of Venice* .. ,. 1872
RUSKIN: *Munera Pulveris*, New York 1872
W. KOENIG: *Ueber Shakespeare*, Leipzig 1873
KARL ELZE: *Essays*, trans. by Miss Schmitz, London 1874
MINTO: *Characteristics of English Poets* 1874
R. PROELSS: *Kaufmann von Venedig*, Leipzig 1875
EARL OF SOUTHESK: *Saskatchewan* 1875
A. W. WARD: *History of English Dramatic Poetry* 1875
G. H. LEWES: *On Actors and the Art of Acting* 1875
J. WEISS: *Wit, Humour, and Shakespeare*, Boston 1876
H. ULRICI: *Shakespeare's Dramatic Art*, trans. by Miss Schmitz .. 1876
F. G. FLEAY: *Shakespeare Manual* 1876
G. FREYTAG: *Technik des Dramas* (ed. iii), Leipzig 1876
W. OECHELHÄUSER: *Der Kaufmann von Venedig*, Weimar 1877
D. G. SNIDER: *System of Shakespeare's Dramas*, St Louis 1877
R. MORRIS: *Legends of the Holy Rood* (E. E. T. Soc.) 1878
A. ROFFE: *Handbook of Shakespeare Music*, London 1878
W. HERTZBERG: *Libell of Englishe Policie* 1878
EDWIN BOOTH: Prompt-Book of *The Merchant of Venice* 1878
H. FRITSCHE: *Der Kaufmann von Venedig, erklärt*, Berlin 1878
S. J. HERRTAGE: *Gesta Romanorum* (E. E. T. Soc.) 1879
C. M. INGLEBY: *Centurie of Prayse* 1879
THE COWDEN-CLARKES: *The Shakespeare Key* 1879
J. G. HERR: *Scattered Notes, &c.,* Philadelphia 1879
J. E. MURDOCH: *The Stage*, Philadelphia 1880
A. C. SWINBURNE: *A Study of Shakespeare* 1880
M. D. CONWAY: *The Wandering Jew* 1881
A. PIETSCHER: *Jurist und Dichter*, Dessau 1881
C. K. SALAMAN: *Jews as they Are*, London 1882
F. F. HEARD: *Shakespeare as a Lawyer*, Boston 1883
GEO. MACDONALD: *The Imagination*, Boston 1883
JOS. KOHLER: *Shakespeare vor dem Forum der Jurisprudenz*, Würzburg .. 1883
J. MEISSNER: *Die Englische Commoedianten, &c.,* Wien 1884
C. K. DAVIS: *Law in Shakespeare*, St Paul 1884
T. PARRY: *Merchant of Venice*, Longmans' Series 1884

J. W. HALES: *Notes and Essays* 1884
D. P. CASSEL: *Litteratur und Symbolik*, Leipzig 1884
HALLIWELL-PHILLIPPS: *Outlines of the Life of Shakespeare* (ed. v) 1885
LADY MARTIN: *Shakespeare's Female Characters* 1885
H. HEINEMANN: *Shylock und Nathan*, Frankfurt, A. M. 1886
R. G. WHITE: *Studies in Shakespeare* 1886
J. PAYN: *Boccaccio* (Villon Society) 1886
J. MUIRHEAD: *Hist. Introd. to the Private Law of Rome*, Edinburgh .. 1886
F. G. FLEAY: *Life and Works of Shakespeare* 1886
R. v. IHERING: *Der Kampf um's Recht* (ed. viii), Wien 1886
PROF. H. CORSON: *Privately Printed Notes* .. .. n. d.
R. S. DAVIES: Act IV, Scene i (Brown's Series), Hull .. .. .. n. d.
F. J. FURNIVALL: *Forewords to Q_1 & to Q_2* .. .. n. d.
J. D. MORELL: *Merchant of Venice*, London .. .. n. d.
REV. D. MORRIS: *Merchant of Venice* (Collins' Eng. Classics) .. .. n. d.
W. C. RUSSELL: *Representative Actors* .. .. n. d.

DICTIONARIES

COOPER'S *Latin Dictionary* 1573
FLORIO: *His firste Fruites* 1578
BARET'S *Alvearie* 1580
FLORIO'S *Worlde of Wordes* 1598
COTGRAVE: *Dictionarie of the French and English Tongues* 1611
MINSHEU: *Guide Into Tongues* 1617
BULLOKAR: *English Expositor* 1621
MINSHEU'S *Spanish Dictionary* 1623
NARES: *Glossary* (ed. Halliwell and Wright, 1867) 1822
RICHARDSON'S *Dictionary* 1838
HALLIWELL'S *Archaic Dictionary* 1847
EASTWOOD and WRIGHT: *Bible Word Book* 1866
WEDGWOOD: *Dictionary of English Etymology* (2d ed.) 1872
SCHMIDT: *Shakespeare Lexicon* 1874
LATHAM'S *Johnson* 1882
SKEAT: *Etymological Dictionary* 1882
MURRAY'S *New English Dictionary* 1884

JOURNALS:

The Academy	*Jahrbücher der deutschen Shakespeare*
The Architect	*Gesellschaft*
The Athenæum	*Monthly Chronicle*
Blackwood's Magazine	*New Shakspere Society*
Albany Law Journal	*Notes and Queries*
Cornhill Magazine	*Overland Monthly*
Edinburgh Review	*Shakespeariana*
Fraser's Magazine	*Temple Bar*
Gentleman's Magazine	*The Theatre*
Jewish Advance	*Young Israel*

INDEX

473